Geography
of the Pacific

Pacific Ocean Island Groups

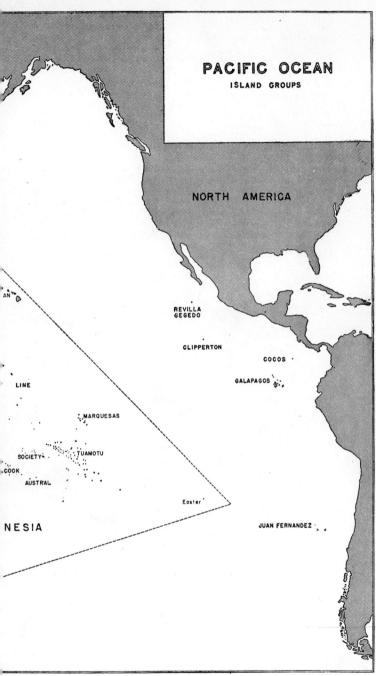

PACIFIC OCEAN
ISLAND GROUPS

NORTH AMERICA

REVILLA
GEGEDO

CLIPPERTON

COCOS

GALAPAGOS

AN

LINE

MARQUESAS

SOCIETY   TUAMOTU

COOK

AUSTRAL

Easter

JUAN FERNANDEZ

NESIA

n by C. A. Manchester, Jr.)

Geography
of the Pacific

OTIS W. FREEMAN, Editor

New York · JOHN WILEY & SONS, *Inc.*

London · CHAPMAN & HALL, *Ltd.*

Copyright, 1951

BY

JOHN WILEY & SONS, INC.

All Rights Reserved

This book or any part thereof must not be reproduced in any form without the written permission of the publisher

PRINTED IN THE UNITED STATES OF AMERICA

Contributors

NEAL M. BOWERS	University of Hawaii
ROBERT G. BOWMAN	University of Nebraska
EDWIN H. BRYAN, JR.	Bernice P. Bishop Museum, Pacific Science Board, and South Pacific Commission
JOHN WESLEY COULTER	University of Cincinnati
CHARLES M. DAVIS	University of Michigan
KENNETH P. EMORY	Bernice P. Bishop Museum and University of Hawaii
OTIS W. FREEMAN	Eastern Washington College of Education
WALTER R. HACKER	University of California and San Francisco State College
CURTIS A. MANCHESTER, JR.	University of Hawaii
LEONARD MASON	University of Hawaii
ANTHONY E. SOKOL	Stanford University
JOSEPH E. SPENCER	University of California, Los Angeles
CLIFFORD M. ZIERER	University of California, Los Angeles

Preface

"The Mediterranean is the ocean of the past, the Atlantic, the ocean of the present, and the Pacific, the ocean of the future." This statement, made in the closing years of the last century by John Hay, secretary of state for the United States, is on the threshold of realization.

The United States has had commercial interests in the Pacific since the foundation of the republic, and in the days of sail her clipper ships and whaling vessels coursed over the Pacific in great numbers. A half century ago Hawaii was annexed, and the Philippines were secured from Spain. Soon after this territorial expansion Japan rose to importance as a world power, and after the First World War she was given control of the Mariana, Caroline, and Marshall islands. The end of the Second World War, however, found the United States and her allies victorious in the Pacific, and America assumed the government, under trust from the United Nations, of the former Japanese-mandated territories. The independence promised the Philippines was granted on July 4, 1946. American responsibilities in the Pacific, together with more than three years of war in that region, have given students in American universities and colleges a keen interest in the Pacific area.

A wealth of information has been compiled about the Pacific, but much of it is not readily available. It is in response to this need for text and reference books on the Pacific islands that over a dozen contributors have joined to prepare the *Geography of the Pacific.* The Pacific is so vast that it would be a huge task for any one individual to become so familiar with the entire area that he could be considered an authority of the whole; hence a division of the work has seemed to be the logical answer. All the authors of these regional studies have done field work in their areas, and most of these specialists have lived in the regions about which they write for periods of time varying from several months to many years.

The *Geography of the Pacific* deals with the mightiest of all oceans, its climates, currents, and features, together with the islands that rise above its surface and the people, resources, and industries found in these lands. Australia is included in the book, but the other continents are considered only as the terminals of the transpacific routes, as markets, as sources of immigrants, and as points of strategic or political interest. The geography of Asia is thoroughly covered by several books about that continent, and separate countries, like Japan, have also been adequately treated in other books; therefore that nation is omitted from the *Geography of the Pacific* although it is an island kingdom. An extensive literature on the Americas is also available. In contrast, source materials on the Pacific area are widely scattered, and many are scarce and inaccessible to both students and teachers. The need, therefore, for a comprehensive book dealing with the Pacific geography is great.

Besides geographers, the contributors to the *Geography of the Pacific* include anthropologists and area specialists. Several are members of the college and university faculties; others are connected with the Bernice P. Bishop Museum in Honolulu or with government agencies. A majority of these men were in the service of the United States during the Second World War in some capacity that dealt with the Pacific. Many have recently completed concentrated research within the islands they describe.

The book begins with a description of the geographic setting of the Pacific, followed by discussions of the native peoples and the exploration and settlement of the Pacific lands in historic times. The environment of the islands of the Pacific and the continent of Australia are described also, and there are descriptions of the human, economic, and political geography. The closing chapter of the book deals with the trade routes, local problems, and possible future of the Pacific lands and peoples.

Otis W. Freeman, Editor

January, 1951
Cheney, Washington

Acknowledgments

CREDIT FOR ASSISTANCE RENDERED SHOULD BE GIVEN TO MANY INDIVIDUALS, government agencies, institutions, and corporations. Among the individuals are Professor Harold S. Palmer, geologist, and Professor Harold St. John, botanist, both of the University of Hawaii, who critically read Chapter 1; Dr. Kenneth P. Emory, anthropologist of the Bernice P. Bishop Museum and University of Hawaii, who critically read Chapter 13 (Eastern Polynesia); and Professor S. S. Visher of Indiana University, who contributed the discussion on tropical cyclones.

Photographs have been secured from a variety of sources, and credit is given with the illustrations. Many individuals helped with the cartographic work, including Douglas Carter, Curtis A. Manchester, Jr., Edwin H. Bryan, Jr., D. W. Burgess, Jr., and John Richardson.

O. W. F.

Contents

xi

The Ocean

Roll on, thou deep and dark blue Ocean, roll!
Ten thousand fleets sweep over thee in vain;
Man marks the earth with ruin, his control
Stops with the shore; upon the watery plain
The wrecks are all thy deed, nor doth remain
A shadow of man's ravage, save his own,
When, for a moment, like a drop of rain,
He sinks into thy depths with bubbling groan,
Without a grave, unknell'd, uncoffin'd, and unknown.

.   .   .   .   .

Thou glorious mirror, where the Almighty's form
Glasses itself in tempests; in all time,
Calm or convulsed,—in breeze, or gale, or storm,
Icing the pole, or in the torrid clime
Dark-heaving;—boundless, endless, and sublime—
The image of Eternity,—the throne
Of the Invisible; even from out thy slime
The monsters of the deep are made; each zone
Obeys thee; thou goest forth, dread, fathomless, alone.

LORD BYRON

I

Geographic Setting of the Pacific

OTIS W. FREEMAN

THE PACIFIC IS THE BIGGEST AND DEEPEST OCEAN OF THE WORLD, AND the largest single earth feature. Most regional studies are devoted to continents on which the water area is small and the land is all important, but the geography of the Pacific is concerned with a huge water area in which the amount of land is comparatively small.

Many scientific expeditions, casual navigators, and individuals have contributed to man's knowledge of the Pacific Ocean. Before the dawn of history rugged "Vikings of the Sunrise," as they have been aptly named by Sir Peter Buck, made long voyages on the Pacific Ocean and discovered and peopled most of the islands, no matter how distant. Centuries later came the Europeans—Balboa, Magellan, Mendaña, Quiros, Torres, Tasman, Cook, Vancouver, Bering, and Bougainville—and in the nineteenth century there were many Americans, most prominent of whom was Wilkes. The names of ships used on expeditions, for example, the *Endeavour, Discovery, Beagle, Challenger,* and *Albatross,* have become romantic words and symbols of scientific discoveries. Peculiarities of the native plants and animals and their distribution, the curious islands called atolls, the origin of the deeps and submarine canyons, and other problems associated with the Pacific have been challenges to the ability of scientists to formulate satisfactory explanations for the occurrences and the phenomena.

The Second World War introduced the Pacific to many Americans. The end of the war left the United States with many new responsibilities in the Pacific and with possible expansion of trade and investments. All these factors make for continued interest in the area and have increased the demand for information about it.

DIMENSIONS

The Pacific Ocean covers more than one-third of the surface of the globe. This area is greater than all the land above sea level on the

1

earth.   The northernmost edge of the Pacific is at Bering Strait, which
is 56 miles wide and of rather shallow water, the maximum depth being
about 300 feet; and here the boundary line between Asia and North
America runs between the two Diomede Islands located near the middle of Bering Strait.   The eastern border of the Pacific is the coast of
the Americas, and the western follows the shorelines of the Asiatic
mainland, Indonesia, New Guinea, and Australia.   Authorities differ
regarding the southern limits of the Pacific Ocean.   Some take the
latitude of 40° south; others include the Southern Ocean to the Antarctic Circle (latitude 66½° south) between the longitude of Southeast Cape on Tasmania and the longitude of Cape Horn.   The concept of the southern limit as the Antarctic Circle will be followed in
this book.   Within the boundaries given, the Pacific Ocean encompasses 68,634,000 square miles, inclusive of the seas adjacent.   Stopping at latitude 40° south would give an area of 55,624,000 square
miles to the Pacific Ocean.   This greatest of all seas measures 10,000
land miles across along the equator and about 12,500 miles, half the
distance around the earth, from Panama to the Malay Peninsula.   The
ocean extends 9300 land miles from Bering Strait to the Antarctic
Circle, or, if latitude 40° south is considered the southern boundary,
the north-south distance becomes 7350 miles.   One of the important
geographic factors in the Pacific is the great distances involved.   Distance affects the migrations and activities of man as well as limits the
spread of plants and animals.

The average depth of the Pacific Ocean is about 14,000 feet, with
an extreme depth of approximately 35,400 feet between Guam and
Mindanao.

The area of those portions of the continents that drain into the
Pacific is estimated at 7,500,000 square miles, only a quarter of the area
that is tributary to the Atlantic Ocean.

THE COASTS

In shape the Pacific Ocean is roughly triangular with its apex at
Bering Strait.   It is enclosed by mountain barriers studded with
scores of active volcanoes arranged in a horseshoe loop around the
basin.   The coasts of the western Americas are generally regular, except those of southern Chile and of North America from Puget Sound
to Alaska, which being drowned have numerous inlets, protected channels, and coastal islands.   The Gulf of California is the largest fringing sea.   On the north the arc of the Aleutian Islands extends nearly
to Siberia and bounds Bering Sea on the south.   In general the mountains on the mainland of eastern Asia are lower than those of the

Americas, and extensive fluvial plains lie between mountainous regions that have rolling, rather than rugged, surfaces. Major islands rise off this western shore of the Pacific and extend from the Kamchatka Peninsula north and northeast of Australia. Here they join with the island arcs of Indonesia, which are formed by crustal folds entering the region from the Malay Peninsula. All the chief islands contain sedimentary, metamorphic, and deep-seated igneous rocks considered to have originated on Continental land masses, in contrast to the lavas and reef limestones found on the remote oceanic islands. Between the islands and the mainland, or amidst the islands themselves, are a series of fringing and semi-enclosed seas, chief of which are Okhotsk, Japan, Yellow, East China, South China, several seas within and adjoining the East Indies, and the Coral Sea. Festoons of islands, which surmount partially submerged mountain ridges, continue into the western and southern Pacific Ocean far beyond the major groups. The trend of the last two arcs in the southwest Pacific is towards the bifurcation of the North Island of New Zealand, and the uplift that continues into South Island is the last of the big mountain arcs toward the south.

Submarine canyons, which resemble extensions of river systems, are located off the shores of California, Washington, and part of eastern Asia. Geologists are much interested in how they originated, but no proposed theory to account for the features has yet received wide acceptance.

Tides are a factor affecting the use of harbors by shipping. Some coasts show a large range between high and low tides, notably the coast of Korea, where tides range between 15 and 30 feet at different stations, and the coast of Alaska, on which tides of 45 feet have been recorded at Cook's Inlet and 30 feet at Skagway. Most of the islands in the central Pacific have only a small tidal range; for example, at Midway the tide shows only an 11-inch range.

THE OCEAN FLOOR

The floor of the Pacific Ocean is flat over vast areas, but there are many submarine cones or seamounts (guyots) besides platforms and ridges, some of which are capped with islands, especially towards the north and west margins of the basin. For convenience of description, the Pacific Ocean can be divided into an eastern and a western portion along the meridian of longitude 150° west.

The eastern Pacific, as thus defined, is nearly devoid of islands except near the margins of the Americas, and the major portion has a fairly uniform depth of nearly 18,000 feet. A broad, ill-defined submarine platform of less depth (about 13,000 feet), called the Albatross Plateau, is located west of South America, and branches of the platform extend north toward Costa Rica, west to the Tuamotu Archipelago and Marquesas Islands, and southward in the direction of Antarctica. Above the platform rise lonely Easter Island and Sala-y-Gomez. Closer to Chile is the Juan Fernandez group, and to the north are the Galapagos Islands, with Cocos Island rising from the branch that

FIGURE 1.   Birth of an island, located 200 miles south of Tokyo at 31° 58.8′ north latitude and 139° 57.75′ east longitude.   When this volcanic eruption occurred in 1946 the steam and sulfur fumes rose hundreds of feet into the air.   The island later disappeared, but other eruptions may make a permanent island.   Official U.S. Navy photograph.

approaches Costa Rica.   These volcanic islands are located near the margins of the Albatross Plateau and presumably are situated along fracture lines, with the Galapagos and Marquesas groups at the intersection of major fissures at opposite ends of the platform.

The western Pacific is characterized by multitudinous islands, generally arranged along arcs.   Typically the islands rise from submarine platforms, some of which are probably constructed by outpourings of lava from rifts on the flat ocean floor and others from deformation of the earth's crust. Many islands represent the summits of mountain ranges, most of which are below sea level. Some volcanic islands have been built up from extreme ocean depths and without apparent help from crustal uplifts. For example, Mauna Kea (13,784 feet) and Mauna Loa (13,679 feet) on the island of Hawaii rise, in a distance of 50 miles, from ocean depths of 18,000 feet, making them higher mountains from the sea bottom than Mount Everest is above sea level. Within the tropical Pacific are thousands of coral islands and reefs, which are sometimes interspersed with those of volcanic origin and sometimes separated by hundreds of miles from any neighbor.

FIGURE 2. Summit of Mauna Loa, Hawaii, showing the summit crater of caldera type called Mokuwoweo, in winter after a snowstorm. Photograph, U.S. Navy.

THE DEEPS

The ocean floor near the margins of the Pacific, especially in its western portion, contains many elongated troughs, some of which are the deepest known on the earth. These deeps, or foredeeps, are parallel to mountain uplifts or to the platforms that support curving rows of islands, and apparently have resulted from the subsidence of the foreland beneath the folded mountains. A deep, to be called such, must exceed 18,000 feet in depth. Important deeps (Fig. 7) include Kurile-Japanese (Tuscarora Deep, 32,644 feet deep); Ryukyu (24,479 feet) east of the islands of that name and east of the Bonins (Ramapo

Deep, 34,626 feet); Philippine Trench east of north Mindanao (Mindanao Deep has the greatest depth known in any ocean, 35,410 feet); deeps east of Palau (26,700 feet), east of Yap (24,732 feet), southeast of Guam (Nero Deep, 32,177 feet), and between Wake and Midway (Bailey Deep, 20,591 feet); Bougainville Trench south of New Britain (Planet Deep, 30,865 feet); west of the New Hebrides (24,837 feet); and the Kermadec-Tonga Trench (Aldrich Deep, 30,930 feet, and Tonga, 30,132 feet) between New Zealand and Samoa. In the north Pacific the greatest depth is found in the Aleutian Deep (25,194 feet), southwest of Attu; and in the southeast Pacific is the Atacama Trench (24,216 feet deep) off the coast of Peru and Chile. The combined areas of great depth in the Pacific are small. All the deeps are elongated and lie parallel either to present coasts and mountains or to the coasts of earlier continents that have largely sunk beneath the sea. The central floor of the Pacific is only about half as deep as the troughs around its margin.

DIVISIONS OF THE PACIFIC

For convenience of description, that part of the Pacific between the tropics of Cancer and Capricorn will be called central Pacific, the area to the north being known as north Pacific, and that south of the tropic of Capricorn, the south Pacific. However, the equator is used to divide the Pacific area into north Pacific and south Pacific by the International Hydrographic Bureau. As previously mentioned, the meridian of 150° west divides the eastern from the western Pacific.

The term *South Sea* has been loosely used, often for the Pacific south of the equator, but it originated with the Spaniard Balboa, who named the Pacific Ocean at Panama "South Sea." For many years South Sea continued to be applied to anything south of the sailing route followed by the galleons on their voyage from Manila to Acapulco, Mexico. This route passed north of Hawaii in order to avoid the northeast trades and to take advantage of the prevailing westerly winds.

The international date line coincides with the 180° meridian, except for zigzags to give the same date to politically related areas a little distance on either side.

For descriptive purposes the customary divisions of the Pacific islands, including the waters around them, are Melanesia, Micronesia, and Polynesia (see Frontispiece). These names are based on the character of the islands or their native peoples. Melanesia (black islands), named from the complexion of its natives, includes the islands south of the equator and north and northeast of Australia, including New Guinea, the Bismarck Archipelago, and the Solomon, New Hebrides, Admiralty, Santa Cruz, New Caledonia, Loyalty, and Fiji islands. Micronesia (little islands) includes the Marianas, Caroline, Palau, Yap, Marshall, and Gilbert islands. Polynesia (many islands) is a huge triangular area, 5000 miles from north to south and 400 miles from east to west. It extends from Hawaii on the north to New Zealand on the southwest and Easter Island on the southeast. It includes the Marquesas, Tuamotu, Society, Samoa, Tonga, Cook, and other islands and groups. The natives of Fiji are of the Melanesian stock but possess much Polynesian culture.

Oceania commonly refers to the Pacific islands, including New Guinea, and some authorities would include and some exclude Australia and the East Indies.

CLIMATE

The climates of the Pacific Ocean area are responsible for many of the differences in crops, products exported, and manner of life of the people on the various islands and coasts. The climates are primarily those to be expected for the latitudinal spread of the Pacific, with modifications mainly resulting from the distribution of land and water and the altitude of the islands. The huge size and currents are other factors affecting climates of the Pacific.

THE WIND BELTS

The doldrums or belt of equatorial calms is near the equator, followed in order by the trade winds, horse latitudes, and prevailing westerlies in both hemispheres going away from the equator. The whole system of wind belts shifts north in the northern summer and south in the southern summer (northern winter). In the western Pacific towards southeast Asia the monsoon winds are in control, and the normal types of wind for the latitudes appear only for a short time during the spring and fall months.

TROPICAL WINDS AND CLIMATES

The *doldrums* coincide with the heat equator that receives the maximum average insolation (heat from the sun). This results in an expansion of the air and the development of a low pressure belt in the doldrums, where the winds are usually light and variable. Winds blow towards the equatorial calms from regions of higher pressure in both the north and the south Pacific, and by the effect of the earth's

rotation are deflected to the right in the northern hemisphere to become the northeast trades, and to the left in the southern hemisphere to
become the southeast trades. The expansion of the rising air in the
doldrums causes condensation of moisture typically associated with
local thunderstorms, which in the western Pacific supply abundant
rainfall. Mean annual temperatures are close to 80° F, with slight
variation between the coldest and warmest month and with only
about 10° F range between the temperatures of day and of night.
This everlasting sameness of weather—frequent showers and even
temperatures—is a chief characteristic of doldrums climate.

The doldrums in the eastern Pacific are nearly always north
of the equator, with the southeast trade wind blowing beyond the
equator the entire year but to a less extent in winter than in summer
of the northern hemisphere. The southeast trades lie between about
latitude 25° south and a few degrees north. In contrast the northeast trades usually remain the entire year in the northern hemisphere,
on an average between the latitudes of 5° and 25° north. In the
eastern Pacific the belt of calms, or doldrums, is only 200 to 300 miles
wide, and the trade winds commonly blow parallel to each other from
the east. There is a minimum expansion and rising of the air, and
conditions for rainfall are therefore unfavorable, so that some islands
in this belt receive only 20 to 30 inches of rainfall annually. This
light rainfall has permitted the accumulation of guano there, which
would have been washed away if the customary heavy rainfall characteristic of most of the doldrums had occurred. Some of the dry,
equatorial islands are situated in the southeast trades for all the year,
or nearly all of it. This is also unfavorable for much rainfall.
Another possible factor promoting continued dryness is that dry islands
have few plants, and the bare sand and rock radiate much heat, causing
the relative humidity of the lower part of the air column above the
islands to be reduced and lessening the chance for rain. The air expands from the heat and as a consequence is cooled, but a cumulus
cloud forming high over the island rather than rain is the usual result.

In the western Pacific, as compared to the eastern Pacific, the zone
of the doldrums widens considerably because of the greater area of
land in the tropics to the west, which promotes more heating of the
atmosphere and development of local storms and condensation of
water vapor. In the Australian area the doldrums shift south of the
equator during the southern summer (December to February).

The *trade winds*, whether northeast or southeast, are not constant
in physical characteristics but may vary in temperature, velocity,
humidity, and density. Then instead of the two trade winds blending

together to form the doldrums, the trade wind having the colder and denser mass underrides the warmer, lighter, and usually more humid mass of trade-wind air and forces it to rise, with resulting cooling and condensation. Frequently weak lows or cyclones develop that may furnish heavy precipitation.   Under these conditions the doldrums are absent.   The junction of the trade winds, whether or not there are

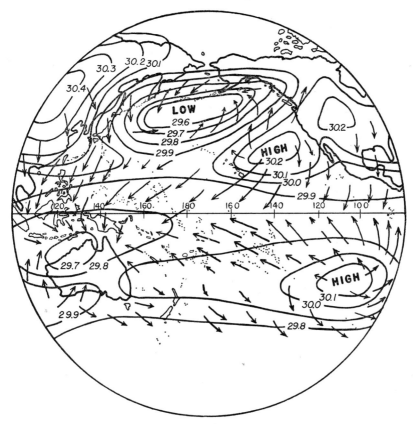

FIGURE 3.   Pressure and winds over the Pacific Ocean in January.

doldrums present, is called the *intertropical front.* In the summer the intertropical front may be latitude 10° or 12° north in the western Pacific.

The southeast trades are strongest in winter in the southern hemisphere and tend to be light and variable in summer from the Tuamotus westward to Australia.

In both the trade-wind belts temperatures show small range through-

out the year and are usually between 70° and 80° F. The rainfall
is light (under 30 inches annually) and variable over the oceans and
on low islands but is very heavy on the windward side of high islands,
declining to a small amount on the leeward side of mountain barriers.

High-pressure areas or anticyclones are features of the eastern
Pacific between approximately the latitudes of 20° to 40°, and these

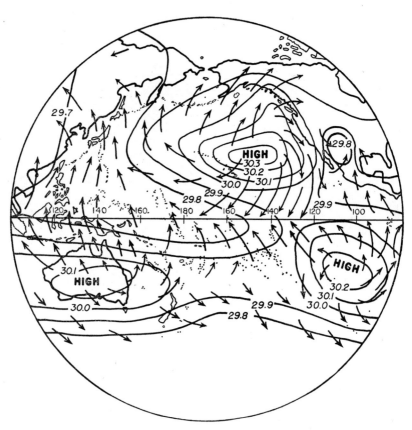

FIGURE 4.   Pressure and winds over the Pacific Ocean in July.

areas or cells of dense, descending air help control the weather and
circulation of the winds. The generally fair weather in these highs,
sometimes called the horse latitudes, is favorable for the operation of
aircraft as is also the steady wind spiraling outwards from the anticyclones. The trade winds blow from these subtropical highs towards the intertropical front.

Monsoons. The monsoons, with their annual reversal of winds, from the ocean to the land in summer and from the land to the ocean in winter, dominate the climate of the north Pacific on the west as far north as southern Japan and Korea.

Differences in the rate of heating and cooling between the oceans and the big continent of Asia account for the monsoon winds. On Asia in summer the pressure is low and in winter high, because land heats faster and cools quicker than water, and the pressure of the air is responsive to the heat balance. In summer, because the pressure is high over the cooler ocean and low over the hot land, the surface winds blow towards Asia. In the Indian Ocean and sometimes in the far-western Pacific, the intertropical front disappears or only small patches of it remain, and the southeast trade wind continues across the equator and joins other masses of air to form the summer monsoon.[1]

North of the equator, the southeast trade wind, or monsoon, is deflected to the right and becomes a southwest monsoon in Borneo and the Philippines. On approaching Asia, however, it is deflected again and pours on to the continent towards the low pressure in the interior as a southeast wind. In winter the monsoons do not extend far out to sea, and the intertropical front persists in the Indian Ocean and into the Australian sector. At this season, December to March, Australia is hot when Asia is cool, and the winter monsoon continues across Indonesia as a northwest wind, bringing precipitation to northern Australia, New Guinea, and Indonesia from the tropical seas to the north. In these same land areas the monsoon from April to October comes in general from the east and is relatively dry. For several weeks in the spring and fall the northeast trades blow from the western Pacific sector southeast of Asia. The winds of these transition seasons are usually weak and variable, although local thunderstorms and typhoons may occur that have winds of high velocity.

Some island groups towards the west in the central Pacific have hot temperatures and abundant precipitation with no particular rainy season, but in the regions dominated by the monsoons the maximum rainfall comes in summer. The exception to this generalization occurs when the winter monsoon has blown across a wide sea against a mountainous coast, resulting in winter rainfall. Examples are portions of the eastern and northern Philippines, the coast of Indo-China, and as mentioned previously Indonesia and New Guinea. Japan receives monsoonic rains in summer, but its winter rainfall is related mostly to cyclonic storms in the prevailing westerlies.

[1] E. H. G. Dobby, "Winds and Fronts over Southern Asia," *Geogr. Rev.*, Vol. 35, pp. 204–218, April, 1945. He describes conditions well but avoids using the word monsoon.

Temperature and Rainfall. The Pacific Ocean largely controls the temperature of the isolated islands and windward coasts, giving to both of them the maritime type of climate with small annual and diurnal range of temperature. When invaded by continental air masses, the ocean soon modifies their low temperature and low relative humidity, so that any air masses, whether coming from the tropics or from the polar regions, become filled with moisture after crossing the ocean and supply most of the rain that falls on the continents. The circulation of ocean water, to be described later, modifies the climate over the surface of the sea and that of adjacent coasts, especially those in a windward location. East coasts in the prevailing westerlies partake of the continental climates, having large ranges of temperature. The contrast between San Francisco, which has a 10° F range between the coldest and warmest month, and Tokyo in the same latitude with a 40° F range is striking in this respect. On an average the temperature of the ocean drops about ½° F for each degree of latitude. Mean air temperatures closely follow those of the ocean surface, and the annual range is around 10° F, which is much less than on the continents.

Most tropical Pacific islands have rather uniform warm temperatures between 70° and a little over 80° F with a daily range of 9° to 16° F and a mean annual range of 1° to 9°, the least range being close to the equator. Surface temperatures of the equatorial western Pacific Ocean are close to 82° or 83° F throughout the year; in the eastern Pacific, February temperatures along the equator are 75° to 77° F, and in August the surface temperature of the ocean at the Galapagos Islands is 66° to 68° F, increasing rapidly northward and less rapidly westward. This coolness results from the cold Peru or Humboldt Current.

Rainfall in the tropical Pacific is highly variable both daily, seasonally, and annually. The maximum amount occurs on the windward side of high mountains in the trades and monsoon winds—the leeward slopes being dry. In the tropical eastern Pacific the rainfall is more associated with the trades and in the Western Pacific with the monsoons. Because of the seasonal shifting of the intertropical front, the period of maximum rainfall in Micronesia and most other islands north of the equator is in the summer and early fall (July to October), and south of the equator between November and April, which is summertime in that hemisphere. The rainfall is light on low islands that in the trade winds the year around. Islands like Hawaii, which are located near the edge of the tropics, may have their maximum rainfall in the winter because of the precipitation accompanying cyclonic disturbances that affect their latitudes.

In the doldrums the relative humidity is nearly always high, which makes the heat there more noticeable. In the monsoon regions the relative humidity in summer is high (80 to 90 per cent) and in winter low. In the zone of the trade winds the relative humidity at sea level is usually lower than in the doldrums.

Tropical cyclones or typhoons are born in the hot tropics where air is rising by convection, but the fundamental cause that starts the winds in motion has not been definitely determined. Once well started, a hurricane is dragged along by the upper winds like a whirlpool in a stream, and continues in force over the tropical waters, but the storm disintegrates from loss of energy when it meets land or a mass of cold air.

TROPICAL CYCLONES OF THE PACIFIC*

More than 130 tropical cyclones occur each average year somewhere within the tropical and subtropical parts of the Pacific Ocean. Collectively they affect appreciably much of this vast region and its borders. Although in a single year only a small percentage of the total area is notably damaged by storms, nevertheless over a period of years the damage is widespread. Moreover, tropical cyclones significantly affect a much larger area than is damaged. A careful consideration of the evidence justifies the conclusion that most of the people of this vast region are at least appreciably influenced by tropical cyclones, some of them quite frequently.

The accompanying generalized map (Fig. 5) shows the general distribution of severe tropical cyclones in this region. Table 1 presents a summary of average frequency in certain areas.

Tropical cyclones vary widely in strength and in other respects. The severe storms that occur in the Far East are now generally called typhoons; similar storms are known as hurricanes in the south Pacific and in the eastern Pacific (and also in the Atlantic and Indian oceans).

Although the destruction caused by severe typhoons and hurricanes often is terrible, tropical cyclones always benefit a much wider belt than they devastate. They do this chiefly by bringing rainfall to large parts of the tropics that otherwise would be too dry. They also bring advantageous weather changes. Relatively few tropical cyclones are notably destructive; the weaker ones usually do little harm and much good. Distant or incipient cyclones set up air currents that induce

* This section on tropical cyclones was written by Stephen S. Visher, professor of geography at Indiana University, author of "Tropical Cyclones of the Pacific," *Bulletin* 20 of the Bernice P. Bishop Museum of Honolulu, published in 1925 and long out of print. This bulletin contains numerous details of occurrence and effects of these tropical storms.

convectional overturning, giving rise to thunderstorms and other rain-fall. Much, if not most, of the rainfall of the tropical and subtropical belt of the Pacific is induced by cyclonic disturbances, often distant or weak.

Tropical cyclones are whirling storms that vary in intensity from mild disturbances to violent hurricanes. They average about 300

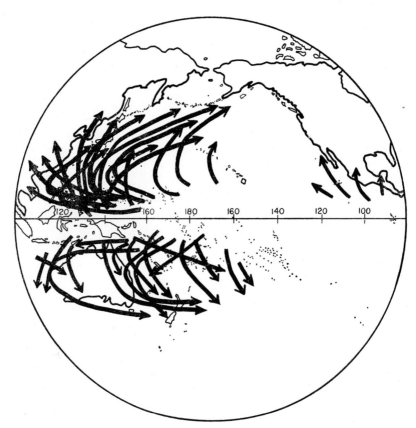

FIGURE 5.   Paths of hurricanes in the Pacific.

miles across, but many are only a score or twoscore miles wide and some are more than 1000 miles across in the tropics and 1500 after leaving the tropics. They develop chiefly in latitudes 10 to 20° and travel generally roughly westerly in the tropics, pushed by the trade winds. They also commonly move into progressively higher latitudes until they die away or leave the tropics. If they reach mid-latitudes, they generally slowly recurve and are carried eastward by the prevailing westerlies, and then are called lows. Most tropical cyclones travel rather slowly, generally averaging only about 10 miles an hour, but sometimes only a third that fast and sometimes four times that fast. Commonly they gain speed as they progress, except when recurving, when they may move very slowly.

The winds that spiral around the center, however, have velocities commonly ranging from about 15 to more than 75 miles per hour. A few have had measured velocities of about 150 miles an hour. The destructiveness caused by the stronger winds is due partly to their sudden variations in velocity and direction. The zone of greatest wind destruction is usually only 10 to 30 miles wide, that passed over by the "eye of the storm."

Typhoons and hurricanes are often destructive in the Pacific because of the strength of their winds. Upon the land the wind may damage or even demolish houses, break off palm and other trees, shred the leaves of the banana, plantain, and other large-leaved plants, and break off branches of many trees. Fruit-laden trees are likely to have much of their fruit shaken off. The damage done in breaking branches is increased by fungus infections that commonly develop at the wounds. When even twigs of the rubber tree and certain other trees are broken, "bleeding" commonly occurs, seriously injuring the tree. The damage that the wind does is increased by flying objects; for example, the sheet-iron "tin" roofs of houses frequently whirl through the air, sometimes affording veritable swords of disaster. Tornadoes occasionally develop in hurricanes, adding to the destruction caused by the wind. Severe hurricane damage to buildings is so common that illustrations are hardly necessary. Part of the damage done by gales is indirect, especially by rain being driven horizontally into buildings.

Strong winds over the water often produce high and tumultuous waves. There are many records of much damage done to ships and on land by storm waves, some of which attain great heights. For example, numerous low islands have had waves sweep across them, carrying away much of what had been on their surface and moving large blocks of coral. One island in which the highest land was 46 feet above mean sea level was entirely covered over, as was shown by the scouring away of the soil and other objects. There are records that the only human survivors from hurricanes on some low islands were persons who climbed trees and tied themselves thereto.

Most tropical cyclones cause torrential rainfalls. Indeed the amounts of rain occasionally received seem almost incredible to most citizens of the United States, who are accustomed to annual totals of 25 to 50 inches. Tropical cyclones in the Pacific region often cause falls of 10 inches of rain within 24 hours. Occasionally more than 20 inches falls within 24 hours, a considerable share of it within a few hours; for example, 25.5 inches fell at Haiku on Oahu on January 16, 1949. There are a number of records within the Pacific region of 30 inches or more in 24 hours; one record from Queensland, Australia, of 63 inches in 3 days and one from the Philippines is of 88 inches in 4 days. It is obvious that torrential rainfalls of large proportions cause much damage not only to cultivated land, roads, bridges, buildings, and other structures but also by drownings.

TABLE 1

FREQUENCIES OF TROPICAL CYCLONES

Average Annual Numbers	*Hurricanes*	*Gales*	*Lows*
Western north Pacific (110° E to 140° E)	10	20	30
Central north Pacific (140° E to 140° W)	2	4	7
Eastern north Pacific (east of 140° W)	3	3	8
Australia and coastal seas (110° E to 160° E)	5	8	10
South Pacific (160° E to 130° W)	5	8	10

Average Annual Number by Island Groups
(Many strike more than one group. Severe or fairly intense storms.)

Japan	10	Tonga	2
Formosa	5	Fiji	2
Philippines	9	New Hebrides	2
Northern East Indies	3	Solomons	0.2
Hawaii and vicinity	1	New Caledonia	3
Marianas	1	Cook	0.5
Marshalls	0.2	Tahiti	0.2
Samoa	2	Timor	0.2

Monthly Distribution, Average Number

	Jan.	Feb.	Mar.	Apr.	May	June	July	Aug.	Sept.	Oct.	Nov.	Dec.
Developing east of the Philippines (125° W to 160° E)	0.7	0.2	0.8	0.5	0.3	1.5	1.8	3.2	4.5	4	3	0.5
Developing north of the Philippines (18° N to 30° N)	1.5	3.5	4	3.7	1.7	2.5	0.7	1.5	0.3	1	1	0.7
Developing west of the Philippines	0.3	0.3	0.7	0.3	0.7	1	0.3	1	0.5	...	0.2	0.6
Developing in the central north Pacific	1.5	0.7	1.8	0.8	0.5	...	1.2	2.2	1.8	1.2	1	1
Developing in the south Pacific (percentage of annual total)	30	20	20	6	0.6	0.6	0.3	0.3	1	2	7	12

Although severe hurricanes are rare near the equator, numerous records of storms with their centers 5° to 8° from the equator are known. In the Gilbert Islands, only 3° N, all the houses but one were blown down on December 5, 1927; the wind had an estimated velocity of 80 to 100 miles per hour, blowing from the equator. On September 8, 1925, in latitude 4° 23′ N, 92° 13′ W, a ship encountered a southerly hurricane. The Marshall Islands (6° N) had a severe hurricane on June 30, 1905; the storm wave reached a height of 46 feet. Northern Borneo (6° N) was crossed by a very destructive typhoon on October 31, 1904. The waves dislodged rocks as much as 3 cubic meters in size. Ellice Islands (5½° to 11° S) experienced a very severe hurricane in February, 1891.

Conclusion. Tropical cyclones of varying intensity occur at least occasionally in almost all parts of the Pacific region. The records from various areas are few partly because the regions contain few persons qualified to record them properly. For example, large fractions of the Pacific Ocean have no islands and perhaps are seldom crossed by a ship. However, a considerable amount of evidence is presented in detail elsewhere that such storms occur.[2]

In addition to the storms that have violent winds, tropical cyclones are significant in numerous other ways, sometimes far from their centers. Examples are the rains that they cause, the "tidal waves" set in motion, and the stimulating effects of changes of weather; the effects elsewhere of remote disasters are also often appreciable.

CYCLONIC WEATHER AND CLIMATE OF THE PREVAILING WESTERLIES

The prevailing westerly winds blow in both the north and the south Pacific beyond the latitudes of about 30° in winter and 40° in summer of the respective hemispheres. The weather in the zones of prevailing westerlies is highly changeable because of the prevalence of cyclones, named for the spiraling of the winds around the storm center, counterclockwise in the northern and clockwise in the southern hemisphere. These extratropical disturbances are far more numerous than the tropical cyclones and are the chief cause for the characteristic variable weather, but the climate of the prevailing westerly zones in the Pacific is largely determined by the ocean itself. Between the latitudes of 30° and 60° the mean annual air temperatures range from about 65° F or 60° F to 30° F in both hemispheres, with summer temperatures

[2] See Visher's "Tropical Cyclones of the Pacific" (reference list at the end of this chapter) and references given there; *Hurricane Notes,* U.S. Weather Bureau, July, 1948, 210 pp. (mimeographed), and the numerous references to recent publications listed there; and I. R. Tannehill's *Hurricanes* (reference list at the end of the chapter).

about 10° F higher and winter temperatures 10° F colder. The moderate annual range shows the marine influence of the Pacific Ocean. The mean annual rainfall over the Pacific in the zone of the prevailing westerlies is not known but probably is between 30 and 50 inches, the least precipitation towards the trade winds and the greatest in higher latitudes.

Storms of the local thunderstorm type are rare in the westerly winds except in the interior of continents during the warm season.

Cyclones of the intermediate and high latitudes develop at the contact between cold air masses from polar regions and warm air masses from the tropics. This gives to the cyclones of these latitudes a cold and a warm front. In the northern hemisphere the warm front is to the east and south of the storm center, and the cold front to the west and north. In the southern hemisphere the warm front is to the east and north, and the cold front to the west and south. In both hemispheres the storms move in general to the eastward within the prevailing westerlies at a usual speed of several hundred miles a day. The diameter of a cyclone is from a few hundred to over 1000 miles, but the thickness is only 5 to 7 miles, the storm being restricted to the lower air (troposphere). Cyclones are most numerous and strongest during the winter in their respective hemispheres. These storms account for most of the rain and snow that falls over the ocean and along the coasts in the latitudes frequented by them.

The edge of the cold air of the Arctic region is called the polar front, and from this at intervals extend tongues of southward-moving cold air. Sooner or later the cold air mass comes in contact with northward-moving warm air, which is filled with moisture because it has come from the tropics where high temperatures have encouraged large evaporation of water. The cold air mass, being heavier than the warm moist air, underrides it like a wedge and forces the warm air mass to rise. Adiabatic cooling causes the moisture in the rising warm air mass to condense and makes rain or snow, depending upon the temperature. The condensation of moisture liberates energy, which helps to maintain the storm.

The warm air masses associated with cyclones bring abundant precipitation to the west coast of North America when the cyclones reach those shores. The cyclones that bring rain to California usually originate well south of the Aleutians and sometimes are tropical cyclones that have veered north. Cyclones may be severe enough to endanger shipping, especially along coasts, and damage trees and buildings but are seldom as terribly destructive as hurricanes. The cyclones of the southern hemisphere are severe in the "roaring forties" and generally less severe at latitude 30° south or less. The temperatures in cyclones that reach Australia and New Zealand in the southern hemisphere are seldom so cold as those in cyclones occurring in winter in similar latitudes over the continents of the northern hemisphere because of the vast southern ocean over which the air masses moved before reaching the southern lands.

CURRENTS

Movements of the ocean water include the tides, currents, and waves caused by the wind, and the slow creep of ocean water at different temperatures, in which the warmer rises and the colder sinks. These and other movements of ocean water affect man in many ways. They influence the climate, the distribution of plants and animals, especially those that are found on remote islands, the sea routes followed by man in his explorations and migrations, and the erosion and deposition of material along shorelines.

The relative temperatures of masses of ocean water affect the temperatures of the lower air, which in turn markedly affect atmospheric pressure. Cold surface water tends to be surmounted by high atmospheric pressure, and warm-water areas by lower atmospheric pressure. In turn the weather of continents, especially on their windward side, often depends on the great offshore areas of high and low air pressure that affect the temperature, precipitation, windiness, and cloudiness. Another weather factor is the temperature of the currents along windward coasts that have important influences upon land temperatures. Likewise the food supply for fish is related to the temperature and movements of ocean currents. Abundant food supplies for fish are found in cold currents, especially those in which water is welling up from the depths.

The surface circulation of ocean water depends mainly on prevailing winds, rotation of the earth, and location of the continents. Subsurface movements are slow and might best be referred to as creeping of the water. They result chiefly from heating of the water in the tropics and chilling in the polar regions. The chilled water creeps slowly toward the tropical regions where surface water is heated and moves on top of the ocean toward higher latitudes. Small differences in salinity result locally from large surface evaporation, heavy precipitation, and inflow of big rivers of fresh water.

The trade winds and prevailing westerlies start drifts of the ocean water that the rotation of the earth and north-south running coasts of the continents help to divert into gigantic eddies (Fig. 6). The drift in the north Pacific is divided at about the longitude of

Hawaii into two circulating drifts that have a clockwise motion, and of which the western is much the larger. The similar drift in the south Pacific moves counterclockwise. The water of the main North Pacific Drift comes chiefly from the westward-flowing North Equatorial Current. This current was set in motion by the northeast trade winds, which in low latitudes blow nearly from

FIGURE 6.   Currents in the Pacific.

an easterly direction. The water is warm because of being heated during its passage for 10,000 miles through the tropics; therefore, the western and northern parts of the North Pacific Drift have temperatures above normal for the latitudes. Where this warm water moves by Japan it is called *Kuroshio* or the Japan Current. Part of this water may reach the coast of North America. The North Pacific Drift carries enormous quantities of warm water from the tropics into the temperate zone. The influence of the South Pacific Drift is less obvious than its counterpart in the northern hemisphere partly because there are no large land masses to be affected by it in the colder latitudes. Most of Australia is closer to the equator than the United States or Japan. The current is also scattered by the many islands in the western Pacific through which it flows.

The trade winds cause an Equatorial Current to flow westward both north and south of the doldrums. When these two currents reach the islands north and northwest of New Guinea the water piles up. Part is deflected north to feed the North Pacific Drift, and part returns eastward through the calm doldrums to form the Equatorial Countercurrent. Both the Equatorial Current and the Equatorial Countercurrent are warm and steady in their flow.

In the great southern ocean that extends around the world without interference from continents a current develops that flows towards the east and is called the West Wind Drift. Along the west coast of South America is the cold Peru (Humboldt) Current, which flows north almost to the equator. This in part represents a portion of the West Wind Drift that has been deflected north, and in part a welling up of cold water from the depths when the southeast trades blow away the warm surface water. The south-flowing Kamchatka Current (Oyashio) off northeast Asia comes from the Bering Sea and hugs the east coast because of the deflective effect of the earth's rotation. Offshore winds and resulting welling up of cold water help account for its being a cold current. The southward-flowing California Current off the Pacific coast of the United States is another cold current whose temperature, low for the latitudes, results from offshore winds and the welling up of cold water after the warmer surface water is blown away. North of the North Pacific Drift is an eastward-flowing cold current called the Aleutian whose water is doubtless a mixture from the Kamchatka Current and the North Pacific Drift.

The location of the cold currents is of importance in that they contain abundant food for fish so that the best fishing grounds coincide with cold waters. The great fishing grounds of northeast Asia and northwest North America are examples of such association with regions of cold currents.

On desert islands in the Peru Current off the coast of Peru there live millions of sea birds that consume fish for food. The guano formed from bird waste is an excellent fertilizer. Each bird deposits several dollars' worth of guano per year, making the birds among the most valuable in the world. Occasionally it happens that the Peru Current is replaced by a southward-flowing warm current called El Niño (literally, *The Child*), because this warm current is likely to flow farthest south about Christmas time. When this happens the supply of fish food decreases and the fish migrate or die in vast numbers, and flood-producing rains may fall on the coastal desert because warm moist winds replace the usual cool, dry winds.

GEOLOGY

THE ANDESITE LINE AND ITS IMPLICATIONS

In the islands north and east of Australia, as far as the Carolines and Fiji, are occurrences of ancient metamorphic rocks like schist, gneiss, slate; sediments such as coal, clay, and sandstone; intrusive granite and siliceous eruptive rocks such as andesite, all of which are characteristic of continents. The volcanic islands in the north Pacific short of the Aleutians, and the eastern Pacific to the mainland, are predominantly composed of dark and heavy basalt, which is thought to underlie the broad, deep ocean there. The name *andesite line* or *sial line** (Fig. 7) has been given to the boundary between the islands whose volcanoes extrude andesite and other sial rocks, which are on the west side of the Pacific, and those in which basalt is the chief lava in the eastern and mid-Pacific. In the opinion of many geologists the andesite line represents the farthest outer limits of a continental mass that once extended into the Pacific area. This hypothetical southern continent is supposed to have connected Australia, New Zealand, Fiji, the Solomons, New Hebrides, New Caledonia, and New Guinea with Asia and may have begun sinking in the late Mesozoic era; possibly the process continued to affect the fragments of the continent through the Cenozoic to the present. The andesite line is the boundary between the continental blocks of Asia and Australia and the Pacific basin.

The andesite or sial line follows the eastern edge of New Zealand, Fiji, Solomons, Bismarck Archipelago, New Guinea, Yap, Marianas, Japan, Kamchatka, and south of the Aleutians. Authorities differ as to whether Truk is west or east of the sial line. The island arcs west of the andesite line, and the Pacific coast ranges of North and South America, show marked deformation of the bedrock, which is folded,

---

* Geologists use the word *sial* to describe rocks high in silica and aluminum that underlie the continents and are of less density than *sima,* which is high in magnesium and iron and is assumed to underlie ocean basins. Granite and andesite are sial rocks, basalt is an example of sima.

faulted, and frequently strongly metamorphosed. The real Pacific basin lies within the horseshoe rim of the mountain uplifts whose deformation began in the Tertiary and in some sections has continued to the present.

FIGURE 7. Seismic zones, andesite (sial) line, and deeps in the Pacific. Seismic and volcanic zones are dotted. The andesite line is a broken line. Principal deeps are black shaded: 1, Aleutian; 2, Kurile; 3, Japan (Ramapo); 4, Bonin; 5, Mariana; 6, Ryukyu; 7, Mindanao; 8, Tonga-Kermadec; 9, Bougainville–New Britain; 10, Atacama; 11, Byrd.

VOLCANIC AND SEISMIC BELTS

A belt of instability or zone of weakness of the earth's crust encompasses the Pacific Ocean on the east, north, and west (Fig. 7). Evidences for the unstable character of the Pacific rim are: frequent earthquakes; thousands of volcanoes, of which nearly 300 are still active, situated along rifts in the bedrock; fault scarps; raised beaches; and young, still rising mountains. The location of the fractures of the earth's crust determine the sites of volcanoes, which perch in rows upon the mountain ridges or more commonly along mountain arcs that are typically convex towards the Pacific Ocean basin. The volcanoes develop at appropriate vents through which the magma (molten rock) emerges, either quietly as lava flows or explosively as pumice, tuff, and ash (Fig. 1). The active and extinct volcanoes occur mainly along a horseshoe-shaped belt from Antarctica, where there is an active volcano, Mt. Erebus, along the west coast of the Americas, across to Asia through the Alaska Peninsula and Aleutian Islands, then south off the east coast of Asia via the Kamchatka Peninsula, Kurile Islands, Japan, Bonin Islands, and Philippines to the East Indies; and the belt continues through New Britain, the Solomons, New Hebrides, and Tonga Islands to New Zealand. This volcanic and seismic (earthquake) zone is generally on the ocean side of old lands, which presumably serve as the resistant masses against which the earth's forces mash, fold, and thrust over each other the beds of sediments and other weak rocks to form upheaved mountains. Frequently, in apparent compensation, on the basin side of the young mountain arcs are foredeeps or submarine trenches paralleling the ranges.

Submarine earthquakes are the cause for powerful tsunamis (seismic waves), which are popularly called *tidal waves* but have nothing to do with the tides. A series of earthquake waves, some of which may have been 100 feet high, caused by the eruption of Krakatoa volcano in the Strait of Sunda in 1883, drowned more than 30,000 people. Several in Japan have drowned thousands of persons and destroyed millions of dollars' worth of property. Tsunamis have ravaged portions of the coast of Chili. On April 1, 1946, a tsunami hit the coast of the Hawaiian Islands, killed more than 150 people, and did $25,000,000 worth of property damage, being especially destructive at Hilo and along the northern coasts of Oahu, Kauai, and Maui.

EROSION

No sooner has land appeared above the sea than it is attacked by agents of weathering and erosion, chief among which in the Pacific are the waves, beating rain, and running water. Wave erosion, by a process of undercutting the bedrock at sea level, accounts for the precipitous cliffs that rise from exposed windward shores of many high islands whose lava slopes once descended into the sea at moderate degrees. This process, called marine planation, produces submarine banks adjacent to the islands subject to attack by the sea, and if continued long enough the waves can completely truncate an island, leaving the bank as sole proof that land ever existed there.

Rapidity of erosion on the land above sea level depends chiefly on the character of the rock and soil, rate of weathering, degree of slope, amount of rainfall and the manner of its precipitation, and the cover of vegetation. New lava flows and cinder beds hardly allow erosion by running water because of their porosity, which permits rapid sinking of the rain. Only after soil has formed by weathering do surface streams develop and erosion by running water commence. Comparative resistance or weakness of the rocks to weathering and erosion, the location of joints (cracks) and faults (slips) in the bedrock, and the relative exposure of surfaces to rain, streams, and the waves account for the marked differences in stage and degree of erosion that occur in different locations on the same island or mountain.

One of the remarkable features of high islands are large, deep valleys with amphitheater heads that rise steeply from a nearly flat valley floor, for example, in Tahiti and in many of the Samoan, Marquesas, and Hawaiian islands (Fig. 107). Cliffs of amphitheater-headed valleys on Tahiti and windward Molokai are over 3000 feet high. Waterfalls are a characteristic of the amphitheater heads, and one in Typee Valley on Nukahiva, one of the Marquesas Islands, drops 2000 feet to the valley flat. According to Stearns,[3] the development of amphitheaterheaded valleys is determined by heavy rainfall and by the slope and structure of the bedrock with alternate resistant and nonresistant beds on which waterfalls can develop and by their headward erosion and coalescence help to form cliffs rising from a flat floor.

CONTINENTAL AND OCEANIC ISLANDS

The Pacific islands are often classified as continental and oceanic types, but scientists are not always agreed on the meaning of the terms. The geologists commonly consider an island to be continental if it contains rocks like gneiss, schist, or granite, believed to have been formed under conditions of great heat and pressure that occur only on the continents or along their borders. By this definition New Caledonia and the larger islands of Fiji would be continental islands because of the metamorphic or deep-seated igneous rocks found there. The oceanic islands would be those remote from continents and would be essentially of volcanic and coralline origin. The biologist bases his division of islands into continental and oceanic on floristic

[3] Harold L. Stearns, "Geology of the Hawaiian Islands," *Bull.* 8, pp. 7–8, Division of Hydrology, Territory of Hawaii, Honolulu, 1946.

and faunistic evidence. If floras and faunas closely resemble those of a near-by continent the island is called continental, whereas if there is dissimilarity in life forms, including some *endemic* (local) species on the island, it is considered oceanic.

CORAL ISLANDS

In the central and south Pacific there is a striking contrast between the "high" islands of volcanic origin and the "low" islands built of reef limestone. Special interest has been aroused by the curious coral atolls, which typically are of a ring shape around a central lagoon.

Reefs are made by different types of lime-secreting organisms, including: (1) polyps, which are the most important coral-forming animals and the chief source of coral reefs; (2) the soft corals, *Millepora* and *Heliopora*, which are varieties of hydroids; and (3) some of the bryozoans, which, although of small importance today, in rocks of the Paleozoic era made up more than half the volume of some limestone beds.

The remains of the lime-secreting animals are consolidated into rock by deposits made by organisms and chemical precipitation from solution. The chief living and growing part of a coral reef is the outer side, which is but a small part of the total volume of the reef. On the inner side of the reef there is relatively little living coral; rather there are likely to be many boulders broken off by waves from the outer edge. Erosion of material from the reef and its distribution seaward by the waves make a slope on which corals can establish themselves and grow, thereby extending the reef oceanward.

Coral reefs are called fringing when they form a platform, which may be hundreds of feet wide, between the shore and deep water. A barrier reef is at a distance from the shore, from which it is separated by a lagoon that may be several miles wide or only a few hundred feet. Barrier reefs are commonly interrupted by passages or channels, sometimes deep enough for boats. Sometimes fringing and barrier reefs grade together. The Great Barrier Reef of Australia extends more than 1200 miles along nearly the whole length of Queensland to reefs off the coast of New Guinea. The barrier reef of New Caledonia extends beyond the limits of the island and is almost 400 miles long.

Atolls vary greatly in size but are similar in their low elevation and narrow width of land surrounding a central lagoon. Many atolls are only a few miles in diameter, but a few are huge affairs as much as 50 to 100 miles across. Kwajalein in the Marshall Islands is about 90 miles long in a curving line by 20 miles wide. Atolls as small as 1 to 2 miles in diameter are rare. Atolls are rarely circular; generally one diameter is longer than another. For example, Canton Island (Fig. 9), one of the Phoenix Islands and used as an airbase, has a central lagoon that measures about 4 miles by 9 miles. Eniwetok in the Marshall group is a near circle with a diameter of 20 miles. Many atolls are highly irregular in shape; Butaritari in the Gilberts and Christmas in the Line Islands are examples. Jaluit, in the Marshalls, is triangular in shape and about 12 by 30 miles in dimensions. Very few atoll rings are unbroken. Most of the rings are composed of many *motus* (islets) connected by reefs, some of which are permanently submerged though others are submerged only at high tide. The majority of the motus are on the windward side of atolls. The land is everywhere narrow compared to the width of the lagoon—a few yards or hundreds of feet for width of the land compared to miles of lagoon water. Since the ground above sea level consists of narrow strips, the area of land in an atoll is inconsiderable compared with that of its lagoon. Manihiki, one of the Cook Islands, is a typical atoll with a lagoon about 5 miles across and has a land area of 2 square miles. Names are commonly given to the motus or fragmental islets composing an atoll as well as to the atoll itself. Wake Island has three islets: Wake, Wilkes, and Peale. Tarawa has eight islets, and Funafuti has a score or more of islets, each of them named, around its 10-by-15-mile lagoon.

Because of their low altitude the problem of drinking water is acute on atolls, and any ground water available is in scant supply and often brackish in quality. The potable water is merely a thin lens of reasonably fresh water floating on the denser salt water that impregnates the rock at and below sea level.

Numerous raised atoll islands are known. The central lagoon has disappeared from such islands, although it may be represented by a hollow, and there is a greater land area, deeper soil, more vegetation, and usually more adequate and fresher ground water than on an atoll of the same diameter. Makatea (Aurora) in the Tuamotus, Nauru, Ocean, Johnston, Baker, Howland, and Marcus are examples of such islands. Given the same rainfall, man finds living conditions much more favorable in raised islands than on atolls. Some atolls have been only partly raised, and in Wake a portion of the lagoon has survived. Mangaia, one of the Cook Islands, has a central hill of basalt surrounded by a cavernous terrace of raised coral reef.

Some high islands of volcanic or other origin contain limestone as the result of the raising of coral reefs—proof that the land has been elevated. Guam is an example.

Some authorities have applied the term *complex island* to types like

Truk in the Carolines in which volcanic islands rise from the lagoon inside the reefs and islets of an atoll rim, but others have called this type an *almost-atoll*.

THE ORIGIN OF ATOLLS

Authorities differ in their ideas about the origin of coral atolls. Among the leading theories is Charles Darwin's (Fig. 8). His theory

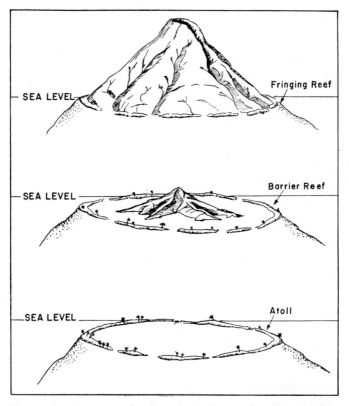

FIGURE 8. Stages in the formation of a coral atoll, according to Darwin's theory. Top, an island surrounded by a fringing reef. Middle, the island sinks and the fringing reef becomes a barrier reef. Bottom, the island has disappeared by sinking, and the reef has become an atoll with a lagoon occupying the site of the former high island.

supposes three stages. (1) The coral builds a fringing reef around a tropical high island, which if volcanic would customarily have an oval shape. (2) The island slowly sinks, and the coral reef grows upward as fast as the rate of sinking to form a barrier reef separated from the shore by a lagoon. (3) Continued subsidence of the island causes it to disappear by submergence, and the growth upward of the coral perpetuates the reef, which becomes an atoll with a lagoon occupying the former land area whose outline is reflected in the roughly oval rim of land. The late William Morris Davis was a strong supporter of Darwin's theory and pointed out, as Dana had previously done, that many islands surrounded by barrier reefs show

FIGURE 9.   Canton Island, a representative central Pacific atoll, seen from the air.   The dark ribbon, edged on both sides with white, is the fringing reef on the ocean side.   The narrow rim of land lies just within this.   The central lagoon appears dark, crossed by lines of coral reef.

drowning of the lower parts of valleys. This condition is best explained by submergence of the island. A boring at Funafuti found nothing but coral rock to depths of more than 1000 feet, which is below the limit of growth of reef corals and thus supports Darwin's theory of subsidence. In 1947 a drillhole on Bikini atoll was carried to a depth of 2556 feet, wholly in calcareous materials, some of which carried fossils of the Tertiary age. From geophysical evidence Ladd and Tracey[1] state that the depth to the basement on which Bikini is built would be about 8000 feet. If coral has grown to such a thick-

[1] H. S. Ladd and J. I. Tracey, *Science*, Vol. 107, pp. 51–54, Jan. 16, 1948.

ness as the area slowly sank, it appears that a profound sinking of the ocean floor has taken place in this part of the Pacific.

Examples of high islands with barrier reefs whose coastlines are embayed, possibly by subsidence, are New Caledonia and some of the Fiji, Society, and Cook islands. However, not all the Pacific area has sunk. Stearns found evidence of both rising and sinking in Hawaii, and Fiji has raised beaches and reefs.

Another theory, which received support from Alexander Agassiz, is that of Sir John Murray, who believed that coral grew upward from shallow submarine mounds or banks that were supposed to represent the accumulated debris or skeletons of lime-secreting organisms. The maximum growth would be on the outside of the reef, and the foundation on which the reef grows would in part be talus broken from the reef itself. Murray explained the central lagoon as formed largely by solution because the coral toward the center of the lagoon would lack food and die and the dead coral could be dissolved to form the lagoon. No change in sea level is necessary according to this theory. Murray suggested that around high islands the reefs grew outward from the shore on the talus and that the lagoons were formed by sea water dissolving the inner, dead portion of the reef. However, from studies of the Florida keys, Vaughn[5] concluded that lime deposition rather than solution was taking place and that, because of the absence of dissolved carbon dioxide in the sea water, solution of the coral limestone by virtue of free carbon dioxide would be impossible.

It has been suggested by Daly that during the glacial period the level of the sea was lowered when millions of cubic miles of ice were locked up on the land in the vast continental glaciers. The temperature of ocean water might then have been too low for coral to live in areas where it now flourishes, and without their protective coral reefs certain islands could be eroded away below sea level by the waves, especially since storms may have been more frequent and powerful in the tropics then than now. When the glaciers melted, the ocean rose perhaps about 200 feet, the banks were submerged more deeply, river mouths were drowned, and where islands had been truncated by marine erosion the corals were reestablished as the water became warm enough for them, and the coral reefs then grew upward from the banks. Daly considered the coral deposits to be merely a veneer on top of the eroded surface of other rocks, but the borings on Funafuti and Bikini do not support his hypothesis. On the other

[5] T. W. Vaughn, *Corals and the Formation of Coral Reefs*, Smithsonian Report for 1917, p. 225.

hand the extreme flatness of the floor of the lagoons is what would be expected from marine planation.

It seems probable that not all coral atolls are formed in the same way, and that at least some of the curious islands have been formed by other methods or combinations of them.

MINERAL RESOURCES

The geology of the past controls the distribution of the mineral deposits of the present. Veins and lodes of metals have been found only in association with rocks of continental origin, for example, granite and various metamorphic rocks that have been subjected to great heat and pressure and especially to the work of hot solutions. Recent lavas rarely contain workable deposits of metallic minerals. The continent of Australia, the islands of Indonesia, the Philippines, New Guinea and New Zealand, and the supposed fragments of a former continent, like New Caledonia, some of the Louisiade Archipelago, and part of the Fiji Islands possess metallic deposits. Coal and oil are associated only with sedimentary rocks. Excluding Japan and the Asiatic mainland, the coal so far mined has come principally from Australia and New Zealand, and the petroleum from Borneo, Java, and Sumatra.

The only valuable mineral sometimes found on coral islands is phosphate rock. Deposits of guano have been exploited on numerous low islands that were the breeding grounds for sea birds and where the light rainfall was insufficient to wash away the manure from which guano is formed. The phosphate rock is supposed to have been formed by the interaction between the lime of the coral bedrock and phosphoric acid leached from the guano. Commercial deposits of phosphate rock are worked extensively on Nauru, Ocean, and Christmas islands, all near the equator, which supply one-tenth of the world's demand for phosphate rock. Angaur Island in the Palaus, several islands in the western Carolines, and Makatea, in the Tuamotus north of the Society Islands, also mine phosphate rock.

Guano has come from scores of islands but is now largely exhausted in the mid-Pacific area. Under an old law, ship captains of the United States could claim sovereignty for their country over any unclaimed island valuable for guano. This law permitted a discoverer to mine guano with legal protection from others. Under this law about 70 islands were claimed for the United States between 1858 and 1880 and many were occupied for a time. Although claims to many lapsed through non-occupancy, title to Howland, Baker, Johnston, and Jarvis were secured in this way. Other nations had laws similar to our guano act, and some islands had several claimants, each of whom might put a different name on the map, which naturally led to confusion.

The soils developed in the Pacific islands depend on many factors, including the original soil materials, temperature, rainfall, drainage, slope, natural vegetation, and the kinds of bacteria and other organisms present. For example, soils recently formed from volcanic ash and those developed on the floodplains of streams are generally very fertile, but those developed on low-lying coral rock are likely to be very poor.

The volcanic islands have complex soil conditions because of differences in rainfall, temperature, plant life, rate of weathering, etc., with altitude and exposure to the winds. Under conditions of high temperatures and rainfall the parent lava rock weathers quite rapidly to depths of many feet, and the soil materials undergo changes, chief of which is laterization. In this process the soluble bases and silica in the soil are leached out, and the iron and aluminum compounds remain until by this concentration the soil chemicals become chiefly these. Lateritic soils are usually red in color from the increase and oxidation of the iron and are high in content of clay. However, the presence of much humus and the character of the chemical changes make the soil more porous to water than its content of clay would ordinarily indicate. On the well-drained lowlands and lower gentle slopes the products of weathering are removed in the order of their solubility; hence these soils may become in maturity generally deficient in nutrients and unbalanced in the elements present. The soils on the islands have seldom developed into true laterites, which may have low fertility, but they are called lateritic and possess moderate to high fertility. They are formed from rather recent lavas, and elements are still being liberated by the weathering of these rocks. On steep slopes erosion keeps pace with soil formation, and the soils are thin. Under tillage the original humus and soluble plant food are quickly exhausted by crops. Some foods grown on depleted soils are deficient in minerals needed by man, and those who consume the plant foods may suffer from malnutrition.

All the soils of coral islands have about the same character. Upon the sterile rock or sand are small amounts of humus and plant debris from decaying vegetation. But this layer is rarely over a few inches thick, its water-holding capacity is low, and frequent rains are necessary for sustained plant growth.   Soil fertility is low, and there may be deficiencies in soil elements.   The thinness of these soils and their excessive porosity to water are unfavorable to plants.   Gardens are possible only when the soil has been improved with plant trash and waste of all sorts.

ENVIRONMENT AND LIFE

Nearly every speck of land in the Pacific, no matter how isolated, has ultimately become a home for plants and animals.   The value to man of the Pacific islands is related to many natural factors, for example, size, relief features, soil, climate, and minerals; but among the leading factors of environment are the plants and animals that have been introduced, both by nature and by man himself.

The Pacific Ocean itself has many marine faunas and floras, which are adapted to different food supplies, temperatures, pressures, etc. Even the deposits made at great depths on the ocean floor are named from the relative abundance of certain organisms, many of which are microscopic in size.   The geologic history and the present distribution of life in the Pacific area are intimately related.

SPREAD OF LIFE IN THE PACIFIC

The geologic history of the Pacific area has to be largely worked out by inference, because exposures of bedrock above sea level are few compared with the vast extent of water.   The conclusions of geologists have been reached by studying the types and character of the rocks, surveying the relief features and depths of the ocean floor, and considering the evidence shown by fossils and the existing distribution of the flora and fauna.

It is generally agreed that in the past there were land links by which Indonesia and probably Australia and other adjacent islands were joined to Asia, and in addition a land connection existed to the north, probably at Bering Strait, which tied North America and Asia together for long periods.   Conversely, some present isthmuses were once covered by the sea; for example, several straits in the past divided central America into an archipelago.   At intervals there may have been land bridges from the supposed south Pacific continent to South America, possibly via Antarctica, over which primitive plants and animals may have migrated.

Without land connections, winds and currents are the principal means by which living forms reach islands.   Usually the number of species present in the flora and the fauna of remote islands is small compared to the number in mainland locations and in islands close to continents. Oceanic islands have no native mammals except bats that can fly, seals and the like that swim, and pigs, rats, and mice that intentionally or accidentally were introduced by man. Sea birds have wide distribution because of their powers of flight, but land birds, lizards, and snails have curious locations, apparently from some happening in the past. It is conceivable that great storms of strong upward draft and high, powerful winds may carry land birds, insects, seeds, and the eggs or very young of toads and small reptiles considerable distances. Small mammals and reptiles might survive by floating on logs drifting to a new island. Migratory birds may introduce plants by dropping seeds from fruit that they have eaten, and water fowl may carry spores and seeds of water plants in the mud sticking to their feet. However, the transportation of plants and animals from the continents over the wide ocean to the Pacific islands is difficult to account for by known means, and some scientists therefore fall back upon the possibility of land connections in the past. Most geologists, however, are skeptical of past land connections for oceanic islands that rise from great depths and are remote from continents. In this connection it should be remembered that numerous high islands have disappeared by erosion or been reduced to little atolls, and hence in the past organisms might not have had to migrate as long distances across the ocean as a cursory examination of the present map would seem to indicate as necessary.

The absence of large modern-type mammals from all the native fauna of the oceanic islands indicates that such islands either have never been connected with continents or have been separated at least from the early Tertiary when such forms originated. Australia has a heavy preponderance of primitive marsupials among its mammals, and New Zealand includes in its native fauna only lizards, birds, and aquatic mammals. Until trout were recently introduced, even the rivers of New Zealand lacked edible fish other than eels, which, being catadromous (descending rivers to spawn), migrate from their spawning grounds in the ocean. Judging from the animal life, Australia has been isolated from Asia since the Miocene period, and New Zealand much longer, probably from the late Mesozoic era.

DISPERSAL OF ISLAND LIFE

Various geographic factors affect the characteristics of organisms and the types of plants and animals that colonize islands. Some factors are subject to change, notably so in respect to land connections and sea barriers, and to some extent there is evidence of climatic modifications.

A moderate drop in sea level could bring about a great change in the geography of the distribution of land and water in the Pacific area. A lowering of the ocean by a few hundred feet would unite Australia and New Guinea, would join Java, Sumatra, and Borneo to Asia, and would make an isthmus of Bering Strait. Such drops in sea level occurred during the glacial period, and during that time plants and animals could migrate across what is now water. Australian plants and some animals invaded New Guinea, and Asiatic species spread into Indonesia. Celebes contains mostly representatives from Asia along with a few from Australia, showing that at intervals it has been connected with both continents.

Wallace's line, named after Alfred Russel Wallace, an English contemporary of Charles Darwin, separates, in general, Asiatic from Australian flora and fauna. It was originally drawn between Bali and Lombok and north between Borneo and Celebes (Fig. 137). Later studies by naturalists seem to show that the boundary between the zones in which Asiatic or Australian-Papuan life forms predominate should be farther east, and what is called *Weber's line* has been tentatively drawn starting on the north between Celebes, which has an estimated 20 to 40 per cent Papuan forms, and the northern Moluccas on the east, which possess 80 to 90 per cent Papuan elements. Southward the authorities have difficulty in deciding the exact location of Weber's line, but it is now generally placed to the east and south of Timor. Wallace's line is still recognized as a faunal boundary. Tigers, squirrels, and other mammals found in Bali are absent from Lombok, and the land birds differ greatly on opposite sides of the Lombok Strait. Borneo has a rich Asian fauna, but the Australian marsupial, phalanger, is found on Celebes. Probably the best way to look at the matter is to consider that the islands between Wallace's and Weber's lines represent a transition zone between Asiatic and Australian-Papuan faunas and floras since much of the evidence is contradictory. Farther east there are successively other "lines" that divide the Asian and Australian floras and faunas from the Oceanic ones.

Animals and plants that colonized oceanic islands have been subjected to varied environments, and the longer the elapsed time since their introduction, the more the local conditions bring about modifications in the flora and fauna. For example, on a high island, temperature, moisture, and soil conditions vary with the altitude and exposure to the winds from the ocean, and representatives of the same family, by adaptation to different local conditions, are modified into new species, each of which is best fitted to thrive in a certain environment. In general, oceanic islands have few families represented in the flora and the fauna but have many species in each family. Some of these species may be *endemic* (peculiar to one island only); for example, the species of land snails may vary from island to island and even from valley to valley on the same high island.

Insects are very numerous in the Pacific islands; it has been estimated that there are over 100,000 existing species. Malaria mosquitoes (*Anopheles*) are found in New Guinea, New Britain, the Solomons, New Hebrides, and some other places. They are absent from Fiji and Polynesia. Other species of mosquitoes transmit dengue fever and the trypanosomes that cause elephantiasis, and the yellow-fever mosquito (*Aedes aegypti*) is common in some islands although the disease has not been imported. In Melanesia and New Guinea burrowing mites cause scrub itch, and stinging flies, hornets, poisonous centipedes, and scorpions may make life miserable for human beings. On some islands, plant insect pests, some of which have been carelessly introduced by man, injure many planted crops and trees.

THE FLORA

There are numerous environments on the Pacific lands, each with its plant associations, that have become adapted to the natural conditions. Most widespread are the strandline or seashore association of trees, shrubs, vines, and herbs, some of which bear seeds or fruits capable of floating far in salt water without losing the power of germination. Other seeds have been carried by the wind and by birds. The strand flora occurs as a band along most shores and is the only type on low coral islands, but the density of the vegetation varies with the rainfall. For example, on rainy Palmyra Island it forms a jungle (Fig. 10), but on dry Canton Island there are only a few coconut trees and bushy thickets. Trees growing along coasts include the mangrove on the tide flats (Fig. 11) and on the drier land the coconut (mostly artificially planted), screw pine (*Pandanus tectorius*), ironwood or she-oak (*Casuarina equisetifolia*), India barringtonia (*Barringtonia asiatica*), Indian almond (*Terminalia catappa*), the primitive palmlike cycad (*Cycas circinalis*), the tree heliotrope (*Messerschmidia argentea*), and the linden hibiscus (*Hibiscus tiliaceus*). The nipa palm (*Nipa fruticans*) grows naturally only in the western Pacific. Other common plants are shrubs, especially the half-flower (*Scaevola frutescens*), creeping vines like the beach morning glory

(*Ipomoea pes-caprae*), and herbs. In all about fifty families are represented in the seashore flora, with the greatest number in the western Pacific and the fewest families on the more remote Oceanic islands. The paucity of the flora on low atolls is largely the result of there being only one environment. However, it is partly due to the salinity of the ground water and soil, which prevents the survival of any introduced plants except salt-tolerant ones. On the low islands

Figure 10. Vegetation on Washington atoll. Although growing on coral sand only a few feet above sea level, the heavy rainfall makes possible a luxuriant growth of ferns, herbs, and trees. Photograph, C. K. Wentworth. Courtesy of the Bernice P. Bishop Museum.

and strandline of the high islands the coconut is easily the most valuable plant to man.

The high islands possess several plant zones above that of the shoreline, which usually include valley bottoms and low coastal plains, rainforests, grassy uplands, semi-arid leeward slopes, and, if high enough, summit bogs and rocky peaks, each of which has plant associations adapted to the conditions. The high oceanic islands may have many endemic plants that have evolved under special conditions and never have spread from their place of origin. For example, 80 per cent of the 2500 species of flowering plants in New Caledonia and

68 per cent of the 1000 species of New Zealand are endemic. About half of some 9000 flowering plants on the continent of Australia are endemic.

The virgin rainforest has a great mixture of species with some huge, dominant trees with flaring buttressed trunks, many smaller trees barely reaching the branches of the big trees, and a ground growth of seedlings, palms, bamboo thickets, rattan vines, pandanus, various shrubs, tree ferns, and herbs. On the forest margins, and along the stream banks, are such dense screens of verdure that they are difficult to penetrate, but travel through the forest itself is somewhat easier. The forest floor is in twilight, and here only shade-tolerant ground

FIGURE 11. Mangroves on Uman, Truk group. Photograph, C. A. Manchester.

plants can grow well. There are many orchids and other epiphytes in the western Pacific area, but the orchids are few on the Oceanic islands. When cleared for primitive agriculture and then abandoned, a secondary forest springs up that is of jungle character. Repeated burnings of the forest may transform some areas to savannas covered with tall grasses. In the highest mountains the trees disappear at 8000 to 10,000 feet, and only grasses, stunted shrubs, and herbs continue to the summits or the snowline if such is present as on a few New Guinea peaks. It should be noted that much greater differences occur between the floras of the upper forests on the high islands than between the plants of the strandline, most of which are widely dispersed.

Birds, being capable of flight, comprise most of the vertebrate fauna on remote Pacific islands.   The sea birds are naturally quite similar throughout the tropical Pacific and are most numerous on uninhabited islands where they resort for breeding purposes.   Among the common sea birds are albatrosses, boobies, terns, petrels, gulls, shearwaters, and cormorants.   The migratory birds include ducks, golden plover, and the curlew.   Land birds are very abundant on the high islands of the western Pacific, where they include cockatoos, parrots, birds of paradise, pigeons, swallows, kingfishers, hornbills, honey suckers, etc.   In the central Pacific endemic species of land birds are fairly common. In both Australia and New Zealand are found species of flightless land birds, for example, the moa and kiwi of New Zealand and the emu and cassowary of Australia, a species of the cassowary also occurring in New Guinea.   Originally flightless rails of different species lived on Laysan Island and Wake Island; the Laysan species was introduced on Midway and survives there but is probably extinct in its native haunts.

The only native mammals outside of New Guinea and Australia are bats and rats.   Some land reptiles, mostly small lizards, are native to certain Oceanic islands, and a very few amphibians are found.   Large monitor lizards live on Komodo and a few other islands of the eastern Indies, and a good-sized species is found in New Guinea.   Snakes are common in New Guinea and include a few poisonous species. The big island also has crocodiles and the manatee, a harmless aquatic mammal.   Harmless snakes live in Samoa and Fiji, and snakes become more numerous in the Solomons and the Bismarck Archipelago.

Cattle, pigs, goats, deer, rabbits, mongooses, and rats have been introduced by man on some islands, and sometimes the newly introduced animals have become pests that have destroyed much of the native plant and bird life and may injure gardens and crops.

MARINE RESOURCES

Animals living on the sea bottom in shallow water and along the shore supply both food and commercial materials.   Invertebrates used for food in the Pacific include spiny lobsters or crayfish, crabs, shrimps, clams, oysters, prawns, and other shellfish.   The sea cucumber, an echinoderm, is dried, and under the name of trepang or bêche-de-mer is esteemed by the Chinese for making soup.   The roe of the spiny sea urchin is eaten as a delicacy by some people. Spiny lobsters are taken for South American markets in the Juan

Fernandez and Galapagos Islands. The king crab, true crabs, and shrimp are canned for market in Alaska. Crabs and shrimp are also marketed in quantity from the coasts of Korea, Japan, and Siberia. Clams, mussels, abalones, conchs, and periwinkles are used for food, and the canning of clams is important in the Pacific Northwest. The coconut crab is eaten by many tropical islanders. Oysters are grown for market in Puget Sound, Willapa Bay, Coos Bay, and Gray's Harbor in the Pacific Northwest, and in coastal waters of Japan and Australia. The octopus is relished by Japanese, Hawaiians, and many other peoples.

Seaweed is eaten by Japanese and Polynesians and also serves as fertilizer and for other purposes. The Hawaiians are reported to have eaten about seventy different varieties of limu (seaweed).

Pearls come mainly from shellfish called oysters, though they are not true members of that species of animal. In the Pacific, pearl fishing is carried on in shallow waters near northern Australia, the lagoons of atolls, in the Tuamotus, and around other islands. In Japan the raising of culture pearls is a skilled industry. Pearl shell is collected from several species of mollusks, mainly pearl oyster, green snail, and trochus shell, living in shallow water near tropical Pacific islands and is shipped by the ton to be manufactured into pearl buttons or toilet articles or used for decorative purposes. Tortoises are caught both for food and their shells, which are made into many small articles. Coral is sold for souvenirs and decorative purposes. Shells of *Tridacna* (a giant clam), some of which are 2 or 3 feet long, were formerly used on the low islands along with shark's teeth and pieces of human bone for the making of implements because no stone harder than the soft coral was available. The high islands had hard basaltic rock from which better tools and weapons could be made by a people in the stone age of culture.

Commercial fishing is carried on in only certain parts of the Pacific, and it is very probable that other fishing grounds can be discovered and extensively utilized. The anadromous (ascending rivers to spawn) salmon are caught in the lower courses of rivers and near shores of North America from Oregon to Alaska and in Siberia. They are marketed fresh, frozen, smoked, salted, and canned. The halibut fisheries are located on offshore banks from Washington to the Gulf of Alaska. Pilchards (sardines) and herring are often found in enormous schools and are taken in quantity in this same area along with cod, mackerel, and other fish. Sharks are prized for their livers, which are high in vitamins and are a substitute for cod-liver oil. Tuna are caught at sea from off Oregon to Central America, and are canned at Astoria, Los Angeles, San Diego, and Monterey. Tuna are also found in the central Pacific and are canned in a small way in Honolulu, and a cannery is planned for Samoa. Investigations of the tuna and other fisheries of the Micronesian areas governed under trust by the United States are now in progress. Fisheries near Japan are among the most valuable in the Pacific and are important to the food supply and economy of that country.

Fisheries in the southern hemisphere are little developed. Those near Australia, New Zealand, Peru, and Chile supply only small quantities of fish for local consumption, but it is believed that they are capable of considerable expansion.

Among the tropical islands there are hundreds of species of fish, many of which are brilliantly colored, but the number of any one species is so limited that the quantity that can be taken in a day is small. In contrast the cold-water areas of the Pacific may have few species, but they are found in enormous schools that permit large catches by nets and traps. The abundance of plankton and other fish food accounts for this abundance of fish. As a result most of the commercial fish caught for market are secured near the coasts in the north Pacific. There may or may not be a lack of fish in tropical waters, but most of those caught near islands are for local food and few are processed for export. Swordfish, sailfish, marlin, and dolphin are caught in the Pacific both for food and sport. Flying fish are common in tropical waters.

There are many species of whales, some of which are the largest living mammals, and several species of these creatures (sperm, black, right, humpback, and blue, sometimes 100 feet long) were once widely distributed in the Pacific but are now rare in the low latitudes and are captured mainly in the cold waters of the southern ocean. Norwegians lead in the whaling industry.

Warm-blooded mammals in the Pacific include sea elephants or elephant seals, sea lions, seals, walrus, dolphins, and porpoises, besides whales. The big gentle sea elephants are easily slaughtered by man, who makes oil from their blubber, and they now survive in only a few localities such as the Auckland Islands in the south Pacific. Closest to the United States is the herd on the Mexican-owned Guadeloupe Island west of Baja California. Once they were numerous in South Georgia and South Orkney Islands, and there were also herds in the Bering Sea area that have long been exterminated.

Sea lions live along the Pacific coast from California to Alaska and are also found in the south Pacific. The fur seal is really a sea lion. The fur seals were once common in both the north and the south

Pacific, but the only remaining herd of large size is that which resorts during the summer to the fog-bound Pribilof Islands in Bering Sea for its breeding grounds. The southern fur seal was originally widely distributed, but only a few small herds survive.

REFERENCES

Agassiz, A., *Observations of a Naturalist in the Pacific*, Macmillan, London and New York, 1903.

—— "The Coral Reefs of the Tropical Pacific," Museum of Comparative Zoology, *Harvard University Memoirs*, Vol. 28, pp. 135–167, 1903.

Betz, Frederick, Jr., and H. H. Hess, "The Floor of the North Pacific Ocean," *Geogr. Rev.*, Vol. 32, pp. 99–116, 1942.

Bridge, Josiah, "A Restudy of the Reported Occurrence of Schist on Truk, Eastern Caroline Islands," *Pacific Sci.*, Vol. 2, pp. 216–222, 1948.

Chamberlain, Rollin T., *The Geological Interpretation of the Coral Reefs of Tutuila, American Samoa*, part of Publication 340, Carnegie Institution, pp. 147–148, Washington, 1924.

Chubb, L. J., "The Structure of the Pacific Basin," *Geol. Mag.*, Vol. 71, No. 841, July 1, 1934, London.

—— "Geology of the Marquesas Islands," *Bernice P. Bishop Museum Bull.* 68, pp. 1–71, Honolulu, 1930.

—— "Geology of the Galapagos, Cocos, and Easter Islands," *Bernice P. Bishop Museum Bull.* 110, pp. 1–44, Honolulu, 1933.

Coker, R. E., *This Great and Wide Sea*, University of North Carolina Press, Chapel Hill, 1947.

Daly, Reginald A., "Pleistocene Glaciation and the Coral Reef Problem," *Amer. Jour. Sci.*, Vol. 30, pp. 297–308, 1910.

—— "Problems of the Pacific Islands," *Amer. Jour. Sci.*, Vol. 41, p. 177, 1925.

—— "Swinging Sea Level of the Ice Age," *Bull. Geol. Soc. Amer.*, Vol. 40, pp. 721–724, 1929.

—— *The Floor of the Ocean*, University of North Carolina Press, Chapel Hill, 1942.

Dana, J. D., *Corals and Coral Islands*, Dodd, Mead, & Co., New York, 1879.

Darwin, Charles, *Coral Reefs*, 3d Ed., D. Appleton, New York, 1897.

Davis, W. M., *The Coral Reef Problem*, American Geographical Society Special Publication 9, New York, 1928.

Day, Albert M., "Old Man of the Pribilofs (Fur Seal)," *Sci. Monthly*, Vol. 68, pp. 329–342, May, 1949.

Gardiner, J. Stanley, *Coral Reefs and Atolls*, The Macmillan Co., London, 1931.

—— "Studies in Coral Reefs," *Bull. Museum of Comparative Zoology*, Harvard University, Vol. 71, pp. 1–16, 1930.

Gregory, J. W., "The Geological History of the Pacific Ocean," *Quart. Jour. Geol. Soc.*, Vol. 86, Part 2, pp. 72–126, 1930.

Hobbs, W. H., *Fortress Islands of the Pacific*, J. W. Edwards, Ann Arbor, 1945.

Ladd, H. S., and J. I. Tracey, "Drilling on Bikini Atoll, Marshall Islands," *Science*, Vol. 107, No. 2768, pp. 51–55, Jan. 16, 1948.

Marshall, P., "Geology of Mangaia," *Bernice P. Bishop Museum Bull.* 36, pp. 1–48, Honolulu, 1929.

——— "Geology of Rarotonga and Atiu," *Bernice P. Bishop Museum Bull.* 72, pp. 1–75, Honolulu, 1930.

Mears, Eliot G., *Pacific Ocean Handbook*, Dekin, Stanford University, 1944.

Murphy, R. C., "Oceanic and Climatic Phenomena along the West Coast of South America during 1925," *Geogr. Rev.*, Vol. 16, pp. 26–54, 1926.

——— *Bird Islands of Peru.* G. P. Putnam's Sons, New York, 1925.

Murray, John, "Narrative," *Challenger Report*, Vol. 1, Part 2, pp. 776–800, 1885.

——— "On the Origin and Structure of Coral Reefs and Islands," *Proc. Roy. Soc. Edin.*, Vol. 10, p. 517, 1880.

Osborn, Fairfield, *The Pacific World*, W. W. Norton and Co., New York, 1944.

Setchell, W. A., "Phytogeographical Notes on Tahiti," *University of California Publications in Botany*, Vol. 12, No. 8, pp. 291–324, 1926.

Shepard, F. P., *Submarine Geology*, Harper and Brothers, New York, 1949.

Stearns, Harold T., "Geology of the Hawaiian Islands," *Bull.* 8, Division of Hydrology, Territory of Hawaii, Honolulu, 1946.

Sverdrup, H. U., "The Pacific Ocean," *Science*, Vol. 94, No. 2439, pp. 287–293, Sept. 26, 1941.

——— M. V. Johnson, and R. H. Fleming, *The Oceans*, Prentice-Hall, New York, 1946.

Tannehill, I. R., *Hurricanes*, Princeton University Press, 1944.

Vaughn, T. W., *Corals and the Formation of Coral Reefs*, Smithsonian Institution, Report for 1917, pp. 189–276, 1919.

Visher, S. S., "Tropical Cyclones of the Pacific," *Bernice P. Bishop Museum Bull.* 20, Honolulu, 1925.

Wentworth, Chester K., "Geology of the Pacific Equatorial Islands," *Bernice P. Bishop Museum Occasional Papers*, Vol. 9, No. 15, Honolulu, 1931.

Williams, Howel, "Geology of Tahiti, Moorea and Maiao," *Bernice P. Bishop Museum Bull.* 105, pp. 1–89, 1933.

Williams, M. Y., *Distribution of Life around the Pacific*, Proceedings 5th Pacific Science Congress, 1934.

Wood, Gordon L., and P. R. McBride, *The Pacific Basin* (revised), Oxford University Press, London, 1946.

Zimmerman, Elwood C., *Insects of Hawaii*, Vol. 1, *Introduction*, University of Hawaii Press, Honolulu, 1948.

2

The   Native   Peoples   of   the   Pacific

KENNETH P. EMORY

FROM ANCIENT TIMES THE GREAT ISLANDS CLOSE TO SOUTHEAST ASIA have drawn forth its people and converted them into seafarers. As these people developed skill and daring they struck out eastward across the seas, eventually reaching the most remote islands in the vast Pacific. The farther east they pushed, the smaller and more widely scattered were the islands they found. Nevertheless, the islands formed a loose chain serving as steppingstones from Asia.

DISTRIBUTION AND PROBABLE ORIGIN OF RACES

On the eastern side of the Pacific, no islands in profusion stood off the coasts of the Americas. The American shores were more sparsely populated and from more recent times. Except for the Galapagos Archipelago and a few isolated islands several hundred miles off the Americas, uninhabited and with no traces of the near-by American Indians or the distant Polynesians, the Pacific ocean stretched westward wide and empty for several thousand miles.

The islands of Indonesia close to Asia were inhabited from very early times, probably before man appeared in America. But the islands of Polynesia, in the middle of the Pacific, were the last favorable lands to be occupied by man.

The people who first entered the Pacific and the earlier of the succeeding waves of settlers differed considerably from each other in physical type, language, and culture. We know that even precursors of modern man, that is the Java ape-man, *Pithecanthropus*, and the more evolved Solo man, roamed Java many thousands of years ago. In their time land bridges existed between Indonesia and Asia.

The first varieties of men like ourselves were probably the ancestors of the small, heavy-browed, dark, but wavy-haired Australian aborigines (Fig. 12A). In Indonesia they have been practically obliterated, but archeologically they are represented by two skulls found at Wadjack in Java. Clear traces of their blood appear here and there in Melanesia, notably in the south part of New Ireland, in northern New Hebrides, and in New Caledonia. It is doubtful, however, that they reached the eastern Melanesia islands until they had become mixed with later comers of higher culture.

A *B*

FIGURE 12. *A.* Australoids. Australian aborigines. *B.* Negrito. Pygmy from the interior of Malaita Island, Solomon Islands. Photograph by Martin Johnson.

Dark, woolly-haired, round-headed, pygmy Negroids, whom we call Negritos (Fig. 12B), were also very early in the western Pacific, judging from their distribution. They are to be found all through the mountainous interior of New Guinea, of the larger islands of the Philippines, and of the Malay Peninsula. They also live in the Andaman Islands in the Bay of Bengal. The Negritos may have preceded the Australoids, but if so it is doubtful that they went as far as Australia. It has been suggested that these people came into the islands during the last ice age, about 25,000 years ago, when the sea was lower and some land bridges existed.

The Oceanic Negro (Fig. 13), taller and more advanced culturally than the Negrito, has been in New Guinea and adjacent islands for a very long time, long enough to evolve numerous local languages quite unrelated to one another. His presence is quite a mystery, for no trace of him seems to exist in western Indonesia. Is he, by any chance, an Australoid-Negrito hybrid? By mixture with the Australoids the Negrito could have gained a larger stature, and by mating with the Negritos the Australoids could have taken on the frizzly hair of the Oceanic Negro, sometimes called the Papuan.

FIGURE 13. Oceanic Negroes of New Guinea. Papuans of the upper Ramu River District, at Kainantu, elevation 5300 feet. They are carrying branches of the Cordyline plant as a sign that their mission is peaceful. Photograph by Dr. C. E. Pemberton, Hawaiian Sugar Planters' Association.

Another theory, however, explains the Negrito as being an Oceanic Negro, dwarfed as a result of generations of living in the mountains and jungles as a refugee. But if we accept this explanation, to which some physical anthropologists find objection, we are left without one for the presence of the Oceanic Negro.

A recognizable physical type appearing in the swamplands of Sumatra, in parts of Borneo and the Celebes, and as far east as Ceram is the Veddoid, only a little taller than the Negrito but lighter in skin color and having wavy hair. People like them live in the interior of Ceylon (The Veddas), in India (Dravidian tribes), and in the Malay Peninsula (the Sakai). All of them are primitive people who have been pushed away from favorable lands. They come the nearest to being living representatives of the Australoids in the Indies. Their frailness has been attributed to mixture of Australoid with the less coarsely molded people who came into the area. It is difficult to place them racially or in point of time. They represent an archaic stock, however.

Two varieties of Oceanic Negro are discernible: (1) a woolly-haired, long-headed, more Australoid, homely individual called the Papuan, and a frizzly-haired, less long-headed, more Indonesian type called the Melanesian (Fig. 14A). The Melanesians crowd the islands to the north, east, and southeast of New Guinea and are well established along the north, east, and southeast coasts of this great island. The Papuans occupy in largest numbers the coast of New Guinea not taken by the Melanesians and the interior of this and many of the other islands. The Papuan type is also dominant in New Caledonia and quite strong in some of the islands of the New Hebrides. The term Melanesian is applied by some to both types of Oceanic Negro.

The Indies and the Philippines together are today populated by nearly a hundred million small, brown-skinned, black-haired Mongoloids, with a few remnants or traces of their predecessors, the Negritos and Australoids. These predominant people, called Indonesians, speak languages belonging to the same family. Like the Oceanic Negro they fall into two types; one is darker, less Asiatic than the other, and, from its distribution in less favorable areas, clearly the earlier. This earlier type has been designated the Proto-Malay (Fig. 16A), and the later type the Malay or Deutero-Malay (Fig. 16B). Caucasoid features such as wavy hair, high nose bridges, and wide-open eyes run through the Proto-Malay element and even the Malay. The Proto-Malays began filtering into the Philippines and the Indies 8000 to 10,000 years ago. They eventually spread over the entire area, exterminating or driving into less desirable lands the Australoids and Negritos who were probably living in small scattered groups. These Indonesians carried with them and firmly established languages that belong to the Malayo-Polynesian family of languages. The degree to which they exhibited Caucasoid physical traits must have varied, and they certainly intermarried with some of the previous inhabitants. Out of this varied and mixed group, some people of extra large size, from some place, perhaps the Celebes or Borneo, moved to the western fringe of Polynesia and became the ancestors of the Polynesian people.

On the heels of the Proto-Malays came the lighter-framed, lighter- or yellower-skinned Malays, with straighter hair, many of them with the Mongolian eye fold. They came in increasing numbers, in time overrunning the earlier population, especially in the west and along the coasts. Mixing with the previous inhabitants, they formed the people we call the Malays. They have also been called Deutero-Malays. No sharp lines can be drawn between the Proto-Malay and the Malay people now, and the degree of intermixture is most haphazard.

The Malays and some of the Proto-Malays before them possessed large double-outrigger, ocean-going sailing canoes. In the early part of our Christian era these craft were crisscrossing the seas of Indonesia, carrying on trade as far as China, Indo-China, and India.

From Indonesia, whether by expulsion, driven by storm lured by prospects of trade, or spurred by the spirit of adventure, the brown people moved constantly into the islands farther east. Melanesia they found already well occupied. In settling there they became in time more or less absorbed by the earlier population. But they profoundly affected the people they met, creating through intermarriage the typical Melanesian: frizzly-haired, often lighter of skin, finer featured than the Papuan (Fig. 14B). They deeply influenced, also, the languages of those they met, altering many until they became, superficially at least, Malayo-Polynesian languages.

Most of the tiny islands of the far-flung Micronesian archipelago may have been inhabited when the first of the brown-skinned Indonesians came ashore, but some of the islands may have had settlers of Oceanic Negroes. Micronesia, at the door of Indonesia, would certainly have been settled before the distant islands of Polynesia. The first settlers, finding the islands uninhabited, would have been able to establish themselves, their language and culture, without opposition. From then on, canoe loads of people reaching islands from Indonesia, Melanesia, and, later, Polynesia, especially if they came frequently, would have been able to modify the physical types and culture and, to a less degree, the language. But the original physical types, language, and culture could be expected to exert the dominating influence. Today the Micronesians appear to be predominately Proto-Malay, with outcroppings of Negroid blood in the form of dark skin and frizzly hair. In the west of Micronesia there are more people who look like the Indonesians of the Philippines, and in the eastern part of Micronesia more people who resemble Polynesians.

Sometime after the peopling of Micronesia, Polynesia was reached

A   B

C   D

FIGURE 14. A. Oceanic Negro. Melanesian from the Solomons. B. Micronesian from West Carolines. C. West Polynesian from Samoa. D. East Polynesian from Mangareva.

by the people who became the Polynesian race (Figs. 14C and 14D). Just where did they originate, by what routes did they come, and when? How often these questions have been put, and how varied the answers. This we know. The dispersal of Polynesians within Polynesia has been so recent that they still have little difficulty in understanding one another's tongue. Their languages belong to the Malayo-Polynesian family, now sometimes called the Austronesian,

FIGURE 15. Polynesian from Hawaii. Photograph by R. J. Baker, Honolulu.

which spread from Indonesia westward as far as Madagascar off the east coast of Africa and eastward as far as Easter Island, 2000 miles from South America. All the Polynesian domesticated animals—the pig, fowl, and dog—and all except one of their important domesticated plants are of Indonesian origin. But the Polynesians exceed in stature and bodily frame the people to the west of them; and those in the most easterly of the Polynesian islands, beyond the reach of later comers from the west, lack in their blood the B and AB blood groupings, are a little longer-headed, and seem more Caucasoid than their western brothers.

It may be thought that in moving towards South America the first Polynesians met with settlers from South America and that mixture with them would account for the make-up of the Polynesians. The fact that botanists are agreed that the sweet potato, which was being grown throughout eastern Polynesia at the time of its discovery by Europeans, is of South American origin gives a valid basis for such speculation. The lack of B and AB blood groupings among many Indian tribes might seem to be further evidence. However, the Australian aborigines also lack the same blood groupings, indicating that this absence may have been original in the islands to the west.

Then, too, no unmistakable evidence of people existing in Polynesia prior to the Polynesians has been produced. If some of the islands had been previously occupied by Melanesians or Indians from America, their former presence would have been revealed by recent research in Polynesia. The most that can be said of the influence of South American people and culture on Polynesia is that it must have been post-Polynesian and, except for the introduction of the sweet potato, slight.

The fundamental cultural relationships between the island groups of Polynesia is brought out by a comparison of their vocabularies. These reflect the total culture of each group and indicate that Polynesia can be divided into two subcultural areas. One includes Samoa, Tonga, and adjacent islands and may be called West Polynesia; the other includes French Oceania, Easter Island, Hawaii, and New Zealand, and may be called, for convenience, East Polynesia. West Polynesia is believed to have been settled first and for a rather long time before there was an expansion to East Polynesia. Tahiti and the other islands of the Society Group were the cradle of East Polynesian culture. The Marquesas were settled before New Zealand, New Zealand before Hawaii, and both Easter Island and Mangareva were settled from the Marquesas. After the first dispersals from Tahiti, contacts took place between island groups, but the fundamental relationships at the time of first settlement have probably not been altered. The Hawaiian people, culture, and language are still more like Tahitian than are the Maori, because the first Hawaiian settlers left the Tahitian homeland later than the first Maori settlers.

Judging from genealogies going back to the time of early settlements and from the amount of change in the dialects since settlement, the great dispersal in East Polynesia would seem to have begun not later than A.D. 900 and to have ended not later than about A.D. 1250. For East Polynesia to develop the characteristics held in common that differentiate it from the rest of Polynesia, the stay in the Tahitian homeland before scattering may well have been 500 years. Likewise, the pause of the Polynesians in West Polynesia is likely to have been even longer. There, evidently, the Polynesians and their culture assumed the characteristics that distinguish them from all others. If the Polynesians as we are accustomed to think of them, and their culture, had existed farther west (excepting the Polynesian outliers settled from Polynesia proper), then we should be finding some definite traces of them. All we find are prototypes.

It is admitted that the Polynesians are a mixed race, but the mixture is rather uniform except for some east and west differences that can be explained on the basis that those who remained in West Polynesia were modified by some later additions, or simply diverged in isolation.

All native types now in the Pacific are certain to survive for centuries to come, but mixture among these people themselves and with the Whites and Asiatics who have come into the region is proceeding at a rapid pace and will continue. Eventually most of the people in Oceania and Indonesia will be a blend of the white and the black or brown races.

THE NATIVE CULTURES

The cultures of the native peoples of the Pacific stem ultimately from Asia and more immediately from Indonesia. The original heritage of those who moved away from the homeland has been so attenuated by time and by the changing of conditions that we can do little more than trace a number of features back to Indonesia. The Australian aborigines probably retain, in a general way, important elements of culture that flourished in Indonesia in the beginning. Melanesians undoubtedly preserve numerous features of later culture in Indonesia, and the Polynesians, still later development. Therefore, through the cultures of the people who moved eastward into the Pacific and through survivals of early culture in Indonesia itself, an approximate idea can be acquired of life in Indonesia before Oriental civilizations, using metal and employing writing, broke in upon the island world at the beginning of our Christian era. Their influence, in the realm of religion, trade, and government, while profound in the East Indies and the southern Philippines, had spread no further than the western outskirts of Melanesia and Micronesia, and here feebly, when Europeans first entered the Pacific in the sixteenth century.

THE CULTURE OF THE AUSTRALOIDS, NEGRITOS, AND PAPUANS

The Australoids, epitomized by the Australian aborigines, live in small, independent groups. Within the group in which they live they divide themselves into kin groups having animal and plant totems, and employ much of their time in initiation rites and magic ritual intended to protect themselves and increase their food supply. Bands of Australians wander in search of the kangaroo and the ostrichlike emu, which they hunt with boomerangs. They keep themselves mobile by doing without clothing, permanent houses, and food gardens. They move ceaselessly over a large area in search of roots, grubs, reptiles, and the kangaroo and are ready to repulse any intruder with spears or boomerangs. Through long centuries of roaming the desert they have become remarkably adapted to it, even to its intense heat and cold.

The Negritos also hunt, but with the bow and arrow. Throughout

mountainous New Guinea they live in independent hamlets and cultivate taro, sugar cane, bananas, and, since their introduction, sweet
potatoes and tobacco. They also raise pigs. Little is yet known
about their social organization except that the dwellers in many
villages belong to either one or the other of two groups, each of
which is named for a totemic animal. A member of one group mar-
ries someone in the other group. Although they sometimes war upon
each other, they are not headhunters or cannibals like their larger
Negroid-Australoid neighbors who occupy more favorable lands and
have access to the sea.

The clothing of the Negrito, like that of all New Guinea natives
in general, is scant and aimed at adornment and some bodily protection rather than concealment. A gourd penis cover serves for the
men, and a fringed-leaf apron for the women. The septum of the
nose is pierced to receive a boar's tusk.

A stone axe consisting of a smooth blade mounted in a socket at
the end of a stout handle is still their main tool. Food is cooked
by placing it with stones that have previously been heated and covering it with leaves and more hot stones. Fire is produced by rubbing
a length of rattan thong around a dry stick.

As throughout most of Oceania there is very little restriction on
sexual intercourse before marriage, the women marry very early.
When a person dies, relatives may cut off a joint of the finger as a
token of their grief and to propitiate the spirit. Spirits of the dead
are much feared. To protect themselves against these spirits, feasts
are held for the dead, accompanied by singing and simple dancing.
Bodies are cremated.

The language of the Negritos of the Philippines is apparently bor-
rowed from their neighbors. It is quite possible that the unstudied
languages of the Negritos of New Guinea will prove to be our first
records of original Negrito speech.

The culture of the taller Papuans, who surrounded the Negritos in
New Guinea, is not much advanced over that of the Negrito except
when influenced by the Melanesians who encompass them in the
islands north and east of New Guinea and have nearly encircled New
Guinea. It is difficult now to determine what culture the Papuans
originally had. The Papuans are hunters and agriculturists rather
than fishermen. They grow the same foods as the Negritos. The
starch in the trunk of the sago palm is an important element in the
diet of those who live in the lowlands. Pigs are very important to
them. Their social and political organization is extremely simple. A
few villages or hamlets may join together for strength in dealing with

enemies, but otherwise they may be quite independent, their affairs being managed by the family heads with perhaps the oldest able-bodied man as the chief. The kin groups are clans, that is, they belong to either their mother's family or their father's family; and they usually believe themselves descended from a totem, an animal or plant forbidden to them as food. A man gains prestige by collecting heads of enemies and strangers and may rise to chieftainship by giving feasts. Through the help of clansmen a man can buy himself into secret societies and rise in grades in the society. Certain of these societies possess the magic over specific sources of food. By donning elaborate masks, members of a secret organization impersonate their gods at important ceremonies. These are the people who sometimes build tree houses. Those who have come under Melanesian influence construct large clubhouses for the men.

Some Papuans go naked. Others cover themselves in a variety of ways, from penis covers to loin clothes and even wrap-arounds, or tapa kilts, for the men; and for the women a bunch of grass drawn between the thighs and attached to a belt, also loin clothes or tapa kilts.

The dead are wrapped in a mat and exposed on platforms, the skulls eventually being kept in the houses. Death is frequently blamed on sorcery, which is practiced much as was once done in Hawaii. Hair or fingernail clippings from the intended victim are procured, and over these death spells are cast.

Languages of the Papuans show little or no relationship among themselves. Some seem to be connected with languages of northern Australians. They lie quite outside the Malayo-Polynesian family of languages except when influenced by them.

THE CULTURE OF THE MELANESIANS

The Melanesians are decidedly more enterprising than the Papuans. Among them fishing and trading by canoe are quite important. Certain tribes make pottery and trade it with those who do not. Although in the islands east of New Guinea, natives undertook long trading voyages in large sailing canoes, no tribal chiefs held jurisdiction over more than a few villages. Each tribe was interminably raiding neighboring tribes. The skulls of victims were painted and put on view in the large clubhouses used exclusively by men.

Magic is rampant wherever we find Melanesians. Through knowing incantations and symbolic acts, magicians are thought to have control over the growth of yams, diseases, love emotions, in fact, almost anything of importance to the people. Consequently, magicians are paid handsomely in pigs, shell money, or other desirables, either for invoking their power or for passing on their knowledge. This is about the extent of the religious practices of most Melanesians. The general absence of offerings to supernatural beings in order to gain their favor distinguishes Melanesian culture from Micronesian and particularly Polynesian.

The Melanesians, as with so many of the primitive tribes in Indonesia, are chewers of the *areca* nut mixed with powdered coral-lime and wrapped in a leaf from the *betel* plant. In Polynesia, where the Areca palm does not grow, *kava* drinking takes its place. The root of the kava plant, a kind of betel, is reduced to fine particles, steeped in water, the particles strained out, and the drink proffered. The kava plant, when any part of it is chewed, is peppery to the tongue and numbs it like cocaine. Kava, which is a narcotic and not an alcolohic beverage, has a soothing and refreshing effect. Some Melanesians grow *taro* as their staple food; others, the yam. Chickens, and particularly pigs, are important foods.

Cooperative ventures are carried out by matrilineal or patrilineal kin groups, and these clan members gather at the time of birth, puberty, marriage, or death rites of a member. Men's clubhouses reach their highest development in Oceania among the Melanesians. Dances by the men in gorgeous masks and headdresses mark festivities of secret organizations. The carving of masks, bow and stern pieces of canoes, drums, and handles of implements is superior to that in Micronesia and most of Polynesia. Tattooing appears as fully developed as in Micronesia and Polynesia. Among the Papuans, scarification is common, but tattooing rare.

Dress and ornamentation among the Melanesians differ little from those of the Papuans. Universal is the piercing of the septum of the nose and the lobes of the ears to receive ornaments. Endless variation and a great range of differences of culture within the Melanesian area make generalization even more difficult than in Micronesia or Polynesia.

POLYNESIAN CULTURE

The culture of the Polynesians, simple in its material equipment, was evolved socially, politically, and religiously far beyond what we would expect of a stone-age people. The heights they achieved in social graces when entertaining, in the imagery of their songs, in concepts of how the world came to be, and the political wisdom of their chiefs, the skill of their experts in building and navigating ocean-going crafts, the energy they put into the worship of their gods, and some of the stone monuments they have left behind have given an impression of participation in a higher civilization. Some believe a civilization foundered in the Pacific with the sinking of a continent or archipelagoes of large islands. But sober students give ear to the geologists who say that no significant changes have taken place in the disposition of the islands in Polynesia since man is likely to have appeared in the Pacific. They look for other explanations.

It does appear that the ancestors of the Polynesians left Indonesia late enough to carry with them the germs of budding Asiatic civilizations but still too early to know about such things as rice and the loom. This in itself should put their departure anterior to the Christian era. Therefore, Polynesians can be considered as carrying on in isolation and under changed conditions a culture that was rather highly evolved in their Indonesian homeland but some of whose complexity was of necessity shed en route. A detailed comparative study of many of the high points of their culture, however, does reveal a considerable amount of development from simple beginnings in Polynesia itself, and a capacity to create, invent, and elaborate. For all their isolation, the Polynesians and their culture were not degenerating. There is danger of robbing them of credit by assuming that they did not, by their own unaided efforts, and in the islands as they were, achieve some of the things we admire. The great stepped-platform tombs of Tonga and the stepped-platform temples of Tahiti owe nothing to Indonesian or Central American pyramids, as they were constructed quite recently when certainly no communication was going on between Polynesia and these regions. The beautifully fabricated and ornamented bark cloth of East Polynesia may be superior to any that has been made elsewhere in the world. The circular fishhooks of Polynesia, operating on the opposite principle from our hooks, but effectively, and affording protection against snagging on the coral bottom, are an example of one of a number of ingenious inventions that may be Polynesian.

The Polynesians lived in simple, one-room houses thatched with local materials. In some of the islands the people built large and more elaborate meeting houses. They subsisted mainly on fish and a few cultivated plants such as taro, the sweet potato, and yams. But the fruit of the breadfruit, pandanus, or the coconut was the staple food in some of the islands. Their domesticated animals, the dog, pig, and fowl, were important for feasts but were not a part of the daily diet. Their clothing of bark cloth, matting fibers, or leaves was scant but quite sufficient for the environment. Only the chiefs donned elegant feather headdresses or feather cloaks. Chiefs of rank were elaborately tattooed and possessed the finest belongings.

Absence of metal tools and pottery has been put down as evidence of the undeveloped state of Polynesian culture, but lack of ores and suitable clay would have forced their abandonment if the ancestors of the Polynesians knew of them. With an abundance of coconut shell and gourds for containers and with the ground oven for cooking, pottery vessels were not at all necessary. Coconut leaves and pandanus leaves provided an unlimited source of material for mats and baskets in the tropical islands of Polynesia. Where these were lacking, as at Easter Island and New Zealand, the people turned to reeds or flax.

As fishing was so vitally important, the making of outrigger canoes, fishing nets, and fishing hooks and tackle occupied much of the men's time. Canoes were the means of travel and transport around the shores of islands and between island and island within a group and often between groups. The canoes for ocean sailing required the services of carefully trained and highly skilled men. The chiefs employed and supported these men. These canoes enabled the Polynesians to reach and spread over the whole of the vast Pacific area and to maintain life at a high level at their island homes. They offered a means of escape, too, in times of defeat in war. Therefore, it is not surprising that some of their best efforts were bestowed on their canoes.

In East Polynesia the places of worship were impressive assemblages of buildings, altars, and images set apart from the habitations. In West Polynesia single houses for the gods stood upon or beside the village green, and it was the platform-tombs of the chiefs that were elaborated. Both had to do with the veneration of the spirits of the ancestors, whom they worshipped. The offerings frequently included human sacrifices. Women were precluded from the main sacred rituals, but in secular affairs they enjoyed considerable status, some even occupying the position of high chieftainship.

The chiefs were a hereditary class; the highest-ranking member in East Polynesia was the eldest son of the previous highest chief. The carefully memorized and guarded genealogies of the chiefs went back to the gods. In Hawaii, with the title of supreme chief went the ownership of all the land in the domain and complete autocratic powers. The social organization was feudalistic: commoners cultivated the land as tenants and paid tribute to the chief assigned to their district. He kept a portion of the tribute and passed the rest on to the chief above him.

Throughout a large part of Polynesia, however, the independent groups regarded themselves as descended from a common ancestor and their chief as the most directly descended in the senior, male line from this ancestor. The chief represented the people to outsiders and was looked up to as their father, their leader in war and peace, and their high priest.

The Polynesians stood in sharp contrast to the Melanesians and Micronesians in the complete absence of clans. The Polynesian family, as with us and many Proto-Malays in Indonesia and the Philippines, is bilateral, counting, as the cooperative family group, relations through both the father and the mother, whereas the clan groups reckoned descent either through the female line alone or through the male line alone.

CULTURE OF THE MICRONESIANS

The Micronesians, like the Polynesians, speak languages belonging to the Malayo-Polynesian family. The languages are more diversified than in Polynesia, undoubtedly as a result of longer settlement or of settlement by different people.

This is the area of the fast, ocean-going, sailing canoes that amazed the Spanish discoverers. Through the invention of a triangular sail, which can be quickly shifted from one end of the canoe to the other, the balancing outrigger-float can be kept always to windward. Because the Polynesians lacked this invention, they could fare forth on the ocean in safety only by resorting to the double canoe, far slower and less maneuverable than a single outrigger canoe. The double canoe, however, had great carrying capacity.

The smallness of the Micronesian islands and the fact that most of them are coral atolls have restricted their plant food. The coconut, pandanus, and breadfruit are the staples in the low islands, but a limited amount of taro is grown. Fish supplied all the protein food until the introduction of the pig and the fowl. These were present in some of the western islands before the advent of the Europeans. Of great help in the diet is the drinking of coconut toddy, the sugary sap from the coconut blossom. In the western islands the areca nut is chewed with betel leaf. The Ponapeans of the East Carolines knew the Polynesian kava drink. Southwest of Ponape lie two small atolls, Kapingamarangi and Nukuoro, inhabited by people whose physical type, language, and culture are Polynesian. This is the farthest west Polynesians have been found.

Loom weaving, using fibers of the banana and the hibiscus plants, diffused from Indonesia as far east as Kusaie. From there eastward, mat or fringed-leaf kilts took the place of woven kilts.

Micronesians pierced their ears and extended the ear lobes by inserting large plugs in the piercings. From their ears they hung shell ornaments. Into their hair they thrust elaborate wooden combs. Around their necks they placed necklaces of coconut rings, and about the waist belts of shell beads. Delicate tattooing covered the body.

As in Polynesia the people were divided into nobles and commoners. The chiefs were members of high-ranking matrilineal clans. The clans were graded according to their age or the number of men and amount of land they owned. At the most, chiefs extended their power over not more than a few small islands or several districts of a large island.

A   B

FIGURE 16.   A. Proto-Malay.   B. Malay.

In every village were clan houses for the men and menstrual houses for the women. The men's clubhouses in the west were large and ornamented with carvings and paintings. About these houses at Yap were set great disks of limestone that served as money. They were pierced in the center with a hole and, except for size, resembled the Melanesian individual disks of shell money. Wealth, not descent from the god, bolstered prestige in Micronesia.

PRESENT STATE OF THE NATIVE CULTURES

In the present era, the impact of foreigners, both Asiatics and Whites, bringing modern civilization, has been tremendously upsetting and often disastrous to the native peoples throughout most of

Oceania.   However, because of the large areas and great populations in Indonesia and the Philippines, and the longer and slower exposure to drastically different existence patterns, the people of these areas have successfully absorbed and in many ways benefited by the change. The Polynesians have already gone through the most difficult part of the transition that they are obliged to make and are emerging as westernized individuals in Hawaii and New Zealand and to quite an extent in Tahiti and Rarotonga.   Elsewhere the native heritage is still strong because it is so well adapted to meeting the local needs. The Micronesians have been struggling with every degree of foreign influence, from Guam, one of the first islands in the Pacific to be settled by Europeans, to Ifaluk atoll, which is still native.   American trusteeship now offers a respite from foreign exploitation.   The natives of Melanesia seem due to undergo a vast impoverishment of their own cultures with prospects of taking on modern civilization in combinations that will be far from satisfactory for a long time to come.   Yet all the native peoples in the Pacific have devised so many means by which all the necessities of life can be extracted from their immediate surroundings and have discovered so many ways of living and working together that they can and doubtless will make a lasting and important contribution to future culture in the Pacific.

REFERENCES

Howells, William, *Mankind So Far,* Doubleday & Co., New York, 1945.

Kessing, Felix M., *Native Peoples of the Pacific,* The Macmillan Co., New York (revised), 1949.

Kroeber, A. L., *Anthropology,* Chapters 4 and 17, Harcourt, Brace & Co., New York (revised edition), 1948.

Stirling, M. W., *The Native Peoples of New Guinea,* Smithsonian Institution War Background Studies No. 9, Washington, 1943.

3

The Exploration and Mapping
of the Pacific

CURTIS A. MANCHESTER, JR.

THE PEOPLES OF MICRONESIA, MELANESIA, AND POLYNESIA EXPLORED the Pacific long before the Europeans sailed upon it, but the Pacific was the last major portion of the earth's surface to become known to other than local inhabitants. Greek geographers, without actually knowing of such an ocean, reasoned that it must exist and named it the Eastern Ocean to balance the Western Ocean or the Atlantic. Arabian geographers learned much more about this ocean and re-named it the Green Sea. Marco Polo and his contemporary travelers brought back to Europe evidence that this ocean existed and descriptions of some of the islands close to Asia such as Japan and the East Indies. The Arabian and medieval travelers found that the ocean was traveled by Chinese vessels. How far back this Chinese navigation extends cannot be determined from present information, but it is evident from archeological evidence that the Chinese had contact at least with Java, the Philippines, and Japan as early as the Han Dynasty (200 B.C. to A.D. 221).

Before the Age of Discoveries, European geographic speculation placed a great ocean extending unbroken from Europe to the shores of Asia. This is shown on the Martin Behaim globe of 1492, which represents the concepts of the world developed by speculation on the part of Greek, European, and Moslem geographers up to the time of Columbus's voyage. As a result of Marco Polo's voyages Sumatra appears as Java Minor and Java as Java Major on the globe.

With the Age of Discoveries, the Americas were soon found to impose a barrier between the Eastern and Western oceans. On September 25, 1513, Vasco Núñez de Balboa crossed the isthmus of

Panama and was the first European to see the Eastern Ocean from the New World. Since Balboa sighted the ocean to the south of a point where the isthmus of Panama runs east and west, the ocean was named the South Sea, and this name has continued to be applied to part or all of the ocean from the Arctic to the Antarctic. At about the same time, the ocean was entered from the other side. The Portuguese who had reached Malacca in 1509 pushed on from there, and in 1512 two of their captains, Abreu and Serrano, sighted New Guinea, although it was not until 1526 that Meneses actually visited its shores. The Portuguese pushed up the coast of Asia, reaching Canton in 1514 and Japan in 1542.

THE SPANISH PERIOD

MAGELLAN

The sixteenth century in the Pacific belonged to the Spanish. In 1520 Ferdinand Magellan, a Portuguese, sailing under the Spanish flag, found the strait at the southern end of South America that bears his name, and on leaving it sailed into the South Sea. The Pacific received its misleading name from the unusually calm weather Magellan experienced while crossing it. Sailing into this unknown sea, Magellan established for the first time the fact that it was a great ocean (Fig. 19). By bad luck, Magellan managed to cross the Pacific without sighting any fertile islands before reaching the Marianas. Although these islands may seem numerous on a modern chart, they are actually few and far between. The expedition suffered from an acute shortage of fresh water and food that could have been relieved if inhabited islands had been found. The only islands sighted were low, waterless islands, probably some of the northern Marshalls, which Magellan named St. Paul and Shark Islands, and, because of their unfortunate nature, grouped them together as the Desaventuradas.

These islands presented for the first time a major problem that was to plague the cartographers of the Pacific until the time of Captain Cook. Although the navigational instruments of this period permitted the navigators to fix latitude with some degree of accuracy, they were unable to fix their longitude except by dead reckoning. Serious errors were made in estimating the actual distance traveled until the circulation of both the winds and the currents was understood. It was not until 1736 that John Harrison invented an accurate chronometer that permitted navigators to fix longitude accurately, and even then it was not used in the Pacific until the second voyage of Captain Cook in 1773.

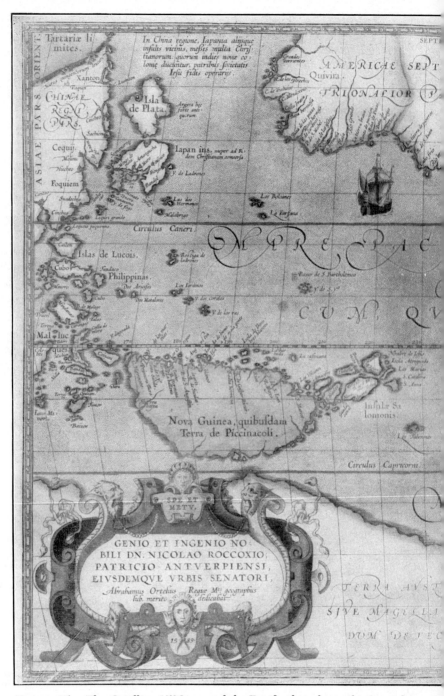

FIGURE 17.   The Ortellius 1598 map of the Pacific that shows the Spanish conce
of H

MARIS PACIFICI,
(quod vulgò Mar del Zur)
cum regionibus circumiacentibus, insulisque in eodem
passim sparsis, novissima descriptio.

MARIS ATLANTICI,

SIVE MAR DEL NORT

PARS.

Noua Hispania.

Bermuda

Cuba
Spagnola

VVLGO

Caribana.

Quito

Circulus Aequinoctialis

AMERICAE

MERIDIONA-

Peru.

LIOR PARS.

Charcas.

Chili.

DEL

Prima ego velivolis ambivi cursibus Orbem,
Magellane novo te duce ducta freto.
Ambivi, meritoque vocor VICTORIA: sunt mi
Vela, alæ: precium, gloria: pugna, mare.

ZVR.

Patagones.

Archipe-
lagus in-
sularum.

Fretum Magellanicum

Mar
del Nort

Tierra del Fuego.

period.   Photograph courtesy of William H. Spalding Map Collection, University
ary.

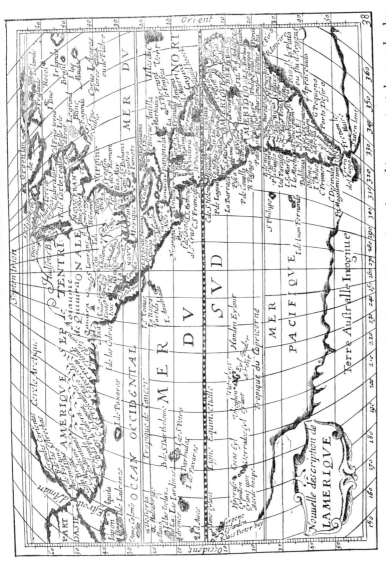

FIGURE 18. Map of the Pacific, published in 1667 in *La géographie pour tout le monde*, by Pierre du Val, showing the three most common names that have been applied to the ocean: Eastern Ocean (*Ocean Occidental*), South Seas (*Mer du Sud*), and Pacific Ocean (*Mer Pacifique*). (CAM.)

One of Magellan's pilots misestimated the width of the Pacific by about 3000 nautical miles. His successors continued to guess the position of land that they discovered or rediscovered. In time the Pacific charts were filled with islands that were incorrectly charted.

On March 6, 1521, the starving sailors sighted fertile islands. Magellan named these the Islands of the Lateen Sails, but they were renamed the Ladrones or Isles of Thieves because of the misunderstanding between the natives and the Europeans over property. Eventually they were named the Marianas after the wife of Philip IV, Queen Maria Anna, who financed missions there. Magellan sailed westward to the Philippines, which eventually received their name in honor of Philip II. Magellan became embroiled in a local quarrel and was killed on a small island near Cebu. Sebastian del Cano, the second in command, took the surviving ship, the *Victoria*, back to Spain, completing the first circumnavigation of the globe. While authorities differ as to the exact numbers, it appears that only 18 of the approximately 268 men who originally sailed from Spain returned on the *Victoria*. This attrition, of course, was to be typical of long Pacific voyages until Captain Cook overcame scurvy.

There was considerable question in Europe, in view of the problems concerning longitude and the actual size of the earth, as to whether these islands as well as the Moluccas fell on the Portuguese or the Spanish side of the Papal Line of Demarkation as modified by the Treaty of Tordesillas of 1494. The Spanish sold their claim to the Moluccas but retained the Philippines.

THE SPANISH PACIFIC

The Spanish were interested in developing only their discoveries on the eastern and western sides of the Pacific. The intervening islands lacked the type of wealth desired by the Spaniards. Because of the danger to shipping, routes were developed to avoid the known islands. Coastal shipping routes were established connecting Peru with Panama and Mexico on the eastern side of the Pacific. On the western side a settlement was established in the Philippines in 1565 and Manila was founded in 1571. The Marianas were not permanently occupied until 1668, when a desire to spread Christianity coincided with a desire to keep English and other pirates out of these islands, which were strategically located on the route of the Manila galleon.

After Magellan's crossing other navigators followed him, taking advantage of the northeast trades to cross the Pacific from east to west. They were unable to beat their way back to the Americas, however, because of their lack of knowledge of the general wind circulation. It was not until 1565 that Andres de Urdaneta found the westerlies and made a successful crossing at about 42 degrees north latitude. For the next 250 years the Manila galleon and other vessels followed "Urdaneta's Passage" between the Philippines and Acapulco, Mexico.

MENDAÑA AND QUIROS

The Greek geographers had postulated that there must be a great southern continent to balance the land masses in the northern hemisphere. This idea of a large southern mass of lands known as Terra Australis Incognito long persisted and appears on the maps drawn by European armchair geographers. It was finally narrowed down to the approximate size of the actual continent of Antarctica by Captain Cook, late in the eighteenth century. Although this continent remained elusive, there were those who believed in it firmly. It appears on Fig. 17 as *Terra Australis Nondum Detecta* (the southern continent not yet discovered). At various times Australia, the Solomons, the New Hebrides, and New Zealand were hopefully labeled as part of this continent. Some of the last Spanish expeditions of pure exploration were conducted by Mendaña and Quiros in search of this continent. The first of these expeditions, under Alvaro de Mendaña in 1567, managed to sail between the Tuamotus and the Marquesas as well as near the Society Islands without sighting land. They finally sighted one of the Ellice Islands. From here they sailed on to islands that were later named the Solomons because of stories of fabulous wealth told by the returning seamen. The Solomons were not rediscovered until 1767 and continued to be one of the many groups of semi-mythical islands that cluttered up the charts. After abandoning an attempt to establish a colony there, Mendana turned northward, skirting the western side of the Gilberts and Marshalls until he reached Urdaneta's Passage and was able to return to the Americas with the aid of the westerlies. Wake was discovered on this voyage, although not revisited until 1796.

After many disappointments Mendana again sailed onto the Pacific with Pedro Fernandez de Quiros as his pilot in 1595. This expedition discovered and named the Marquesas after the wife of the Viceroy of Peru, the Marquesas de Mendoza. The Santa Cruz Islands were at first mistaken for the Solomons. Mendana died after an unsuccessful attempt to found a colony, and the survivors proceeded to Manila with much difficulty.

In spite of the failure of the previous expedition, Quiros was fired

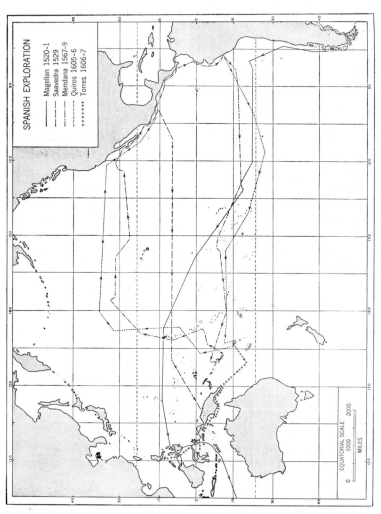

FIGURE 19.   Spanish explorations in Pacific.

by zeal to bring Christianity to the natives of the Pacific and to discover the unknown southern continent. He pestered the Viceroy of Peru, the Council of the Indias, the King of Spain, and the Pope until he was given command of an expedition that sailed from Callao in 1605. Quiros, an idealist, issued orders that there was to be no swearing, no gambling, and no blaspheming. Daily services were to be held, and the natives were to be treated with humanity. After discovering some small islands near Tahiti, thus contributing more semi-mythical islands to the Pacific charts, he finally, in 1606, discovered the New Hebrides.

A colony was founded on Espiritu Santo, named Australia del Espiritu Santo. The colony was called New Jerusalem; the town, Vera Cruz; the river, Jordan; and the bay, St. Philip and St. James, names that reflect the religious zeal that now took complete possession of Quiros. The colony broke up because of mutiny, native troubles, and disease. Quiros returned to Acapulco by Urdaneta's Passage while his chief pilot, Torres, continued exploration westward. Torres discovered and sailed through the strait between Australia and New Guinea that bears his name. The fate of this discovery illustrates a new phase of Pacific cartography. The Spanish empire had by this time passed its zenith and wished to hold what it possessed without the development of new discoveries. As a result, the discovery of Torres Strait was buried in the archives and did not become known to the world until much later when the English, in 1762, captured a map in Manila showing New Guinea to be an island, and the geographer Dalrymple labeled the passage Torres Strait.

During the Spanish Period, English and French pirates or freebooters made some discoveries that appeared on charts. Sir Francis Drake, in 1578, raided the Spanish settlements in the Americas and crossed the Pacific on his return to Europe. His real contribution to cartography was the discovery of a route south of Terra del Fuego. Other raids, of which that of Thomas Cavendish in 1586–1588 is outstanding, contributed to the general knowledge of the Pacific; but as a result the Spanish became even stricter in their release of information regarding the Pacific.

THE DUTCH PERIOD

THE ARRIVAL OF THE DUTCH

The Dutch shared in the early Pacific developments because their country was part of the heritage of the King of Spain. Dutch seamen and navigators also gained experience in southern and southeastern Asia where they were employed by the Portuguese. After the Dutch revolted against Philip II of Spain in 1568 they published charts on the Far East that became the basis of cartographical representation of the areas for many years.

A Dutch fleet established direct trade relations with the East Indies in 1597. The following year five expeditions, containing twenty-two vessels, left Holland for Eastern Asia. In 1602 the United East Indies Company was established to end the ruinous competition between various Dutch companies in the exploitation of the East Indies.

DUTCH EXPLORATION

The Dutch were more interested in profits from trading in well-developed lands and quickly lost interest in new areas if opportunities for trade were limited. However, there were a few notable exceptions that added measurably to the world's knowledge of the Pacific. Dutch merchants who were jealous of the East Indies Company's monopoly of the trade tried to reach the East Indies from Holland by sailing south of Tierra del Fuego. Drake had made this voyage but his exploit had been questioned by later cartographers. The Dutch vessels under Jakob Le Maire and piloted by William Schouten in 1616 sailed around Cape Horn, which they named after their native town of Horn. They passed through the Tuamotus, discovered Hoorn Island, between Fiji and Samoa, and skirted the shores of New Ireland and New Guinea, discovering the Admiralties and Schouten groups. Other Dutch navigators, soon after Schouten, established the fact that Staten Island, which is separated from Tierra del Fuego by the Le Maire Strait, was an island and not part of the southern continent.

TASMAN

In 1636 a new Governor General, Anton Van Diemen, arrived in Batavia and initiated the most ambitious program of general exploration planned by the Dutch. He planned to solve some of the cartographical mysteries surrounding the New Guinea area, explore the waters in the vicinity of Japan, and settle the question of whether the land now known as Australia, which had appeared on some Portuguese and French maps and had been briefly touched by some Dutch navigator, was actually part of Terra Australis Incognita. The first expedition to explore the southern continent came to a quick end on the coast of New Guinea in 1636 when the commander of the expedition was killed by natives. In 1639 Janszoon Tasman was sent into Japanese waters to look for the Gold and Silver Islands, which had long appeared on European maps. This expedition failed to find much but water although it did serve to erase some non-existent lands from the Pacific charts.

In 1642 Tasman was sent to explore the southern land and find whether it was possible to sail south of it. Tasman discovered the land south of Australia that bears his name today, although it was first named Van Dieman's Land and thought to be part of Australia. He proceeded eastward and discovered New Zealand, which was thought to be part of the southern continent. Turning northward, Tasman was probably the first European to discover the Tonga or Friendly Islands and the Fiji Islands.

In 1644 Tasman explored the northern coast of Australia, mapping the Gulf of Carpenteria and the northwestern coast of Australia as far as Willems River. Van Dieman died soon after this voyage, and the East Indies Company was unwilling to continue costly exploration that promised to bring little return in profits.

The next major voyage of the Dutch that resulted in exploration was that of Mynheer Jakob Roggeveen, who, in 1722, discovered and named Easter Island.

Unlike the Spanish, the Dutch were fairly free in releasing the information gained from their explorations. Accounts of Tasman's explorations were published, and maps were quickly released showing the new lands. The maps published by the Bleau family and others, representing some of the major achievements of cartography up to this time, quickly reflected the new information about the Pacific.

THE FRENCH AND THE ENGLISH PERIOD

BUCCANEERS

French and English interest in the Pacific was revived by a group known variously as filibusters, sea rovers, freebooters, and pirates, late in the seventeenth century. During the numerous wars of this period both England and France commissioned their sailors to raid Spanish shipping in the Americas. During intervals of peace, these sailors, who had developed experience and knowledge of the best means for despoiling the Spanish New World, continued their activities unofficially. Although many of the expeditions were poorly recorded, some of the freebooters were prolifically literate and inspired general interest in the Pacific. It has been estimated that there were over one hundred English and French voyages into the Pacific between 1695 and 1726.

William Dampier, who appeared in the Pacific at different times as a buccaneer, officer of the Royal Navy, and merchant navigator, touched many parts of the ocean during his career (Fig. 20). He visited Guam, the Philippines, Australia, New Guinea, New Ireland, and New Britain, where he discovered the passage between New Britain and New Guinea that bears his name. The accounts he published concerning his voyages not only provided much detailed information, which was widely read, but also caused a flood of South Sea novels. This interest led directly to the great French and English scientific voyages of the nineteenth century. Dampier's description of native life on idyllic Pacific islands aided the development of the European version of the "noble savage," a concept that continues to influence thinking and policies concerning Pacific problems. In the Second World War, many an American soldier was disappointed when he did not find life in the Pacific as it had been pictured in a long line of literature inspired by Dampier.

The French were first attracted to the Pacific by the opportunities for Spanish loot. These activities contributed some additional knowledge concerning the Strait of Magellan and Tierra del Fuego, but the voyages seldom extended west of the Galapagos. Information thus gained was put to use in more peaceful activities. Frondac in 1709 took advantage of the north Pacific westerlies on his return to France from a trading voyage to China. He was followed by other French vessels engaging in the Chinese trade. Explorations of Lozier Bouvet, during 1738 and 1739, in search of the southern continent resulted in the discovery of what is now known as Bouvet Island, but at the time this was thought to be actually part of Terra Australis. This discovery influenced Captain Cook's southern exploration.

ANSON'S VOYAGE, 1740–1744

Lord Anson's circumnavigation of the globe during the War of the Austrian Succession marks the beginning of the scientific exploration of the Pacific. Although the voyage resulted in much plunder and another idyllic description of Saipan and Tinian (Fig. 58), the geographical results were disappointing. However, one tangible result of importance to later Pacific voyages was a study of scurvy published by James Lind. Scurvy took a severe toll of the men on the expedition as it had on every long Pacific voyage since Magellan. Of the 1955 men sailing on seven vessels, 1051 died of scurvy. The loss of life on the Spanish fleet sent to intercept Anson was even worse; only 100 out of 3000 men survived. Scurvy results from a deficiency in vitamin C, which was missing from the diet on long voyages owing to the lack of fresh vegetables. Cook profited from Dr. Lind's study, and his men largely escaped the disease by his issuance of lemon juice and his securing fresh provisions wherever possible.

RUSSIAN EXPLORATION IN THE NORTH PACIFIC

While the other European countries were reaching the Pacific because of their interests in the Americas or Eastern Asia, the Russians were advancing across Siberia, and in 1639 they reached the Sea of Okhotsk. From 1725 to 1728 an expedition under the command of Titus Bering explored the coast of Kamchatka and Asia as far north as 67° 18' but did not sight the North American coast. Bering's second expedition (1733–1743) explored the Aleutians and discovered Alaska.

Fur trade with the newly discovered lands followed immediately. In 1784 a permanent settlement was made on Kodiak Island, and in 1798 the Russo-American Company was given a monopoly of trade in Alaska. The manager of this company, A. A. Baranov, had visions of the Pacific as a Russian lake, but his ideas were ineffective; for example, the Russians made an abortive attempt to seize the Hawaiian Islands in the early nineteenth century. Although Bering failed to establish definitely the existence of a strait between Asia and North America, his expeditions established the probability that such a strait did exist. Results of Russian exploration were presented to the world on Deslile's maps.

BYRON

The Treaty of Paris in 1763 brought a period of peace to Europe that resulted in the scentific exploration of the Pacific. Expeditions, backed by governments or scientific societies, explored the Pacific with the objective of solving geographical problems. As a result of these voyages new islands were discovered, old discoveries were accurately fixed on the charts, and the southern continent was whittled down to the approximate size of Antarctica. Britain led in this exploration with the voyage of Commodore John Byron in 1764. Byron surveyed the Falkland Island in preparation for the establishment of a naval base and described in detail conditions on some of the lesser islands of the Tuamotus and Gilberts. He found Saipan and Tinian in the Marianas much less attractive than they had been portrayed by Lord Anson. As far as new discoveries were concerned, this voyage was disappointing. However, an example was set by the publication of charts and detailed descriptions of the flora, fauna, and peoples of the islands.

WALLIS AND CARTERET

A few months after the return of Byron in May, 1766, another expedition to the Pacific set out under the command of Captain Samuel Wallis. This expedition added much more to the knowledge of the Pacific than Byron's. Wallis, on the *Dolphin*, explored the Tuamotus, where he named the numerous islands after members of the royal family until that source of names was exhausted and he was forced to turn to the list of admirals. On June 19, 1767, Wallis sighted Tahiti. The name that he selected, "King George III," has not survived. The sailors had a pleasant stay here, and their description further strengthened the "noble savage" myth. The description of the different moral standards encountered helped to make Tahiti a favorite rendezvous point for Pacific navigators.[1] Wallis also visited Tinian and Saipan for fresh supplies.

Carteret, on the *Swallow*, was separated from Wallis while passing through the Strait of Magellan and followed a more southerly route across the Pacific. Carteret's voyage was important for the rediscovery of the Solomons (although this was not known until later) and his exploration of the Bismarcks. His most important discovery was St. George's Channel between New Britain and New Ireland. New Hanover, in this group, and the Admiralty Islands were mapped and named by Carteret (Fig. 20).

BOUGAINVILLE

Count Louis Antoine de Bougainville was one of the outstanding Pacific explorers. He also established a precedent for later Pacific exploration by taking along qualified scientists, including a botanist and an astronomer. In 1766 Bougainville started on his circumnavigation of the world. He reached Tahiti only eight months after Wallis's departure and received a most cordial reception. The description published of this stay further strengthened the reputation of Tahiti as being the Garden of Eden.

In May, 1768, Bougainville discovered the Samoan Islands, and from there went on to the New Hebrides. He continued westward until he encountered the Great Barrier Reef, which caused him to alter his course without discovering the east coast of Australia. He turned northward and became entangled with the islands east of New Guinea and the Solomons. He mapped and named the Louisiade Archi-

[1] John Hawkesworth (ed.), *An Account of the Voyages Undertaken by the Order of His Present Majesty for Making Discoveries in the Southern Hemisphere,* Vol. 1, p. 481, London, 1783.

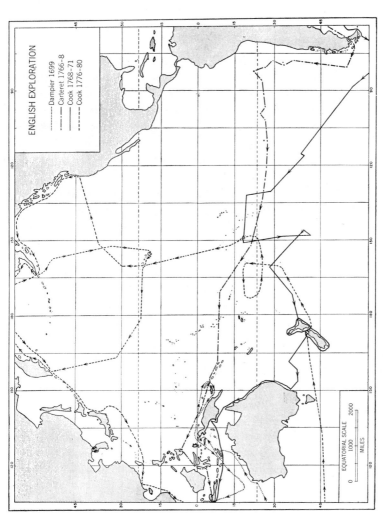

FIGURE 20. English explorations in Pacific.

pelago, Choisel, Buka, and other islands in this area. Bougainville, the largest island of the Solomons that he mapped, was later named in his honor. He had intended further exploration in this area but, like Carteret, was forced to hurry to Batavia because of the toll that scurvy was taking of his crew.

CAPTAIN COOK

James Cook (1728–1779) well deserves the title of the greatest explorer of the Pacific. Cook made a few original discoveries during his years of exploration, but when he started his work the Pacific charts were cluttered with non-existent or incorrectly located islands and a great non-existent continent was shown over a large section of the southern hemisphere. By the time of Cook's death on his third voyage, the main island groups were fixed in their correct positions and the southern continent was restricted to the approximate size of Antarctica. This was not by mere chance. Cook was a capable sailor, navigator, and cartographer.

COOK'S FIRST PACIFIC VOYAGE (1768–1771)

Voyages just completed had renewed interest for Britain in the problems still unsolved concerning Pacific charts. The British Admiralty was interested in whether or not there was a great southern continent. If there was, as was thought probable by the leading geographers, the Admiralty wished to secure bases similar to the Falkland Islands to protect British routes to the new area of exploitation. The Royal Society wished to have an observation of the transit of Venus across the sun made from one point in the south to correlate with similar observations to be made on Cape North of Norway and in the Hudson Bay area. These projects received the active backing of George III. Cook was finally selected as the man best fitted to command the expedition on the basis of his reputation as a sailor and leader of men as well as for his ability as a scientist, which he had demonstrated by his work in charting North American waters and his previous recording of an observation of an eclipse of the sun on Newfoundland.

On August 25, 1768, Cook sailed from the Thames on the *Endeavour* with seventy officers and men, twelve marines, and twelve landsmen. Cook was interested in the problem of preventing scurvy, which had brought disaster to so many of the previous expeditions. Wherever possible he secured fresh food and carried live animals. He also insisted on clean quarters and dry clothing. In January, 1769, Cook rounded Cape Horn and, after sailing to 60° south latitude without finding the unknown continent, proceeded northwestward to Tahiti (Fig. 20).

Tahiti was sighted on April 10, 1769, on the parallel reported by Wallis but considerably eastward of Wallis's estimated longitude. The expedition did not leave until the middle of July, which gave the Tahitians and the Europeans considerable time to get acquainted. Unlike such encounters in the past, the current European ideas about the noble savage aided in making the encounter friendly (Figs. 21 and 22). While awaiting the opportunity for the astronomical observation, Cook charted the waters of Tahiti and some of the neighboring islands.

Figure 21. Webber's painting of *Oheitepeha Bay*, Tahiti, made during Captain Cook's second voyage. Photograph courtesy of the University of Hawaii Library.

After leaving Tahiti, Cook sailed southward to 40° south latitude looking for Terra Australis without success. This was as far south as he had been ordered to go. His attainment of this southerly point wiped off the contemporary maps a large section of the supposed continent. From here he proceeded westward to find the east coast of Tasman's New Zealand. The Maori of New Zealand were found less hospitable than the Tahitians. Cook sailed slowly around the islands, roughly charting the coast as he went. He discovered the strait that bears his name between North and South Islands. His work definitely established that New Zealand was not part of Terra Australis.

Cook sailed across the Tasman Sea to explore the unknown east coast of New Holland. The name Australia was not applied to this continent officially until 1817. He proceeded up the coast, discovering Botany Bay, and became entangled with the Great Barrier Reef. On June 11, 1770, the *Endeavour* struck a coral ledge of the Great Barrier Reef and sustained serious damage. After making temporary repairs, Cook proceeded to Batavia by way of Torres Strait, completing the first known navigation on this strait after Torres's original discovery. More men were lost at the disease-ridden port of Batavia than had died on the entire voyage up to this time. Repairs were finally made, and on July 10, 1771, the *Endeavour* returned to England via the Cape of Good Hope.

COOK'S SECOND VOYAGE (1772–1775)

Although Cook had demonstrated on his first voyage that the hypothetical Terra Australis could not be as large as some had thought, the possibility of a large land area with a mild climate had aroused

FIGURE 22.   Webber's painting of the natives of the Tonga or Friendly Islands made on Cook's second voyage.   These paintings were later reproduced in Europe as engravings.   Photograph courtesy of the University of Hawaii Library.

interest in southern bases. In 1770 France, Spain, and Great Britain had quarreled over possession of the strategically located Falkland Islands. As a result, the British Admiralty was interested in finally solving the age-old mystery of the southern continent. Soon after his return from the first expedition Cook began preparations for his second voyage, which was to find the land or disprove its existence. The encounter with the Great Barrier Reef had demonstrated the desirability of two vessels. Cook fitted out two colliers, the *Resolution* and the *Drake;* they were of the same type as the *Endeavour*, which had performed so well on the first voyage. Cook, in command of the *Resolution,* sailed from Plymouth on July 13, 1772. He proceeded southward from Capetown and in January, 1773, crossed the Antarctic Circle. At 67° south latitude pack ice was encountered that would

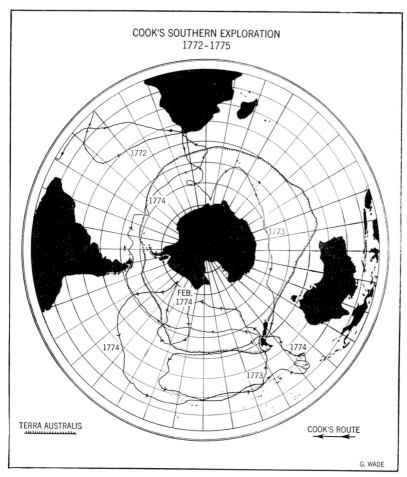

FIGURE 23.   Cook's southern exploration 1772–1775.

not permit the ship to make higher latitudes. So far as is known this was the first time anyone had crossed the Antarctic Circle. If it had been possible to proceed a little farther east, Enderby Land, part of the continent of Antarctica, would have been discovered (Fig. 23).

The *Resolution* worked eastward between the fiftieth and sixtieth parallels to about 150° east longitude and then turned northeast to

New Zealand. About one-third of the circumference of the earth was covered on this section of the voyage without discovering land. Cook suspected that land did lie farther south because of the icebergs and birds that were encountered. However, any land farther south would not be of commercial interest. In July Cook reached Tahiti, where he picked up fresh food before making another effort to find land in the south. He was stopped again by pack ice in position 71° 10′ south latitude, 106° 54′ west longitude. From this position he turned northward, fixing the location of Juan Fernandez, Easter Island, and the Marquesas. Proceeding westward, the *Resolution* again visited Tahiti and fixed the positions of the southern Fiji Islands, New Hebrides and New Caledonia. After a stop in New Zealand Cook returned to the Atlantic, sailing between the fiftieth and sixtieth parallels. Crossing the south Atlantic in the same latitudes, he sighted South Georgia, the Sandwich Group, and Bouvet Island, and crossed the track of his outgoing voyage. The expedition arrived at Portsmouth on July 29, 1775.

This expedition solved the great mystery that had plagued cartographers and geographers for more than 2000 years. It was definitely established that there was not a great southern land mass extending north of 60° south latitude. If there was land to the south, as Cook suspected, it was a cold land that offered few opportunities for man. The chronometer of John Harrison was proved accurate, and henceforth it was possible to fix longitude accurately. The methods Cook had adopted in fighting scurvy were proved successful, as no men were lost on account of this disease on the *Resolution* during the long voyage. Men were lost on the *Adventure,* whose captain did not follow Cook's orders strictly. In addition, many Pacific islands were accurately charted for the first time.

COOK'S THIRD VOYAGE (1776–1780)

Cook's first two voyages had removed most of the major mysteries regarding the south Pacific. One large section of the Pacific remained to be charted, the northeast. This section remained on the charts in much the same state it had been after the early cartographical interest of the sixteenth century. A map of the Pacific published between the second and third voyages shows the islands of the south and west Pacific in correct positions, little different from the most recent maps. This map shows the northeast Pacific with the same names applied to vaguely located islands as were shown on the sixteenth-century maps of Mercator and Ortelius.

The decline of the economy of the Caribbean possessions of Britain and the interest in the newly acquired areas in Canada had led to interest in the northwest coast of North America. Bering had already established the strait that bears his name, but little was accurately known of the area between the strait and what is now northern California. The Spanish had done some exploration as far north as Nootka Sound but had not made this knowledge available to the world. The Admiralty was sufficiently interested in the coast to send Cook on another expedition.

On July 12, 1776, Cook sailed from England on the *Resolution,* accompanied by the *Discovery.* Cook proceeded by way of Cape-

FIGURE 24. Webber's painting of *Taloo Harbor*, Murea or Emeo Island, in the Society group. Photograph courtesy of the University of Hawaii Library.

town, Tasmania, and the Cook Islands to Tahiti, where he arrived in August, 1777. At Tahiti, Cook landed the cattle, sheep, and horses, which were gifts from George III to the Tahitians. In December he left the Society Islands and sailed northward. On December 24 a small low island was discovered and named Christmas Island.

On January 18, 1778, Niihau and Kauai, the westernmost of the large Hawaiian Islands, were discovered. Brief landings were made on Niihau and Kauai to secure fresh provisions, and Oahu was sighted, but Cook did not stay long enough to explore the islands thoroughly and map them. His orders made it clear that he was to explore the northwest coast of North America before developing incidental discoveries. The islands were named the Sandwich Islands in honor of the Earl of Sandwich, who was then the First Lord of the Admiralty and an important backer of Cook's Pacific explorations.

The question immediately arose concerning prior Spanish discovery of the Hawaiian or Sandwich Islands. Cook's contemporaries gave credit for the original discovery to the Spaniards. This credit has recently been questioned.[2] Pacific maps from as early as 1569 had shown islands in the approximate position of the Hawaiian Islands. The discovery of these islands has been commonly attributed to a little-known Spanish explorer, Juan Gaetano, who was a pilot on the Villabos expedition, 1542–1545.[3]

Cook found the Hawaiians in possession of a few pieces of iron that they valued highly. Iron was unknown in other parts of Polynesia before the arrival of Europeans, and the Hawaiians had been without contact with the rest of Polynesia since pre-Spanish times. However, the possibility of Japanese origin of the iron has been advanced. Some years after Cook's visit legends were collected that would seem to indicate that the Hawaiians had traditions of earlier visits by Europeans. Whether or not Cook was the first European to set eyes on the Hawaiian Islands, he does deserve the honor of being the first to record the position of the islands clearly and to describe their inhabitants.

In March, Cook sighted the coast of North America a few degrees south of the present United States–Canadian border. He sailed northward along the coast and through the Bering Strait to a position 70° 30′ north latitude, where his further poleward exploration was blocked by ice. For the first time this coast was clearly established. As winter approached, Cook decided to carry out his work of exploration in southern waters and returned to the Hawaiian Islands. He was now free to explore them in detail, having fulfilled the Admiralty's orders to first chart the northwest coast of North America.

Maui was sighted on November 25, 1778, and the big island of Hawaii soon after. Between November 30 and January 17, Cook sailed around the island of Hawaii (or, as he recorded it—Owhyes), charting the coast without making a landing. On January 17, 1779, he finally anchored in Kealakekua Bay. While the ship sailed around the island there was mounting excitement ashore, and the *kahunas*,

[2] John F. G. Stokes, *Hawaii's Discovery by Spaniards, Theories Traced and Refuted*, Hawaiian Historical Society Papers No. 20, pp. 38–113, Honolulu, 1939. *Contra:* James A. Williamson, *Cook and the Opening of the Pacific*, pp. 200–201, The Macmillan Co., New York, 1948.

[3] James Burney, *A Chronological History of the Discoveries in the South Sea or Pacific Ocean*, Vol. I, pp. 226 ff., Luke Hansard, London, 1803.

or priests, had time to work out an explanation for the visit. The ships were associated with the god Lono, who, according to tradition, had sailed away, promising to return. The kahunas explained to the people that this was Lono returning. When Cook landed he received an embarrassingly friendly reception. Provisions desired for the ships were supplied by the Hawaiians, and gifts were exchanged with the kahunas and chiefs.

At last the ships departed on February 4 without any serious friction between the Hawaiians and the Europeans. The *Resolution* was damaged in a storm, and the expedition returned to Kealakekua Bay on February 11 for repairs. The reception was not as enthusiastic as before. Supplying food had been a severe strain for the common people. The chiefs were jealous of the kahunas. Friction developed, and the number of thefts increased. The friction reached a climax with the theft of a large ship's boat, which the Hawaiians broke up for its nails. On February 14 Cook landed with nine marines and a lieutenant, intending to take a chief as hostage for the return of the boat. Cook almost accomplished his purpose, but trouble suddenly developed. In a few minutes Cook and four of the marines were dead. Some reprisals were taken, and part of Cook's body was recovered. Finally, on February 22 the *Resolution* and *Discovery* departed.

The expedition continued under the command of Captain Clerke. Following the orders of the Admiralty, Clerke sailed across the Pacific to Kamchatka and through Bering Strait. The expedition was again blocked by ice in a position 70° 33′ north latitude on July 5, 1779. The *Resolution* and *Discovery* returned to England by way of Japan, Formosa, Sunda Strait, and Capetown, arriving on the Thames in October, 1780.

Cook is one of the oustanding explorers of all time. When he began his Pacific explorations, this great portion of the earth's surface was but poorly known. The maps and charts were dotted with vague islands, which were often incorrectly located, and the south Pacific was portrayed as possessing a great land mass that rivaled Asia in size. When Cook died the major mysteries of the Pacific were solved and the principal island groups fixed in their correct positions.

THE POLITICAL DIVISION OF THE PACIFIC

THE FIRST OUTSIDE IMPACT

Cook's expeditions were followed by a number of expeditions that were sponsored by various governments. Their work was largely a refinement of Cook's. Vancouver, Perouse, D'Urville, Wilkes, and others continued to fix the positions of islands and report their cultural and natural features. However, within a few years after Cook's death, the native cultures in many places had been dealt a shattering blow by a constantly growing tide of whalers, traders, missionaries, and blackbirders.

Whalers. The whalers were the first to arrive. Even before Cook's last voyage, London whalers were reported off the coast of Peru. About 1800, American and European whalers were operating in the waters between New Zealand and Australia, and by 1819 off the northeastern coasts of Japan. Their effect was felt everywhere from New Zealand to the Hawaiian Islands. These whalers, operating out of New England, the ports of England, and France, for the most part, were a long way from their home ports and required fresh provisions that they secured from the natives of the Pacific islands. In return for the various products of "civilization," the natives sold the whalers firewood, fresh vegetables, pork, beef, potatoes, sugar cane, and fresh water. The New England whaling industry had received a setback during the Revolutionary War, but, in 1791, seven New England whalers rounded the Horn. In spite of a further setback during the War of 1812, the number of American whalers in the Pacific continued to increase. In 1818, eleven whalers were reported at one time in Kealakekua Bay and twenty-three in Honolulu harbor. The whalers moved from one group of islands to another as the whaling grounds changed and as they received better treatment in other islands. The number of whalers stopping at any one island varied greatly from year to year. In the year 1844, 490 whalers stopped in the Hawaiian Islands, 220 in 1851, and 549 in 1859.

The impact of the whalers contributed to the breakdown of native cultural patterns. There is a saying that the sailors hung their morals on the Horn as they passed. The natives were introduced to new vices, and venereal disease began to reduce the population of most islands. The time required to prepare supplies for ships diverted natives from their normal cultural patterns. The chiefs acquired a taste for foreign goods, which was to keep them bankrupt. This extravagance led to further exactions on their people. The natives who served on ships as seamen returned to their homes with acquired habits that were greatly deplored by the missionaries.

Traders. The Chinese trade brought merchants to the Pacific. As a result of the voyages of Cook and Vancouver to the northwest coast of North America, British, French, and American vessels picked up furs, especially the sea otter and seal, along the coast of northwest

North America and sold them at Canton. These ships, coming from distant ports, required supplies. The Hawaiian Islands were well located to furnish supplies for northbound vessels as well as for those on the run to China. In 1791 it was discovered that the Hawaiian Islands could supply sandalwood, which was highly prized in China. For a brief period, until the sandalwood ran out, the mountains were combed by Hawaiians searching for it. When the Hawaiian sandalwood gave out the traders moved to other islands in other parts of the Pacific where it grew.

Besides sandalwood, other Pacific products found markets. Tortoise shell and sea cucumbers (also known as bêche-de-mer, trepang, dri, and *Holothuria*) were collected and sold in China. The Royal Navy found excellent pine spars in New Zealand. New Zealand also exported dried human heads for European collectors. Captains would select the heads and specify the tattooed designs desired on the dried head when it would be picked up some months later on the return voyage. About 1800, Tahiti began to export salted pork to the convict colony in New South Wales. From about 1850, copra, coconut oil, and coir were important exports of the Pacific islands. As a result of the American Civil War some of the Pacific islands, such as the Fiji, had an opportunity to develop cotton exports. However, cotton raised in the Pacific was unable to compete with cheaper American cotton. The first Europeans found sugar cane widely distributed throughout the Pacific, and there was some export soon after Cook's voyages. The industry did not become important in any of the islands until it was put on a plantation basis.

These commercial activities contributed to the breakdown of the native way of life. Everywhere the people were taken from their accustomed tasks to perform duties so that their chiefs could purchase foreign luxuries. The raising of agricultural products for sale to the whalers and traders kept them from their normal pursuits. The traders also contributed to the spread of new diseases and vices. The introduction of plantations in many islands meant the loss of land to the natives.

Beachcombers and Blackbirders. Deserters from ships and escaped convicts from Port Jackson soon added a new and undersirable element to the Pacific. These individuals quickly spread throughout the whole area. Sometimes they were kept as useful pets by chiefs because of their ability to repair firearms and cast bullets. At other times they set themselves up as petty dictators and terrorized the natives. Everywhere they contributed to the spread of disease and the breakdown of the native systems of morality.

Blackbirding developed soon after the beginning of the nineteenth century. The exploitation of the guano deposits of Peru required cheap, docile labor. Pacific natives were kidnapped from their homes and slowly worked to death in Peru. Whole islands such as Easter Island, as well as the islands of the Ellice group, were nearly depopulated. As sugar plantations developed in Queensland, Fiji, Samoa, New Hebrides, labor was "recruited" with face-saving contracts but the old methods. In spite of long protest on the part of missionaries and others, this system was not entirely abolished until after the First World War.

Missionaries. Missionary work started in the Pacific with the Spanish, and missionaries accompanied the first Spanish explorers on their voyages. Their efforts were mainly directed toward the Philippines and the Marianas, with occasional attempts in the Carolines. The renewed interest in the Pacific, after the late eighteenth-century voyages, brought fresh missions. In 1797 the *Duff* landed representatives of the London Missionary Society on Tahiti and Tonga. Rival groups followed. After the Napoleonic Wars, French Catholic missionaries entered the field. American missionaries from Boston reached the Hawaiian Islands in 1820. The missionaries championed the natives against the abuses of the traders, whalers, and blackbirders. From their arrival they fought for standards of moral decency. However, they probably contributed more than all the other contacts to the breakdown of the native cultures. Too often they taught uncritically that anything native was bad, while Christianity meant Mother Hubbards and Western cultural patterns. On some islands the children of the missionaries or even some of the missionaries themselves acquired land from the natives and established plantations, further contributing to the destruction of the native way of life as well as the natives themselves. A few missionaries like Ellis made explorations and published the information thus gathered. Also the reduction of native tongues to written forms was a contribution of the missionaries.

COMIC-OPERA MONARCHIES

A common feature of early trade contacts was an intensification of tribal warfare. Many chiefs were quick to realize the possibilities that firearms offered for strengthening their power. Warfare became more bloody and more decisive. Kamehameha in the Hawaiian Islands, Cakobau in the Fiji Islands, Pomare in Tahiti, Taufa'ahau in the Tonga Islands, Hongi Ika in New Zealand, and many other chiefs attempted, with varying success, to extend their rule and establish kingdoms on European models.   The more successful ones introduced European court ceremonies, even though the crown might be made of pasteboard.   These monarchies were expensive, and the debts of the kings led to intrigue that resulted in increased foreign control.

ENGLISH AND FRENCH RIVALRY

By the time of the great eighteenth-century voyages in the Pacific, Spain had ceased to be a major power.   She secured the Carolines and Marshalls and made a few efforts to secure Tahiti but did not offer much competition in the rivalry for Pacific islands that developed in the nineteenth century.   Britain and France, the two most powerful European nations, had led in the exploration of the Pacific and ac-quired, during the nineteenth century, most of the more desirable islands.   The explorers of both nations had made conflicting claims to their discoveries.   The traders and others who followed continued to make claims.   Missionaries and planters were loud in their cries for assistance from their home governments in their troubles with natives and nationals of other countries.   This rivalry long delayed annexation, as neither of the home governments in Paris or London considered the Pacific islands worth a war.   French attention to New Zealand in the 1820's and the 1830's brought British colonists and annexation in 1840.   France took advantage of local troubles to establish a protectorate over Tahiti in 1842 although she did not annex the Society Islands outright until 1874.

The French barely nosed out the British in New Caledonia.   The island was discovered by Cook in 1774, but he did not leave a very impressive account of it.   The next visitor was the French navigator D'Entrecasteaux, who gave a more favorable description.   In due time the French government began to take an interest in this part of the Pacific.   In 1843 some missionaries were sent on a warship and the French flag was raised.   The missionaries proved too anxious in securing land and were mistreated by the natives.   When word of this reached France there was agitation for annexation.   The French heard a well-founded rumor that the British were about to annex the island in 1853 and sent an order to their Pacific squadron to annex the island if the British had not already done so.   The British captain was slow and, as a result, the French secured the island and its great mineral resources.

THE GERMANS AND THE JAPANESE

France and Britain had secured title to most of the important Pacific islands when the Germans appeared on the scene.   German interest in the Pacific was first represented by commercial companies located in Bremen and Hamburg. During the 1840's German vessels began to appear in the Pacific with increasing frequency. The Hamburg firm of Godeffroy, the most aggressive of these, had branches in Hawaii, Fiji, Samoa, and New Guinea. After the unification of the German Empire in Europe, Bismarck was finally won over to the policy of securing colonies. In 1884 Germany annexed northeastern New Guinea and the New Britannia (now Bismarck) Islands over the bitter protests of Australia. She managed to secure a few additional islands in the part of the Pacific that Britain and France had not already effectively occupied. German interest in the Carolines and Marshalls brought Spanish colonies to those islands during the 1880's. However, Spain lost the Philippines and Guam in the Spanish American War and had no interest in such poor and remote islands. In 1899 Germany was able to buy them for $4,000,000 and to divide the Samoan Islands with the United States.

Japan appears to have had some contact with the Carolines and Marianas through fishermen before Magellan crossed the Pacific. However, her first real action came in 1890 when she forced a chief on one of the Marshall atolls to apologize for the murder of shipwrecked Japanese fishermen. In the same year the first of some small Japanese trading firms was established in the Carolines. By 1912 Japanese traders were established in Palau, Truk, Ponape, and the Marianas. In 1914 Japan, with the agreement of Great Britain, seized the German islands north of the equator. After the war these were given to her as a mandate from the League of Nations. Australia received the German possessions south of the equator with the exception of western Samoa, which went to New Zealand.

THE UNITED STATES IN THE PACIFIC

The United States was a latecomer to the Pacific. By the time the revolution was over most of the islands had been discovered and claimed many times. American seamen and guano workers did discover some minor islands and lay the basis for claims to others that became important with the advent of transoceanic planes. As was true of other nations, American naval officers and citizens claimed islands and worked to have them annexed to the United States but received little backing from the home government. During the War of 1812 Captain David Porter, U.S.N., raised the American flag over Nukahiva, one of the Marquesas. There is some question whether the natives understood the treaty that they signed. Porter's annexation was not followed up.

Early American interest in the Pacific centered around the whaling industry. Between 1839 and 1842 an American squadron, under command of Lieutenant Charles Wilkes, U.S.N., carried out an extensive scientific expedition in the Pacific. The main objective of this expedition was to aid the whaling industry. The Perry expedition (1852–1854) resulted in the opening of Japan to outside contacts. Perry strongly recommended that the United States acquire naval bases in the western Pacific, but again nothing was done.

During the 1870's there was increasing American interest in the Samoan Islands. Through the efforts of local American citizens, a treaty of annexation was drawn up but not ratified by the United States. In 1877 the United States did accept Pago Pago as a naval base. In 1899 the United States annexed eastern Samoa in order to keep the Germans out.

Because of the activities of the missionaries, the United States long held a dominant position in the Hawaiian Islands. In 1893 a group of Americans overthrew the native monarchy with an idea of annexation by the United States. President Cleveland did not approve of the methods employed, and annexation was delayed until the strategic importance of these islands was demonstrated in the Spanish American War. They were finally annexed in 1897. As a result of the Spanish American War, Spain ceded the Philippine Islands and Guam for $20,000,000. The Philippines were granted their independence on July 4, 1946. The United States occupied the Japanese mandated islands during the Second World War and afterwards received them as a trust territory from the United Nations.

REFERENCES

Amherst of Hackney, Lord, and Basil Thomson (ed.), *The Discovery of the Solomon Islands, by Alvaro de Mendana in 1568*, The Hakluyt Society, London, 1901.

Anson, Lord George, *A Voyage Round the World in the Years 1740, 1741, 1742, 1743, 1744; Compiled from Papers and Other Materials by Richard Walter*, London, 1748. (Many other editions.)

Beaglehole, J. C., *The Exploration of the Pacific*, Adam and Charles Black, London, 1934.

Brookes, Jean I., *International Rivalry in the Pacific Islands 1800–1875*, Berkeley, University of California Press, 1941.

Burney, James, *A Chronological History of the Discoveries in the South Sea or Pacific Ocean*, 5 Vols., Luke Hansard, London, 1803–1817.

Cook, Captain James, and Captain James King, *A Voyage to the Pacific Ocean Undertaken by Command of His Majesty for Making Discoveries in the Southern Hemisphere, etc.*, 3 vols. and Atlas, London, 1784. (Many other editions.)

—— *A Voyage towards the South Pole and Round the World, Performed in H. M. Ships the Resolution and Adventure, 1772–1775*, 2 vols., London, 1777. (Many other editions.)

—— *Views in the South Seas from the Drawings of the Later James Webber, Draftsman on Board The Resolution, Captain James Cook, from the Year 1776 to 1780*, Boydell and Co., London, 1808.

Hawkesworth, John, *An Account of the Voyages Undertaken for Making Discoveries in the Southern Hemisphere, and Successively Performed by Commodore Bryon, Captain Wallis, Captain Carteret and Captain Cook, drawn up from the Journals, etc.* 3 vols., London, 1773. (Various other editions.)

Heawood, Edward, *A History of Geographical Discovery in the Seventeenth and Eighteenth Centuries*, Cambridge University Press, London, 1912.

Henderson, G. C., *The Discoveries of the Fiji Islands*, John Murray, London, 1933.

Hildebrand, J. R., "Columbus of the Pacific: Captain James Cook," *Natl. Geog. Mag.*, Vol. LI, pp. 85–132, January, 1927.

Jenkins, James T., *A History of the Whale Fisheries*, Witherby, London, 1921.

Kuykendall, Ralph S., and A. Grove Day, *Hawaii: A History*, Prentice-Hall, New York, 1948.

Lloyd, Christopher, *Pacific Horizons, the Exploration of the Pacific before Captain Cook*, Allen and Unwin, London, 1946.

Markham, Sir Clements (ed.), *The Voyages of Pedro Fernandez de Quiros, 1595 to 1606*, 2 vols, The Hakluyt Society, London, 1904.

Morgan, Theodore, *Hawaii, A Century of Economic Change, 1778–1876*, Harvard University Press, Cambridge, Mass., 1948.

Scott, Ernest, *Australian Discovery*, 2 vols., J. M. Dent and Sons, London, 1929.

Stanley of Alderley, Lord (ed.), *The First Voyage Round the World by Magellan*, The Hakluyt Society, London, 1874.

Williamson, James A., *The Age of Drake*. Adam and Charles Black, London, 1946.

—— *James A. Cook and the Opening of the Pacific*, The Macmillan Co., New York, 1948.

Wroth, Lawrence C., "The Early Cartography of the Pacific," *The Papers of the Bibliographical Society of America*, Vol. XXXVIII, No. 2, pp. 87–268, 1944.

4

Australia: the Physical Framework

CLIFFORD M. ZIERER

AUSTRALIA IS THE DOMINANT LAND MASS IN THE SOUTHWEST PACIFIC. Its area of nearly 3,000,000 square miles is small when compared to the Pacific, but it is large in comparison with even the combined land area of all the islands. The continent lies antipodal to the north Atlantic and near the center of the world's water hemisphere. It is the only inhabited continent that lies entirely within the southern hemisphere.

About 6500 miles of ocean lie between Australia and California, and it is approximately 7500 miles from Sydney to the Panama Canal. London is 12,500 miles distant from Sydney by way of Panama, and it is about the same distance from London to Perth around South Africa. These great distances between the main centers of European colonial expansion and Australia contributed not only to its late discovery but also to the lag in its exploration and settlement by Europeans.

Although only about 4000 miles lay between Australia and the great centers of population of India, China, and Japan, no great overseas expansionist movement took place from those comparatively near-by Asiatic countries. As a result of Occidental discovery and settlement, Australia has long been the "isolated" continent to Europeans and Americans.

Air travel has now brought Australia nearer to America and Europe in terms of travel time. It is only 40 hours' travel time between California and Sydney. Eighteen or more days are required between those ports for the usual ocean vessels. Travel between England and Australia involves three to four days by air and several weeks by ship. Thus the degree of isolation and its many effects are being appreciably reduced. Increasing attention is also being paid to the relative "closeness" of Australia to Asiatic countries. Thus the "outpost of Europe" is becoming the "near neighbor" of Orient in many important respects.

GENERAL PHYSIOGRAPHIC FEATURES OF THE CONTINENT

The continent of Australia probably assumed its present topographic form about a million years ago after undergoing many significant changes in outline and elevation during the very long geologic period

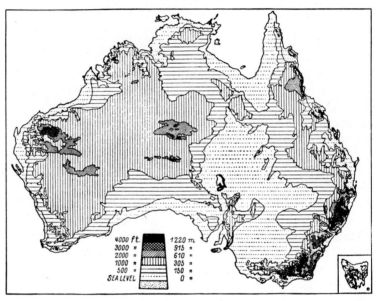

FIGURE 25.   Elevation map of Australia.   From *Climatology of Australia,* by Griffith Taylor, in Köppen and Geiger, *Handbuch der Klimatologie,* Gebrüder Borntraeger, Berlin, 1932.

that preceded the Pleistocene. The ancient land mass was finally reduced over most of its area to heights not far above sea level. During the early Pleistocene period the western portion was elevated about 1000 feet and the eastern portion was raised to heights varying from 2000 to 7000 feet. The intervening land remained near sea level and thus separated the raised western plateau from the higher eastern blocks and folds.

Reduced ocean levels during the glacial epoch eliminated the straits separating Australia from New Guinea on the north and from Tasmania on the south, thus permitting the migration of fauna and flora.

These straits were subsequently restored, and the gradual dissection of the uplifted land masses has proceeded under progressive desiccation of the continent. Minor local uplifts, subsidences, and volcanic outflows are responsible for many of the minor land-form features such as marine terraces, the drowned estuaries of the south coast, and the scattered basalt flows throughout the eastern highlands. Erosion has made substantial progress in dissecting the uplifted portions of the continent only where rainfall is sufficient. Large parts of the interior plateaus have changed but slightly since their major uplift, because of aridity. Large deposits of erosional detritus have accumulated in the central lowlands, but its surface has not been changed substantially in recent geological times.

The present-day surface of Australia is generally low and monotonous in appearance, averaging less than 1000 feet above sea level, and only about 180,000 square miles, or 6 per cent of the continent, lie above the 2000-foot contour line. No continent has a form that is more compact or a coastline that is more smooth (Fig. 25).

Despite these broad elements of uniformity in the form of the continent, significant contrasts exist among three major land-form regions, and many lesser differences occur among the score of minor divisions. Many of these land-form variations are reflected in the patterns of distribution and qualities of climates, soils, vegetation, water supply, and other physical conditions.

The three major land-form divisions of Australia are (1) the Eastern Highlands, (2) the Central Lowlands, and (3) the Western Plateau. These three major regions will be discussed in turn, and some of the characteristics of the lesser divisions will be described at the same time.

THE EASTERN HIGHLANDS

The Eastern Highlands include about one-sixth of the continent or nearly 500,000 square miles of area. It is a complex region of uplifted blocks and folds with intervening lowlands and a narrow, discontinuous coastal plain. The highland region parallels the eastern and southeastern coast for a distance of nearly 2500 miles. The width varies from about 100 miles at each end to as much as 250 miles in the middle portions.

The Eastern Highlands reach their greatest elevations in the southeastern corner of the continent, where, near the border of New South Wales and Victoria, Mt. Kosciusko rises to 7328 feet (the highest point in Australia). Mount Bogong (elevation 6508 feet) is the highest point in Victoria. Elevations above a mile are also reached on the New England Plateau in northeastern New South Wales and on the Atherton Plateau in northeastern Queensland. Most of the Eastern Highland has elevations between 1000 and 3000 feet. About 80,000 square miles lie above the 2000-foot contour line.

The existence of parallel ranges with intervening uplands along with broad uplifted blocks, deeply dissected by streams, produces a wide variety of land forms and exposures. The coastal plain is narrow and discontinuous because extensions of the uplands reach the sea at many points.

Four important plateau areas stand out conspicuously in the Eastern Highlands sometimes called the great Dividing Range, because of their superior elevation and considerable extent. These divisions from north to south are: (1) the Atherton Plateau, (2) the New England Plateau, (3) the Blue Mountain Plateau, and (4) the Monaro Plateau. A number of less significant uplands include the Buckland Tableland, the Toowoomba Upland, the Warrumbungle Range, and the Liverpool Range.

Atherton Plateau. The Atherton Plateau has an area of about 13,000 square miles above the 2000-foot contour line, and the highest point reaches 5438 feet in Mt. Bartle Frere. The elevation of the Atherton Plateau makes its climate much more attractive than that of the adjacent lowlands. The plateau rises precipitously from the narrow coastal plain, and deep gorges have been cut into its eastern margin by the Barron, Mulgrave, and Russell rivers.

New England Plateau. The New England Plateau has an area of about 23,000 square miles above the 2000-foot contour, and Ben Lomond and several other knobs approach 5000 feet in elevation. The Darling Downs in Queensland include about 5000 square miles above the 2000-foot contour just across the state boundary. The highest margin of the New England Plateau faces the sea, and its margin has also been deeply carved by the Macleay, Manning, and Bellinger rivers. The narrow coastal plain is crossed by those streams in their quick descent to sea level. The New England Plateau, like the Atherton Plateau, is comprised principally of granites, but volcanic materials have been ejected in numerous places. A narrow coastal plain lies along the eastern margin of the New England Plateau.

Blue Mountain Plateau. The Blue Mountain Plateau rises to a height of 3000 to 4000 feet, and it has about 15,000 square miles above the 2000-foot contour. Although the plateau makes direct contact with the interior somewhat difficult, residents of Sydney make full use of the upland for resort purposes. The Grose and Cox rivers have cut spectacular bottleneck valleys into the steeply rising eastern flank of the upland. Vertical sandstone cliffs 1000 to 2500 feet in height make these broad, flat-floored valleys useless as approaches to the plateau surface.

The coastal belt to the north and the south of Sydney has been uplifted in places as much as 500 to 1000 feet, and streams have carved gorges with intricate patterns. Subsequent drowning has made the lower courses of these rivers useful for harbors, as at Sydney and Jervis Bay. The Illawarra coastal plain, 50 miles south of Sydney, provides a suitable lowland for agricultural development and for industrial sites.

Although the Blue Mountain Plateau lies athwart Sydney's direct route into the interior, suitable gaps at the north and south ends of the plateau are available. The Hunter River valley provides an easy route to the west from Newcastle, and near Goulburn the railroad passes around the southern end of the Blue Mountains.

Monaro Plateau. The Monaro Plateau is on the New South Wales-Victoria border. About 13,000 square miles lie above the 2000-foot contour line. It is the highest upland region in Australia, and several peaks rise above 6000 feet with Mt. Kosciusko reaching 7328 feet. Several thousand square miles of the Monaro Plateau lie above the 5000-foot elevation and provide a readily accessible tract of snow-covered country for winter sports during the months of June to September. The most important rivers of the continent rise in this high southeastern plateau region. The Commonwealth Federal Territory is situated on the northern margin of this upland at an elevation of about 2000 feet.

Victoria Highland. The Victorian Alps, closely associated with the Monaro Plateau, include about 8000 square miles of moist mountain land above the 2000-foot contour. General elevations are similar to those of the Monaro Plateau.

Victoria Lowland. The extensive coastal lowlands of Victoria lie on the south side of the Monaro Plateau and its western upland continuation. The Victoria lowland stretches for more than 150 miles to the east of Melbourne as the Gippsland district, and as far to the west in the form of a basalt-covered plain. A convenient gap at Kilmore in the east-west segment of the highland enables Melbourne to tap the Murray basin. Port Phillip Bay represents the drowned middle portion of the Victorian lowland, and at its head is situated the city of Melbourne.

Tasmanian Land Forms. Tasmania, although separated from the mainland by Bass Strait (about 150 miles in width), is essentially an outlier of the Eastern Highlands. The dominant feature of the island is the western plateau, which attains a general height of about 3500 feet. About 4000 square miles lie above the 2000-foot contour. Several peaks rise from its western and southern margins to heights of nearly 5000 feet, and Mt. Cradle attains a maximum of 5069 feet. Although the margins of the plateau are deeply dissected, the central portion consists of an old undulating surface. Several large natural lakes occur on the upland, among them Lake Sorell and Great Lake, that are the source of the island's hydroelectric power.

The plateau descends on the east by a series of step faults ("tiers") to a central lowland. Launceston is situated near the north end of this lowland, and Hobart, on the Derwent River estuary, is at the southern end. The eastern margin of the island is occupied by ranges of mountains, which in the northeast corner exceed 5000 feet in height. The eastern highland merges with the western plateau at Oatlands in a range of hills that separates the drainage of the Derwent River from that of the Tamar River.

Coastline in Eastern Australia. The coastline associated with the Eastern Highlands and Tasmania consists of alternating rocky headlands and sandy beaches or embayments. In many places narrow coastal plains lie between the surf and the uplands, and numerous rivers have been drowned in their lower courses. Islands are numerous in the shallow Bass Strait and also along the Queensland coast, where coral reefs help to preserve them.

The Great Barrier Reef of Queensland is the most notable shoreline feature of Australia. The reef and associated islands extend for 1250 miles from a point off Rockhampton to Torres Strait. The reef lies more than 100 miles offshore at the southern end, but it approaches within a few miles of the mainland along much of its northern portion.

THE CENTRAL LOWLAND

The Central Lowland of Australia includes the gently sloping western flank of the Eastern Highlands and also the low-lying basins tributary to the Gulf of Carpentaria on the north and to Spencer Gulf on the south. An area of about a million square miles or one-third of the continent is included; most of it lies below the 500-foot contour, and nearly all is less than 1000 feet above sea level.

The Central Lowland experienced no major geologic change in recent times as did the Eastern Highlands. Large amounts of alluvial material have been brought down by streams from the adjoining uplands and deposited over its ancient surface. Winds have moved much of this material about from place to place. The northermost part of the Central Lowland has been submerged to form the Gulf of Carpentaria. Its margins are shallow and muddy and should be avoided by even small ships. The southern end of the Central Lowland has likewise undergone partial submergence, and Spencer Gulf and the Gulf of St. Vincent penetrate deeply in the direction of Lake Torrens and Lake Eyre. Lake Eyre has an elevation of 39 feet below sea level

The Central Lowland is divided into several drainage basins by low saddles or uplifts that connect the Eastern Highlands with the Western Plateau. The Cloncurry (Mt. Isa) uplift separates the drainage area tributary to the Gulf of Carpentaria from the Lake Eyre basin. In similar fashion the Cobar–Broken Hill uplift separates the Darling River basin from that of the Murray River in the south. The Great Artesian Basin underlies all the Central Lowland to the north of the Cobar–Broken Hill uplift. It includes an area of 550,000 square miles and is the greatest example of its kind in the world.

The Mt. Lofty–Flinders Range extends northward from Adelaide for a distance of nearly 400 miles, thus further separating the Darling-Murray rivers basin from the Spencer's Gulf–Lake Torrens subdivision. The area tributary to Lake Eyre is extremely dry, and much of the watershed of the Darling River is likewise subjected to arid-land erosional processes. Even the Murray River and its important tributaries, the Murrumbidgee and Lachlan, are unable to carry the loads of sediment that reach their courses. As a consequence, their channels shift about continuously through the intricate maze of "billabongs" (anabranches), swamps, and marshes that parallel the drainage courses.

THE WESTERN PLATEAU

The Western Plateau contains about 1,500,000 square miles, or half the area of the continent. It includes essentially all Western Australia and Northern Territory along with the western half of South Australia. Most of the plateau is elevated about 1250 feet above sea level, and it retains the characteristic surface features of a very old land mass. Ancient granites and metamorphic rocks are characteristic. The margins of the plateau have undergone considerable dissection in the moist northern and southwestern sections, and hills and valleys are characteristic land forms.

At various points low mountain peaks and ranges rise above the monotonous plateau surface. The Macdonnell and Musgrave ranges rise to heights of 4800 to 5200 feet near the center of the continent.

The Hammersley and Wiluna ranges approach 4000 feet in the west. In the far north the rugged Kimberley district displays elevations between 2000 and 3000 feet. The Stirling Range, in the extreme southwest corner, rises abruptly to heights of 2000 to 3000 feet from the surrounding plain along its 50-mile length. About 100,000 square miles of the Western Plateau rise above the 2000-foot contour line. The Macdonnell Uplands, near the center of the continent, include half of this higher country; the other half is divided among the Hammersley, Flinders, Musgrave, Wiluna, and Ashburton uplands.

Nullarbor Plain. The Nullarbor region that borders the Great Australian Bight is distinctive because of its uniform surface, lack of streams, and absence of tree growth. Its thick limestone beds are filled with underground drainage lines and caves. High cliffs mark the southern margin of the Nullarbor Plain either at the ocean front or at the inner edge of a narrow coastal plain. The Nullarbor Plain rises from 200 to 400 feet in the south to 1000 feet in the interior, where it merges with the ancient rocks of the plateau.

The Salt Lakes district in the southwest corner of the Western Plateau contains numerous large and small ephemeral lakes. It is an area of interior drainage, but the lakes are loosely strung together along former drainage lines. Drifting sand has blocked many of the old drainage courses, and the lake beds are covered with salt deposits and dry mud during most of the year. Low monadnocks rise above the plateau surface in places. Gravel-filled channels of ancient streams, known as "deep leads," have proved to be important sources of alluvial gold, as at Kalgoorlie.

Sand Ridge Desert. The Sand Ridge Desert occupies over 400,000 square miles of the Western Plateau region, extending across its center from Ooldea in the southeast to Ninety Mile Beach in the northwest. The ridges vary in height from a few feet to 50 or 60 feet, and they show a remarkable degree of parallelism as well as a high degree of uniformity in spacing (one-fourth mile apart, usually). Their orientation is generally from southeast to northwest, but the direction varies from place to place, depending upon the prevailing winds. The principal source of sand is the surface sandstone strata of the region. Stream patterns are lacking, and there is no permanent surface water.

Coastal Margins. Narrow coastal plains border the Western Plateau principally on its western and southern margins. The coastlines about the margins of the Western Plateau vary from a high degree of uniformity along the Nullarbor region to one of extreme irregularity in the northern Kimberly and Arnhem districts. Recent slight submergence of the deeply dissected north coast accounts for its island-fringed and indented characteristics, but high cliffs along the sound margins make them useless for harbors.

The west coast is generally smooth, but the construction of sand bars by the northward-moving currents has produced numerous bays with openings to the north. The good natural harbors at Perth and Albany are the result of submergence. Ninety Mile Beach owes its smooth curve to the abundant supply of sand made available on the beach by land winds. Submerged coral reefs border the northwest coast for hundreds of miles.

CLIMATE AND WEATHER

The generally low relief of Australia and the arrangement of its major land forms are reflected in the patterns of distribution of many climatic features. The distribution of rainfall is strongly affected by the Eastern Highlands. Australia's small size among the continents permits even the most interior location to be only about 550 miles from one of the oceans. Isotherms extend principally in east-west directions and reflect normal latitudinal differences.

Australia's climatic characteristics are also fundamentally related to the fact that the entire continent lies between 10° and 40° south latitude. This position places portions of the continent in the belt of the southeast trade winds throughout the year, within the belt of tropical monsoon rainfall in the summer, and within the westerly wind system in the winter. The climates of Australia are as a consequence characterized by abundant heat and drought and by significant differences in the seasons of rainfall. Tasmania has a relatively cool and moist climate because of its position several degrees to the south of the mainland.

The traditional seasons of the northern hemisphere are, of course, reversed in Australia. Since the seasonal range of temperature is not great in most parts of the continent, the season of drought and the season of rain may be more significant divisions of the year, particularly in the lower latitudes. As the three major wind systems shift to the north and the south with the seasons, individual regions experience the annual sequence of weather conditions (Fig. 26).

SUMMER PERIOD

During the warmer half of the year (November to April) most of Australia except the north coast is under the influence of the southeast trades. These winds bring considerable rainfall to the windward slopes of the Eastern Highlands, but they are drying winds to the great interior areas of low relief.

The north coast is dominated during this season by the northwest monsoon, which brings as much as 50 to 60 inches of rainfall to parts of the tropical coastal region.   Tropical hurricanes bring heavy rainfall and destructive winds to the northwest coast near Broome and to the northeast coast near Cooktown in summer.   The summer rainfall diminishes rapidly toward the interior desert regions.   The southern coastal region receives little or no effective rainfall during the six

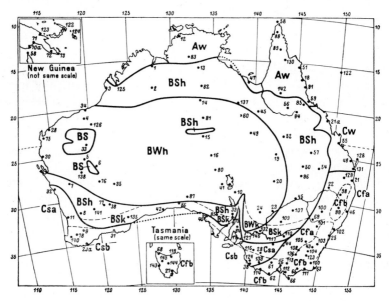

FIGURE 26.   Climatic regions based on Köppen system of classification. From Köppen and Geiger, *Handbuch der Klimatologie,* Gebrüder Borntraeger, Berlin, 1932.

warmer months, but the east coast usually receives considerable moisture from the southeast trades as they rise over the Eastern Highland.   High temperatures are experienced throughout the continent, but Tasmania offers some relief from both heat and drought.

Because of the low absolute humidity that prevails over much of Australia during the hotter months, relatively few uncomfortable days occur each year despite the high temperatures.   The combination of heat and humidity along the north coast and along the northeast coast, however, produces much uncomfortable weather for white inhabitants.   On the other hand, the cooler season in tropical Australia is no more uncomfortable than the warmer season along the southern coast.

During the six cooler months (May to October) the north coast is dominated by the southeast trades, producing a long season of drought. The trades continue to bring moisture to the northern portion of the east coast and drought to the interior desert regions.

During the cooler half year the southern part of Australia is affected by the northward seasonal migration of the Antarctic cyclonic belt. During July and August the eastward-moving storms have reached their greatest intensity and also their deepest penetration of the continent. The intensity, position, and rate of movement of these storms largely explain the variable cooler season weather conditions that prevail over the southern third of the continent. Rainfall as great as 40 or 60 inches comes to parts of the southwest and southeast coast and to Tasmania during the winter months. The amount rapidly diminishes, however, toward the north. Thus it is seen that the interior desert regions receive little rainfall from any of the three major sources from which various portions of the continent are benefited.

Winter temperatures are comparatively mild in all parts of Australia except at higher altitudes. Snowfall does not occur in Perth, Adelaide, or Melbourne along the south coast. The Monaro and Tasmania uplands receive abundant snowfall and freezing temperatures every winter. Snow sometimes falls in the Blue Mountain, New England, Flinders, and Southwestern uplands. Frosts have occurred in practically all parts of the continent except the northern quarter. Even the sugar-growing districts of southeastern Queensland suffer frost damage occasionally.

Rainfall is most reliable along the southern and northern margins of Australia and least reliable in the central desert region. The wettest areas in Australia are on the Atherton Plateau and in Tasmania, and the driest area is in the vicinity of Lake Eyre. Evaporation exceeds rainfall in nearly all parts of Australia. South winds are usually cool and north winds are normally hot as experienced by most Australians. Sunshine is most abundant in central Australia and least abundant in Tasmania and in the southeastern and southwestern corners of the continent.

NATURAL VEGETATION

Before the arrival of large numbers of British settlers, most of Australia was covered with vegetation, unique in nature and well adapted to local soil and climatic conditions. The bringing of sheep, cattle, horses, and rabbits introduced a new element that has led to widespread alteration of natural cover in many parts of the continent. The continued expansion of cultivation has also resulted in the nearly complete destruction of natural vegetation over many millions of acres. Forest industries and man-caused fires have changed the cover on additional large areas. Native vegetation has thus undergone many significant changes in 150 years of vigorous occupation by a people whose livelihood has been won in large measure from the land, although much of Australia is still covered with some semblance of its original plant cover.

GENERAL VEGETATION PATTERN

In its most general aspect the pattern of natural vegetation in Australia shows first a rim of eucalyptus forests along the north, east, and south coasts (Fig. 27). Inside this "horseshoe" is a somewhat wider belt of grasslands dotted with eucalyptus and acacia trees (Fig. 28). A central area of sand ridges and flats supports only sparse desert vegetation.

Australia is a hot and dry continent, and only a very small part of its area was originally covered with dense forests. Less than 30,000 square miles of land are available today for commercial timber production. The extreme southwest corner of the continent and the Eastern Highlands, including Tasmania, contain the best forest lands. Large tracts of open eucalyptus forests of poorer quality occupy less favorable sites in the highlands and along the northern coast. Isolated tracts of dense tropical hardwood forests occupy favorable soils along the moist eastern Queensland coast.

Eucalyptus Forests. About 400 species of eucalyptus trees occur in Australia, ranging from the giant trees of the Victorian mountain forests to the dwarf mallees of the south coast (Fig. 28). Their gray-green foliage is the dominant color in the landscape of most coastal regions. In moist regions a rich ground cover of ferns is commonly associated with the dense tree growth. In drier areas the eucalypts occur as an open forest growth with an intermixture of woody shrubs and grasses. They are also found growing as gallery forests along the banks of rivers in the interior, such as the Murray and its major tributaries (Fig. 30).

Many of the eucalypts are highly inflammable, and some of the most valuable species have been seriously damaged by forest fires. Eucalypts provide the bulk of wood used in Australia for ordinary construction purposes and fuel. Large areas of eucalyptus forests have

FIGURE 27. Dense growth of valuable eucalyptus forest, tree ferns, and associated plants covers the high and rugged uplands of eastern Victoria.

FIGURE 28. These clumps of mallee illustrate the essential characteristics of this dwarf eucalyptus growth that covers vast areas in southern Australia.

been destroyed by "ring-barking" operations in order to extend the pasture and crop areas. The various species of eucalyptus are known to Australians by a variety of common names such as ironbarks, gums (smooth barks), half barks (boxes), stringybarks, and peppermints. The brilliant red flowers of certain eucalypts in Western Australia are conspicuous for their beauty in contrast to the small white flowers of most eastern species.

Outstanding among the eucalyptus timber trees are the so-called mountain ash (*Eucalyptus regnans*) of the Victorian uplands and the karri (*Eucalyptus diversicolor*) and jarrah (*Eucalyptus marginata*) forests of Western Australia. The 4,000,000 acres of karri and jarrah forests comprise one of the most important forest regions in Australia.

The forests of Tasmania resemble those of the highlands in Victoria. However, in addition to large stands of eucalyptus, dense growths of myrtle beech (*Nothofagus*) forests occur on the western uplands.

The mallee is a species of dwarf eucalyptus characteristic of a wide belt along the south coast from Victoria to Western Australia. Bushy growths, 20 feet or less in height, cover large areas of sub-humid sandy land. The mallee is often cleared by wheat farmers by rolling it down and burning the tangled growth. Serious soil drift often follows such operations. The bulky roots of mallee are commonly used as firewood (Fig. 28).

Tropical Forests. Along the east coast of Queensland, where precipitation is most abundant, are scattered tracts of Malayan or tropical rainforest. Among the characteristic trees are red cedar (*Cedrela*), rosewood (*Synoum*), hoop and bunya pines (*Araucaria*), Kauri pine (*Agathis*), and Queensland maple (*Flindersia*). All are useful as cabinet woods, and they support an important lumber industry. Vines, ferns, and orchids are abundant in these mixed tropical forests. Certain members of the tropical forest association, such as cabbage palms (*Livistona australis*), are also found along the New South Wales coast.

Open Forests. Inland from the principal coastal forests are stands of open stunted forests of eucalyptus and acacia species. The eucalypts occupy the western slopes of the Eastern Highlands as well as a wide belt along the north coast. Not only are all these trees able to stand a low average rainfall but they also survive severe droughts extending over several successive seasons. On the western flanks of the highlands of New South Wales and Queensland are extensive growths of cypress pine (*Callitris*). It grows in open stands and reproduces rapidly. In recent years it has been milled extensively, in part because it resists termites.

FIGURE 29. Characteristic sheep and wheat country near Wagga, New South Wales.

FIGURE 30. The Murray River fills its channel from bank to bank at Renmark because of the series of low dams that impound its flow.

Acacia Species. There are more than 600 species of acacia in Australia, and most of them are found in the hotter and drier interior regions. Acacias usually appear as scattered trees in grass- and shrub-covered areas and are low, spreading trees with relatively thin foliage. They are of little commercial significance because of their small size. They are commonly called mulga, brigalow, or wattle by Australians. The seed pods of acacias are an important type of fodder for sheep, and in times of drought even the foliage is utilized. The golden bloom of the acacia provides much color for the interior plains and hills and for desert stream courses during late winter and spring months. One species of acacia, known as blackwood (*Acacia melanoxylon*), grows to log size in Tasmania and provides excellent cabinet wood.

Shrub Growth. Among the best-known and most valuable types of shrub growth in Australia are saltbush (*Atriplex*) and bluebush (*Kochia*). They are common along the south coast from New South Wales to western Australia. Considerable amounts of annual forage are available between the perennial shrubs, but in times of drought sheep feed on the succulent foliage of both ˙saltbush and bluebush. These growths resemble the sage brush of the United States in many respects.

Native Grasses. One of the most valuable native grasses is Mitchell grass (*Astrebla*), which covers considerable areas in central Queensland and adjacent portions of New South Wales and Northern Territory. It occurs in scattered perennial clumps, and after rains much ephemeral forage grows on the intervening ground. The uncertain nature of rainfall, however, results in wide variations in the amount of vegetation from season to season. Growth takes place after the brief period of summer rains, and a long dormant period occurs during the drier winter season.

Desert Vegetation. The native vegetation of the desert regions consists entirely of drought-resisting plants and trees. Acacias (mulga and brigalow) are most common, but dwarf eucalypts appear near the margins. Stream courses are defined by lines of tree growths, such as the she oak (*Casuarina*). Spinifex (*Triodia*) is a tough spiny grass that grows in large clumps in sandy desert areas. Spinifex and mulga provide most of the feed for sheep in some of the driest pastoral areas of the continent.

SOILS

The distribution and nature of soils in Australia are related to geological, physiographic, climatic, and vegetational conditions. The widespread occurrence of hard granitic and metamorphic rocks rather than soft sedimentaries has not favored the development of deep fertile soils. The large extent of mountains and hill lands in the moist areas has resulted in rapid soil wastage on steep slopes. Desert types of soils are especially widespread, owing to inadequate rainfall in most of the interior of the continent. Characteristic differences between grassland and forest soils appear in Australia as in other continents. Pedalfer soils are found in the moister coastal zones whereas pedocals occupy the bulk of the continent (Fig. 31A).

PODSOLIC SOILS

A wide band of podsolic soils parallels the north, east, and southeast coast from the Kimberleys to western Victoria. Tasmania and the southwest corner of Western Australia also have badly leached podsol-type soils. This belt of soils corresponds generally with the more rugged parts of the continent, the wettest areas, and the more heavily forested districts. These podsolic soils are not very fertile because most plant nutriment has been removed by leaching, and soils do not accumulate easily on steep slopes underlain by hard rocks.

Patches of better-quality soils have developed in the highlands where basalt flows and softer sedimentary rocks of certain kinds weather rapidly into productive soils. Fertile soils are also usually associated wth alluvial deposits along the many rivers that enter the sea along these coastlines.

The Hunter River lowland has long been famous for its productive soils. Similar soils occur along the lower courses of the Clarence and Macleay rivers in northeast New South Wales. Some of the best soils in Tasmania are along the floodplains of the Tamar River at Launceston and along the Derwent and Huon rivers near Hobart. The best soils along the north coast of Australia are to be found along the lower floodplains of the Adelaide, Daly, Victoria, and Roper rivers. Marsh soils along the lower Murray River are notable for their productivity. Coastal lowlands underlain by sterile sandstones, as near Sydney, however, are notably unproductive.

The deep reddish soils characteristic of the basalt areas of northern Tasmania, the Darling Downs, the Atherton Plateau, and elsewhere are also notable for their fertility. The basalt plain to the west of Melbourne, however, is so rocky that it is practically useless for cultivation although it produces an excellent cover of grass. High moor soils, consisting of fine black peat overlying weathered rock fragments and clay, are characteristic of the uplands of Tasmania and portions of the Monaro Plateau. The presence of large tracts of lateritic soils in the southwest corner of Australia represents a fossil soil that developed during a geologic time characterized by much greater rainfall than the present.

Superphosphate fertilizer has assisted in making favorable tracts of

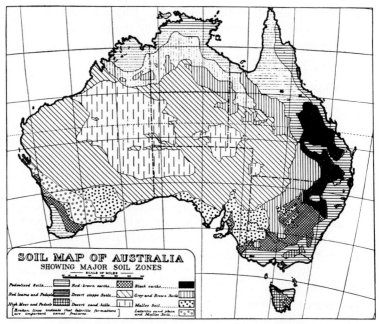

FIGURE 31A.   Major soil regions of Australia.   Prepared by J. A.
Prescott, "The Soils of Australia in Relation to Vegetation and
Climate," *C.S.I.R. Bulletin* 52, Canberra, 1931.

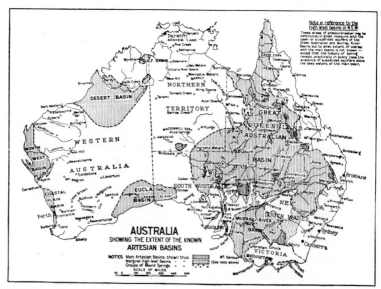

FIGURE 31B.   Artesian basins and location map.   From *Commonwealth Yearbook.*

podsolic soils somewhat more productive. As soon as the lime and phosphate deficiency is overcome, clover and other legumes may be established successfully. Much excellent pasture has been constructed in this manner along the east coast where rainfall is usually ample throughout the year.

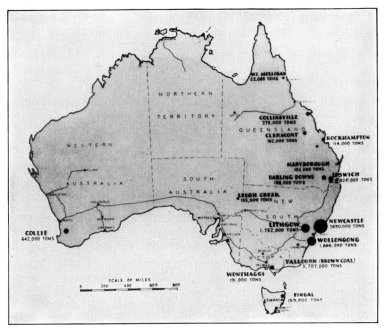

FIGURE 31C. Principal coal-producing localities. From *Coal Mining in Australia*, by H. S. Elford and M. R. McKeown. Reproduced by permission of Tait Publishing Co., Ltd., Melbourne, 1947.

PEDOCAL SOILS

The richer soils of Australia occur in a nearly continuous "horseshoe" belt (open to the west coast) inside the coastal podsol zone. This belt corresponds somewhat closely with the tree-dotted grasslands and brushlands that nearly enclose the central desert region. The rainfall of this soil belt diminishes from the coastal margins toward the interior, as does the quantity of vegetation. Because of the relatively light rainfall, soil leaching is not a problem in this district. Rainfall is the principal limiting factor in agricultural productivity. As is characteristic of most Australian soils, there is usually a phosphate deficiency. In some districts small amounts of copper and zinc sulphate must be supplied along with the superphosphate to correct mineral deficiencies.

These important intermediate soils (between the coastal podsols and the interior desert soils) include gray-earths in the north, gray-earths and black-earths in the east, and chestnut-earths and mallee soils in the south. All these soils receive annual rainfall varying from about 35 inches to about 10 inches. The humus content ranges from an abundant supply in the black-earths to a scant amount in the mallee soils. Vegetation cover varies from savannah woodland and savannah to mallee scrub. The chestnut-earths in the south represent an extension southward of the northerly black-earths. Summer rainfall is characteristic in the black-earth region, and winter rainfall is typical in the chestnut-earth region. Mallee soils are characteristic of the lower Murray basin, Eyre Peninsula, and the western Nullarbor region. They are light in color, sandy, and subject to blowing when cultivated.

The seasonal distribution of rainfall has important effects upon soil types in Australia. In regions of summer rainfall soils resembling the true chernozem are developed; in zones of winter rainfall soils with surface horizons leached of clay and lime, but still retaining the oxides of iron, are characteristic. In Queensland, podsolic soils usually develop along the coast, black-earths develop inland under wooded savannah conditions, brown and gray soils arise under open grassland and shrub steppe, and desert sandhills lie in the extreme west. In southwestern Australia the normal sequence is forested podsols along the coast, red-brown earths with savannah woodland, pinkish-brown mallee soils, red soils with mulga and saltbush, and desert sandhills in the interior. Lateritic soils occur as cappings of iron oxide and alumina in old peneplain surfaces of low relief especially in Western and Northern Australia.

DESERT SOILS

Wind action is a dominant factor in determining the nature of soils in arid Australia. Wind strongly affects evaporation, it influences the accession of cyclic salt by the soil, and it is a powerful factor in the distribution of soil-forming materials. Desert surfaces include vegetation-covered sandhills, stony plains, and rock surfaces. It is likely that spinifex-covered sandhills were more widespread before the arrival of pastoralists in the arid and semi-arid regions. Gibber plains or stony deserts (serir) are formed by the removal of fine soil particles by wind and the leaving of polished pebble surfaces. Rock deserts (hamada) are characteristic of the Nullarbor Plain, where massive limestone outcrops.

SOIL EROSION

Australians, like most Americans, have become generally aware only recently of the seriousness and extent of soil erosion. The widespread deterioration and removal of natural vegetation cover are largely responsible. The production of wheat on dry marginal areas, the extensive use of the fallow system, and the occurrence of dry years have provided the combination that permits dust storms to carry away the top soil from the subhumid interior farming districts. Overgrazing by sheep, rabbits and other livestock has removed the grass and brush cover that once protected the soil. Careless cultivation and fallowing of the rich red soils of the Darling Downs have led to their serious gullying, even on gentle slopes. Apple production on steep slopes in Tasmania has resulted in serious sheet wash and gullying of the podsol soils. Many soils in the Eastern Highlands erode seriously after the removal of timber cover.

Dust storms and muddy streams, gullies and rock exposures, reduced yields, and smaller carrying capacities are the usual evidences of soil destruction. Very little has been done thus far by either individuals or government to check the losses on a large-scale basis.

WATER RESOURCES

Only one-third of Australia, or 1,000,000 square miles of area, receives more than 20 inches of rainfall annually. Another third receives between 10 and 20 inches each year, and the final third receives less than 10 inches. The average annual rainfall for the continent is estimated to be only about 17 inches.

Severe droughts were experienced in Australia in 1866, 1876, 1888, 1902, 1914, 1929, and 1944, or at 10 to 15-year intervals. Some of these droughts lasted for two or three successive years. The 1944–1945 drought was perhaps the most disastrous because of the unprecedented expansion of agriculture into the drier districts, many of which are characterized by light soils.

Although rainfall is fairly well distributed throughout the year in the eastern portion of the continent, precipitation in a wide belt along the north coast is limited to the summer season, and that along the south coast comes in winter. To make matters worse, there is a wide variation in the amount of rainfall from year to year. In years of severe drought two-thirds of the continent receives less than 10 inches of rainfall. In years of moderate drought one-half of the continent receives less than 10 inches. In many years of drought even the better-watered portions of the continent receive only half or two-thirds their normal rainfall, and hence these regions also suffer important losses. As a result of all these conditions water supply is relatively scarce in most parts of the continent, and it is the major limiting factor in the general development of most regions.

SURFACE WATERS

The scarcity of water is reflected in the scant number and ephemeral nature of streams and other surface-water bodies. Perennial streams are found only along the north, east, southeast, and southwest coasts of Australia and in Tasmania. Many of them are subject to large flows during the summer rainy season and to severe diminution during the long season of drought. No rivers occur in a vast area in the interior or in the Nullarbor Plain. Rivers along most of the west coast and those in the Lake Eyre and Darling River basin flow only occasionally. Even the Murray has on rare occasions practically ceased to flow. On these bases the continent may be divided into large regions with (1) *no* runoff, (2) *internal* drainage, and (3) *external* drainage. Numerous significant facts about water supply, climatic conditions, and soil and vegetational responses are intimately related.

Numerous lakes appear on the physical maps of Australia although they scarcely exist in reality. The large lakes appearing in South Australia, such as Eyre, Torrens, and Gardiner, are really only lake beds ("playas," "salt pans," or "clay pans") covered by a shallow layer of water after occasional wet periods and by glistening salt deposits during most of the year. The salt-lake region of Western Australia and its hundreds of "lakes" present the same picture. In all these instances not only is surface water ephemeral but also its saline character makes it of little use for plant, man, and beast. Small accumulations of water are available on the Western Plateau in rock basins for brief periods after rains.

ARTESIAN BASINS

Fortunately, some portions of Australia that lack surface water supplies have substantial amounts of underground water that may be tapped by wells and bores. The Great Artesian Basin of Queensland and portions of adjoining states is well known. The basin extends southward from the Gulf of Carpentaria to the Broken Hill–Cobar uplift and thus includes the Lake Eyre and Darling River drainage.

It has a total area of 550,000 square miles, and in places the water-bearing strata are more than a mile deep. The intake for the artesian strata lies among the moist highlands to the east. Temperatures of the artesian water increase at the rate of 1° for each 20 to 50 feet of depth, depending on the locality. Salinity increases generally toward the west or in the principal direction of underground movement. Under natural conditions the artesian basin drained slowly through saline springs in the vicinity of Lake Eyre (Fig. 31*B*).

The most important portion of the Great Artesian Basin is in Queensland, which claims nearly two-thirds of its area. The first deep bore was completed at Blackall in 1888 to a depth of 1663 feet. By 1900 there were 524 artesian bores, with an average depth of 1475 feet, producing 224,000,000 gallons of water daily. By 1910 state laws regulated the tapping and use of artesian water. By 1914 artesian water flow in Queensland reached a maximum of 355,000,000 gallons daily from about 1200 bores. Flows have decreased slowly since 1914, and despite the fact that there were over 2000 bores in 1945 the year's flow amounted to only 225,000,000 gallons.

By 1945 about one-third of Queensland's 2000 bores had ceased to flow. The average depth of bores was between 1500 and 1600 feet, and the average yield was about 160,000 gallons for each 24-hour period. An annual average decline in flow of 1¾ to 2 per cent may be expected at each bore because of diminished pressure. Water may be pumped after a bore ceases to flow, but that increases costs.

The greatest concentrations of bores in Queensland occur to the east of Cloncurry and to the west of Jericho. In New South Wales most of the bores are found to the north and east of Bourke. There are a few wells near Charlotte Waters and Oodnadatta in South Australia along the route between Alice Springs and Port Augusta.

Artesian water finds its principal use in watering stock and for domestic purposes. The bores make possible the use of pastures that lack surface water but have adequate feed. There is insufficient water to meet the needs of irrigation, and its high mineral content also tends to prohibit such use. Artesian water is usually distributed by ditches for stock-watering purposes. Since the ditches are not lined, seepage losses are great, and some water is also lost by evaporation. It is estimated that less than 5 per cent of the water delivered from the well is actually consumed by livestock. It is claimed, however, that the cost of distribution by pipe lines would not be justified by the returns from the pastoral industry. The present waste of water is enormous.

IRRIGATED LANDS

Australians irrigate about 885,000 acres of crop land, of which two-thirds are in Victoria and one-sixth is in New South Wales. The acreage varies considerably from year to year, depending upon rainfall and the amount of stored water. The larger irrigation projects are associated with the Murray River and its principal tributaries. Smaller projects are in the Inkerman and Dawson Valley districts of Queensland and at Harvey and Davesbrook in Western Australia.

The Murray River and its principal southern tributaries, the Goulburn, Lodon, and Mita, provide most of the water for irrigation in Victoria. The Murrumbidgee and Lachlan rivers are the most important sources of water for irrigation in New South Wales. Burrinjuck, Hume, Waranga, Eildon, and smaller reservoirs on these rivers provide a combined storage capacity of about 2½ million acre-feet of water. The capacity of several of these storages is being increased.

The catchment area of the Murray River and its tributaries includes over 400,000 square miles, but only the higher lands adjacent to the headwaters (158,000 square miles) contribute runoff. The contributing watershed has 20 to 40 inches of rainfall; most of the non-contributing area has 10 to 20 inches, and a small part has less than 10 inches. In its original condition, the Murray spread its muddy waters over hundreds of square miles of lowland during times of flood, and during times of drought it was little more than a succession of water holes stretching through its semi-arid middle and lower basin.

Irrigation was begun as early as 1882, when the Echuca and Waranga shires joined forces in the establishment of the Goulburn-Waranga irrigation system in Victoria. In 1886 the passage of an irrigation act in Victoria, which vested in the Crown the right to use water from any stream, lake, or swamp for irrigation, marked the beginning of several important projects along the Murray. The important irrigation communities of Mildura and Renmark were established by the Chaffey brothers from Southern California during the late 1880's.

In 1906 the Victoria State Rivers and Water Supply Commission was established to control and direct the use of Murray River water for irrigation. Storage reservoirs have been constructed, and irrigated land has been steadily expanded through the efforts of that group. In 1915 the Commonwealth and the three states involved in the flow of the Murray agreed on a program of future development. A system of locks and weirs was designed to improve the navigation of the river without interfering with irrigation interests. Continued decline of navigation in competition with railroad and highway transport gradually brought about a shift in emphasis to irrigation, flood control, and power development. The Murray River Agreement also led to the construction of several large storage reservoirs to regularize the flow of the river.

Hume Reservoir, near Albury, New South Wales, comprises the largest artificial fresh-water storage on the continent with its 50 square miles of water surface and 1,250,000 acre-feet of storage. Plans are being made to increase its capacity to 2,000,000 acre-feet. Water is backed up the Murray for 40 miles and up the Mitta for 20 miles.

The total flow of the Murray River at Euston (below the junction with the Murrumbidgee) was 5,330,000 acre-feet in the year 1946–1947. In 1945–1946, the amount of water passing into South Australia amounted to 5,500,000 acre-feet after New South Wales and Victoria had extracted 2,600,000 acre-feet for irrigation. These facts indicate that the effective use of Murray River water has only begun.

The Darling River, principal tributary of the Murray, has been little developed. It drains an area of about 250,000 square miles in New South Wales and southern Queensland. It has failed to flow only occasionally, as during periods in 1902 and 1919, despite the fact that most of its drainage basin has less than 10 inches of rainfall. The flow at Menindee has ranged from none to 11,000,000 acre-feet per annum since measurements began in 1885. The average flow is about 1,250,000 acre-feet yearly.

EVAPORATION LOSSES

Evaporation losses in Australia are enormous, and this fact detracts greatly from the effectiveness of water stored in surface reservoirs. Evaporation losses from open-water surfaces in areas having less than 10 inches of rainfall are estimated to average about 7 feet per year. Shallow reservoirs are almost useless in arid country, for during a 2-year drought practically all the water would be lost by evaporation alone. One of the great advantages of artesian basins is that they are free from evaporation losses.

STOCK WATER SYSTEMS

In Victoria the total area of land supplied with water for domestic and stock purposes and for irrigation (exclusive of metropolitan areas) amounted to 15,376,000 acres in 1945–1946. In that year the irrigated crop land amounted to 657,000 acres, but much additional pasture land was watered. The Wimmera-Mallee Domestic and Stock Water

Supply System provided water for 12,000 farmers living in the drier parts of the state and occupying nearly 15,000,000 acres of land. Thousands of miles of ditches deliver water to storages on these holdings at selected times of the year.

MINERAL RESOURCES

The occurrence and distribution of mineral resources in Australia are obviously related to the geologic character of the continent. The widespread distribution of Paleozoic and Precambrian rocks in the western two-thirds of the continent, along with isolated patches in the east and in Tasmania, accounts for the importance of Australia's resources of gold, silver, lead, tin, copper, and related minerals. The fact that these ancient rocks lie exposed at the surface over wide areas has facilitated prospecting. The sparseness of vegetation in most of these areas has likewise made mineral discovery easy, although in places surface deposits of sand have been a handicap. Some minerals, such as gold and tin, have accumulated in placer deposits after the disintegration of the source rocks.

PRECAMBRIAN MINERAL DISTRICTS

The Western Australian gold fields, from Halls Creek, Pilbara, and Marble Bar in the north to Kalgoorlie and Phillips River on the south, are related to surface exposures of Precambrian rocks. Minor occurrences of copper, chromium, lead, and tin also are involved.

The Spencer's Gulf–Broken Hill mineral district of South Australia and New South Wales owes its existence likewise to the presence of these ancient rocks. The lead-zinc deposits of Broken Hill, the formerly important reserves of copper at Burra, Kapunda, and Wallaroo-Moonta, and the rich iron ores of the Iron Knob district lie near the southeast corner of the ancient Western Plateau.

Within the north margin of the plateau are the Yampi Sound iron deposits, the Kimberley gold fields, the copper deposits of Cloncurry, the lead-zinc-copper ores of Mt. Isa, and many smaller scattered deposits of gold, silver, tungsten, lead, and tin in Northern Territory.

PALEOZOIC MINERAL DISTRICTS

The Eastern Highlands of Australia contain Paleozoic rocks that are mineralized from York Peninsula on the north to Tasmania in the south. The highlands of Queensland and northeastern New South Wales are almost continuously mineralized. Tin and gold are important in the north at Herberton and Croydon; gold and copper are more significant at Mt. Morgan; and tin is important on the New England Upland. The Cobar uplift in New South Wales has gold and copper, and the gold deposits of Bendigo and Ballarat of Victoria are well known. The older mineralized rocks of western and northeastern Tasmania have produced copper, lead, zinc, tin, and other metals.

MINERAL FUELS

Although Australia does not rank among the countries having great reserves of mineral fuels, it does have sufficient coal deposits to meet the needs of the southwest Pacific region for many generations (Fig. 31C). The presence of important supplies of natural petroleum has still to be demonstrated. Bituminous coal occurs principally in several large basins in southeastern Queensland, between Bowen and Brisbane, and in eastern New South Wales, between Port Stephens and Port Kembla. Large deposits of lignite occur in the Gippsland district of southern Victoria. Small deposits of bituminous coal exist in eastern Tasmania, at Collie, Western Australia, and elsewhere. Some lignite is found at Leigh Creek, South Australia. The bituminous coal resources of Australia are estimated to be about 10,000,-000,000 tons, and the lignite reserves are believed to be as much as 40,000,000,000 tons.

PRINCIPAL COAL FIELDS

The principal coal basin of New South Wales occupies about 16,500 square miles, and an additional area extends beneath the ocean. The coal seams outcrop about the margins of the basin at Newcastle in the north, Lithgow in the west, and Bulli in the south. The seams underlie Sydney at a depth of nearly 3000 feet.

In Queensland the coal measures extend for 500 miles north and south, and appear to have a much greater extent than the New South Wales field. The principal lignite deposit of Victoria occurs in a basin about 40 miles long and some 15 miles wide. The lignite deposit is 100 to 240 feet thick and is covered by only about 40 feet of gravel and clay.

SCARCITY OF PETROLEUM

Despite several decades of effort to locate commercial deposits of natural petroleum, Australia is still almost entirely dependent on imports. Drilling has been conducted particularly in the great Central Lowlands, as at Longreach and Roma in Queensland. Oil shale deposits occur in association with the coal measures of the Eastern

Highlands, and their possible usefulness as an emergency source of petroleum products has been demonstrated.

FISHERIES

A wide variety of fish characteristic of both temperate and tropical waters is available in Australia, but the quantity caught for market is small in comparison with the number caught in many other countries, in large part because of the abundance of meat available.

The principal commercial fishing areas include the coastal waters and associated river mouths, bays, and estuaries between Cairns, Queensland, and Ceduna, South Australia, and between Esperance and Geraldton, Western Australia. Onshore fisheries are commonly associated with tidal river mouths. The northwest and north coast between Shark Bay, Western Australia, and the Cape York Peninsula is also important for its tropical pearl-shell fishery.

Demersal fisheries are conducted principally on the southeastern continental shelf between Crowdy Head and Cape Everard, off the north and east coasts of Tasmania, and off the southwest corner of the continent. Pelagic fishing grounds, producing Spanish mackerel, occur between Cairns and Coff's Harbor, with the industry centering at Townsville. Barracouta are taken in Bass Strait and off eastern Tasmania. Tuna are known to occur at various points but are not significant commercially.

Oysters are found along the eastern Queensland coast, and they are extensively cultivated in shallow estuaries in New South Wales. Prawns (or shrimp) are found off the temperate portion of the east coast, and crayfish are common on the reefs along the southeast and southwest coasts. Whales occur in the cooler waters off the southern coastline and for some distance northward along both the east and west coasts. A whaling station is situated at Albany, Western Australia, in order to exploit the Indian Ocean area, and another is planned for Shark Bay, Western Australia, near the Tropic of Capricorn.

A wide variety of fishing boats and gear is employed, but increasing emphasis is being placed on modern trawlers and seine boats. About 12,000 men are normally employed in the fisheries.

Most of the Australian catch is marketed fresh in the large metropolitan market centers. Fishing activity tends, therefore, to be concentrated in those waters lying within easy reach of those markets whereas distant grounds are only lightly fished. The canning and curing of fish are not extensively developed.

The pearl shell fishery of the north coast was formerly conducted principally with Oriental labor, but during the Second World War the industry ceased almost entirely. Aborigines may assume a larger place in the conduct of that industry as it is gradually restored. The principal centers of activity have long been Broome, Darwin, and Thursday Island. Pearl shell is the commodity that supports the industry rather than pearls. The pearl-shell oysters are gathered by divers from the sea bottom at depths of 5 to 20 fathoms. Bêche-de-mer and tortoise shell are also accessory products of the north-coast fisheries. Practically all these commodities are exported. About 200 boats and 2000 men were employed during the years of maximum prewar development.

REFERENCES

Dare, H. H., *Water Conservation in Australia,* Simmons, Ltd., Sydney, 1939.

Fenner, Charles, *South Australia—A Geographical Study,* Whitcombe & Tombs, Melbourne, 1931.

Gentilli, J., *Australian Climates and Resources,* Whitcombe & Tombs, Melbourne, 1946.

Holmes, J. M., *Soil Erosion in Australia and New Zealand,* Angus & Robertson, Sydney, 1946.

Jose, A. W. (ed.), *The Australian Encyclopaedia,* Angus & Robertson, Sydney, 1927.

Madigan, C. T., *Central Australia,* Oxford University Press, London, 1944.

Official Yearbook of the Commonwealth of Australia, Government Printer, Melbourne.

Taylor, Griffith, *Australia—A Study of Warm Environments and Their Effect on British Settlement,* Methuen & Co., London, 1949.

5

Australia: the Cultural Development

CLIFFORD M. ZIERER

AUSTRALIA WAS FIRST APPROACHED BY PORTUGUESE EXPLORERS, AND later it might easily have been a Spanish colony. The Dutch rejected it in favor of the more attractive East Indies, and the British were first to occupy it shortly after the American Revolution. Such, in brief, is the account of early European contact with this continent.

The exploration by James Cook in 1770 of the previously unknown east coast of Australia, then called New Holland, became the real basis of British interest in that continent. Cook sighted the southeast coast of New Holland at Cape Everard on April 20, 1770. He coasted northward and entered Botany Bay, where Joseph Banks, the botanist, became familiar with the distinctive flora. The expedition continued its mapping activities northward along the coast and, after being shipwrecked at Cooktown, sailed through Torres Strait for Java and eventually England. The name New South Wales was applied by Cook to the east coast because of its assumed resemblance to his native coast of Wales.

A great deal of interest was aroused in England by the accounts of Cook and Banks regarding New South Wales as a place for settlement. The need for a new convict-receiving center after the American Revolution led in 1788 to the arrival at Botany Bay of the First Fleet.

BRITISH SETTLEMENT IN 1788

The commander of the First Fleet, Captain Arthur Phillip, was less favorably impressed with Botany Bay than was Cook, and, as a result, the first settlement was established at Sydney, six miles to the north. The site at Sydney Cove provided deep water along shore, ample

118

supplies of timber, stone, and fresh water, and several small tracts of cultivable land. A rigid system of military control was established to supervise the convicts and most other activities. Sydney was a penal establishment and not a colony of free settlers. From time to time additional consignments of convicts arrived, and the post was largely dependent on imported foodstuffs and supplies. Some detailed knowledge of the coastline to the north and south of Sydney was gained by small exploring parties although the main objective was to restrict expansion rather than to encourage such effort. The name Australia gradually replaced the earlier name New Holland.

ESTABLISHMENT OF OUTPOST SETTLEMENTS

The arrival of additional convicts made necessary the establishment of convict outposts in Van Diemen's Land, at Newcastle, at Brisbane, and on Norfolk Island. The expiration of prison sentences and retirements from the military force also created a free population interested in establishing homes in the new land. Business enterprises arose, and expanding opportunities in agricultural and pastoral pursuits were recognized. In due time free citizens came to outnumber the convicts, and efforts were made to prohibit the arrival of more convicts. A total of about 160,000 persons was transported to Australia during a period of 80 years for major and minor offenses.

Convict shipments to the east coast ceased before 1850. Van Diemen's Land received no convicts after 1853, at which time its name was changed to Tasmania in an effort to remove the stigma attached to the former name as a major convict center.

PENAL COLONIES BECOME FREE SETTLEMENTS

Without any well-defined plan, the original penal establishments at Sydney, Hobart, Newcastle, and Brisbane were thus gradually transformed into centers of normal settlement, trade, and industry. The separate colony of Van Diemen's Land was proclaimed in 1825, being the first separation from the eastern half of the continent that was annexed by Cook in 1770. Settlement pushed beyond the prison-camp confines largely under the stimulus of the pastoral industry. Autocratic rule under the military governors was replaced by democratic process.

ESTABLISHMENT OF OTHER FREE SETTLEMENTS

Not all the principal centers of population in Australia were initiated under the penal system. In 1829 a shipload of British settlers arrived at Perth to insure control of that strategic and promising corner of the continent. Progress was discouragingly slow during the next 20 years, which led to the request in 1849 for convicts to provide a labor force.

The late establishment of colonies in the vicinity of Melbourne is most surprising. After an unsuccessful attempt in 1803 to establish a colony at the entrance to Port Phillip Bay, more than 30 years intervened before the establishment of settlements at Portland in 1834 and at Melbourne in 1835. Discovery of the rich pastoral resources in Southeast Australia thereafter led to the rapid colonizing of the territory between Sydney and Melbourne. In 1850 Victoria was recognized as a colony separate from the Mother Colony of New South Wales.

In 1836 two shiploads of settlers arrived at Kangaroo Island off the south coast of Australia to establish a colony based on the Wakefield idea of introducing both a land-owning aristocracy and a worker group. Finding the island unsatisfactory, the colony moved to the near-by mainland and established the town of Adelaide. Years of struggle to make a living from the soil were followed by the successful establishment of the pastoral industry by the "overlanders" from New South Wales.

EXPANSION OF SETTLEMENT THROUGH PASTORAL INDUSTRY

The exploration of the continent of Australia, after the delimitation of its exterior boundaries by sea, was closely related to the development of the pastoral industry. As early as 1796 considerable interest was displayed in Sydney in the establishment of the Merino wool industry. By 1813 a road was pushed over the Blue Mountain Upland from Sydney to Bathurst, the first town to be established in the interior. Bathurst lay at the edge of a vast grassland, interspersed with trees, which stretched far to the west, north, and south. Explorers pushed out in all directions from Sydney and later from Adelaide to observe the nature of the continent. The pastoralists followed closely on their heels wherever suitable pasture lands were discovered.

Thus, by 1830, Australia entered upon the squatting era, and for some decades the rugged pastoralists drove their flocks beyond the original confines of the settlements to encompass the most favorable portions of the continent. Government followed the squatters and usually confirmed the rights to land that they had pre-empted. The sheepmen became the aristocracy of the new land, and their influence is still characteristic of the continent.

GOLD PROVIDES A NEW BASIS FOR SETTLEMENT

Although the occurrence of gold in Australia was indicated 10 years before the California discovery, it was fully confirmed only after the return of certain Australians from the California diggings in February, 1851. Within a few months the rush of the "diggers" to Bathurst, 150 miles west of Sydney, was in full swing. Gold was soon found in even larger quantities in Victoria. Bendigo, Ballarat, Castlemaine, and other centers experienced all the features associated with hectic mining activity by thousands of new arrivals. Melbourne boomed as the principal point of entry to the Victorian gold fields. Within 10 years the population of Australia rose from 400,000 to 1,145,000. A strong, vigorous, and new group of people was injected into the population of the continent, and mining was firmly established as a major occupation of Australians. Although early gold mining based on scattered alluvial deposits inevitably diminished in importance, the continuing interest in mining eventually turned to copper in South Australia, gold at Mt. Morgan, silver at Broken Hill, silver-lead in Tasmania, and eventually to the rich gold finds in Western Australia after 1890.

DISCOVERY OF NEW RESOURCES

Although Australians were interested principally in wool and gold before 1860, many new areas were occupied and their varied resources were exploited between 1860 and 1900. The population of the continent expanded from little more than 1,000,000 to nearly 4,000,000 during those decades.

The occupation of the drier central portions of the continent as well as the tropical northern districts was investigated and undertaken after the decline of the early gold rush in 1860. Explorers pushed their way into the interior and to the north coast, but their reports were not very encouraging to the grazier and farmer. Nevertheless, both groups pushed steadily into the marginal districts. The moist eastern coast of Queensland afforded opportunities for tropical farming, and the dense forests furnished attractive cabinet woods. Lumber interests also were attracted to the rich forests of jarrah and karri in the extreme southwest and to the blackwood and mountain ash of Victoria and Tasmania. Sandalwood from Western Australia provided a commodity for export to the Orient. Pearls and pearl shell provided a new source of wealth along the north coast. These decades were also characterized by the establishment of the states in essentially their present form, the adoption of the framework of the modern railroad pattern, the establishment of systems of widespread land ownership and leasing arrangements, the introduction of large-scale wheat raising as a basic primary industry, the creation of early water conservation and irrigation facilities, and the steady growth of cities with their associated activities and problems.

CREATION OF THE COMMONWEALTH

Climaxing these decades of growth and progress came the establishment of the Commonwealth. Before 1900 each colony proceeded along its own lines of development with only limited consideration of its relationships to neighboring states. Long-seated jealousies rather than mutual interests sometimes dominated discussion of matters of common concern. Great distances between the small settlements on the west coast and the principal eastern centers of population presented a major problem to confederation. The huge areas in the north with almost no white population also presented a major challenge to the states. Even the matter of locating the new federal capital posed problems that required many years to compromise. Even after formal confederation, experience was only slowly acquired in the application of the principles on which confederation was based. Two world wars provided the emergencies to accelerate unified action and thinking. Near the close of the first half century, it may be claimed not only that Australia has learned to work effectively on a national basis but also that the Commonwealth is exerting an important influence among the nations of the world.

LAND OCCUPANCY AND OWNERSHIP

Only slightly more than 1 per cent of the area of Australia, or 23,000,000 acres, is devoted to cultivated crops. Irrigated acreage amounts to 885,000 acres, or less than 0.1 per cent of the crop land. In contrast to the United States, most land in Australia has not been alienated. Less than 10 per cent of the continent's 2,000,000,000 acres has passed into private ownership, more than 50 per cent is leased, and nearly 40 per cent is reserved or unoccupied land (Table 1).

Lands devoted exclusively to pastoral pursuits occupy about three-fifths of the area of Australia. The choice grazing lands are commonly in private hands, but the great bulk or about 80 per cent is leased to graziers by the state and Commonwealth governments. Forest lands, aboriginal reservations, and reserves for other public purposes occupy substantial areas also, but they are of small extent in comparison with the pastoral lands.

About 2,000,000 square miles of Australia are occupied, chiefly by farmers and pastoralists, and about 1,000,000 acres are largely unoccupied. The occupied areas include pastoral leases and holdings, crop land, forest lands, and urban areas; the unoccupied lands consist chiefly of desert lands and areas set aside as aboriginal reserves and for other public purposes.

UNOCCUPIED LANDS

Nine-tenths of the unoccupied area is located in Western Australia, Northern Territory, and South Australia. This large area includes chiefly the sand-ridge deserts and bordering lands. Most of the unoccupied area lies within the 10-in-rainfall line except in the north, where areas with greater amounts of summer precipitation are included. Most of the Nullarbor Plain to the south is also included because its occupancy is difficult owing to the scarcity of surface water. Some extremely rugged land is unoccupied in Arnhem Land and in the Kimberlies.

TABLE 1

LAND TENURES IN 1945–1946 (MILLIONS OF ACRES)

State	Private Lands		Crown Lands		Total Acreage
	Alienated	In Process of Alienation	Leased	Other	
New South Wales	51	16	115	16	198
Victoria	29	3	15	9	56
Queensland	22	6	355	46	429
South Australia	12	2	135	94	243
Western Australia	20	12	212	381	625
Tasmania	6	1	3	7	17
Northern Territory	1	0	203	131	335
Total	141	40	1038	684	1903

OCCUPIED LANDS

The occupied area includes two major types of land, (1) the pastoral country and (2) the land suitable for crop production, forests, improved pasture, and close settlement. Many sheep are grown in both divisions, but beef cattle are restricted chiefly to the pastoral

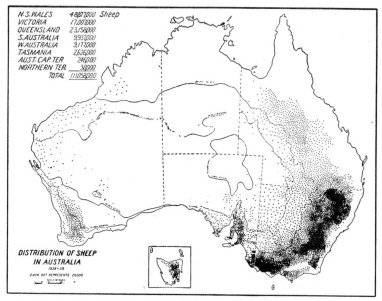

FIGURE 32A.   Distribution of sheep.   From *Commonwealth Year-book.*

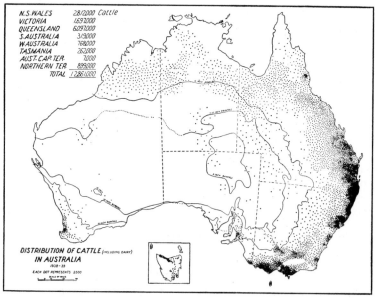

FIGURE 32B.   Distribution of cattle of all kinds.   From *Common-wealth Yearbook.*

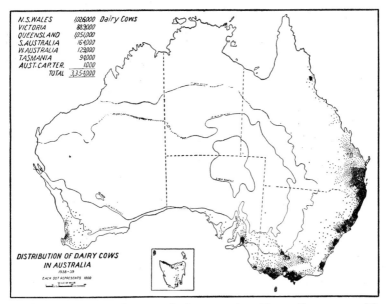

FIGURE 32*C*. Distribution of dairy cattle. From *Commonwealth Yearbook.*

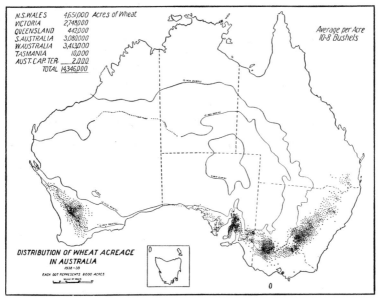

FIGURE 32*D*. Distribution of wheat acreage. From *Commonwealth Yearbook.*

districts. Farmers are tempted in times of high prices and sufficient rainfall to expand into the pastoral country. Pastoralists are tempted under similar circumstances to push their way into the normally unoccupied areas. Those boundaries are zones of advance and retreat, and brief success is commonly followed by quick defeat. It now appears that both farmers and pastoralists have pushed their boundaries too far into the dry lands, and a gradual retreat might be the desirable direction for the immediate future. There is little prospect that many more people can be supported by animal and crop production in these interior districts. The hope for future settlement lies instead in the intensification of output in the best pastoral and agricultural districts.

SIGNIFICANCE OF PASTORAL INDUSTRIES TO AUSTRALIA

The great pastoral industries involving both sheep and cattle provide the only available means for the economic occupation of a large part of the continent.

SHEEP RAISING

The overwhelming importance of wool in the Australian economy is the result of 150 years of experiment and progress. Although a few sheep arrived at Botany Bay with the first fleet, Spanish Merinos were not introduced until 1805. By 1810 there were 34,000 sheep in the colony, in 1820 there were 156,000, and by 1850 there were more than 12,000,000.

TABLE 2

GROWTH OF SHEEP RAISING IN AUSTRALIA*

Year	Millions of Sheep	Ratio of Sheep to Population	Wool Production, Millions of Pounds in Grease	Wool Exports, Millions of Pounds in Grease
1860	20.1	17.6	59.0	. . . . .
1870	41.6	25.2	173.5	. . . . .
1880	62.2	28.9	354.1	329.2
1890	97.9	31.1	462.4	468.3
1900	70.6	18.8	445.1	391.4
1910	98.1	22.2	787.5	738.4
1920	81.8	15.1	625.2	551.2
1930	110.6	17.1	912.9	863.7
1940	122.7	17.0	1141.8	591.4
1945	96.4	13.0	932.9	881.1
1949	103.0	12.6	. . . . . .	. . . . .

* *Source:* Commonwealth Bureau of Census and Statistics.

The development of sheep production is shown in Table 2, but the wide variations in numbers from years of good feed to years of drought are not fully indicated. Six major periods of loss include 1877, 1883–1884, 1892–1902, 1918–1922, and 1942–1945. After the protracted drought of 1892–1902, when flocks numbering 106,000,000 were reduced to half, it took 30 years to restore the number to the previous high and a further 10 years to reach 125,000,000 in 1942. The flocks were then reduced by nearly 30,000,000, or 24 per cent, during the drought seasons that followed.

DISTRIBUTION OF SHEEP

About 85 per cent of Australia's sheep are found today in a crescent-shaped interior area extending from southern Queensland across New South Wales and Victoria to the South Australian border. Fifty per cent of the Commonwealth's sheep are found in New South Wales alone. Outside this crescent most of the remaining 15 per cent are nearly equally divided between coastal South Australia and the southwest corner of Western Australia. The central lowland of Tasmania has about 2,000,000 sheep, and the Northern Territory has only about 25,000 head (Fig. 32A).

Most of Australia's sheep are found in the areas having a predominant winter rainfall between 15 and 20 inches annually. Considerable number of sheep also are found in areas having between 10 and 15 inches of winter rainfall, but very few occur in areas receiving less than 10 inches annually. Sheep are not important in the areas having similar amounts of predominantly summer rainfall. Most of the wool and mutton is produced in the more favorable third of the continent, where sheep often compete with crops for the use of the land.

About three-quarters of Australia's sheep are Merinos, and they predominate in the crescent area of greatest concentration. Most of the remaining quarter are crossbreeds developed in the coastal districts to produce fat lambs, mutton, and wool.

SIZE OF FLOCKS AND STATIONS

The wool industry is no longer based on the huge sheep stations of the past century but on the successful handling of about 100,000 smaller flocks. Subdivision of large properties has proceeded steadily, and the most profitable flocks are commonly those consisting of only 1000 or 1500 animals. In 1940 there were only 38 stations with more than 50,000 sheep each, but there were 75,000 flocks with fewer than

1000 sheep. The size of flocks varies widely, depending upon feed conditions and methods of management. In Queensland the average flock contains 4266 sheep, in Tasmania only 528, and in Australia, as a whole, 1205 head.

The size of land holdings is also significant because it is related to quality of forage and other conditions. Grasslands with 25 inches of rainfall may support one sheep per acre whereas 4 acres may be necessary with 15 inches, and on the saltbush plains, with only 10 inches of rainfall, 12 to 30 acres may be required per head. Typical sheep holdings in Queensland average 18,000 acres; in New South Wales, Western Australia, and South Australia 1000 to 5000 acres; in Tasmania and Victoria, 100 to 500 acres; and in the Commonwealth, 4700 acres. Carrying capacities range from Queensland's 5½ acres per sheep to Tasmania's 1⅕ acres and 4 acres per sheep for the Commonwealth.

KINDS OF FORAGE

The Australian sheep industry is based almost entirely on native forage except in the moist southeastern section where improved pastures are common. Little or no supplemental feed is available for most sheep when drought strikes. Losses of many millions of sheep (30,000,000 in 1942–1947) occur from time to time. It is estimated that drought losses if spread over the good years would be represented by an annual 10 to 15 per cent increase in the cost of wool production.

SHEARING OPERATIONS

Shearing operations in Queensland begin in June and continue until September. They take place in New South Wales from July to November, in Victoria from August to December, and in Tasmania from October to December. South Australia and Western Australia shear during the period July to November. A long period of activity is thus assured the shearing gangs, which migrate from station to station and also from state to state. Shearing on individual stations is frequently spread out over several months as the different classes of sheep are shorn. An average of about 9 pounds of wool is shorn from each mature sheep annually.

WOOL SHIPMENTS

Shipment of wool to storage and sales centers proceeds throughout the year with some time variations among the states, as shown in Table 3.

TABLE 3

AVERAGE PERCENT OF THE WOOL CLIP ARRIVING AT SALES CENTERS, 1938–1939 TO 1947–1948 SEASONS*

	July–Aug.	Sept.–Oct.	Nov.–Dec.	Jan.–Feb.	Mar.–Apr.	May–June
Queensland	20.0	23.8	11.2	7.5	17.8	19.7
New South Wales	17.6	39.2	22.6	7.2	6.3	7.1
Victoria	6.9	46.5	34.7	5.6	3.0	3.3
Tasmania	1.6	5.5	71.5	15.3	4.7	1.4
South Australia	15.8	44.2	21.3	3.6	6.6	8.5
Western Australia	11.2	49.0	27.2	4.2	3.0	5.4
Commonwealth	14.4	39.0	24.7	6.6	7.1	8.2

* Data from National Council of Wool Selling Brokers of Australia.

SHEEP AND LAMBS FOR SLAUGHTER

Approximately 19,000,000 sheep and lambs were slaughtered each year before the Second World War. The number rose to 25,000,000 in several war years but fell to 17,000,000 in 1945–1946. Thirty-six per cent of Australian mutton and lamb is produced in New South Wales, 36 per cent in Victoria, 18 per cent in South Australia, and 10 per cent in the remaining states. Victoria gives greater emphasis to meat than any other state, and Britain is the chief buyer of the exports.

WOOL MARKETING

Australia produces about a billion pounds of wool, or one-fourth of the world's production of all grades, but it grows nearly three-fifths of the world's Merino wool. New South Wales has always been the principal wool-producing state with about 47 per cent of the crop.

Twelve market centers in Australia (Sydney, Albury, Newcastle, Goulburn, Melbourne, Geelong, Ballarat, Brisbane, Adelaide, Perth, Launceston, and Hobart) sell 90 per cent of the shorn-wool crop to domestic and foreign buyers. Sydney sells more than a million bales of 350 pounds each year, and it is the world's largest wool-auctioning center. Sales usually begin in Sydney at the end of August and continue until the following June. Thirty-two firms of wool-selling brokers act as agents for the growers.

WOOL IN THE AUSTRALIAN ECONOMY

The importance of wool to the Australian economy is indicated by the facts that during the five years preceding the Second World War wool accounted for 35 to 40 per cent of the value of foreign trade or more than the export of all other primary goods combined. Wool accounts for 12 per cent of the total national income. It contributes in a most important way to the maintenance of domestic railroad systems as well as overseas shipping because of its ability to pay relatively high rates. Ten per cent of the annual wool crop supplies woolen-manufacturing plants in Australia.

The rapid development of synthetic fibers has caused considerable concern among wool growers in all parts of the world. A tax of 2 shillings is collected on every bale of wool produced in Australia to support research and to promote the production and use of wool. Promotional organizations are located in the major wool-buying countries to further the appreciation and use of this ancient staple of the clothing industry. Any major decline in the world's utilization of wool would result in major repercussions in the land-use patterns and business of Australia.

CATTLE PRODUCTION

Between 13,000,000 and 14,000,000 cattle are pastured in Australia, and three-quarters of them are beef cattle. About 50 per cent of all the cattle are found in the northern half of the continent, and Queensland ranks as the principal cattle-producing state with 6,000,000 head. Pastoralists usually grow cattle only when the more profitable sheep are unsuited to local conditions. On the basis of five sheep being equivalent to one head of cattle in terms of feed consumption, it is evident that cattle are about two-thirds as significant as sheep in Australia.

DISTRIBUTION OF BEEF CATTLE

Beef cattle occupy those tropical grasslands and woodlands in the north that are unsuited to sheep because of the coarseness of the forage and the moist summer climate. Cattle are also able to occupy large sections of the interior more effectively than sheep because of their ability to travel longer distances to water. In dingo (wild dog) country cattle are able to survive, but sheep and lambs are easily killed by these marauders. Newer types of cattle, such as Herfords and Brahmas, seem better able to withstand poor feed, difficult climatic conditions, and pests than earlier types of cattle grown in Australia. Severe droughts have caused the loss of tens of thousands of cattle from time to time because little supplemental feed is available (Fig. 32B).

NATURE OF FEED AND STATIONS

Cattle raising in Queensland is based almost entirely on natural grass, with the result that the condition of the stock shows marked variation from summer with its usually abundant feed to winter with its scarcity of both feed and water. Cattle fatten rapidly during the months of the monsoon rainfall and for a short time thereafter. They lose weight steadily during the long season of drought. This annual occurrence establishes the normal time in each district for marketing and slaughtering operations.

Although there are hundreds of cattle stations in Queenland, which graze thousands of head, most of the stations graze only a few hundred animals. A few cattle stations in Northern Territory count their cattle in tens of thousands and their grazing leases in hundreds of thousands of acres. Most of the cattle industry of Queensland operates on land held on lease from the Queensland government.

MARKETING OPERATIONS

Problems of marketing also exert a limiting effect upon the operation and expansion of the northern cattle industry. Most cattle are grazed far from established railroads and market centers. It is customary to drive cattle several hundred miles from the remote districts along public "stock routes" that may be supplied with bore water and pasture at established intervals. Considerable numbers of cattle are driven southward annually for further feeding and slaughter in adjoining states. Slaughtering plants are distributed along the northern coast at Wyndham, Darwin, and Normanton, and along the east coast of Queensland at Cairns, Townsville, Bowen, Rockhampton, Gladstone, and Brisbane. Australia consumes three-quarters of its beef production, and the remainder goes principally to Britain as frozen beef, chiefly from Queensland ports.

DAIRY INDUSTRY

Beef cattle are found in areas having as little as 20 inches of rainfall, often poorly distributed, but the majority of dairy cattle are concentrated in areas having 30 or more inches favorably distributed throughout the year. Most Australian dairy cattle, like beef animals, depend upon pastures. Droughts affect the dairy industry despite its predominant location along the normally moist coastal districts of the east, southeast, and southwest. Victoria, New South Wales, and Queensland have 1,000,000 to 1,500,000 dairy cattle each, and South Australia and Western Australia each have about 250,000 (Fig. 32C). Jersey and Guernsey cattle are most common. The mild coastal climates make it unnecessary to provide expensive housing and feed storages for dairy cattle.

Butter and cheese production dominates the industry except in metropolitan districts, where whole-milk consumption expands steadily. Butter factories in each district receive the cream or milk from neighboring farms to convert into marketable foodstuffs. Pig raising is a characteristic subsidiary of dairying, and the bacon factory is commonly situated in the vicinity of the butter factory.

WHEAT PRODUCTION

Wheat has long occupied the bulk of the cultivated acreage in Australia, one-half to two-thirds of the total in recent years. It has also been a major export crop since only about one-third of the normal harvest of about 150,000,000 bushels is consumed at home. Wheat growing has been conducted in an extensive manner with a minimum of man-hours expended per acre. Yields on the choice lands of the Wimmera district of Victoria and on the Yorke Peninsula of South Australia have usually been between 20 and 30 bushels per acre. National yields have been about 12 bushels per acre, and marginal lands have produced as few as 5 or 6 (Fig. 32D).

PROBLEMS OF OVEREXPANSION

General optimism during the 1920's led to extension of wheat farming into the increasingly dry lands and on the poorer soils. High prices, development of new machinery, favorable rainfall, and government encouragement contributed to this expansion. At the close of the decade and during the 1930's unfavorable growing conditions and decline in prices brought about serious losses and general discouragement. High prices during the early 1940's gave renewed hope, but the severe drought of 1944 reduced the acreage drastically, and the yield dropped to about 50,000,000 bushels or just enough to meet the domestic needs for milling, fodder, and seed.

There is evident need to reduce the wheat acreage from 14,000,000 acres to about 12,000,000 in order to move the marginal acreage subject to most serious wind erosion and lightest yields. Further encouragement to diversification on the better lands is needed. Wool and lamb production provides an ideal accessory source of income, a means of maintaining soil fertility, and a further basis of crop rotation through temporary pastures and forage crops. The best wheat land in Australia is also the best sheep land, as shown by the general overlapping of the two great crescent areas.

Wheat production in Australia is limited mainly to the belt of 12 to 25 inches of winter rainfall. The dry summers permit the grain to mature on the stalk, and the wheat is gathered and threshed in a single operation. Although some of the grain still goes to market in 3-bushel bags, facilities are now available in New South Wales and Victoria for bulk handling. This system permits important savings to the grower because he need not buy expensive bags, and grading of the wheat is facilitated. Modern storage silos have sprung up in country towns and at the major seaports to handle the bulk wheat crop.

CANE-SUGAR INDUSTRY

Cane-sugar production began in Australia in 1863 as a plantation industry based on recruited labor from southwest Pacific islands. After several decades the industry was reorganized, Kanaka labor was prohibited, and sugar production became an independent small-farm undertaking. Production moved northward along the moist east coast, and after 1900 the industry became the Commonwealth's implement for encouraging settlement in the tropics. The record sugar output of 928,000 tons was manufactured in 1939, and the production of 1948 was about 800,000 tons. Average annual sugar consumption in Australia amounts to about 450,000 tons.

DISTRIBUTION OF CANE PRODUCTION

Queensland contains about 95 per cent of the Australian acreage, and the state government has carefully controlled the industry since 1923. The sugar districts are scattered at intervals along the coastal plain, utilizing the richer soils. Most of the crop is not irrigated. The harvest proceeds from May to December, thus giving the 33 mills a long season of operation. Italians and Slavs are important groups among the cane-field workers.

GOVERNMENT REGULATION

The Queensland Government secures control of the raw sugar at the mills, supervises the refining process in the large plants located in each of the capital cities, and directs the finished product into domestic and overseas markets. Growers are guaranteed fixed prices but must accept assigned acreages. Australian consumers buy sugar at fixed prices that are adjusted to balance losses on exports. Production costs are higher in Queensland than in many other parts of the world, and export sugar is usually sold at a loss.

FRUIT INDUSTRIES

Commercial production of many kinds of fruits is possible in Australia because of the wide range in climatic conditions. Fruit markets in the capital cities afford choices ranging from papayas, bananas, oranges, and pineapples, on the one hand, to apples, pears, grapes, and peaches.

TROPICAL AND SUBTROPICAL FRUITS

The Brisbane area and adjacent portions of New South Wales are the principal sources of commercial tropical fruits. Plantings of bananas, pineapples, passion fruit, and papayas are commonly situated on gentle slopes facing the sea where danger of frost is reduced to a minimum. Citrus fruits are grown principally in the irrigated districts of the Murray River system, where varieties, cultural practices, and marketing procedures are almost identical with those of southern California. Oranges are also grown near Newcastle and Sydney.

HARDY FRUITS

Temperate-latitude fruits are especially characteristic of the southern margin of the continent and Tasmania, although apples, pears, and cherries also thrive on the New England Plateau. Apple production reaches important dimensions in Tasmania, where orchards occupy favorable districts accessible to both the south and north coasts (Fig. 33). Export apples from Tasmania, Victoria, and Western Australia reach European markets from March to June. Australia's 1946 apple production amounted to 14,000,000 bushels, of which only 2,000,000 bushels were exported as compared to exports of 5,000,000 bushels before the Second World War.

Grapes are the principal horticultural crop in Australia. Four times as many grapes are grown as apples. Wine production is one of the oldest industries, although Australians prefer beer and ale to wine. About 500,000 tons of grapes are produced annually, of which one-fourth is converted into wine, two-thirds are dried for currants and raisins, and the remainder is consumed fresh (Fig. 34).

The principal centers of grape production are in the Murray Valley irrigated districts and on the slopes of the Mt. Lofty Ranges near Adelaide. The importance of the grape-drying industry restricts most of the vineyards to regions of light rainfall and hot, dry summers,

FIGURE 33. Fertile fields and orchards make the Launceston district one of Tasmania's most productive agricultural localities.

FIGURE 34. Productive vineyards occupy the gentle west slopes of the Mt. Lofty Range near Adelaide. The winery on the right processes the grapes of this vineyard.

such as the Mildura and Renmark irrigation districts. The Barossa Valley south of Adelaide is the principal center of the wine industry and here 20,000 acres of vineyards are operated.

Considerable quantities of bush berries and other fruits are converted into jams and marmalade (using Queensland sugar) for domestic consumption and export. Commercial canning of peaches, pears, and vegetables received an important stimulus in several irrigated districts during the Second World War.

The total acreage devoted to fruits and commercial gardens in 1945 was in excess of 250,000 acres. Acreages increase steadily in the vicinities of the major metropolitan centers despite the fact that soil conditions and topography may be unfavorable. Easy access to the large Sydney market, for example, encourages sandy and sterile soils in its environs to be intensively cultivated in market gardens. Rich basalt soils make the north coast of Tasmania one of the outstanding potato-growing areas in the Commonwealth.

RECLAMATION OF PRICKLY PEAR LAND

A notable example of land reclamation has taken place in Queensland and adjacent portions of New South Wales in recent decades. About 25,000,000 or 30,000,000 acres of land recently occupied by dense growths of prickly pear cactus have been restored to pastoral pursuits and crops. The land lies principally in southeast Queensland, 40 to 100 miles inland and extending southward from Mackay into northeastern New South Wales. An additional 30,000,000 acres is still available for occupation in the upland areas.

Several varieties of cactus were introduced to Australia more than a century ago. By 1900 these plants had spread over 10,000,000 acres of good grazing land, and by 1920 they occupied 60,000,000 acres. Growths were so dense that the land could not even be grazed. The introduction of an insect from the Argentine, known as *Cactoblastis cactorum*, in 1925 and its systematic dissemination through the cactus-infested regions led to a remarkably rapid destruction of the pest. Within a few years large tracts of land that were hopelessly occupied by cactus were completely freed and made available to farmers and stockmen. A community near Chinchilla, Queensland, gratefully erected a memorial community hall to *Cactoblastis*.

FUTURE AGRICULTURAL EXPANSION

The greatest opportunities for future agricultural expansion in Australia lie in the more favorable occupied lands rather than in the "open spaces." Considerable land now devoted to extensive cultivation and grazing is capable of more intensive utilization by either livestock or crops. In areas of favorable rainfall and soil more farmers and stockmen could make a living through an intensification of effort. The further application of the techniques of irrigation, drainage, diversification, and fertilization, along with the extension of heavier yield crops, is needed. There is no likelihood that important numbers of people will ever be able to make a living by agriculture or stock raising in the interior arid portions of Australia.

The Australian tropics present a challenge for future white settlement. About 200,000 white persons now reside in the northern third of the continent, but the great bulk of them live along the east coast of Queensland. If markets can be found for larger quantities of sugar, tropical fruits, and cotton, many more persons could make a living in those areas of relatively uniform and abundant rainfall.

Despite a half-century of effort to establish permanent white settlements along the north coast of the continent, there is relatively little to show for such experimentation. Hot and humid summers followed by dry and warm winters, together with poor soils, remote situation, and much rugged relief, present a difficult situation for both stockmen and cultivators. Extensive cattle raising is at present the only important activity of the region. Partially successful experiments in farming have been based on peanuts and millets.

FOREST INDUSTRIES

FOREST LANDS

The area of land available for commercial timber production in Australia has been estimated by foresters to be 19,500,000 acres, or only about 1 per cent of the area of the continent. The area of state forests now reserved in perpetuity approximates this acreage, but a considerable portion is not suited for timber production. Hence there is need for further additions to the reserved area as well as need for impoving forest conditions on most tracts. The idea of conserving timber is relatively new to most Australians, and in many localities forest-land destruction continues, particularly through bush fires.

The principal commercial forests are found in the east and southeast coastal regions, including Tasmania, and in the extreme southwest corner of the continent between Perth and Albany. The southern forest regions have a rainfall of 30 or more inches annually, and those of tropical Queensland have twice that amount. Although most of the best forests are on the ocean side of the Eastern Highlands in Queensland, New South Wales, and Victoria, important stands of smaller timber are available on the western flanks of the ranges. Some trees of commercial significance are found along the banks of the Murray and its tributaries. Vast acreages of stunted trees are scattered over the northern coastal districts and over much of the less dry interior. This timber serves many valuable purposes, such as fuel, fence posts, and rough building material.

The scarcity of softwoods, a condition characteristic of the southern hemisphere generally, comprises one of Australia's major forest problems. Probably 90 per cent of the native timber of the Commonwealth consists of hardwoods, chiefly eucalyptus.

SOFTWOOD SUPPLY

Australia's principal native softwoods include hoop, bunya, and kauri pines of the northeast coast, cypress pine of the western slopes of the Eastern Highlands, and the Huon, King William, and celery top pines of Tasmania. Hoop and bunya pine supply valuable timber for plywood, veneers, and cabinet work. The original stand of these pines has been estimated at 850,000,000 cubic feet, but less than 50,-000,000 remain, an amount sufficient for less than another decade. Plantations of both species are being established in Queensland, and hoop pine is being planted in New South Wales. Kauri pine sometimes attains a diameter of 6 to 7 feet and is fairly abundant in northeastern Queensland, although many accessible stands have been removed. The large trees are commonly used for plywood manufacture.

In Tasmania, King William pine (*Athrotaxis*), Huon pine (*Dacrydium*), and celery top pine (*Phyllocladus*) are scattered over much of the moist western uplands. All are slow-growing, but they produce high-grade timber. Cypress pines occur in many parts of Australia, but the largest compact stands occur in the 20- to 30-inch rainfall belt of central New South Wales and south central Queensland. The timber is resistant to termites, and as a consequence it is valuable in many kinds of construction work.

HARDWOOD SUPPLY

Proper management of Australia's relatively adequate acreage of eucalyptus forests will provide sufficient hardwood timber for future basic construction needs. Although it is possible that only 10,000,000 acres are ideally suited for the production of prime hardwoods, large amounts of poles, firewood, pulpwood, and small logs may be produced on the second-quality hardwood-forest lands. Eucalyptus forests are particularly susceptible to serious fire damage in dry years. Most "bush fires" are due to carelessness, and it is only recently that the public has come to realize the seriousness of these recurring burns.

FOREST FIRES

One of the most disastrous forest fires occurred in Victoria during January, 1939, near the close of a long dry season. It swept through some of Victoria's finest timber stands destroying as much material as would have been required to build 100,000 homes. Seventy lives were lost along with many homes, lumber mills, bridges, and thousands of sheep and cattle. Three and one-half million acres of watersheds were seriously damaged, and a huge acreage of timber was killed. Increasing efforts are being made to reduce fire losses by the installation of spotting and communication systems, improving forest access, acquisition of modern fire-fighting equipment, and minimizing fire hazards.

SOFTWOOD PLANTATIONS

In order to reduce the Commonwealth's dependence upon imported softwoods, extensive pine plantings of American and European species have been made by the various states. Nearly 300,000 acres have been planted, and these tracts of dark green stand out in striking contrast to the gray-green of the native forests. Proposed plantings will double or treble this acreage within the next few decades.

TIMBER MILLS

Sawmills in Australia are generally small and unable to produce a large volume of lumber, owing in part to the irregular nature of hardwood logs. The mills are distributed in approximately the same pattern as the stands of merchantable timber. Larger mills are commonly situated on the waterfronts of principal cities where imported softwood logs are milled. Modern plywood mills are situated near the source of large softwood peeling logs in Queensland.

PAPER MANUFACTURING

Australia was long dependent on foreign sources for paper until it was discovered, about 1935, that eucalyptus timber could be employed in paper manufacture. Two mills have been in operation in Tasmania since about 1940, one on the north coast at Burnie and the other at Boyer on the Derwent River in the south. Other paper mills are operated at Maryvale, Victoria, and Millicent, South Australia. Newsprint and wrapping paper have been the chief products made from these short-fiber hardwoods, but a substantial part of the domestic needs for fine printing and writing papers is also being met by these plants.

RELATION OF FORESTS TO WATER SUPPLY

The various state forestry departments, which now control permanently a substantial share of Australia's best timber lands, manage these properties not only for timber production but also for water conservation. Many of the timber reserves lie at the headwaters of streams that supply water for irrigation, stock purposes, and metropolitan centers. Reforestation is frequently connected with the improvement of critical watersheds. After the disastrous fire of 1939 in Victoria, serious water shortages occurred in many small communities, and even residents of Melbourne were subjected to restricted water consumption.

MINING INDUSTRIES

Mining has long been one of the important aspects of Australian economic development. Gold discoveries brought about large increments in population a century ago. Mineral discoveries and development have been responsible for the establishment of many segments of the railroad pattern, thus facilitating the subsequent establishment of pastoral and agricultural industries. The distribution of population and secondary industries is related in many instances to mineral deposits. Certain minerals have long been important among the raw materials exported to other parts of the world.

GOLD PRODUCTION RANKS FIRST

Gold has been the most valuable mineral produced in Australia during most years in the past century. In 1948 the Commonwealth produced 888,429 fine ounces, worth $31,600,000. For a half century Western Australia has been the principal producer, although Victoria outranks all the states in total accumulated production during the century.

The increased price of gold, beginning in 1931, stimulated gold production in many parts of the continent. The principal center of production, however, continues to be Kalgoorlie, the normal ouput of which exceeds that of all other districts combined. Less important gold fields lie to the south of Kalgoorlie at Norseman and to the north at Leonora, Murchison, and East Murchison. The Bendigo field in

Victoria, which produced sensational amounts of gold in the 1850's, continues to produce from newly discovered leads. In Queensland the principal centers are Charters Towers, Mount Morgan, Cracow, and Gympie. Mount Morgan is also a copper mine.

COAL—THE MOST SIGNIFICANT MINERAL

Coal, although normally second to gold in value, is Australia's most significant mineral. A total output of nearly 15,000,000 tons of bituminous coal has been achieved in recent years. In addition, about 5,-000,00 tons of lignite are extracted annually. These minerals produce most of the energy to run factories and railroads and to illuminate towns and cities, and they furnish fuel for ships, metallurgical plants, and homes. Australia has large reserves of coal but only a limited amount of water power and little or no natural petroleum. Coal assumes, therefore, a position of major importance in the industrial structure (Fig. 31C).

NEW SOUTH WALES COAL FIELD

The most important coal field lies in eastern New South Wales centering upon Sydney. No coal is mined at Sydney, however, because of the great depth of the seam. Outcrops to the north at Newcastle, west at Lithgow, and south at Bulli provide easy access, and these localities are the major mining districts. Nearly 12,000,000 tons of coal were produced in New South Wales in 1947, or four-fifths of the Commonwealth's output. Because of the high quality of this coal, 2½ million tons were shipped to other Australian states. These interstate shipments move entirely by coastwise collier.

COAL PRODUCTION IN OTHER STATES

Queensland produces about one-tenth of Australia's bituminous coal, most of it coming from the Ipswich field near Brisbane and several smaller fields in the vicinity of Rockhampton. The recent opening of the large Blair Athol strip mine on the Clermont Field 130 miles inland from Rockhampton may enable Queensland to assume a much more important position in the coal industry in the future.

Victoria produces only a small amount of bituminous coal at Wonthaggi, but it mines 5,000,000 or 6,000,000 tons of lignite at Yallourn, 100 miles to the east of Melbourne. The beds of lignite are 180 to 200 feet thick and overlain by 30 to 40 feet of overburden. Mining is done by huge bucket machines operating on two levels. Most of the brown coal is converted into electricity in a plant at the pit margin, although a substantial part of the output is made into briquettes. The state-operated electric plant is the key unit in a system providing electricity for most parts of Victoria.

South Australia is producing a subbituminous grade of coal at Leigh Creek, 380 miles north of Adelaide. The only important coal mine in Western Australia is south of Perth at Collie. The Fingal district in Tasmania supplies about two-thirds of that island's coal requirements.

MAJOR USES FOR COAL

Nine-tenths of the electricity used in Australia is produced from coal. Each year these plants utilize more than 2,500,000 tons of bituminous coal as well as most of the lignite mined in Victoria. One of the largest electric generating plants on the continent is operated by the city of Sydney at Botany Bay, and it consumes more than 600,000

FIGURE 35.   A portion of the array of surface structures along the lode
outcrop at Broken Hill.

tons of bituminous coal each year. Major consumers of coal are manufacturing establishments, railroads, artificial gas plants, and domestic consumers. New South Wales coal is also suitable for the manufacture of coke for metallurgical purposes. Most of that used by the Newcastle and Port Kembla steel plants is made in close proximity to the mines (Fig. 36).

SHALE OIL

Although considerable effort has been made to find natural petroleum in commercial quantities, little success has thus far been achieved.   Central Queensland and the Kimberley district of Western Australia have shown some signs of oil.

Large quantities of oil shale occur in New South Wales, and a plant at Glen Davis in Capertree Valley (25 miles north of Lithgow) has been producing about 10,000,000 gallons of gasoline yearly from crude shale oil.   About 350,000 tons of shale are processed annually, yielding 65 gallons of crude oil per ton.

IRON-ORE PRODUCTION

The principal iron-ore-producing district in Australia is situated some 30 miles inland from Whyalla on the west side of Spencer's Gulf.   The high-quality hematite ore is secured from open cuts in several low hills that rise above the surface of the surrounding plains.   The ore is de-

FIGURE 36.   Blast furnace and associated steel plant at Port Kembla, N.S.W.

livered by railroad to Whyalla for shipment by sea to blast furnaces at Newcastle and Port Kembla on the east coast.   During the Second World War a blast furnace was constructed at Whyalla in order to decentralize this important industry.   Since 1900 the South Australian iron-ore output has totaled 30,000,000 tons.

High-grade iron-ore deposits on Irvine, Koolan, and Cockatoo islands in Yampi Sound (northwest coast) are being developed to supplement the Whyalla ore supply.   The Yampi Sound ore lies several hundred feet above sea level on the islands and within easy reach of vessels.   The Yampi Sound deposit is 3200 miles from Whyalla by sea.   Australia is not rich in iron ore, but there is an ample supply for many years.

LEAD, ZINC, AND SILVER

Australia ranks among the world's most important producers of lead and zinc. Broken Hill is one of the spectacular mining centers in the arid interior and one of the most important lead and zinc producers in the world (Fig. 35). It has been in operation since 1883, and the end of mining is not yet in sight. Essentially all the materials used in these mines as well as in the town must be brought in from the outside. The lead concentrates are shipped to Port Pirie for smelting and refining. Zinc refining is done near Hobart, Tasmania, by electrolysis. Cadmium, cobalt, and silver are by-products of these processes. Sulphur secured from the roasting of zinc ores aids in the manufacture of superphosphate fertilizers in various parts of the continent. Raw phosphate rock is imported in large quantities from Nauru and Ocean islands.

Zinc and lead ores are also produced at the Read-Rosebery mines in western Tasmania, at Mt. Isa in northwest Queensland, and at the Captain's Flat Mine in southeastern New South Wales. Captain's Flat was a gold-mining center at the start of the century, and Broken Hill was most famous for the silver output during its early years.

OTHER MINERAL INDUSTRIES

Sufficient copper is produced in Australia to meet normal domestic needs. Mines at Moonta and Wallaroo, South Australia, were important producers many years ago. Today copper is produced in a number of widely distributed localities, including Mt. Isa, Mt. Morgan, and Cloncurry, Queensland, Cobar, New South Wales, and Mt. Lyell, Tasmania. Electrolytic refining of copper is done at Mt. Lyell with cheap hydroelectric power and at Port Kembla where copper-fabricating plants are situated.

Small amounts of tin have been produced from placer and lode deposits for many years. The New England Plateau, the Mt. Bischoff district in western Tasmania, and the Herberton district in Queensland are most important. Like copper mining, tin mining is subject to wide fluctuations because of the difficulty of meeting outside competition when business conditions are normal.

Large quantities of clay are used in the manufacture of bricks and tiles near each of the larger cities. Cement works are situated in relation to raw materials as well as major markets. Great quantities of limestone are quarried near Melrose, Tasmania, for flux in the blast furnaces at Newcastle and Port Kembla. Flux for the furnace at Whyalla comes from Rapid Bay, South Australia.

MANUFACTURING

Manufacturing or secondary industries have made notable progress in Australia during the last several˙decades. The periods of the two World Wars were particularly significant for their rapid industrial expansion. One in three workers now depends upon secondary industry for a living. Manufacturing employs more than 800,000 workers as compared with 625,000 before the Second World War. Some 2000 new manufacturing projects were added during the period 1940–1945. Shortage of overseas balances has spurred local industries to meet domestic needs for manufactured goods since 1945. The advanced nature of Australian living standards makes its concentrated groups of urban residents particularly attractive markets for many kinds of manufactured products.

Australia has now attained the position of being self-sufficient in respect to most kinds of factory goods, and it could easily provide quantities of many items for export to neighboring areas. Some manufactured commodities are likely to be imported in the future because of Australia's inability to produce them in quantity and in effective competition with other countries. Government policy has provided protective tariffs for most of the secondary industries. The government has joined with private interests in the establishment of industries regarded as strategic or of basic importance.

The marked concentration of manufacturing in the major cities, and especially in New South Wales and Victoria, is significant. There has been a long-time trend for manufacturing to concentrate in the major port cities where state railway systems came to a focus and where large population groupings provided not only a labor pool but also the chief markets. In Newcastle the industrial development was particularly related to the abundant and high-quality coal resource. Tasmania has attracted several significant industries to the island mainly because of its supply of cheap hydroelectric power.

IRON AND STEEL INDUSTRY

Before 1915 Australia imported most of its iron and steel. Today it supplies nearly all its domestic needs, and it exports certain products from an annual output of about 2,000,000 tons. The entire industry is operated by a single combine, the Broken Hill Proprietary Company, Ltd., and its subsidiaries and affiliates. The B.H.P., as this company is generally called, opened its modern Newcastle plant during the period of the First World War, choosing that site because of the availability of an abundant supply of coking coal. In 1928 a company that had previously engaged in iron and steel manufacturing at Lithgow began operating a modern steel plant at Port Kembla on the southern coal field. Both these plants have smelted ore obtained from the Eyre Peninsula in South Australia. In 1941 a blast furnace was blown in at Whyalla, South Australia, the port through which iron ore was shipped to east-coast plants. Ore boats brought coal 1200 miles from the east coast on the return trip. During the first three years of operation the furnace produced 400,000 tons of pig iron for shipment to east-coast steel plants. It has been proposed that a complete steel plant be installed at Whyalla. Plans are now being drawn for a blast furnace in Western Australia utilizing Collie coal and Yampi Sound iron ore. Expansion of the Port Kembla plant is also nearing completion.

A wide array of subsidiary plants has been developed or is in prospect at each of the blast-furnace centers. At Newcastle, these plants include plate mills, wire works, pipe plant, railway wheel and axle foundry, and ship yards. Ship yards are also located at Brisbane, Sydney, Melbourne, and Whyalla. By-products of coke ovens at Newcastle and Port Kembla include tar, benzol, naphtha, metallurgical coke, and gas. About 25,000 men are employed in the steel industry, which represents an investment of probably 100,000,000 dollars. It is claimed that the Australian industry is able to produce steel at a price comparable with that in other major centers of the world.

LIGHT-METAL PRODUCTION

The importance of aluminum and magnesium in the manufacture of airplanes and many other kinds of equipment was brought forcefully to the attention of Australians during the Second World War. Adequate resources of bauxite have been proven in Tasmania as well as on the mainland. The availability of large quantities of hydroelectric power in Tasmania has led to the decision to establish an aluminum industry in the vicinity of Launceston. Small amounts of magnesium are produced in New South Wales from magnesite.

AUTOMOBILES AND AIRCRAFT

Automobile assembly plants of American and British manufacturers have been in operation in the principal cities of Australia since about 1930. There has been a steady trend toward the supplying of an increasing share of parts from local sources. By gradual stages it is planned to arrive at the point where an all-Australian car, designed to meet local needs, will be produced on a mass basis.

Airplanes were manufactured at Melbourne and Sydney plants as early as 1939, and during the war these factories delivered about 3500 aircraft of different types. Probably 50,000 persons were employed in the aircraft industry at its peak wartime development. A rapid decline occurred in Australia as in other countries at the close of hostilities.

TRANSPORTATION

Australia is a country of great distances, small and highly localized population, and relatively limited freight tonnage and passenger travel. Since each state tends to be somewhat self-sufficient, the amount of interstate transport is not great. The bulk of the freight and passenger transport within each state, therefore, is carried by the local systems of railroads and highways. Transcontinental and interstate haulage is much less significant than in the United States. Since most of the transportation of goods and people takes place in the coastal districts, instead of the interior, water transportation comes into direct and effective competition with land transport.

RAILWAYS

Most of the railroads are owned and operated by the state. Of the 28,000 miles of railways open for general traffic, more than 25,000 miles are owned by the states, 2200 miles belong to the Commonwealth, and about 700 are privately owned. The difficulties that have resulted from the different gauges in the several states have long been recognized. The high cost of integrating the systems on a national basis delayed major improvements for several decades. The Second World War, however, clearly demonstrated the disadvantages of the old system in time of national emergency.

A comprehensive plan to connect all the mainland capitals with standard-gauge railways is proposed. All the important broad-gauge railways of Victoria and South Australia are to be converted to standard width. The main line between Kalgoorlie and Perth and also between Broken Hill and Port Augusta will be converted to standard gauge. A new railway will be extended northward from Bourke, New South Wales, across central Queensland and Northern Territory to Darwin. The approach to Darwin from Queensland is to replace all former plans of completing the railway between Adelaide and Darwin. The new railway will provide the promising Barkley Tableland with railway connections, improve the railway service for all interior Queensland, and connect Darwin with the important east coast at Townsville, Brisbane, and all points to the south. The project involves the conversion of 8500 miles of existing railways and the construction of 1600 miles of new lines. More than 25,000 railway cars and loco-motives will also have to be modified to fit the new gauge.

About 42,000,000 tons of freight have been carried annually by gov-ernment railways or about 1500 tons per average mile of line. More than 500,000,000 passengers were carried each year, or about 20,000 per average mile of line. New South Wales railways accounted for about half of both kinds of traffic. Wheat and flour, coal and other minerals, wool and livestock, and lumber and other manufactured goods comprise the major items of railway tonnage. Modernization of the railways, originally patterned after the British system, proceeds slowly, and there have been few important additions to mileage in several decades.

COASTWISE WATER TRANSPORT

Since the main centers of population lie along the coast at great intervals (500 miles between Brisbane and Sydney, and Melbourne and Adelaide) water transportation becomes a most important factor in interstate-trade relationships. Distances by water are frequently less than by land, and the rates on bulky commodities are lower. Furthermore, the state railway systems were never designed to ac-commodate traffic of that kind. Some of the principal commodities moving by coastal vessels are coal, iron ore, other concentrated ores, timber products, and raw sugar. Coastwise trade is regulated by the Commonwealth and is limited to Australian vessels. The railroads involved in interstate shipments, of course, are usually under the con-trol of the states. Air transportation, in all its aspects, comes under Commonwealth supervision.

ROADS

Half a million miles of roads give access to the settled parts of Aus-tralia. Only about 20,000 miles, however, may be classed as modern roads, another 100,000 miles are slightly improved, and 380,000 miles are scarcely more than "tracks." The better country roads are usually maintained as main intercity routes by the state highway departments. Local governments are largely responsible for the others. Most of the main roads are surfaced with bitumen or asphalt.

About 900,000 automobiles, trucks, and motorcycles are in service in Australia. Relatively high initial costs and heavy taxes make auto-mobiles more difficult to own and operate than in the United States. Great numbers of urban dwellers depend entirely on public transporta-tion. In rural areas, where long distances must be covered, motor cars are a great convenience or even a necessity. Most goods are moved in metropolitan districts by motor truck. In many centers railroads do not provide direct contact between wharves, warehouses, and distributing centers, thus necessitating trucking operations. Longer hauls of goods and people by truck and bus are not encouraged in order to preserve that business for the established publicly owned railways.

RIVER TRANSPORTATION

Inland-water transportation is of very little significance in Australia because even its major stream, the Murray, has a navigable depth in places of only a few inches during much of the year. Riverboats, however, still operate along the lower river, as at Murray Bridge, where a few bulky commodities are assembled for railway shipment. A small amount of river traffic also is found on the Brisbane River and other east-coast streams whose lower courses have been drowned.

AVIATION

During the period 1946–1947 Australian commercial airlines flew about 23,000,000 miles and carried 860,000 passengers without a single fatality. Flying conditions are generally favorable, owing to the absence of high mountains and the occurrence of cloudless skies during much of the year over most of the continent. Long distances between centers of population also stimulate air travel. It takes a week or more to travel by coastal steamer from Sydney to Perth and several days by railway, but only 10 or 12 hours are needed to cover the intervening 2300 airline miles. Essendon airport at Melbourne, Mascot in Sydney, and Ipswich field near Brisbane are major centers in a nationwide airfield pattern.

FOREIGN TRADE

Australia has long been recognized as an important contributor of raw materials to world-trade channels. Its exports have consisted principally of a few important products of the range, farm, and mine produced in competition with other continents. Its close ties with Great Britain and other nations in the Empire are reflected by the direction of Australian trade and by its trade agreements and preferences. Although Australia has become progressively more urban and industrial, it has been able to maintain large outputs of primary goods through mechanization of her large-scale agricultural, pastoral, and mining industries. It is likely that Australian trade relationships in the future will become closer with her near neighbors in southeast Asia and perhaps shift from the Atlantic to the Pacific basin.

TRADE FACILITIES

Most of Australia's foreign trade is conducted through the ports of the capital cities and a few other centers such as Newcastle, Geelong, and Albany. These major centers alone provide the facilities for handling large overseas vessels and providing them with outgoing cargoes. Most of these major ports have been developed on natural harbors, and the associated urban centers constitute a large part of the Australian market.

Specialized facilities for handling exports are provided at these ports. Modern bulk-handling equipment is now available at several centers such as Sydney, Newcastle, and Geelong. Wool warehouses and export facilities are important features at every major Australian port. Plants for slaughtering, freezing, and storing meats are available at many centers. Specialized machinery is important at Newcastle, Port Pirie, Whyalla, Port Kembla, and elsewhere to facilitate the handling of coal, ore, and stone shipments. Large general cargo and passenger docks are available at each of the capital city ports. Australia has scores of outlying harbors that serve local coastal districts and share in the coastwise trade of the continent.

EXPORT COMMODITIES

Wool continues to be Australia's most important export. About 2,500,000 or 3,000,000 bales move into world-trade channels each year. Sydney alone ships more than 1,000,000 bales annually, making it the leading wool-export center of the world. Wheat and flour, butter and other dairy products, along with mutton and beef, constitute the other major agricultural export commodities. Products of lesser significance from farms include sugar, apples, pears, wine, and dried fruits. Exports of gold, lead, zinc, and lesser minerals are likewise important among Australia's surplus production.

IMPORTS

Among the principal agricultural imports are cotton and tobacco, in both of which the domestic production has been wholly inadequate to meet home demand. Imports of tropical products, such as tea and rubber, also assume importance and may be the means of developing future important reciprocal trade with southeast Asia.

There is a widespread feeling among Australians that exports are good and imports are bad because the one provides jobs at home and the other calls for outside payments that may threaten home standards of living and jobs. If Australia expects to sell surplus primary products abroad it will be necessary for her to buy certain manufactured goods or raw products from other parts of the world.

ABORIGINAL POPULATION

It is estimated that Australia was formerly occupied by 250,000 or 300,000 aborigines. Their numbers varied from very few in the dry interior to close groupings along the coastal margins. The moist regions provided better hunting, fishing, and gathering for those primitive folk. It is generally agreed that they came to Australia from the north before the landbridges were severed and that their primitive character is related to their long separation from those land areas and the associated evolutionary processes.

Since the time of White arrival in Australia the number of aborigines has declined very greatly. They were completely exterminated from Tasmania in the process of settlement. On the mainland their number has been reduced to about 75,000, two-thirds being full-blood and one-third mixed-blood. Most of the city-dwelling Whites of Australia rarely see or have much concern about the aborigines.

Most of the aborigines live in the northern half of the continent where large areas have been set aside as reserves for their exclusive use. The Arnheim Aboriginal Reserve in Northern Territory, for example, includes 31,200 square miles of territory with an estimated population of 4000 nomadic Blacks. On these reserves natives fend for themselves, and little supervision is provided. Some of them live in a manner not greatly different from that of their ancestors. Most have felt the impact of civilization, however, in one way or another.

The Aboriginal Census of June 30, 1944, indicated that nearly one-third of these people are still living on a nomadic basis chiefly in the northwest quarter of the continent. About one-fourth of the total number is employed, and a quarter lives in supervised camps or settlements. Only one-third of the aborigines live in the southern half of the continent. In New South Wales the entire aborigine population abandoned the tribal way of life decades ago, and only about 5 per cent is full-blood.

The aborigines now contribute to the Australian economy principally through supplying common labor to rural industries. They have also contributed to the Australian scene hundreds of geographic names for towns and localities. The vocabulary of Australians has also been enriched by words of aboriginal origin, such as billabong, wallaby, kangaroo, kookaburra, and corroboree.

WHITE POPULATION

The poulation of Australia (excluding full-blood aborigines) is nearly 8,000,000 (estimated 7,710,000 in 1949). The population of New South Wales is over 3,000,000, and of Victoria more than 2,000,000. The rural population is slowly declining; it was estimated to be 2,353,000 in 1948. The major seaboard cities contain over half the total population. Australia has more than 100 towns with populations of less than 10,000 and 37 cities with more than 10,000 persons each. Its two largest cities together claim one-third of the entire population

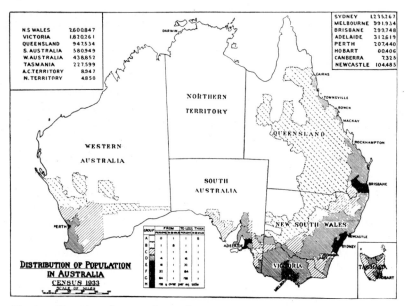

FIGURE 37.   Distribution of population.   From *Commonwealth Yearbook*.

of the Commonwealth. The six capital cities of the states have a combined population equal to that of half the entire Commonwealth (Fig. 37).

The postwar entry of tens of thousands of displaced persons from continental Europe will reduce only slightly the vast preponderance of population of British extraction. The average rate of population growth for the Commonwealth has amounted to only about 1 per cent annually since the start of the century. More than 90 per cent of the population of Australia is native-born. There is a widespread hope that the Australian population may be doubled before the close of the century by natural increase and by selected immigration. In order to attain this growth, it is probable that about 50,000 immigrants will have to be secured every year.

The Australian population is predominantly urban with 5,357,000 in 1948, or 70 per cent of the total, living in cities and towns. In each of the mainland states the bulk of the population is concentrated in the capital city (Figs. 38 and 39). The cities continue to expand, and the further mechanization of farming enables fewer farmers to care for the limited amount of cultivable land. The continued expansion of manufacturing contributes to further urban growth. It is not likely that a substantial part of industrial expansion can be encouraged to

FIGURE 38.　Adelaide Street is one of Brisbane's most important shopping districts.

locate in interior towns. The city offers too many attractions that appeal to the average Australian—an ordinary job with considerable security, an abundance of leisure time, and a wide variety of ways in which to spend those leisure hours.

THE POPULATION PROBLEM

The desirability of securing a population of 15,000,000 or 16,000,000 for Australia in the relatively near future is widely proclaimed. It is probably felt that the continent should be able to support a population of twice the present number without serious reduction in the standard of living. It is insisted, however, that the "White Australia Policy" be continued in the future, although Australians stand ready to assist Asiatics and others in the improvement of conditions in their home-lands. Australians recognize that unless their continent is fully uti-lized it may attract the interest of crowded Asiatic peoples and gov-ernments intent on expansion.

Australians insist that future immigrants be of European extraction and capable of assimilation into the prevailing social, economic, and political systems. Australians argue that they do not wish to exclude any racial group but merely those who are not likely to become merged with the present population.

FIGURE 39. Flinders Street stores and offices are convenient to the large interurban railway station through which thousands of shoppers and workers move in and out of the center of Melbourne every day.

Australians also recognize that a doubling of their own population and productive capacity not only will strengthen their hold on the continent but will also enable them to assume a more advanced posi-tion economically and politically among the nations of the world. The restricted home markets make it difficult or impossible to produce many kinds of complex manufactured products in competition with industrial nations having assured home markets of large size. An ex-pansion of the home market would enable Australian manufacturers to produce additional types of goods on a competitive basis with large established industrial nations. Australian industry could then enter into competition with other industrial nations for its share of world markets.

CHARACTER OF AUSTRALIAN PEOPLE

Give the average Australian a comfortable cottage, a motor car, and a reasonable income, and he is content. He does not require luxuries, and he sees no point in wearing himself out quickly in the search for wealth. Advanced social legislation is an important part of Australian life. The trade union was established early among the sheep shearers and coal miners. The closed shop and collective bargaining are accepted principles. A comprehensive system of social security is in force. Wealth and income are more evenly distributed than in the United States.

All kinds of outdoor sports are popular. Horse racing is a national sport, and most Australians participate in state-operated lotteries. In all the coastal cities and town surf bathing is extremely popular. Tennis, bowling, yachting, skiing, and similar sports have large followings. A maximum of holidays with week ends beginning at Saturday noon provide much time for gardening, sports, and relaxation. An abundance of waterfront and other land has been set aside by each population center for public recreation purposes. Movies and radio provide entertainment and education for millions. One of the strictest voluntary radio codes in existence is in effect.

Life in Australia is very much like life in the United States and Canada, whether it be in the city or in the country. Australian conditions are particularly like those in the southwestern United States, where large modern cities are in close juxtaposition with farm and range country as well as with large tracts of unoccupied land. The recent occupation of both areas by similar people and also the similar physical environments help to make Australia like the American Southwest.

REFERENCES

Daniel, H., and M. Belle, *Australia the New Customer, a Commercial and Economic Guide for American Business Men*, Ronald Press Co., New York, 1946.

Fitzpatrick, Brian, *The Australian People, 1788–1945*, Melbourne University Press, Melbourne, 1946.

Grattan, C. H., *Introducing Australia*, John Day Co., New York, 1947.

Grattan, C. H. (editor), *Australia*, University of California Press, Berkeley, 1947.

Hancock, W. K., *Australia,* E. Benn, Ltd., London, 1945.

Holmes, J. M., *The Murray Valley,* Angus and Robertson, Sydney, 1948.

Shann, Edward, *An Economic History of Australia,* Cambridge University Press, London, 1930.

Wadham, S. M., and G. L. Wood, *Land Utilization in Australia,* Melbourne University Press, Melbourne, 1939.

Wood, G. L., *Australia—Its Resources and Development,* The Macmillan Co., New York, 1947.

6

Northern Melanesia:
New Guinea and the Bismarck
Archipelago

ROBERT G. BOWMAN

Northern Melanesia is one of the most backward and least-known regions in the world. Geographically it embraces the northern and western islands of the great archipelagoes that rim the Pacific Ocean basin to the north and northeast of Australia, just south of the equator. Ethnically the term refers to the sausage-shaped, insular realm of Melanesia, where melanin, or dark skin pigment, is a prevailing and conspicuous racial characteristic of some two million Pacific Islanders. Most of the culturally retarded peoples of Melanesia are of Papuan or Melanesian racial stocks, or blends of the two. At the western extremities of Melanesia, however, infusions of Malay stock are revealed in the generally lighter skin color of the people, especially along the coasts of western New Guinea and the islands adjacent. In the eastern islands (eastern Fiji) Polynesian infusions of blood account for the lighter color of some groups. In the interior of Dutch New Guinea, moreover, there are a number of valleys inhabited by relict Negrito or "little Negro" tribes; in the more important coastal towns, on neighboring plantations, and in the mining districts live small numbers of Whites, and on some of the islands Indians, Chinese, Javanese, and others.

The islands that comprise northern Melanesia extend from the immediate vicinity of the equator to 12° south latitude, and from 130° to nearly 155° east longitude (Fig. 40). The more important of these are New Guinea, together with its western outliers such as Waigeo, Japen, and the Schouten group, and its eastern outliers, which include the Louisiade Archipelago, the D'Entrecasteaux group, and lesser

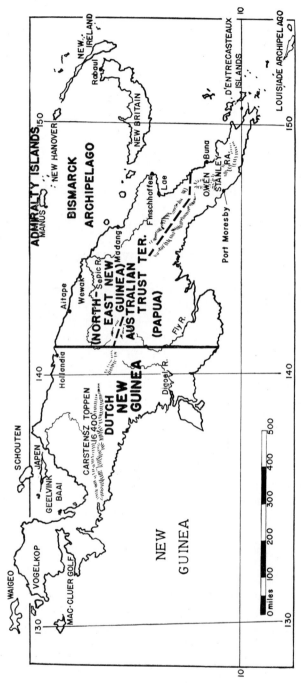

FIGURE 40.   Sketch map of New Guinea and the Bismarck Archipelago.

near-by islands; the Bismarck Archipelago, dominated by New Britain and New Ireland; and the Admiralties, of which Manus is the largest and most important island.   The larger islands are mostly quite rugged, with elevations up to 9000 feet on New Britain and over 16,000 feet in western New Guinea.   Some of the smaller islands—primarily those of volcanic origin—are hilly to mountainous, but many of the others are low, flat, and swampy, or else low, relatively flat, and sandy or rocky.   The climate of the lower elevations (below about 3000 feet) is mostly warm to hot and humid to wet.   In places and at times, however, the equatorial heat is tempered by monsoon winds and land-and-sea breezes.   Southern New Guinea in the vicinity of Port Moresby has a subhumid climate resulting, apparently, from rain-shadow effects and the direction of the monsoonal air flow that parallels the coast much of the time.   Intermediate elevations (3000 to 7000 feet) range from warm to cool and from humid to wet, depending chiefly on their degree of exposure to wind and sun.   Higher elevations (above 7000 feet) are likely to be rather wet, cloudy, and cold.

The vegetation pattern of northern Melanesia reflects the diversity of its surface configuration, climates, soils, and cultural or human activities.   Rainforest and swampforest prevail in the lowlands and on the mountain slopes up to 5000 feet or more, except where native clearing and cultivation or commercial plantation enterprises have modified the indigenous plant associations.   Relatively pure stands of pine and other softwoods are found in places on the mountain slopes above 5000 feet, whereas mossy forest dominates most of the higher, wetter elevations.   Above 15,000 feet in western New Guinea, perpetual snow and ice prevent the development of any type of flora; elsewhere, rock outcrops, recent volcanic activity, sour soils, coastal sands, and poor drainage modify the pattern locally.   Wherever cultivation has taken place, significant changes have been wrought in the vegetation landscape.   Thus instead of rainforest on some of the humid coastal lowlands, we now find coconut and other plantations (including cacao and citrus), or grasslands composed of coarse, tall, tropical grasses induced by the shifting cultivation practices of the natives.   Such grasslands also extend into many of the remote interior valleys of highland New Guinea.   Finally there are a number of specialized plant associations in addition to the above, such as halophytic beach plants in the immediate vicinity of the coasts where salt spray restricts rainforest development; sago palm forests spottily distributed through the lower, wetter rainforest; mangrove swamps in the vicinity of the larger river mouths; and bamboo and pandanus thickets in the intermediate mountain zone.

The native fauna of northern Melanesia, like the flora, is essentially a composite of Asian, Australian, and indigenous elements. In the fauna, as in the flora, profound local changes have resulted from human occupation, both native and European. Among the more curious or more widely publicized forms of animal life that preceded man into this Melanesian environment are: cassowaries, or large, ostrichlike birds; snakes, including the giant pythons that are capable of swallowing a live pig or a man; lizards, the most impressive of which is the iguana, which may attain a length of 3 or 4 feet; the gorgeously plumed but raucous-voiced birds of paradise, of which the rust-red and the white species are the most numerous and the azure blue perhaps the rarest and most-sought-after for its feathers; the

Figure 41.   Native carriers crossing a river some-where in New Guinea.   Signal Corps Photograph.

wallaby, or small kangaroo; the kangaroo rat; the cuscus, a unique marsupial; the snow-white cockatoo; the crocodile that infests the larger rivers; giant, night-flying moths; the "flying-fox," a kind of bat; and a myriad of lesser animal forms.   In terms of nuisance value, there can be little doubt that honors go to certain insects, such as the malaria mosquito (*Anopheles punctatum*), the mite that spreads the deadly scrub typhus, leeches, fleas, lice, and the common housefly, although the natives on the whole have more fear of crocodiles and pythons, and a variety of snails, leaf-chewing and juice-sucking insects cause more damage to crops.   Wallabies are an important source of native food, as are also other marsupials, birds, snakes, lizards, and various rodents.   Fish, shellfish, turtles, and other forms of sea life such as sea-slugs, the sea-cow, (dugong or manatee), sea-worms, and the like are also used for food by natives living along the coasts, and trepang, pearls, pearl shell, and tortoise shell are commercial exports from the region. Natives are said to have taken fish larger than a man from the Membaramo River in western New Guinea.

NEW GUINEA

SIZE, SHAPE, AND OUTLINE

New Guinea is not only by far the largest island in Melanesia; it is also the second largest island in the world, with an area estimated at about 312,000 square miles. It is approximately 1300 miles long—nearly half as great an east-west spread as the United States and nearly one-third that of all Melanesia—and in its widest central portion it is nearly 500 miles wide. In outline it resembles a giant bird, with its open beak and long, slender neck outstretched toward Borneo and its graceful, tapering tail curving southeastward toward New Zealand. There are several deep indentations of the shoreline, notably MacCleur Gulf and Geelvink Bay in the west—both rather broad, shallow embayments fringed with mud flats and swampy shores—and Huon Gulf, Collingwood Bay, Milne Bay, and the Gulf of Papua in the east, all of which are deeper and have more approachable shores. Offshore coral reefs and sandy beaches line the coast in places, the coral providing numerous hazards to navigation as well as extensive, protected anchorages inside the reefs, where deep-water channels transect the obstructions and give access to the sheltered waters within. The spacious roadstead off Finschhafen and Lae in northeastern New Guinea could accommodate the combined fleets of the entire world, and so, too, could the immense basin rimmed and protected by the Bismarck Archipelago and Admiralty Islands just to the north. Both functioned as Allied naval bases for a time in 1944 during the Second World War, just as earlier Port Moresby and Milne Bay accommodated great Allied fleets, and later Hollandia, in Dutch New Guinea.

RELIEF AND DRAINAGE

The most distinctive feature of the topography of New Guinea is the towering cordillera that dominates the skyline of the interior of the island practically throughout its length, together with the dissected plateaus that lie within its central regions. This great mountain system—one of the most impressive in the world—is composed of a number of roughly parallel mountain ranges in the broader parts of the island, narrowing to a single line of hills in the "neck" of the birdlike peninsula (Vogelkop) and to a lofty sierra, the Owen Stanleys, in the southeast. Among the higher and more important ranges, in addition to the Owen-Stanley, are the Oranje and Schneegebirge (Snowy) ranges in Dutch New Guinea and the Mt. Hagen, Bismarck, Musgrave, and Kratke ranges in Australian (eastern) New Guinea. The highest known peak in Dutch New Guinea is Carstensz Toppen, whose gleaming, snow-capped summit rises some 16,400 feet above sea level; highest of the eastern chain as far as surveys now show is Mt. Wilhelm in the east-central part of the island near Chimbu, which rises a little over 15,000 feet and is occasionally dusted with snow. All the snow-capped peaks lie within 8° (550 miles) of the equator.

In the main body of the island to the north and south of the inland ranges lie vast, swampy lowlands most of which are densely forested

FIGURE 42. Native canoe used for wire laying during the war along the coast of New Guinea. Signal Corps Photograph.

and carry only sparse native populations. Those of the northern area appear to be geosynclines, like the Mamberamo, Idenburg, and Sepik lowlands, although the Markham-Ramu valley may well be a combined geosynclinal-rift valley form. The southern lowlands are essentially delta plains formed by the three major rivers of the southern slope, the Digoel, Fly, and Purari. Elsewhere elongate coastal or delta plains and low river or marine terraces interdict the coastal hills and ranges in places. Among the more extensive of these are the lowlands about MacCleur Gulf, where producing oil wells are now located; the Geelvink Plain fringing Geelvink Bay; the western extensions of the Digoel-Fly lowland; the crescent-shaped lowland about the head of the Gulf of Papua, and the Buna-Collingwood lowlands southeast of Lae on the northeast coast. Plateaus other than the one mentioned above in the eastern interior include the interior of the Vogelkop or "bird's head," the Bomberai Peninsula southeast of MacCleur Gulf; the volcanic plateau northwest of the head of the Gulf of Papua; and the low Oriomo Plateau inland from the south-central shores of the island.

Along and inland from the north coast of the island rise several linear mountain ranges. These are all composed of rocks and rock structures older than those of the interior ranges or adjacent lowlands, and at one time in the remote geologic past may have been linked with Asia through Japen Island, the northern mountains of the Vogelkop, Celebes, and Borneo. The highest peaks in this group lie in the Saruwaged and Finisterre ranges, where several summits reach to 12,000 feet and a few slightly exceed 13,000 feet.

New Guinea contains the only large rivers in Melanesia, and these are neither very long compared to the Amazon, Mississippi-Missouri, Nile, or Yangtse nor well known outside New Guinea. Nevertheless some of them are mighty rivers in their own right, in terms of navigable length, volume, and hydroelectric potential. The Fly is navigable by steam launch to a distance of 500 miles above its mouth, and the Sepik over 300. The Purari and Markham are bordered in places by floodplains of rather unusual fertility for equatorial lowlands. In their lower extremities the Fly, Digoel, Ramu, Sepik, and Memberamo are wider than the lower parts of the Mississippi River, as deep in places, and scarcely less impressive. After exceptionally heavy rains in the interior they may flood hundreds of square miles of lowland, form great, shallow, temporary lakes, and color the sea with muddy water to a distance of many miles out from the shoreline.

SOIL AND MINERAL RESOURCES

Little is known about the soils and useful minerals of New Guinea, for soil surveys are almost entirely lacking except for a few small localities along the coast, and much of the interior remains unexplored and hence unprospected. For these reasons it is rather meaningless to say that the soils of New Guinea are "poor" or conversely that they are "rich"; or that mining opportunities are "good" or "insignificant." The plain fact is that we do not have enough information to pass final judgments of this sort as far as New Guinea is concerned. In the early 1930's some geologists were inclined to take a rather pessimistic view of mining opportunities in New Guinea. Then prospectors turned up the fabulous gold placers of the Wau-Bulolo valleys south of Lae, which are so rich that it pays to fly the dredges in and the gold out by plane. Just before the Second World War these placers were yielding over 10,000,000 dollar's worth of gold a year! Not many years ago it was also said that the petroleum outlook was not encouraging, but there are now wells yielding "black gold" in profitable quantities in the Vogelkop, and several large oil concerns have been test-drilling in what is now considered to be a "promising" area near Aitape on the north-central coast. Coal has been picked up in several river beds, and at times in the past, copper, zinc, lead, osmiridium, graphite, and other minerals have been mined. The big island may not turn out to be as rich mineralogically as New Caledonia, its Melanesian neighbor to the southeast, but it may yet be found to contain some extremely valuable surprises.

FIGURE 43.   Mangrove swamp, New Guinea.   Signal Corps Photograph.

If most of the soils of New Guinea are deficient in one respect or another (what soil isn't?), some of them are surprisingly productive. Three successive bumper corn crops have been taken from the same piece of land in a single year, without the addition of fertilizer. Army farms during the Second World War in the vicinity of Port Moresby, Lae, and Gusap produced exceptional yields of a variety of fruits and vegetables, and many of the native gardens both in the lowlands and the highlands seem unusually productive. It may well be that yields on such land would decrease rapidly after a year or two of cultivation without resort to fertilizers, as would appear to be true of tropical soils in general. But there is no adequate basis as yet for forecasting low yields for either the lowland or highland regions of New Guinea, or for any specific crop. Ultimately some of the swampy lowlands (of which there is hardly a shortage!) might prove to be excellent for rice growing, although costs of reclamation of such land will undoubtedly be high regardless of whether it is done by native hand labor or heavy machinery. Some of the mountain country seems well suited to coffee, tea, citrus, and a variety of other subsistence or commercial crops. The fact that coconuts have been the dominant plantation crop in the past is no indication of lack of opportunities in other lines of specialization.

FOREST RESOURCES

The forest resources, like the soil and minerals, are hardly well enough known to allow useful forecasts of their economic value and utility. The lowland forests are known to contain a variety of useful timber trees in certain areas, but mostly these species are scattered and unavailable or unprofitable to cut and remove. Markets are remote, operational costs are high, native labor is scarce, and there is still hardwood timber of suitable quality in more readily accessible parts of the world. Still there were several successful sawmills in operation near Lae and Finschhafen just before the Second World War. As valuable tropical hardwoods become scarcer in other parts of the world, and as roads are extended into the back country of New Guinea for one reason or another, it seems likely that increasing use of the lowland forests of the island will be made.

FISHERIES

Fish abound in New Guinea waters, but most species are not favored in commercial markets overseas. Natives in the immediate vicinity of the coasts make use of the more desirable species, as well as various shellfish, the palolo worm, sea-slugs, turtles, and other marine fauna. Commercial fishing prospects remain largely unsurveyed, but the experience of Army fisheries units in the vicinity of Huon Gulf during the Second World War and aerial photographs of shoals of fish in Torres Strait—possibly tuna—suggest that there may be long-neglected possibilities in this field.

NATIVES

The natives of southeastern New Guinea and parts of the eastern interior are predominantly Papuan stock, speaking a variety of local dialects. Those of northeastern New Guinea, the Bismarck Archipelago, and the Admiralties are essentially Melanesian, speaking a variety of quite unrelated and often mutually unintelligible dialects. Those of western New Guinea appear to be blends of these and Malay elements in the lowlands and more or less undiluted Negritic elements in the interior mountain valleys.

No census has been taken of the native populations of New Guinea, but it seems probable that the total native population does not greatly exceed a million. Of these some 200,000 live in the interior valleys of eastern New Guinea between Wau and Mt. Hagen, where population densities range up to 100 persons per square mile in some locali-

FIGURE 44. Army camp site near Port Moresby, New Guinea. Signal Corps Photograph, 1943.

ties and where there is already noted a marked pressure of population on the land for the supply of food, clothing, and shelter. The lowlands, in most instances, are sparsely populated except in the vicinity of the larger ports or where native village concentrations are favored by better soils or superior plant and animal resources. Lowland natives appear to be less energetic and less healthy than highland tribes of the eastern interior, but whether this is the direct or indirect result of climate, altitude, diet, more frequent contacts with the outside world and with each other, or some other "conditioning" influence cannot be accurately determined.

Native economy varies somewhat both in degree of specialization and in the nature of specializations. Coastal peoples naturally derive a substantial part of their food supply from the sea; riverine settlements depend in part on fresh-water fish. The Negritos of the western interior rely on pandanus fruit to a marked extent, and the lowland swamp-dwellers are heavy eaters of sago, a starchy food made from the pith of the sago palm. All the natives of the island, however, appear to place more emphasis on primitive agriculture (hoe culture with shifting cultivation or rotation of fields instead of crops) than on hunting, collecting, fishing, or other pursuits. The sweet potato is the main food staple of most parts of the island, although coconuts, sago, and pandanus are local substitutes where for one reason or another (mainly soil and soil-moisture conditions) sweet potatoes are difficult or impossible to grow.

Most of the natives live in small villages ranging up to about 50 families. Houses are either closely grouped around a central open space or else strung out along the inner edge of a beach, along a trail, or atop a ridge crest. The size of the villages is probably restricted by the amount of land available as tribal or village property, and by the relatively large amount of land needed in a shifting-cultivation type of economy.

The *strassendorf* or linear type of village along a beach is fairly easy to explain. Coconuts, fish, and shellfish thrive in the vicinity of these beaches, and there are strict geographical limits to which coastal settlements of this type can expand inland or toward the sea; hence the spread along the shore.

The preoccupation with ridge crests in most parts of the interior (except on the larger, richer valley floors) can probably be traced to better water drainage, defense advantages, and relief from the damp, chill night air that settles in the valleys of the interior and against which the ill-clothed, ill-housed natives have little protection. Some of the native huts in the highlands are rather well suited to the cool highland climate, being low, thick-walled, and well-thatched, but there are good reasons for believing this is due to cultural habit rather than climatic adaptation. This last also appears to be true of the varying shapes and interior fixtures of native dwellings in New Guinea. There seems to be no other explanation of the fact that in one highland area the houses are predominantly round and in another square; in one valley the population is grouped in villages, and in another (such as east of Chimbu) there are dispersed farmsteads; and in one village elevated, bamboo sleeping platforms are used inside the huts but in another the family sleeps on the ground. In general, however, the lowland houses are built on piles, as in most parts of Indonesia and the Philippines; in the highlands most houses are built on the ground (that is, without elevated wooden floors). Another generalization quite safe to make is about the highland houses: nearly all are poorly ventilated (one small door and no windows), smoky, ill-smelling, and the favored haunt of rats, fleas, lice, and flies.

PORTS AND TOWNS

All but one of the towns of New Guinea are located on or immediately adjacent to the seacoast, the gold-mining center of Wau in the eastern interior being the sole exception. Chief ports are Port Moresby on the eastern shores of the Gulf of Papua, Lae on the western shores of Huon Gulf, Finschhafen on the Huon Peninsula to the north of Lae, Madang and Alexishafen on the north coast west of the Huon Peninsula, Aitape and Hollandia on the north-central coast, and Merauke on the south-central coast. (Strictly wartime developments, such as Nadzab and Gusap in the Markham Valley, Sausapor on the northern shores of the Vogelkop, Milne Bay in the extreme southeast, and Dobodura between Milne Bay and Lae in the northeast, are not included for the reason that they ceased to exist as towns after military operations passed beyond New Guinea. Nor is it certain that such towns as Buna and Salamaua on the northeast coast, which were obliterated by bombing during the Second World War, will be reconstructed, for easier and more dependable access to the interior is now provided via Lae to the west.)

POLITICAL CONTROL

New Guinea is shared about evenly between the Netherlands and Australia, the boundary between their territorial acquisitions in New Guinea passing through the approximate center of the island from north to south. Until 1947 the eastern half of the island was administered in two separate sections by Australia: Papua and the Mandated Territory of New Guinea. Papua was turned over to Australia toward the end of the nineteenth century by Great Britain, and New Guinea, formerly a German colony, was occupied by Australians in 1914 at the outbreak of the First World War and mandated to Australia in 1921 according to terms of the Versailles Treaty. The two colonies are now administered as a single unit by Australia under a United Nations trusteeship. In the western half of the island the Netherlands retains control, and the area is not yet included in the Republic of Indonesia.

BISMARCK ARCHIPELAGO

LOCATION, COMPONENTS, GENERAL FEATURES

The Bismarck Archipelago consists of two fairly large, mountainous islands, New Britain and New Ireland, and a considerable number of smaller islands and islets that together with their larger neighbors ring the Bismarck Sea on the south, east, and northeast. Their combined area is about 19,200 square miles, most of which is accounted for by New Britain, the largest in the group, and by New Ireland, the second largest. These two islands are long, relatively narrow, and curve within a few miles of each other at their eastern extremities. Off the northern shore of New Britain are several isolated volcanic cones, roughly circular in outline; off northwestern New Ireland lie a number of low, nearly flat, irregularly shaped coral islands and reefs extending westward toward the Admiralty group. Elsewhere a scattering of small islands, some volcanic and some primarily marine in origin, complete the picture.

SURFACE CONFIGURATION

The surface of New Britain is dominated by a number of large volcanoes. From the westernmost part of the island to its northeastern promontories in the vicinity of Rabaul, these volcanoes form the more elevated parts of the skyline, but their slopes often coalesce in the interior and reach the sea toward the periphery of the island. The higher peaks rise to elevations of 7000 to 9000 feet, and with infrequent exceptions the insular divide stands above 4000 feet. In the northeast recently active volcanoes ring the magnificent natural harbor of Rabaul and the city of Rabaul, which until its complete destruction in the early Pacific phases of the Second World War was the finest port and largest city of northern Melanesia as well as the capital of the Mandated Territory of New Guinea. This was the second time within a decade, incidentally, that the city had suffered destruction, volcanic explosions late in the 1930's accounting for the earlier catastrophe.

The lowlands of New Britain are small, scattered, and coastal in distribution except where a few valleys extend into the interior in the eastern part of the islands. In consequence of this and the wet, cloudy climate of the higher elevations in the interior, most of the population is strung out along the coasts or concentrated in a few widely spaced villages at or near the coast. Plantations have a similar distribution, mostly because of the unfavorable climate and steep slopes of much of the interior. In the east, where the topography is somewhat more favorable for cultivation, plantations and native gardens extend well into the interior in spots.

New Ireland is somewhat more favored by topography as far as settlement and agriculture are concerned, being in general lower and, in the vicinity of the coasts, rather flatter and drier. Its crestline is dominated by metamorphosed sedimentary and igneous rocks rather than massive, solitary volcanic cones. The coastal plains that fringe the island, especially on the west, are narrow but fairly continuous and on the whole rather well suited to coconut plantations, the principal industry of the islands.

CLIMATE, SOIL, AND VEGETATION

Except in the more sheltered coastal lowlands such as the north shore of New Britain, the protected valleys of the northeastern part of that island, and along the west coast of New Ireland, the climate of the archipelago is not very favorable for agriculture and human settlement, although clusters of natives are found at intervals along all coasts and small numbers of natives manage to eke a living, if a poor one, off the mountainous, forested interior. The southern slopes of New Britain are exceedingly wet, the annual rainfall at Gasmata in the south-central region averaging about 250 inches a year. This coast is wet principally because it is fully exposed to the southeast monsoon for half the year and receives a considerable carry-over of rainfall from the northern side of the island during the northwest monsoon the other half of the year. The eastern shores of New Ireland are less wet because the winds during both monsoons blow more or less parallel to the coastline a good part of the time, and the lower interior produces less orographic lifting of the air masses that do penetrate into the interior. The more exposed coasts of the islands are normally breezy places, especially during the height of the monsoonal air flow. This is a definite advantage from the standpoint of human comfort in these low latitudes where a still atmosphere is a hot atmosphere; but from the agricultural point of view this is a disadvantage because of higher rainfall.

The soils of the two main islands are neither uniformly poor nor exceptionally fertile. Some of the volcanic soils, notably those derived from certain basalts, are highly productive when properly handled. But it is by no means true that all volcanic soils are good soils. Some of the poorest soils on the islands are of this type, for they are little more than accumulations of recent ash showers from the volcanoes. Except for the local influence of parent materials, we may generalize perhaps to the extent of saying that the higher the rainfall in this region the poorer the soils, for high rainfall means rapid leaching of the upper soil profile. Again, the north coast of New Britain and the west coast of New Ireland are the favored localities for agriculture.

The natural vegetation of the Bismarck Archipelago is somewhat similar to that of New Guinea, except that rainforest extends to the summits of most of the higher mountain peaks, and there are fewer indications of Australian elements in the plant associations. The rainforest, as in New Guinea, consists of a multi-storied assemblage of tall, buttressed, forest trees of varied species; medium-high growth of lesser trees; and lower growth of various shrubs, ferns, and other plants; all levels being densely interlaced by climbing vines and embellished by a wide range of parasitic and epiphytic forms. Some of the giant liana vines, indeed, grow to the very tops of the forest in their struggle for sunlight, throttle the host tree, and assume the nature of trees themselves.

THE NATIVES

The natives of these islands are not very different in appearance from their Melanesian cousins in New Guinea, as would be expected in islands in such close proximity with rather frequent cultural contacts across the narrow, intervening waters. Dialects, tribal customs and traditions, and the life vary somewhat, but the western shores of New Britain, the eastern shores of the Huon Peninsula, and the intervening islands have all developed a common culture pattern.

PRODUCTS

Copra, or the dried meat of the coconut, is by far the most important commercial product of the archipelago. Its future in the sphere of plantation agriculture, however, does not seem very promising, owing to competition from other sources of supply, labor difficulties in the region, and the increasing use of vegetable-oil substitutes, such as cottonseed oil and peanut oil. Just before the Second World War the Agricultural Experiment Station at Rabaul was experimenting with a variety of other plantation crops, but the outlook at the time was not very hopeful as far as finding other mainstays was concerned. Coffee, tea, derris root (for the insecticide *rotenone*), and a new variety of sisal from East Africa were thought to have possibilities. The war, however, put an end to these experiments, and the task of rebuilding is still far from complete. On the whole, it would seem that these islands enjoy certain advantages over New Guinea in the matter of fertile, volcanic soils, but suffer from rough topography, wet climate, and the absence of valuable mineral resources. The capital of the Territory of New Guinea will probably remain at Rabaul in spite of its vulnerable situation close to an active volcano, although a shift to Lae has been proposed.

ADMIRALTY ISLANDS

The Admiralty Islands are of much less importance and interest economically, ethnically, strategically, and in other respects than the Bismarck Archipelago and New Guinea, although closely related geographically and geologically to these islands. They lie athwart the northern approaches to the Bismarck Sea to the northwest of New Ireland and northeast of the Huon Peninsula. The main axis of the group, which is a composite of igneous, sedimentary, and metamorphic rocks, extends east and west. Manus is the most important island in the group, being the largest, the best endowed with natural resources, especially cultivable soil, and the most populous. During the Second World War the group functioned as an advanced Allied air and naval base for a time (early 1944), but with the Allied occupation of Hollandia in Dutch New Guinea the Admiralties were quickly relegated to the status of a staging area and subsequently a rear base with the reconquest of the Philippines. As before the war, the group is of little interest except to the Melanesian natives who dwell there, to a handful of white administrators who consider assignment on Manus a pleasant but not very important tour of duty, and to a few stray scientists who occasionally venture into out-of-the-way places.

REFERENCES

Bowman, Robert G., "Army Farms and Agricultural Development in the Southwest Pacific," *Geogr. Rev.*, Vol. 36, July, 1946.

———— "Acclimatization in New Guinea," *Geogr. Rev.*, Vol. 39, pp. 311–314, April, 1949.

Commonwealth of Australia Official Yearbook, Canberra.

Handbook of the Territory of Papua, Government Printer, Canberra.

Hogbin, H. Ian, "Tillage and Collection: a New Guinea Economy," *Oceania.* December, 1938, and March, 1939.

Keesing, Felix M., *Native Peoples of the Pacific* (revised), The Macmillan Co., New York, 1949.

Krieger, Herbert, *Peoples of Micronesia and Melanesia,* Smithsonian Institution, War Background Studies No. 16, Washington, 1943.

New Guinea Agricultural Gazette, New Guinea Department of Agriculture.

Taylor, Griffith, *Australia,* Methuen & Co., London, 1949.

7

Eastern Melanesia

JOHN WESLEY COULTER

EASTERN MELANESIA IS NOT A VERY CLEARLY DEMARCATED REGION geographically or politically. A distinction can be drawn, however, between the area included under this title and the myriad islands to the east, especially with reference to population and resources. The Lau Islands, easternmost of the Fijian Archipelago, comprise a transition area anthropologically between Melanesia and Polynesia. A great wealth of agricultural and mineral resources characterizes eastern Melanesia, an area that includes from west to east the Solomons, Santa Cruz Islands, New Hebrides, New Caledonia, Loyalty Islands, and Fiji.

The islands in this part of the southwest Pacific have various origins. Some are volcanic, built up from vents in the ocean floor; for example, Bagana on Bougainville in the Solomons is still active, and great eruptions have occurred on Ambrim (1894, 1913, 1929, and 1937), Tana, and Lopevi Islands in the New Hebrides. Others are coral atolls less than the height of a man above sea level. Several have complicated structures due to uplifts and the action of several earth-building agencies. Most of the islands are surrounded by coral reefs. The tops of the high mountainous islands are often obscured in clouds; they are all clothed with various kinds of forest; all abound in food for the native people, and are remarkable for grand and picturesque scenery. The atolls support little natural vegetation other than coconut, pandanus, and shrubs characteristic of the strandline.

Lying within the tropics, these bits of land have a uniformly warm temperature and generally heavy rainfall. The rainfall, however, varies considerably from one archipelago to another, and sometimes from one island to another in the same group. The southernmost islands, strongly affected by the trade winds, have rainy windward sides and drier lee coasts.

Melanesians, a dark-skinned people as compared with the brown Polynesians to the east, are blackest in the Solomons and other islands in the extreme southwest of the Pacific. In Buka and Bougainville in the Solomons their skins are as black as those of the blackest African negroes. Contacts of Melanesians with people from the outside world before the Second World War varied from almost none on islands like Buka to everyday associations of Fijians near the ports with Europeans and Asiatics.

FIGURE 45. Two belles in Natewa, an isolated village in Fiji—hostesses to J. W. Coulter. Photograph by J. W. Coulter.

The natives of eastern Melanesia are in general farmer-fishermen. Perhaps the most striking thing about these occupations is the sameness of the products and the similarity in ways of obtaining them. In the volcanic islands, taro, breadfruit, and bananas are staples. On coral atolls the same foods are raised, but with more difficulty, and the people there depend more on coconuts and pandanus. Of course there are other crops of local importance: cassava in Fiji, and yams in various islands.

On volcanic islands the forest-clearing type of agriculture is practiced. In an open space, hacked in the forest with long bush knives, taro, cassava, or some other crop is planted with a pointed, hardwood stick or similar native implement. Two or three crops are generally raised in about two years, at the end of which time the soil has been so depleted of its plant nutrients that the land is abandoned. A new clearing is hacked in another part of the forest, and the agricultural process is repeated.

FOREIGN RELATIONSHIPS

The islands, like most of those in the Pacific, were brought to the attention of the western world by gradual and sometimes haphazard discovery. The commercial value of sandalwood, copra, pearls, and tortoise shell was early recognized and attracted to some of them more and more foreigners, among whom were deserting sailors, escaped convicts, and other unscrupulous persons who committed many abuses against the natives. Thousands of Solomon islanders were "blackbirded"' to Queensland, Australia, to enforced labor on sugarcane plantations. On some of the larger islands tracts of good land, especially those adjacent to ports, were secured by foreigners.

Sometimes the resentment of natives against newcomers broke out in open revolt. In New Caledonia there were several uprisings because of the encroachment of settlers on land used by the natives, and because damage caused by colonists' cattle, which roamed at will throughout the island and destroyed gardens and other plantings.

Various forms of administration in these islands have arisen from the diversity of circumstances under which they were acquired by European nations and Australia. Bougainville, Buka, and several atolls in the northern Solomons are part of a trusteeship of Australia. The major part of this archipelago, with the Santa Cruz group, form the British Solomon Islands Protectorate, a territory under the jurisdiction of the British High Commissioner for the western Pacific. The New Hebrides are ruled jointly by Britain and France as a condominium. New Caledonia and its dependencies are a French colony. Fiji is a crown colony of Great Britain governed through the British Colonial office in London.

The government of the natives in all these islands is by a system of indirect rule. At first it was the most expedient way of dealing with native tribes and governments for administrations that in earlier years had little knowledge of the native peoples. It has continued to be necessary in view of the small number of British, French, and Australian administrators scattered through the islands. Under indirect rule old native systems retain their basic structure and sometimes are elaborated to accommodate the needs of the administration. Codes of native regulations for governing according to native communal social systems are drawn up and given the force of law.

European residents of these islands distinguish between those born in the mother countries and expecting to return there, and those born or permanently settled in the islands. In the French islands the former are called *metropolitans*. The more influential people from the homeland are usually government officials, missionaries, and representatives of big business firms. Missionaries generally stay a long time in the islands and are in very close touch with the natives. Many of them are able men, and governments cooperate with them in devising measures for the welfare of the natives. Occasionally both Protestant and Roman Catholic missionaries acquire an influence that government officials cannot rival.

For 150 years, more or less, contacts with Europeans, especially where close and continuous, have been bringing about a gradual modification of the traditional manners and customs of the natives of these islands. Whalers, traders, adventurers, and missionaries have contributed to the gradual changes in island civilizations. The Second World War was a quickening factor, the like of which had never before been experienced by the indigenous populations. Parts of the Solomon islands were devastated by the conflict. A native labor corps was formed in the days when the Japanese were being driven from Guadalcanal. Chief Ngatu received the British Empire Medal for the invaluable help he gave in organizing resistance to the Japanese during their occupation of the northern Solomons.

Wherever in eastern Melanesia there is exploitation of the soil by Europeans, it is characterized by plantation agriculture. In establishing plantations in many of the islands, Europeans found the natives unsatisfactory as laborers. The native culture had no place for individualism, private enterprise, and the accumulation of a surplus. In meeting the labor needs for the expansion of the copra industry, a system of indentured native labor has been employed by which natives, generally recruited for 1 to 2 years, could be punished for breaking their "contracts." To develop the sugar-cane industry in a few larger islands and mining in others, dependence has been placed mostly on imported Oriental labor, which, at first, was also indentured.

THE SOLOMON ISLANDS

The Solomon Islands lie to the east of New Guinea and to the north of the New Hebrides. The main group comprises a double chain of islands, stretching roughly from north-west to south-east (Fig. 46). It includes seven major islands: Bougainville, Choiseul, Ysabel, New Georgia, Malaita, Guadalcanal, and San Cristobal; between 20 and 30 smaller islands, and numerous islets. Many islands in this archipelago are very mountainous, but Rennell Island, a raised atoll, is nearly flat.

Several smaller groups of islands, also isolated, are usually considered as part of the Solomons Archipelago. They include: to the south, the large island of Rennell and its smaller neighbor, Bellona; to the southeast, the Santa Cruz group of Ndeni, Vanikoro, and Utupua; the Reef and Taumako groups, and the small isolated islands of Tikopia, Anuta, and Fatutaka; and, to the east and north, a num-

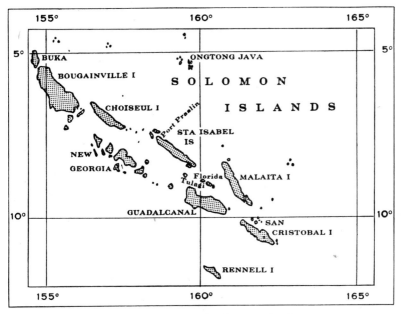

FIGURE 46.   Map of Solomon Islands.

ber of atolls of which the most important are Ontong, Java, and Sikaiana.

For administrative purposes the major part of the group forms the British Solomon Islands Protectorate, a territory under the jurisdiction of the British High Commissioner for the Western Pacific. Bougainville, Buka, and several atolls in the north of the group, however, fall within the limits of the trusteeship territory of New Guinea, of which they constitute the Kieta District; they are administered by the Commonwealth of Australia. The area of the Protectorate is 12,400 square miles and of the Solomon Islands in the trusteeship 4100 square miles.

The Solomons, predominantly of volcanic origin, are a link in the larger chain of volcanic ranges and islands stretching from southeast Asia through Sumatra, Java, and New Guinea and continuing beyond the Solomons into the New Hebrides. The cores of the main islands are ancient lavas, many of which are overlain by recent deposits, both volcanic and sedimentary. Active volcanoes exist at each end of the group, on Mts. Balbi and Bagana, in Bougainville, and in Tinakula in the Santa Cruz group.

TABLE 1

PRINCIPAL SOLOMON ISLANDS

Island	Area, Square Miles	Dimensions	Population (Partly est.)
Bougainville	3880	127 miles long Maximum breadth 49 miles	40,000
Guadalcanal	2500	90 miles long Breadth about 30 miles	14,200
Ysabel (Santa Isabel)	1802	92 miles long Maximum breadth about 19 miles	4,200
Malaita	1572	104 miles long Maximum breadth 23 miles	34,000
San Cristobal	1177	70 miles long Maximum breadth 24 miles	5,000
Choiseul	981	90 miles long Maximum breadth 20 miles	4,000
New Georgia	680 (est.)	50 miles long Maximum breadth 5 to 30 miles	12,000
Ndeni (Santa Cruz)	370	23 miles long Breadth 11 miles	1,800
Rennell	318 (est.)	42 to 50 miles long Maximum breadth between 8 and 10 miles	500

The economic resources of the Solomons, only slightly exploited, are imperfectly known. The islands first became of economic importance as a source of labor for the sugar-cane plantations of Queensland and Fiji. As a field for tropical agriculture, they did not attract attention until the beginning of the twentieth century, when individual settlers and large firms began to take up land for coconut plantations. To avoid too great dependence on a single crop, subsidiary crops were tried, but the quantities grown were small.

The igneous rocks of the main islands probably contain minerals of economic value. Gold has been found in Bougainville, New Georgia, Vangunu, and Guadalcanal. Tin has been reported in south

Bougainville. Phosphate deposits, of poor quality, however, have been found on Rennell.

The military occupation of the Protectorate by Allied forces continued until March 31, 1946. The islands are still in the reconstructional stage, and neither employment, production, exports, nor imports are more than small fractions of the figures obtaining in the years before the Second World War.

FIGURE 47. Mt. Bagana, Bougainville, an active volcano. Signal Corps Photograph.

The production of copra has been the most important industry of the Solomons since about 1900, when Europeans first established plantations. Before then nearly all of it was the produce of native groves, but shortly afterwards plantation copra became much more important. Exports rose steadily until about 1928, from which time the annual export remained about 20,000 tons until 1940.

Insect pests have seriously menaced the industry, especially by causing the young nuts to fall before reaching maturity. Attempts to control the pest, an active bug, have so far been unsuccessful.

The seriousness of the menace is evidenced by comparing the average yield of three-fourths of a ton per acre in the unaffected Russell Islands with that of one-tenth of a ton per acre in Guadalcanal and other affected islands.

The natives of the Solomons have customarily earned small amounts of money by selling copra (of a poor quality) from their own groves to European and Chinese dealers. The government has attempted to improve the quality by encouraging the building of better copra kilns. Native production is more affected by fluctuations in prices than that of European plantations, for the Europeans, especially the large firms, have sufficient capital to tide them over slump periods. To natives, however, copra production is only one of several ways of obtaining cash, and, when prices are very low they, like most natives of the Pacific islands, turn their attention to other sources of income.

The native population forms by far the majority of the inhabitants of the Solomons. The total for the group, comprising the protectorate and what was formerly a mandate but now a trusteeship, is difficult to assess, but was probably about 145,000 in 1940. Except in several marginal islands to the north, east, and south of the main group, the natives are Melanesians. In a few outer islands they are Polynesians. There are a few hundred Europeans and Chinese in the islands.

TABLE 2

POPULATION OF THE
BRITISH SOLOMONS ISLANDS PROTECTORATE, 1947

Europeans	118
Melanesians	90,930
Polynesians	3,808
Chinese	109
	94,965

TABLE 3

EXPORTS OF BRITISH SOLOMONS ISLANDS PROTECTORATE, 1941–1942

Principal Exports	Quantity	Value
Copra	15,660 tons	£95,721
Trochus shell	253	8,500
Timber	1,174,497 square feet	35,717
Gold	1,648 ounces	17,221

BOUGAINVILLE

Bougainville, the largest island in the whole group, is the northernmost except for little Buka, from which it is separated by a channel only about half a mile wide. The interior, imperfectly known, contains at least one massive mountain range following its length. Two active volcanoes, Balbi and Bagana, are respectively 10,171 and 9850 feet. The island is heavily forested. Some of the coastal areas are fertile, and there are a few copra plantations. Roads are rare, and usually only trails connect the settlements. The native population, in 1940 estimated at approximately 39,000, is more dense in the south than in the north. In the south the villages are relatively large and the inhabitants are knit together into strong political and social systems. Tribal fighting still occasionally occurs between the natives of the interior and those of the coastal areas. A government post is located at Buin near the southern end of the island.

GUADALCANAL

Guadalcanal, the largest island in the protectorate, is mainly of volcanic formation with an irregular and very rugged chain of mountains following the southern shore fairly closely, but separated from the north coast by gently sloping plains. The highest peak, Popomanasiu, 8005 feet, is near the center of the south coast. Numerous rivers follow direct courses to the sea. The whole island is densely wooded with the exception of the western part of the northern plain, where there are extensive areas covered with *alang-alang* grass.

The population is concentrated mainly on the north coast, where the natives depend mainly on fish, yams, and coconuts; taro is the staple crop of those still living in the interior. Before the Second World War, Guadalcanal had been more developed than most other large islands in the Solomons, and large coconut plantations were located along the fertile north coast, but these have suffered severely from immature nutfall. The new capital of the Solomon Islands Protectorate is at Honiara on the north coast near Henderson airfield. It has an established road net and is centrally located with reference to the copra industry. During the Second World War fierce fighting took place on the island and in the seas adjoining Guadalcanal, and the first important victory over the Japanese was won there.

YSABEL

Structurally Ysabel is a single chain of volcanic mountains, which, in most parts, dips gently to a low-lying coastal strip. The whole island is forested. It is believed that Ysabel has been considerably depopulated, and formerly the inhabitants were subjected to headhunting raids from New Georgia. The more important areas of settlement are in the extreme southern and northern parts of the island,

and here are found several coconut plantations.   At the northern end
of Ysabel a complex group of islands extends northwestwards, and
the Gijunabeana islands extend 4 or 5 miles off the east coast.

MALAITA

Malaita, known locally as Mala, is separated by a narrow, tortuous
passage from Little Mala.   The island is basically of volcanic forma-

FIGURE 48.   Solomon Islanders from Malaita.
Photograph by *Yank*, the Army Weekly.

tion with superficial deposits of coral limestone on the lowlands near
the coast.   Forested mountains, with elevations up to 4275 feet, follow the main axis, but the interior is mostly unsurveyed.   The population, estimated at about 35,000, consists of vigorous natives who
have a reputation both as fighters and workers, and there are still
occasional reports of tribal warfare.   Most of the villages of this
island have contacts with Europeans through young men who are
laborers on coconut plantations, mostly on other islands.

FLORIDA

The Florida or Nggela group lies between Guadalcanal, Malaita, and Ysabel islands. Florida, the largest island of the group, is about 25 miles in length by 8 to 10 in breadth. The coast is very irregular with good harbors. Close to the south shore of Florida on a little island is Tulagi, a trading port and former seat of government in the Solomons Protectorate.

CHOISEUL

Choiseul is narrow for its length and its center consists of a long ridge, level-topped and devoid of outstanding peaks. The island is nearly surrounded by reefs. Coconut plantations have been established about Choiseul Bay and in other well-drained parts of the coastal belt and on off-lying islands. Planted areas are separated from each other by stretches of marsh and mangrove swamp. The population of about 4000 is concentrated entirely in the coastal areas.

NEW GEORGIA

New Georgia is the largest of a considerable group of islands. There are many harbors, including Marovo and Roviana lagoons. New Georgia was the site of a Japanese airbase and was recaptured by the Americans in 1943. Gizo, on a little island of the same name, is a port and government station near the center of the New Georgia group. Copra is the principal export.

RENNELL

Rennell and Bellona are two raised limestone islands about 100 miles south of Guadalcanal. They are about 15 miles apart. Rennell, between 40 and 50 miles long, is a former atoll that has been uplifted about 400 to 500 feet. The population of approximately 1500 consists of Polynesians with some admixture of Melanesians. The people have little contact with the outside world and retain much of their primitive culture. They raise yams and taro, and collect shellfish and wild fruits for food. Bellona, about 6 miles long and fertile, has a population of 500 of Polynesian origin.

OTHER ISLANDS

Other islands associated with the southern Solomons are: the Stewart Islands, an atoll about 110 miles east of Malaita; Ontong Java (Lord Howe's group), an atoll of several islets about 160 miles north of Ysabel whose inhabitants are largely Polynesians; and the

Shortland Islands, Treasury Islands, and Faure Islands, west of Choiseul and south of Bougainville.

Little scientific work has been done in the Solomon Islands. A recent outline of physical geography is listed among the accompanying references. There are works on physical and social anthropology dealing with scattered parts of the area. No full account of the history of the islands exists. Information on administration is found in the official publications of the governments concerned.

SANTA CRUZ ISLANDS

The Santa Cruz group, about 240 miles east of the southern Solomons, was discovered in 1595 by Mendaña. Most of the islands are small and of volcanic origin. The largest island, Ndeni, known locally as Santa Cruz, is 25 by 14 miles, and roughly rectangular in shape. On the north, east, and south densely wooded hills rise from the sea to a maximum elevation of 1800 feet. Numerous bays indent the steep and rugged coast along which the population is concentrated in coastal villages. The government station for the Santa Cruz District is at Peu, one of the better anchorages on the island of Vanikoro. The total population of the Santa Cruz group is about 5000. Some copra is exported.

THE NEW HEBRIDES

The New Hebrides, including the Banks and Torres islands, are northeast of New Caledonia and southeast of the Solomons (Fig. 49). Much of the land, generally mountainous, is covered by dense tropical forest. A few of the islands, like some of the Solomons, contain active volcanoes. The New Hebrides proper have an area of about 5700 square miles and comprise 12 major islands, 18 lesser islands, and between 30 and 40 small islands and islets distributed around their coasts. They are dispersed in the form of a Y, of which the southern islands form the tail. Among the principal islands are Espiritu Santo, Malekula, Eromanga, and Efate.

The New Hebrides were discovered in 1606 by De Quiros, then forgotten until they were explored in 1768 by Bougainville. The islands were charted by Cook in 1774. During the nineteenth century the natives suffered through contacts with whalers, sandalwood traders, pirates, and "blackbirders" who recruited labor for plantations. In 1887 Great Britain and France signed an agreement for a dual government in the islands, and in 1906 a formal condominium was estab-

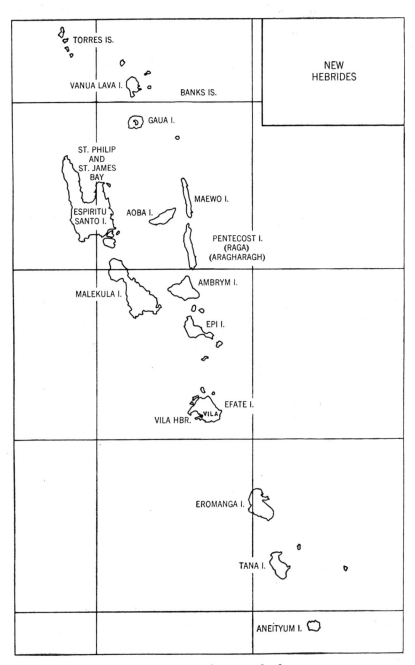

FIGURE 49. Map of New Hebrides.

lished. The administrative structure of the New Hebrides is unique in the Pacific because of the complex division of powers between the Anglo-French condominium administration and the separate British and French administration. In general, the national administrations have jurisdiction over their respective nationals, and the condominium over natives and where the interests of British and French do not coincide.

A complete census has never been taken in the New Hebrides, but a rough estimate for the native population is 47,000. The European population is about 1000 (935 in 1938), of whom three-fourths are French and most of the remainder British. There are over 2000 Asiatics, mostly Indo-Chinese, almost all laborers brought in under indenture or members of their families. The degree to which the native population has been affected by contact with Europeans varies considerably. Many near the coast are fully "missionized," though their understanding and practice of Christianity are generally superficial. A considerable number have been recruited for labor on copra, cocoa, and coffee plantations. The inhabitants of poorly accessible interiors of the larger islands were little affected by modern contacts until the Second World War.

TABLE 4

PRINCIPAL NEW HEBRIDES ISLANDS

Island	Area, Square Miles
Espiritu Santo	1500
Malekula	450
Eromanga	330
Efate	300
Ambrim (Ambrym)	160
Tana	150
Raga (Pentecost)	125
Omba (Aoba)	105
Epi	100
Maewo	90
Vanua Lava	85
Gaua	85
Malo	70
Aneityum	40

The New Hebrides generally have fertile soil developed from volcanic materials, and the abundant rainfall and warm temperatures favor the growth of dense forests and of planted crops. The economy of the islands is based primarily upon agriculture. Coconuts, cacao, cotton, coffee, and maize are among the exports. Sandalwood is still gathered in small volume from the forests, and shell from the coastal waters. Cattle do well where grass is available, and sheep are raised for wool and meat on Eromanga Island. The natives raise starchy roots, bananas, and vegetables for themselves and keep pigs and chickens for food. The islands are capable of large expansion in plantation crops if labor, capital, and markets all become favorable. Formerly, sulphur deposits on the island of Vanua Lava were worked commercially. It is commonly believed that these islands, like neighboring New Caledonia and Fije, contain valuable mineral deposits, but so far no significant discoveries have been made, and no organized prospecting has been carried out.

Copra has long been the principal export of the archipelago. In 1938 the area in plantations operated by Europeans was about 50,000 acres, of which 33,000 were in coconuts, 9000 in cacao, and 7000 in coffee. The majority of these are in French hands.

Since the Second World War plantation economy has been struggling to get on its feet. In New Hebrides, as in many other parts of the Pacific, one of the principal barriers to the extension of European enterprise is the shortage of labor.

ESPIRITU SANTO

Espiritu Santo, known locally as Santo, is the largest island in the New Hebrides, is of irregular shape, and about 76 by 46 miles in dimensions. It consists of two widely different regions. The eastern half of the island, largely a plateau of raised coral limestone with a general elevation of 300 to 600 feet, culminates in Mt. Turi, 1760 feet. The western half of the island is mountainous, rising to 5566 feet at Santo Peak (Iaiiriiri) and 6195 feet at Mt. Tabwemasana. This part has a well-developed drainage system. The largest river, the Yora, rises near Santo Peak and flows northeastward to St. Phillip and St. James Bay, locally called Big Bay. The mountains are heavily forested, and trees include the valuable kauri pine. Sandalwood was once common, but this resource has been much reduced by cutting.

The southeast coast of Espiritu Santo and the adjacent islands of Aore and Malo constitute one of the more important regions of European settlement in the group. Along both shores of Segond Channel, which separates Aore from the larger island, there are almost continuous stretches of plantations, and on the mainland shore is the French administrative, commercial, and missionary center of Luganville. During the Second World War, Espiritu Santo was developed as a military base that included a large airfield in the northern part. The British government agency was formerly at Hog Harbor in the northeast part of the island, and British-owned coconut plantations and missions are located here and on St. Phillip and St. James Bay.

MALEKULA

Malekula, known to the French as Mallicolo, the second largest island in the group, is about 46 by 23 miles in maximum length and breadth. It is formed largely of limestones that have been penetrated in some districts by lava. The surface is hilly, and there are several peaks, Mt. Penot, 2925 feet, being the highest. Vegetation, everywhere dense, in the southern and central parts consists mostly of thick forest, matted together by numerous lianas and creepers. Coral terraces in the north are thickly covered with cane grass. Malekula is still the most populous island in the New Hebrides, in spite of a considerable decline during the last century. European enterprises consist mainly of several French and British coconut plantations largely confined to the east coast, which has some good harbors, including Port Stanley and Port Sandwich.

EROMANGA

Eromanga, known to the French as Erromango, is 35 by 25 miles in size and the largest of the southern islands of the New Hebrides. It is composed mainly of lavas and volcanic agglomerates with terraces of raised coral on the lowlands. The interior is mountainous. The island is fertile but underdeveloped, the absence of good harbors being a handicap. Furthermore, the natives were originally unfriendly to settlers, and labor is scarce because the island has been largely depopulated. Sandalwood, at one time the sole export, is still found in some districts.

EFATE

The island of Efate, known to the French as Ile Vate, is of volcanic origin, but is almost completely encrusted with coral limestone. Rivers have cut through the limestone to penetrate the weak volcanic tuffs and soft metamorphic rocks beneath. The eroded material has been deposited to form alluvial flats in their lower reaches. A sharp-crested mountain chain follows the northwest coast a few miles inland, its highest peak attaining 2203 feet. The southern part of the island is a plateau 200 to 300 feet high, intersected with coral ridges. The whole island is densely wooded except for a peninsula in the southwest, which for the most part is covered with grass. The majority of the European and Indo-Chinese people are in or near Vila, the administrative and commercial center of the New Hebrides. Nearly all the Tonkinese work on French plantations. Native New Hebrideans live in scattered coastal villages and on small islands off the coast. A supply base and airfield were established in Efate by the Allies during the Second World War.

Vila on Mele Bay, a protected harbor in southeast Efate, is the sole port of entry for the New Hebrides. Its population is about 1500, including several hundred non-natives.

The eastern chain of the New Hebrides north from Efate includes the Shepherd Islands, Epi, Ambrin, Raga (Pentecost), and Maewo. South of Efate are Tana and Aneityum. Raga or Pentecost is a long, narrow island, 39 by 7½ miles, fertile, and supports about 6000 natives and many white planters. The natives on the north end are Polynesians, those to the south Melanesians. Tana is mountainous, some 32 by 15 miles in size, is fertile and has a comfortable climate. The island supports 6500 natives and several plantations.

BANKS ISLANDS

The Banks Islands, of volcanic origin, are situated about 50 miles northeast of the main New Hebrides. The vegetation is luxuriant, the rainfall abundant, and the soil fertile. The chief islands are Vanua Lava, which has an active volcano, and Gaua, both of which have an area of about 85 square miles.

The Torres Islands, a chain of small islets, are northwest of the Banks group. The largest isle is 10 by 2 miles in greatest dimensions. The natives are Polynesians, of whom only about 200 now remain as the island has been seriously depopulated.

NEW CALEDONIA

The archipelago of New Caledonia (including the Huon Islands, the Belep Islands, and the Isle of Pines) and the Loyalty Islands and little Walpole Island (150 miles southeast) lie about 900 miles east of Australia and 1000 miles northwest of New Zealand. Also attached to New Caledonia for administrative purposes are the Chesterfield Islands, 285 miles west of the Huon Islands (Fig. 50).

New Caledonia, locally often referred to as "the mainland" (la Grande-Terre), is a large island 248 miles long with an average breadth of 30 miles. Its total area is about 6200 square miles. The area of its dependencies amounts to about 800 square miles. The climate is pleasant and healthful and suitable for European settlement. The temperature is moderate for its latitude, mean monthly averages varying between 65° to 72° F, and the weather is tempered by fresh trade winds. The annual rainfall is about 40 inches, and the relative dryness is favorable for Europeans and for livestock of European origin. The island has an irregular coastline with numerous bays and is nearly surrounded by a barrier reef about 5 miles offshore. The reef continues north to the Huon Islands and has a length of over 400 miles.

New Caledonia was discovered and named by Cook in 1774, but the British did not establish a claim to the island, and after negotiations agreed to its annexation by France in 1853. It was a penal colony from 1864 to 1894, and during these years about 40,000 prisoners were transported. The natives, who were Melanesians mixed with some Papuan and Polynesian blood, were originally estimated to number between 60,000 and 100,000, but are now reduced to less than 20,000. With settlement of the country, trouble began with the natives, who were crowded off from much of their land. A great insurrection of natives in 1878–1879 lasted 9 months and was put down only after much bloodshed and property damage. Another insurrection came in 1881, and parts of New Caledonia have never recovered from the effects of these wars. The natives raise taro, sweet potatoes, breadfruit, bananas, manioc, beans, corn, and other crops. Abandoned terraces, once planted in taro, record the decrease in native population.

Politically, New Caledonia and its dependencies, a French colony, are administered by a Governor, who also acts as High Commissioner (Commissaire général de la République Française dans le Pacifique) in charge of French interests elsewhere in the western Pacific, including those in Uvea and the Hoorn islands, and in the condominium of New Hebrides.

TABLE 5

POPULATION OF NEW CALEDONIA (LA GRANDE-TERRE)

Europeans at Noumea	10,450
Europeans in the Interior	8,050
Aborigines	18,000
Others (chiefly Asiatics)	9,000
	45,500

GEOLOGY

The geological structure of the island is important in relation not only to the relief features but also to its valuable mineral resources. Metamorphic and sedimentary formations are found extensively. The metamorphic rocks fall into two major groups, gneiss and schists, and serpentine. The principal outcrop of gneiss constitutes the Ignambi

FIGURE 50.   Map of New C

Drawn by E. H. Bryan, Jr.

chain, about 40 miles long in the northeast part of the island. There are several main summits, of which Mt. Panie, 5387 feet, is the higest point in New Caledonia. On the seaward, to the east, the mountain chain slopes steeply to the coast with scarcely a break, and the streams that flow in its narrow valleys fall in a series of cataracts, one of the notable of which is at Tao. On the landward side, to the west, the descent is also steep, to the valley of the Diahot River. The mountain masses in the rest of the island show a confused series of peaks and ranges, not arranged in any major chain. The schists, hard and crystalline, occupy an area from the east-central part of the island northwest to the extreme north; their relief is extremely irregular and broken. The second group of metamorphic rocks, composed largely of serpentine, attains its chief development in the south of the island, though from there it extends in a series of progressively more isolated massifs to the extreme northwest.

Sedimentary rocks are confined to a zone a few miles broad extending along the west coast from the south of the island for about three-quarters of its length. They are the most important factors in the relief of broad, gently undulating plains, with some steep-sided hills that do not reach a great elevation.

TABLE 6

Value of Nickel Matte Exports,
78 Per Cent Nickel

Year	(in Thousands of Francs)
1939	112,600,000
1940	107,100,000
1941	132,000,000
1942	87,000,000

TABLE 7

Year	Nickel Ore Mined (Metric Tons)	Nickel Matte Processed (Metric Tons)
1942	256,555	6,600
1943	210,697	7,025
1944	231,850	7,248

The metamorphic rocks of New Caledonia yield copper, gold, and argentiferous lead and zinc; the serpentine of the northwest and the southeast yields nickel, chrome, cobalt, and iron, and the sedimentary earths provide some manganese, antimony, and coal.

New Caledonia holds second rank in the world in the production of nickel ore. But though the export of this metal in various forms represents a very important item in the country's trade, it does not supply a high proportion of the world's output. The major share is contributed by Canada, which supplies 90 per cent, and New Caledonia, which furnishes 7 per cent. The nickel resources of the island show no sign of exhaustion. In 1936 the exports of nickel represented 45 per cent of the total value of exports from the colony; by 1939 they had risen to 68 per cent. The ore occurs in various forms, and at first it was all exported for treatment abroad. In 1910, however, the treating of the lower-grade ores in local furnaces began at Noumea, thus diminishing greatly the cost of freight in export. The treated product, in which the metal is concentrated into a sulphide, is known as *matte*, and is usually sent to France for refining.

New Caledonia is an important source of chromium, formerly taking fifth or sixth place among the world's producers. But though the volume of production has not changed markedly, New Caledonia has dropped to seventh or eighth place. Most of the chrome is taken by the United States.

Among the less important resources, iron ore is probably the most abundant. However, much of it is of low grade, and for want of local coal suitable for coke it has been little exploited. Cobalt, occurring in rich deposits on the summits of many of the serpentine hills, was extensively mined in the past; but, with the discovery of more lucrative deposits in the Belgian Congo and Canada, mining of this metal in New Caledonia has almost ceased. Copper, occurring principally in the Diahot valley in the north, has negligible importance commercially. Coal, large in quantity, is poor in quality, and imports of better grade, largely from Australia and New Zealand, have increased with the growing demands of nickel smelting.

On the whole, the exploitation of most of the mineral resources of New Caledonia, despite optimistic hopes entertained for them, has proved disappointing owing to the distance from overseas markets and the competition of more extensive and richer deposits elsewhere. The extraction of nickel and chrome, however, has proved of great value.

TABLE 8

PRINCIPAL EXPORTS OF NEW CALEDONIA, 1938

Nickel { Bars	8,031	
Nickel { Ore	32,492,000 kilograms	
Chrome	42,271,000 kilograms	
Copra	2,945,000 kilograms	
Coffee	1,763,000 kilograms	

Kilogram = 2½ pounds

The flora of New Caledonia has affinities with the flora of Australia and New Zealand and is less tropical in appearance than that in the

Solomons. The kauri grows to good size for timber, and the abundance of *Araucaria* on the Isle of Pines gave the name to that island. Waxy-leaved tamanaas add to the beauty of the forest. The niaouli (*Melaleuca viridiflora*) is a shrub eucalyptus whose stalks, bark, and oil are all used by man. The growth of sandalwood, once common, was cut out long ago. Introduced guava and lantana have spread widely. Some of the native trees have brilliant red blossoms, and climbing vines occur in the damper forests. There are extensive and excellent grasslands utilized for grazing cattle. There were originally no native mammals except rats and bats, but deer were introduced and have greatly increased. Numerous birds include pigeons, doves, parrots, ducks, and kingfishers. A flightless bird, the kagu (*Rhinochetus jubatus*), is found only in New Caledonia.

In the earlier years of the mining industry, labor was supplied by convicts hired out from the local penitentiary for a nominal fee, and also by natives from the New Hebrides. Later Japanese were imported to help replace decreasing convict labor, and after them Annamite and Tonkinese convicts. Chinese, Javanese, Arabs, and Solomon islanders have been among other laborers imported under indenture. Near the end of the Second World War the contract system of labor in New Caledonia was abolished. Minimum pay for the freed Asiatics is now three times their indentured wage. Hundreds of former indentured laborers have started retail stores, laundries, and other small business ventures. The French, dismayed by the prospect, maintain that, without indentured labor, the economic exploitation of the island's resources has been arrested.

AGRICULTURE

The value of agricultural products of New Caledonia is much less than that of minerals. Colonization of the island by French farmers has met with indifferent success. Failures of various organized attempts have been due to one or all of several factors, small size of farms, lack of capital, insufficient preparation to receive immigrants, and absence of accessible markets. There is a small influx of French colonists, but shortage of labor is now a serious problem.

Coffee, introduced in 1856, was cultivated especially from 1895 on, the time of the "Feillet" colonization, called after the governor who organized it. That colonization was characterized by an obligation on the part of the settlers to raise coffee trees. The coffee industry, in spite of various economic difficulties, has maintained itself to this day and is a mainstay of farming. Farmers on the humid east coast raise the *Robusta* variety; those on the drier west side, *Arabica*.

The quality of the coffee is good. Most of it is prepared for the French market on the farms and plantations by simple methods involving depulpers, hullers, and graders. Production reached its height in 1937 with about 1900 metric tons.

A considerable area of unimproved land in New Caledonia, on dry uplands, is grazed; about 15 acres maintain one head of cattle. The pastoral industry, taking advantage of large savanna areas with native grasses, has occupied a prominent position since the early days of the colony. Cattle number over 160,000 and are mainly crossbred from Australian and French stock. They furnish the local meat markets and also supply a meat-packing plant at Ouaco. The greater part of

Figure 51. Natives of New Caledonia working with bullocks in rice fields close to a modernized village. Signal Corps Photograph.

the product is exported in France, French colonies, and the New Hebrides.

Copra, for many years an important agricultural product, has recently taken second place to coffee. During the decade before the Second World War the average annual export was 2425 tons. New plantations have been largely native-owned, and the native share in the copra export is about 70 per cent.

The economic life of the natives of New Caledonia is based on agriculture and fishing. Yams and taro are the more important food crops raised.

The demands of the French colonists for land have resulted in confinement of the natives to reserves, some of which are small. For several reasons this has resulted in the destruction of old forms of social organization. Present-day natives, largely Christianized, imitate the ways of Europeans. Native crafts have been mostly abandoned, cotton garments are worn; houses of sawn timber with corrugated iron roofs have almost entirely replaced thatched and bark-walled houses. Many eat canned food instead of native products, and cook in kerosene cans.

TABLE 9

CROPS OF NEW CALEDONIA, IN ACRES

Wheat	375
Corn	1,250
Rice	375
Beans, peas	250
Yams, manioc, taro	1,500
Sweet potatoes	375
Potatoes	175
Bananas	2,500
Coffee	12,500
Coconuts	12,500
Improved pasture	175,000
Total	206,800

NOUMEA

Noumea is the capital, largest city, and most adequately equipped port in New Caledonia and in fact is the only port of entry in the colony. It is located on a superior harbor, land-locked and encircled by low hills and well sheltered by an offshore island. The city has a population of about 11,000, and is second to Suva among the south Pacific island towns. It was founded in 1854, and its streets, laid out on a rectangular plan, are wide and lined with trees. The government buildings are of stone or concrete; the residences are mainly wooden structures. There are churches, barracks, hospitals, and many businesses, including the publishing of several journals and a daily newspaper. Industrial establishments include the nickel smelter and a sawmill. Steamship service is available to France via the Panama Canal, to several of the south Pacific islands, and by small craft to the coastal towns of New Caledonia. Air transportation is also available.

LOYALTY ISLANDS

The Loyalty group consisting of three large islands and a number of reefs and islets, is arranged in a chain that parallels the length of New Caledonia about 70 miles to the northeast. The large islands are: Mare, 20 miles long, population about 3000; Lifu (Lifou) of irregular shape, 33 miles in greatest length and 28 miles in greatest width, and with a population of nearly 6000; and Uvea, which is an atoll and supports about 2,000 inhabitants. Mare and Lifu are of uplifted limestone formation. Uvea atoll is low and has its main island on the east side of the lagoon; the latter is 22 miles long with 3 miles at greatest width. The climate resembles that of New Caledonia, but because of the low altitude the rainfall is sometimes deficient. The bedrock is too pervious for surface drainage; water is secured from wells but is often brackish in quality. Trees include the coconut, pandanus, banyan, pines, and several types of hardwoods. The inhabitants are mainly Melanesian. The natives, expert fishermen, raise taro, yams, and a variety of vegetables. They live in dozens of little hamlets that are connected. Copra is the chief export.

THE FIJI ISLANDS

The Fiji Islands lie midway between Samoa and New Caledonia. They comprise the two large islands of Viti Levu and Vanua Levu, the lesser islands of Taveuni and Kandavu, and nearly 260 small islands, mostly in the Lau group, to the southeast of Vanua Levu. The total land area is 7055 square miles, of which Viti Levu occupies 4053 square miles and Vanua Levu 2137 square miles. Only about 100 of the islands are inhabited. Fiji has been a British colony since 1874 (Fig. 53).

The rocks of Fiji represent a longer period of geological history than those of most Pacific islands and include a great variety of formations. They include rocks of metamorphic and volcanic origin; some of the volcanic rocks were formed above the sea and others laid down below sea level. The topography, in general fairly rugged, includes mountains of moderate height. There are several large rivers and many smaller streams.

Gold is found in association with a type of crystalline rock called porphyritic andesite on Viti Levu and Vanua Levu. Gold mining began in 1932, and the extraction of this metal now ranks second to sugar among exports of the islands, being worth about $5,000,000 annually (£1,288,780 in 1947, £ = $3.47). Most of the production has come from three mines in the Tavua district on Viti Levu.

The climate of Fiji, generally hot and rainy, is favorable to the growth of heavy forests, which occupy a large part of the interior and include both hardwoods and softwoods. One of these, *dakua*, resembles the kauri of New Zealand, and another, *buabua*, is widely utilized for house posts because of its extreme durability.

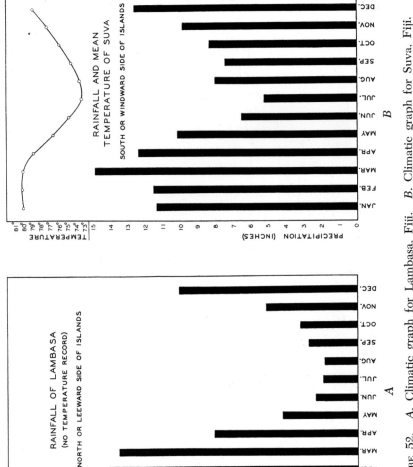

FIGURE 52. A. Climatic graph for Lambasa, Fiji. B. Climatic graph for Suva, Fiji.

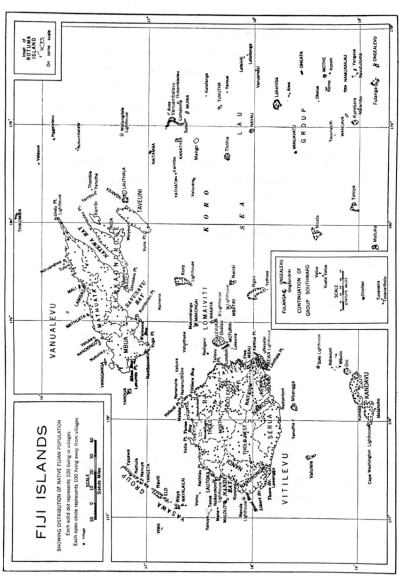

FIGURE 53.   Map of Fiji Islands.   Distribution of native Fijians.   From J. W. Coulter's *Little India of the Pacific*, courtesy of the University of Chicago Press.

TABLE 10

POPULATION OF FIJI, 1947

Race	Total
Europeans	5,376
Part-Europeans	6,341
Fijians	121,249
Polynesians, other Melanesians, Micronesians	3,823
Indians	125,674
Rotumans	3,403
Chinese	2,891
Others	517
	269,274

TABLE 11

PRINCIPAL ISLANDS OF THE FIJI GROUP

Area in Square Miles

Viti Levu	4053
Vanua Levu	2137
Kandavu	169
Yaveuni	168
Gau	54
Ovalau	40
Koro	40

INHABITANTS AND THEIR ECONOMY

With metal-bearing rocks, its damp, tropical climate, and rich, volcanic soil, Fiji possesses a wealth of economic resources ranging from gold and timber to sugar, bananas, and copra. Historically there have been considerable changes in the types of agriculture in Fiji. Native Fijian agriculture, based originally on subsistence and local exchanges, has become a mixed economy. With the introduction of cash and the inclusion of the group within the orbit of world trade, a growing though still relatively small part is played by native production for world markets. Indians, introduced originally as indentured laborers, have now gained their economic independence and become small farmers. In terms of scale, organization of production, and value of products, Indian farming is more important than that of the Fijians.

Sugar is the leading export crop of Fiji, and its production under the plantation system began in the 1870's. Indians and other non-Caucasians were brought in as laborers. In the 1940's about 53,000 acres were planted to cane and 5 mills were in operation, all owned by the Colonial Sugar Refining Company. Production is about 200,000 tons (131,294 in 1942) annually. Other crops include bananas, rice, cacao, coffee, citrus fruits, cotton, and rubber. Production of copra and coconut oil is important.

The East Indians in Fiji are commanding more attention than Asiatics in any other Pacific islands. The future of Orientals there is receiving a good deal of anxious thought, and the eyes of other governments in the South Seas are focused on the situation that the Indians have brought about. From indentured laborers they have developed into good farmers, raising sugar cane, rice, and nearly all the other commercial crops of the colony. They are tenant farmers, laborers, mechanics, store keepers, business and professional men, and politicians.

TABLE 12

PRINCIPAL EXPORTS OF FIJI, 1947

Export	Quantity	Value, in Pounds
Sugar	112,433 tons	2,840,307
Gold bullion	134,922 ounces	1,288,780
Copra	27,490 tons	966,246
Coconut oil	6,570 tons	440,189
Bananas	242,206 bunches	72,867
Biscuits	955,756 pounds	29,345
Molasses	21,982 tons	21,982
Canned pineapple	551,488 pounds	15,896
Hides	12,411	12,645
Bêche-de-mer	1,007 hundredweight	9,168
Silver bullion	34,933 ounces	7,291
Trocas shell	105 tons	6,525
Pineapples	7,176 cases	4,303
Rubber (raw)	60,380 pounds	3,670

VITI LEVU

Viti Levu comprises more than half the area of the Fiji group, and, though smaller than Hawaii or New Caledonia, is one of the larger islands in the Pacific. The island has four types of surface features: (1) the high central Rairaimatuku plateau, (2) the mountain ranges, (3) large areas of hilly uplands, much dissected by rivers, and (4) the coastal areas, consisting of low-lying plains near the coast, the deltas of the principal rivers, and low rounded hills farther inland. The largest river, the Rewa, near Suva, is navigable for 60 miles, and drains one-third of the island. Its floodplain and portions of the delta are devoted to sugar cane. The coast is surrounded by an extensive barrier reef, linked by patches of detached coral reefs to the reefs of neighboring islands. Viti Levu has more than two-thirds of the total population of the group.

Suva, capital of Fiji, and seat of the High Commissioner for the Western Pacific, is situated on a reef-locked and sheltered harbor in the southeast of Viti Levu. It is a cosmopolitan city, and with its suburbs has a population of about 17,000, including Europeans, Indians, and Fijians. It was the development of cotton growing, now replaced by sugar, in the Rewa valley from 1860 onwards that drew attention to the advantages of Suva, and in 1882 the capital was moved there from Levuka. The town extends inland from the wharves; the business section adjoins the waterfront and the residential section for Europeans is situated on higher ground. Suva is the most important of the three ports of entry of Fiji. The great majority of overseas vessels call at Suva even if they also visit Lautoka, on the northern coast of Viti Levu, or Levuka, on the small island of Ovalau. Ex-

FIGURE 54. A kava ceremony at Ngolan village, Fiji. Signal Corps Photograph.

ports and imports of Suva are over half the total trade of the colony, almost all the remainder going through the port of Lautoka. Vessels calling at Fiji include cargo steamers to carry away sugar and copra, liners, and oil tankers. Smaller boats handle the inter-island trade with other Fijian Islands and the Tonga group. Air connections are offered to Hawaii, North America, New Zealand, and Australia. From Suva a highway makes a circuit of the island and narrow-gauge railways serve the sugar industry. Suva has several educational institutions including a medical school with a four-year course for native practitioners, an experiment station devoted to tropical agriculture, hotels, churches, and a variety of business establishments, including sawmills, a soap factory, and coconut-oil mill. Near Suva are sugar mills set among the cane fields and a dairy farm of 10,000 acres with 1000 cows.

FUTURE DEVELOPMENT

Fiji, in some ways similar to the Hawaiian Islands, is less fully developed. Its further output as well as that of other islands in Melanesia and the Pacific in general is difficult to prognosticate. Insistence on economic development is great. If it is well conceived, it benefits the natives as well as the outside world. If, however, development by European capital in the European interest is pushed too fast, at the expense of the native communities, or if Occidental and Oriental settlement encroaches too much on native lands, the natives suffer.

All the islands of Melanesia, like many others in the Pacific, are included under the title of Non-Selfgoverning Territories and Trusteeships. The United Nations Organization in its charter has signified its intention of going far in respect to measures for the solution of problems of native peoples in places in this and other parts of the world that come under that designation. Three chapters of the charter were devoted to dependent areas. Basic principles of far-reaching significance embodied in those chapters were: first, that nations responsible for the administration of dependent territories should recognize that they are accountable to the world community for the well-being and development of the peoples under their authority; second, that the political, economic, social, and educational advancement of dependent peoples is a primary concern; and third, that dependent territories must be administered in such a manner as to contribute to the maintainance of peace and security.

OCEANIC ISLANDS OF AUSTRALIA

The Commonwealth of Australia owns Lord Howe Island and Norfolk Island, which are isolated remnants of volcanic islands that rise from submarine banks about midway between New Caledonia, Australia, and New Zealand. They were uninhabited when discovered, and the present inhabitants are chiefly of English ancestry. Lord Howe Island has 200 inhabitants, and Norfolk about 800, many of the latter being descendants of the *Bounty* mutineers moved from Pitcairn Island. This Lord Howe Island must not be confused with one of similar name in the Santa Cruz group, or with Lord Howe Islands (Ontong Java) northeast of the Solomons.

Lord Howe Island (latitude 31° 35′ south, longitude 159° 04′ east) is about seven miles by one mile in size and attains an altitude of 2840 feet. Cliffs 800 feet high have been cut in nearly horizontal lava flows and furnish proof of profound wave erosion. The seeds of the native kentia palm (*Howea belmoveana*) form the chief export. The seeds are bought by florists the world over because of their hardiness, and the palms grow indoors with ease.

Norfolk Island (latitude 29° 04′ south, longitude 167° 56′ east) has an elevation of 1050 feet and covers 13 square miles of land. Subsistence crops are raised, and formerly bananas were the chief export; now the pulp of passion fruit, guavas, and bean seeds are exports. The Norfolk Island pine (*Auracaria excelsa*) has been widely planted abroad for decorative purposes.

REFERENCES

Solomon Islands

British Solomon Islands Protectorate Blue Book, Suva, Fiji (published annually by government of the British Solomon Island).

Davis, Charles M., "Coconuts in the Russell Islands," *Geogr. Rev.,* Vol. 37, pp. 400–413, July, 1947.

Hogbin, H. I., *Experiments in Civilization,* Routledge, London, 1939.

———— "Coconuts and Coral Islands (Ontong Java)," *Natl. Geog. Mag.,* Vol. 65, pp. 265–298, March, 1934.

Lever, R. J. A. W., "The Geology of the British Solomon Islands Protectorate," *Geol. Mag.,* Vol. 74, pp. 271–277, London, 1937.

———— "The Physical Environment, Fauna and Agriculture of the British Solomon Islands," *Trop. Agric.* Vol. 14, pp. 281–285, Trinidad, 1937.

Villiers, Alan, *The Coral Sea,* Whittlesey House, McGraw-Hill Book Co., New York, 1949.

New Hebrides

Buxton, P. A., "The Depopulation of the New Hebrides and Other Parts of Melanesia," *Trans. Royal Soc. Tropical Medicine and Hygiene,* Vol. 19, pp. 420–454, London, 1926.

Mawson, D., "The Geology of the New Hebrides," *Proc. Linnean Soc., New South Wales,* Vol. 30, pp. 400–485, Sydney, 1905–1906.

Robson, R. W. (editor), *The Pacific Islands Handbook, 1944,* Pacific Publications, Sydney, North American edition, Macmillan and Co., Toronto, 1946.

New Caledonia

Compton, R. H., "New Caledonia and the Isle of Pines," *Geogr. Jour.,* Vol. 49, pp. 81–106, London, 1917.

Parsons, J. J., "Coffee and Settlement in New Caledonia," *Geogr. Rev.,* Vol. 35, January, 1945, pp. 12–21.

Santot, H., "New Caledonia," *Scot. Geogr. Mag.,* Vol. 58, pp. 105–108, Edinburgh, 1942.

FIJI

Coulter, J. W., "Environment, Race and Government in South Sea Islands," *Scot. Geogr. Mag.*, Vol. 63, No. 2, pp. 49–56, Edinburgh, 1947.

—— *Fiji: Little India of the Pacific*, University of Chicago Press, Chicago, 1942.

Davis, W. M., "The Islands and Coral Reefs of Fiji," *Geogr. Jour.*, Vol. 55, pp. 34–45, 200–220, 377–388, London, 1902.

Derrick, R. A., *The Geography of the Fiji Islands*, Ndaviulevu, 1938.

Fiji, *Handbook of the Colony*, Suva, 1941 (special wartime issue), 1943.

Thompson, Laura, *Fijian Frontier*, Institute of Pacific Relations, American Council, New York, 1940.

Walker, Nancy, *Fiji: Their People, History and Commerce*, Witherby, London, and Ryerson Press, Toronto, 1936.

LORD HOWE

Clark, H. L., "The Paradise of the Tasman," *Natl. Geog. Mag.*, Vol. 68, pp. 115–136, 1935.

8

The Mariana, Volcano,
*and Bonin Islands**

NEAL M. BOWERS

THE MARIANA, THE VOLCANO, AND THE BONIN ISLANDS ARE A PART of that great series of arcuate islands that can be traced across the Pacific from Alaska to New Zealand.[1] They lie south-southeastward from Japan, forming the central and southern portions of a chain extending from the Izu Peninsula through Guam. All are high pelagic islands. Measured against world total they are of microscopic importance in total area, population, and resources. Location, however, gives them a major place in the spatial relations of global geography. Aviation technology may some day outdate the need for stopping points along the Pacific air routes. But, at present, over an ocean of such vast distances and one in which the total island area is small as compared with total water surface, the islands, their location, and their geographic nature are of vital importance in commercial and military aviation.

During the Second World War the various islands in the Marianas and Volcanoes were captured or bypassed in the steppingstone offensive towards Japan. Some of the larger ones were developed as staging areas to be used in the final attack against the enemy. The precipitous end of the war, following the atomic bombing of Hiro-

---

* This study is drawn from materials collected by the author as a participant in the 1947–1948 CIMA Program (Coordinated Investigation of Micronesian Anthropology) under the auspices of the Pacific Science Board of the National Research Council, the U.S. Navy, and other contributing groups.

[1] The Marianas lie between 13° 14′ and 20° 33′ north latitude, and 144° 54′ and 146° 05′ east longitude; the Volcanoes, between 24° 14′ and 25° 26′ north latitude, and 141° 16′ and 141° 28′ east longitude; and the Bonins, between 26° 30′ and 27° 45′ north latitude, and 142° 05′ and 142° 13′ east longitude.

shima and Nagasaki, left the islands unused for their intended purpose, but they still remain of crucial strategic value to the United States.

HISTORY AND POLITICAL GEOGRAPHY

In the some four hundred years that these islands have been known to Western man, they have been administered wholly or in part by the Spanish, the Germans, the Americans, and the Japanese. The Bonin and the Volcano islands were drawn into the Japanese sphere by colonization in the nineteenth century. Spain established early control over the Marianas on a basis of discovery and occupation but lost them in 1898, when Guam was ceded to the United States and the remaining islands were sold to Germany. In 1914 Japan, as an Allied Power, captured the German Marianas. Retention was permitted by the League of Nations and a Class C Mandate granted; control was not relinquished in 1935, when Japan withdrew from the League. American capture in the Second World War brought the islands under the jurisdiction of the United States.

After American acquisition the islands were placed under Naval Military Government. This terminated in Guam in May, 1946, and in the remaining Marianas in July of the following year. Guam reverted to its status as an unorganized United States possession under the jurisdiction of the Navy, which it had before the Second World War. In 1949 administration of the island was shifted to the U.S. Department of the Interior, and the first civilian governor was appointed by President Truman. The remaining Marianas were organized as the Saipan District of the Trust Territory of the Pacific Islands under a United Nations trusteeship.[2] The local administration functions under powers delegated to a Civil Administrator by the Deputy High Commissioner at Guam and the High Commissioner in Hawaii. Government of the Trust Territory under the Navy was established as an interim measure in 1947. The Bonin and Volcano islands still remain under U.S. Naval Military Government and are administered from the headquarters of the Saipan District.

United States trusteeship differs in several aspects from the Class C mandate under which they were administered by Japan. The most important modification deals with defense. The whole of the Pacific Trust Territory is designated as a strategic area and is under the jurisdiction of the Security Council of the United Nations rather than the

[2] United States trusteeship was approved by the Security Council of the United Nations on April 2, 1947, and was accepted by the U.S. Government on July 18, 1947.

General Assembly. The islands may be fortified[3] and their man power and resources used to aid the territory in participating in maintenance of international order.[4] All members of the United Nations are to receive equal social, economic, and commercial treatment within the area but not to the detriment of the inhabitants or to world peace.[5]

AREA

Because of their linear arrangement, the land area of the Mariana, Volcano, and Bonin islands is small as compared with groups of scattered pattern such as the Carolines. All the islands in the three groups are diminutive in size (Table 1). Guam, the greatest in area, is also the largest between Hawaii and the Philippines.

TABLE 1

AREAS OF THE MARIANA, VOLCANO, AND BONIN ISLANDS°

Name of Island	Area, Square Miles	Group Total
A. Bonin Islands (Ogasawara-guntō)†		
Mukoshima-rettō (Parry Group)		
Kitano-shima	0.14	
Muko-shima	1.34	
Nakadachi-jima	0.72	
Yome-shima	0.39	
		2.59
Chichishima-rettō (Beechey Group)		
Ototo-jima	2.01	
Ani-shima	3.09	
Nishi-shima	0.19	
Chichi-shima (Peel Island)	9.50	
Higashi-jima	0.11	
Minami-jima	0.10	
		15.00
Hahajima-rettō (Baily Group)		
Haha-jima	8.17	
Mukō-shima	0.53	
Hira-shima	0.12	
Mei-jima	0.48	
Imoto-jima	0.56	
Ane-shima	0.32	
		10.18
		27.77

[3] Article 5, United Nations, Trusteeship Agreement for the Japanese Mandated Islands.
[4] Article 84, Charter of the United Nations.
[5] Article 76, Charter of the United Nations.

TABLE 1 (Continued)

Name of Island	Area, Square Miles	Group Total
B. Volcano Islands (Kazan-rettō)†		
Kita-iō-jima	2.07	
Iwo Jima (Iō-jima)	7.79	
Minami-iō-jima	1.45	
		11.31
C. Mariana Islands (Ladrones)‡		
Farallon de Pajaros	0.79	
Maug		
East Island	0.36	
West Island	0.26	
North Island	0.18	
Asuncion	2.82	
Agrihan	18.29	
Pagan	18.65	
Alamagan	4.35	
Guguan	1.61	
Sarigan	1.93	
Anatahan	12.48	
Farallon de Medinilla	0.35	
Saipan	46.58	
Tinian	39.29	
Aguijan	2.77	
Rota	32.90	
Guam	215.50	
		399.11

* The island groups and the islands within are arranged from north to south; numerous islets associated with the Bonins have been omitted.

† Original figures, in kilometers, are from the U.S. Navy, Office of Chief of Naval Operations, *Izu and Bonin Islands*, Civil Affairs Handbook, Washington, D.C., 1944.

‡ Figures from Edwin H. Bryan, Jr., "Geographic Data," Vol. II of *An Economic Survey of Micronesia*, United States Commercial Company, unpublished, 1946.

GEOLOGY

The Mariana, Volcano, and Bonin Islands (Fig. 55) are grouped along rising mountain ranges, or great curving anticlines, which on the convex side of their arcs towards the Pacific Basin are parallel to elongated deeps resulting from subsidence of the ocean floor. A generalized cross-section of an island group would show the surface rising from the ocean floor in a huge fold, along the top of which volcanics, coral growth, and uplift had resulted in the formation of islands.

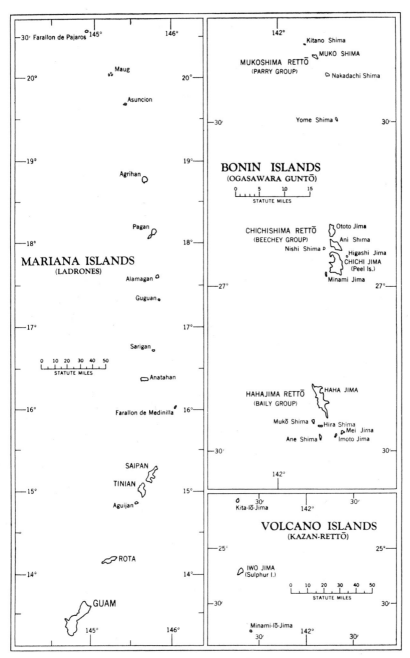

FIGURE 55. Map of Mariana, Bonin, and Volcano Islands.

During quiescent periods in the mountain-forming process, wave-cut terraces develop, which when later uplifted give the islands a stair-step appearance.   The terraces are most strongly developed along the eastern coasts, which are subjected to more intensive wave action owing to the direction of the prevailing winds.   Subsequent faulting may have somewhat modified the original island structure, resulting in surface tilt and secondary levels.   A second modification has occurred on those islands on which the volcanic base was capped with coral growth; later uplifted, the limestone surface eroded into karst features. The coasts are generally cliffed and are characterized by wave-cut benches, notches, and sea caves.

CLIMATE

This area is dominated throughout the year by tropical maritime air.   In the summer equatorial air masses invade the region, bringing increased temperatures and higher humidity.   In the winter polar continental air masses occasionally move out over the islands from Asia.   These are much modified by the time they reach the Bonins, and they arrive in the southern Marianas as weak cold fronts bringing greater precipitation and cloudiness.   In the Bonins, however, they result in a wider range of temperature.

Because of the area's attenuation, the climate can best be generalized by a consideration of the meteorological records of the northernmost and southernmost stations in the chain.[6]   Owing to the warm Kuroshio and the mitigating influence of the ocean waters, temperature variability over so extended an area is not so great as might be expected.   The average annual temperature at Sumay, Guam, is 80.9° F, and the annual range is 3.3° F; at Omura, Chichi-shima, the average annual temperature is 72.9° F and the annual range 18.2°F. Rainfall decreases from south to north, ranging from 89.4 inches at Sumay to 64.4 inches at Omura.   Prevailing winds throughout the entire area are easterly.   In Guam and Saipan wind direction is predominately northeast; in the Bonins east winds prevail, but only by a slight percentage over winds from other quadrants.

In general summary, the climate of the southern islands is tropical maritime, and that of the Bonins is subtropical.[7]   In the northern islands temperatures decrease, annual and diurnal ranges increase, and rainfall decreases but is more effective because of lower temperatures and more even distribution.

[6] Statistics are from the U.S. Weather Bureau, Washington, D.C.
[7] Sumay is classified as "Ami" according to the Köppen system, Omura as "Cfa."

SOIL

On a generic basis, three categories of soil may be distinguished: volcanic, coralline, and coralline-volcanic. On the geologically recent volcanic islands much of the lava surface is bare or covered with volcanic detritus. On gentle slopes and in the valleys fine clay soils of fair fertility have formed from a few inches to several feet in depth. The coralline soils, occurring on the raised terraces, are often shallow and with occasional outcrops of limestone. When fully developed, these soils are reddish brown, fine-textured, and claylike, and they usually contain pieces of undecomposed coral throughout the profile. The water-holding capacity of these soils is slight, and during the dry season vegetation growth is retarded. Volcanic-coralline soils occur in valleys and over other areas where alluvial action has resulted in a mixture of the other two soil types. These soils are heavy clay, fine-grained, but sometimes contain coral chunks. All these soils are lateritic, having evolved under high temperatures and heavy rainfall.

VEGETATION

The native vegetation is tropical and shows a generic relationship with the plant life of Malaysia. Only in the Bonins is there any indication of northern elements, and these are few in number. According to the early explorers the original cover was forest and grass. The entire area lies within the zone of coconut palms, but in the Bonins the tree is believed to have been introduced by man. Elevations are not of sufficient height to result in zoning, and, dependent upon soil conditions, strand plants may be found on the highest points. Several ecological associations occur, resulting largely from edaphic factors:

1. *Mangrove.* Found in Guam, and to a very limited and weak extent in Saipan.
2. *Beach.* A complex of vines and low shrubs, with breadfruit, coconut palms, Formosan koa (*Acacia confusa*), and Australian pine or Polynesian ironwood (*Casuarina equisetifolia*) along the beach ridge.
3. *Upper strand.* Vines, short, coarse, grass, and low shrubs; a treeless association occurring on thin, rocky soils at the top of seaside cliffs and within range of salt spray. Most highly developed along exposed eastern coasts.
4. *Secondary forest.* No part of the primary forest remains undisturbed. Cliff sides and deep ravines, covered with a tangle of vines, ferns, and trees, give some impression of the former native

jungle. Nearly all the timber trees have been removed, and the second growth is small. Japanese reforestation projects have covered some areas with fast-growing Australian pine and Formosan koa.

5. *Marsh.* Limited in extent and consisting of grasses, ferns, and sedges.

6. *Grassland.* In the southern Marianas this is frequently made up of wide stretches of sword grass with cutting scabrous edges. This grass is chiefly associated with volcanic soils, but its area has been extended as the result of native practices of burning.

Because of the isolation of the islands and their recent geological formation, the number of indigenous genera and species is small. Plants with adaptations for migration over so wide a water area as separates these islands from the mainland are few. Accidental or intentional introduction by man has resulted in modifying the greater part of the plant life in the islands; on Guam, for instance, 58 per cent of the vegetation has been introduced.

Repatriation of the Japanese has left much land unused and has resulted in vigorous competition among the plants for capture of the formerly cultivated areas. Sugar cane has strongly resisted invasion, and it still dominates the vegetation landscape on Tinian, on Saipan, and to a lesser extent on Rota. The other fields are invaded first by hardy and tolerant weeds, two or three species of which tend to become dominant before trees begin to encroach on the area.

FAUNA

As is characteristic of pelagic islands, indigenous fauna is limited. The only mammal native to the islands is the bat, two species of which are found in the Marianas, and one in the Bonins. One of these, the fruit bat, is used as food in the Marianas; it is caught in the forest and along the cliffs at night with long-handled nets. Geckos are found throughout the entire chain, and the iguana in the Marianas. The only land snake is a small, harmless burrowing variety about 5 inches in length and resembling an earthworm. Sea snakes are common and a constant hazard to wading fishermen. Insect and bird life is abundant. Introduced rats have become a major problem. Agriculturally, the two chief parasites are the coconut beetle, which has damaged the palms on Saipan, Tinian, and Rota, and the African snail, which attacks all types of plant growth.[8]

[8] Through cooperative efforts, the National Research Council and the Navy have introduced a wasp from Java that is a parasite of the coconut beetle. Work under the same agencies is being conducted to find an enemy of the snail.

NATIVE PEOPLES

Both the Bonins and the Volcanoes were uninhabited at the time of discovery. The Marianas were occupied by the Chamorros, a race of Mongoloid stock but of obscure origin. They were described by Pigafetta[9] as having "blacke beardes and blacke heare on theyr heades which they weare longe downe on theyr wastes. They are of the same stature that we are, and well made, of coloure lyke vnto an olyue. Theyr women are well fauored with blacke and thick heare on theyr heades reachynge to the grownde."[10]

Specifically when, by what route, and from what area the first inhabitants of the Marianas came is unknown. Study of their cultural traits as reported by early voyagers indicates that the ancestors of the Chamorros probably came from the Malayan area, that their movement was late in the Pacific migrations, and that they moved by way of western Micronesia and perhaps the Philippines. Some racial elements may have also been added by way of the island routes from Japan. At the time of discovery, the natives practiced a gardening, fishing, and collecting economy. Evidence of their material culture includes neolithic stone tools, bone implements, pottery, and the "latte," double rows of capped pillars, which are believed to have served as supports for houses and canoe sheds.[11]

The prehistoric landscape was largely a wooded one broken here and there by villages and garden lands. Settlement was mainly along the coast in villages of 50 to 150 huts; interior villages were smaller, seldom consisting of more than 20 buildings. The houses were raised on piles and constructed with thatched roofs of coconut leaves. Rice was grown in the stream valleys and marshes; bananas, sugar cane, breadfruit, taro, and coconuts on the higher land. Though rice was a preferred food, land suitable for its growth was limited. It apparently was grown only on Guam, Rota, and Saipan. Fire was probably used in clearing, and the fields were abandoned as the soil became depleted. Tillage was accomplished with digging sticks and a kind of stone-bladed hoe. In their limited and restricted island area, the Chamorros

[9] Antonio Pigafetta, who sailed with Magellan, kept a journal of the voyage, abstracts of which are still available. Magellan's personal journals have been lost.

[10] Edward Arber, editor, "A Briefe Declaration of the vyage or navigation made abowte the worlde. Gathered owt of a large Booke wrytten hereof by Master Antonie Pygaffetta Vincentine, Knyght of the Rhodes and one of the coompanye of that vyage in the which, Ferdinando Magalines a Portugale (whom sum caule Magellanus) was generall Capitayne of the nauie," *The First Three English Books on America*, (?1511)–1555, Being chiefly Translations, Compilations, etc., by Richard Eden, Archibald Constable and Company, Westminister, 1895, p. 254.

[11] Laura Thompson, "The Native Culture of the Mariana Islands," *Bernice P. Bishop Museum Bull.* 185, p. 12, Honolulu, 1945.

pressed every possible item of their environment into use within the limits of their culture level. Edible foods such as yams and arrow-root were collected from the jungle; birds and bats were captured for food; fish, crabs, and turtles formed part of their diet.

Today no pure-blooded Chamorros remain, and their culture has been profoundly altered. The native peoples are a mixture of many strains, chiefly Spanish and Filipino, but also German, Japanese, and American, with traces of other nationalities added during the whaling days. In the long period of Spanish rule, acculturation brought many changes in the native manner of living. Some original culture forms such as language have persisted, and certain personality traits remain. American ideas have been strong on Guam. In the other Marianas, German rule was brief and left little cultural imprint. The Japanese sought to reshape native attitudes and habits to fit into the socio-economic structure established on the islands with colonization and commercial development. The natives became a minority group surrounded by the Japanese and an imported culture, but the total amount of influence was small. Throughout the Mariana area, the pattern of life is still basically a combination of Spanish and native elements.

AREA PROBLEMS

The islands within this area have never been self-supporting within the period of modern history. The Marianas were important to the Spanish only because they lay across the line of traffic between Mexico and the Philippines. Lacking gold or other quick material wealth, they held no special attraction to Spanish interests. Germany held the islands too briefly for development of their economic program. The Japanese colonized and fully exploited the islands under their control, but commercial enterprise was heavily dependent upon subsidy. Full use of resources in Guam has lagged.

The Second World War destroyed all facilities, leveled the towns, and demolished the farmsteads. American administration was faced with the immediate problem of providing food, clothing, and shelter for the displaced native and Japanese civilians. Repatriation of the Japanese removed eight-ninths of the population from the islands north of Guam, giving the area a frontierlike aspect in that there are too few hands to utilize the area fully. Former industries are no longer economically feasible, and destruction of the economy has turned the people back to a subsistence level. Land titles are unclear as the result of military use of the land, loss of deeds, death of owners, and destruction of boundary markers. On some islands development of the major resources, the soil and the sea, must compete with wage-earning possibilities at American installations.

Transportation difficulties are a major problem in connection with the export of any commercial crop that may be developed. Though aviation has reduced the significance of distance within the Pacific area, exports must depend largely upon water transport, and the mileages are not to be underestimated. The Marianas are 1400 miles from the Philippines, 1350 from Japan, and 5000 from the United States.

THE MARIANAS

DISCOVERY

The Marianas were first made known to the Western world by Magellan, who discovered the islands March 6, 1521, after his hazardous voyage across the Pacific. The island chain was christened in honor of St. Lazarus, but before sailing away Magellan changed the name to "Las Islas de las Ladrones" (The Isles of the Thieves). After the ships had anchored, the natives had come crowding aboard, taking everything that could be carried away. Eventually this led to bloodshed, beginning the modern history of the Marianas with a violence that eventually almost terminated the native population.

THE MARIANA CHAIN

During the Second World War the Marianas provided an island road for American advance northward to Japan. The seventeen islands in the group, three of which make up the island cluster, Maug, extend over a distance of 440 miles, roughly the airline mileage between Boston and Washington, D.C. The islands are arranged along two lines, which, if extended, would parallel each other. Along the eastern line, and making up the northern portion of the chain, are nine small volcanic islands, among which Pagan, Asuncion, and Farallon de Pajaros are still active. The southern islands, located along the western line, are larger, coral-capped, terraced, and fringed in part with coral reefs. Youthful karst features characterize the geomorphologic landscape: sinkholes, caves, and disappearing streams. The vegetation patterns are mainly those imposed by man. Under the Japanese, clearing for commercial agriculture and the cutting of trees for timber have left little native cover. Only on the rocky cliffs and ledges of Rota is there still preserved some trace of the original forest, a dense growth of ferns, vines, shrubs, and trees. The five southern islands have a total area equal to about five-sixths that of the entire group, whereas Guam has an area greater than that of all the other islands combined.

CLIMATE

Climatically the year falls into two seasons with very little temperature variation but pronounced rainfall differences. The annual range, less than 5° F, reflects the nearness of the thermal equator. Diurnal range seldom varies more than 10° to 20° F. Approximately 60 per cent of the rain occurs during the months of July, August, September, and October when the zone of convergence between the trades lies over the islands. Guam receives an annual rainfall of about 90 inches, Saipan about 82 inches, Tinian, being less elevated, 72 inches. Total rainfall varies considerably from one year to another, sometimes becoming a critical factor in crop production. Annual precipitation extremes range from 60 to 130 inches.

Until American occupation, rain supplied the main source of drinking water, and each home was provided with a surface of underground cistern. On the larger islands most of the settlements are now supplied with water by pumping systems, but in the rural sections the islanders are still dependent upon catchment.

HISTORY AND ECONOMIC DEVELOPMENT

Spanish Period. Over a hundred years passed after Magellan's discovery before the Spanish occupied the area. In 1668 missionary activity was initiated and, after first meeting with every success, aroused an opposition that led to open revolt against the priests and the Spanish troops. Sporadic conflict continued until 1694, when, as a last measure, the inhabitants of all the islands were transported to either Guam or Saipan. Those on Saipan were removed to Guam in 1698. War, famine, and disease so reduced the Chamorros during the first three centuries of Spanish control that, of the original population, estimated between 40,000 and 90,000, only 3760 remained in 1710, the year of the first census. By 1764 the number was 1654. The islands were generally known by this time as the Marianas, having been renamed in honor of the Spanish Queen, Maria Anna, widow of Henry IV and patroness of the first missionaries.

Long before the beginning of missionary activity in the Marianas, Guam became a supply station for Spanish galleons plying between Acapulco, Mexico, and Manila in the Philippines. The ships, only one a year during the early colonial period, were dispatched from New Spain in February, and, taking advantage of the trades, made the reckoned 70-day journey to Guam without altering their sails, and arrived in the Philippines before the beginning of the westerly monsoon. Guam, the only stop along the route, supplied fresh water, and equally important in those days of scurvy-plagued ocean travel, fresh vegetables and fruits, which were obtained by barter with the natives. This early importance as a way station, beginning before Spanish occupancy, increased as trade expanded in the Pacific, and reached an apex during the whaling period.

The economy of the Marianas did not rise much above the subsistence level during the entire Spanish period. The small Spanish population consisted largely of administrators, soldiers, and churchmen. Native farms supplied food, the seas a limited catch. Probably the major economic advantage of Spanish rule was the introduction of domesticated animals and new vegetables and fruits. There was also acceptance by the natives of certain Latin cultural patterns.

After the Spanish American War Guam was acquired by the United States under the terms of the Treaty of Paris, December 10, 1898. The island was already in our possession, having been captured almost incidentally in the previous summer. Because of the slow communication, the Spanish governor had not learned that a state of war existed, and he was surprised to learn that the American cruiser in the harbor was not saluting the port. Hard pressed financially, Spain sold the remaining Marianas and the Carolines to Germany for $4,500,000 in 1899.

German Period. The Marianas proved an economic liability to the Germans, costing far more in government expenditure than value returned. Efforts were made to expand the area commercially by building up the copra industry and stimulating local food and livestock production. German population, mostly administrative and religious, never numbered more than seven. At the beginning of the First World War the German possessions were captured by the Japanese, and after 1920 they were held by them as a Class C mandate.

Japanese Period. The Japanese were the first to utilize the islands fully. All resources were surveyed and, if commercially feasible, were brought into production. Colonization, exploitation of resources, Japanization of the natives, and, later, militarization were major drives in the Japanese program. Easy accessibility, space for an expanding population, and the need for food imports at home were factors motivating Japanese development of the area.

Sugar production dominated the economic scene, setting the tempo of island life with its seasons of planting, harvesting, and manufacture. The industry was controlled by the South Seas Development Company

(Nanyo Kohatsu Kaisha), which leased government and private land and rented it to tenant farmers. Sugar manufacture was heavily subsidized by the Japanese government as part of its policy of colonial expansion. No income or business taxes were paid, grants were given for the clearing of land, initially no rental was charged for government land, and until 1936 shipping subsidies were granted. Production in 1937 was 58,582 metric tons. Annual tonnage made up 4 to 6 per cent of the Japanese Empire's sugar supply. Molasses and alcohol were important by-products of the industry. The subsidy program also included other enterprises: vegetable production, cassava, livestock, coffee, cotton, fishing, and numerous commercial activities.

Fishing was the second most important activity. Production in 1937 amounted to 3900 metric tons, approximately one-half of one per cent of the entire catch made within the Empire. Commercial fishing was a Japanese monopoly based chiefly upon tuna and bonito. Native fishing was subsistent and restricted to the shore and lagoon areas by Japanese regulation. Except on Saipan, where a fishing association has been organized, fishing still remains an adjunct of household economy, and every family possesses the needed equipment of nets, spears, hooks, lines, and traps.

Japanese colonization and commercial enterprise brought a complete change of landscape to the Mandated Marianas. The forest was cleared, and all the arable land plotted to fields. Mainly because of damage by the coconut beetle, but also because of expansion of sugar plantings, the coconut groves were cut. Japanese settlements were established; Japanese farmsteads dotted the countryside. Roads were extended, and narrow-gauge railroads constructed to transport cane. Factories were built, port facilities developed, regular shipping schedules maintained. The native population, 3398 according to the first Japanese census taken in 1920, became a minority group in an alien culture. By 1937 the total population of the Japanese Marianas was 46,708.[12] The standard of living was low; that of the Chamorros compared well with the average Japanese but was superior to that of the Carolinians.

Chamorro Farm Practices. Although the Chamorros in the Mandated Marianas lived within the Japanese economic system, they did not take an active part in its functioning. Their contribution to the total commercial agricultural production of the islands was small; less than twenty Chamorro families were engaged in raising sugar cane. Most of the Chamorros rented their land to the Japanese, retaining only a small portion to supply food needs, employing tradi-

[12] The ratio between native and Japanese population was 1:11.3.

tional farm methods. In Guam, agricultural techniques have been somewhat modified through the influence of agricultural programs, but old methods and customs are still commonplace.

Chamorro farm practices are hand methods adapted to small plots. The farmers live in villages and make trips to their "ranchos" three or four times a week. Occasionally they remain at their farm three or four days, but always return to the village to attend church on Sunday. Travel is by foot, by oxcart, and, in some areas, by farm association truck. The average farm size is 5 to 10 acres. The chief farm tools

FIGURE 56. Preparing the soil for planting is an arduous task with the crude plows used by the Chamorros on their small farms. Cattle are the common draft animals.

are the machete, employed for clearing, and the fosino, a long-handled thrust hoe, used in planting and weeding. Cows serve as the common draft animal, but on Guam the carabao is sometimes seen. The soil is turned with an iron-tipped plow. Corn, which is used as food, occupies over 50 per cent of the cultivated farm land; sweet potatoes, the second crop, about 10 per cent. Yearly rainfall distribution controls planting. Most of the fields are seeded in late September and early October, and the crop matures before the wet season fully declines; a second and smaller planting is made in May or early June and is harvested before the wet season reaches its peak.

The farm is regarded chiefly as a unit for home production. There is always something to harvest and to carry home for the weekly food supply. The farmhouse, usually a less well-constructed building than the village home, is built on the same plan as urban dwellings, raised on piles and with a detached or semi-detached cook house. No barns are needed as the cows are tethered, but pigs are generally penned, and sometimes the chickens sheltered at night. Surrounding the farmhouse, ofttimes with plantings almost up to the door, is a complex and highly varied storied garden culture made up of fruits and interplanted vegetables. A few bananas, papayas, coconuts, mangoes, breadfruit, citrus, and avocados are usually found in the door yard and planted unsystematically throughout the farm area. Between the trees or, if the shade is too dense, in open gardens is a large variety of plants that add to the daily diet: pineapples, melons, corn, taro, beans, peppers, eggplant, and other vegetables. Farther away from the house there may be solid fields of corn and sweet potatoes, or banana and coconut groves, but, except for sweet potatoes, these too may be interplanted. About one-third of the farm is allowed to lie fallow, and the area is utilized for pasture. Fertilization is not a Chamorro farm practice, and, although familiar with its advantages, the cost is prohibitive to most farmers.

Some commercial farming has been stimulated among the natives in Guam by the Americans, and since the Second World War in the other islands. The Japanese also were active in increasing native agricultural produce that found a ready local market. Marketing now constitutes a major problem. There is some interisland sale; Guam, with its larger population, is the main buying center.

GUAM

Guam, somewhat peanutlike in shape, is 28 miles long and varies in width from 4 to 8 miles. It was captured by the Japanese on December 9, 1941. The island was unfortified, lightly garrisoned, and entirely surrounded by Japanese possessions. Plans for defense had been vetoed because the island's limited mass would have required elaborate installations far out of proportion to the United States intended use of the area.

Physiographically the island of Guam (Fig. 57) is divided into two sections, a northern plateau and a higher southern mountain area. The northern plateau is coral-capped and 200 to 600 feet in elevation, with three low volcanic hills, all of which are under 900 feet in altitude. The plateau surface slopes southwestward toward the lowland

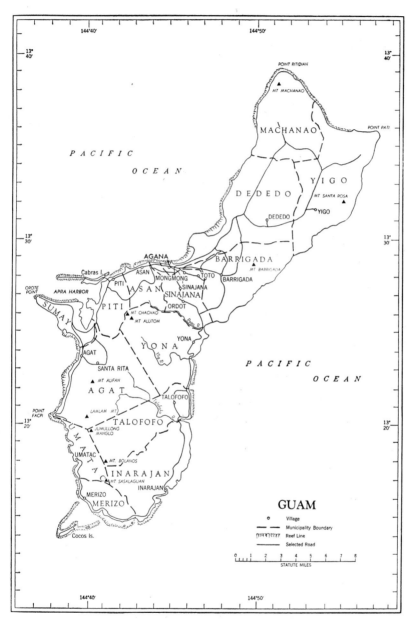

Figure 57. Map of Guam.

area drained by the Agana River, and, because of the porous lime-stone bedrock, this section is crossed by no permanent streams since the few brooks soon disappear in the coralline soil. Soils over the plateau are of relative fertility, but thin and with numerous madre-poric outcrops. Forest and scrub cover the area, broken only by a few farm clearings and the cuttings made for roads. The seaward edges of the plateau drop directly to the water on the northeast, and to narrow discontinuous plains separated by rocky headlands on the north and west. On the south an area of low hills marks the descent to the Agana River valley.

An area of volcanic hills lying across the central portion of the island sharply separates the southern region from the northern plateau, and continues southward as a line of peaks along the western coast. The highest, Lamlam Mountain, rises to 1334 feet. On the western side the range descends to a narrow broken coastal plain; on the east it drops through a 500- to 300-foot plateau, and falls to the sea in cliffs and steep slopes. Five east-flowing streams cross the plateau, and with their tributaries have cut the area into valleys and uplands. Erosion has been extreme, and the limestone that once covered the slopes of the peaks has worn away. Vegetation cover over the vol-canic area is chiefly sword grass and unsuitable for forage. Forest occurs between Mt. Alifan and Mt. Lamlam, and extends eastward across the island connecting with a belt along the east coast. Numer-ous small bays indent the southern portion of the island, and the ad-jacent river valleys and plains are sites of small agricultural villages.

On the west side of the island Apra Harbor, enclosed between Orote Peninsula and Cabras Island, has been greatly improved since the war, and serves as a naval base. Piti, the port of entry, is located at the north end of the harbor area. About five miles northeastward along the coast is Agana, the capital, situated on a low sandy plain at the mouth of the Agana River. Before the Second World War Agana was a compact, crowded town of 10,000, restricted from further expansion by cliffs that rise a short distance inshore. Bombing, shelling, and fighting through the town left scarcely a building stand-ing. Rebuilding is progressing, and the population in 1946 was about 800. Sumay, prewar population of 1200, was the second largest settlement and the site of the Pan-American Air Base. In 1950 Sumay had a population of 6131. According to the census of 1950, the largest municipality was Barrigada with 11,532 inhabitants.

Three major demographic changes have occurred since American occupation in 1898: a growth of Guamanian population, an increase in the number of non-residents, and a change in the distribution of native population.* According to the first census taken by the Naval Administration in 1901, the Guamanians numbered 9676; in 1947 there were 24,139, an increase of 149 per cent in 46 years. Racial composition over the same period remained approximately the same, 97.4 per cent Chamorro in 1901, 97.9 in 1947. The relationship between Guamanian and non-resident population has changed enormously since the Second World War. In 1941 the non-residents numbered about 600; in 1947 there were 36,388, mainly Army, Navy, and Marine forces, their dependents, Civil Service personnel, and contractors' employees. In both the Spanish and the pre-1941 American era, native population was concentrated in Agana and the Apra Harbor area. As part of the process of pacification, the Spanish required the Chamorros to abandon their small villages and to resettle in seven designated towns. Eventually Agana and Apra Harbor attracted the greater part of the island's inhabitants. This concentration continued under the Americans, although many farmers moved to the rural areas. The Second World War leveled all the settlements in the densely populated zone, and, of necessity, much of the land was taken over for military installations. The resultant demographic redistribution brought an increase in all the municipalities outside of Agana except Piti. The postwar pattern of settlement shows the heaviest densities in the municipalities adjacent to the former zone of concentration.

Occupationally, the population structure of Guam resembles that of a governmental capital. Most of the people are supported either directly or indirectly by wages paid by the United States government. In 1946, 25 per cent of the population over 16 years of age was employed at government installations.[13]

Nearly every family possesses a "rancho" or plot of ground that is cultivated to supplement wage income. Corn, vegetables, fruit, chickens, and eggs add to the household economy, and occasionally supply a surplus for sale in local markets. In 1946, 1300 acres were under cultivation. Corn, introduced from Mexico, is the main cereal under cultivation, occupying over half the cultivated area. Rice was formerly grown on the alluvial soils in the river valleys and marsh areas, but production has not been revived since 1945. Copra provided the main prewar export; in 1938, 2500 tons were shipped. In the same year coconut groves occupied 12,700 acres.

At the time the Americans acquired Guam, every family was pri-

---

* According to the preliminary figures for the 1950 census the population of Guam was 58,754.

[13] U.S. Navy, *Information on Guam Transmitted by the United States to the Secretary-General of the United Nations,* 1947, p. 29.

marily self-sufficient. With increase in population, young people looked for opportunities other than farming, and the trend away from agriculture was accelerated after the Second World War. The inflow of non-Guamanian population required services that ended the unemployment problem and attracted laborers from other islands. Guam became less self-sufficient; in 1940, 2812 persons were listed as farmers according to the United States census; in 1946, only 435 persons were so listed.[14]

Marketing constitutes a major problem. Products must compete in price with imported foods, which in some instances can be bought at prices below the cost of Guamanian production. Cost of local transportation adds further difficulties.

Livestock production and fishing are small-scale. Most of the stock is for draft purposes, or home food supply. Commercial fishing is of little importance; the industry engaged only 71 persons in 1946, and the catch for the 7 months following reestablishment of Island Government (1946) was 284,536 pounds.[15]

ROTA

Rota is the only island in the Marianas other than Guam that has had a history of continuous Chamorro occupancy. When the inhabitants were removed by the Spanish in 1694, a few families escaped capture by hiding in caves. Their escape is reflected in the local language, which has a high pitch and contains words unfamiliar to other Chamorro groups. Also a larger number of original place names have been preserved than elsewhere in the Marianas.

Rota is 10 miles long and 3 miles wide (Fig. 58). It consists of coralliferous limestone on a volcanic base. On the southeast, an extensive area of the andesitic base rock is exposed and has been eroded into ridges and ravines. The maximum elevation is 1625 feet. The upland is covered with sword grass, and the valleys are marked by dense tree growth. From early Chamorro settlement through the Japanese era, the permanent streams in this section have been utilized to irrigate rice paddies; but production has not revived since the war.

The Japanese did not begin to develop Rota until about 1930. One-third of the island's acreage was devoted to sugar cane. Owing to edaphic factors, yield per acre was below that of Saipan and Tinian. Papayas for the preparation of papain held second place in agriculture. Sheltered areas were planted to cacao, but production was small be-

[14] *Ibid.*, p. 24.
[15] *Ibid.*, p. 25.

cause of insects and plant diseases. Both guano phosphate and manganese were mined. Phosphate was obtained on the southern plateau and transported by aerial tramway to a drying plant at Terusan on the southern coast. Five-sixths of the estimated deposit has been removed. The manganese ores were of low quality, and mined as a war measure to meet deficiencies within the Japanese Empire.

The island was by-passed during the war, but all facilities were completely destroyed by repeated bombings. The former population of 7621 was concentrated chiefly in the sugar-mill town of Songsong (Rota Village), on the isthmus, and the native village of Tatacho on the west coast.

Repatriation of the Japanese in 1946 left about 800 Chamorros whose numbers have since been reduced to 672 because of lack of economic opportunity. Some 400 acres were under cultivation in 1947, as compared with 8000 under the Japanese. Former fields are rapidly becoming covered with scrub. Shipping is irregular, and marketing of the small agricultural surplus difficult. The inhabitants have rebuilt their homes on the isthmus among the ruins of Songsong, the main site of pre-Spanish Chamorro settlement.

TINIAN

Tinian (Fig. 58) is unique among the southern Marianas in that, after removal of the inhabitants by the Spanish, the island never again became important in the Chamorro sphere of occupancy. The savanna-like nature of the vegetation cover provided good range, and the Spanish set the area aside as a game preserve. Frequent expeditions were sent from Guam to hunt wild cattle and to jerk the beef for the Spanish garrison in Agana. Small shipments were also made to Manila. Native population, largely transitory, was small. In 1939, after Japanese colonization, only 25 of the 14,900 inhabitants were natives. None of them owned land.

Under the Japanese Tinian became a gigantic sugar plantation. The island, 10½ miles long and 5 miles wide, is composed of two plateaus separated from each other by a valley that has a NE-SW axis. All elevations are under 600 feet, and 80 per cent of the area is arable. In 1938 four-fifths of the cultivated land was in cane; the remainder was largely in vegetable crops. The cane was processed at two mills in Tinian Town, located on the southwest coast. Sugar production outranked that of Saipan and Rota.

The pattern of Japanese occupancy was best developed on Tinian since there were no interrupting native land holdings. The island was divided into rectangular plots that were leased to tenant farmers. Rural settlement was dispersed, but with a tendency towards grouping of two or three houses at crossroads.   The farm homes, constructed of wood and thatch, were destroyed, but the ruins of cement barns and cisterns remain.   Each barn, and its associated pig pens, was constructed to form a fertilizer unit.   All waste drained into a compost pit to which was added bagasse from the sugar mill.   Night soil was also used for fertilizer.   The main road pattern was irregular, following the contours from one bench level to another, but the secondary system formed a regular network conditioned by the field arrangement. Windbreaks bordered the roads and separated the fields of cane.

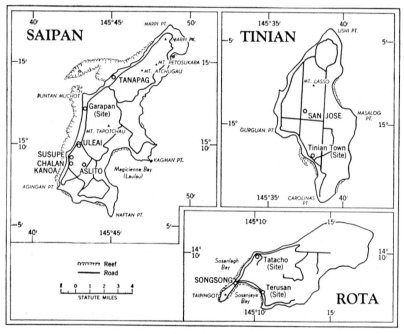

FIGURE 58.   Maps of Saipan, Tinian, and Rota.

Tinian Town, population 4695, and five small villages provided urban services.

Tinian was left without native population after the removal of the Japanese.   The island has now been opened for homesteading to any native inhabitant of the Trust Territory.   In April, 1948, a group of Chamorros from Yap, descendants of migrants who left the Marianas in the Spanish and German eras, established a settlement in the north central part of the island. Their village, San Jose, has a population of 292.

SAIPAN

Saipan (Fig. 58) was unoccupied for over a century after the removal of the Chamorros by the Spanish. In 1810 a few Americans and several Hawaiians started a plantation to supply whaling vessels, but the project was without official sanction and was broken up by Spanish troops. About 1815 a small group of Carolinians, driven from their homes by a typhoon, settled on the island. Persuaded by the Spanish, others followed to collect coconuts and dry the meat for copra. A few Chamorros came in from Guam late in the Spanish period, and the German census in 1902 recorded 1631 native inhabitants.[16]

The island was the first in the Mariana chain to be colonized and exploited by the Japanese. As under the Germans, it continued to serve as an administrative and commercial center. Population in 1939 was 23,682, composed mainly of Okinawan tenant farmers induced to migrate by the South Seas Development Company. Cane occupied 68 per cent of the cultivated land, tapioca 15 per cent, and vegetables, sweet potatoes, papayas, cotton, bananas, and coffee the remaining percentage in the order named. Sugar was milled at Chalan Kanoa, a town of 3300 population, on the southwestern coast. Garapan, 4 miles northward, was the main port and largest town in the Mandated Marianas. Its population of 12,000 was engaged in administration, commerce, fishing, and the processing of fruits, vegetables, and marine products. Five smaller villages served the island as local collection and distribution points and minor government centers. All these settlements were destroyed during the American invasion.

Saipan is 12½ miles long by 5 miles wide. It divides itself into four surface regions: a rugged northern upland occupying about two-thirds of the island area, the southern plateau, a coastal lowland on the southwest, and Kagman Peninsula.

Native population in September of 1948 was 4962, composed of 3890 Chamorros and 1072 Carolinians. The former sugar-mill town of Chalan Kanoa, destroyed during the war, has been rebuilt and expanded and has become the main settlement on the island. Four smaller villages have been developed.

[16] William Safford, *The Useful Plants of Guam*, Contributions from the United States National Herbarium, Vol. IX, Smithsonian Institution, Washington, D.C., 1905, p. 138.

Farming, working at American government installations, fishing, and small commercial and handicraft enterprises are the chief occupations. During the 12 months following July, 1947, 343,314 pounds of farm produce and 174,466 pounds of fish were sold.

MINOR MARIANAS

The minor Marianas, lying to the north of Saipan, are rocky islands rising abruptly from the sea. Because of small areal extent, thin soils, and deficiency of level land, the islands offer few opportunities for occupancy. The area was first explored by Spanish missionaries, who reported making conversions but left no records of total population.

The economic development of the minor Marianas is largely a history of copra production. Beginning about 1870, Carolinian laborers were sent to the islands to harvest coconuts, and a few remained as settlers. Further settlement occurred as a part of the German copra program. The first German census (1902) listed a total of 185 persons on Pagan, Agrihan, Alamagan, and Sarigan.[17] The other islands had no permanent inhabitants, but were leased for mining guano and catching sea birds.

Japan's interest in the minor Marianas was both commercial and strategic. Copra was developed to its fullest extent, but required only a transitory population. Permanent inhabitants were few; in 1939 only 382 persons were reported on the smaller northern islands.

Alamagan and Agrihan were resettled by Carolinian groups in 1948. Alamagan, a 2441-foot inactive volcanic cone, forms an almost circular island, 4½ miles in area. There are two small villages with a combined population of 139. Agrihan, double-peaked, 6 miles long and 3 miles wide, has an elevation of 3166 feet, the highest in the Marianas. The more gentle lower slopes and a few higher plateaus offer level land for farming, but most of the island is steep and cut by deep ravines. The two newly founded villages have a population of 116. Small areas on both islands have been brought under subsistence cultivation, but settlement is chiefly based on copra drying. The coconuts of the northern islands have not been infested by the coconut beetle and, besides serving as an economic resource for the new communities, have supplied plantings for Saipan, Tinian, and Rota.

Maug consists of three islands, remnants of a partially submerged caldera. The enclosed harbor area is 1½ miles in diameter.

Pagan, the largest of the northern Marianas, consists of two rugged volcanic areas connected by a narrow isthmus. The northern portion of the island, Mt. Pagan, is an active volcano, 1670 feet in elevation,

[17] William Safford, *op. cit.*

its head usually shrouded in smoke and clouds. The southern portion consists of several smaller cones, two of which are active. The last eruption on the island occurred in 1922. Communication is difficult between the two sections of the island because of intervening cliffs. The only level land is a small plateau north of the isthmus; it was used by the Japanese for an airfield. Population in 1939 was 220, mostly Carolinian. An agricultural experiment station was maintained by the South Seas Development company for research in cotton and sugar cane.

VOLCANO ISLANDS

(Kazan-rettō, Sulphur Islands)

Spain claimed jurisdiction over the Volcano Islands on the basis of discovery by Bernard Torres in 1543. The claims, however, were never pressed, and the islands remained unoccupied. They were not explored until an official Japanese party visited the islands in 1887. Annexation followed four years later, after settlement by a small colony of farmers from the Izu-shichito.

Commercial development was slow. Cotton production, upon which colonization was based, did not prove successful, and a shift was made to sugar about 1910. Production reached a peak during the sugar shortages of the First World War. The agricultural decline that followed was somewhat relieved by a small production of coco, coffee, indigo, and medicinal plants. Fishing was never developed on a commercial scale.

The Volcano Islands were of more strategic than economic importance to the Japanese. The three small islands are located in an 86-mile chain. Total land area is small, less than 12 square miles. The civilian population was removed during the Second World War and the islands left in control of Japanese troops. In 1950 they were still unpopulated. Minami-iō-jima, the southernmost, is square, about a mile in width, and has an elevation of 3181 feet; it has never been occupied. Kita-iō-jima, at the northern end of the chain, is a ridge of peaks with deeply cut ravines along the lateral slopes; elevations range up to 2630 feet. The former population, 103 in 1939, was composed mainly of tenant farmers engaged in sugar production. One hundred and eighty-four acres, 12 per cent of the island's area, were under cultivation. The cane was shipped to Iwo Jima for processing.

Pear-shaped Iwo Jima (Fig. 59), 5 miles long and 2½ miles wide, became ours during the war by one of the bloodiest battles the Marine Corps ever experienced. Less rugged than the other islands, it was the site of two Japanese airfields from which planes intercepted our B-29 flights to Japan, and made raids on Saipan and Tinian. Prewar population numbered about 1000, Farming was the main form of land use; every possible bit of arable land had been brought under cultivation. Seven hundred and forty-four acres were planted

FIGURE 59. Iwo Jima. Mt. Suribachi in the foreground. U.S. Navy Photograph.

to sugar cane, coco, coffee, and vegetables. Some sulphur had been mined early after Japanese acquisition, but workings had been abandoned.

The terrain of Iwo Jima was ideal for defense, and the island was made into one of the strongest forts ever constructed. The northern portion of the island is a ravine-cut dome. This descends southward through a rough plateau, and is connected by an isthmus to Mt. Suribachi, a steep-sided, 554-foot crater on the southwest. The 22,000

Japanese held the island under orders to fight until dug out and killed. American landing was made February 19, 1945, on a beach of black volcanic sand on the southeastern coast. Fighting continued over the 8 square miles of area until D-35 day. By April Iwo Jima was a busy United States forward fighter base and a rescue station for damaged B-29's returning from Japan.

THE BONIN ISLANDS

(Ogasawara-guntō)

Discovery of the Bonin Islands is attributed to the Spanish explorer Villalobos in 1543. Spain, however, never pushed her claims, although the islands lay along the route of the galleons between the Philippines and Mexico. The Japanese colonized the islands in the nineteenth century, claiming ownership on the traditional discovery by Daimyo Ogasawara Sadayori in 1593. He is credited with holding the islands as a fief from the Emperor of Japan, and of founding a colony that continued until 1624. Apparently the islands were then forgotten, as they were noted as a new discovery when visited by a Japanese ship blown off its course in 1675. The name "Bonins" is believed to be derived from "Bunin-shima," applied by the storm-driven sailors to denote the island's lack of population.

The islands first acquired importance during the Pacific whaling period. Claims of sovereignty were made for several countries by visiting ship captains, but none of these was followed through, until the British consul in Honolulu sent out a party of colonists in 1830.[18] Settlement was made at Port Lloyd (Omura) on Peel Island (Chichishima). The group included two Americans, one of whom, Nathaniel Savory, became the recognized leader, and was elected governor after the death of the appointed British representative. Perry visited the islands in 1853, made proposals for the establishment of a coaling station, and delegated one of his officers to proclaim formally the sovereignty of the United States over Haha-jima (Fig. 60). Both these actions drew protests from the British government. However, neither government protested in 1861 when the Japanese established a hundred colonists across the bay from Port Lloyd.[19] This venture failed within 15 months for lack of suitable land for rice cultiva-

[18] The party consisted of two Americans, an Englishman, a Dane, a Genoese, and twenty or more Hawaiian men and women.

[19] The United States at the time was involved in the Civil War, and the British in the crisis of Anglo-American relations that culminated in the Trent Affair.

tion. In 1875 Japan, after an official visit by government representatives, announced ownership of the islands, and both the United States and Great Britain acceded the claim. Further settlement was restricted to Japanese immigrants, and the early colonists were soon outnumbered. Because of their checkered history of discovery and

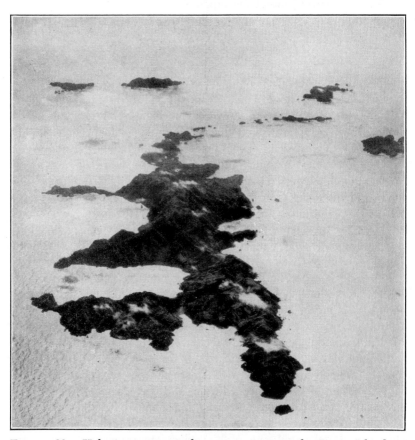

FIGURE 60. Hahajima-rettō, southernmost group in the Bonin Islands, is steep and rocky and offers few opportunities for agriculture. Japanese population was 1905; today the group is uninhabited. U.S. Air Force Photograph.

settlement, all the islands have English and American as well as Japanese names.

The chain, extending over a distance of 85 miles, is made up of three island clusters, Mukoshima-rettō (Parry Group) Chichishima-rettō (Beechey Group), and Hahajima-rettō (Bailey Group), each occupying the central portion of a submarine ridge. All the Bonin Islands are irregular in shape, with cliffed shores, abrupt slopes, and few areas of level land. Beaches occur only at the head of coves. Altogether there are ninety-seven islands and islets in the chain, but their total area is less than 30 square miles. Early descriptions of the Bonin Islands report luxuriant tropical vegetation from water's edge to the highest peaks. Most of the timber trees have been cut, and the remaining woodland, about 50 per cent of the island area, is scrubby and thicket-like owing to thin soils and strong winds. Predominant trees are palms and pandanus, which grow up to an elevation of 650 feet. Tall grass covers the ridges and steep slopes, and the tree growth reaches its most vigorous development in the sheltered and more fertile valleys. Most of the streams are intermittent. The underlying rocks are andesitic lavas, tuffs, and agglomerates capped with coral limestone.

The early settlers traded with the whalers, exchanging vegetables and fruits for whatever manufactured goods the ships might have to offer. Although money was sometimes accepted, it had no local use. Under the Japanese, sugar, truck, and fruit production were developed on a commercial basis, but these industries were declining because of competition with more favored areas. Only 11 per cent of the area is arable. Farms were small, averaging about 6½ acres, and they were often broken into scattered irregular plots adjusted to the contours. There was some dispersed settlement along the coastal roads, in the valleys, and at clearings in the forest, but most of the farmers lived in the villages. Approximately 60 per cent of the farmers were tenants brought in by development companies. Fishing was the major industry, supplying an export as well as an important item in the local diet. In 1936 shipment of marine products to Japan amounted to 206 metric tons. Salted whale, dried, salted, and canned tuna and bonita made up the greater part of the export that also included dried seaweed and canned turtle and oysters.

MUKOSHIMA-RETTŌ (PARRY GROUP)

The northernmost group in the chain consists of four islands and a number of islets extending over an area 21 miles long and 7 miles wide. Muko-shima, the largest, is the least rugged of all the Bonin Islands. It consists of a southern plateau and a hilly northern section; all elevations are under 300 feet. Most of the island is covered with tree growth; the soil is thin and of little value for agriculture, and the population in 1939 only 46.

CHICHISHIMA-RETTŌ (BEECHEY GROUP)

Situated 21 miles southward from Muko-shima is Chichishima-rettō, composed of six islands and numerous small islets occupying an area 12 miles long and 6 miles wide.

Chichi-shima, the largest island (5 by 2½ miles), encloses, on the northwest, Futami-ko, the most spacious harbor in the entire chain, protected by the sheltering walls of an extinct volcano. The island's rugged surface rises to numerous peaks and ridges to a maximum elevation of 1069 feet. This is the only occupied island in the Bonin Group. After the Second World War the Japanese were removed from all islands in the chain. Chichi-shima's prewar population was 4300; in 1950 it supported some 130 persons, descendants of the original colonists. Japanese blood has been added to their racial mixture, and their European and American names are in contrast to their somewhat Oriental appearance. Their economy, based upon agriculture and fishing, is on a subsistence level.

HAHAJIMA-RETTŌ (BAILY GROUP)

Hahajima-rettō (Fig. 60), located about 30 miles south of Chichishima, is compassed within an area of 55 miles. The cluster is composed of Haha-jima, 9 miles long and 5 miles wide, and five smaller islands. These are the highest islands within the Bonin chain. A mountain axis extends the length of Haha-jima, rising to elevations of 1000 feet in the north, reaching a 1500-foot peak in the central part, and descending to 500 feet in the south. About half the island is covered with forest.

The Japanese population of Haha-jima was 1905, divided between two villages, Okimura (1478) on the southwest coast and Kitamura on the north. Both were located at the head of coves and were hemmed in by hills and mountains. About 1200 acres, approximately 23 per cent of the island's area, was under cultivation, largely in sugar cane. Many of the slopes used, however, were too steep for good agricultural practice. Windbreaks were needed to protect the growing crops.

REFERENCES

Cholmondeley, Lionel B., *The History of the Bonin Islands from the Year 1827 to the Year 1876 and of Nathaniel Savory, One of the Original Settlers,* Constable and Co., London, 1915.

Morehouse, Captain Clifford P., *The Iwo Jima Operation,* United States Marine Corps, Historical Division, Quantico, Va., 1946.

Robertson, Russell, "The Bonin Islands," *Trans. Asiatic Soc. Japan,* Vol. IV, pp. 111–140, 1876.

Safford, William E., *The Useful Plants of Guam,* Contributions from the United States National Herbarium, Vol. IX, Smithsonian Institution, Washington, D.C., 1905.

Thompson, Laura, *Guam and Its People,* Princeton University Press, Princeton, 1947.

———— *Native Culture of the Mariana Islands,* Bernice P. Bishop Museum *Bull.* 185, Honolulu, 1945.

United States, Department of the Navy, *Information on Guam Transmitted by the United States to the Secretary-General of the United Nations,* Washington, D.C., 1947.

———— Office of Chief of Naval Operations, *Izu and Bonin Islands,* Civil Affairs Handbook, OPNAV 50 E 9, Washington, D.C., 1944.

———— Office of Chief of Naval Operations, *Mandated Mariana Islands,* Civil Affairs Handbook, OPNAV P 22–8, Washington, D.C., 1944.

Wilson, E. H., "The Bonin Islands and Their Ligneous Vegetation," *Jour. Arnold Arboretum,* Vol. I, pp. 97–115, October, 1915.

Yoshiwara, S., "Geological Age of the Ogasawara Group," *Geol. Mag.* (London), Vol. IX, New Series, pp. 296–303, July, 1902.

9

The Caroline Islands

CURTIS A. MANCHESTER, JR.

THE CAROLINE ISLANDS ARE SCATTERED OVER A WIDE AREA OF SEA, extending roughly from 3° to 10° north latitude and from 131° to 163° east longitude (Fig. 61). This is a great sea area covering almost 1,300,000 square miles. However, the islands, which Bryan has estimated to number approximately 936, contribute very little dry land. The total land area in all these islands is estimated to be only 461 square miles. With only 33,000 people on the many islets scattered over this vast area, the establishment of communications to connect the many isolated islands becomes one of the major problems of the area.

The Caroline Islands have been called the New Philippines and the Carolinas in the past. For the smaller groups and individual islands the list of alternate names is almost endless. Various explorers in the past felt free to name islands that they had discovered or rediscovered. The general tendency today is to use the native names for the islands.

Politically the islands have been divided into the eastern and western Carolines along meridian 148 west. The eastern Carolines are subdivided into the Truk District and the Ponape District for administrative purposes. Formerly the western Carolines were divided into the Palau District and the Yap District, but the two districts have been consolidated into the Palau District for administration, although the former districts are sometimes referred to as areas. Each of these administrative centers for which the districts are named is a high island and the largest of the district.

THE GEOLOGIC SETTING

The division between the eastern Carolines and the western Carolines represents a major geological division. The major islands and

236

TABLE 1
CAROLINE ISLANDS*

Island	Lagoon, Statute Square Miles	Land, Statute Square Miles
Kusaie	. . . .	42.316
Pingelap	0.465	0.676
Mokil	2.608	0.478
Ponape Islands	68.885	129.040
Ant Atoll	28.70	0.718
Pakin	5.523	0.421
Ngatik	30.342	0.674
Oroluk	162.348	0.192
Nukuoro	10.52	0.644
Kapingamarangi	22.01	0.521
Nomoi Group:		
Etal	6.252	0.731
Lukunor	21.246	1.090
Satawan	147.524	1.757
Namoluk	2.972	0.322
Losap	10.577	0.396
Nama	. . . .	0.289
Hall Group:		
Murilo	135.082	0.497
Nomwin	112.573	0.716
East Fayu	. . . .	0.144
Truk (all islands):	822.916	38.56
Tol		13.188
Moen		7.297
Fefan		5.105
Dublon		3.375
Udot		1.902
Uman		1.816
Kuop	34.89	0.19
Namonuito	723.9	1.710
Pulap	12.093	0.383
Puluwat	0.600	1.313
Pulusuk	. . . .	1.083
Pikelot	. . . .	0.036
Satawal	. . . .	0.505
West Fayu	2.178	0.024
Lamotrek	12.166	0.379
Elato	2.888	0.203
Olimarao	2.419	0.085
Gaferut	. . . .	0.043
Faraulep	0.902	0.163
Ifalik	0.939	0.569
Woleai	11.354	1.749
Eauripik	2.286	0.091
Sorol	2.74	0.361

TABLE 1 (Continued)

Island	Lagoon, Statute Square Miles	Land, Statute Square Miles
Fais	. . . .	1.083
Ulithi	183.135	1.799
Yap (all islands):	10.00	38.670
Yap		21.680
Tomil-Gagil		11.129
Map		4.109
Rumung		1.659
Ngulu	147.707	0.165
Palau (all islands):	477.8	188.269
Babelthuap		153.299
Urukthapel		7.373
Peleliu (and adjacent islets)		4.877 (?)
Koror		3.618
Eil Malk		3.438
Angaur		3.250
Sonsorol	. . . .	0.735
Pulo Anna	. . . .	0.313
Merir	. . . .	0.349
Tobi	. . . .	0.228
Helen Reef	39.078	0.761

Total   3283.127 square miles   461.441 square miles

* Edwin H. Bryan, Jr., *Maps of the Islands of Micronesia under Administration of U.S. Naval Military Government Pacific Ocean Areas,* United States Commercial Company Economic Survey, Pearl Harbor, 1946. These figures were compiled by Colonel Bryan, from a series of 1:100,000 charts of the islands, using a planimeter and cross-section paper.

island groups of the western Carolines are the tops of submerged mountain ranges that rise above the surface of the sea. The Palau group, Yap, Fais, and Sorol, at least, are elevated portions of great ridges that are wrinkles in the continental shelf and are similar in origin to the areas nearer Asia, such as Japan and the Ryukyus. All these islands are west of the sial or andesite line, which marks the edge of the continental shelf. They are recent elevation, and the process of elevation is still going on, as is proved by recently elevated marine terraces and by earthquakes. The islands of the eastern Carolines stand on a great submarine shelf that is fairly stable, although there may be some subsidence in the western portion. Truk shows signs of subsidence whereas Ponape and Kusaie do not.

There are three main types of islands: the high volcanic islands, the low coral atolls, and raised atolls. Each of these types presents its own peculiar setting as a home for man. There are five volcanic islands or island groups: the Palaus, Yap, Truk, Ponape, and Kusaie.

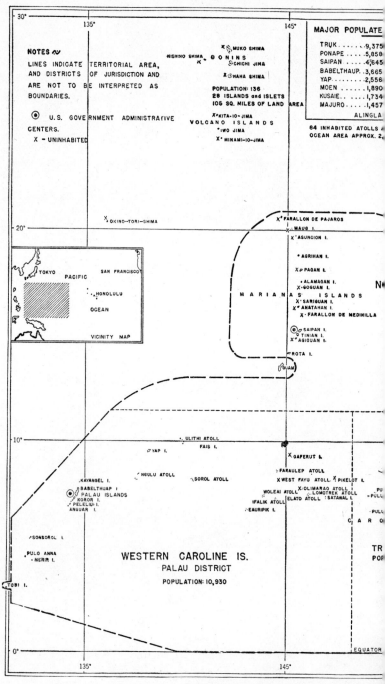

X ⬡ MUKO SHIMA

NISHINO SHIMA ⊙ O N I N S
X ⬡ CHICHI JIMA

X ⊙ HAHA SHIMA

POPULATION: 136
28 ISLANDS and ISLETS
105 SQ. MILES OF LAND AREA

X ⬡ KITA-IO- JIMA
VOLCANO ISLANDS
⊙ IWO JIMA
X ⬡ MINAMI-IO-JIMA

MAJOR POPULATE

TRUK	9,375
PONAPE	5,858
SAIPAN	4,645
BABELTHAUP.	3,665
YAP	2,556
MOEN	1,890
KUSAIE	1,734
MAJURO	1,457
	ALINGLA

64 INHABITED ATOLLS A
OCEAN AREA APPROX. 2,

X ⬡ FARALLON DE PAJAROS
X ⬡ MAUG I.

X ⬡ ASUNCION I.

⊙ AGRIHAN I.

X ⊘ PAGAN I.

⊙ ALAMAGAN I.
X ⬡ GOGUAN I.

M A R I A N A S   I S L A N D S   N⬤

X ⬡ SARIGUAN I.
X ⬡ ANATAHAN I.
X ⬡ FARALLON DE MEDINILLA

⊙ ⊘ SAIPAN I.
⊘ TINIAN I.
X ⬡ AGIGUAN I.

⬡ ROTA I.

⊘ GUAM

X , OKINO-TORI-SHIMA

X , FARALLON DE PAJAROS

PACIFIC
TOKYO   SAN FRANCISCO

. . HONOLULU

OCEAN

VICINITY MAP

. , ULITHI ATOLL
⊘ YAP I.   FAIS I.

⊘ NGULU ATOLL

. , SOROL ATOLL

. KAYANGEL I.

⬡ BABELTHUAP I
⊙ ⬡ PALAU ISLANDS
⬡ KOROR I.
. PELELIU- I.
. ANGAUR I.

. SONSOROL I.

. PULO ANNA
. MERIR I.

TOBI I.

X GAFERUT I.

. FARAULEP ATOLL
X WEST FAYU ATOLL X PIKELOT I.

WOLEAI ATOLL X OLIMARAO ATOLL
. , LOMOTREK ATOLL
. IFALIK ATOLL ELATO ATOLL . SATAWAL I.
. EAURIPIK I.

PU
PULL

PULL
C A R O

WESTERN CAROLINE IS.
PALAU DISTRICT
POPULATION: 10,930

TR
POP

EQUATOR

30°   135°   145°

20°

10°

0°

135°   145°

FIGURE 61. Trust Territory of the M

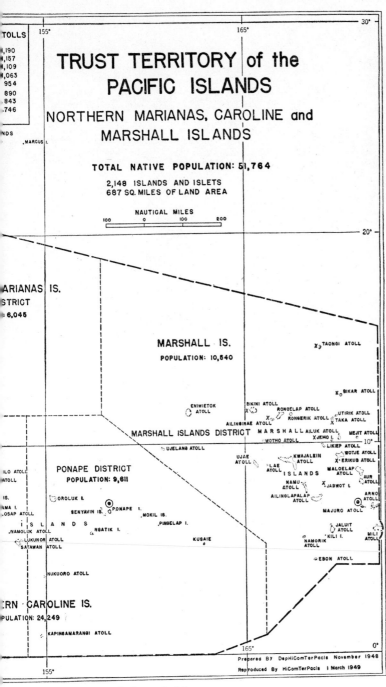

nds.   Map courtesy of the U.S. Navy.

The Palaus and Yap are composed of recent volcanic lavas and ancient metamorphic rock that testify to their continental nature. Truk, Ponape, and Kusaie are composed chiefly of basaltic lavas. Some of these volcanic islands have elevations of more than 2000 feet above sea level. The low coral atolls seldom rise to more than 6 or 8 feet above sea level. The partly raised atolls, such as Fais and Angaur, have elevations up to about 60 feet and usually contain phosphate deposits.

CLIMATE

Although there are slight climatic variations over this large area, the low latitude and oceanic location combine to produce uniform conditions at any one station during the entire year. Although the climate is oceanic in character, it is dominated by the northeast trades except in the area west of about 145° east longitude, where the effect of the Asiatic monsoon is felt during the summer months. From November to April the prevailing winds over the whole area are from the northeast or east. In the northern summer, the southeast trades are dominant over the southern Carolines and occasionally reach as far northward as the Marianas.

Typhoons, or tropical cyclones, do considerable damage in the Carolines. They can occur in any month, but they are most common from July through November, with the highest frequency in September. There is an average of 25 typhoons each year. Originating in the Carolines and Marianas, they may occur anywhere west of 160° east longitude and 5° north latitude. Although they are commonest between Yap and Guam, at rare intervals one strikes as far east as the Gilberts.

In general the rainfall is heaviest in a belt between 1° 30' and 8° 30' north latitude, which marks the zone where the northeast and southeast trades meet. The rainfall is usually over 120 inches in this belt (Fig. 62). However, there is orographic influence on the high islands that results in heavier rainfall on the windward side. The 2000-foot mountains of Kusaie produce as much as 255 inches on their windward (west) side whereas on the leeward side the annual rainfall is only 177 inches. The low coral atolls do not produce this orographic effect and are much drier.

Temperatures are uniform throughout the area (Fig. 62). The mean monthly temperatures are seldom less than 79° F or more than 83° F. The difference between the means of the summer and winter months is rarely more than 2°. The daily range usually amounts to about 9° or 10° F. Day temperatures vary from 83° to 89° F, and

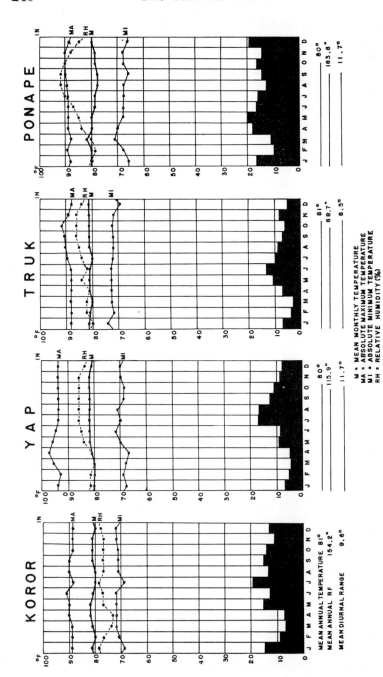

FIGURE 62.   Climatic graphs for Koror, Yap, Truk, and Ponape.

night temperatures from 74° to 77° F. The mean relative humidity is high throughout the year. The early morning relative humidity varies from 85 to 95 per cent; the early afternoon readings may vary from 70 to 80 per cent. There is little variation in the humidity from month to month.

SOILS

Great contrast exists between the soils of the high volcanic islands and those of the low coral islands. On the coral isles the soils consist of group-up coral and shells with an accumulation of humus near the surface. This is seldom very thick and is speedily lost under cultivation. These soils do not retain moisture well as the rainfall quickly soaks through the sand and is lost in the porous coral beneath.

There is greater variation on the volcanic islands. The parent material is more varied, and there is an accumulation of fairly fertile alluvium on the coastal plains and in the stream valleys. However, the frostless year with high rainfall is favorable to leaching and alluviation, with the result that tropical laterites or lateritic soils with little fertility are common. These may give good yields for a few years under cultivation, but, unless humus or fertilizer is added, yields soon decline. The soil scientists who have worked in the area since the Second World War have strongly recommended that the phosphate being shipped from Angaur to Japan be conserved for use by the people of the Trust Territory.

VEGETATION

As is true throughout the Pacific, there is considerable contrast between the vegetation of the coral islands and the volcanic islands. The indigenous flora is of Indo-Malayan origin, although there are a few endemic species, and many new plants have been introduced since the coming of the Europeans to the Pacific. In general the low coral islands with their poor soil offer a very limited environment and have a much more restricted plant life than is found on the volcanic islands that have a much more varied physical environment.

The plants of the low coral islands are limited to a small number of species that tolerate high salinity. The flora of the low islands has been so changed by human occupancy that it is impossible to establish the nature of the original vegetation cover. Even the characteristic coconuts were probably introduced by man.

The high islands of the eastern and western Carolines fall into two general groups of natural vegetation. The eastern islands of Kusaie,

Ponape, and Truk have fairly heavily forested interiors whereas the western islands of Yap and Palau have interiors that are mainly covered with savanna grass, the trees being concentrated near the coast and along streams. The more even rainfall in the eastern islands has been advanced as a reason for this difference, although there is a possibility that the savannas were culturally induced.

In both the Yap and Palau islands the practice of burning off the sword grass in order to produce tender shoots for grazing cattle and to clear the ground for agriculture frequently results in fires escaping from control and burning large areas. Since the American occupations some forested areas have been replaced by sword grass.

FAUNA

Before the arrival of the Europeans there were only a few species of mammals in the Carolines—pigs, rats, and bats. Dogs, deer, and cattle have been introduced to some of the islands by various outsiders increasing variety since the beginning of the nineteenth century. The reptiles are better represented. Crocodiles are found in the swamps of the Palau group and occasionally have been blown to some of the eastern islands but not in sufficient quantity to maintain themselves. A species of iguana is found on Yap. There are many species of lizards and the abhorred toad. Two species of snakes are known in the Palau group. The house fly is all too common as well as other insects. There are also centipedes, scorpions, and spiders.

MINERALS

The Caroline Islands possess fairly important deposits of bauxite and phosphate and minor deposits of a few other minerals. Bauxite is found on Babelthuap, Yap, Ponape, and Kusaie. The deposits in the Ngardamau area of northern Babelthuap are by far the most important. It has been estimated that there are bauxite reserves here of about 50,000,000 tons that run from 52 to 55 per cent aluminum and 20 per cent iron. The Japanese mined about 2,000,000 tons.

The Angaur phosphate deposit ranks as one of the major phosphate deposits of the Pacific. Angaur is a partly raised atoll with phosphate occurring in the old lagoon. It has been estimated that there are about 1,650,000 tons of high-grade phosphate remaining. In 1939 the Japanese mined 143,420 tons at Angaur, 43,821 tons at Fais, 26,303 tons at Peleliu, and 4269 tons at Tobi. There are also phosphate deposits on Sonsorol, Pulo Anna, and Gaferut.

Lesser deposits of other minerals occur on the high islands. Manganese is found on Babelthuap and Yap. Some low-grade coal occurs on Babelthuap near Airai and along the west coast. Some traces of gold have been reported on Babelthuap. The Japanese mined some iron ore on Yap and Ponape. Yap also has minor deposits of copper, zinc, and asbestos.

HISTORY

EARLY EUROPEAN CONTACTS

In a series of voyages after Magellan's Pacific crossing, most of the islands of the Carolines were discovered. As little wealth was found, the islands were neglected and, as they were a hazard to navigation, were avoided as much as possible during the sixteenth and seventeenth centuries. Spanish missionaries made a few unsuccessful attempts to convert some of the natives early in the eighteenth century.

New England whalers followed the sperm whale into the Marshalls and eastern Carolines in the 1840's and brought close outside contact to the natives of Kusaie, Ponape, and Truk. The traders and whalers, who came in increasing numbers, brought smallpox and other disastrous new elements to the entire area.

The missionaries were not far behind the sailors, and in 1852 the American Board of Commissioners for Foreign Missions established bases on Ponape and Kusaie. Hawaiian missionaries followed soon after. From the original bases on Ponape and Kusaie, the missionaries branched out into the Marshalls and other sections of the Carolines.

THE SPANISH PERIOD

The 1870's saw increased German commercial activity in these islands as in other parts of the Pacific. Spain's jealousy was roused, and she attempted to claim sovereignty that brought her into conflict with both Germany and Great Britain. The matter was referred to the Pope for arbitration in 1885, and he ruled in favor of Spain.

The Spanish immediately occupied Yap and in 1887 established a settlement, Colonia de Santiago, on Ponape. The occupation of Ponape resulted in trouble with both natives and well-entrenched American missionaries. The trouble with the natives, which was expensive and also costly in lives, continued even after the missionaries were removed. In 1898, as a result of defeat in the Spanish American War, Spain ceded Guam to the United States and in the following year sold the rest of her Micronesian possessions to Germany.

The Carolines, during the German period of occupation, were under the jurisdiction of the governor of German New Guinea. After 1911 they were divided into the western Caroline district, which was administered from Yap, and the eastern Caroline district, which was administered from Ponape.

Although there were never many German administrators or settlers in the area, this was a period of rapid economic and political change. Copra became the economic foundation of the islands although they were never self-supporting. The Germans reduced the power of the chiefs and made changes in the forms of land tenure. Roads were constructed with native labor, public buildings built, and some of the harbors improved. The Germans paid some attention to native health and sanitation, with the result that in some places the decline of the native population was checked. Schools were left largely in the hands of the missionaries. The changes did meet some resistance from the natives, especially from the chiefs, who lost some of their prerogatives.

One of the outstanding accomplishments of this period was the laying of the Pacific cable in 1905. Yap was made the center for the lines connecting Japan, Asia, and the south. Control of Yap was later to be a source of international friction.

In 1914 the Japanese navy took over the German possessions in Micronesia and ruled the islands until 1922, when a civilian government was placed in charge. In 1919 Japan received the islands as a class C mandate from the League of Nations. The type C mandate was administered as an integral part of the mandatory state, and eventual independence of the territory was not contemplated. After Japan's withdrawal from the League of Nations in 1935, the islands were retained, with the Japanese military playing an increasing part in their administration.

The headquarters of the Japanese government for the entire mandated area was set up on Koror in the Palau group. The Governor had executive, legislative, and some judicial powers. Before 1941 he was under the Japanese Ministry of Foreign Affairs, but after that date he was responsible to the Greater East Asia Ministry. Through most of the Japanese occupation the Carolines were divided into four districts, which were administered from Koror, Yap, Truk, and Ponape.

The Japanese followed a policy of economic development that was

intended eventually to make the islands pay for themselves and supplement the Japanese economy by the production of tropical commodities that could not be produced in Japan, by the development
of such minerals as were present, and by securing fish that play an
important part in the Japanese diet. Although the islands did form
an outlet for some of Japan's growing population, it was always
recognized that the islands were too small to absorb more than a
small part of the increase. However, by the outbreak of the Second
World War, the number of the Japanese in the whole of the mandated territory exceeded that of the natives.

The following list shows the distribution of the Japanese within the
Carolines and the rapid influx between 1930 and 1940:[1]

District	*1920*	*1930*	*1940*
Yap	97	241	1,933
Palau	592	2078	23,768
Truk	601	749	4,128
Ponape	425	689	8,048

During the Japanese expansion the interests of the natives were
protected, and, with a few exceptions, the natives do not look upon
the occupation as having been oppressive. The natives enjoyed many
material advances under the Japanese, and eventually they will judge
the American occupation by the degree to which these material gains
are continued or expanded.

An important part in the program of economic expansion was played
by the Tropical Industries Experimental Station, with experimental
farms at Palau and Ponape, and by the Marine Products Experimental
Station at Palau. There were experimental and demonstration farms
on other islands. The experimental station on Ponape was developed
until it was the second most important botanical farm in the tropics,
exceeded only by one in the Netherlands Indies. The Ponape Experimental Station suffered from neglect after the occupation, but in
1948 action was taken to save and expand this station. Many of the
plants and commercial trees growing here are found in no other place
under the American flag and can be of considerable importance to
Hawaii and the American possessions in the Carribean.

THE AMERICAN PERIOD

In 1944 the U.S. Navy became active in the Marshalls and the
Marianas. During the spring and the summer various islands of the

---

[1] These figures are taken from Table 3, p. 55, Vol. I, *Economic Survey of
Micronesia Conducted by the U.S. Commercial Company for the U.S. Navy 1946*,
typescript, microfilm, Library of Congress.

Caroline group were under air attack, and in the fall Palau and Ulithi were taken. The rest of the Carolines were bypassed, although air raids continued until the end of the war. Both Palau and Ulithi played an important part in the operations against the Philippines and the Ryukyus. After the Japanese Emperor's surrender on August 15, 1945, the bypassed islands surrendered and were occupied by the U.S. Navy.

The allies agreed in both the Cairo Declaration of December 1, 1943, and the Potsdam Declaration of July 26, 1945, that Japan should be permanently stripped of her mandated islands. The United States received these as a Trust Territory from the United Nations on April 2, 1947. Since then the islands have been under the administration of the Secretary of the Navy, and the High Commissioner has been the Commander in Chief of the Pacific Ocean area. The Deputy High Commissioner has been an admiral with his headquarters at Guam. The President has ordered that the administration of the Trust Territory will be turned over eventually to the Department of the Interior.

The Carolines were divided into four administrative centers with headquarters on Ponape, Truk, Yap, and Koror. However, as the American personnel is very small, the Yap and Palau districts were consolidated in 1948 into the Palau district.

The destruction of the war and the repatriation of the Japanese settlers brought the economy of the islands to a standstill. The standard of living that the natives had acquired during the nineteenth century and that they wished to retain almost vanished. To cope with this situation, a federal agency, the United States Commercial Company, was established and financed by the Reconstruction Finance Corporation in 1945. The corporation was given the extremely difficult job of trying to revive the economy and trade of the islands. Any profits made by the company were to benefit the natives. Although foreign capital was barred from the area, the program was devised so that native private enterprise could take over when ready. This has already happened in a few cases. The company was reorganized as the Island Trading Company of Micronesia in January, 1948.

A health service program has been established that includes medical care, dental care, and the training of native medical practitioners and nurses. The native medical practitioners receive 4 years of medical training on Guam. Part of the health program involves a complete physical examination of every native of the Trust Territory.

An educational program is well under way. It includes a teacher training center on Moen island, known as PITTS (Pacific Island Teacher Training School), where the equivalent of a high-school education is given to the teachers of the Trust Territory. Student teachers are brought to this center from all the islands and atolls of the Carolines and Marshalls to receive basic training and refresher courses. Educational facilities are now available for all children between the ages of 8 and 14 who desire an education. On the elementary level all instruction is in the vernacular, with English gradually introduced as a secondary language. By the time the students have reached the secondary level they have sufficient command of English to receive instruction in it.

POPULATION

THE NATIVE PEOPLES

The Micronesians are not homogenous in culture or race. They are basically of Indo-Malayan origin, but have strong traces of Melanesian and Polynesian blood. The western Carolines have received some admixture from the Philippines. The islanders have received substantial elements of European, Negro, and Japanese blood. In general, the Micronesians are of medium height and well built. Their skin is light brown and their hair usually straight or wavy, although the Melanesian frizzy hair may occur. The peoples of the western Carolines show some mongoloid characteristics; those in the Ponape district show caucasoid features that they may have received from European and Polynesian admixtures. The people of the islands south of the Palau show the strongest Melanesian traces, whereas the atolls of Kapingamarangi (Fig. 75) and Nukuoro represent an almost pure Polynesian racial and cultural intrusion.

DISTRIBUTION OF POPULATION

One of the major problems for the various administrations in the islands has been the distribution of the population in many small clusters spread over a great ocean area. This has made administration of the islands and their economic development difficult. The greatest population clusters are found on the high islands. Because of the greater concentration of people, it has been possible to accomplish more here in improving the medical and health situation, with the result that these islands today show a greater rate of population increase than the low islands. During the nineteenth century, with the first strong outside contacts, their population declined sharply.

The 1900 population of the islands has been estimated as 75 per cent less than that of 1800. The introduction of modern medicine and concepts of sanitation during the German and the Japanese occupation checked the decline, and on some of the islands the population is increasing today. This increase has been more noticeable on the high islands, with the exception of Yap, where about 80 per cent of the population is over the age of 15, than on the low islands, as shown by the figures in the table.

Palau		Yap			Truk		
1800	about 50,000	1783	40,000	(est.)	1827	35,000	(est.)
1862	10,000 (est.)	1896	12,000	(est.)	1877	12,000	
1882	4,000	1899	7,808		1901	12,000	
1900	3,750	1903	7,156		1907	13,514	
1908	4,321	1910	6,328		1914	11,000	
1920	5,605	1935	3,479		1935	10,344	
1930	5,794	1946	2,805		1946	9,895	
1937	5,749	1948	2,744		1948	9,510	
1946	5,634						
1948	5,900						

Ponape		Kusaie		Tobi		Pulusuk	
1820	15,000	1824	c.3000	1832	c.400	1819	900
1844	8,000	1852	c.1700	1878	200	1850	350
1877	5,000	1855	1106	1930	183	1901	300
1880	2,000	1868	500	1935	171	1909	177
1891	1,705	1874	379	1946	130	1930	226
1900	3,165	1888	350	1948	141	1935	194
1904	3,279	1895	400			1948	202
1914	4,401	1905	516				
1930	5,320	1927	800				
1935	5,601	1930	990	c. = uncertain			
1946	5,639	1935	1189				
1948	5,735	1946	1558				
		1948	1652				

LANGUAGE

Language is another major problem of the area. The approximately 33,000 people of the Carolines speak eight distinctly different languages, and each of the languages is subdivided into dialects. On Kapingamarangi and Nukuoro a dialect of Polynesian is spoken. The Palauan language is thought to be of Indonesian origin, but it shows definite affinity with some of the Philippine languages. The language of the islands southeast of Palau and the Yapese, Uilithian, Trukese, Ponapean, and Kusaiean languages show close relationship to the languages of the northern Melanesian islands. There is no common language, although individuals, according to their age group, may speak Spanish, German, Japanese, or English. Everywhere the natives express a desire to learn English as rapidly as possible. They say that in the past they could not handle their rulers until they had command of the language of the new administrators.

Efforts to reduce the languages to writing have increased the confusion. Rival missionary groups have their own forms of grammar and spelling, each of which has considerable emotional backing among the natives. The efforts of government linguistic experts in the area since the end of the Second World War have in some cases resulted in merely another form of grammar and romanization rather than a generally accepted standard.

HOUSES

The traditional Micronesian house is rectangular, with a wooden frame and mat or wicker walls (Fig. 69). The roofs were formerly thatched, although the corrugated steel roof is more common today. The houses were generally raised on a stone platform, which might be, as on Yap, very elaborate. The clubhouses built for men and other community meeting houses are much more elaborate than the ordinary residence. In general the clubhouses are much more elegant in the western Carolines than in the eastern Carolines. The framework is usually made from breadfruit trees and lashed together by coir.

The Japanese administration felt that there was a definite connection between the declining birth rate and this traditional type of house. The houses were dark and damp inside. The dirt or coral floors and the thatch roofs were conducive to holding moisture as well as vermin. Before outside influences had introduced tuberculosis and other heretofore unknown diseases the houses had been satisfactory. But, with the innovations, they were death traps. By means of subsidies the Japanese encouraged the building of houses with elevated wooden floors and corrugated steel roofs. These, being drier, discouraged diseases. The corrugated steel roofs also trapped a safe supply of much-needed fresh water. The new houses are by no means as esthetically attractive as the old houses, and, even under the Japanese administration, there were those who mourned the passing of the picturesque; but the death rate did decline as the new houses became more common. As with all outside influences, the new type of house is more common on the high islands than on the low islands.

The Caroline Islands are noted for the use the natives make of stone. House foundations, dancing platforms, and graves are commonly made from stone. Elaborate stone causeways connect islands and cross bays in the high islands. On Yap, stone money was imported from quarries on Babelthuap. On Ponape and Kusaie, elaborate cities and fortifications were constructed from stone. The ruins of Nan Matal, or Metalanium, cover about 9 square miles. The ruined city consists of a number of small natural and artificial islands that are protected by a breakwater. Some of the ruined walls are 10 feet thick and 20 to 30 feet high. Excavations have proved that

FIGURE 63. Stone ruins at Nan Matol, Ponape. These large basaltic crystals were transported about thirty miles to their present position by the ancestors of the present Ponapeans. Photograph courtesy of the Bernice P. Bishop Museum.

the culture of these people did not differ materially from that of their descendants of the nineteenth century.

NATIVE ORGANIZATION

The basic social unit is the family, but each family is part of a well-developed clan system governed by chiefs. Except in the islands southwest of the Palaus, descent was through the female line, but under German, Japanese, and missionary influence this custom is breaking down. The modern period also has seen a lessening of the influence of the chiefs, especially among the young men in areas of outside influence. A counter tendency under German and American rule has been a strengthening of the position of the chiefs because of the lack of foreign administrative personnel. It is much easier to relay orders through responsible chiefs, and under American rule an atoll chief has been introduced in places where one did not exist before.

FIGURE 64. Avenue of stone money on Yap. These coins, brought with difficulty from Palau, are still highly prized by the Yapese. The Yapese are conservative and cling to their traditional dress more than the people of the other islands. Photograph by U.S. Navy.

AGRICULTURE

SUBSISTENCE AGRICULTURE

Subsistence agriculture supplies the natives with most of their food. This source is supplemented by the products of the fisheries, some livestock, and, in the areas of greatest outside influence, by importing foods not grown in the islands. The agricultural products are much more varied and numerous on the high islands than on the low islands, where the beach environment limits variety in the plants and the amount of cropland.

On both the high and the low islands the natives grow root and tree crops. The principal tree crops on the high islands are coconuts, breadfruit, papaya, citrus fruit, bananas, and mangoes. The leading root crops are wet and dry taro, arrowroot, yams, sweet potatoes, and cassava (Fig. 68). On the low islands there are not as many varieties and the natives are much more dependent on the pandanus, which is eaten on the high islands only when other foods fail.

The distribution of yams and sweet potatoes varies. On Truk and Kusaie the sweet potato is a staple food whereas yams are of little importance. The situation is reversed on Ponape, Yap, and in the Palaus. Ponape is noted for its yams. More than 156 native varieties are known; one is said to attain a length of 9 feet and a diameter of 3 feet.

FIGURE 65. The Turtle Dance being performed on Ngulu. The people of the low islands tend to their traditional dress more than the people of the high islands. Photograph by U.S. Navy.

During the Japanese occupation other crops were introduced such as rice, new types of sugar cane that crowded out the older eating varieties, corn, sorghum, and tobacco. Of these, tobacco is the only one that the natives are continuing to raise in quantity, although they became familiar with the others and will purchase them in the stores when they are available.

Method of agriculture have been little influenced by outside contacts. The digging stick and a long bush knife are still the principal farming tools. There is some desire on the part of the natives for mechanical aid in restoring the wet taro patches that were destroyed during the Second World War, but, on the whole, they are satisfied and successful with the traditional methods.

COMMERCIAL AGRICULTURE

Copra has been important in the Carolines and continues to be the chief industry and source of income for the natives. Coconut plantations are prominent on both the high and the low islands. This industry suffered severely during the Second World War, and by 1950 had not been restored to its prewar level. In the Palaus the rhinoceros beetle has been a factor in cutting production. The total production for the mandated islands was 14,938 tons in 1939, but amounted to only 5,000 tons in 1947. In 1938 the Ponape district led the Carolines with a production of 3517 tons of copra, followed by the Truk district with a production of 2458 tons, the Yap district with 1090 tons, and the Palau district with 600 tons. Coir continues to be a by-product of the coconut industry.

Although sugar was raised in the Carolines, the industry was in only an early stage of development in 1941, and the production never approached that of the Marianas before the war. The sugar raised in the Carolines was largely used in manufacturing alcohol. This industry has suffered a complete eclipse since the Second World War.

The production of manioc as a source of tapioca starch increased rapidly in the 1930's. Although some was produced on all the high islands, Ponape led with a production of 11,177 short tons of manioc roots in 1937 and the Palaus followed with a production of 5,173 tons. Manioc does well on the more fertile soils of the high islands. As most of the labor was Japanese, the industry has lapsed under the American occupation.

A number of minor agricultural industries, including the production of pineapples, coffee, and vanilla, were in an early stage of development immediately before the Second World War. Truck garden vegetables were also becoming important as the Japanese population increased. All of these have become war casualties.

FISHERIES

Fishing is an important part of the native subsistence economy, and under the Japanese was an important commercial industry of the islands. Traditionally the natives have secured an important part of their diet from the lagoons and reefs and to a lesser extent from deep sea fishing. On the reefs they catch marine snails, clams, trepang, mollusks, and lobsters. In the lagoons and on the reefs they catch many species of fish with hooks and lines, spears, weirs, and stone traps. Trochus and pearl shell is collected. Outside the atolls they troll for bonito, shark, and other fish.

The Japanese fleet of small fishing boats, based on Koror, Truk, Ponape, and Yap, had built up a major deep-sea fishing industry, important for bonito and tuna.   The Japanese fishing boats, gear, and cannery were destroyed during the Second World War and the Japanese fishermen have been repatriated.   It will require training and capital to equip the natives for commercial deep-sea fishing as they had not participated in this industry under the Japanese.

LIVESTOCK

The Caroline islanders have long raised pigs and poultry.   With the advent of Japanese settlers there was an increased demand for livestock.   Pigs, cattle, and poultry played an important part in the diet of the natives during the Japanese period.   Carabaos were used as draft animals instead of horses.

War was especially hard on livestock, whose numbers were disastrously reduced by hungry garrisons, natives, and invaders.   The number of pigs dropped from an estimated prewar total of 20,400 to 3260 in 1946.   A similar reduction occurred to the other livestock.   In spite of the desires of the natives, the postwar restoration of livestock in the Carolines has progressed slowly.   The curtailment of this accustomed source of protein was one of the most serious of the postwar dietary deficiencies.

THE WESTERN CAROLINES

THE PALAU GROUP

The Palau arc is about 125 miles long and 25 miles wide, and the administrative center of this group in Koror (7° 20′ north latitude, 134° 28′ east longitude).   The islands are 706 nautical miles southwest of Guam and 1044 nautical miles east of Manila.   There are an estimated 243 islands, but only 8 are of significant size.   The total land area is about 188 square miles, with about 478 square miles of enclosed lagoon (Fig. 67).

The main islands, Babelthuap, Koror, Ururthapel, Eil Malk, and Peleliu, are surrounded by a coral reef, about 70 miles long, that fringes the eastern shores but widens out on the western side.   The lagoon on the western side of the islands is about 40 miles long and 8 miles wide.   This reef is difficult to cross, except in a few places, even by the native canoes.   To the north of the main islands there is an atoll (5 by 2 miles) with four low, sandy motus, the Kayangel Islands, which rise a few feet above the water.   To the south of the main islands there is a raised atoll, Angaur, which has important phosphate deposits.

Babelthuap, the largest island of the Palau group, is a pear-shaped island that is widest toward the southern end and narrows down to a slender peninsula on the north. It is about 23 miles long and varies in width from 4 to 8 miles. The total area of Babelthuap is about 143 square miles. The island has several lines of hills with a maximum elevation of 713 feet. Babelthuap is composed of volcanic rock

FIGURE 66. *Abai* (house occupied by men only) of Arai Village, Bebelthaup. This is one of the few old *abai* to survive the war. The gable has been repainted to show the American conquest of the Palaus. Photograph by C. A. Manchester, Jr.

except for some uplifted coral in the south. The coastal lowlands are covered with mangrove while most of the hilly interior is wooded except for some savanna cover.

POPULATION

The Japanese left Babelthuap in the hands of the natives except for a few administrators and those engaged in mining. The total population of the Palau islands in 1946 was 6500, most of whom lived on Babelthuap. The native villages are concentrated on the

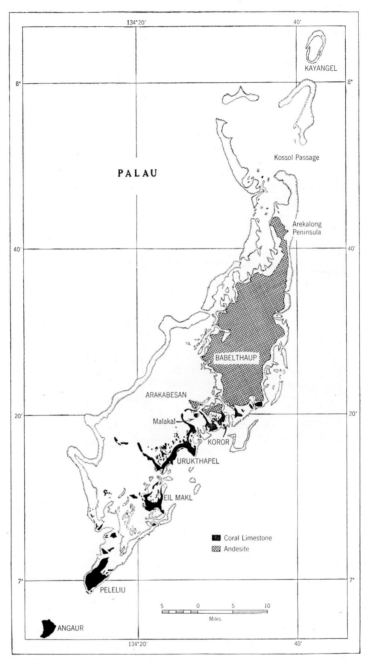

FIGURE 67.   Map of Palau.

eastern coast. The largest village, Airai, had a population of about 700. The natives are supported by subsistence farming and fishing, and produce copra for sale. During the Japanese period some natives found employment working on the roads and in the mines. Under the Japanese about 235 acres were devoted to the commercial production of vegetables, 900 acres to manioc, and 1000 acres to pineapples. This commercial agriculture has been abandoned since the war.

THE YAP GROUP

The Yap (pronounced Wop or Uop) group (9° 25′ and 9° 46′ north latitude, 138° 03′ and 138° 14′ east longitude) consists of four

FIGURE 68. House showing strong outside influences on Neon Island, Truk. The typical foods of the Carolines surround the house: taro in the foreground, banana tree on the left, and breadfruit and coconuts in the background. (CAM)

principal islands, Yap or Rull, Gagil or Gagil-Tomil, Map, and Rumung, and about ten small islands. These are located on one triangular submarine platform and surrounded by a fringing reef (Fig. 70). The reef varies in width from one-half to 2 miles. The islands enclosed by the reef make a compact group 16 miles long and 8 miles wide. The total land area has been estimated to be about 38½ square miles, whereas the reefs enclose about 10 square miles of lagoon.

These islands represent the top of a great underwater ridge, similar in formation to the island arcs of Palau, the Ryukyu, and Japan. Like them they rise from the continental shelf and west of the sial line, and the eastern side of Yap is marked by a deep trench in the ocean floor. The core of the island group is of metamorphic rock, but the eastern portion is composed of weathered lava. The greatest elevation, and consequently the greatest erosion of this ridge, was on the eastern side. Subsequent subsidence has resulted in the ocean invading the old erosional valleys. Coral growth has been unable to keep pace with the subsidence of the valleys, and as a result these estuaries form natural channels throughout the reef today. Tomil, the commercial harbor, is on the southeastern side of the group. Although it is the best harbor of the group, it has a narrow, dangerous entrance. The coral-free channel of 6 fathoms depth is only 100 yards wide. Yap-Colonia, which appears on some maps as Yaptown, is the chief administrative center of the Yap Islands and is located on the western side of Tomil Harbor.

FIGURE 69. House on Pis Island, Truk, which reflects the lesser outside influence on the low islands. (CAM)

The largest of the individual islands, Yap, is about 12 miles long and 3 miles wide. The highest elevation of the whole group, 585 feet above sea level, occurs near the northern end of Yap. These northern hills lose elevation toward the south, and most of the southern portion of the island is low, with occasional mangrove swamps.

Yap and Gagil-Tomil were almost separated, except for a narrow neck of land, by the subsidence that formed Tomil Harbor. This separation was completed when the Germans dug the Tageren Canal.

POPULATION

The Yap natives are of the general stock that originated in the islands of southeastern Asia and migrated into this area. However, there appears to be a strong mixture of Mongolian, Melanesian, and Polynesian blood.

Local customs have prevented the mixing of native blood with that of the Japanese and Americans who have resided in the islands to a much greater extent than on other Micronesian islands with a similar history of foreign contacts.

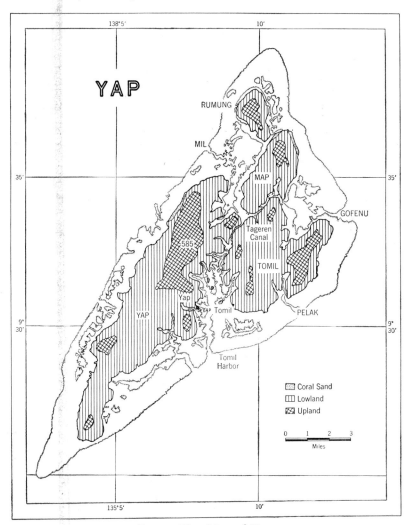

FIGURE 70. Map of Yap.

Because the Yapese people have rejected western clothing, have clung to some of their old institutions, and have continued to prize their stone money they have acquired a reputation of being backward and stubborn. Americans who have had real contact with the people since the American occupation and who have gained the confidence of the people have not found this reputation to be justified. The CIVADREP, Richard J. Umholfer, Lieutenant USNR, said to the author of this chapter, in September, 1949:

> These people are not stubborn or resistant to change but rather are highly selective and discriminating in their process of adapting Western techniques and artifacts to their own culture. Unlike other areas within the Trust Territory, the Yapese have not gone overboard in adopting exotic ways of life in order to please or emulate their administrators. It appears that common sense has been mistaken for stubbornness, and a policy of "wait and see" has been interpreted as evidence of backwardness and uncooperativeness.

Most of the Yapese have rejected western dress because they consider it to be too warm. They have continued to build their homes and all-men's houses, *falu*, according to traditional styles. During the centuries they have built many miles of stone roads and causeways that connect the villages and agricultural lands. These roads are lined with stone coins that are made from stalactites and stalagmites imported from Babelthaup and to a lesser extent from Guam. These factors combine to give the islands the pre-European appearance that misled so many observers in the past.

THE EASTERN CAROLINES

TRUK

The Truk (pronounced Chuk) group (151° 22′ to 150° 04′ east longitude, 7° 7′ to 7° 41′ north latitude) is about 900 miles north of Rabaul and 650 miles southeast of Guam. Truk is an almost, or complex, atoll with a barrier reef that varies from 30 to 40 miles in diameter (Fig. 71). There are about 40 small motus on the reef, but only one of these, Pis (pronounced peace) Island, is permanently inhabited. The lagoon has a circumference of about 140 miles and contains 6 fairly large high islands and many lesser ones. About 100 of the lesser islands of the lagoon bear names. The total dry land of the island group is about 39 square miles. Tol, or Ton, is the largest of the islands and has the highest elevation, 1483 feet. The other important islands in order of their size are Moen, Fefan, Dublon, Udot, and Uman. Elevations on these islands vary from about 950 feet to a little more than 1000 feet.

Truk is the deeply eroded summit of a great volcanic dome that rises from a submarine plateau. Although the islands of the eastern part of the plateau appear to be fairly stable, there has been some recent subsidence of Truk as is evidenced by drowned river valleys.

Moen, the center of the American administration, possesses the only operational airfield in the island group. Dublon was the seat of the Japanese administration and was the site of a well-developed Japanese city that was wiped out during the Second World War.

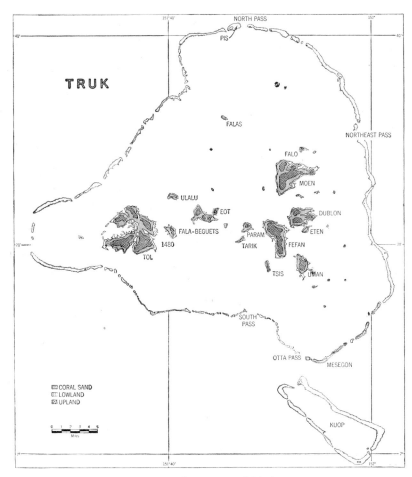

FIGURE 71.   Map of Truk.

Tol is the most densely populated of the islands, but native life on it has been less disturbed than on the other high islands. The natives of Tol live in small scattered villages; those on the other high islands were concentrated into larger villages during the German and Japanese occupations.

PIS ISLAND

Pis is a small motu on the northern side of the Truk barrier reef and typical of the low coral islands of the Carolines. The low coral sand island, never more than about 4 or 5 feet above sea level, possesses about 150 acres of dry land. The approximately 140 people who live on this island have been under much less outside influence than those who live on the near-by high islands within the Truk lagoon. Their houses show much less outside influence. Most of the houses have thatched roofs, breadfruit tree frames, and pandanus mat sides. Traditional outrigger canoes are still used to a much greater extent than on the high islands.

Breadfruit, coconuts, pandanus, and fish form the core of the diet of these people, although some taro, arrowroot, and other foods are raised. Nearly every plant or tree that is not essential to the lives of the people has been eliminated, with the result that the island presents a parklike appearance.

The population of the island is concentrated along the southern shore. The center of the village is a community house and a trading store. Houses and boathouses are scattered on either side of these along a narrow coral road that runs around the island near the shoreline. One of the boathouses is used as a school house.

Some income is secured from the sale of copra and native handicraft. People in the States can order especially beautifully woven pandanus mats and goods from a mail-order catalog.

THE PONAPE DISTRICT

The Ponape district consists of the Caroline Islands east of 154° east longitude. The district contains the high islands of Ponape and Kusaie and a number of small low islands. The total native population was estimated in 1947 to be 9577, over half of whom were located on Ponape. The natives are basically Micronesian, although Kapingamarangi and Nukuoro represent a Polynesian intrusion.

PONAPE

Ponape (6° 53′ north latitude, 158° 14′ east longitude) is a volcanic dome similar in origin to Truk, but less advanced in subsidence. It is about 14 miles from north to south and 16 miles from east to west (Fig. 72). The island is surrounded by about 25 small islands of both coral and volcanic origin. The whole complex is surrounded by a barrier reef that encloses a narrow lagoon. The total land area has been estimated at 129 square miles. Ponape and the near-by atolls of Ant and Pakin are sometimes called the Senyavin Group.

The interior of Ponape consists of a series of sharply eroded peaks and deep valleys. Three peaks that are located near the center of the island rise to more than 2500 feet. Faulting has produced steep cliffs in the columnar basalt. A cliff on Jokaj Island rises 900 feet

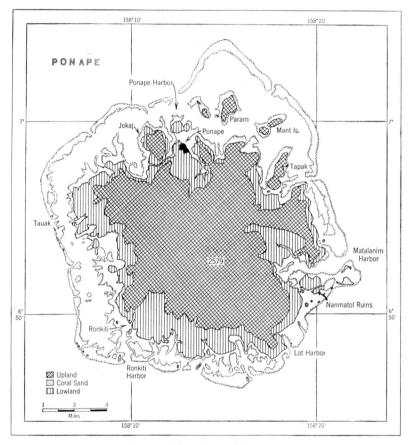

FIGURE 72. Map of Ponape.

from sea level. The principal flat areas are found along the coasts and up some of the river valleys.

The town of Ponape or Colony was the center of a Japanese population of about 8000. Most of the Japanese were engaged in local industries and the production of the chief exports of Ponape: bauxite, copra, ivory nuts, manioc starch, and dried bonito. The coastal plains and an interior plateau made Ponape one of the most promising lands for commercial agriculture under the Japanese.

Because of the large Japanese population the native Ponapeans have received strong influences from outside. Some of the training has been retained, as shown by the fact that they have repaired and maintained in operation the hydroelectric plant installed by the Japanese.

KUSAIE

Kusaie, which is located in a position approximately 5° 20′ north latitude and 163° 00′ east longitude, is the easternmost of the Caro-

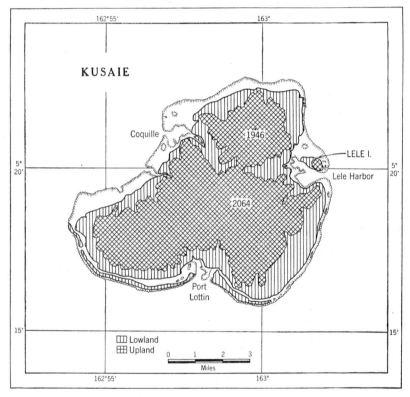

Figure 73. Map of Kusaie.

lines and the third in size. The island is roughly 8½ by 10 miles, with an area of about 42 square miles (Fig. 73). The main part of Kusaie is made up of two rugged basaltic mountain masses whose sharp ridges and V-shaped valleys are characteristic of a youthful

stage of erosion. Mount Buache, elevation 1943 feet, occupies the
northern part of the island and is separated from the southern mountains by a low valley. The southern range forms a compact mass in
the center of the island with numerous peaks. Mount Crozer, eleva-

FIGURE 74. Yap farmhouse. Most Yap homes are built in the
traditional manner. These strongly constructed buildings resist
typhoons better than most modern buildings. The stone foundations are used as a wall to display the stone money that the
family possesses. The small courtyard is stone-paved. The
courtyard is surrounded by coconut trees, bananas, and other
useful tropical trees.

tion 2061 feet, is the highest. Both mountain masses are surrounded
by an alluvial coastal plain of varying width. The coastal plains have
a dense cover of mangrove and coconut palms. The mangrove
swamps are so dense that landing is difficult except where they have
been cleared. Back of the mangrove there is a belt of coconuts,
mango, and breadfruit trees. There are patches of nipa palms at
the mouths of the streams.

Most of the original forest that occupied the interior has been destroyed and replaced by a secondary forest of trees 30 to 40 feet
high. These are mixed with shrubs to produce an almost impassable
tangle. There are some openings with a high grass cover.

In 1935 the native population was 1189, and in 1948 it was 1652.

The natives are all Christians of a very devout nature. They do not smoke and are extremely modest. They will not work cargo on Sunday. This is the result of the work of the Boston Missionary Society, which has continued on this island without serious interruption through the periods of Spanish, German, and Japanese occupation. Another result has been to make Kusaie an educational center for the

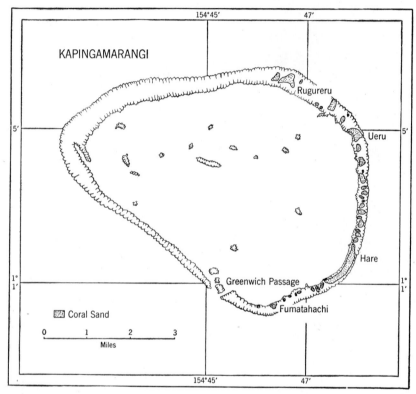

FIGURE 75. Map of Kapingamarangi.

eastern Carolines and Marshalls. This, in turn, has resulted in the diffusion of English through the neighboring islands.

The chief occupations of the natives are subsistence agriculture and fishing. Some copra is exported. The Japanese started a small sugar plantation that has been abandoned since the American occupation. This also happened to the fishing industry, which had been started by Okinawans with motor sampans.

The native houses are rectangular in form, and the better ones built on raised stone platforms. There are ruins of a stone city on Lele Island that are similar to the stone ruins at Nan Matal on Ponape. These consist of walls built from large basaltic columns, rising in places to a height of 20 feet.

FIGURE 76. Yapese mother and daughter. The people of Yap have resisted Western clothes as being too warm for their humid climate. Photograph by C. A. Manchester, Jr.

REFERENCES

Bascom, William R., *Ponape: a Pacific Economy in Transition, 1946,* Typescript, Microfilm, Library of Congress.

Bridge, Josiah, *Mineral Resources of Micronesia, 1946,* Typescript, Microfilm, Library of Congress.

—— "A Restudy of the Reported Occurrence of Schist on Truk, Eastern Caroline Islands," *Pacific Sci.,* Vol. II, No. 3, pp. 216–222, July, 1948.

Bryan, E. H., *Geographic Summary of Micronesia, 1946,* Typescript, Microfilm, Library of Congress.

—— *Maps of the Islands of Micronesia, under Administration of U.S.*

Naval Military Government Pacific Ocean Area, United States Commercial Company Research Section, Pearl Harbor, 1946.

Christian, F. W., *The Caroline Islands,* Methuen & Co., London, 1899.

—— Exploration in the Caroline Islands, *Geogr. Jour.,* Vol. XIII, No. 2, pp. 105–136, February, 1899.

Clyde, Paul H., *Japan's Pacific Mandate,* The Macmillan Co., New York, 1935.

Coolidge, Harold J. (editor), *Conservation in Micronesia,* National Research Council, Washington, 1948.

Coulter, John W., "The United States Trust Territory of the Pacific," *Jour. Geogr.,* Vol. XLVII, No. 7, pp. 253–267, October, 1948.

Fosberg, F. R., "Atoll Vegetation and Salinity," *Pacific Sci.,* Vol. III, No. 1, pp. 89–92, January, 1949.

Furness, William Henry, *The Island of Stone Money: Yap of the Carolines,* J. B. Lippincott Co., Philadelphia and London, 1910.

Gantt, P. A., *Livestock Survey of Micronesia, 1946,* Typescript, Microfilm, Library of Congress.

Graves, F. C., "The Health Services Program in the Trust Territory of the Pacific Islands," *Naval Medical Bull.,* November–December, 1948.

Hobbs, William H., *Cruises along By-ways of the Pacific,* The Stratford Co., Boston, Mass., 1923.

—— *The Fortress Islands of the Pacific,* J. E. Edwards Brothers, Ann Arbor, 1945.

—— "In the Japanese Mandated Islands, a Visit Soon after the Japanese Took Possession," *Quarterly Michigan Alumnus,* pp. 104–111, Winter, 1943.

Karig, Walter, *The Fortunate Islands,* Rinehart & Co., New York, 1948.

Lyman, Richard Jr., *Livestock Report on the Marshalls, Carolines, and Marianas, 1946,* Typescript, Microfilm, Library of Congress.

MacMillan, H. G., *Report on Agricultural Conditions in Micronesia, 1946,* Typescript, Microfilm, Library of Congress.

Murdock, George P., and Ward H. Goodenough, Social Organization of Truk, *Southwestern Jour. Anthropology,* Vol. 13, No. 4, pp. 331–343, Winter, 1947.

Murphy, Raymond E., "Landownership on a Micronesian Atoll," *Geogr. Rev.,* Vol. XXXVIII, No. 4, pp. 598–614, October, 1948.

—— "'High' and 'Low' Islands in the Eastern Carolines," *Geogr. Rev.,* Vol. 39, pp. 425–439, July, 1949.

Navy Department, Civil Affairs Guide, *Agriculture in the Japanese Mandated Islands,* OPNAV P 22–17, 1944.

—— Civil Affairs Guide, *The Fishing Industry of the Japanese Mandated Islands,* OPNAV 50 E–20, 1944.

—— Civil Affairs Handbook, *Administrative Organization and Personnel of the Japanese Mandated Islands,* OPNAV 50 E–4, 1944.

—— Civil Affairs Handbook, *East Caroline Islands,* OPNAV P 22–5, 1944.

—— Civil Affairs Handbook, *West Caroline Islands,* OPNAV P 22–7, 1944.

—— Civil Affairs Studies, II, *The Languages of the Japanese Mandated Islands,* OPNAV 50 E–15, 1944.

———— *Handbook on the Trust Territory of the Pacific Islands, 1948*, Washington, 1949.

Nugent, L. E., Jr., "Emerged Phosphate Islands in Micronesia," *Bull. Geol. Soc. Amer.*, Vol. 59, No. 10, pp. 977–994, October, 1948.

Oliver, D. (editor), *Summary of Findings and Recommendations, U.S. Commercial Company Survey, 1947*, Typescript, Microfilm, Library of Congress.

Pelzer, J. K., Agriculture in the Truk Islands," *Foreign Agriculture*, Vol. 11, No. 6, June, 1947.

Pelzer, K. L., and E. T. Hall, *Economic and Human Resources—Truk Islands, 1947*, Typescript, Microfilm, Library of Congress.

Price, Willard, *Pacific Adventure*, Reynal and Hitchcock, New York, 1936.

Rogers, O. G., *Report on Soils of Micronesia, 1946*, Typescript, Microfilm, Library of Congress.

St. John, Harold, "Flora and Vocabulary of Pingelap," *Pacific Sci.*, Vol. II, No. 2, pp. 97–113, April, 1948.

United States Department of the Interior, Board on Geographical Names, Decision List No. 4414, *The Caroline, Marshall, and Mariana Islands (except Guam)*, Washington, 1944.

United States Navy, *An Outline of the Activities in the Trust Territory of the Pacific Islands under Naval Administration to 1 October 1948*, Pearl Harbor, 1948.

Useem, J., *Economic and Human Resources, Yap and Palau, Western Carolines, 1947*, Typescript, Microfilm, Library of Congress.

Wright, Carleton, "Trust Territory of the Pacific Islands," *U.S. Naval Institute Proc.*, Vol. 74, No. 549, pp. 1333–1341, November, 1948.

Yamasaki, Naomasa, *Micronesia and Micronesians*, Second Session (Honolulu) of the Institute of Pacific Relations, Institute of Pacific Relations (Publishers), New York, 1927.

Yanagihara, Tadao, *Pacific Islands under Japanese Mandate*, Oxford University Press, London and New York, 1940.

10

Micronesia: Marshalls, Gilberts, Ocean Island, and Nauru

LEONARD MASON

THE ISLANDS OF EASTERN MICRONESIA, COMPRISING THE MARSHALLS, GILberts, Ocean island, and Nauru, lie scattered over half a million square miles of Pacific ocean (Fig. 77). Jaluit Atoll, in the Marshalls, is fairly central within this area and lies nearly 5000 miles southwest of San Francisco. At the same time it is the center of a large triangle, the corners of which rest in Japan to the northwest, in Hawaii to the northeast, and in Australia to the southwest, each about 2000 miles distant from Jaluit. The islands are roughly located along a southeast-northwest axis between 2° 45′ south and 15° 00′ north and between 161° 00′ east and 177° 00′ east. The area has been, and still is, off the beaten path of commercial air and steamer transport. But for the events of the Second World War, the islands and their peoples would be practically unknown to the rest of the world.

ORIGIN OF THE ISLANDS

The Marshalls and the Gilberts, unlike the rest of Micronesia, where high volcanic islands are a common phenomenon, consist entirely of low coral islands, usually clustered in atoll pattern. The phosphate-bearing islands (Nauru and Ocean) represent yet another type of formation, in which the coral foundation has been raised to considerable height above sea level.

EARLY DISCOVERY

The sixteenth was the first century to witness the penetration of eastern Micronesia by Spanish voyagers from the New World. They reported contacts with islands, now included among the Marshalls.

During the succeeding two centuries, Spanish galleons sailing from Mexico to the Philippines undoubtedly had opportunities for contact with inhabitants of the coral atolls. For the most part, however, this period in eastern Micronesia is a blank page in Pacific islands history.

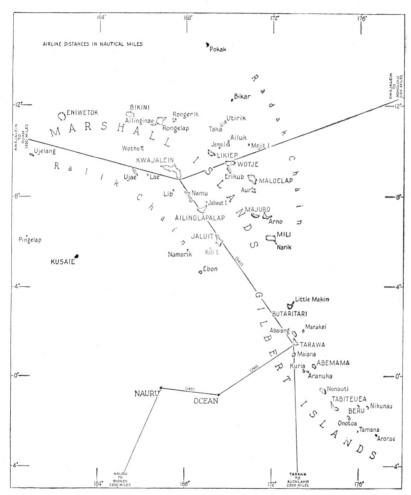

FIGURE 77. Marshalls, Gilberts, Ocean Island, and Nauru. (Source: Army Map Service No. 1201, Sheet 8, 1st ed., 1945.)

The islands were rediscovered in the eighteenth century. Admiral John Byron, commanding the British *Dolphin* and *Tamar*, sighted Nikunau Atoll in the southern Gilberts in 1765 but was unable to make anchorage. Two years later, in the northern Marshalls, the

English navigator Wallis was reported to have touched at Rongerik, an uninhabited atoll that 180 years later was the temporary home of Marshallese displaced from Bikini Atoll by American atomic bomb experiments. The two major archipelagoes acquired their present names when Captains Gilbert and Marshall, of the *Charlotte* and *Scarborough*, respectively, explored the islands briefly in 1788 en route to Canton from Australia. Two raised coral islands south of the equator and west from the Gilberts, and valued today for their wealth in phosphate, welcomed the first European visitors only toward the close of the eighteenth century. Thus, in 1798, Captain John Fearn of the British *Hunter* stopped at Nauru, experiencing such pleasure with the island and its native inhabitants that he called it Pleasant Island, a name that persisted on nautical charts for many years. Its companion, known to islanders as Banaba, was discovered in 1804 and named after the ship *Ocean*, which touched there briefly in that year.

European traffic in the atolls increased considerably during the next 50 years as whalers of several nations carried on their operations in these whale-frequented waters, accompanied by adventurous traders who gambled their goods against their ability to maintain friendly relations with the warring natives. From those early years to the present, inhabitants of the low islands have known beachcomber, missionary, trader, scientist, and government administrator, each playing his own role in carrying Western civilization to this underdeveloped backwater of the Pacific world.

GENERAL CHARACTERISTICS

Practically all the Marshalls and Gilberts are coral atolls, each with a number of small low islands rising clear of the sea to encompass a placid lagoon of varying size and shape. Some atolls possess as few as two islets; others soar past the hundred mark. Lagoons range in size from only one square mile to nearly 850. Land is scarce, less than 250 square miles of it distributed in approximately 1500 pieces over 500,000 square miles of ocean. With an average population density of 200 and with facilities for agriculture at a premium, human habitation is made possible by the vast food resources available in the lagoon, on the reef, and in the deep waters beyond. Indeed, in the culture of the islanders, lagoons figure perhaps even more prominently than the land since there are on the average about twenty-five parts of lagoon to one of land. Here and there in the archipelagoes are a few isolated islands that have no lagoon, and in consequence are usually uninhabited.

Available soil lacks the proper qualities for efficient agricultural production on a large scale. Native animal life is non-existent, if one excepts the rat, although introduced animals include cat and dog, pigs and poultry, some goats, and a few cows. There are seasons when food becomes scarce, and also water to drink. Storms, hurricanes, and tidal waves occasionally threaten the existence of small communities as they wait under sparse tree cover along the lagoon beaches. But advantages do exist. The area is free from malaria, yellow fever, and similar scourges found to south and west, the cooling trade winds relieve the otherwise humid and oppressive tropical atmosphere of high islands, and the tempo of living guarantees a minimum of high blood pressure.

TABLE 1

*ISLANDS, AREAS, AND POPULATIONS**

Area Name (Alternates)	Land Area, Square Miles	Lagoon Area, Square Miles	Native Population
Marshall Islands (34)	69.84	4,506.87	10,553 (1948)
Radak (Ratak) chain			
Pokak (Taongi, Gaspar Rico)	1.25	30.13	. . . . . .
Bikar (Dawson)	0.19	14.44	. . . . . .
Utirik (Kutusov, Utrik)	0.94	22.29	166
Taka (Suvarov)	0.22	35.96	. . . .
Mejit (New Year, Mejij)	0.72	. . . .	299
Ailuk (Tindal, Watts)	2.07	68.47	319
Jemo (Tyemo)	0.06	. . . .	. . . . . .
Likiep (Count Heiden)	3.96	163.71	568
Wotje (Romanzov)	3.16	241.06	328
Erikub (Bishop, Junction)	0.59	88.92	. . . . . .
Maloelap (Kaven, Calvert)	3.79	375.57	457
Aur (Ibbetson)	2.17	92.58	418
Majuro (Arrowsmith)	3.54	113.92	1473
Arno (Daniel, Peddlar)	5.00	130.77	1071
Mili (Mille, Mulgrave)	5.77	293.38	279
Narik (Narikrik, Knox)	0.38	1.32	. . . . . .
Ralik chain			
Eniwetok (Brown)	2.26	387.99	. . . . . .
Ujelang (Arecifos, Providence)	0.67	25.47	142
Bikini (Eschholtz)	2.32	229.40	. . . . . .
Rongerik (Rimski-Lorsakoff)	0.65	55.38	. . . . . .
Rongelap (Pescadore)	3.07	387.77	95
Ailinginae	1.08	40.91	. . . . . .
Wotho (Schanz)	1.67	36.65	31
Ujae (Katherine)	0.72	71.79	244
Lae (Brown)	0.56	6.82	138
Kwajalein (Menschikov)	6.33	839.30	1043
Lib (Princessa)	0.36	. . . .	84
Namu (Musquillo)	2.42	153.53	341
Jabwot	0.22	. . . .	. . . . . .
Ailinglapalap (Elmore, Odia)	5.67	289.69	705
Jaluit (Bonham)	4.38	266.31	960
Kili (Hunter)	0.36	. . . .	184

TABLE 1 (*Continued*)

Area Name (*Alternates*)	Land Area, Square Miles	Lagoon Area, Square Miles	Native Population
Namorik (Baring)	1.07	3.25	461
Ebon (Boston)	2.22	40.09	747
Gilbert Islands (16)	114.12	· 777.60	27,709 (1947)
Northern District			
Little Makin (Makin Meang, Pitt)	2.80	....	965
Butaritari (Makin, Touching)	4.50	103.68	1821
Marakei (Matthew)	3.94	7.57	1797
Abaiang (Charlotte)	11.05	89.78	2803
Central District			
Tarawa (Knox, Cook)	7.73	132.67	3529
Maiana (Gilbert, Hall)	10.39	63.57	1422
Abemama (Hopper, Roger)	6.57	51.12	1171
Kuria (Woodle)	4.98	....	313
Aranuka (Henderville)	5.97	9.21	366
Southern District			
Nonouti (Sydenham)	9.83	143.00	2000
Tabiteuea (Drummond)	19.00	141.00	3778
Beru (Francis)	8.15	15.00	2225
Nikunau (Byron, Nukunau)	7.00	....	1591
Onotoa (Clerk)	5.21	21.00	1490
Tamana (Rotcher)	2.00	....	883
Arorae (Hope, Hurd)	5.00	....	1555
Ocean Island (Banaba)	2.30	....	1809 (1947)
Nauru (Pleasant)	8.22	....	1545 (1948)†

* *Marshall Islands.* Land and lagoon areas were measured by E. H. Bryan, Jr., using calibrated cross-section paper and U.S. Hydrographic Office Charts. Population estimates are those reported by the Civil Administrator (U.S. Navy), Marshalls district, for the last quarter of 1948. *Gilbert Islands* (*including Ocean Island*). Land areas and population estimates are quoted from an official statement from the Western Pacific High Commission (Suva, Fiji), from the census of June, 1947. The Ocean Island population represents laborers recruited from the Gilberts, and does not include 113 non-natives employed by the Phosphate Commission, nor the indigenous Panabans who were relocated in 1946 at Rambi Island, Fiji. Lagoon areas were computed by the writer, using planimeter and U.S. Hydrographic Office Charts.

† *Nauru.* Population is that of June, 1948, as taken from Australia's first annual report to the United Nations on Nauru administration. It includes 1448 Nauruans and 97 Gilbertese; in addition there are 1370 Chinese laborers and 247 Europeans, most of whom are associated with the phosphate industry.

ENVIRONMENT

CLIMATE

A visitor from the United States mainland would doubtless regard the climate of these islands as pleasant though monotonous. Although humidity and temperatures are high, life in the atolls is definitely more comfortable than in the high islands of the Carolines. This is due in great part to the cooling effect of the trade winds, which flutter the thatch of low-island dwellings nearly every day of the year. The newcomer finds it difficult at first to distinguish between seasons in the Marshalls-Gilberts area, for the differences are slight and depend largely upon wind direction and precipitation. Rainfall is heavy, with some seasonal variation, but work habits are adjusted to the conditions of the moment.

Winds are important in the routine of native life. The seasons are often labeled according to prevailing winds. This region of the Pacific appears to be a meeting ground for trade winds, northeast and

FIGURE 78. Approaching a village from the lagoon. Outrigger canoes are hauled up on the shelving sandy beach or remain anchored in the shallow waters offshore. Back of the beach line, under coconut and pandanus trees, are thatched dwellings and outhouses of Likiep Village on the island and atoll of the same name. Marshall Islands. Photograph by Mason, 1946.

southeast, and capricious westerlies. In the Marshalls, which are north of the equator, "winter" is a season of strong northeast winds that raise whitecaps on the blue waters outside the lagoon from December through April. This is a period of heavy rainfall in the northernmost Gilberts and southern Marshalls. At the same time natives in the southern Gilberts and the phosphate islands are experiencing "summer" with its unsteady east and southeast blows, interspersed with periods of clear, dry weather or with sudden squalls from almost any quarter of the compass. Nauru is strongly influenced by weather conditions in the west, and exhibits an extremely variable climate in this respect from one year to the next; the westerly or "bad weather" season usually occurs from November to February.

Contrariwise, from May to November the wind pattern in the islands undergoes considerable change as the heat equator moves northward. Northeast trades in the Marshalls diminish, and winds shift around to the east and southeast, with occasional westerlies bringing storms to liven up the customary calm weather. This is "winter" in those Gilbert Islands lying below the equator, and southeast trades grow steady and strong to provide fine sailing weather for outrigger canoes. Throughout the islands, gales of hurricane force happen infrequently; indeed they have occurred so rarely as to provide a convenient calendar for older inhabitants to recall events in the uncounted years of their childhood and youth.

Atoll inhabitants are concerned about rainfall because the water supply of low islands is derived almost entirely from that source. Catchment basins and cisterns of concrete have been constructed to conserve the precious water, wherewith to supplement a brackish supply from shallow beach wells. At intervals of about 7 years the marginal areas north and south experience extremely dry conditions, or droughts, at which times water becomes scarce, crops fail, and the populations require subsistence relief. In eastern Micronesia the terms "wet" and "dry" must be used in a relative sense, for the mean annual rainfall in the northern atolls, such as Ujelang, is about 75 inches as compared with a "wet" atoll like Jaluit, which customarily receives about 160 inches. In general, rainfall tends to decrease from west to east, reflecting the influence of westerlies. Thus at Nauru as much as 180 inches of rain has been recorded in a year when westerlies were frequent and strong, whereas only 15 inches were received during another year when these winds occurred but rarely. In the wet islands of the southern Marshalls and northernmost Gilberts, some rain falls on one or two days out of three, and with less variation monthly than in the dry islands. Throughout the low islands wet weather appears to be correlated with proximity of the heat belt and shifting winds, especially westerlies. Trade winds by comparison are dry winds.

Monotonous regularity from day to day and from month to month is an outstanding characteristic of temperature in these islands. The annual mean for most of the area is about 81° F, with no more than 1 or 2 degrees variations from that in the mean of any month. Exceptions to this generalization may be found in some of the Gilbert Islands where temperatures average several degrees higher. Daily temperatures are more variable, but even so, the average range is only 10 to 12 degrees. The maximum temperature recorded in the islands is 101° F, the minimum is 68° F. Although midday is frequently scorching, relief is readily available in shaded areas, and human activity assumes a slower pace to conform with the weather. Evenings are frequently cool enough to warrant a blanket or mat covering for the sleeper. Natives, accustomed as they are to an even temperature, shiver visibly when a sudden decrease of only a few degrees is experienced, such as often follows a heavy thunderstorm.

SOILS AND MINERALS

The low islands have poor soil, and minerals are non-existent except for certain deposits of phosphate and phosphatic-guano. The limestone reef-rock base of the low islands is covered with only a shallow layer of coral sand and decomposed vegetable matter. This soil lacks those elements necessary for profitable cultivation of more than a limited number of food products, such as coconut, pandanus, and some coarse taro. It is exceedingly porous, and rainwater quickly soaks through to the coral rock below. Occasionally areas in the interior of larger islands possess a richer humus 7 or 8 feet deep. Fertile earth has sometimes actually been imported by canoe and ship from adjacent high islands in Micronesia and Polynesia. Under European direction, natives have also tried to build better soil by burying dead leaves and decayed timbers in pits located at intervals in the plantation area. Breadfruit, bananas, and papayas are planted in the compost accumulated in these pits.

Guano, the droppings of birds that frequent outlying uninhabited islands, is to be found here and there in the area, and some low-grade phosphate exists on certain low islands, such as Ebon in the Marshalls. Nauru and Ocean Island, of course, afford exceptional instances of high-grade phosphate deposits worthy of commercial exploitation on a large scale.

NATURAL VEGETATION

Although relatively little work has been done on the flora of the Gilberts, Ocean Island, and Nauru, available evidence indicates a remarkable resemblance of plant life to that of the Marshall Islands, which has been more adequately described. The low coral islands are covered with a strand or seacoast type of vegetation. Salty air, brackish ground water, and inadequacies of soil constitute an environment in which few plants can survive. The trees, shrubs, vines, herbs, and grasses of a strand flora are well adapted to such unfavorable conditions. For example, as protection from salty spray blown over the island from the outer reef, leaves of many plants are very leathery or fleshy, and the seeds and fruits are specially constituted to withstand long immersion in salt water and yet be capable of germination when cast ashore on another island.   Although as many as fifty families may be represented in a low island flora, the variety of plant life is meager when compared with that of high islands.

Sparse, bushy, scrubby forest is the typical plant cover in the drier northern Marshalls. Along the outer beach above high-tide limits occurs the low bush *Scaevola frutescens,* together with the creeping *Triumphetta procumbens* and *Boerhavia diffusa.*   Inland from the beach, brush is mixed with the hardwoods *Pisonia grandis* and *Messerschmidia argentea,* all of them festooned and tangled with vines. Coconuts have usually been planted throughout the island by native inhabitants, and almost anywhere *Pandanus tectorius* provides fruit for food, leaves for thatch and mats, and wood for building.   Arrowroot is also common.   The southern Marshalls atolls have more luxuriant plant life and numerous species that are quite absent in the less fortunate isles, including breadfruit, hibiscus, and taro.   Around their dwellings, native residents have planted other food producers, such as papaya, banana, lime, breadfruit, coconut, and pandanus. Occasional mangrove swamps may be found on the wetter islands.

LAND FAUNA

Without the many species introduced by foreign agency, the land fauna of the islands would be extremely limited.   Almost all the birds are of the shore and sea variety, such as the pigeon, heron, cuckoo, curlew, turnstone, wandering tattler, plover, sandpiper, and other migratory birds, and the booby, frigate-bird, tropic-bird, noddy, white "love bird," and other terns.   Insect life is abundant, although relatively mild.   There are butterflies, beetles, grasshoppers, dragonflies, mosquitoes (but not the malaria-bearing *Anopheles*), ants, spiders, lice, scorpions, and centipedes.   The European housefly has become a distinct pest in many islands, and other introduced insects from Asia or the Americas threaten the existence of certain food crops. The only indigenous mammal is the rat, although it has been supplemented since by several species of European rodent.   The islands are free of snakes, but a few small lizards are found, including the gecko and an iguana introduced by the Japanese into the Marshalls. Dogs and cats are common pets, and the islanders raise pigs, chickens, and ducks for festival food.   Goats and cattle occur in limited numbers on some islands, but the return on labor expended is usually deemed insufficient by the natives to warrant expansion of this activity.

MARINE FAUNA

In describing the physical environment up to this point, much emphasis has been placed on the limited or marginal nature of soils, of drinking water, of vegetation, and of animal life on land. In striking contrast to this, the visitor to the coral atolls will discover practically limitless numbers and varieties of fishes and shellfish in the quiet lagoons, on the shallow reefs along the shore, and on the fringing reefs around the islands. This vast marine resource, from the small tropical fishes of home-aquarium type to the fighting game fishes that weigh several hundred pounds, has great significance for island peoples, who could not subsist on the restricted resources of land alone. Some of the fishes that frequent the warm waters of reef and shore include angel-fish and butterfly-fish, demoiselles, eels, flounder, flying-fish, goatfish, lizard-fish, Moorish idols, mullet, parrot-fish, puffers, rays, rudder-fish, scorpion-fish, groupers, sharks, squirrel-fish, surgeon-fish, threadfish, trigger-fish, and wrasses, to mention the more important ones. In deeper waters outside the reef, native fishermen seek the albacore, barracuda, oceanic bonito, crevalles, yellow-fin tuna, wahoo, and swordfish, as much for sport as for food. Some fishes are poisonous, but the natives known the edible quality of each fish in their home waters so that they are rarely ever poisoned.

Next to fish, probably the most important source of protein in the native diet is the shellfish and other marine invertebrates. At low tide fishermen eagerly search the reefs for crabs, spiny lobsters, clams, squid, and octopuses. Of these the giant clam (*Tridacna gigas*) is a spectacular creature weighing 400 to 500 pounds. Often its shell is 2 to 3 feet long. Certain mollusks are more valuable for their shell than for their flesh. For example, the cowries once used by natives for money are now strung together in souvenir belts and necklaces; the many varieties of *Murex, Conus, Pterocera,* and *Spondylus* are valued by tourists as bric-a-brac; the pearl oyster furnishes mother-of-pearl for inlay work in other tourist handicrafts; *Trochus niloticus* is harvested in some islands as an export item for the button trade; and conchs and cowries are still adapted by islanders as useful articles for everyday use in their homes. Sea cucumbers were once dried and shipped to China as trepang, or bêche-de-mer, a prized delicacy for the table, but their value has decreased considerably. In some atolls sponge culture offers possibilities for increasing local cash income, and the Hawksbill turtle supplies a large horny shell that can be utilized in the handicraft industry of the islands.

THE ISLANDERS

When describing the islanders and their manner of life one must recognize the existence in eastern Micronesia of certain groupings of people, founded upon differences and similarities that are the product of historic accident and the relationship between individuals and their total environment.   Thus the Marshallese are a fairly homogeneous people in their physical constitution, their langauge, and their customs.   The Gilbertese form another grouping, in most respects not

Figure 79.   One narrow street for each village.   Household units are spaced at intervals along both sides of the single, sanded village street.   This view of the temporary home of Bikinians at Rongerik Atoll, Marshalls, illustrates the arid conditions of the northern islands under which most tree growth is limited to coconut and pandanus.   Photograph by Mason, 1946.

greatly dissimilar from their northern neighbors but sufficiently so to deserve separate treatment.   Regional differences within the group may be discerned, as between Ralik and Radak in the Marshalls and between northern and southern Gilbertese; and yet the Radak people are more like those from Ralik than are any of the Gilbert islanders. The indigenous populations of Ocean Island and Nauru each possess certain diagnostic traits that compel the observer to establish two more categories, Banabans (Ocean Island) and Nauruans.

RACE

Further investigations are necessary in the physical anthropology of the coral-isle inhabitants, but available studies indicate an exceedingly mixed population. Basically there is evidence for a primitive Caucasoid (White) strain dominating one of very early Negroid character, possibly with some Mongoloid elements also present. The islanders, in what constitutes a transitional area, are closely related to Polynesians as well as to other Micronesians. Polynesians are judged to be a blend of Caucasoid, Negroid, and Mongoloid, with more White characteristics dominant than in most Micronesians. It is related that Polynesians from Samoa in recent centuries migrated northward into the Gilberts, and from thence on to Ocean Island and Nauru, mixing in varying degree with the indigenous populations. In general the Marshallese, and also the northern Gilbertese, are distinguished by medium stature, slender build, dark skin, brown eyes, broad and flat noses, straight-to-curly black hair, full and rather everted lips, and sparse body hair. By contrast, in those islands invaded by Polynesians the inhabitants tend to be taller, heavier, lighter of skin, with narrower nose, and hair that is more often wavy and dark brown.

LANGUAGE

The indigenous languages of the area are all interrelated, though studies of Marshallese, Gilbertese, Banaban, and Nauruan have not been sufficiently intensive to establish the exact nature and degree of their relationship. It is agreed, however, that all belong to the Micronesian branch (together with Carolinian languages of Kusaie, Ponape, and Truk) of an extensive Malayo-Polynesian family. Certainly the common language of the Marshall Islands is Marshallese, with its two dialects of Ralik, or western chain, and Radak, or eastern chain. As between Ralik and Radak, speech differences are mainly those of pronunciation and vocabulary, and so slight that Radak speakers have no difficulty in understanding those from Ralik. If Marshallese were compared with English, for example, the Ralik-Radak distinction would find a parallel in the differing dialects of New England and the Deep South in the United States. Furthermore, just as speakers of English find German unintelligible, so do Marshall islanders regard Gilbertese. In the Gilberts and at Ocean Island, Gilbertese of some sort is spoken by all, with possibly three dialect areas; northern and southern Gilberts and Ocean Island. Nauruan,

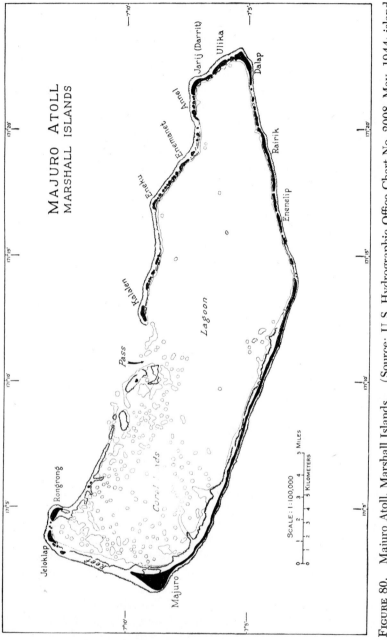

FIGURE 80.   Majuro Atoll, Marshall Islands.   (Source: U.S. Hydrographic Office Chart No. 2008, May, 1944; island names from Marshallese informant.)

although it contains many Gilbertese loan words, is a language separate from both Gilbertese and Marshallese. At Kusaie before the Second World War native students from many parts of Micronesia came together to study at the American mission school. There Banabans and Gilbertese understood each other with no trouble, but could not communicate with Marshallese and Nauruans; the Marshallese, in turn, could comprehend the speech of no other group.

ECONOMIC LIFE

Upon a provident sea and an infertile soil is founded the economy of the islands, which even today is largely self-sustaining. The islanders, classed among the primitive world's best fishermen, skillfully and daringly exploit the bountiful resources of the ocean with a score of devices, including spear and line, trap and net. In the atolls a proper meal, roasted over hot coals or steamed for hours in the ubiquitous earth oven, must contain both flesh and vegetable foods. Fish and shellfish provide the first element of this formula, although pigs and poultry are popular on festival occasions. Vegetable food means either fruits or tubers. Coconut and pandanus are old reliables, supplemented by breadfruit in season and by bananas and papayas in more fortunate islands. Tubers include taro, sweet potatoes, and arrowroot. Island dwellers, when thirsty, generally drink the sweetish milk of green coconuts, or fresh toddy bottled a drop at a time from slashed inflorescences of coconut trees.

Well adapted to a tropical environment was the dress of former years when bare foot, bare head, and naked waist enjoyed favor with all. Garments of cloth have now displaced kilts and skirts of matting and leaves in most islands; new standards of modesty have been successfully introduced by missionaries. Tattooed bodies and pierced ears, once prime requisites of the properly attired, are in evidence today only among the aged. Still persistent and flourishing in more youthful circles is the delightful custom of wearing brightly hued blossoms in the hair, back of the ears, or neatly strung in floral crowns and necklaces.

To be self-sufficient in the coral atolls implies a certain skill in the working of wood and fibers. Wall panels, floor and sleeping mats, basketry, and souvenirs for the tourist are deftly plaited from pandanus and coconut leaves by women. The breadfruit tree and several native hardwoods are laboriously felled and shaped with ax and adze into canoe hulls and building timbers. No nails or screws pierce the mortised house joints, which are bound firmly with strong lashings of coconut cord or sennit. Formerly the men ground pieces of shell into fishhooks and adze blades, but iron and steel imports have rendered this industry obsolete. Lacking in the islanders' repertoire of skills are stonework, pottery making, loom weaving, and metal work.

As might well be expected of people surrounded by leagues of open water, atoll inhabitants are skilled in navigation and seamanship. Their single-float outrigger canoes are models of craftsmanship that bring joy to the hearts of true seafarers. Knife-bladed hulls, carefully hewn from the breadfruit logs or stitched together from odd-sized planks where larger timbers are unavailable, cut sharply through the waves with a power provided by large triangular sails. Ashore the only aids to transportation are narrow foot trails that join village to village the length of the narrow islands.

Settlements are not large, several hundred persons at most and scattered along shore, preferably on the lagoon side. A single street strewn with coral sand and pebbles is flanked on either side by saddle-roofed rectangular dwellings, thatched with pandanus and built on short piles or directly on the ground. As in the surrounding yard, huts are often floored with coral gravel beneath large mats of pandanus leaf. Little other furniture exists nor is it needed. All meals are cooked outside under a thatched lean-to. Every household comprises a working unit of closely related individuals who eat and sleep together. Within the community, where everyone is a jack-of-all-trades, the household or extended family cooperates with other similar units in larger work projects, such as house building, canoe construction, community fishing, and the like. Each village has a common meeting place, which in the Gilberts attains the magnificent proportions of the *maneaba,* a thatched structure at times exceeding 100 feet in length.

SOCIAL CUSTOMS

The average American visiting these islands observes with envy the personal security that is a social heritage of native children. At birth the natives automatically acquire membership in a family, a clan, a local group, and a social class, each providing them with the comforting feeling of belonging. An islander is first and foremost affiliated with his family group, which traditionally is much more extensive than its Western counterpart. This basic unit of island society is not limited to parents and siblings, but may also include grandparents, aunts, uncles, and cousins, as prescribed by local custom. Such a

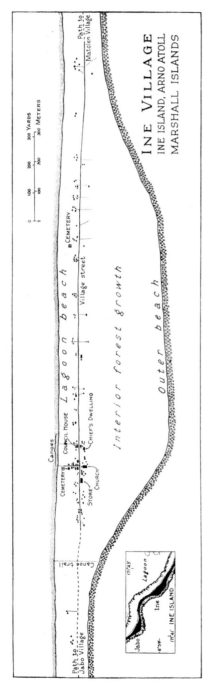

FIGURE 81. Ine Village, Arno Atoll, Marshall Islands. (Sources: author's notes, May, 1946; U.S. Hydrographic Office Chart No. 6004, 1st ed., May, 1944.)

kin group, numbering fifteen to twenty persons, may occupy a single dwelling or, if space is restricted, is split into two or three adjacent households. Economic, social, and political activities of each extended family are directed by a headman, usually the oldest living male member.

An islander also belongs to a local group, either hamlet or larger village. A customary local group in eastern Micronesia comprises a number of extended families not uncommonly interrelated through generations of inbreeding.

Considerable importance is attached to blood relationship. Although kinfolk in both male and female lines are recognized, more attention is directed to those of one line only. In the Marshalls and Nauru the system is matrilineal (descent through the female line); in the Gilberts and Ocean Island the tendency is to favor the male side (patrilineal). Inheritance of property, succession to office, and clan affiliation are all determined according to this unilinear principle. A clan is a group of people claiming to be descended through either the male or the female line from a common ancestor who usually has become legendary. Obligations between clansmen include the offer of food, shelter, and other assistance to visiting members from other islands, thus providing a kind of reciprocal hostel service.

Stratified groups of nobility and commoners persist in most of the atolls. A half century ago, when island feudalism was strongest, nobles could be distinguished from those of common birth by differences in dress and diet, living facilities, and mode of recreation. At the summit of the socio-political hierarchies were paramount chiefs each independent of the others and each exercising absolute control over life and property within his respective domain. The masses worked as tenants on the land, supervised by persons of higher rank who were accountable, and often closely related, to the paramount chiefs. A portion of all produce from land and sea was rendered as tribute to the ruling class. The privilege of birth was accompanied by a responsibility for organizing and maintaining a strong fighting force, well equipped with clubs, slings, and spears, food provisions, and canoe transport, because the atolls at that time were continually shaken by bloody combat between petty feudal states seeking to seize more land or avenge an insult. The autocratic character of those political regimes has largely disappeared under pressure from missions and foreign administrations, but subtle qualities of the period linger, though not readily apparent to casual visitors. A more Western type of community government operates, island councils cooperating with native magistrates, scribes, and policemen.

RELIGION

For nearly a century the untiring efforts of Protestant and Catholic missionaries have influenced native religious life, with the result that Christian taboos, hymn singing, daily prayer, and regular church attendance have all but eradicated the ancient practices in most communities. The Marshallese have probably changed more in this respect as evidenced by their opinions about the "heathen" Gilbertese to the south. Even in the Marshalls, however, Christianity is in many ways a veneer of formal practices thinly laid over persisting beliefs and attitudes of paganism. The aboriginal ritual, often indistinguishable from rites of magic and sorcery, was intimately bound up with food production, social control, treatment of illness, and almost every facet of daily living. The external world was conceived to be populated with numberless gods and spirits dwelling in the sea and the soil, in animals, trees, and inanimate stones.

ADJUSTMENT TO WESTERN CIVILIZATION

Island cultures received their first shock from the rough and brutal behavior of early nineteenth century whalers and adventurers. From 1850 on, recovery was aided by the sincere efforts of missionaries and administrators, but inevitably changes continued. At first native populations declined rapidly as trade guns provoked more deadly civil wars, as slavers on "blackbirding" voyages removed able young men to plantations in Central America, and as introduced diseases drew heavy toll from a people lacking immunity. That downward trend of population reversed after 1900 as the result of more efficient medical service and of law and order established under foreign administration.

Although the total number of Whites in the islands does not equal 1 per cent of the aboriginal population, activities of foreigners have been effective in altering the old customs. Traders satisfied new cravings for imported foods, for metal tools and utensils, for sailcloth and fishing tackle, kerosene, and clothing materials. To pay for these goods, natives increased their coconut plantings and processed copra for export; tourist handicrafts, marine products, and wages have provided supplementary income in some islands. Under German, British, Japanese, and American administrations, autocratic island monarchies have been giving way to government by village councils and tax-supported native officials. Catholic and Protestant missions not only modified indigenous patterns of religious activity and moral values but also contributed much in terms of elementary education for island children. Nearly 100 per cent of the people are literate in their own tongue, although programs for advanced training are few and undeveloped. Selected students have gone to Suva, Guam, and other Pacific centers for special work in medicine, carpentry, navigation, and teacher training.

In the Second World War occupation by Japanese forces and destructive attacks by Allied aircraft brought hardship and death to island peoples. After the battles of Tarawa, Kwajalein, and Eniwetok, the atolls revealed tremendous losses in capital goods and natural resources. Native communities were uprooted to make way for military installations. Since the war, economic and psychological recovery in eastern Micronesia has been slow, as elsewhere in the world. The problem demanding greatest attention in the islands relates to the balance between increasing populations and limited economic resources. Extensive readjustment of island economies seems to be required; however, the problem is not simple.

ECONOMIC DEVELOPMENT

The phosphate resources on Ocean Island and Nauru save eastern Micronesia from being classed as an economic liability. Native produce for export is limited practically to copra, the dried meat of coconuts. In prewar years marine products were available in minor quantities, but fishery experts agree that commercial fishing in the area will never be a major industry. Island handicrafts for sale to tourists have possibilities that deserve further exploration. Phosphate mining is a non-native enterprise, supported by British capital and imported Chinese and native contract labor. The quality and extent of Nauru and Ocean deposits have qualified these two islands as one of the wealthiest production areas in the Pacific. Land rents and royalties on mined phosphate provides the native communities a handsome income as compared to that of non-phosphate islands. Provisions and manufactured goods are primary imports, in the consumption of which the native population participates in proportion to its cash income. A high percentage of manufactures shipped to Ocean Island and Nauru is, of course, consigned to the phosphate interests.

COPRA PRODUCTION

Copra affords practically the only source of income for natives in the coral atolls. The main expenditure is labor, since essential equipment is limited to machetes, cutting knives, drying racks, and storage facilities. Coconut plantings in regularly spaced rows were started in the late nineteenth century under European management, although nearly every plantation in the islands today is owned and operated by native producers on a family basis. Men husk the mature brown fruit and with machetes crack the exposed nuts in half. The firm white flesh, pried from the shells in pieces of varying size, is spread

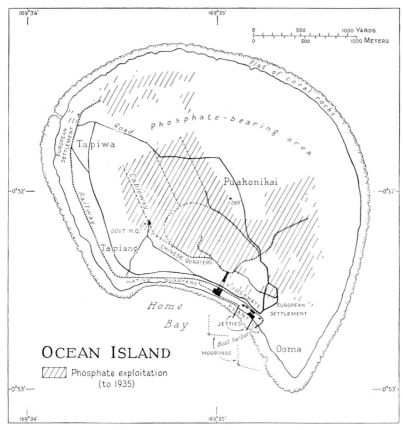

FIGURE 82. Ocean Island. (Sources: A. F. Ellis, *Ocean Island and Nauru*, end map, Sydney, 1936; U.S. Hydrographic Office Chart No. 2179 [C], 6th ed., August, 1944.)

on mats or wire-mesh racks to dry in the sun or over low-burning fires, depending on existing weather conditions. When sufficiently dried, copra is sacked and stored to await the trader's arrival, at which time the product is graded, weighed, and purchased from native producer or through cooperative marketing societies. Companies in Europe and America purchase copra for use in manufacturing soap, margarine, and glycerin. Prior to the Second World War an estimated 50,000 acres in the low islands were planted to coconuts, and more than 10,000 tons of copra were produced annually in peak years. During the war copra production ceased entirely. Many islands were rendered unfit for future planting because of bombing damage and conversion into coral-packed airfields, groves became choked with heavy undergrowth among the coconut trees, and production and marketing organization was disrupted. By 1948 high prices for copra had done much to rehabilitate the industry.

PHOSPHATE INDUSTRY

Inextricably bound up with the history of Ocean Island and Nauru is the development of the phosphate deposits on these small isolated

FIGURE 83.   Cutting copra, Gilbertese method. Mature nuts are chopped in half, the ripe coconut meat being extracted in small pieces with a knife. Marshallese usually husk the nuts first, cut the shells in two, and expose the meat to the sun for a short time, after which the coconut may easily be removed in one piece.

islands. Modern methods and efficient equipment resulted in an annual export just prior to the Second World War of 1,250,000 tons of phosphate. German and Japanese offensives from 1940 on, together with Allied air retaliation culminating in recovery of the islands from Japan in late 1945, brought about almost complete destruction of plant facilities. The task of reconstruction in postwar years has been gigantic, but both islands toward the end of 1948 were reported as again producing, sometimes at the high rate of 700,000 tons per

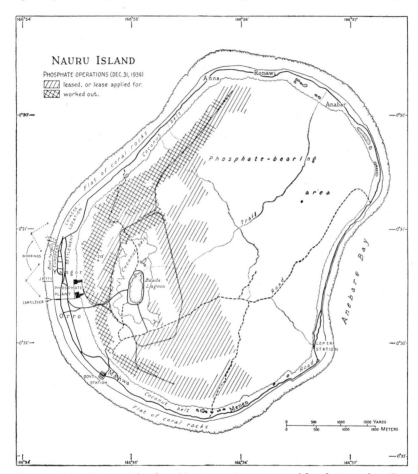

FIGURE 84. Nauru Island. (Sources: Commonwealth of Australia, *Report to the Council of the League of Nations on the Administration of Nauru for 1939*, end map, Canberra, 1940; A. F. Ellis, *Ocean Island and Nauru*, end map, Sydney, 1936; U.S. Hydrographic Office Chart No. 2179 (B), 6th ed., August, 1944.)

annum. If prewar output is maintained once the industry is rehabilitated, it is estimated that phosphate reserves on the two islands will hold out for another fifty to sixty years.

The natural wealth of the two islands was first exploited by the

Pacific Phosphate Company (formerly the Pacific Islands Company) until 1919, when at a cost of £3,500,000 the company was bought out by Australia, New Zealand, and the United Kingdom. These three governments agreed to establish the British Phosphate Commissioners to manage production and export of the phosphate. Native land-owners were protected in their hereditary rights by guarantees of rents on lands being mined and of royalties on every ton of the exported product. Hand methods of production have been discarded for more effective mechanized equipment, and Chinese laborers recruited at Hongkong on a contract basis supplement casual native labor. Steam shovels load phosphate at the quarries into trucks and small railways transport the material to wet bins at the plateau edge. The rock next slides down inclines to storage bins on the low coastal foreland, being crushed and dried mechanically en route. Loading of vessels has always been a difficulty at Ocean Island and Nauru for lack of normal harbor facilities. This problem was neatly solved at Nauru by constructing a huge cantilever loader that extends a quarter-mile offshore beyond the reef. Under normal weather conditions vessels are brought under the cantilever and moored while their holds are quickly filled with an endless stream of phosphate brought from storage on long conveyor belts (Fig. 86). Once loaded the freighters head south to fertilizer plants in Australia and New Zealand where the crude product is treated with sulphuric acid, producing superphosphate that is soluble in water and can then be used to enrich the soils of farmlands Down Under.

THE MARSHALL ISLANDS

On July 18, 1947, the Marshall Islands became a part of the Trust Territory of the Pacific, a strategic area trusteeship under the United Nations with the United States designated as administering authority. Thus the Marshallese entered one more phase of foreign government, which began in 1885 when Germany declared a protectorate over the islands. These thirty-four atolls and isolated islands, eleven of which support no permanent population, are divided geographically and culturally into the Radak (sunrise) chain and the Ralik (sunset) chain, which parallels the former about 150 miles to the west. More than 10,000 natives live there in over 100 small communities scattered over 70 square miles of land; the average population density is 150. Although the northern islands possess better fishing possibilities, the southern area is favored in terms of climate, soils, and vegetation.

When Protestant workers of the Boston Mission entered the Marshalls in 1857, responding to rumors that whalers and beach combers were demoralizing the natives, they encountered a number of petty warring states led by paramount chiefs who exercised absolute control over the common people. Under foreign influence this feudal system has withered, but the strong matrilineal family and clan organization of Marshallese society continues to function.

Japan, an American ally in the First World War, occupied the Marshalls in 1914 and sent the Germans home. The islands prospered economically as part of the mandate assigned to Japan by the League of Nations in 1920. Then, about 1937, in violation of the mandate, Japan began to fortify the area. Jaluit, Mili, Maloelap, Wotje,

Figure 85. Islanders make expert seamen. The island outrigger canoe is being supplemented by larger native-built sailing craft of foreign design. This five-ton sloop is owned and operated by the people of Ailuk Atoll, Marshalls. Photograph by Mason, 1946.

Kwajalein, and Eniwetok developed into strong air bases and dispersal points for Japanese troops destined to invade the south Pacific after the Pearl Harbor attack. During the Second World War the Marshallese suffered, innocent though they were, and they welcomed the Americans who in January, 1944, struck hard at Kwajalein and Eniwetok to secure the islands as one more step in the advance toward Japan. American military government strove to assist the natives in recovering health and economic security. With the advent of United Nations trusteeship, military government gave way to civil administration.

Kwajalein remains the military center of the islands as well as an essential stopover for trans-Pacific military air traffic; Majuro has been established as the seat of civil administration.   In 1946 the Marshalls again made the headlines when atomic bomb experiments were held at Bikini, and two years later the experiments were repeated at Eniwetok.   The future happiness of the Marshallese rests with them and their American advisers.   The Americans have an active cooperative educational program directed at helping the Marshallese to live a fuller, more secure existence in their changing physical and social environment.

THE GILBERT ISLANDS

When the Japanese Marines occupied Makin, Tarawa, and other islands of the Gilberts in the tumultuous months after the attack on Pearl Harbor, they interrupted an era of British rule that began in 1892 when a protectorate was proclaimed in the Gilberts and in the Polynesian Ellice Islands trailing away to the southeast.   Undisturbed as that half century of paternalistic administration had been it contrasted sharply with the vengeful feuds and bloody civil wars that characterized the Gilberts of earlier decades.   Other Pacific islanders still see in the Gilbertese a proud and sensitive people, intensely jealous of their women and quick to anger at real or supposed affront.   Culturally, the group is divided; the "people of Makin (of the north)" possess a long history of expanding autocratic monarchies akin to those in the Marshalls and the "people of Beru (of the south)" reflect much of Polynesian influence in their more democratic village councils and social organization.   Throughout prevails a tradition of patrilineal inheritance and succession to office as well as a respect for individual rank and clan affiliation.

All sixteen atolls and islands of the Gilbert archipelago are densely populated, most of them subject to periodic destructive droughts. Indeed overpopulation is a pressing problem because 114 square miles of dry land, though more than in the Marshalls, actually supports three times the number of people.   The British were impelled in 1938 to relieve the pressure, at least temporarily, by relocating some 2000 Gilbertese in the uninhabited Phoenix Islands away to the east.   In addition several hundred Gilbertese, some with their families, are recruited each year to work as contract labor on copra plantations in the Line Islands (Fanning, Washington, and Christmas).

The British protectorate acquired the status of Crown Colony in 1916, and eventually came to include not only the Gilberts, Ellices, and Ocean Island, but also the Line Islands and the Phoenix group. The Resident Commissioner, who sits at Tarawa, is responsible to the British High Commissioner of the Western Pacific at Suva, Fiji.

Conditions in the Gilberts during Japanese occupation were harsh, especially in the northern atolls. With American forces, which in late 1943 invaded Tarawa, Makin, and Abemama, went British civil servants to pick up the threads of administration that had been severed two years earlier. Recovery of the islands since the war has been delayed, as elsewhere, by inadequacies of shipping and imports. Copra continues to be the only colony export, excepting Ocean Island phosphate. Elementary education for island children has been resumed by the personnel of the London Missionary Society and the Mission of the Sacred Heart, under government supervision as to standards of curriculum and teacher training.

NAURU AND OCEAN ISLAND

Fifty years of phosphate exploitation have bound Nauru to Ocean Island although culturally and politically their histories remain distinct. Both of them were neglected in the century after discovery. Nauru was brought under the German Marshall Islands protectorate in 1888; Banabans continued alone until 1901, when, recognizing the Ocean's potential wealth, Britain added it to the Gilbert and Ellice islands protectorate.

The First World War by-passed Ocean Island but brought international status to Nauru. In 1914 Australians occupied Nauru and evacuated all Germans to stake a claim, which after the war the League of Nations honored in mandating Nauru to the British Empire; Australia was assigned administrative responsibility. Between 1920 and 1940, under management by the British Phosphate Commissioners, Nauru and Ocean prospered as two of the richest islands in the Pacific. Income from phosphate properties insured a sound educational program, an efficient medical service, and economic security seldom enjoyed by other islanders. The earlier link between Nauru and the Marshalls was parted, and both isolated islands experienced increasing contacts with the Gilbert Islands. As time passed, however, the smaller of the islands, which lacked the natural advantages of Nauru, watched the phosphate workings encroach upon native settlement areas. The British, just before the Second World War, considered the advisability of relocating the Banabans. With this in mind, they purchased Rambi (Rabi) Island in the Fijis with Banaban trust funds, but further action was postponed by the advent of war.

In August, 1942, months after most Europeans and Chinese had been evacuated, Japanese troops seized both islands without resistance. During the war the Japanese removed all natives from Ocean Island

and scattered them to Nauru, Tarawa, and Kusaie in the Carolines. About a thousand Nauruans were transferred in 1943 to Truk, also in the Carolines, to relieve the growing pressure on Nauru. This tragic uprooting of native peoples was brought to an end in 1945 when British troops raised the Union Jack once more on Nauru and Ocean. Three main tasks demanded the attention of occupying forces. First, all Japanese were removed. Second, engineers and imported Chinese and Gilbertese labor set about reviving phosphate production to satisfy the acute fertilizer needs of Australia and New Zealand. Third, thousands of natives awaited repatriation; February, 1946, saw the

FIGURE 86.   Loading phosphate at Nauru cantilever.   The lack of normal harbor facilities at Nauru and Ocean islands presents a problem in transporting over the reef.   This cantilever loader, by which the phosphate is carried on rubber belt conveyors from storage areas on shore to the vessel moored in deep water, replaces the former system of employing punts and lighters.   Nauru.   Photograph by British Phosphate Commissioners, 1931.

successful completion of this last task.   Surviving Nauruans were returned home from Truk.   Some thousand Banabans and Gilbertese relatives were assembled at Tarawa from wartime residences of Nauru, Kusaie, and atolls of the northern Gilberts.   As one group, they sailed south to Rambi to begin life anew on an island with flowing streams, plenty of coconuts for profitable copra production, and an acreage ten times that of the barren rock island that had been their home for centuries.

A postwar sequel in Nauruan history has to do with its new status as a Trust Territory when, on November 1, 1947, the United Nations General Assembly approved a trusteeship agreement for the island, with Australia continuing as administering authority.

REFERENCES

Australia, Governor-general, *Annual Reports to the General Assembly of the United Nations on the Administration of the Territory of Nauru*, Canberra.

———— *Annual Reports to the League of Nations on the Administration of Nauru*, Canberra.

Ellis, Albert Fuller, *Ocean Island and Nauru: Their Story*, Angus and Robertson, Sydney, 1936.

———— *Mid-Pacific Outposts*, Brown and Stewart, Ltd., Auckland, 1946.

Great Britain, Colonial Office, *Annual Reports on the Social and Economic Progress of the People of the Gilbert and Ellice Islands Colony*, London.

Grimble, Arthur, "From Birth to Death in the Gilbert Islands," *Jour. Royal Anthropological Inst.*, Vol. 51, pp. 25–54, 1921.

———— "War Finds Its Way to the Gilbert Islands," *Natl. Geogr. Mag.*, Vol. 83, pp. 71–92, January, 1943.

Japan, South Seas Bureau, *Annual Reports to the League of Nations on the Administration of the South Seas Islands under Japanese Mandate*, Tokyo.

Mahaffy, A., *Western Pacific—Report on a Visit to the Gilbert and Ellice Islands, 1909*, H. M. S. Office (Gt. Brit. Parl.), Command Paper 4992, London, 1910.

Mason, Leonard, *The Economic Organization of the Marshall Islands*, U.S. Commercial Company, Economic Survey of Micronesia, Vol. 9 (microfilm copy in Library of Congress), Honolulu, 1947.

Maude, H. E., *Culture Change and Education in the Gilbert and Ellice Islands*, papers and addresses presented at a seminar conference on education in Pacific countries, 2 vols. (mimeographed), Honolulu, 1936.

Maude, H. C. and H. E., "The Social Organization of Banaba or Ocean Island, Central Pacific," *Jour. Polynesian Soc.*, Vol. 41, pp. 262–301, 1932.

Moore, W. Robert, "Gilbert Islands in the Wake of Battle," *Natl. Geogr. Mag.*, Vol. 87, pp. 129–162, February, 1945.

———— "Our New Military Wards, the Marshalls," *Natl. Geogr. Mag.*, Vol. 88, pp. 325–360, September, 1945.

Rhone, Rosamond Dodson, "Nauru, the Richest Island in the South Seas," *Natl. Geogr. Mag.*, Vol. 40, pp. 559–589, December, 1921.

Spoehr, Alexander, "The Marshall Islands and Trans-Pacific Aviation," *Geogr. Rev.*, Vol. 36, pp. 447–451, July, 1946.

Stephen, Ernest, "Notes on Nauru," *Oceania*, Vol. 7, pp. 34–63, September, 1936.

United States Department of the Navy, *Annual Reports to the United Nations on the Trust Territory of the Pacific*, Washington, D.C.

Wedgwood, Camilla H., "Report on Research Work in Nauru Island, Central Pacific," *Oceania*, Vol. 6, pp. 359–391, June, 1936; Vol. 7, pp. 1–33, September, 1936.

———— "Notes on the Marshall Islands," *Oceania*, Vol. 13, pp. 1–23, September, 1942.

Woodford, C. M., "The Gilbert Islands," *Geogr. Jour.*, Vol. 6, pp. 325–350, July–December, 1895.

11

The Philippine Islands

JOSEPH E. SPENCER

THE SEVEN THOUSAND AND EIGHTY-THREE PHILIPPINE ISLANDS FORM A portion of the long line of island arcs that border the western Pacific Ocean (Fig. 87). Only a third of them bear names. Only 11 contain over 1000 square miles each, 462 measure over one square mile, and most are uninhabitable rocks. Luzon and Mindanao together total two-thirds of the area. The archipelago stretches from Y'ami, 65 miles south of Formosa, to Salwag, 30 miles off the northern coast of Borneo, a distance of 1152 miles. The whole mass is perched uneasily on the edge of the greatest of the oceanic deeps, the Mindanao Trough, just east of the southern Philippines. Active and extinct volcanoes, coral reefs, folded and faulted mountain ranges, and deep alluvial basins have been thrown together into a complex assemblage of landscapes. The many islands are quite unequal in value, in degree of utilization, and in density of population.

LANDSCAPE AND ENVIRONMENT

PHYSICAL GEOGRAPHY

The major physical trends of the archipelago run north-south, with a variable alignment of the structural skeleton. There are at least five structural lines displayed in the southern and central islands. These merge in southern Luzon, causing that island to be chiefly a group of peninsulas joined along a double backbone. This double line dies out in the small Batanes island chain stretching toward Formosa. There are six sections to the full archipelago. From north to south these are the Batanes Islands of the far north, Luzon and minor coastal islands, the central or Visayan group, Mindanao and as-

298

TABLE 1

AREA AND POPULATION OF LARGER PHILIPPINE ISLANDS

Island	Rank by Area	Area Square Miles	Population Totals		Rank by Population
			1918	1948	
Luzon	1	40,420	5,000,000	9,020,000	1
Mindanao	2	36,527	870,000	2,450,000	2
Panay	6	4,445	915,000	1,445,000	3
Negros	4	4,904	540,000	1,430,000	4
Cebu	9	1,702	770,000	1,040,000	5
Leyte	8	2,785	536,000	915,000	6
Samar	3	5,049	320,000	660,000	7
Bohol	10	1,492	320,000	523,000	8
Mindoro	7	3,757	50,000	166,000	9
Masbate	11	1,262	48,000	164,000	10
Catanduanes	12	620	62,000	112,000	11
Jolo	17	323	6,000	111,000	12
Basilan	13	488	2,200	108,000	13
Marinduque	15	367	56,000	86,000	14
Palawan	5	4,549	9,000	65,000	15
Tablas	19	278	32,000	64,000	16
Camiguin, South	32	90	37,000	60,000	17
Biliran	22	207	32,000	55,000	18
Siquijor	27	130	56,000	48,000	19
Guimaras	21	227	27,000	40,000	20
Ticao	29	123	16,000	37,000	21
Siargao	24	180	12,000	33,000	22
Dinagat	16	326	8,000	31,000	23
Panaon	36	70	19,000	30,000	24
Bantayan	42	40	24,000	25,000	25
Sibuyan	23	183	14,000	22,000	26
Total of 26 islands		110,544	9,774,000	18,740,000	
Total for Philippines		115,600	10,314,310	19,234,182	

There are 31 islands with areas of over 100 square miles each. Those not given in the above list each have populations under 20,000. They are, in rank by size: Busuanga, 14th; Polillo, 18th; Tawi Tawi, 20th; Burias, 25th; Culion, 26th; Dumaran, 28th; Balabac, 30th; Samal, 31st.

sociated minor islands, the Palawan-Cuyo chain, and the Sulu Archipelago in the far south.

There is a basic similarity of major physical conditions. The east coasts of Mindanao, Samar, and Luzon are rugged, irregular, and rocky coasts exposed to wind and sea during the period of the north-

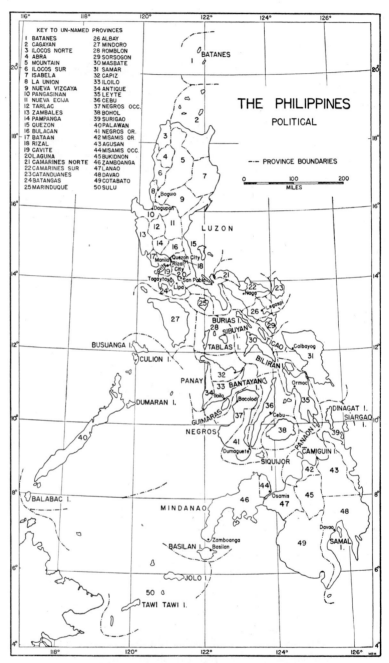

KEY TO UN-NAMED PROVINCES

1 BATANES	26 ALBAY
2 CAGAYAN	27 MINDORO
3 ILOCOS NORTE	28 ROMBLON
4 ABRA	29 SORSOGON
5 MOUNTAIN	30 MASBATE
6 ILOCOS SUR	31 SAMAR
7 ISABELA	32 CAPIZ
8 LA UNION	33 ILOILO
9 NUEVA VIZCAYA	34 ANTIQUE
10 PANGASINAN	35 LEYTE
11 NUEVA ECIJA	36 CEBU
12 TARLAC	37 NEGROS OCC.
13 ZAMBALES	38 BOHOL
14 PAMPANGA	39 SURIGAO
15 QUEZON	40 PALAWAN
16 BULACAN	41 NEGROS OR.
17 BATAAN	42 MISAMIS OR.
18 RIZAL	43 AGUSAN
19 CAVITE	44 MISAMIS OCC.
20 LAGUNA	45 BUKIDNON
21 CAMARINES NORTE	46 ZAMBOANGA
22 CAMARINES SUR	47 LANAO
23 CATANDUANES	48 DAVAO
24 BATANGAS	49 COTABATO
25 MARINDUQUE	50 SULU

THE PHILIPPINES

POLITICAL

--- PROVINCE BOUNDARIES

FIGURE 87. Political subdivisions of the Philippines.

east monsoon. The west coasts of Palawan, Panay, Mindoro, and central Luzon almost repeat the rocky irregular east coast, here swept by the southwest monsoon. Small island chains lie both north and south of the major islands. From the Visayas southward, uplifted coral reefs and marine terraces are common. Here many of the smaller, offshore islands are built-up coral basements. A great many islands show narrow coastal plains encircling mountainous cores that reach somewhat uniform elevations. Many islands are fringed by tidal marshes and swamps. Extinct and active volcanoes are scattered throughout the archipelago; the active volcanoes form the highest mountains. Some volcanoes rise above dissected mountain ranges. Others are set on coastal plains close to sea level. Many of the extinct volcanoes have blown away their tops in past geological times. Earthquakes are common, and about a dozen volcanoes are currently active, causing considerable damage to crop lands and settlements.

Throughout the two major islands, Luzon and Mindanao, deep alluvial basins are set between the mountainous structural timbers of the archipelago. Five of them form wide and cultivable basins. The Cagayan Valley of northeastern Luzon, the Central Plain of Luzon, the Agusan Valley of northern Mindanao, the Davao Gulf Basin of the southeast, and the Cotabato Valley of southwestern Mindanao comprise the list. The main mass of northern Luzon is a rugged mountainous region with deep and narrow canyons. Central southern Luzon is a flat-to-rolling bench containing a large shallow lake, the Laguna de Bay, and dotted with numerous old volcanoes. Northern Mindanao contains extensive plateau lands capped by volcanic materials and topped by a series of volcanic peaks.

These varied features combine to form landscapes that vary in detail from place to place but that form many fundamentally similar environments. The Zambales coast of western Luzon and the western coast of Panay are very similar landscapes, as are the slopes of Mount Apo in southeastern Mindanao and those of Taal Volcano in southwestern Luzon. The fishing villages on the coast of northern Panay and around the northern shore of Manila Bay are set amid the same type of nipa palm and mangrove swamps. But each regional landscape is put together in such a way that it is not reproduced exactly elsewhere. Masbate Island differs from near-by Bohol Island in detailed landscape patterns though the two show many similarities. The narrow northwest coast of Luzon, with its fringe of coastal sand dunes, is like no other island coast anywhere in the archipelago. Naturally there are a few regions that really differ from other parts of the islands. The volcanic Bukidnon-Lanao Plateau of northern Mindanao is not duplicated elsewhere, nor is the massive but rugged landscape of Mountain Province of northern Luzon.

CLIMATIC ZONATION

The Philippine lowlands possess a tropical marine climate. With elevation it gradually changes into mild tropical highland climate. Regional climatic irregularities and local differences are numerous. Except for northern Luzon and the Bukidnon-Lanao Plateau of northern Mindanao, the area of tropical highland is small, scattered, and confined to mountain ranges or isolated volcanic peaks. In the lowlands high temperatures and high humidities are common the year around, though the pronounced dry seasons of some local regions show lower humidities. Annual ranges of temperatures are low, though most Filipinos make a real distinction in sensible climate between the hot and the cold seasons. During the winter, occasional masses of cool air from the Asiatic continent are brought as far as Luzon, producing lowland minimum temperatures below 65° F and bringing the local equivalent of a cold wave. Climatic graphs (Fig. 88) show the variable elements for several typical stations.

Precipitation totals range between about 50 and 180 inches per year (Fig. 88). Local differences in relief and exposure to prevailing winds cause great irregularity in rainfall totals within short distances. The chief physiographic lines of the islands run north-south, and the chief wind movements cross these lines at variable angles. Involved are the northeast monsoon, the southwest monsoon, the northeast trades, and the southeast trades, all regular except for typhoons. The result is precipitation regimes that trend north-south. Generally speaking, the east coast is the rainier, whereas the western half of the islands is somewhat drier, except for exposed positions and suffers a more pronounced dry season. The first three normal wind movements provide the chief seasonal elements in the annual rainfall and weather regimes. The typhoons, however, form the chief climatic threat in the islands. South of a line from the northern tip of Mindanao to the northern tip of Palawan, typhoons are rare and cause little damage. North of a line connecting southern Samar and southern Mindoro, typhoons are numerous and cause severe damage almost every year. The northern half of Luzon and the Batanes Islands suffer the most from these storms. The normal typhoon season is from early August through October, but a few storms come as early as May and some of the most damaging occur during November and December. Seven to 25 typhoons a year sweep out of the western Pacific, across the islands, and north over Formosa and the North China Sea. High

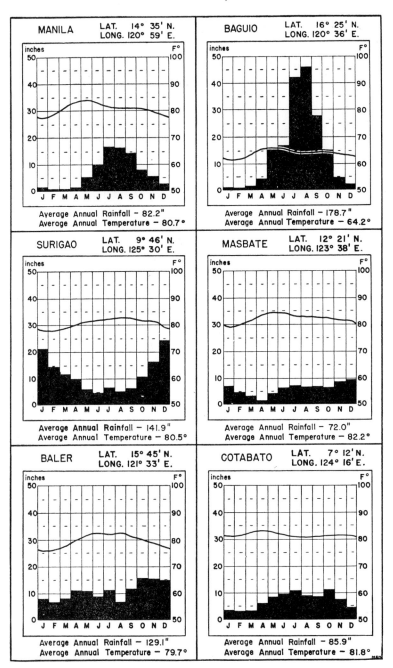

FIGURE 88. Climatic graphs.

winds blow down buildings and trees, and torrential rains cause heavy floods that tie up transport and destroy crops.

The three most important sets of climatic lines for the Philippines are the north-south lines that distinguish the different rainfall regimes, the horizontal contour lines that distinguish temperature regimes, and the northwest-southeast lines that mark the frequency of occurrence of typhoons. All these have repeatedly been plotted by meterologists. Climatologists, however, have not tried defining climatic subregions within the islands.

THE SOILS

The Filipino farmer has taken the soil for granted as a fixed resource in his environment that needed neither thought nor care. Consequently, soil erosion and soil depletion have taken a heavy toll throughout the islands. The pressure upon the land is becoming noticeable in many regions, and areas long occupied by the farmer are wearing out. There are many areas of land remaining idle that have not been depleted by clearing for exploitative farming. Some of these areas possess very rich agricultural soils that produce excellent crops during the first 3 or 4 years of cultivation. If properly farmed, they could continue high productivity rather than decline rapidly in quality.

With quite a varied landscape and a complex regional pattern of climate, it is natural that the soils are varied in composition and irregular in distribution. Most soils lie somewhat on the acid side, and many soils are deficient in lime and the phosphates. For rice culture a slightly acid soil is to be preferred, but rice covers not more than 40 per cent of the cultivated land of the islands. Brown to black clays and clay loams predominate on the lowlands; depleted red and brown clays and stony clays are common on the uplands. Volcanic soils occur widely at all elevations, varying from high to low quality. Many specific soil types are to be found on many different islands in similar situations. The Philippine government is engaged in surveying its soils, and it appears that the final soil map of the islands will be a patchwork affair of many small areas of different soil types.

PLANTS AND ANIMALS

Most of the domesticated plants and all the animals now in the islands have been brought in by immigrants sometime since the first Neolithic farmers appeared. Most of the well-known crops of the world's tropics and subtropics are now grown in the islands. Only the commonest of the domesticated animals are kept in large numbers. There are a great many valuable plants native to the islands that were, in earlier periods, wild and semi-wild plants, never truly domesticated. The appearance of a commercialized, foreign-trade economy has caused the abandonment of many such forest plants. Both the purely wild flora and the fauna are of varied and mixed types, clearly indicating plant and animal migration along the land bridges of southeastern Asia during the glacial periods.

In the original wild state the Philippines were covered by a complex and heavy growth of forest and jungle, pieced out here and there by rank tropical grasses and aquatic plants. It was a forest rich in botanical species, with a wide variety of fruits, fibers, and gums useful to early hunting-gathering cultures. The very heavy and multi-

FIGURE 89.   Harrowing plowed rice fields in August in central Luzon preparatory to transplanting rice.   Animals are carabaos.

canopied forest was a handicap to the primitive farmer, however. And the rank tropical grasses that took over his small clearings, made by the slash-and-burn technique, were even harder to cope with. Such grasses, with other weeds, caused constant abandonment of old farms and the clearing of new lands. This shifting agriculture, termed *caingin* (cay'-ing-in), has significantly reduced the forest cover and promoted the increase of grasslands of rather low value. Commercial forests still cover 44 per cent of the islands' area and form a large economic resource that has not yet been tapped by the commercial production of lumber, rattan, and the gum-resins.

ISLAND REGIONALISM

In a multiple island world unity, sectionalism, and regionalism are complex matters. Out of the 7083 islands less than fifty are large enough to be really important in this connection. The six physically separated island groups mentioned above form the simplest basis for regional distinction. Within these limits further divisions can be made by varied physical and cultural criteria. In general, regionalism is on about the same plane in the islands as in the United States. The Philippines are not yet a mature cultural realm with a well-developed cultural core and distinct local regionalisms that clearly divide the country. A Malaysian-Indian underlayer is covered with a thick veneer of Spanish culture and a variable top crust of American culture that still is being applied. The islands today are in a culturally mobile and changing state. That naturally affects local custom and regionalism quite as much as do the fixed elements in the environment.

Within Luzon there are three rather clear geographic regions that stand apart on both natural and cultural grounds. The northwest coastal lowland, from its people known as the Ilocano country, forms the clearest geographic region of the islands. Its landforms, climate, house types, agriculture, farming customs, handicrafts, lack of decorative flourishes, and its economic and social psychology set off the area and its people. The central highland of northern Luzon, politically combined into Mountain Province, is another fairly clear region based on climate, landforms, people, and culture. The Bicol Peninsula of southeastern Luzon can be similarly set apart, though the distinctions are less clear. In the rest of Luzon cultural and environmental contradictions and confusions prevent division into effective regions.

Certain distinguishing features within the Visayas are clear, others are less tangible. Western Negros and Panay are somewhat similar in agriculture, language, social custom, and economy, but eastern Negros, Cebu, Siquijor, Bohol, and Masbate fall into another group. The separation of many small islands promote detailed local differences. Mindanao, as an active frontier zone of colonization, is changing so rapidly that any clear differentiation is almost impossible. Five or six regional divisions so far depend upon landforms alone, but these major units and some minor ones are taking on agricultural and cultural differences that will, in time, distinguish them fairly clearly. The homeland of the formerly militant and dangerous Moros is becoming filled with Ilocanos, Visayans, and Chinese town-dwelling merchants, so that the Moros and the pagan tribes are becoming submerged. The Sulu Archipelago, as a small-island world of sea-faring Moslem peoples, remains one of the sections least touched by modern occidental culture.

THE DIRECT USE OF THE LANDSCAPE

EARLY AGRICULTURE, FORESTRY, AND MINING

The oldest island hunters wandered over much of the archipelago. Their use of the forest and mineral ranges was limited to selected fruits, rattans, leaf and fiber producers, special kinds of wood, a few animals and birds, and a few sources of stones and shells. Selection of required volumes from the abundant supply was easy. The resources were never exhausted of natural growth or supply in any locality. Only when the neolithic farmer and his bronze and iron

FIGURE 90. Forest half-cleared for caingin farming on the colonial frontier in southern Mindanao. Some small patches had been cropped once already.

age successors came along, with their slash-and-burn technique of clearing the land for simple caingin agriculture, did man begin to alter the composition of the natural plant cover. Tropical grasses spread behind the slash-and-burn farmer and often seriously reduced the value of many local landscapes, and soil depletion followed steadily in the wake of the shifting farmer. But long before the arrival of the Spanish, local subsistence agriculture had worked out crop patterns and farm sequences for most parts of the islands.

At least by the early centuries of the Christian era the islands were a source of selected commercial woods that were shipped to China and as far as India. The islands also were a source of plant fibers long before the Spanish discovered the Philippines. This early exploitation, by Chinese and Malaysian traders, led to the modern trade in *abaca* (the manila hemp used in ropes).

When the knowledge of minerals, mining, and smelting finally came to the islands, just prior to the Christian era, copper, gold, and iron were the only metals produced. Apparently imported tin was used to make bronze. Many of the modern sources of gold and copper were spotted and mined. Low-grade iron ores in small volume are fairly common throughout the islands. The islands were one of the early eastern sources of trade gold, but the discovery of much modern mineral wealth is a contemporary matter.

CONTEMPORARY AGRICULTURE

Since late in the nineteenth century crop yields have not kept pace with the growth of the population, and the Philippines now import much foodstuffs. Yields per acre are low, farm practices are inefficient, farm equipment is primitive, losses from pests are great, and many regions have seriously depleted soils. A progressive shift from the old subsistence agriculture toward commercial crops has been coupled with changing food habits. American supervision did little to encourage scientific improvement in island agriculture. Efforts to correct the situation are beginning to achieve results, but it will be some years before the islands feed themselves and many years before the productive level of Philippine agriculture becomes adequately lifted. About 17,000,000 acres are included in the 1,700,000 farms, but only about 12,000,000 acres are cropped each year, including double cropping. About 22 per cent of the total area is in farms. About 9,000,000 people are engaged in agriculture, some 40 per cent of whom are tenants.

The chief crop is rice, even though production does not meet demand. There are hundreds of varieties, grown under varying conditions on different kinds of fields. They range from well-irrigated and carefully tended lowland tracts through casually planted upland slopes to forest clearings in which rice still is grown by traditional caingin methods. Yields vary accordingly. The total crop covers almost 5,000,000 acres per year, requiring about half the farm-labor force. It is grown in every province, but central Luzon, southeastern Luzon, southern Panay, and central southern Mindanao are the chief surplus regions.

About one-fourth the population subsists chiefly on corn, coarsely ground and cooked like rice. The crop covers about 2,000,000 acres in most years, grown in one to four crops per year. Yields are low since plant pests often are serious. Some corn is grown everywhere, but the eastern Visayan coral limestone islands not suited to rice, and northeastern Luzon, are the main producing regions.

Sweet potatoes lead a group of root crops that include manioc (for cassava or tapioca), yams, taro, white potatoes; and peanuts are grown almost all over the islands. The northern Luzon highland grows almost no manioc or taro but has a large area of sweet potatoes, and vegetables are produced in variety. Among the fruits, bananas, grown everywhere except on the higher mountain lands, are the commonest and cheapest fruit and are important in island economy. Other widespread and common domesticated fruits are the mango, papaya, lanzone, avocado, jackfruit, and breadfruit. Both coffee and cacao are widely but sparingly grown for home use. The total of the root, vegetable, and fruit crops annually amounts to over 1,000,000 acres.

Allowing for a temporary setback caused by wartime destruction of sugar mills, sugar is the chief export crop (Fig. 91). Negros, central Luzon, eastern Panay, and northern Cebu are the large producers of export and domestic sugar. Elsewhere small acreages of cane are put through small plants to yield brown sugar. The sugar acreage has reached about 500,000 acres, largely under the stimulus of free entry into the American market. Domestic consumption normally is about 12 per cent of the annual crop, amounting to perhaps 20 pounds per person.

Coconut products, taken together, are increasing in volume and may become the chief export crop. From central Luzon southward every island grows coconuts. Plantations are common, but most of the crop is harvested by small planters who do not use efficient techniques in growing, harvesting, or preparing their product. The export leaves the country as copra, coconut oil, desiccated coconut, and coconut meal. About 140,000,000 trees cover about 2,500,000 acres, with about 100,000,000 trees of bearing age.

Abaca was the chief export crop until sugar and coconut surpassed it. The islands still hold a monopoly over the world's supply of manila hemp fiber, but may soon lose it to Middle America and the East Indies. Southeastern Luzon, Leyte, and southeastern Mindanao are the chief producers, though some abaca is grown throughout the Visayas, Mindanao, and Sulu. Prior to 1941 the crop averaged about 725,000 acres. Postwar liquidation of Japanese plantations in southeastern Mindanao has reduced the acreage to about 650,000 acres. Reduced productivity and altered basis of production are

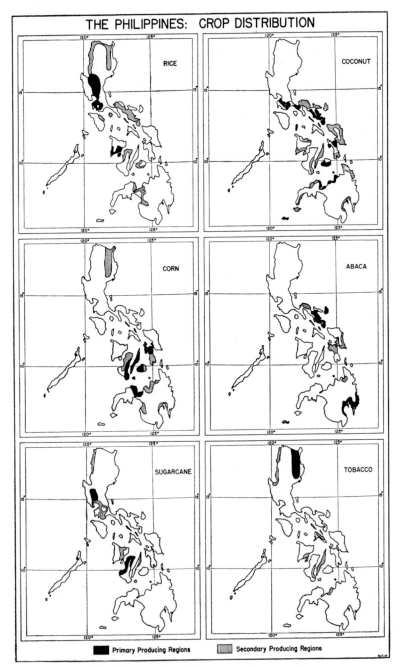

FIGURE 91.   Agricultural products of Philippines.

factors in the possible loss of the monopoly in the face of large world demand.

Tobacco once was a leading export, but, under American competition, the islands now import more tobacco products than they export. Grown in small patches almost everywhere, northeastern Luzon and Cebu are leading producers, with the total crop about 150,000 acres. Pineapple is widely grown as a minor home crop but, on an American-managed plantation in northern Mindanao, is becoming an important export crop.

The ten major Philippine crops, ranked by value of product, are rice, sugar cane, coconut, corn, abaca, bananas, sweet potatoes, manioc, tobacco, and the mango. Ranked by acreage they are rice, coconut, corn, abaca, sugar cane, sweet potatoes, bananas, tobacco, manioc, and the mung bean.

Wartime slaughtering of animals set the islands back many years. The animal population supplies neither adequate draft power nor a sufficient meat supply. Filipinos eat more meat than most orientals, though much less than the average American. In order of rank, hogs, carabao (the island term for the water buffalo), cattle, and goats, with chickens and ducks, are the only numerous members of the animal and fowl groups.

FOREST UTILIZATION

The area of commercial forest in 1949 amounted to about 32,000,-000 acres, widely distributed over the islands and almost entirely government-owned. This was supplemented by about 10,000,000 acres of non-commercial second growth and cutover lands. With the exception of the central lowland of Luzon and the islands of Panay and Cebu, no populous regions lack easy access to timber. The usual lack is for facilities in turning timber into usable lumber. In many heavily settled areas too little timber remains to justify modern-powered sawmills. Inadequate transportation prevents easy distribution of finished lumber. Hand sawing of remaining timber resources still goes on in many local areas, producing beautiful slabs of wood for home use. The present state of forest utilization is the combined result of wartime destruction of lumber mills and the natural state of affairs in a country lacking economic maturity. Northern Negros, Mindoro, and northeastern Mindanao are the chief sources of commercial lumber.

Though no accurate timber survey has been made, the volume of commercial timber has been estimated at 450,000,000,000 board feet, about half of which is reasonably accessible. The annual growth rate probably exceeds 3,000,000,000 board feet per year. Over 3000 species of trees grow to more than one foot in diameter. Forest destruction by caingin cultivators and colonial settlers is serious. Most commercial lumber now marketed represents about sixty species, sold under about twenty separate wood names. The annual lumber cut has seldom gone above 1,000,000,000 board feet per year, now insufficient to satisfy the reconstruction demand and the foreign-trade market. There is every reason to believe that the foreign-trade market can grow to become a valuable part of the international trade pattern.

The islands are an important source of rattans, now increasingly entering domestic and export markets. There is a growing shift from the export of raw rattan to the export of finished rattan furniture. From a widespread swamp fringe around many islands comes a large annual cut of mangrove firewood and a variable cut of nipa palm fronds for building cheaper houses. A wide assortment of gums, resins, and extracts are produced all over the islands for domestic use and a small foreign-trade volume. In many regions wild fruits are important in local food economy. A variety of woods for tools and agricultural implements, many medicinal agents, and other items of domestic use are forest-derived but on a local and quite unorganized basis. Philippine forests possess a considerable number of useful plants, not now being exploited, that could be developed into important products.

FISHERIES

The annual per capita consumption of fish in the islands runs well above 50 pounds, though it is unequally divided between coast and interior. Rice and fish are the two most important items in the average menu. Despite this emphasis on fish in the diet, the fishing industry of Philippine waters has not been highly developed by Filipinos. Japanese fishermen, prior to 1941, supplied a considerable share of the fresh and salted supply, and American and Japanese canneries supplied a tinned volume for consumers in island interiors. The lakes, marshes, irrigated rice fields, canals, and rivers, all over the islands, give up a volume of small fish for home use. Every island coast is fringed by fishing villages, from which small craft work the immediate coastal waters by trap, net, and hook-and-line. There are almost no large, deep-water fishing craft owned by Filipinos. An intensive survey and developmental program are in progress in an attempt to make the islands self-productive and self-sufficient in one of its special food deficits.

The Filipinos have highly developed one aspect of the fishing industry, catering to urban markets. This is the raising of one fish, the bangos, in diked ponds in the mangrove swamp fringe of many tidal estuaries and bays. In 1948 about 155,000 acres of swamp and marsh had been converted to fish ponds.

CONTEMPORARY MINING

The Philippines are newcomers in the ranks of important mineral producers. Native artisans have mined and worked with gold, copper (and bronze by preparation), and iron for centuries in small amounts. Many reports of numerous minerals turned up during Spanish times, but little activity occurred beyond gold mining. It was not until the early 1930's that real development began in the mining industry. The value of mine products jumped from just under $2,000,000 in 1928 to over $47,-000,000 in 1940, the last prewar year of full records. Destruction during the war set miners back several years, and, by 1949, the industry had only partially recovered its losses. In coming years the mining industry should continue to grow more productive, of real value to island economy. However, the known range of minerals is not as broad as is needed to turn the islands into a strong, industrialized country. Thorough mineral surveys, in progress, will require several years to complete.

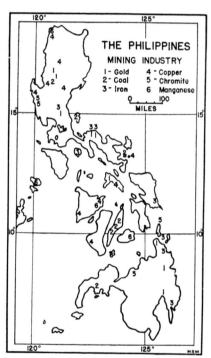

FIGURE 92. Mining industry of the Philippines.

The precious metals are the most valuable in financial return and are spectacular in their upward production trend. Gold is the metal sought, and silver is the frequent by-product. Although a small amount of gold is derived from stream gravels, lode mining is the only form conducted on a large scale. Northern and southern Luzon, Masbate, and eastern Mindanao have a number of productive ore ranges being developed. Gold mining is almost entirely a corporation enterprise that will yield profitable returns to large-scale operations. Gold production in 1940 was valued at $39,151,000.

Iron ores have been mined for handicraft use for centuries. But until the Japanese began buying Philippine ores there was no large market and no industrial mining. 1940 was the peak year, with 1,-230,000 tons of ore produced. Ores are of various types, all rich enough for present-day smelting techniques, and they are fairly widely distributed from central Luzon to southern Mindanao (Fig. 92). Reserves are sufficient to permit considerable sale abroad and still supply the home market for many years, even when modern industrial production of iron and steel begins.

The two ferro-alloys chromium and manganese are widely scattered throughout the islands, though only partial survey work has been done to determine the commercial value of numerous sites. Neither was seriously produced prior to the middle 1930's, whereas in later years each became an item for strategic stock piling by the United States. In 1941 chromite production hit a peak of over 300,000 tons; the manganese peak production was the 62,000 tons mined in 1940. The islands have no immediate large volume demand for either alloy, so that production of each depends upon foreign industrial interest.

Coal deposits are scattered over the islands. Unfortunately most of them are small deposits, are often difficult to mine, and consist largely of mid-Tertiary lignites and soft coals of non-coking nature. These conditions are handicaps to future island industrialization, since they lessen the economic and technical chances for the development of heavy industry. Until 1946 production never exceeded 60,000 tons per year, frequently being under half that. Petroleum, the other power source and raw material of heavy industry, still is an unknown quantity in island economy. There is extensive evidence of petroleum occurrence, but so far no sizable yields have been proved. It is too early, however, to dismiss the island potential in petroleum as insignificant.

Copper is the only other known mineral of importance now being produced. A part of the yield is a by-product of gold mining; copper is also mined directly in a number of places. The production record is somewhat erratic, rising and falling with gold mine activity.

TRADE, TRANSPORT, AND MANUFACTURE

THE OLDER PATTERNS

In the centuries before the Spanish came there were many participants in the water-borne interisland and foreign trade of the Philippines. Arabs, Indians, Bornese, and Chinese were the chief merchants who dealt with the islands; but Japanese, Javanese, Sumatrans, Malaccans, and Chams from southern Indo-China were represented. Filipino sea traders themselves wandered rather far afield. As typical trade goods, one may note the cotton textiles, high-grade iron utensils and tools, copper utensils and religious sculptures, glass beads, jewelry and precious stones that came from India, the slaves, various spices and tin ores from Malaysia, or the silks, copper ware, porcelains and pottery, medicines, wines, and salt fish brought by the Chinese. Exports of the islands were such things as betel nuts, coconuts, abaca in both raw and cloth forms, timber, rattans, kapok, vegetable waxes and resins, shells, pearls, gold, and slaves.

THE SPANISH PERIOD

During the first decades of Spanish occupation there were no restrictions on trade. Manila, as the administrative center, soon became the port of call for the merchants of many countries who gathered to sell their products to Spanish merchants and officials. Manila quickly became one of the chief entrepôts of the Orient. Philippine products were less in demand than were the cream of the handicraft goods, spices, perfumes, and rare products from other parts of the East. These goods went to the Spanish colonies in the Americas and to Spain itself, from a new group of merchants who were in direct competition with older merchant groups in Spain. The protective ideas of sixteenth century mercantilist theory were invoked by the Spanish to protect their vested interests, and by the middle of the seventeenth century a great many restrictions upon Philippine trade were being enforced. The few small vessels that annually sailed in the "Manila Galleon" trade with Mexico from 1703 to about 1812 carried the only officially sanctioned exports of the islands to Mexican markets, monopolized by Spanish officialdom and the clergy. These restrictions stifled native trade and the home handicraft industries. The Spanish never were interested in manufacture themselves. Administrative policy was to tie down the native population to fixed residences. The Chinese soon took over the ranking position as the handlers of all kinds of trade goods.

By the early nineteenth century, changing economic theory finally carried Spanish policy with it. Between 1810 and 1860 most restrictions upon trade and upon foreign and native participation were withdrawn. First Manila and then Cebu, Iloilo, and Zamboanga were opened to foreign commerce. After 1830 roads began to be built into island interiors, and the rules of Filipino fixed residence were lifted.

Products of the Philippines, rather than the choice goods of the rest of the Orient, began to be important in trade. The sugar and abaca industries were the first to respond. The tobacco trade had been made into an official monopoly in 1782, a pattern continued for exactly a century, but its volume nevertheless gradually increased. Coconut products began to be of interest to foreign traders, and the first commercial plantings were made about the middle of the century. Manila remained the chief port and became again an entrepôt as it had been in the first decades of Spanish rule.

THE AMERICAN PERIOD

The Growth of Transportation (Fig. 93). Spanish efforts in transportation did not achieve very much, though in 1892 a British-built railway was opened from Manila to Lingayen Gulf across the central plain of Luzon. Extensions were made to this line early in the American period, and two short lines were built on Panay and Cebu. In 1941 they amounted to about 850 miles of line, in all, but wartime destruction caused the abandonment of the Cebu line. The real problem facing railways in the linear-shaped Philippines is the parallel competition from roads and inter-island ships. It is not likely that a large railroad system will ever be built up.

Roads, on the other hand, are constantly being increased in mileage and improved in quality. The highway system totals about 15,000 miles of paved and all-weather roads. They form a skeleton system over most of the islands, but there is a very great need for additional secondary roads and improvement of trunk roads. American supervision failed to develop transportation adequately, following needs rather than opening opportunities. Mindanao, Mindoro, Palawan, and northern and eastern Luzon are the regions most lacking in road transport. There were about 75,000 vehicles in 1949. Almost every major region has operating bus systems, but neither passenger nor freight services are adequate to the constantly expanding volume of traffic.

There are ample inter-island shipping services that cover the ports of all the major islands throughout the archipelago. Most small ports are open only to inter-island ships, but there now are eleven ports open to international shipping. Air services rather adequately connect every large island and every important city with Manila, so that in a few hours one can get to almost any part of the islands.

Trade and Industry. The Americans inherited the Philippines just when they were beginning to participate actively in foreign trade and to revive their domestic trade. Local handicrafts then were less

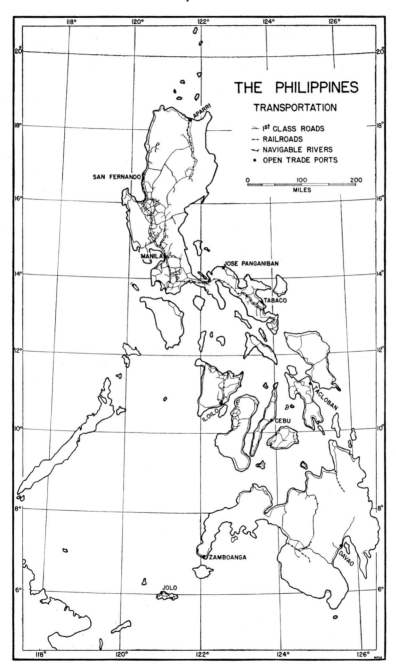

FIGURE 93.   Land transportations and ports of the Philippines.

varied and less productive than in many other parts of the Orient. Under the American administration domestic free trade and industry developed within an American protective tariff framework. The legal terms of trade have been constantly revised as the islands have been given more and more freedom. These arrangements greatly stimulated commercial agriculture and the exports of certain crops. They provided a guaranteed market for island exports. They also provided an ample supply of American manufactured goods for the island market. But they did not adequately guide and stimulate the redevelopment of handicraft industries, and they did not effectively sponsor the growth of modern local industry. However, the islands are afforded a traditional period of trade adjustment, extending until 1974, in which gradually increasing American tariffs on island exports to the United States will make the two countries totally separate.

In 1899 the total island trade amounted to about $34,000,000, imports being slightly larger than exports. By 1941 this total had changed to a figure of almost $300,000,000, with exports slightly leading imports. The 1947 trade volume, swollen by high prices and large reconstruction imports, reached $775,000,000, imports being double exports. The 1947 per-capita trade figure was about $40.00, some eight times the 1899 total. During most of this half century the islands have had a favorable balance of trade. Once American-Philippine trade patterns had developed, the United States took the bulk of island exports and supplied almost all the imports. By the 1947 returns, thirty-six countries did more than $1,000,000 total trade with the islands. The leaders are the United States, in a class by itself, followed at a distance by Canada, France, China, Great Britain, Denmark, Italy, Belgium, and the Indies, in that order. Allowing for wartime destruction and the slow return to more normal patterns, the leading exports are sugar, coconut products, gold, abaca, tobaccos, embroideries, timber and rattan, iron ore and the ferro-alloys, and canned pineapple. In the same sense the leading imports are cotton goods, iron and steel, petroleum, tobaccos, paper and its products, grains and preparations, rayons and other synthetic fibers, automobiles and tires, meats and dairy products, and chemicals, drugs, and cosmetics. Manila is the major port, by far. Cebu, Iloilo, and Davao are next in importance. Table 2 gives selected trade statistics, but it should be noted that 1947, owing to war-damage reconstruction and a high world price level, is hardly a normal year.

American and Filipino concerns handle the bulk of the foreign trade, both import and export. Between these large concerns and the small retail shops and market stalls run by Filipinos in the towns and villages all over the islands there is a very wide gap. This is the field cultivated by the Chinese. Their concerns have more capital and trade skill than the small Filipino enterprises. They are the large and small wholesalers, the distributors for most of the imports once they leave the major ports, and the middlemen for much of the outgoing produce before it reaches the major points of export. Their invested capital exceeds that of the Americans, and their numbers and their penetration into Filipino economy have grown steadily throughout the American period.

The islands lack industrial power, technical skills, and management abilities. They process a good deal of their agricultural exports, but they need to expand this phase greatly. The processing and the

TABLE 2

SELECTED PHILIPPINE TRADE STATISTICS IN PESOS*

VALUE OF TOTAL TRADE

Year	Imports	Exports	Totals
1855	₱4,235,814	₱6,121,623	₱10,357,437
1895	25,398,798	36,655,727	62,054,525
1899	38,385,972	29,693,364	68,079,136
1909	62,168,838	69,848,674	132,017,512
1916	90,992,675	139,874,365	230,867,040
1920	298,876,565	302,247,711	601,124,276
1929	294,320,549	328,893,685	623,214,234
1933	134,722,926	211,542,105	346,265,031
1937	218,051,490	302,532,500	520,583,990
1941	271,182,780	322,269,981	593,452,761
1946	591,716,481	128,375,049	720,091,530
1947	1,022,700,608	531,096,704	1,553,797,312

DIRECTIONAL TRADE PATTERN FOR 1947

Country	Imports from	Exports to	Total Trade	Share of Total, %
U.S.	₱879,999,624	₱304,379,829	₱1,184,379,453	76.0
Canada	27,624,606	11,198,831	38,823,437	2.5
France	35,256,801	1,815,000	37,071,801	2.4
China	28,535,866	2,843,113	31,378,979	2.0
Gr. Brit.	6,199,018	17,021,583	23,220,601	1.5
Denmark	425,942	20,128,916	20,554,858	1.3
Italy	669,188	15,603,599	16,272,787	1.0
Belgium	4,859,784	10,992,708	15,852,492	1.0
Indies	4,627,898	9,738,250	14,366,148	0.9

TABLE 2 (Continued)

LEADING COMMODITY IMPORTS AND EXPORTS FOR 1947

Commodity	Imports	% from U.S.	Exports	% to U.S.
Cotton goods	₱153,442,326	90.9		
Grains and manufactures	98,834,050	68.6		
Silks and rayons	90,584,900	99.6		
Meat and dairy products	53,061,820	82.9		
Automobiles and products	51,414,052	99.0		
Iron and steel	46,144,372	87.4		
Tobacco products	43,962,246	99.9		
Paper and products	38,887,246	84.9		
Petroleum products	36,842,052	41.3		
Fish and products	31,883,484	?		
Chemicals, etc.	29,623,320	90.2		
Miscellaneous commodities	358,457,388	?		
Coconut products			₱391,812,007	74.0
Abaca			63,435,874	70.7
Gold bullion			94,074,653†	?
Tobacco products			4,382,982	29.5
Sugar			4,081,188	100.0
Embroideries			2,835,116	82.0
Iron ores			4,077,472†	0.0
Maguey			3,294,883	?
Pineapple			3,001,381†	100.0
Rope and twine			2,904,420	?
Timber and products			528,414	100.0

* Normal exchange rate is ₱2.0 to $1.0.
† 1941 data.

manufacture of consumer goods have begun and are steadily growing, but they have not yet reached a large volume. Government corporations operate in a number of lines, such as sugar refining, coconut and abaca products, rice and corn milling, fresh and tinned fish, shoe manufacture, cotton textile production, and the manufacture of cement. Plans indicate development of hydroelectric power, fertilizers, and metals production via government corporations. Ostensibly these developments are in lines in which insufficient domestic capital is available to undertake home production.

For years Filipinos discouraged American capital investment on the ground that it would postpone independence. Now that their country is independent they are discouraged because American capital does not rush in, since existing laws provide Americans equal opportunity with Filipinos in island investment. Government preemption of many lines that would invite American funds is an important factor in this reluctance. Possible nationalistic and prohibitory labor legislation and rapidly rising labor costs are other factors. The lack of coal, petroleum, and electric power are serious handicaps. There are some excellent hydroelectric sites, but they will be costly to develop and tardily available under government development. Technical and managerial skill in the handling of corporate endeavors is not yet available in the volume needed, and yet the manufactured output of the islands is swelling. The steady increase in the level of consumer demand contributes to the impression of domestic insufficiency. Another generation in which to develop the momentum, skill, and resources mandatory to a balanced economy will considerably alter the situation.

THE PEOPLES OF THE ISLANDS

RACE AND LANGUAGE

The modern Filipino is racially a blend resulting from the mixing of nearly a dozen different elements. Table 3 presents approximate details of these origins. Most of these elements are Mongoloid, though of different ages. The mixing process has been active for at least 4000 years, but in the multiple-island environment nature seldom repeated her proportions exactly. There still are some 25,000 Negrito scattered over the islands, not yet amalgamated into the blend. There are slight differences in the physical build, personality, and psychology of many natives that only the experienced Filipino recognizes easily. Moslem immigrants settled only certain parts of some southern islands, and the Spanish neither conquered nor converted the Moros.

The variable mixing process in the islands resulted in language complexity. More than eighty different languages and dialects are spoken, ranging from tongues used by a few hundred people only up to English, which, as the real *lingua franca* of the islands, is spoken by more than 8,000,000 people. Of the native languages, the Cebuano dialect of the Visayan language group is perhaps spoken by more people than any other. Its home is Cebu, but it is found on eastern Negros, on Siquijor, and quite widely in northern Mindanao. Tagalog of central Luzon is the native tongue of almost as many people as Cebauno, and it has been chosen the national language of the islands. Through being taught in the schools and heard on the radio and in moving pictures, Tagalog is spreading widely, and in coming years it will be known by most educated Filipinos. Ilocano is a widely scattered language, largely because a great many natives of crowded northwest Luzon became colonists in other parts of the islands.   Spanish is widely spoken by the elder generation, and local corruptions have become almost like regional dialects.   Earlier, a great many Spanish words were adopted by many local dialects, a process today happening with English.   It is not uncommon to hear both Spanish and English words used in one native language sentence.

In 1950 there were about 10,000 Americans, some 3200 Spanish, 1600 British, 1600 Indians, and perhaps 10,000 known members of scattered nationalities living in the islands.   Numerous Bornese have been filtering into Sulu and Mindanao without tabulation.   The Chinese form the largest alien group, though data concerning their numbers are of little value.   By official count the 1948 figure was 136,000, but illegal entries are known to be large and unofficial estimates run as high as 450,000.   In addition there are well over a million part-Chinese natives of the islands.

TABLE 3

APPROXIMATE COMPOSITION OF THE
PHILIPPINE POPULATION*

Age and Group	Date of Arrival	Share in 1948 Population, Percentage
Paleolithic		
Negrito	30,000 to 20,000 B.C.	0.5
Proto-Malay	15,000 to 10,000 B.C.	9.0
Neolithic		
Indonesian A	6000 to 2000 B.C.	12.0
Indonesian B	1500 to 500 B.C.	18.0
Copper-Bronze		
Indonesian B	800 to 100 B.C.	3.0
Iron Age		
Malaysian	500 B.C. to present	37.0
Indian	300 B.C. to present	4.0
Arab-Persian-Indian	300 B.C. to present	2.5
Chinese-Japanese	A.D. 600 to present	10.0
Occidental (Spanish, American, miscellaneous)	A.D. 1521 to present	4.0
Total		100.0

* After H. Otley Beyer.

THE RURAL AND THE URBAN SCENES

Filipinos live everywhere.   Their homes are scattered in the fields from high tide to the mountain tops.   They live in long and straggling lines along roads, rivers, lake shores, and island coasts.   There are many small towns with formal plans built around a Spanish plaza.

Most fields are rectangular when conditions permit, but the farm landscape lacks the precise and well-trimmed air one finds in many parts of China and Japan. Homesteads also are somewhat casual in arrangement and in construction. Bamboo and nipa palm form the most common materials, but many special materials are used when local resources favor. Houses usually are raised a few feet off the ground on posts. Animals, fowls, tools, and crops often are quartered on the ground level, under the house. Improved light and water facilities usually are lacking, except in cities and in towns, and many domestic arrangements are most casual. Houses seldom seem large enough to shelter all the children, animals, tools, crops, and possessions that belong to one family.

FIGURE 94. Two rural homes built of nipa palm thatch and bamboo in long-inhabited coconut landscape of southeastern Luzon.

The larger towns and cities have expanded mostly around old Spanish towns. These additions often are straggling and at variance with the original formal plans. Zoning seldom is applied, and often residences, shop, tiled mansion, factory, and poor thatched hut flank or face one another. Most cities and larger towns have electricity and piped water systems. One finds electric refrigerators, radios, cold-drink machines, "juke boxes," tiled bathrooms, and other modern equipment in many homes and shops of these towns.

The chief cities and ports in most cases are those that were leaders in pre-Spanish times. Among the ports of Manila, Cebu, Iloilo, Davao, Zamboanga, Tacloban, and Legaspi only Davao is a creation of the modern period. Manila, with its excellent bay and its role as the

Spanish and American capital, has outstripped all other island cities.[1] Its political unit is limited in area, but the metropolitan settlement is one of the world's great cities with a population of about 1,330,000, as of October 1, 1948. Its traffic problem compares with that of crowded cities elsewhere. It is the chief port of the islands, the hub of inter-island transportation, the largest trading center, the region doing most of the manufacturing, and the center in which most alien populations are gathered. Urbanization is increasing, but there are not yet many large cities. Counting the Manila metropolitan region as one city, there was but one other above 100,000 in 1948, the city of Cebu. Six more, Iloilo, Bacolod, Davao, Cavite, Dagupan, and Legaspi, exceeded 25,000. Perhaps another twenty cities exceeded 10,000 each. The total number of urban residents slightly exceeds 2,000,000, just over 10 per cent of the total population.

GROWTH IN POPULATION

Both at the time of Magellan's exploratory visit in 1521 and when the Spanish returned in force in the 1560's most parts of the islands appeared to be lightly populated, and a figure of about half a million people has been accepted as a reasonable estimate for 1521. By 1800 this figure had grown to 1,561,000, and by 1845 the total had jumped to 3,488,000. A considerable share of this growth came in Luzon and Panay. The Visayas generally were subjected to constant raids by Moros from Sulu and Borneo, with a restraining effect on population growth and colonial settlement. By 1903 the total population had grown to 7,635,000. In this period the Visayan islands expanded greatly in population as a result of the cessation of Moro raids, and the colonization of Mindanao had informally begun, through the migration of Visayans.

The 1939 census indicated a population of 16,000,000, and that of October 1, 1948, totaled 19,234,000, despite the effects of the war. Much of the increase in this short period has been in Mindanao and the less crowded parts of Luzon, certain parts of the Visayas actually decreasing.

BORDERLAND POLITICAL GEOGRAPHY

GROWTH OF A POLITICAL SYSTEM

The Spanish found varied tribal political-social systems in use upon their arrival, those of the Moros being the most advanced. The

[1] Quezon City, really a suburb of Manila, is to be the future capital of the islands.

Spanish aim was to transform the native mobile society into a sedentary society in order more easily to Christianize and control it. Since they regarded the native social systems as un-Christian, all were rejected and replaced by their own. But the Spanish retained the local political unit (barrio) and the chief (teniente), corresponding to the ward and the lieutenant of American party politics. Above the barrio the Spanish finally placed the municipio or municipality. It consisted of a fixed town settlement and such religious and administrative personnel as were required to handle affairs of the surrounding district, comprising many barrios. Gradually provinces were established, and island administration was centered in Manila. The Roman legal system replaced customary tribal law.

The Americans retained the whole of the Spanish administrative system, but they replaced important parts of the Roman legal code by American codes based on English common law. And they tried to infuse a great deal of democracy into the Filipinos, intangible though much of it is. Unfortunately our island students learned much of the bad with the good, and it may well be that half a century is too short a period in which to absorb the intricate operations of social and political democracy.

The Filipinos, now that they are independent, are groping for some fusion of old customary procedure, the Spanish and the American systems. They have inherited serious problems resulting from inadequacies in both Spanish and American systems. Theirs is not yet a full-fledged democratic system. The future is somewhat unpredictable, and their system undoubtedly will have features unfamiliar to the American.

PROBLEMS OF A NEW REPUBLIC

Both the United States and responsible Filipinos for years worked steadily toward the ultimate independence of the islands. In 1934 this goal was definitely set for the middle of the next decade. Philippine Independence Day was July 4, 1946. Formidable problems are in the path of progress. There are faults in education, agricultural advancement, transport development, and foreign-trade distribution that have been inherited from the American and Spanish administrative past. Others may be grouped as political, economic, and strategic problems.

Beginning operations in the aftermath of a period of war that seriously damaged the whole of the Philippines, the new government is hampered by a decline of political morality that engenders too little confidence among the people and may require several years to surmount. The very speed of the movement toward independence has left great inequalities in the preparedness of Filipinos to use and protect their liberties and to fulfill their duties. Education still has a long way to go to bring all the people of the islands into full participation in modern Philippine society.

The possibly too-rapid increase in the material standard of living of many people may drain off funds that could better go into capital improvements in island economy. Related are the several topics of island export trade, American quotas on island goods, possible increased American tariffs, and, in the end, competitive world trade. After the Second World War the United States distributed large war damages and war-time back pay throughout the islands, to be completed in 1952. The ending of the payments to the Filipinos will leave the islands with a dilemma, both political and economic. How will adequate foreign funds and technical aid for industrialization be secured in the future, and to what extent should the government preempt the place of private industry?

In a separate category are the strategic problems of military, naval, and air bases of interest to the United States, island defense, and general moral responsibility for the future of the islands. The increasing role of the Chinese in island affairs has behind it implicit political, social, and economic dangers for a small country with a long and undefended coastline. The Philippines form a small island world perched on the edge of the oriental realm far from the United States. With tremendous social, political, and economic change certain to affect a good share of that realm in the next two generations, the islands are both in and out of the realm. Their own transition to independence was completed peacefully, and culturally they form the least oriental section of the realm. But they are certain to be affected by adverse currents of events, without their former full recourse to American assistance.

REFERENCES

Alip, E. M., *Philippine History, Political, Social, Economic,* Alip & Brion, Manila, 1948.

Beyer, H. O., and J. C. de Veyra, "Philippine Saga," *Evening News,* Manila, 1948.

Cady, J. F., P. G. Barnett, and S. Jenkins, *The Development of Self Rule and Independence in Burma, Malaya and the Philippines,* American Institute of Pacific Relations, New York, 1948.

Facts and Figures about Economic and Social Conditions of the Philippines, Bureau of Census and Statistics, Manila, 1948.

References 327

Hainsworth, R. G., and R. T. Moyer, *Agricultural Geography of the Philippine Islands*, U.S.D.A., Office of Foreign Agricultural Relations, Washington, 1945.

Hayden, J. R., *The Philippines, A Study in National Development*, The Macmillan Co., New York, 1942.

Kolb, A., *Die Philippien*, Koehler Verlag, Leipzig, 1942.

Kroeber, A. L., *The Peoples of the Philippines*, American Museum of Natural History, revised edition, New York, 1943.

Mining Industry of the Philippines, Information Circular No. 5, Bureau of Mines, Manila, 1947.

Pelzer, K. J., *Pioneer Settlement in the Asiatic Tropics*, American Geographical Society Special Publication No. 29, New York, 1945.

Proposed Program for Industrial Rehabilitation and Development of the Republic of the Philippines, H. E. Beyster Corporation, Detroit, 1947.

Yearbook of Philippine Statistics, 1946, Bureau of Printing, Manila, 1947.

12

Hawaii   and   American   Island   Outposts

OTIS W. FREEMAN

THE HAWAIIAN ISLANDS ARE ECONOMICALLY WELL DEVELOPED AND HAVE strategic importance because of their location at the crossroads of steamer and airplane routes in the north Pacific. The Territory of Hawaii includes all the Hawaiian chain except Midway, which is a separate possession of the United States.   For administrative purposes Palmyra Island is included in the Territory, but it is not a part of the Hawaiian chain.   Hawaii has about 500,000 people living on the 6435 square miles of the main islands, seven of which are inhabited.   Although only one-sixth of the Territory is called tillable and less than 8 per cent is cropped, yet the land under cultivation is so productive that nearly $150,000,0000 worth of sugar and pineapples are produced annually.

LOCATION AND CHARACTERISTICS

The Hawaiian Islands rise above an elongated submarine platform or ridge that stretches for almost 2000 statute miles in a southeast to northwest direction, between the parallels of 18° 40′ to 28° 40′ north, and, the meridians of 154° 30′ to 178° 40′ west.   The platform is supposedly constructed of volcanic materials that were erupted from a zone of fissures on the ocean floor; besides the visible islands there are several submarine peaks and numerous banks.

The Hawaiian chain (Fig. 95) can be divided into three sections based on the nature of the islands and the stage of erosion.   The southeastern portion is about 400 miles long, and embraces eight high volcanic islands that are only moderately reduced by erosion.   These islands are Hawaii (4030 square miles), Maui (728), Lanai (141), Kahoolawe (45), Molokai (260), Oahu (604), Kauai (555), and

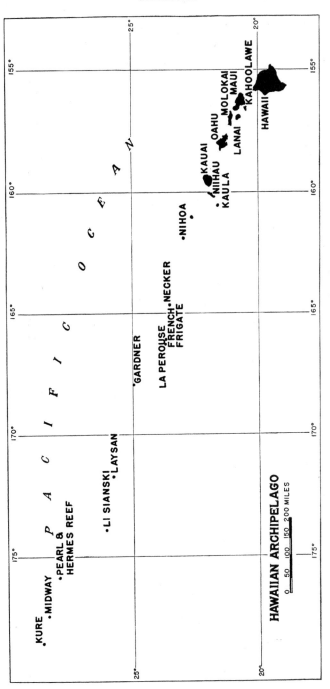

FIGURE 95. Hawaiian Archipelago.

Niihau (72). The seven largest islands contain all the population of the Territory, Kahoolawe now being uninhabited (Table 1).

The middle segment is nearly 800 miles long, from little Kaula near Niihau to beyond Gardner, and includes five islets or stacks of volcanic

TABLE 1

HAWAIIAN ISLANDS

Islands	Area Square Miles	Altitude, Feet	Estimated Population, Exclusive of Military
Hawaii	4030	13,784 (Mauna Kea) 13,680 (Mauna Loa)	74,000
Maui	728	10,025 (Haleakala)	47,000
Molokai	260	4,970	5,000
Kahoolawe	45	1,491	0
Lanai	141	3,370	3,800
Oahu	604	4,025	370,000
Kauai	555	5,170	35,000
Niihau	72	1,281	200
	Acres		
Kaula	120	550	0
Nihoa	155	895	0
Necker	40	276	0
French Frigate Shoal (La Perouse Pinnacle)	60	122	0
Gardner Pinnacles	3	170	0
Laysan	1000	40	0
Lisianski	450	40	0
Pearl and Hermes Reef	300	10	0
Midway (atoll)	2000	43	30
Kure (atoll)	300	20	0
	Square Miles		
Area eight main islands	6435		535,000 (est.)
Outlying islands	7.5		
Entire chain	6442.5		

rock, Kaula, Nihoa, Necker, La Perouse Pinnacle, and Gardner Pinnacles, besides French Frigate Shoals and several banks that have resulted from the erosion of volcanic islands. Both Necker Island (41 acres) and Nihoa Island (155 acres) show evidence of a former occupation by man but were abandoned before the arrival of Europeans. La Perouse Pinnacle rises from the bank of French Frigate Shoals. During the Second World War an airfield was developed on the low land within the reef of the shoals, but it was deactivated after the close of the conflict.

The northwestern section, which is about 700 miles long, consists of low atolls, sandy islets, reefs, and shoals wih no visible volcanic rock because the upper portion of the volcanoes that once existed have been eroded below sea level, and their truncated cones form the platform on which coral grew to form reefs and islands. From east to west the islands are Laysan, Pearl and Hermes Reef (an atoll), Midway, and Kure or Ocean Island. Laysan and Kure are included in the Hawaiian Islands Bird Reservation, which comprises all the islands as far east as Nihoa. None of these islands contains permanent human inhabitants except Midway. Guano has been mined on Laysan, which once supported millions of sea birds, now much reduced in numbers.

VOLCANIC ACTIVITY

All the high islands in the Hawaiian chain are of volcanic origin, but the only active craters are on Hawaii, the last island toward the southeast. With some exceptions, volcanic activity seems to have begun on the ocean floor at the northwest end of a series of roughly parallel fissures and to have moved progressively toward the southeast. Usually the completeness of erosion and its stage have proceeded in the same direction, because the volcanoes in the northwest section have been eroded below sea level, those in the middle section largely eroded with only a few surviving stacks, and in the southeast the volcanic domes have been only partially eroded with the last island, Hawaii, affected least of all.

The main islands were constructed of flow after flow of basaltic lava one above the other, with the flows first erupting from fissures and vents on the ocean floor, and later continuing from major craters above sea level until lava domes or shields rather than cones were built high above the ocean. For example, Mauna Kea on Hawaii is 13,784 feet and Haleakala on Maui is 10,025 feet above sea level. Beds of volcanic ash, pumice, and tuff, all products of explosive eruptions, may lie between some lava flows, but these have small volume compared to the masses of lava. The larger lava domes may be 10 to 60 miles in diameter at sea level, and they rise to heights of thousands of feet. Two domes rise 2½ miles above the sea from depths that are 3½ miles below the surface of the ocean within 50 miles of the coast. At least 90 per cent of the lava is hidden below the water surface.

Associated with the domes are numerous cinder cones that resulted from minor eruptions on the slopes and margins of the major volcanoes. As a result of collapse of the summit and the enlargement of the resulting crater by stoping (fusion of wall rock), huge calderas (caldrons) develop on top of the lava domes, for example, Mokuweoweo on Mauna Loa (Fig. 2) and Halemaumau, the firepit of Kilauea.

Nearly 1,500,000,000 cubic yards of basalt have erupted from Mauna Loa in little over a century, far more lava than has come from any other active volcano in the world during that time. During the last

FIGURE 96.   Windward Oahu from the Nuuanu Pali.   Photograph courtesy of the Hawaii Visitors Bureau.

150 years Mauna Loa has erupted on an average of once every 3½ years and has had a lava flow every 6 years. The flow of 1859 was 35 miles long and lasted for 10 months, and several flows have reached the ocean in historic times. Eruptions occurred in 1926, 1933, 1935, 1940, 1942, 1944, 1949, and 1950.

DEVELOPMENT OF THE RELIEF FEATURES

The present relief features result mainly from erosion of the volcanic mountains by running water and waves combined with changes in elevation of the islands in respect to sea level. There is little evidence for folding of the bedrock, but faulting has been common. The slopes of a lava dome initiate a radial drainage pattern, but in the areas of heavier rainfall the greater erosion there causes the development of deep canyons with amphitheater heads that contrast strongly with the smaller and less incised valleys found on the dry slopes. Both rising and sinking of the land areas have taken place, particularly on Oahu. Elevation of this island has resulted in raised beaches and terraces along the foot of the mountains, whereas the sinking of the land or rising of the ocean has caused the drowning of valleys to form Pearl Harbor and the deposit of silt in valleys like that of lower Manoa.

GROUND-WATER SUPPLIES

Ground water is needed for irrigation and domestic use in Hawaii, and its occurrence depends upon the geology. Clay is an impervious

FIGURE 97. West Maui near Lahaina, showing the narrow zone of tillable slopes mostly planted to sugar cane, between the mountains and the ocean. Photograph, Hawaiian Airlines, Ltd.

material, and where it has been deposited above pervious lavas and gravel beds, and then the whole has sunk by some hundreds of feet, the clay forms a capping to the pervious beds so that fresh water will be retained in them under hydrostatic pressures. Several artesian areas within the limits of Honolulu have this origin and supply great quantities of water; some of it comes from flowing wells, but most of it is pumped. Difficulty arises if more water is pumped out than enters the ground from rain, because then the salt water, on which the fresh water rests, will rise and pollute the supply, sometimes to such an extent that wells have to be abandoned. Dikes of lava that are dense and impervious to water may cross more open volcanic rocks and seal them to hold supplies of ground water perched at quite high elevations in the mountains. When tapped by tunnels and wells driven into the dike complexes, these supplies of water become important sources for irrigation and municipal needs. About $45,000,000 has been invested in Hawaii's irrigation works, about half of which are on Oahu.

CLIMATE

The climate of the Hawaiian Islands chiefly depends upon their insular location just within the Tropic of Cancer over 2000 miles from the mainland in the zone of the northeast trades, the altitude, and the effects of cyclonic fronts that pass generally to the northward.

The temperatures are pleasantly mild, averaging about 72° F for all available stations, because the steady blowing trade winds have crossed a moderately cool ocean for thousands of miles (Fig. 100). Differences between the warmest months, August and September, and the coldest months, January and February, are 5 to 8 degrees, with the larger range occurring on the leeward side of mountainous islands. The diurnal range of temperature is about 10° F and exceeds the annual range, which for all stations averaged together is 68.7° F in February, the coldest month, and 75.8° F in August, the warmest month. Altitude has marked effects on temperature, which drops about 3° F for each increase in elevation of 1000 feet. Thus Hilo, near sea level, has a mean annual temperature of 72.1° F, and the Volcano House, elevation 4000 feet, 60.6° F. Frost rarely occurs below 4000 feet elevation above sea level, and has never been known lower than 2500 feet. The summits of Mauna Kea and Mauna Loa on Hawaii are covered with snow frequently in winter; snow sometimes falls on Haleakala on Maui. Uncomfortably hot, humid weather is rare and results from the passage north of Hawaii of frontal disturbances that cause replacement of the trades by Kona (southerly) winds of high humidity, thereby bringing heavy rainfall to the ordinarily dry, leeward side of the islands.

The rainfall is closely related to the mountains and exposure to the winds from the ocean (Fig. 98B). On windward slopes rainfall increases from sea level to elevations of 3000 to 6000 feet, after which it declines progressively at loftier heights. On Hawaii the zone of maximum rainfall usually lies between about 2500 to 3000 feet elevation on the windward slope of Manua Kea, where it averages 100 to over 300 inches annually, but on Kauai and the dome of west Maui the rainfall continues to increase upwards almost to the summit. Mount Waialeale, Kauai, at an elevation of 5075 feet, has an annual rainfall of about 460 inches, with 624 inches falling in the rainiest year on record, making it one of the wettest spots on earth. Few places in the world equal the Hawaiian Islands in the great contrasts in annual rainfall between the windward and the leeward slopes of a mountain range or dome. On Kauai the summit rainfall of over 450 inches declines to 20 inches annually 15 miles southwest. The windward side of Haleakala up to elevations of 5000 feet has rainfall of 200 to 300 inches annually, declining towards the summit and lessening down the leeward slopes until, near sea level, the rainfall is less than 20 inches per year. Low islands, like Niihau and Kahoolawe, the low isthmus of central Maui, and the low ends of other islands resemble the leeward side of all the islands in having little rainfall. For example, Lahaina, Maui, has 13 inches of rain annually, and Puako, Hawaii, in 1947 recorded only 4.1 inches. Some of the rainfall is connected with cyclones, and at Midway, which is in a latitude several hundred miles north of Honolulu, most of the rains in winter come as a result of such frontal disturbances. Very heavy local rains sometimes occur during the passage of fronts, and a precipitation of 24 to 30 inches in 24 hours has been recorded at a few stations. Thunderstorms are of moderate frequency and come mostly in the winter.

The huge, volcanic domes on the island of Hawaii are higher than the depth of the trade winds, which are deflected around Mauna Kea and Mauna Loa, and the leeward slopes are large enough to permit the development of a local land and sea breeze. The sea breeze brings rain to the Kona district on the leeward side of Hawaii where a favored strip of land has been developed agriculturally between the elevations of 1000 and 2500 feet because of the ample rainfall there. Below 1000 feet it is too dry and above 2500 it is too wet for raising coffee and other specialty crops.

VEGETATION ZONES

Vegetation zones in Hawaii are related principally to rainfall and altitude. The wet and dry sides of islands have plant associations that differ, depending upon the rainfall. To a considerable extent there is also a correlation between the vegetation and the soils of the

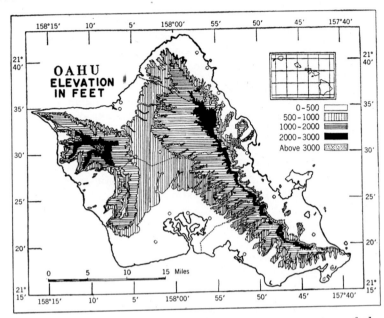

FIGURE 98A. Oahu, elevation in feet. Base map courtesy of the
University of Hawaii.

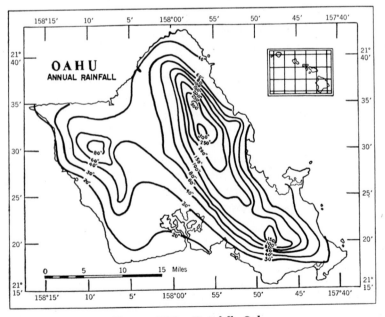

FIGURE 98B. Rainfall, Oahu.

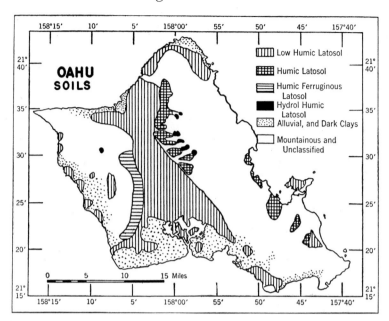

FIGURE 98C. Soils, Oahu.

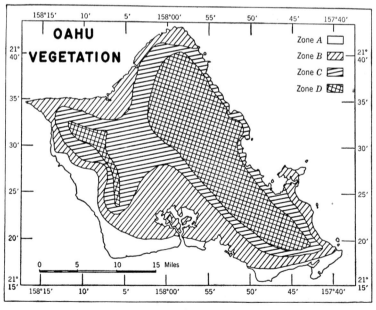

FIGURE 98D. Natural vegetation, Oahu. The altitude of Oahu is too low for zone E to be present.

islands. A lower limit of forest growth determined by low rainfall is found only on the leeward side; the upper limit at about 10,000 feet is related to temperature. Because trees suitable for higher elevations were never introduced, boreal-type plants are few.

The number and the nature of the original plant species were greatly influenced by the wide separation of Hawaii from large bodies of land, and the broad ocean prevented the migration of many species. Of 1729 described indigenous species of seed plants about 85 per cent are endemic. Fosberg[1] believes that the native Hawaiian flora was evolved by differentiation from the introduction of comparatively few parent plants.

The wild vegetation of the present day contains many introduced plants, and the number of such exotic species is estimated at over 2000, which have been brought in during the last 175 years. Examples of introduced plants that have gone wild are guava, algaroba, lantana, and cactus. Introduced plants have become dominant over the native flora on large areas.

Five generalized vegetation zones in Hawaii have been recognized by Ripperton and Hosaka[2] (Fig. 98D). Zone A, on the leeward side of the islands, consists of coastal flats and of slopes from sea level to elevations of 500 feet, except on the dry side of the island of Hawaii where it extends to 2000 feet. It also occupies the low ends of islands and portions of the windward coasts where the rainfall happens to be light. If the land is irrigated, sugar cane can be raised; otherwise it is used mainly for pasture. The introduced algaroba (mesquite), thorny shrubs like koa haole and cactus, and drought-resistant grasses are now predominant. Native trees include the wiliwili (*Erythrina*) and the hola (*Pandanus*).

Zone B, or the lower forest belt, lies above zone A, where zone A is present; and probably the most common tree, along with the koa haole bushes, is the kukui. Shrubs like the ilima form thickets as does also the introduced cactus and lantana. Pili grass, other grasses, and annuals are available for grazing.

The middle forest zone, zone C, is located where the rainfall is about 40 to 60 inches annually, and in elevation the zone rises to 4000 feet and on windward coasts may descend to sea level. The ohia lehua and koa are important trees, and there is luxuriant under-

[1] F. R. Fosberg, "Derivation of the Flora of the Hawaiian Islands," *Insects of Hawaii*, by E. C. Zimmerman, Vol. I, pp. 107–119, University of Hawaii Press, 1948.

[2] J. C. Ripperton and E. Y. Hosaka, "Vegetation Zones of Hawaii," *Hawaii Agr. Exp. Sta. Bull.* 89, University of Hawaii, 1942.

growth, including small tree ferns. In the lower and less rainy sections, guava forms thickets. Bermuda grass, staghorn fern, and lantana often occupy openings in the drier forests. The soil is somewhat leached but generally fertile, and much of this forest land has been cleared and planted in sugar cane and pineapples especially on the central plateau of Oahu. This type of forest originally covered much of Oahu and is common on other islands.

Zone *D* develops in areas of very heavy rainfall, and originally the forests in this belt were of very dense growth. There are some differences in the composition of the forest, depending on altitude. The upper phase begins at about 4000 feet and extends to about 8000 feet and is found only on Hawaii and Maui, which alone among the islands have this upper elevation. On the windward side of the islands the lower zone begins at sea level and occupies ground on which the rainfall is 60 to 300 inches annually. Dense thickets of guava, shrubs, staghorn, and other ferns, ohia lehua, and koa occur. The upper levels are mostly in forest reserves. On Hawaii and to a limited extent on other islands the lower levels have been cleared and planted in sugar cane.

Zone *E* occurs only on Maui and Hawaii and extends from about 4000 to 10,000 feet, which is the tree line. Forest reserves and national parks include much of this area, little of which is for agriculture although there is some grazing. Some sandalwood grows in this zone along with wild strawberries and akala berries. The high tablelands and mountain tops like Mount Kaala on Oahu and Waialele on Kauai have bogs with a peculiar flora related to plants found in New Zealand, the southern Andes Mountains, and the Falkland Islands. Possibly some of these plants were introduced by aquatic wild fowl.

The forests of Hawaii are more useful today for the conservation of ground water, flood control, and prevention of soil erosion than as a source of commercial timber. Originally there were many sandalwood trees, and the export of the logs was among the first industries developed in the islands, but this resource was exhausted in a generation. At present some koa (Hawaiian mahogany), and ohia are used for furniture, interior decoration, and curios. The introduced algaroba (mesquite) covers 100,000 acres of dry lowlands and furnishes blossoms for bee pasture, wood for fuel, and seeds (beans) for stock feed. Some of the wooded land is grazed. Nearly 700,000 acres of Territorial government land and 357,000 acres of privately owned land are included in forest reserves that are located in the mountains of the five largest islands. They amount to 25.6 per cent of the area of the Territory. The city of Honolulu guards the forests on the watersheds used for municipal water supply, and many sugar plantations likewise maintain forest reserves from which comes water for irrigation.

SOILS

The soils of Hawaii have developed from volcanic rocks under a warm tropical climate. The chief parent soil materials are basaltic lava, products of explosive eruptions like volcanic ash and cinders, alluvial deposits made by running water, and the coralline limestone on raised beaches and lowlands that were once the ocean floor. The characteristics of the soils depend upon various factors, among which are nature of the original materials, time available for the development of the soil, rainfall that varies from arid to humid, temperature, surface relief features, drainage, natural vegetation, and the organisms present in the soil. Only about 10 per cent of the area of the islands has deep, well-developed soils because of the youthfulness of some of the volcanic rock and other parent materials and the steep slopes and excessive rainfall of the mountains that permit the rapid removal of weathered materials. The deep, more mature soils are mostly on the surface of ancient lava flows that slope at a moderate degree. On the valley floors and along some coasts there are small areas of alluvial soil, which are too youthful to show much effect of climate and other influences. On recent lava flows the soil is thin but generally fertile; such pasture soils are successfully cropped in several areas, for example, in the Kona district on the island of Hawaii.

The rate of rock decomposition in Hawaii is very rapid largely because of the hot, humid climate but partly because the heavy rainfall and good drainage of the porous soil promote such rapid leaching that minerals, characteristic of mature, zonal soils elsewhere in the world, rarely accumulate. Consequently Hawaiian soils have the *A* zone (topsoil) and *C* zone (weathered original material) but not *B* zone (subsoil) of accumulation. In areas with humid climate the chief soil-forming process is *laterization,* in which silica is leached out, and the oxides of aluminum and iron accumulate as the residual components. These lateritic soils have been named *latosols* by soil scientists. The latosols, developed under very humid conditions, have a high organic content (10 to 35 per cent by volume), possibly because plant materials in the ground are soaked with water that would delay their decay. All the latosols have a high iron content, and those with a low amount of humus are likely to have a large content of manganese. Several hundred soil types have been recognized in Hawaii, but a simplified general classification (Fig. 98*C*), would include low humic latosols, humic latosols, hydrol humic latosols, and humic ferruginous latosols, all developed from basalt flows under a rainfall in excess of 30 inches annually; red desert soils; reddish prairie soils and brown forest soils, but developed from volcanic ash; alluvial soils; bog soils; and lithosols from very rocky materials.

The low humic latosols have under 5 per cent organic matter, were developed under an annual rainfall of 30 to 60 inches, and originally had a cover of moderately open forest.   Huge areas of these soils have

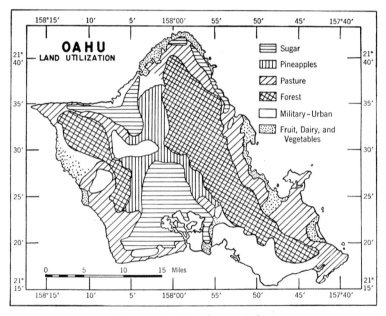

FIGURE 99.   Land use, Oahu.

been cleared for cultivation and are the most widespread Hawaiian soils, comprising much of the land planted to sugar and pineapples, for example, the Wahiawa Plain of central Oahu, west Molokai, Lanai, and portions of the drier slopes on Maui and Kauai.   These soils are friable clays and clay loams with a granular structure, rather uniform texture, high porosity, and an acid reaction.   Their natural fertility is moderately high, and good yields of crops are maintained by the heavy application of fertilizer, which helps to replace the nitrogen that disappears under steady cropping.

The low humic latosols may develop into two end products.   (1) Corresponding to increasing rainfall of 60 to over 150 inches annually, they pass through a transition type of humic latosols (6 to 9 per cent organic matter) into hydrol humic latosols (10 to 20 per cent organic matter), which are high in alumina (Al_2O_3). (2) In places with a wet-dry rainfall regimen they develop into humic ferruginous latosols, which are high in iron and titanium accumulation. The humic latosols have developed on the lower slopes of the rainy Hamakua coast of Hawaii and under similar conditions on Maui and other islands. Much of these soils on Hawaii and Maui has been cleared of dense forests and planted to sugar cane. The hydrol humic latosols coincide with the rainforest that grows in regions of very heavy rainfall, especially on Hawaii, Maui, and Molokai, but except for some sugar fields near Hilo, comparatively little of this soil type is in crops. Much of the humic ferruginous latosols is tilled, for example, on Maui, Kauai, and Oahu.

The soils formed from volcanic ash are reddish prairie soil developed under a rainfall of about 35 inches or less annually and that is mainly for grazing rather than crops, and brown forest soils developed under a rainfall in excess of 35 inches yearly and covered by dense forests, very little of which has been cleared for tillage. These soils are mostly found on Hawaii and Maui. Both types are fertile and low in silica, but because of their location in rather high altitudes they are seldom planted in crops. Another soil type is of alluvial origin. Soils of this type are generally very fertile and much used for taro, rice, and vegetables as well as sugar.

Hawaiian soils are subject to erosion on the uplands and slopes, and farming practices have had to be adapted to reducing the loss of soil in this way. Some grazing lands also show the effects of erosion both by water and by wind. This condition usually is the result of overgrazing or other carelessness.

USE OF LAND

Great changes in land use have occurred in Hawaii since the first European settlers. The native economy was founded on subsistence farming and fishing; the present-day economy on plantation agriculture and services for tourists and the military. The Hawaiians of the past were entirely self-sufficient; the residents of the Territory of the present are dependent upon imports and exports.

Products of the farm and pasture lands in the Hawaiian Islands have an annual value of $100,000,000 to $150,000,000, which is further materially increased by the processing required before sale to consumers. The amount of cropped land is about 307,000 acres, barely

7.5 per cent of the 4,118,400 acres included in the islands, indicating a value of $300 to $400 per acre for the annual yield. About 60 per cent of the area of the islands is in farms. However, much of this is pasture, and it is doubtful if over half a million acres, one-eighth of the island area, will ever be cultivated (Table 2). In addition to cultivated land, other uses are pasture, 1,313,500 acres, about one-third of all land; forest reserves, both public and private, 1,055,000 acres, about one-quarter; waste land, 1,200,000 acres, nearly 30 per cent of the total area; and parks, about 163,000 acres. The remainder is in military and naval reservation, roads, cities, towns, etc.

TABLE 2

RURAL LAND UTILIZATION

(Acres estimated 1948 by county agents)

	Territory	Hawaii	Maui	Molokai and Lanai	Oahu	Kauai and Niihau
Agricultural (farm and grazing) land	1,925,425	1,362,814	144,620	114,934	69,734	233,323
Forest reserves	1,063,777	576,217	156,995	52,805	117,105	160,655
Military use	60,645	728	2,700	285	54,846	2,086
Park	167,679	147,978	17,468	10	613	1,610
Waste and other uses	882,314	485,703	172,297	88,606	134,662	1,046
	4,099,840	2,573,440	494,080	256,640	376,960	398,720

NATIVE HAWAIIAN LAND USE

The Hawaiians, members of the Polynesian race, came to the islands perhaps 1000 to 1500 years ago, and introduced all the food crops and the pig. Under a state of nature only sea food and a few wild plants, for example, the tree fern used as a source of starch, were available.

The Hawaiians lived in villages favorably located for obtaining food, and they preferred sites within sight and sound of the sea. Their houses were rectangular in shape and were thatched with pili grass over a framework of wood. Stone was not part of the construction of buildings except in the heiaus (temples), which were built largely of rocks. The food supply came primarily from planted crops—taro, yams, sweet potatoes, and bananas—and from fishing. Other plant foods were the arrowroot, breadfruit, coconut, sugar cane, pandanus, seaweeds and the tree fern for eating, and kukui nuts for seasoning and oil. Pigs were raised in moderate numbers, but most of their flesh was reserved for feasts. Taro, like rice, is best grown on water-covered patches of ground on the valley floors, and such

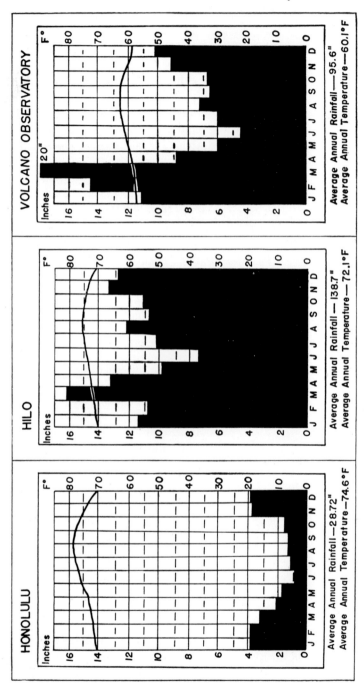

Figure 100. Climatic graphs for Honolulu, Hilo, and Volcano Observatory.

areas were the most thickly populated by the native Hawaiians of any in the islands. Some upland taro was raised without irrigation in rainy locations, and yams and sweet potatoes were planted on moderately dry uplands; but most of the land now in sugar and pineapples was originally covered by forests, and little was cultivated by the natives. In addition to food plants, the paper mulberry was grown, and from its inner bark was made the bark cloth called *kapa* (tapa).

The Hawaiians utilized the forests for timber from which canoes, the framework of houses, and wooden utensils and implements were made; for materials such as olona fiber for making fishline, ti leaves for wrappings, luahala (pandanus) leaves for plaiting mats and baskets, and coir from coconuts for cordage; for the feathers of birds from which robes and decorations were made; and to a small extent for gathering food, although wild animals did not exist. Stone, wood, shells, and bone were manufactured into artifacts, weapons, and household articles because the Hawaiians had no metals.

Fish, shellfish, and other sea food were important to the Hawaiians, who built stone walls into shallow water to enclose scores of ponds in which mullet and other fish were raised. As late as 1853 there were 53 fishponds on Molokai, and many were also found on Oahu, Maui, and Kauai. Some fishponds are still operated.

The ideally situated village possessed low land for taro and a water supply to irrigate the fields; a coastal strip for fishing, fishponds, house sites, and the launching of canoes; some uplands suitable for sweet potatoes and yams; and forested mountains that could furnish timber and feathers. Nearly all the original population, estimated at 200,000, lived along the coastal lowlands and in the valleys. Until after the middle of the nineteenth century Hawaii was the most populous island, but Oahu has ranked first for the last seventy-five years because of the rapid growth of Honolulu. Only Niihau and Kahoolawe have lost population compared with ancient times, although certain sections on other islands have become depopulated, for example, windward Molokai and the Napali coast of Kauai.

HISTORICAL DEVELOPMENT

The islands were discovered by Captain James Cook in January, 1778, and were named the Sandwich Islands. They supplied food and water, and served as a base for the refitting of ships engaged in the fur trade between the Pacific coast of North America and China. The discovery of sandalwood, which was highly valued by the Chinese because of the aromatic oil contained in the heartwood of the slow-growing tree, stimulated trade. Sandalwood logs were the chief export from the islands between 1800 and 1830, being worth $300,000 annually, but careless cutting exhausted this resource by about 1835.

Between 1791 and 1810 the Hawaiian group was united under the rule of King Kamehameha. In Kamehameha's reign feuds and tribal wars were stopped, land was apportioned to the people, and trade with foreigners was encouraged. A few traders established themselves in the Hawaiian Islands before 1800, and by 1818 between 100 and 200 foreigners were residents. In 1820 missionaries began to arrive who helped in the education of the Hawaiians and the evolution of the people into a nation. Hawaii was a kingdom until 1893 and a republic until 1898, when it was annexed to the United States at the time of the Spanish-American War.

From about 1820 until the Civil War in the United States, the whaling fleet, chiefly American, had Hawaii as a base of operations, a source of food and supplies, and a place to rest the sailors and refit the ships. The industry reached its peak between 1840 and 1860, when one hundred to several hundred whaling ships a year visited the ports of Honolulu, Lahaina, and Hilo. Five hundred and eighty-five vessels are reported to have called at the port of Honolulu in 1852.

Young Hawaiian men joined ships as sailors to such an extent, sometimes more than 1000 in a year, that it became a factor in the depopulation of the country, a condition that had been started by introduced diseases and changing circumstances of life after contact with the westerners. In 1832 there were 124,000 Hawaiians; by 1850, there were 82,500; and by 1860, there were 67,000. Intermarriage with other races became common after 1860, and in 1872 a census showed 56,897 people, of whom 51,531 were Hawaiians. The low point in population was probably reached about 1875, after which date immigration from the Orient and elsewhere more than compensated for the decline in numbers of the Hawaiians.

The decades of the 1860's and 1870's were a time of changing economic base. The whaling industry declined because of the reduction in numbers of whales, the destruction of whaling ships by the *Shenandoah* and other Confederate raiders during the American Civil War, the loss of much of the whaling fleet in Arctic ice floes, and the substitution of the kerosene lamp for the whale-oil candle after the discovery of petroleum in 1859. Feeling the need of substantial new industries to take the place of whaling, the Hawaiians undertook to expand the production of sugar cane and rice; and with the signing of a reciprocity treaty with the United States in 1875, the production of these commodities was greatly expanded. Capital became available, and scores of sugar plantations were started. The discovery of artesian water and the construction of canals and tunnels to bring water from the rainy side of islands to dry areas made it possible to grow sugar cane by irrigation on land that otherwise was too arid for the crop. Improved varieties of cane and the lavish application of fertilizer also helped the growth of the industry, which expanded in tonnage of sugar fifteen times between 1875 and 1890. Labor was needed by the sugar plantations, and from 1877 to 1890 more than 55,000 immigrant laborers were admitted, over half of whom were Chinese and about one-fourth Portuguese. Some of the workmen returned home after the end of their period of enlistment, but many of them became permanent residents. Japanese began to come to the islands in numbers in 1885, and continued to come until 1907 when their immigration was restricted by a "gentlemen's agreement." Thereafter Filipinos became a leading source of plantation labor.

THE PEOPLE

Many peoples with different cultural backgrounds have contributed to the present population of the Hawaiian Islands. There has been much intermarriage between the diverse groups that have fused, until Hawaii is frequently cited as an example of a successful melting pot for races. The number of pure-blood native Hawaiians has declined pretty steadily since the discovery of the islands by Captain Cook. However, the number of part-Hawaiians has been increasing for many years, and they now greatly outnumber the full Hawaiians.

Settlers came to Hawaii for various reasons. Americans and Europeans came first as traders and missionaries; and their descendants, along with more recent immigrants, to a great extent manage the plantations, big ranches, banks, factories, mills, and large mercantile establishments. Need for laborers on the sugar plantations account for most of the immigration of Portuguese, Chinese, Japanese, Koreans, Filipinos, and a few from other Pacific islands. Descendants of these former plantation workers now are found operating small farms, running thousands of retail stores, and engaging in service, clerical, and professional occupations.

The population has been increasing since about 1875, and it more than tripled between 1900 and 1950, according to the census, which was taken every 6 years from 1860 to 1900, after which it has been taken every 10 years. Table 4 gives the principal racial elements in the population of Hawaii in 1940, the breakdown for 1950 not being available at the time of publication.

TABLE 3

POPULATION OF HAWAII

1832	130,313	1872	56,897	1910	191,909
1836	106,579	1878	57,985	1920	255,912
1850	84,165	1884	80,578	1930	368,336
1855	73,138	1890	89,990	1940	426,654
1860	69,800	1896	109,020	1950	493,437
1866	62,959	1900	154,001	(preliminary count)	

TABLE 4

RACIAL ELEMENTS IN THE POPULATION OF HAWAII, 1940

Hawaiian	21,165
Part Hawaiian	42,326
Caucasian	115,836
Chinese	28,609
Japanese	158,849
Korean	6,761
Filipino	52,148
Others	960
Total	426,654

SETTLEMENT PATTERN

The pattern of settlement in Hawaii has changed considerably during the last century. In the old days the populated areas formed a fringe along the shoreline of the islands and extended inland only in the larger valleys. Chief gaps in the settled zone came where mountains descended abruptly into the sea, for example, the Napali coast of Kauai. The interior plateaus, plains, and slopes had few residents until the land began to be used for grazing introduced livestock, and the planting of new crops. Forest land has been cleared for sugar mainly since 1875, and the irrigation of dry uplands was chiefly accomplished after 1890. Upland plains and slopes were first planted to pineapples about 1903.

The people of Hawaii live not only along the coasts and in the valleys, but plantation villages also occupy sites on the interior plains and uplands, where also are found small farms and large stock ranches. The settlement of lands for plantation agriculture was an accomplishment of the haole (Caucasian) managers and capitalists. Only high mountains, precipitous slopes, and very rocky or dry ground are uninhabited. In the old days there were many villages but no large cities. Canoes could land on almost any beach, and commerce did not demand large vessels. Few people lived in Honolulu until its harbor began to be used by traders and whalers. Many village sites, important before the advent of Europeans, proved unsuited to modern conditions, and now are either reduced to hamlets or abandoned.

Honolulu, on Oahu, now has about half the population of the Territory, and is built near a small but adequate harbor, which is protected by a coral reef. In 1949 the city claimed a population of over 250,000 (181,000 in 1940). It is the largest city, not only in the Hawaiian Islands but also in all the Pacific islands between the mainland of North America and Japan, Manila and Australia. Honolulu

FIGURE 101. Waikiki Beach and Diamond Head, an extinct volcano. Photograph, Hawaii Visitors Bureau.

has substantial office buildings, large hotels, and modern houses, and except for the tropical verdure there is little difference in appearance between the city and a seaport of similar size in the States. The industrial district is close to the harbor, the resort hotels and stores for tourists are at Waikiki Beach, and the homes of the people are spread out over a large area as most residents live in separate houses rather than apartments. Scores of neighborhood business districts are scattered over the city, each being called by a familiar local name. Kaimuki, Moiliili, Waikiki, Aala, Kalihi, Palama, and Manoa Valley are examples. The city has climbed up the slopes of the Koolau Mountains, and some of the choice residential neighborhoods are on the heights at altitudes of 1000 feet or more. Honolulu is the major seaport and airport in the north Pacific, and a naval base of great strategic importance. Leading industries are those associated with shipping, the wholesale and retail distribution of imports and exports, catering to tourists and the military, canning of pineapples, manufacture of fertilizer, managing headquarters for the plantations, and various service occupations.

Hilo, the second city of the islands, is also a seaport located on a harbor partly protected by a lava flow on the island of Hawaii. It is the chief port of that island and has a population of over 20,000. Other cities of more than 5000 people are Waipahu and Wahiawa in interior Oahu, and Lahaina and Wailuku on Maui. Large communities are also located at Pearl Harbor, Schofield Barracks, and other military establishments on Oahu.

PLANTATION AGRICULTURE

Hawaiian commercial agriculture is predominantly of the plantation type. Plantations of sugar cane and pineapples comprise 95 per cent of the cropped land, and supply nearly all the agricultural exports of the Territory. The large-scale operations of the plantations afford a striking contrast to the small farms on which coffee, taro, bananas and vegetables are grown, chiefly for use within the islands.

SUGAR

Sugar, the paramount industry of the Territory of Hawaii, forms the foundation upon which business in the islands is built. In early years there were difficulties in growing sugar, including lack of experience, scarcity of capital, shortage of labor, and an uncertain market. In 1876 reciprocity with the United States became an accomplished fact, and the sugar industry developed rapidly. Exports of 12,540 tons in 1875 grew to 125,000 tons in 1890. During the 1930's the output of sugar per year averaged 1,000,000 tons; but during the 1940's the usual crop was between 800,000 and 900,000 tons, for example, 835,107 tons were ground in 1948. The value of the sugar raised and manufactured within the Territory has varied from $50,-000,000 to over $100,000,000 annually during the decade of the 1940's, depending on production and the price of sugar. About 9 tons of cane are needed for a ton of sugar, and approximately 8,000,000 to 9,000,000 tons of cane are harvested from about 120,000 acres of the nearly 205,000 acres planted to cane.

The number of plantations, mills, and employees has been declining slowly since the late 1920's when there were 47 sugar plantations, 43 mills, and over 50,000 laborers. In 1950 there were 28 plantations, 26 mills in operation, and about 27,000 employees. The acreage in cane has declined 25 per cent from an all-time high of 276,800 acres in 1917 to 235,110 in 1940, and 215,200 in 1948. However, the annual production has declined less than the acreage, being about one-tenth less than in the peak years of the 1930's. This record was made possible by more efficient use of the land, improved cultural practices, and better varieties of cane.

FIGURE 102. Machine harvesting of sugar cane. Photograph courtesy of the Hawaii Visitors Bureau.

Mechanized methods are used throughout the field and mill operations in the sugar industry. The soil is plowed and worked in preparation for planting by huge tractors pulling plows that turn a furrow two feet deep. Two rows are planted at a time by a machine that digs furrows, deposits fertilizer, lays sections of cane in the furrows for seed, and covers them with dirt. After planting, distribution ditches for irrigation are laid out and lined with concrete slabs or aluminum gutters to prevent loss of water by seepage. Spraying the young cane with weed killer saves labor compared with the older method of hoeing by hand. Machines apply fertilizer as needed, and the young cane is cultivated by machines. In harvest the leaves are burned off to lessen the amount of trash to be handled, and the cane may be knocked over with bulldozer rakes or by crawler-type cranes (Fig. 102), which load it into trucks or little railroad cars for transportation to the mill. Hand cutting of cane is now practiced only on steeply sloping land. Three or four ratoon crops that sprout from the roots can generally be secured before replanting is required at the end of 8 or 10 years. Some plantations, however, replant at the end of a single harvest, when the machinery has taken the roots with the cane. Sugar cane exhausts the soil, but rotation of crops is seldom practiced; instead fertilizer is applied to maintain production.

Hawaiian sugar mills are most efficient. At the mill mechanical unloaders handle the cane a ton at a time. After being washed to remove the dirt, the cane is shredded and crushed to squeeze out the juice, which is sent through heaters, clarifiers, filters, evaporators, vacuum pans, and centrifugals to extract the sugar. By-products from the sugar mills are molasses, used for stock feed and industrial alcohol, and bagasse, the residue from which the juice has been taken, that is used for fuel, and at one plant for making insulating board called canec. Much of the mill machinery is made in Honolulu. Most of the raw sugar is sent to the San Francisco Bay region for refining.

Raising sugar in Hawaii requires much capital, nearly $200,000,000 being invested in the industry, and everything is done on a large and efficient scale. Land has to be prepared for irrigation, sources of water developed by wells, tunnels, reservoirs, and diversion from streams, miles of ditches and pipes built to bring water to the field, a mill and village built, and a great quantity of equipment secured as the industry is highly mechanized.

The sugar industry is concentrated on four islands, Hawaii, Maui, Oahu, and Kauai. In spite of declining acreage, production of sugar cane has been maintained through larger yields made possible by the lavish application of fertilizer, the control of pests, and the introduction of improved varieties of cane.

Insect pests include borers that attack roots and stalks, leafhoppers, and the bettle *Anomala*. Leaf mosaic and other fungus and virus diseases also attack the sugar plant. The insects have been controlled by the introduction of parasites. The tachinid fly from New Guinea lays eggs in the larvae of the cane borers and reduces their depredations by 90 per cent; a wasp (*Scolia*) from the Philippines destroys the *Anomala* by laying its eggs in the bettle's grub, which dies as the wasp develops; and several insects prey on the leafhopper (*Perkinsiella saccharicida*), including a tiny antlike wasp from China whose larvae hatched from eggs imbedded in the side of the leafhopper destroy it by sucking out the body juices, and a minute wasp from Formosa that lays its eggs in the eggs of the leafhopper. A large toad, *Bufo marinus*, from Central America, and possessor of a giant appetite for insects, has been introduced and is proving very useful.

New varieties and strains of cane have been developed at the experiment stations of the Hawaiian Sugar Planters Association and of the University of Hawaii that yield more tonnage per acre, have a higher sucrose content, and greater resistance to insect pests and plant diseases, like root rot, than the types of cane previously planted. The sugar plantations employ entomologists, chemists, plant geneticists, botanists, foresters, geologists, meteorologists, and plant physiologists to carry on needed research. Probably in no tropical region has science been better applied to agriculture.

The sugar industry is favored by natural conditions of soil and climate, lay of the land and sources of water permitting irrigation that makes for maximum and steady yields, introduced laborers, a protective tariff, and highly efficient management that, by using fertilizers, controlling insects and other pests, cooperative refining and marketing, development of new varieties of cane, extensive mechanization, and proper handling of labor has really made the sugar industry what it is today. Sugar production, therefore, is favored by a fortunate combination of natural and human factors.

The management of the plantations is provided by five experienced commercial houses or sugar factors that supervise all but two small plantations.

PINEAPPLES

Pineapples introduced from tropical America rank next to sugar among the industries of Hawaii, and are of increasing importance to the island economy, bringing in over $60,000,000 annually. Only half a century old, the success of the pineapple industry has stemmed from a combination of favorable climate and soil and applied scientific knowledge and sound business judgment.

Pineapples are propagated by planting suckers, slips, crowns, or stumps from selected plants; seeds are used only for experimental breeding. Land being prepared for planting pineapples is plowed deeply, and much trash from previous crops is worked into the ground to provide humus. The fields are divided by roads about 300 feet apart over which the machinery can run, and on sloping land planting is done on the contours (Fig. 103). Plants are inserted into the ground, in double rows through a mulch paper, usually by hand, although planting machines are being tried. The mulching paper helps to conserve moisture, maintain an even temperature, and keep down weeds. The machine that lays the paper also fertilizes and fumigates the ground in the same operation. During growth the pineapples are sprayed, cultivated, fertilized, and weeded by machinery, a minimum of hand work being necessary. Little irrigation is done, pineapples being raised as a dryland crop, but great quantities of fertilizer are applied. The first fruit ripens in about 18 months. All the suckers are trimmed off except two, which grow into fruits in another 12 months; sometimes a third ratoon crop is gathered before replanting. The main harvest season is from July through September. Some fruit

FIGURE 103. Pineapple field from the air showing the rows of fruit planted on the contour of a slope. Photograph, Hawaiian Pineapple Co.

ripens throughout the year, however, and by staggered planting the canning season has been extended. Labor is saved by a harvesting machine with two side booms 50 feet long carrying conveyor belts on which the laborers place the fruit after removing the crown, and the pineapples are carried to a huge crate or dumped into a truck for transport to the canneries.

A pineapple cannery is a model of efficiency. First the pineapples are graded for size and then pass in a continuous stream through a machine that pares and cores the fruit faster than one each second. Next the cylinders of fruit are trimmed by hand if necessary, sliced by machines, and inserted in the cans to which sugar syrup is added before they are sterilized and sealed.

There are nine companies operating thirteen plantations with about 70,000 acres in pineapples, and there are nine canneries in the islands —three on Oahu, three on Maui, and three on Kauai. The number of employees averages about 9000. One of the establishments in Honolulu is reputed to be the largest fruit cannery in the world. The total annual pack is 18,000,000 to 20,000,000 cases, divided into about 55 per cent pineapple and 45 per cent pineapple juice. Shipments of frozen pineapple are increasing ($626,500 in 1947), but export of fresh pineapples to the mainland has been impossible since an embargo was placed against fruit from Hawaii because of the fruit flies found there. The cores and peelings are made into pinapple bran for stock feed. Citric acid is another by-product. The machinery for canning pineapples was invented in Hawaii, and the methods for raising the fruit were perfected there also. The fruit is grown on Oahu (Fig. 99), Maui, Kauai, Lanai, and Molokai, but is not grown commercially on the island of Hawaii. The plantations are usually located above 1000 feet altitude; for example, on Oahu the pineapple fields occupy the upper section of the central plateau and sugar the lower slopes. The variety called Smooth Cayenne is the only pineapple extensively grown for market in Hawaii.

Canned pineapple is not a necessity of life, and must compete with several mainland fruits. To stimulate demand for pineapple products and help in the orderly marketing of the crop, Hawaiian producers spend more than a million dollars a year on advertising and promotion campaigns. The industry is based on production of quality products, good management, and clever advertising, and the value of this combination is proved by the growth of the industry from 2,000 cases in 1903, to 2,000,000 cases in 1913, 6,000,000 cases in 1923, and 12,726,000 cases in 1931. In 1931 because of the economic depression not all the pack could be marketed, and reorganization of the industry became necessary. Renewed demand for canned pineapple and the development of a large market for pineapple juice have again put the industry on a firm basis; by the late 1940's production had made new records.

The pineapple companies maintain an experiment station and employ a large staff of research workers. The soil is analyzed and the growth of the pineapples watched, and if the plants need certain elements these are fed to them. For example, in some soils the iron is held in a compound from which it cannot be obtained by the pineapple plant; such fields are sprayed with iron sulfate to supply the necessary iron. Land is fumigated before planting to rid the ground of harmful organisms, and weeds are in part eliminated by chemical weed sprays. By the use of hormone sprays the growth of plants is stimulated, and the time of fruiting is hastened.   It is expected that other hormones can be developed that will delay maturity of the fruit so that the period of harvesting will be extended.

DIVERSIFIED AGRICULTURE AND RANCHING

In 1948 there were 3650 farmers engaged in raising diversified crops and livestock, the market value of the products sold being a record $30,752,000.   This value, however, did not equal that of pineapples produced by 13 plantations and was only half that of sugar sold from 28 plantations.   Not included in the farm crops are flowers, of which 296,897 packages worth about $2,000,000 were shipped to the mainland in 1948, and more than that value was sold locally.   The market value of all animal products sold by ranchers that year was $21,611,000 and of diversified and miscellaneous crops was $9,141,000.   Hawaii is not self-sufficient in growing fruits and vegetables, and it imports from the mainland annually between 60,000,000 and 70,000,000 dollars' worth of edible animal and plant food products.

Animal products in order of their value are beef, dairy, poultry, and pork.   Sheep and bees are of minor importance.   Island beef comes mostly from large ranches on Hawaii and Maui, one of which on the big island covers 260,000 acres.   Oahu supplies 75 per cent of the fresh milk, and because there is a shortage of grazing land convenient to Honolulu a majority of the cows are stall fed.

Rice was second to sugar among crops of Hawaii for many years, but during the last quarter century it has declined to insignificance. Once 10,000 acres of rich, easily flooded lowlands were planted to the crop by hand methods, but in 1948 only 250 acres on Kauai were in rice.   Importation of cheap rice from the mainland, where it is raised on mechanized farms, was the chief reason for the decline.

Coffee, worth about $2,000,000 annually, ranks third among crops in the Territory, although far behind sugar and pineapples.   Coffee production is shared among 700 small farmers in the Kona district on the island of Hawaii who have 3500 acres in the crop.   Kona is on leeward Hawaii, and the coffee is raised at elevations of 1000 to 2500 on the lower slopes of Mauna Loa.

The climate of Hawaii is favorable for most tropical fruits, and many have been introduced.   In 1948 about 3200 acres were planted to fruit and nuts.   Unfortunately certain pests have come also, notably the melon fly, the Mediterranean fruit fly, and the Oriental or mango fly.   To prevent the carrying of such pests to the mainland an embargo is in effect preventing shipments of fresh fruits from Hawaii so that markets for unprocessed fruit are entirely local. To combat the harmful insects, parasites that prey on them have been introduced and sprays are used; nevertheless much damage is done to many fruits.

Bananas are an important local food and are exceeded only by pineapples in value of fruit, although bananas lag far behind. Production exceeds 9,000,000 pounds annually. More than 1000 acres are in bananas.

TABLE 5

CROP LAND, IN ACRES
(1948, data from County Agents)

	Territory	Hawaii	Maui	Molokai and Lanai	Oahu	Kauai and Niihau
Plantation crops						
Sugar cane	205,293	95,000	32,651	......	35,493	42,149
Pineapple	68,000	....	11,000	31,000	20,000	6,000
Total	273,293		.			
Non-plantation crops						
Vegetables, fresh	5,254	1,764	1,254	77	1,878	291
Coffee	3,500	3,500	......	......	......	......
Nuts, macadamia	1,030	672	6	2	123	227
Taro (for manufacturing)	1,006	247	69	18	453	219
Rice	217	......	......	......	......	217
Total	13,917	7,099	1,719	184	3,941	974
Total cropped land	287,210					
Grazing land	1,638,215	1,260,715	99,250	83,750	10,300	184,200
Farm and grazing land or agricultural land	1,925,425					

Papayas are a very popular fruit, and many varieties are grown. There are nearly 200,000 papaya trees in the islands, and production is over 7,000,000 pounds a year. The bulk of the commercial crop is planted on Oahu.

Among the many other fruits grown are mangoes, breadfruit, avocados, oranges, tangerines, figs, grapes, passion fruit, and coconuts. Guavas grow wild and are gathered in a small way for jelly and preserves. Macadamia nuts, introduced from Australia, are of increasing importance, and more than 1000 acres are planted to this nut tree. No copra is made in Hawaii, although the fruit is used in various ways. Coconut trees are more often considered of worth for shade and decoration than for food.

Taro is used for food; about 1000 acres of flooded land are devoted to the crop. About 6000 tons are harvested annually, about half coming from Oahu. The growing of vegetables is increasing, 5250 acres being in vegetables in 1948 on 1800 farms, from which crops to the value of about $5,000,000 were harvested. Still large quantities of fresh vegetables are imported from California and other mainland areas, and the value of the imports exceeds that of the island vegetables several times over.

NON-AGRICULTURAL INDUSTRIES

FISHING

Several hundred species of fish, including many with bizarre multicoloring, like the butterfly and surgeon fishes, abound in the warm waters around Hawaii. The Hawaiians secured much food from the sea, and they recognized individual rights for fishing along the sea frontage. To increase the available quantity of fish, hundreds of fish ponds were located along low shores and were enclosed by long stone walls that took much time and labor to construct. Only a few of the fish ponds are now in use. Commercial fishing is done principally by the Japanese, who catch the fish with seines and hooks and lines from their sturdy sampans. There are about 1200 to 1500 commercial fishermen in the islands.

In 1948 the catch of fish taken in Hawaiian waters was a record 14,240,000 pounds, with a value of $4,170,000. The most valuable commercial fish are the *aku* (bonito), *ahi* (tuna), *ahipalaha* (albacore), *a'u* (swordfish), *akule* and *opelu*, both mackerels. The *mahimahi* (dolphin), *ulua* (pompano), *he'e* (squid), and many others are also marketed. Tuna are canned in Honolulu, but the others are sold as fresh fish. Shore fishing is carried on both for sport and for food, and, besides fish, shore fisheries supply turtles, spiny lobsters, crabs, octopuses, and small shellfish. Over seventy species of *limu* (algae or seaweed) were used for food by the Hawaiians.

TOURISM

A welcome addition to the economy of Hawaii is the money spent by visitors who come mostly from the mainland. The tourist business is called the "third industry" of the islands, and in 1948 when 42,000 tourists visited the islands they left behind an estimated $35,000,000.

Passengers on boats calling at Honolulu who spend a day or two in port are not counted. Travel depends so much on economic and political conditions that there are large variations in the number of tourists (for example, in 1932 and 1933 there were only 10,000 visitors) and the amount of money they spend, but ordinarily several thousand people in Hawaii gain much of their livelihood from the tourist business. There are two peaks for travel during the year; the greatest activity is during the winter, particularly for two or three months after Christmas, with a somewhat less busy time during the summer. In the spring and autumn seasons visitors are fewest.

The tourists flock to Waikiki beach (Fig. 101), and they are the main support of the resort hotels, many restaurants, travel agencies, transportation companies, curio shops, and amusement centers. Honolulu benefits most from the visitors, but Hawaii, Maui, and Kauai are patronized to a less degree. Attractions include a delightful and healthful climate, the beaches and sea bathing, ocean game fish, volcanoes and lava flows, scenic mountains and forests, abundant flowers, the sugar and pineapple plantations, historical remains of the Hawaiian kingdom, and the diverse character of the population.

THE MILITARY

Money paid for wages, materials, and constructions for the naval, air, and ground forces, including their civilian employees, exceeds that paid to employees of the sugar plantations or any other single industry in Hawaii. During the years of the Second World War there were 27,500 army and navy civilian employees and 13,400 employees of other government agencies, and the amount distributed annually for wages was $180,000,000. In the late 1940's, however, the number of employees and wages had been reduced to about half the totals mentioned. Nearly 90,000 acres of land are used by the military. About 55,000 acres on Oahu, 14.4 per cent of the island, are in military reservations, but other installations are located on Midway, Maui, and other islands. Pearl Harbor, one of the great naval bases of the world, is headquarters for the Pacific fleet. The airports, like Hickam Field and Barber's Point, and the army posts, like Schofield Barracks, are among the largest built by the United States. Constructions include huge storage warehouses, repair shops, and other facilities that are almost cities in themselves. By 1950, because of changed conditions, personnel stationed in Hawaii had been greatly reduced from the peak years, and several airports and other installations had been deactivated or placed on a stand-by basis. The use made of the facilities in the future will depend on affairs outside

Hawaii. The islands serve as a port of call, and a supply and repair center for transpacific transport by water and air for the military. During the war, by leasing and other arrangements, the Army controlled 210,000 acres and the Navy 118,694 acres, and annual rentals amounted to $41,000,000. Much of this land has now been released.

MANUFACTURING

The processing of materials derived from agriculture is the foundation for manufacturing in Hawaii. Examples are the extraction of sugar, the canning of sliced pineapple and juice, the making of jellies, jams, and pickles, the canning of guava and papaya nectars, poi made from taro, meat slaughtering, processing of coffee and macadamia nuts, and the manufacture of mulch paper (called canec) from bagasse. Tuna are seasonally canned at Honolulu, and most of the pack is exported. Many perishable food products are made for local consumption, including baked goods, ice cream, beer, soft drinks, and confectionery.

The commercial importance of Hawaii has led to the manufacture of sugar-mill machinery, the repair of ships, and the building of fishing sampans and other small boats, and the operation of welding and machine shops. Fertilizers (125,000 tons a year) are imported and mixed or otherwise prepared for plantation use. Sport garments are made from island patterns and include Aloha shirts, gowns, and bathing costumes. Some footwear, household utilities, furniture, and building supplies are manufactured for local use, and curios, ukuleles, cosmetics, and other small articles are made both for the tourist trade and for local sale. Printing and publishing businesses are located chiefly in Honolulu and depend mostly on local demand.

During the decade of the 1940's the total annual value of manufactures in Hawaii was about $150,000,000, and the average number of employees throughout the year was about 20,000; but this is exceeded considerably during the summer canning season for pineapples.

COMMERCE AND COMMUNICATION

The commerce of Hawaii is predominantly with the mainland states, and often exceeds $300,000,000 annually. The value of island commodities shipped from Hawaii yearly is about $100,000,000 ($114,-000,000 in 1946), and imports are about $200,000,000 ($271,000,000 in 1947). The excess of imports over exports largely represents goods for the federal government, including construction materials, plus the purchasing power from the wages and salaries of the Armed Forces and the civilian employees of the military establishments. Tourists and interest on investments outside the islands supply other income for purchases. Commerce to and from the mainland states and Hawaii is classified as coastal trade and is a monopoly of the United States flag. Over 90 per cent of the imports are from the States, and 98 per cent of the exports go to the mainland.

Transportation facilities in Hawaii are generally adequate although changes have taken place in recent years in the nature of the transport agencies. Railroads have almost ceased to function, most of the mileage on Oahu and that on the Hamakua Coast of Hawaii have been torn up, and only a few short railways on plantations are in operation. Abandoned rail lines have been replaced by trucks and busses. Much of the cane is now hauled to the mills on huge trucks. The six principal islands are well served by paved highways, and these islands also have good airports. Early in 1949 passenger service by steamship between islands was discontinued, and the inter-island ships and barges carry freight only. Airplanes transport the passengers, mail, and some of the package freight.

OUTLYING ISLANDS IN THE HAWAIIAN CHAIN

Midway is an atoll 1300 miles west of Honolulu, near the end of the Hawaiian chain; only the uninhabited Ocean Island lies farther west. Midway is nearly circular and about 6 miles in diameter within the encircling reef. The lagoon, shallow for the most part, includes two islands, Sand and Eastern, with a combined area of about 2 square miles. Sand Island attains a height of 43 feet and is the site of an air base and cable station. The United States took possession of Midway in 1867, and technically it is not a part of the Territory of Hawaii. In 1935 Midway began to be used as a landing field for trans-Pacific airplanes, and it is an important strategic air base. To the west, in June, 1942, was fought the battle of Midway, which ended in the defeat of the Japanese fleet and was a turning point in the Pacific war. Airplanes are given a treatment for insects before proceeding from Midway.

Except for the Midway Islands, the islands in the Hawaiian chain are a part of the Territory of Hawaii and are included in the county and city of Honolulu, which also includes Palmyra Island far to the south. Honolulu has the greatest distance between its parts of any city on earth.

The islands are of two types. Those that are of lava and therefore erosional remnants are Nihoa, Necker, La Perouse Pinnacle or Rock, and Gardner Pinnacles; the low islands of coral sand are French Frigate Shoal, close to which rises La Perouse Pinnacle, Laysan Island, Lisianski Island, Pearl and Hermes Reef, all east of Midway, and Ocean or Kure Island to the west.

ISOLATED ISLAND OUTPOSTS

Johnston (Cornwallis) Island is situated at latitude 16° 44′ north and longitude 169° 32′ west, about 760 miles southwest of Honolulu. It has been owned by the United States since 1858, when it was claimed under the guano act. Johnston Island is about 3000 feet long and 600 feet wide, and is made of sand and coral that reaches 44 feet above sea level in one place. Together with little Sand Island, it is located in a shallow lagoon about 8 miles long that is surrounded by an irregular coral reef. Johnston Island has very little rainfall, and the vegetation is limited to bunch grass and a few low herbs. Potable ground water is lacking. The island was uninhabited until it was developed as a base for seaplanes and landplanes by the military, which controls all installations and facilities.

Wake Island is an atoll at latitude 19° 16′ north, longitude 166° 37′ east, about 2300 statute miles west of Honolulu, and has been owned by the United States since 1899. The atoll consists of three islets, Wake, Wilkes, and Peale, which enclose a lagoon on three sides. Birds are abundant and include a dozen species of sea birds, several migratory birds, and a flightless rail (*Rallus wakensis*). Fish are plentiful in the shallow water, and rats and crabs on the land. Wake was never permanently inhabited by man until 1935, when it was developed by Pan American Airways, which built an inn, shop, power house, radio, and living quarters for ground employees on Peale Island to serve the company planes on their transpacific flights. Wake Island was later developed as a strategic air base. Captured by the Japanese in December, 1941, after a two weeks' battle, it was not reoccupied by the United States until the end of the war. The Interior Department is now the governing agency on Wake. Both the military services and the civil-operated planes use the facilities for aircraft.

Marcus Island (latitude 24° 34′ north, longitude 154° east), renamed Minamitori Shima by the Japanese, is located about 1000 miles southeast of Tokyo and about 1000 miles northwest of Wake. The island is a raised coral atoll with a maximum elevation of about 75 feet. It is of triangular shape, about 1½ miles north to south and 1¼ miles east and west, and has an area of about 740 acres. A coral reef surrounds the island, whose surface is flat and originally was covered with woods. Marcus is isolated in the north Pacific and hence has high value as an air base, weather station and strategic outpost. Seized by Japan in 1899 for a cable base, it is now occupied by the United States.

REFERENCES

Cline, M. G., *Soils of Hawaii*, U.S. Department of Agriculture, Washington, D.C. *In preparation*.

Coulter, J. W., *Agricultural Land–Use Planning in the Territory of Hawaii*, Agricultural Extension Service, University of Hawaii, Honolulu, 1940.

Elliott, Ralph, *Statistics of Diversified Agriculture in Hawaii, 1948*, Agricultural Extension Service Circular 263, University of Hawaii, 1949.

Freeman, Otis W., *Story of the Hawaiian Islands*, McKnight and McKnight, Bloomington, Illinois, 1935. (Out of print).

Jarrett, Lorna H., *Hawaii and Its People*, Honolulu, 1933. (Out of print.)

Jones, Stephen B., "The Weather Element in Hawaiian Climate," *Annals Assoc. Amer. Geog.*, Vol. XXIX, pp. 29–57, 1939.

Kuykendahl, Ralph, and A. Grove Day, *Hawaii: A History*, Prentice-Hall, New York, 1948.

Leopold, Luna B., "Diurnal Weather Patterns on Oahu and Lanai, Hawaii," *Pacific Sci.*, Vol. II, pp. 81–95, 1948.

MacDonald, G. A., F. P. Shepard, and D. C. Cox, "Tsunami of April 1, 1946, in the Hawaiian Islands," *Pacific Sci.*, Vol. I, pp. 21–37, 1947.

Ripperton, J. C., and E. Y. Hosaka, "Vegetation Zones of Hawaii," *Hawaii Agr. Exp. Sta. Bull.* 89, University of Hawaii, Honolulu, 1942.

Sherman, G. D., T. C. Foster, and C. K. Fujimoto, "Properties of Ferruginous Humic Latosols of the Hawaiian Islands," *Proc. Soil Sci. Amer.*, Vol. XIII, 1948.

Stearns, Harold T., *Geology of the Hawaiian Islands*, Bulletin 8, Division of Hydrology, Territory of Hawaii, Honolulu, 1946.

Territory of Hawaii, Division of Hydrology, Honolulu, *Bulletins* on the geology and water resources of the separate islands, including Hawaii, Maui, Oahu, Kauai, Lanai, Molokai, Niihau, and Kahoolawe, besides other publications.

University of Hawaii, many bulletins, papers, and other publications on the island resources, industries, and people.

Vandercook, John W., *King Cane—the Story of Sugar in Hawaii*, Harper and Brothers, New York, 1939.

Wentworth, C. K., *Geographic Variations in Annual Rainfall on Oahu*, University of Hawaii Research Publication 22, 14 pp., Honolulu, 1946.

Zimmerman, E. C., *Insects of Hawaii*, Vol. I, University of Hawaii Press, Honolulu, 1948.

13

Eastern Polynesia[*]

OTIS W. FREEMAN

MOST OF THE ISLANDS OF EASTERN POLYNESIA SOUTH OF THE EQUATOR ARE included in French Oceania (Établissements Français de l'Océanie), which are the Marquesas, Society, Tuamotu, Austral, Mangareva, Rapa, and Morotini islands. In the eastern part of Polynesia also are the British islands of Pitcairn, Oena, Henderson, and Ducie, and the Chilean island of Easter.

FRENCH OCEANIA

The estimated areas and populations of the islands included in French Oceania are given in Table 1, but these statistics should be looked upon as approximations because authorities differ widely regarding them. The seat of government is Papeete, Tahiti, and the bulk of the trade of the colony also passes through this seaport, which is the only city of importance in the entire colony.

Some of the islands are high and of volcanic origin and are in striking contrast to smaller, low islands made from coral. The coral islands are atolls, except for Makatea in the Tuamotu group, which is a raised atoll and in the luxuriance of its vegetation resembles a high island. The volcanic islands may reach altitudes of several thousand feet and usually are characterized by jagged peaks, deep valleys, steep cliffs, abundant rainfall, running streams, rich soil, and dense and varied vegetation. The atolls are low and flat with small strips of land, no streams and few sources of water, and poor, thin soil. There are few species of trees or other plants, but these are adapted to the atolls and may grow luxuriantly.

[*] This chapter was critically read in manuscript by Kenneth P. Emory, anthropologist, University of Hawaii and the Bernice P. Bishop Museum, Honolulu.

364

TABLE 1

FRENCH OCEANIA

	Number of Islands	Area, Square Miles	Estimated Population, 1950
Marquesas Islands	10	459	2,400
Society Islands	14	593	30,950
Tuamotu Archipelago	76	319	6,580
Austral Islands	5	53	3,190
Mangareva Group	4	11	580
Rapa	1	15	270
	110	1450	43,970

The trade winds are the dominant factor in the climate. They keep the temperatures equable, and most of the rainfall is associated with them. However, tropical cyclones occur and affect some sections severely on an average of once in thirty years. Many atolls suffer disastrously at such times. At sea level in different latitudes mean annual temperatures are between 75° and 80° F, with only a small annual range between the hottest season from December to March, and the coolest from June to August.

The Society Islands were discovered in 1767 by Wallis, visited by Bougainville in 1768, and by Cook in 1769 and on later voyages. The islands became favorite stopping places for traders and whalers, and, after 1820, traders and missionaries settled in Tahiti. In 1842, with the consent of Queen Pomare of Tahiti, the French established a protectorate, and in 1880 the islands, including the western Tuamotus, were formally annexed by France. In early days there were many native wars and some resistance to French rule, but, after such opposition proved useless, the natives accepted the foreign control and inevitable changes in the manner of life. Now they are nominally Christians. The majority of church members belong to the Catholic Church, and most of the remainder are Seventh Day Adventists and Mormons. Churches occupy an important place in community life. The Marquesas Islands were discovered by Mendaña in 1595, but were not visited by any other European until Cook found them in 1774. The islands were annexed by France in 1842. The numerous atolls of the Tuamotu Archipelago were discovered by many explorers, whalers, traders, and missionaries over many years, beginning with Quiros in 1606. France annexed the group in 1880. In Tahiti and the Marquesas Islands France early applied a policy of assimilation, but in the Tuamotus and most other outlying islands indirect rule is the usual custom and the chiefs are invested with the functions of minor civil officials.

The native peoples living in French Oceania are Polynesians, and ten to seven centuries ago the Society Islands served as a center of diffusion into other areas like Hawaii and New Zealand. Dialects differed somewhat, but in general the cultural pattern was similar in all the island groups where corresponding conditions existed.

The natives of eastern Polynesia had well-developed social customs, religion, and material culture. They were practical farmers, and they

FIGURE 104. Borabora, Society Islands. Note the steep mountain slopes that resulted from erosion. Photograph, K. P. Emory, Bernice P. Bishop Museum.

understood irrigation and cleverly constructed terraces, dikes, and ditches for the purpose. They knew their flora intimately, and utilized a large variety of products. From the upland forests they secured the fei (cooking banana), tumeric, arrowroot, kinds of taro, and roots of the tree ferns. Their ancestors had brought with them the bread-fruit, and taro for food, and the paper mulberry used for tapa cloth. Pigs, dogs, and chickens were also introduced. Shellfish were gathered from coastal waters, fish wiers were built, and fish were taken by a variety of other methods and gear. A fermented, narcotic drink was made from roots of the ava. They built substantial thatched houses, some of which were rectangular and others were rounded at the ends. Their canoes were seaworthy, and long voyages were made in those of a double-canoe and outrigger type that were equipped with sails. Tapa cloth and mat garments were worn. Priests occupied an important place in the community and sometimes gave exhibitions of their miraculous power, for example, in fire walking where a priest led a group across a pit filled with white-hot stones. There were many rules of etiquette and conduct followed by the people, including food restrictions on which tapus might be placed by the chiefs.

The title to land has been a problem in the islands. The native attitude towards land ownership is different from the European attitude so that there often is difficulty in obtaining a clear title. Normally a native property has a number of owners with undivided shares who are loath to dispose of their claims, and the process of untangling and evaluating the many interests is very slow and complicated.

Most of the natives are engaged in subsistence agriculture and fishing, and their principal source of cash is copra made for trade to the local merchant, usually a Chinese. Some grow vanilla for sale. In the Tuamotus diving for pearl shell is a seasonal occupation.

France dominates the trade of the colony and buys most of the copra and vanilla, although some of both are shipped to the United States. Before the Second World War Japan was the largest purchaser of phosphate. Some was sent to Australia, New Zealand, and Hawaii. About 1200 tons of pearl shell are produced annually from the Tuamotus. Over 20,000 tons of copra and about 200 tons of vanilla were exported per year before the war, but trade was slowed up for a time after the Second World War largely because of transportation difficulties.

THE SOCIETY ISLANDS

There are fourteen islands in the Society group between latitudes 15° 48′ and 17° 53′ south and longitudes 148° 5′ and 154° 43′ west, divided with respect to the trade winds into the Windward group (Isles du Vent), to the east, and the Leeward group (Isles sous le Vent), to the west. The trend of the islands is northwest to southwest. The high islands are all volcanic, and the bedrock is basalt. Names of the islands are given in Table 2. The area of the Society Islands has not been determined with certainty. Figures found for Tahiti alone varied from 402 to 600 square miles, but the area is conservatively estimated at 593 square miles for the group, with a population of about 31,000 on the eight inhabited islands.

Tahitians, restricting the term to the natives of the Society Islands, are typically a tall, handsome people and closely resemble the Hawaiian type of Polynesian. The Tahitian dialect is softer than in most other parts of Polynesia, and it is marked by the absence of the *ng* and *k* sounds. Tahitians originally had a well-developed social order consisting of (1) chiefs and their relatives, (2) land owners, and (3) commoners without land. The priests belonged to the first two classes. Rank and title to land were hereditary. Large maraes (shrines) were erected to the tribal gods, especially the god of war. Over two hundred ruins of such stone temples have been found. The stone platform of one on Tahiti, described by Captain Cook, was 270 feet long, 90 feet wide, and 50 feet high, rising in ten steps. A temple platform 141 feet long is still standing on Raiatea.

TABLE 2

SOCIETY ISLANDS

Island Names	*Size*	*Origin and Maximum Altitude*
Windward Group		
Tahiti	402 square miles	Volcanic, 7321 feet
Moorea	50 square miles	Volcanic, 3975 feet
Meetia	650 acres	Volcanic, 1427 feet
Tetiaroa	1600 acres	Atoll of 13 islets, low
Tapuae-manu	1200 acres	Volcanic core, 550 feet, and coral flats
Leeward Group		
Huahine	20 miles circumference	Volcanic, 2331 feet
Raiatea	Raiatea and Tahaa are	Volcanic, 3389 feet
Tahaa	joined together by reefs, 23 by 10 miles	Volcanic, 1936 feet
Borabora	6 by 2½ miles	Volcanic, 2379 feet
Maupiti	1½ miles diameter	Volcanic, 698 feet, surrounded by reefs and coral islets
Tubai	Atoll lagoon, 4 by 4 miles	Atoll, 30 feet
Mopihaa	Atoll lagoon, 10 by 4 miles	Atoll, low
Fenua Ura	Atoll lagoon, 7 miles diameter	Atoll, low
Motu One	Atoll lagoon, 3 miles long	Atoll, low

Tahitians make their living primarily by harvesting coconuts, farming, and fishing. Both soil and climate are very favorable for agriculture on the high islands, and subsistence crops can be raised with a minimum of difficulty. Taro, yams, sweet potatoes, bananas, and breadfruit are their principal crops, but a variety of fruits and vegetables are also raised. Cash for the purchase of desired articles is secured by the production of copra and sometimes of vanilla, and by working for foreigners. Trading centers, especially Papeete, provide a market for fish and fruit. Some natives work for wages, but on the smaller and outlying islands there are few opportunities for employment. Houses are built of wood and thatch, and the people live in villages from which they go out to work their land and to harvest crops. The Tahitians are good craftsmen, and, in addition to canoes, sometimes build cutters and sail them to other islands carrying freight and passengers.

TAHITI

Tahiti, with a length of 35 miles, is the largest and most important island of French Polynesia. It has the shape of an hourglass, and consists of two volcanic domes connected with a low, narrow isthmus. Valleys radiate out from each dome, and as the rainfall is heavy, averaging over 72 inches at Papeete, the streams have deeply eroded the domes, until the divides are reduced to knife-edge crests like La Diadéme at the head of Aorai Valley. The valleys have precipitous walls and often end in amphitheater heads where many waterfalls are found. The mountains are very rugged, and many peaks attain elevations of thousands of feet; Orohena, 7321 feet, is highest. In most sections there is a lowland between the mountains and the ocean. This coastal plain has fertile soil, and most of the farms and inhabitants are found there, although it averages only a few hundred yards wide and is of small area compared with the mountainous parts of the island. Other land is cultivated in the lower sections of the major valleys where slopes are gentle. Tahiti is nearly surrounded by a reef inside which there is a protected lagoon where there are many ports and anchorages, safe from any storms except a hurricane. Passes through the reef give access to the ports, Papeete being by far the most important. A highway 100 miles long nearly encircles the island.

The climate is tropical with a range of temperature from 69° F to 84° F throughout the year, with an average of 77° F. Rainfall is adequate everywhere but is heaviest on the windward side.

Vegetation is very luxuriant. If introduced plants are counted, more than five hundred species of vascular plants are known. There are flowering trees and shrubs, ferns, flowers including orchids. The fei or mountain cooking banana (*Musa fehi*) is a favorite food, and guavas form dense thickets. There is a zonal arrangement of vegetation, the mountain flora beginning at altitude of 1500 feet on the dry side of the island, descending to 100 or 200 feet on the rainy, windward side. Living in the forests are doves, pigeons, kingfishers, swallows, and thrushes.

Tahiti had a poulation of 19,029 in 1936; in 1950 it had increased to approximately 30,000. About half the inhabitants are Tahitians, 30 per cent are French and mixed blood, 18 per cent are Chinese, and a few hundred are Americans, British, and of other ancestry. Cook estimated in 1769 that the population of Tahiti was upwards of 120,-000. This figure was likely much too high, but the population then was certainly several times that of the present. Decrease in popula-

FIGURE 105. Papeete Harbor, Tahiti. Some of these boats are used for inter-island trade. Photograph, K. P. Emory, Bernice P. Bishop Museum.

tion resulted mainly from introduced diseases, for example, venereal diseases, tuberculosis, smallpox, and measles, and disruption of the former manner of life by contact with the competitive, highly and differently specialized western culture. As late as 1918, 4000 Tahitians of the scanty population died of influenza.

There are several thousand cattle in Tahiti, and these are locally utilized for beef. Only a small dairy herd is maintained, neither Tahitians nor Chinese using much, if any, milk. Pigs, goats, and poultry are raised for local consumption.

Vanilla is grown both by plantations and individual Chinese and Tahitians and in some years exceeds the value of copra. In the years before the Second World War 100 to 200 tons or more were produced, amounting to about one-fourth the world's crop, but natural vanilla now competes with the cheaper synthetic product and has suffered in consequence. The vanilla plant is related to orchids. The fleshy stems or vines attach themselves to trees by means of aerial roots, and some nutriment is drawn through them, although more of the plant's food is derived from the soil through its own roots. The pods are harvested, and the seeds or beans are extracted and dried and supply the vanilla flavor. Vanilla plants are cultivated mainly in rich, humid valleys, both in Tahiti and in outlying high islands in the group. Exports average several hundred tons per year.

Papeete has a population of about 10,000 (8456 in 1936), and is the largest and only real city in eastern Polynesia. It has adequate port facilities, warehouses, shipyards, many stores, hotels, a bank, several clubs, a hospital, and many churches. There is an electric plant and a water-distribution system. Most of the large business houses are managed by Europeans, but the small shops are generally run by Chinese, who occupy an important quarter of the city. Papeete is a port of call for the Messageries Maritimes between New Caledonia and France, and before the Second World War the Union Steam Ship Company boats stopped there between Wellington and San Francisco. Service on this line became irregular after 1941. Launches, auxiliary sailing boats, and native cutters carry freight and passengers to and from Papeete and the outlying islands of the Society group and the Tuamotus. There is no regular air transportation.

Tahiti has been attractive to tourists, both for those viewing the island on steamer day and for those staying longer. Several artists, of whom Gauguin was the first, and authors (Pierre Loti, Charles Nordhoff, etc.) have lived in Tahiti and have painted or described the native life. However, no one should now go to Tahiti and expect to find a tropical paradise populated by a naïve, generous folk among whom the newcomer can enjoy life without labor. The Tahiti of Wallis and Cook and the Marquesas Islands of Melville have passed away forever. However, the tropical verdure, the fantastic-appearing mountains, the blue ocean, and the calm, pleasant life are still available.

OTHER ISLANDS IN THE WINDWARD GROUP

Moorea, 9 miles west of Tahiti, is a triangular-shaped island whose volcanic mass has been so reduced by erosion that the valleys are wider and the ridge tops lower than in Tahiti. A coastal flat extends around Moorea, and on it are located all the settlements. These are connected by a road 35 miles long that encircles the island. A reef and its lagoon surround the island, and the chief villages are convenient to passes for boats through the reef. The population is over 2000, and 90 per cent are Polynesians, the remainder being Chinese and other foreigners. Meetia (Mehitia), Tetiaroa, an atoll of 13 islets, and Tapuaemanu are other small islands.

THE LEEWARD GROUP

Huahine is a volcanic island about 20 miles in circumference, which at high water is separated into two parts called Huahine Nui and Huahine Iti. At low water the isthmus is dry. The soil is fertile,

FIGURE 106. Home on Borabora, Society Islands. Photograph, K. P. Emory, Bernice P. Bishop Museum.

the climate warm and rainy, and the vegetation luxuriant. Coconuts, taro, bananas, and vegetables are raised on the coastal lowlands, and pineapples and vanilla on the lower slopes of the hills. The population of about 1300 includes 300 Chinese and 50 Europeans. The principal village and port is Fare, from which copra and other products are shipped to Papeete.

Raiatea and Tahaa islands are joined by reefs. Together they are 23 miles long, with an extreme width of 10 miles. Raiatea is about twice the size of Tahaa. Both are volcanic islands whose mountains are well trenched by streams. The alluvial lowland at the base of the mountains is very fertile and forms the cultivated and inhabited part of each island. Raiatea has a population of about 5000 and about 400 more live on Tahaa. Uturoa, administrative center for the Leeward islands, is the second community in size in French Oceania and the chief port of Raiatea. Copra, vanilla, pineapples, and other fruits are exported.

Borabora is of volcanic origin and has a population of 1300, supported by subsistence agriculture, fishing, and the export of copra. Historically Borabora was important to the Tahitians and was once renowned for its warriors and naval conquest. During the Second World War the United States built an airport here, and several thousand United States troops were stationed at the island for several years.

THE MARQUESAS ISLANDS

Mendaña, a Spanish navigator, named the first islands he discovered in 1594 after the lady of the Viceroy of Peru, Las Islas Marquesas de Mendoza, which has been shortened to Marquesas. Captain Cook rediscovered the southeast group in 1774, and an American, Captain Ingraham, discovered most of the northwest islands in 1791. The islands were annexed by France in 1842.

The Marquesas consist of ten islands more than one square mile in area and several islets, divided into southeast and northwest groups, and they are situated between latitudes 7° 50′ and 10° 35′ south and longitudes 138° 25′ and 140° 50′ west. The islands are of volcanic origin except for the doubtful exception of two small "coral" islets in the extreme north that have been described by some as made of volcanic sand rather than coral. No reefs surround the Marquesas Islands, which thus present a strong contrast to the Society group. The French estimate the area of the Marquesas to be 459 square miles, and another authority gives the area as about 490 square miles. The conservative estimate of 409 square miles is shown in the Table 3.

The high islands have been eroded into extremely rugged mountains. Steep, rocky walls almost preclude climbing out of some valleys that often end in amphitheater heads, for example, Taipi Valley on Nukuhiva down whose cliffs descend beautiful waterfalls of great height. Cliffs, sometimes rising for 1000 feet or more, line the shores and may prevent travel from one valley to another except by sea. The absence of a coastal lowland limits the land available for agriculture to the valley floors, a central plain on Nukuhiva, and a few uplands broad enough for cultivation on the divides between the canyons. The sea cliffs seem to have resulted, in part at least, from faulting, in addition to erosion by the waves. The lack of a reef and a protected lagoon makes fishing and voyaging dangerous for canoes. The Marquesans did little of either compared with the natives of Tahiti and the Tuamotus. The absence of reefs is probably the result of occasional inflow of cold water from the Peru Current, although the presence of deep water at the base of the cliffs may help prevent the growth of the reef-forming animals.

TABLE 3

MARQUESAS ISLANDS

Islands	Area, Square Miles	Dimensions, Miles	Highest Altitude, Feet	Estimated Population, 1950
Southeast Group				
Fatuhiva	30	9 x 4½	3670	200
Mohotani	6	5 x 1½	1700	0
Tahuata	20	9 x 5	3280	250
Hivaoa	125	25 x 8	4130	850
Fatuuku	½	1½ x ½	1180	0
Northwest Group				
Uapou	40	9 x 8	4040	380
Uahuka	30	9 x 5	2805	150
Nukuhiva	130	16 x 12	4000	550
Eiao	20	8 x 4	2000	0
Hatuku	7	5 x 2	1380	0

The climate is healthy, partly because of the persistence of the trade winds. The mean annual temperature at sea level is about 78° F, and the range from the coldest month, August, to the warmest month, November, is only 4 degrees. Relative humidity is high, seldom falling below 80 per cent. The rainfall is subject to great yearly variations. In rainy years the precipitation is over 100 inches; in dry years the same station may receive only 20 to 40 inches, and intense periods of drought may last for many months. During droughts the coconut and breadfruit trees suffer severely. Streams are generally short, and many become dry during droughts.

The vegetation of the larger islands may be divided into three zones, determined by altitude and rainfall. (1) From low levels up to 1000 or 1500 feet on windward slopes and 1000 feet higher on the leeward sides of the mountains are found the pandanus, hibiscus, guava, Tahitian chestnut, coconut, breadfruit, grasses, shrubs, and many herbaceous plants. (2) The intermediate zone between elevations of 1000 to 1500 to 2500 feet has dense thickets of hibiscus, many ferns, coarse grasses, and the palm-like tree, *Cordyline terminalis*. (3) The upper zone above 2000 to 2500 feet is shrouded in clouds much of the time and has a dense rainforest of ferns, treeferns, small evergreen trees, and, in the gulches, groves of wild bananas and bamboo. The native flora is typically oceanic, and the number of species is small compared with island groups to the west, like Fiji.

The fauna is limited. There are fifteen species of native land birds and a few lizards, but, until introduced by man, no mammals, not even a bat. Pigs, cattle, horses, goats, and chickens are found wild.

THE MARQUESANS

The number of natives in the Marquesas Islands has declined tremendously since they came into contact with Europeans. Early explorers guessed that between 100,000 and 200,000 persons lived in the Marquesas. Those figures were likely too great, but an estimate made about 1813 of 50,000 and in 1842 of 20,000 seem substantially correct. In 1872 the population was about 6200, and in 1911 it was 3116 (including 146 Caucasians), in 1926 it was 2225 (including 146 Caucasians and Chinese), and in 1931 the population was 2283. Although later census records are not available, the present population is probably approximately 2400. War, introduced diseases, and disruption of the old culture account for a 96 per cent decline in the native population in 150 years. This is the worst depopulation for any major group of high islands in Polynesia and probably in the whole Pacific.

The Marquesans are among the taller and lighter-skinned Polynesians, and even in their decline they appear handsome and muscular. Each valley in the larger islands was inhabited by one or more tribes living in its own village, and they were often at war with one another. The land was held on a tribal basis, although individual ownership of garden plots and fruit trees was generally recognized. Breadfruit was the staple food because conditions favored this tree, and there was a shortage of level land and water for the raising of wet-land crops like taro. Breadfruit was mashed and then preserved in storage pits lined with leaves; they were like a pit silo. The pasty product, called *ma* (or *popoi* when cooked), could be kept for several years, and it served as a provision against famine when the breadfruit crop was damaged by droughts or hurricanes. The mashed fruit packed into the pits lined with leaves underwent fermentation, and the natives learned to prefer the flavor of the preserved article over that of fresh breadfruit. Ordinary pits were about 6 feet in diameter and 2 or more feet deep, but large community pits were also built to store reserve food. At least 33 varieties of breadfruit were distinguished, showing the importance of this crop. The Marquesans recognized 26 different varieties of bananas and 11 varieties of coconuts. Some taro was raised on the valley floors and sweet potatoes on the uplands. Cloth was manufactured from the bark of the breadfruit tree. Pigs were raised, but lack of much food for the animals limited their numbers. Some birds and fish were captured, but there was a shortage of meat in the diet. The Marquesans practiced cannibalism, sometimes for ritual reasons but also from a desire for the flesh.

FIGURE 107. Atuona village and valley, Hiva Oa Island, Marquesas. Note the coconut palms and radio mast. Photograph, Bernice P. Bishop Museum.

Stone was constructed into temples and assembly grounds, carved images, and the platforms on which houses were built. The fact that the surface of the ground was generally sloping made necessary the building of stone terraces for houses and public assemblies.

The Marquesans were clever workers in wood and made many implements and articles of this material, including digging sticks, war clubs, spears, bowls, images, and canoes. Without protection by a reef small craft were unsuited for the heavy swells, and seaworthy double canoes or large ones with outriggers were built for fishing. The natives practiced tattooing, and all adults were thus decorated, many having most elaborate designs on their skins. Today few of the natives live in old-style thatched houses. Most of the dwellings are two-room houses with board walls and corrugated iron roofs. The staple food is popoi, the cooked fermented paste made of bread-fruit, although rice and other imported foods are consumed when available.

The trade of the Marquesas Islands is small. The chief export is copra, and there are small shipments of vanilla and coffee. Cattle are raised, and the abundance of grass would permit an expansion of this industry. Lack of population and labor is a handicap to economic development. Land travel is very difficult, and the footpaths and horse trails that are substitutes for roads are often in bad condition. Vessels of the Messageries Maritimes sometimes call at Atuona on Hivaoa Island, and an irregular traffic with Papeete is maintained by auxiliary schooner. Auxiliary boats and canoes carry on the inter-island communication and freight shipments.

SOUTHEAST GROUP

Hivaoa has the largest population among the Marquesas Islands. The mountains exceed 4000 feet in height, the valleys are deep, and there are waterfalls several hundred feet high. The people live in ten villages and hamlets, located at intervals along the coast. Atuona on the south shore, the largest settlement in the Marquesas, has a population of about 350. It is the place of residence of the administrator and is provided with a hospital, church, and stores, the smaller shops being run by Chinese.

Tahuata once supported a large population, but there were only 253 inhabitants in 1931, distributed among five villages.

Fatuhiva, the southernmost island in the group, appears to be the remains of a double volcanic cone, a new cone having been built up inside the outer and larger crater; the western half of the whole structure disappeared by downfaulting. The island is isolated, and the natives retain some of the old forms of life by making bark cloth and carving wood. Tattoo artists still live there.

NORTHWEST GROUP

Nukuhiva, the largest island in the Marquesas, is very mountainous, with deep broad valleys, one being Taipi Valley, made famous by Hermann Melville in his book *Typee*. The western (leeward) portion of the island is a dry plateau that has been little eroded. Formerly many thousands of people lived on Nukuhiva; now the population is reduced to 550, scattered among seven little villages. The chief settlement, Taiohae, has about 200 inhabitants and is on a bay of the same name on the south coast. It was headquarters of many New Bedford whalers during the middle nineteenth century, and here the French established their principal military post when they first took control of the islands. The government was removed to Atuona in 1904, but still Taiohae is the main center of the northern Marquesas. In 1813 an American, Captain David Porter, took possession of Nukuhiva for the United States. This action, however, was never ratified by the United States government, and France annexed the group thirty years later. Porter describes the lovely fertile valleys of Nukuhiva as the home of many thousands of vigorous, happy people. Now the land is deserted and unused, and the farms and former village sites are abandoned.

Uapou and Uahuka are the other inhabited islands in the northern group. Copra is the main export from all these islands.

THE TUAMOTU ISLANDS

The Tuamotu Archipelago (latitude 14° to 23° south, longitude 135° to 140° west) consists of seventy-six atolls, only one of which, Makatea, is elevated. They stretch from north of the Society Islands in the northwest to the Mangareva Islands in the southeast, a distance of over 1000 miles (Fig. 108). Because of its geographic proximity, Mangareva is often included with the Tuamotus, but its native culture is distinctly apart. The atolls were discovered by slow degrees and by many navigators, beginning with Quiros in 1606 and Le Maire and Schouten in 1616, and some were apparently first described as late as a century ago. Most of the islands bear several names; but the custom is now to return to the native name, which is used in this book. The western islands came under the protection of France in 1842 along with Tahiti. The whole group was annexed in 1880, and the islands have been incorporated into French Oceania (Établissements Français de l'Océanie). They are governed from Papeete. Other names applied to the islands have been Paumotus, which could be interpreted "conquered islands," and was abandoned at the request of the natives who did not like it; the Low Archipelago; and the Dangerous Archipelago. Because the islands are low, many of the reefs are awash, charts are unreliable, and erratic currents among the islets and channels are a pitfall to the unwary navigator, the term Low or Dangerous Archipelago was very fitting.

The atolls have a small land area, consisting as they do of rims of land or of detached motus (islets) rising above the reef. The area

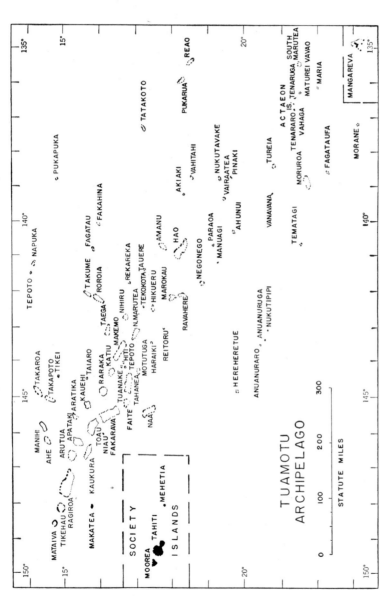

FIGURE 108.   Tuamotu Archipelago.   Map courtesy of the Bernice P. Bishop Museum.

is officially estimated at 330 square miles, but this is probably too high. K. P. Emory estimates the area of land above high-water mark at approximately 75 square miles. Except for Makatea, none of the islands is over 30 feet above sea level. Certain of the lagoons, for example Hao, Fakarava, Rangiroa, and Makemo, have a circuit of nearly 100 miles; others are only a mile or two in diameter. Many of the atolls have passes into the lagoons, mostly on the northwest, north, and northeast sides; others are without entrance, and the land forms a complete ring. In the northwest the islands are arranged along two main lines and are fairly close together, but in the eastern portion they are widely scattered.

In appearance the islands tend to conform to a pattern. First there is the outer edge of the reef, shown by a white line of surf, and along it the waves advance and recede, alternately hiding and revealing the jagged and fissured coral and other marine formations. Then comes a short stretch of smooth, shallow water, or a pitted and rock-covered flattish reef partly exposed at low tide. Following this is a dazzling white beach of coral sand and other detritus, behind which rises a dark wall of cocount palms, pandanus, and other vegetation. Beyond the belt of trees is a second beach and the inner lagoon. Often the reef is topped by many separate islets rather than a continuous ring of land, although such occur. The strips of land in the atolls are always narrow, never exceeding one-half mile wide, and are always low, rarely more than 10 to 20 feet above sea level. Where passages are available the landings are on the inner lagoon, and if the island is inhabited the village is located near by. The houses are irregularly placed in the shade of the palms and have roofs of thatch, or more rarely of corrugated iron. Drinking water is nearly always a problem. A few islands secure potable water from shallow wells, but often ground water is brackish. Rain water is sometimes collected in cisterns, especially from buildings with metal roofs. However, on many islands the best supply is the milk of green coconuts.

The climate is healthy but rather hot, and temperatures average from about 76° F to 81° F in different islands. The cooler season is from May to October, when the trade winds are most regular, and the warmer season from November to April, when the rainier season occurs. Rainfall is adequate for plant growth, but sterility of much of the soil limits the exuberance of vegetation, which has less density and fewer species than on the high islands. Hurricanes are a hazard to the residents of the Tuamotus. Those of strongest force came in September, 1877, February, 1878, January, 1903, and February, 1906,

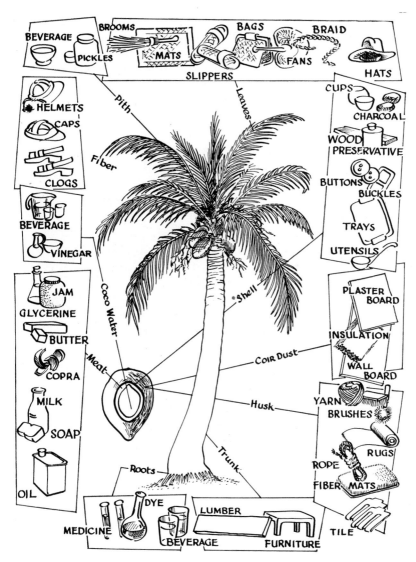

FIGURE 109. Uses of the coconut palm.

and destroyed villages and many lives. On some islands the soil and trees were swept away by the sea, leaving bare areas of broken coral worthless to man.

Coconut palms are prominent on most of the islands and form the cornerstone on which the economy of the natives is built. The natives aided the spread of coconuts by planting them on many islands where they were absent or uncommon. The coconut palm (Fig. 109) supplies both food and material for many sorts of construction. The meat is eaten fresh and is also dried to make copra, from which coconut oil is pressed. Between 3000 and 4500 nuts are required to make a ton of copra. The loss of weight on drying the meat of the split nuts is about 50 per cent. Green nuts are called drinking nuts and are customarily used for that purpose; on some islands, they supply the only available drinking water. The soft immature meat is the first solid food fed to babies. The meat from more mature nuts is grated, squeezed, and strained in fibers to extract the "cream." This

FIGURE 110. Taro growing in an artificial pit at Reao, Tuamotus. Photograph, K. P. Emory, Bernice P. Bishop Museum.

cream is put into puddings before they are cooked, or food is dipped in the cream before being put in the mouth. Coconut cream and sea water are mixed to make a sauce for food. The living crown makes a wonderful salad, hearts of palms, but is rarely available as the trees are killed to secure it. Half shells of nuts may be used for cups. The fiber of husks is made into rope, twine, fish nets, mats, and brooms. Baskets, hats, and mats are plaited from sennit derived from the leaves. The wood of the trunk is not first-class timber, but lacking better material the natives make house posts and dugout canoes of it. Leaves are plaited, and from them natives fashion roof thatch and windbreaks, and along with husks burn them for fuel.

Midribs make excellent brooms, and the bark of mature palms, a good charcoal. In the First World War coconut char was an absorbent in gas masks. A medicine is brewed from the roots.

The pandanus tree is widely distributed, and from this useful plant many things are obtained. The ripe fruit is eaten, and from it also a flour can be made that was available for voyages or kept as a reserve food. The leaves are plaited and made into floor mats, table mats, sails, and baskets. From the fibers of the aerial roots comes cordage.

Considerable labor is sometimes expended on growing other food plants than coconuts and pandanus. A few breadfruit, bananas, and papayas trees are grown on some islands where the poor coral sand has been improved by the addition of plant rubbish to provide humus. Sometimes canoe loads of rich earth from high islands are imported for little gardens. Taro is grown in artificial pits (Fig. 110), excavated in the coral sand to the level of ground water, and then refuse is added to supply fertilizer. With all their labor, there is limited food available on land, and the people turn to the sea for many of their necessities.

The sea supplies fish of many varieties, including moray eels, the octopus, and sharks. There are quantities of turtles, shellfish, including the giant clam (*Tridacna*), bêche-de-mer, and crustaceans. Fish wiers with rock walls were constructed beside the lagoon passes near villages, in shallow channels between islets, and along the shore of the lagoon. Most of the traps were built in a crescent shape and were designed and placed so that the fish following along with the current are led into enclosures from which they do not easily escape and can be readily taken with net and spear. Ownership of the wiers is hereditary. At certain seasons some of the fish from a lagoon may be poisonous, possibly from the algae on which they feed; and care must then be exercised in the selection of fish for food.

The diving for pearl shell and pearls is an industry of importance. The lagoons are favorable for the pearl oysters that are brought up from the beds by divers equipped only with goggles and a basket. The use of diving machines is now prohibited for fear of depleting the beds. Three years are required for the maturing of the shell, and lagoons are designated for diving only after being closed to the divers for that length of time. The population of islands varies widely, depending upon the opening of a lagoon to diving. Shell is the main product, pearls are incidentally produced, and the price for the latter has declined because of competition with culture pearls. The more important pearl fishing lagoons are in Takume, Takaroa, Takapoto, Makemo, Maniki, Arutua, Raroia, Kaukura, Marokau, Hao, and

Apataki. The pearl shell is sold to local dealers and enters world markets via Papeete; the pearls are bought by dealers who follow the diving seasons from one island to another.

Animal food is rare except for that derived from the sea. A few pigs are kept, but their production was always limited by the small amount of food available for the animals. In ancient times many of the Tuamotuans were cannibals. Under the worst conditions human beings were regarded as potential food, and an individual was not safe without protection. It was considered a great disgrace to be eaten! Pigs and human beings (called long pigs) were commonly cooked in an *umu* (underground oven). Sea birds are common, but land birds are rare. There are lizards and rats on all the islands.

MAKATEA

Makatea (Aurora) Island, about 120 miles northeast of Tahiti, is a raised atoll of uplifted limestone, about 5 miles long and 2 miles wide. Its flattish surface has an elevation of about 200 feet above the sea, with the high point attaining an altitude of 372 feet. The center of the island is occupied by a depression, site of the former lagoon. The island is everywhere bordered with cliffs, at the foot of which is a narrow fringing reef. The climate is hot and humid, and water is fairly plentiful, an unusual condition in the Tuamotus. The flora is more abundant than on the low atolls, and has been modified by the introduction of many plants from Tahiti. There is some cultivation of vanilla, taro, arrowroot, and manioc; and papayas, coconuts, breadfruit, and other fruits are grown on the plateau. Pandanus, hibiscus, banyans, and other trees flourish. There are a few native land birds, including pigeons and herons. Land crabs are plentiful.

The island is of commercial importance for its deposits of phosphate rock in the interior that in places are 40 feet thick. Reserves are estimated at 10,000,000 tons, a much smaller number than those on Nauru. Production runs around 120,000 tons per year. A narrow-gauge railway brings the rock to the shore, and the phosphate material is dumped from a cantilever pier into lighters that convey it to vessels lying at mooring buoys offshore. The population of Makatea was about 1000 in 1936, but exceeds that during periods of active mining and export of phosphate rock. About two-thirds of the inhabitants are native.

THE ATOLLS

Anaa, before the hurricane of 1877, from whose effects the island has never entirely recovered, was the most densely populated island in the Tuamotus, having between 1500 and 2000 inhabitants, a number reduced at present to about 400. In the early and middle part of the nineteenth century the Anaa warriors engaged in extensive raids on other islands and brought back captives in considerable numbers. The island, being fertile and well-developed, could support a large population until the hurricanes of 1877 and 1906 destroyed a large part of its great coconut groves on the eleven islets that compose the atoll.

Takaroa, Rangiroa, and Faaite atolls are reported to have 400 to 700 inhabitants, and during the diving season. Hikueru, whose lagoon is rich in shell, may have a temporary population of 2000. However, in general the atolls of the Tuamotus support few people. K. P. Emory says that "on the whole we must picture Tuamotuan culture as carried along by very small groups of from 75 to 250 people," living most of the time on one atoll. Only one island in the Archipelago has a population above 1000, ten have populations between 250 and 500, fifteen atolls support 100 to 200 people, and eighteen islands have a population under 100. The more populous atolls have good coconut groves; usually some taro and breadfruit are raised, and the lagoons are filled with fish. Thirty-two atolls are usually uninhabited but may be visited at intervals by natives from other islands to make copra, to fish, and to collect shell. Most of the islands at the southeastern end of the archipelago are uninhabited. The population of the Tuamotus is thought to be 5000 to 6000 and is officially estimated at 6580. Outside of Makatea there are about 200 Asiatics and a dozen Europeans scattered through the group; the rest are natives. The native tongue is closely related to Tahitian.

MANGAREVA

The islands of the Mangareva group, formerly called the Gambier Archipelago, lie between latitudes 23° and 23° 15′ south and longitudes 134° 50′ and 135° 5′ west, about 900 miles southeast of Tahiti. There are four inhabited high islands of volcanic origin, together with several smaller islets, the whole area amounting to about 6 square miles. The islands are narrow, and their irregular outline is typical of drowned coasts. The group is surrounded by a barrier reef 40 miles in circumference. On the east it contains many motus, but on the west is submerged. Geologically the Mangareva group is an almost-atoll or complex island similar to Truk in the Carolines. The islands appear to have been discovered by Captain James Wilson in 1797. France claimed a protectorate in 1844, and annexed the group in 1881.

Mangareva has a rainy climate with mean temperatures ranging from about 72° F in July to 80° F in January and February. There are no permanent streams, but a few springs exist and rain water is collected in cisterns for drinking. The soil is rocky, and flora is scanty. A tall grass called *aeho* covers much of the islands. Of the plants useful to man, only seven species are indigenous, and about twenty-two species were introduced by the Polynesians. Coconut, breadfruit, banana, taro (Fig. 111), sweet potato, pandanus, and other plants are grown. There are a few birds, but the only mammals are introduced ones like pigs and goats.

FIGURE 111. Taro patch and mountains, Mangareva. Photograph, Bernice P. Bishop Museum.

The population is about 500, including perhaps 50 non-natives. This represents a large decline in a century, the number of inhabitants being estimated at 1500 in 1842. The major god was considered the god of breadfruit, showing the importance of this crop to the people. The chief food now is fermented breadfruit, but various other plants also are eaten. Fish is an essential item, and its importance is shown by the native saying that "The garden of the poor is the sea." The people earn several thousand dollars a year from diving for pearl shell. The chief center and only port is Rikitea.

Mangareva (4 by 1 mile) is the largest island; its high point is

1447 feet. Taravai is 2¾ miles long; Aukena, 2 miles; and Akamaru, 1½ miles. These are the inhabited islands.

Most of the cultivation is done in the short valleys and on the flat land at the head of the bays between the promontories. The inland ridges are worn to narrow crests.

AUSTRAL ISLANDS AND RAPA

The Austral or Tubuai Islands, including Rapa, are south of the Society group between latitudes 21° 45′ and 28° south and longitudes 143° 30′ and 155° west. The total land area is about 67 square miles, of which Rapa occupies nearly 16 square miles. Some authorities give a total area almost twice this amount. Tubuai was discovered by Cook in 1777, and the islands were annexed by France in 1880. The population of the Australs is about 3500, all Polynesians except for a few non-natives, mostly Chinese shop-keepers.

There are five islands in the Austral group. Maria (Hull) Island is an atoll and uninhabited. The other four, Rimatara, Rurutu, Tubuai, and Raivavae, are of volcanic origin; and the mountains exceed 1300 feet in altitude on Rurutu and Tubuai, and attain 1434 feet on Raivavae. Tubuai and Raivavae are surrounded by barrier reefs inside which are protected lagoons containing a plentiful supply of fish. The reefs on Rimatara and Rurutu are of the fringing type.

The climate of the Australs is warm and fairly rainy, but the trades predominate only in summer (November to March). In the winter (May to September) the winds are more westerly, especially in Rapa; this is the stormier and rainier season.

Economic resources are mostly agricultural; and copra, coffee, and cattle are exported mostly by way of Papeete.

Rurutu is about 7 by 3 miles in size and covers about 8500 acres. The population of about 1200 (1931) is Polynesian, except for 30 Chinese and Europeans. Geologically it resembles the Cook group in that an uplifted reef formation of hard limestone forms a terrace a few hundred feet high, surrounding a core of volcanic rock at the center of the islands. Metamorphic slaty rocks have been reported from one valley. There are considerable deposits of iron pyrite that contain traces of gold, as well as small deposits of manganese.

Tubuai is oval in shape, about 5 by 3 miles in size, and consists of two mountain masses separated by a lowland. There are about 1000 people living in five villages, Mataura being the principal one. The soil is fertile, and many crops are raised, including sixteen varieties of taro, twelve kinds of bananas, yams, manioc, and numerous fruits and vegetables. Cattle, pigs, and turkeys are exported to Tahiti. Often fish are caught with a long net pulled by scores of people. This community enterprise serves as the occasion for feasting and sociability. Home industries include building canoes, making sennit cordage from coconut fiber, and plaiting mats, hats, and baskets from pandanus leaves.

Rapa, lying about 380 miles southeast of Tubuai, is a mountainous island with an altitude of 2077 feet and a circumference of nearly 20 miles. It has a small but excellent harbor, and is situated close to the Panama Canal–New Zealand shipping route. The island, a former volcano, has a deeply indented coastline. The head of land-locked Ahurei Bay on the eastern side occupies the former crater and gives the island a horseshoe shape. Rapa is cooler than most of French Oceania, and cyclonic storms are common. Forests are sometimes dense and include the candlenut, pandanus and tree ferns, but fires and the grazing of stock have damaged the forests. Grass now occupies considerable areas that were formerly tree covered. The climate is too cold for breadfruit and papayas, and even the coconut fails to produce fruit. Various subsistence crops are raised, and fish are caught. The population is about 300 (266 in 1935), a great decrease from the 2000 reported in 1826.

On Raivavae and Rapa, are stone statues, different in facial aspect but analogous to those of Easter Island. On Rapa the natives built many forts on hilltops resembling those constructed in New Zealand and the Marquesas.

Marotiri (Bass) Islands (latitude 27° 55′ south, longitude 143° 26′ west), 50 miles southeast of Rapa, consist of nine small rocky islets, with a total diameter of 2 miles for the group and a maximum altitude of 346 feet. Vegetation is almost absent, and the islands are uninhabited, although sometimes visited by Rapa men for fishing.

PITCAIRN AND ASSOCIATED BRITISH ISLANDS

Pitcairn Island (latitude 25° 4′ south, longitude 130° 6′ west) is a British possession along with Oeno, Henderson, and Ducie islands; all lie southeast of the Tuamotu Archipelago.

Pitcairn is a volcanic island of irregular shape, about 2 miles long by 1 mile broad, and rises to an elevation of about 1100 feet. Cliffs descend for hundreds of feet to the shore, and there are only two practicable landings for small boats. The climate is equable, average temperatures being about 82° F in summer and 65° F in winter. The rainfall usually is adequate, but droughts occasionally occur.

There are no streams although there is one spring.   Each house generally has a cistern for rain water.   The soil is fertile, and the greater part of the island is covered with evergreen trees and shrubs.   Useful trees include the coconut, pandanus, breadfruit, bananas, candlenut (*Aleurites moluccana*), paper-mulberry, and purau, the last yielding building timber.   There are many introduced fruits and vegetables, including the white potato.   Only one species of land bird, a flycatcher, is known.   Sea birds, however, are common.   The rat is the only native mammal.   Fish and shellfish are plentiful.   There are no cattle or pigs, but goats and chickens are raised.

Pitcairn was uninhabited when discovered, but stone ruins and stone implements in abundance prove that it was once long inhabited by Polynesians.   It is noted for its connection with the mutineers from the *Bounty*, an English ship commanded by Captain Bligh.   In 1790 nine of the mutineers, together with six Tahitian men and twelve Tahitian women, came to the island, destroyed the *Bounty*, and settled.   Nothing was known about them until an American whaler in 1808 found that the youths spoke English.   In the the interim all the mutineers, except one, and the six Tahitian men had died, most of them by violence, and the people were ruled by the surviving mutineer, John Adams.   He had instituted a patriarchal discipline over the community of mixed blood.   Pitcairn traded supplies to whaling vessels until that industry ended.   As the population grew, famine was feared; and some of the people moved to Tahiti but returned. In 1856 the British government moved 190 natives at their own request to Norfolk Island, but in a few years several families were homesick and went back to Pitcairn.   Today more than 200 persons live on Pitcairn, and more than that number on Norfolk.

The Pitcairners speak an English dialect, all live in the village of Adamstown, and belong to the Seventh Day Adventist Church.   In spite of intermarriage there has been no deterioration of the stock, and except for poor teeth they are healthy and taller than the usual Englishman or Tahitian.   The men engage in farming and fishing, and build large boats of the whaleboat type that are about 36 feet long with 9-foot beam and are manned by 14 oars.   The men are extremely skillful in handling these craft in heavy seas.

There is no regular ship service to Pitcairn or trade from the island. Oranges have been sent to New Zealand, and if transportation were available bananas could be exported.   Pleasure yachts and trading craft occasionally stop, and curios and fruits are traded with the visiting ships for clothing and other needed articles.

Henderson is a raised atoll, 50 to 100 feet high, 105 miles northeast of Pitcairn, whose inhabitants sometimes resort to it for timber and other products. Ducie is a little atoll, 2½ by 1 mile, 290 miles east of Pitcairn; and Oeno is an atoll, about 2½ miles in diameter, 65 miles northwest of Pitcairn. None of the three islands has permanent inhabitants, but certain rights are claimed by the Pitcairn islanders.

EASTER ISLAND

Easter Island (latitude 27° 10′ south, longitude 109° 20′ west) is the most easterly land settled by Polynesians. It was discovered by Roggeveen on Easter Day, 1722, and since 1888 has been a Chilean possession, being officially known as Islas de Pascua or Rapa Nui. The native name, Te Pito o te Henua (the Navel of the Earth), suggests the isolation of the island, which is 2230 miles from Chile and 1100 miles east of Pitcairn, the nearest inhabited land. Easter Island is about 12 by 6 miles and of triangular shape. Its area is variously given as from 45 to 61 square miles.

Being of volcanic origin, Easter has many extinct craters, the three largest standing at the corners of the triangular island. The highest peak, Terevaka, has an altitude of 1768 feet. Within the crater of Rano Kao at the southwest corner is a fresh-water lake nearly a mile in diameter, and there is a smaller pond in the crater, Rano Aroi, on Mount Terevaka. These are the principal sources of water on the island.

The climate of Easter is healthy and devoid of extremes. The mean monthly temperatures range from 60° to 73° F, and the rainfall averages about 54 inches annually for the short time in which records have been kept. The relative humidity is high, being close to 80 per cent. Sea breezes temper the heat during the day, but the nights seem cool, in part because of heavy dews and dampness.

The bedrock and the soil are very pervious, and the rainfall is so quickly absorbed that streams do not exist. Moreover, the water table is low and wells dug near sea level become brackish. However, a well near the settlement, Hanga Roa, has a windmill and supplies potable water. The natives built stone reservoirs to collect rain water in the past.

Vegetation is very scanty. There are only a few small trees, but an abundance of grasses, which are utilized for the grazing of livestock. The island is leased for grazing about 20,000 sheep, besides cattle and horses. The exports consist of wool and hides, but the meat of the sheep and cattle is consumed locally because there are no facilities for handling perishable products. The natives keep a few pigs, dogs, and numerous chickens. Sea birds nest on adjoining islets. A few lizards and a native rat, now exterminated by the European rat, comprised the original fauna.

Native foods in the past included bananas, yams, sweet potatoes, taro, and sugar cane. There was generally a shortage of food, especially of meat, as only the eggs of sea birds and a few pigs were available. An elaborate cult was built around gathering the first egg each year.

During the middle nineteenth century the population of Easter, originally estimated at 3000 to 4000, was decimated by smallpox and other diseases, and by raids for laborers to work on the guano islands of Peru and elsewhere. Today the population is about 600 (577 in 1942), of whom 200 are pure Easter Island descent and the remainder mixtures of many races brought in as laborers, beside a few Chileans and Europeans.

FIGURE 112. Stone statue, Easter Island. Photograph, Bernice P. Bishop Museum.

The Easter islanders were Polynesians, and their culture has aroused great interest among anthropologists. They possessed wooden tablets (*toromiro*) on which glyphs, looking like pictographic script, had been carved. These tablets were held by the learned while reciting the legends and chants of the people. However, it is probable that the characters are mnemonic (aids to memory) and not phonetic or ideographic.

Great interest has been aroused by the many stone statues consisting of a human figure from the waist up, which were all carved essentially of the same model, showing pursed lips, a broad nose, and pendant, distended ears (Fig. 112). The largest statue was 33 feet long, but smaller ones were more common. The statues were carved from a single block of dark volcanic tuff, and a headpiece or crown of red tuff was placed on the head of the statue. The stone images were erected widely over the island, many being placed on stone platforms facing the sea. The carving of the statues with nothing but tools of lava, their transportation without a tree trunk larger than a few inches in diameter being available for levers or rollers, and the erection of the heavy images at sites sometimes several miles away from the quarry must have been a task lasting many years. However, by the time the Easter islanders were seriously questioned about the statues and tablets, the people who had participated in the aboriginal culture had disappeared and their descendants had not bothered to learn what they had known. The paucity of information has encouraged writers to use their imagination. There are several hypotheses to account for the statues, but most anthropologists have no doubt they were erected by the Polynesian ancestors of the inhabitants at the time of discovery and that they are of no great antiquity.

REFERENCES

Aitken, R. T., "Ethnology of Tubuai," *Bernice P. Bishop Museum Bull.* 70, Honolulu, 1930.

Adamson, A. M., "Review of the Fauna of the Marquesas Islands and Discussion of Its Origin," *Bernice P. Bishop Museum Bull.* 159, Honolulu, 1939.

——— "Marquesan Insects: Environment," *Bernice P. Bishop Museum Bull.* 139, Honolulu, 1936.

Buck, Peter H. (Te Rangi Hiroa), "Ethnology of Mangareva," *Bernice P. Bishop Museum Bull.* 157, Honolulu, 1938.

Christain, F. W., *Eastern Pacific Islands: Tahiti and the Marquesas*, Robert Scott, London, 1910.

Chubb, L. J., "Geology of the Marquesas," *Bernice P. Bishop Museum Bull.* 68, Honolulu, 1930.

Crossland, C., "The Island of Tahiti," *Geogr. Jour.*, Vol. 71, pp. 561–585, 1928.

Emory, K. P., "Tuamotuan Stone Structures," *Bernice P. Bishop Museum Bull.* 118, Honolulu, 1934.

——— "Archeology of Mangareva and Neighboring Atolls," *Bernice P. Bishop Museum Bull.* 163, Honolulu, 1939.

Handy, E. S. C., "Native Culture in the Marquesas," *Bernice P. Bishop Museum Bull.* 9, Honolulu, 1923.

——— "History and Culture in the Society Islands," *Bernice P. Bishop Museum Bull.* 79, Honolulu, 1931.

Henry, Teuira, "Ancient Tahiti," *Bernice P. Bishop Museum Bull.* 48, Honolulu, 1928.

Linton, Ralph, "The Material Culture of the Marquesas Islands," *Bernice P. Bishop Museum Memoirs*, Vol. 8, No. 5, 1923.

Melville, Herman, *Typee*, New York, 1876. Reprint Dodd, Mead and Co., New York, 1948.

Metraux, Alfred, "Ethnology of Easter Island," *Bernice P. Bishop Museum Bull.* 160, Honolulu, 1940.

Routledge, C. S., *The Mystery of Easter Island*, Hazell, Watson and Viney, London, 1919.

Russell, Samuel, *Tahiti and French Oceania* [a guidebook], Pacific Publications Limited, Sydney, 1935.

Shapiro, H. L., "The Physical Characters of the Society Islanders," *Bernice P. Bishop Museum Memoirs,* Vol. XI, No. 4, Honolulu, 1930.

—— *The Heritage of the Bounty,* Simon and Schuster, New York, 1936.

Stark, J. T., and A. L. Howland, "Geology of Borabora," *Bernice P. Bishop Museum Bull.* 169, Honolulu, 1941.

Thomson, W. J., *Te Pito de Henua or Easter Island,* U.S. National Museum Annual Report, pp. 447–552, 1889.

Williams, Howel, "Geology of Tahiti, Moorea, etc.," *Bernice P. Bishop Museum Bull.* 105, Honolulu, 1933.

Zimmerman, E. C., "Cryptorhynchinae of Rapa," *Bernice P. Bishop Museum Bull.* 151, Honolulu, 1938.

14

Central and Western Polynesia

EDWIN H. BRYAN, JR.

THE ISLANDS INCLUDED IN THIS CHAPTER FORM THE HUB OF THE PACIFIC. They occupy the central portion of the Pacific Ocean, and most of them lie south of the Equator and east of the 180th meridian (Fig. 113).

The majority are small islands composed of various kinds of geological materials. They include atolls, sandy "pancakes," rugged blocks of raised reef, and volcanic peaks in various stages of dissection. A few have combinations of limestone and volcanic rocks. One, perhaps, is a remnant of more ancient land on the edge of the disintegrating "Melanesian continent." With this one exception, no part of the land is very old in the geologic sense.

Some of these islands rise individually from great depth of ocean. Others are the summit peaks of great ranges of volcanic mountains and can be associated in chains or archipelagoes.

Throughout the area there is great diversity of rainfall, ranging from very wet to very dry. It tends to modify what might otherwise be a marked similarity of fauna and flora in the low islands. On the high islands are found rich rainforests harboring a rich endemic fauna of insects, land snails, and other invertebrates but only a few kinds of birds and almost no native reptiles, amphibians, or mammals.

The indigenous peoples of this area are Polynesians. In these islands live more than 40 per cent of all the persons of Polynesian blood. Many of the other Polynesian peoples—Hawaiians, Marquesans, Tahitians, Austral Islanders, even the Maori people of New Zealand—have intermarried with persons from Europe, America, and the Orient; but the majority of those in central and western Polynesia have remained relatively pure-blooded.

394

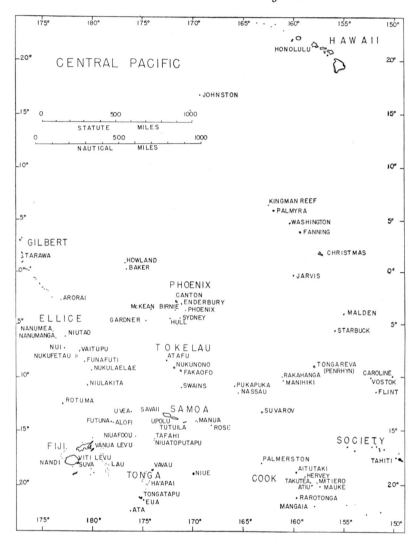

FIGURE 113. Map of central Pacific islands.

These islands have been divided by geographers and government administrators into the groups listed in Table 1. There are 224 islands, scattered over an area of ocean 2000 miles square, with a land area less than that of the little state of Delaware or the single island of Hawaii. They have a combined population comparable with that of the city of New Haven, Connecticut, Grand Rapids, Michigan, or Youngstown, Ohio. They are administered in a variety

TABLE 1

SUMMARY OF CENTRAL AND WESTERN POLYNESIA

Group	Area, Square Miles	Number of Islands	Population (1947–1948) Indigenous	Foreign	Administering Nation
Cook	98.7	15	14,145	311	New Zealand
Niue	100.3	1	4,289	29	New Zealand
American Samoa	72.8	6	20,000	15*	United States
Western Samoa	1,138	4	72,935	677	New Zealand trusteeship
Tonga	268.9	160	43,286	1162	Kingdom under Great Britain's protection
Wallis and Futuna	60.5	3	8,200	40	France
Ellice	9.6	9	4,427	60	Great Britain
Nauru Island†	8.2	1	1,379	1476	Trusteeship, New Zealand, Australia, Great Britain
Ocean Island†	2.3	1	. . . .	2060	Great Britain
Tokelau	3.9	3	1,416	. . . .	New Zealand
Phoenix	11.1	8	903‡	230	United States and Great Britain
Equatorial	263.5	13	409‡	160	United States and Great Britain
Total	2,037.8	224	171,389	6220	

* Not counting naval personnel stationed in American Samoa; indigenous Samoan total is a close approximation.

† Nauru and Ocean Islands lie within this area but are discussed in Chapter 9. Indigenous population of Ocean Island has been evacuated to Fiji.

‡ The "native" peoples in the Phoenix and Equatorial or "Line" islands are not indigenous to them. Most are colonists or workmen from the Gilbert and Ellice groups; others are from Fiji.

of ways by five of the six nations that care for the welfare of peoples in the south Pacific.

The exports of these islands are very important to their inhabitants, for they determine the amount of goods that the inhabitants can afford to import, and to some extent the revenue that they can spend for government, education, health, and public works; but they scarcely make a ripple on the ocean of world trade. During a normal year the combined exports of these central and western Polynesian islands might amount to £750,000 or about $3,000,000, largely agricultural products. The phosphate exported annually from Nauru and Ocean islands is valued at about this same amount. The 177,000 people (men, women, and children) on the average raise produce for export valued at not more than $17.00 per capita each year.

A large proportion of this value comes from copra, the dried kernel of the coconut. It is practically the only product exported from the low islands and also from American Samoa and Wallis and Futuna. The high islands of the Cook group also raise citrus fruits and to-matoes, and Niue produces chiefly bananas. Western Samoa's other crops are cocoa, bananas, and desiccated coconut. In addition to copra, Tonga exports only bananas and a few other fruits. All fruit shipments are dependent upon finding suitable markets and means for shipping, largely to New Zealand. Other tropical crops could be grown but not in competition with other, larger regions, such as Indonesia, the Philippines, or tropical America.

In all these islands the native people depend for subsistence largely on products of the soil and what they can catch in the sea. There are a few pigs and chickens, but they are considered to be delicacies, to be eaten chiefly at feasts. On the high islands the chief food plants are bananas, breadfruit, taro, yams, sweet potatoes, and manioc. On the low islands most of these are scarce or entirely lacking, the starchy foods being coconuts, pandanus fruits, arrowroot, and a very inferior relative of the taro. Many Polynesians have developed a fondness for such foreign foods as canned salmon and beef, rice, tea, sugar, and crackers, thus making them increasingly dependent upon trade with the foreigner. Water is scarce on the low islands, where rain must be caught and stored. Coconut water is a favorite beverage throughout the area. Kava, a non-alcoholic drink, made by mixing the pounded root of the pepper plant (*Piper methysticum*) with water and removing the grit, is a thirst-quenching drink, served with ceremony at gatherings. The coconut is the most valuable plant throughout the area, supplying food, drink, material for shelter and fiberwork, canoe paddles, household utensils, and copra, the chief cash crop.

CLIMATE

The climate of most of the islands of the central Pacific is tropical and humid but modified by the trade winds. The winds blow rather steadily from May to November, from an easterly direction near the equator, from the southeast further south. During the remainder of the year winds are variable with occasional severe storms. Destruc-tive hurricanes occur at intervals in various areas.

There is much uniformity in most elements of the weather through-out the area. Tonga is a little cooler and drier than Samoa, but the humidity is high from January to March, which makes it seem hotter than it really is. Throughout the low islands, nearer the equator, the temperature is higher. There is, however, less humidity, and the nights are cool.

The rainfall is the most variable feature of the climate. Great range of rainfall occurs not only from island to island but also on the same island from year to year. The meager rainfall records, coupled with observations on vegetation, indicate that there are zones of light, medium, and heavy rainfall across the area, roughly parallel to the equator. On the high islands, where the mountains intercept the trade winds, rainfall in general increases about 6 per cent with each 100 feet of elevation. Thus, rainfall in the interior of Upolu Island (3600 feet) averages about 196 inches a year; whereas that in the interior of Savaii (up to 6094 feet) is as much as 275 inches a year.

THE PEOPLE

An account of the various peoples of the Pacific islands is given in Chapter 2. All the indigenous islanders of this central region are Polynesians. Tradition, coupled with similarities of language and physical characteristics, indicates that the majority of them came into the various individual islands and groups by way of a cultural center in the Samoan area, to which they had migrated from southeastern Asia. Some of the Cook islanders, however, may have reached that group from another cultural center in the Society Islands, near Tahiti. This had been the center from which Polynesians had migrated to Hawaii, the Marquesas, Tuamotus, Mangareva, and New Zealand.

An intensive study has been made of the Polynesian culture, especially by scientists from the Bernice P. Bishop Museum in Honolulu. The reader who is particularly interested in this phase of the subject is referred to the publications listed in the bibliography. Suffice it to say here that the Polynesians had a feudal culture in which stone, shell, and bone were the hardest and most durable materials; in which native fibers were employed to make clothing, house thatch, and household necessities, and ornaments. Their worship of supernatural forces and spirits, which so strongly influenced their daily lives, has almost completely disappeared, being replaced by various forms of Christian religion. Navigation was by means of outrigger or double canoes, in which they not only went fishing but also made long voyages between islands.

The people lived in small or moderate-sized villages, usually near the sea. Today there are few places large enough to be called "town": Apia, Samoa; Nuku'alofa and Neiafu, Tonga; and the Pago Pago naval station in American Samoa. Houses have wooden frames, covered with various kinds of thatch. Floors are covered with mats plaited from coconut leaves.

The language throughout the group consists of various dialects of Polynesian, which was not reduced to writing until after contact with foreigners, chiefly missionaries. Some confusion in spelling has resulted from the way in which various groups transcribed the spoken language. For example, in Samoa the sound *ng* was represented by *g*; thus Pago Pago is pronounced *pang'-o pang'-o*. In Tonga *p* and *b* have been used interchangeably by different groups; *s, j,* and *t* also were used to represent the same sound. On March 31, 1943, the spelling was standardized in Tonga, the use of *ng, p,* and *s* being approved, and the insertion of the glottal (') being mandatory.

HISTORY

The history of the Polynesian peoples, handed down as it was by word of mouth prior to the arrival of foreigners in the area, is obscured by a maze of tradition. The history of foreign contact with the south Pacific can be divided into four periods: (1) chance discoveries; (2) exploration; (3) traders, whalers, and missionaries; and (4) international rivalry.

During the first period Spanish and Portuguese navigators voyaged westward from the Americas, and Dutch navigators traveled eastward around Australia from the Spice Islands. They included such men as Alvaro de Mendaña, Quiros, Schouten and Le Maire, Abel Tasman, and Jacob Roggeveen, 1568 to 1730.

The second period occupied the last quarter of the eighteenth and the first quarter of the nineteenth centuries. There were such familiar names as John Byron, Wallis, Bougainville, James Cook, La Perouse, Fanning, Freycinet, and Bellinghausen.

Throughout the third period, which began about 1796, the reaction of traders and missionaries on the native peoples and on each other laid foundations for economic and cultural development quite different from the feudal life, dominated by prohibitions, that had gone before. The "stone age culture" disappeared overnight with the arrival of firearms, iron tools, and foreign clothing.

Many of the scattered atolls and "pancake" islands were discovered by the whalers who visited the area by the hundreds between 1820 and 1850. To make this expanse of uncharted sea safe for navigation, the United States Exploring Expedition covered it systematically from 1838 to 1842. Three ships, as well as whalers and chance visitors, discovered on some of the drier islands a gray, powdery substance called guano—lime phosphate, resulting from the inter-action of dry coral sand with the droppings of myriads of sea birds. Found to be useful as fertilizer, it was dug and shipped from about 1857 to the end of the century. Some forty-eight islands were claimed under the American Guano Act of 1856, but only half a dozen—Baker, Howland, Jarvis, Enderbury, Phoenix, and McKean—were worked extensively by three American guano companies. Other digging was done by British interests, chiefly on Malden Island.

INTERNATIONAL RIVALRY IN SAMOA

The French claimed islands in southeastern Polynesia and in Mel-anesia, and the British extended protection to numerous islands, but international rivalry reached its highest peak within this central area in Samoa. .

During the nineteenth century representatives of Germany, Great Britain, and the United States took advantage of rivalries between patriarchal "families" of the natives to gain certain advantages. Under their stimulus a "kingdom" of Samoa developed, rival candidates for the office of "king" being backed by the different powers. This turned the last few decades of the century into a period of wars and intrigues. In March, 1889, an international conflict might have occurred had not a violent storm struck Apia harbor and wrecked three German and three American warships that lay at anchor there. Various conferences were held. In 1899 the three powers sent a High Commission to Samoa, as a result of which the position of "king" was abolished; and soon after this the islands were divided between the United States and Germany. Those west of longitude 171° west were placed under the administra-tion of Germany, and those to the east under the United States. Great Britain gave up its interests in return for rights elsewhere.

In western Samoa German administration continued, with some economic success, until August 29, 1914. The territory was occupied by New Zealand troops during the First World War. After 6 years of military occupation, the Supreme Council of the Allied Powers, on May 7, 1919, conferred the mandate for western Samoa upon his Britannic Majesty, to be executed by the New Zealand government. This action was confirmed by the Council of the League of Nations, December 17, 1920. When the League of Nations was replaced by the United Nations, the mandate was changed to a trusteeship, under which New Zealand assumed direct responsibility for the administra-tion of western Samoa. This agreement was approved by the United Nations General Assembly on December 13, 1946.

During the years the Samoan people have gradually been given a greater voice in the management of their own affairs. However, in January, 1947, they petitioned the Secretary-General of the United Nations to be given immediate self-government. The trusteeship continues, but by a revised constitution the Samaons were given a majority in their Legislative Assembly, the principal executive authority in the territory. It enacts all laws for the "peace, order, and good government of the Territory," but not for its defense or external affairs, which are attended to by New Zealand.

The administration of the eastern part of Samoa (American Samoa) has been in the hands of the United States Navy Department. The United States was interested primarily in the use of Pago Pago harbor as a naval base. Chiefs of Tutuila and Manu'a acknowledged the "sovereignty and protection of the United States," but the islands have never been formally annexed. The President of the United States only authorized the Navy Department to administer them. Citizenship was not granted to the Samoans; they have only the status of "American-protected persons." Copra and handicrafts have been marketed by the Naval Government, but settlement and trade have been discouraged.

There is considerable agitation for citizenship and a civilian government. There is no special complaint against the Naval administration, health, education, and economic conditions have been improved materially. A naturally proud and independence-loving people simply want a greater say in their own affairs and a more definite political status.

ADMINISTRATION

The islands of western Polynesia are administered by five different governments. Three of them—Australia, New Zealand, and the United Kingdom of Great Britain and North Ireland, generally referred to as Great Britain—belong to the British family of nations. The others are France and the United States of America.

Australia, Great Britain, and New Zealand have joint trusteeship, under the United Nations, over the island of Nauru (discussed in Chapter 9). It is actually administered from Canberra, Australia.

Uvea and the Hoorn Islands are included by France as part of their *Nouvelle-Calédonie et Dépendances,* under the official name, *Îles Wallis et Futuna.* They are administered from Noumea, capital of New Caledonia.

Great Britain, operating through the Colonial Office and the Western

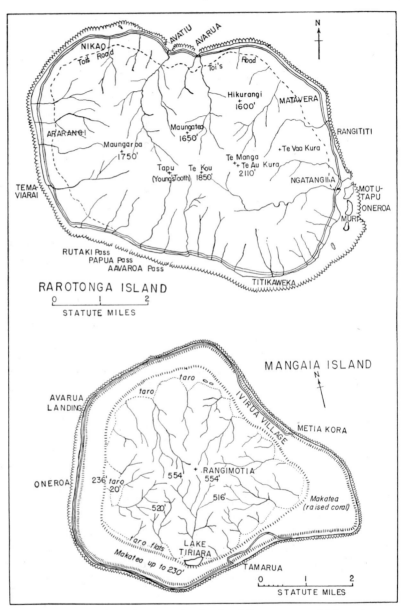

FIGURE 114.   Southern Cook Islands of Rarotonga and Mangaia.

Pacific High Commission, administers the Gilbert and Ellice Islands Colony. This includes the Gilbert and Ellice groups; Ocean Island (see Chapter 10); the eight Phoenix islands, two of which—Canton and Enderbury—are administered jointly with the United States; and the British Northern Line islands (Washington, Fanning, and Christmas). The Western Pacific High Commission also has jurisdiction over the five British Southern Line islands (Malden, Starbuck, Vostok, Flint, and Caroline) and the British Protectorate of Tonga, which is an independent kingdom.

The Cook Islands, Niue Island, and the Tokelau Islands are dependencies of New Zealand, which also has trusteeship over western Samoa, as noted above. All of these are under the Department of External Affairs, Wellington.

The United States, through its Navy Department, controls American Samoa, including Rose atoll and Swains Island. Also under American jurisdiction are the American Equatorial islands (Baker, Howland, Jarvis, Palmyra, and Kingman Reef); and Canton and Enderbury, jointly with Great Britain.

In all these islands where there are indigenous people much of the local administration is left in the hands of their chiefs and leaders. The Resident Commissioners and their assistants are concerned chiefly with the broader aspects of health, education, justice, finance, and economic development.

SOUTH PACIFIC COMMISSION

Because such problems of health, social welfare, and economic development are similar throughout the entire area, the six governments, by an agreement signed at Canberra, February 6, 1947, established an advisory body called the South Pacific Commission. Its headquarters have been set up at Noumea, New Caledonia, with a Secretary-General and staff. Its purpose is to recommend to the member governments means of promoting the well-being of the peoples of these territories. An important part of the Commission's organization is a Research Council, made up of full-time specialists and a group of advisers, chosen for their special knowledge of the problems of the territories. They plan and carry out studies in the fields of health, social development, and economic development. In addition, it is planned to hold every three years a conference of representatives of the fifteen territories, including indigenous inhabitants and their advisers, to discuss their mutual problems; the first was at Suva, Fiji, in April, 1950.

HEALTH

The Polynesians of this area are a people of fine physique. Effective medical service is helping them to counteract the effects of diseases that arrived with foreigners and against which they have no immunity. Each island group has public hospitals at which the native people receive medical and dental treatment, either without charge or at very nominal cost. European doctors and health officers are assisted by native medical practitioners, trained at the Central Medical School in Suva, Fiji. Suva is also headquarters for a South Pacific health service that helps to coordinate public health activities for the entire area.

FIGURE 115. Volcanic hills on Mangaia Island, Cook Group, separated by low swampy ground from the raised reef "makatea" that surrounds the island. Photograph, Sir Peter Buck, courtesy of the Bernice P. Bishop Museum.

These islands are free of many of the diseases that afflict tropical lands. There is no malaria or yellow fever. Hookworm is well under control, as the result of a campaign waged with the assistance of the Rockefeller Foundation. Leprosy is uncommon. The major diseases have been tuberculosis, yaws, filiariasis (elephantiasis), and an eye complaint. Active measures are being taken to combat them. The health of mothers and children, especially, is being cared for in the villages. Systematic sanitary inspection, coupled with group medical examinations, and modern treatment of disease are doing much to improve health conditions in each community.

The establishment of health services, however, has been more than the procuring of doctors, hospitals, and materials. It has been necessary, through education, to change the entire attitude of the native people toward disease. Sickness had been regarded as caused by supernatural agencies. These deep-rooted superstitions had to be replaced by a modern understanding of hygiene, health, pure water, and sanitation. This has been accomplished by trained natives whom the people understood and trusted.

EDUCATION

There is a high degree of literacy throughout the area. Practically all the Samoans and Tongans can read and write their own Polynesian dialects, which constitute the language of daily life and the medium of instruction in the schools. In addition, many natives can speak English fluently and read it well. Higher education also is being provided, and outstanding students are being sent to New Zealand and other places for advanced schooling at the expense of the administration.

SAMOA

The Samoan Islands are the summits of a range of volcanic mountains (Fig. 116.) Savaii, at the western end, is largest, highest, and geologically the youngest. Rose atoll at the other end, 300 miles to the eastward, may long ago have been a high island, but today it consists of a wooded pile of sand and reef rock rising 10 feet above a circular ring of reef. Between these are seven islands, the names, elevations, and areas of which are given in Table 3.

The Samoan Islands were brought to the notice of Europeans in 1722 by Jacob Roggeveen but were not explored by him. That was left to the voyagers who followed. Bougainville (1768) was so impressed by the Samoan sailing canoes that he called the group the "Navigator Islands." In 1830 missionaries of the London Missionary Society arrived and introduced a new era of island life.

The population of the group declined until about 1890, owing to almost constant warfare and the arrival of foreign diseases. With the coming of peace and improved health conditions, the tide turned, and the Samoans have been increasing in number at an accelerating rate. Between 1921 and 1948 the indigenous population of western Samoa doubled (33,336 to 67,149 Samoans). During the same period the number of Europeans decreased from 835 to 316; the number of Chinese laborers from 1290 to 285; and of Melanesian laborers from 465 to 72. In American Samoa, from 1920 to 1950, the indigenous population increased from 7776 to 18,602, including Swain's Island.

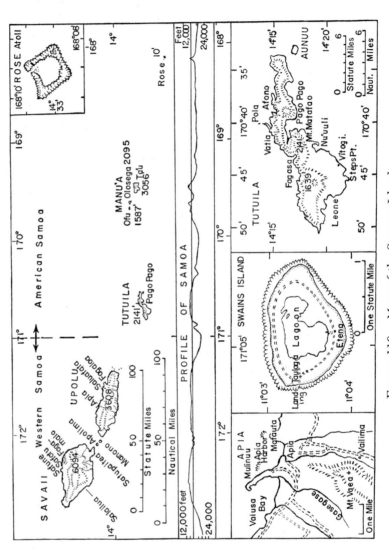

FIGURE 116. Maps of the Samoan Islands.

Apia, with a population of nearly 10,000, is the largest town in the entire area covered by this chapter. The rest of the people of Samoa live in 236 villages, all but a few located near the sea.

There has been considerable effort to encourage Samoans to cultivate crops for export. There are not over thirty-five European copra planters today, the bulk of that industry being in Samoan hands. The raising of cacao has remained in European hands, but bananas are grown principally by Samoans, who also raise most of the pigs, cattle, and poultry. Rubber grows well, but there is too much competition from Malaya. There are no factories in Samoa, but native handicrafts are important, especially in American Samoa, which cultivates only coconuts to make copra for export.

Of approximately 725,000 acres of western Samoa, 125,630 acres are held by the Crown and by Europeans, but only about 18,000 acres are under cultivation. One quarter of the entire area might be considered as waste land.

In American Samoa, out of 45,500 acres, less than 2500 acres have been alienated, leaving at least 43,000 acres for the use of the 20,000 Samoans, about 2 acres each. About 450 acres are used by the U.S. Naval Government, and 360 acres are leased by the Mormon Mission.

TONGA

Tonga's 160 or more islands are distributed in two distinct chains that trend roughly north and south, following a great submarine ridge that connects New Zealand with Samoa, through the Kermadec Islands (Fig. 117). The eastern chain consists of numerous limestone islands, formed of raised reef, some rising as much as 670 feet above the sea, but most of them less than 200 feet high. In contrast, the western chain is formed by a dozen volcanic peaks, the highest (Kao) rising 3380 feet above the sea in a perfect cone. Five of the craters are active periodically; six others have been dormant during historic times, but all are recent in the geologic sense. Fonuafo'ou (or Falcon Island) has been built up by eruptions several times during the past century, only to be worn away again by the sea. Perhaps best known to Americans is Niuafo'ou—"Tin Can Island"—of swimming mailman fame.[1] It experienced such a violent volcanic eruption in December, 1946, that all its population had to be evacuated. To the geologist Eua is the most interesting, for it is believed to contain ancient rocks and to mark the eastern edge of the "Melanesian continent."

[1] Thomas A. Jaggar, "Living on a Volcano: An Unspoiled Patch of Polynesia Is Ninafoō, Nicknamed 'Tin Can Island' by Stamp Collectors," *Natl. Geographic Mag.,* Vol. 68, pp. 91–106, July, 1935.

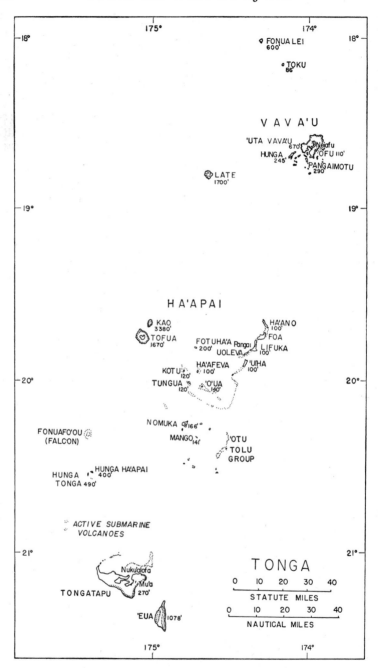

FIGURE 117. Tonga Islands.

Tonga is an independent kingdom, the only one in the Pacific to have survived the period of expansion of the great powers. Genealogical records, handed down by word of mouth, enable Queen Salote (Charlotte), the present ruling monarch, to trace her ancestry back 1000 years or more to the first Tui Tonga, who came to this island group from Samoa. At the height of the little island empire's history, it controlled not only Samoa and parts of Fiji but also islands to the north from the New Hebrides on the west to Tahiti on the east. Archeological sites found by Bishop Museum scientists on Fanning Island, north of the equator, suggest that the Tongans voyaged at least that far north.

FIGURE 118. The Samoan Village of Ana lies at the foot of Mt. Pioa (1717 feet), popularly known as the "rainmaker." Photograph courtesy of the Bernice P. Bishop Museum.

Each of the three principal districts of Tonga—Vava'u, Ha'apai, and Tongatapu—had its own rival chiefs. They were frequently at war until a chief of Ha'apai rose to power in 1820. He championed the missionaries, who arrived in 1828. He was baptized in 1831, adopting the name Siaosi (George) Tupou, and lived until 1893, producing a peaceful, modern, Christian state.

He was succeeded by his great-grandson, George Tupou II, in 1893. When there were financial difficulties Great Britain took the little kingdom under her protection, signing a "treaty of Friendship and Protection" in 1900. By this treaty Tonga left all foreign relations to Great Britain, and the British Agent and Consul were instructed not to interfere in Tonga's internal affairs, except (as was added in 1905) in financial matters. Thanks to the watchful supervision of the British Empire, Tonga has no public debt. Instead, it has a substantial surplus, well invested. The people are thrifty, and the government savings bank, established in 1926, had 3327 depositors by 1946 and credits amounting to £113,335.

FIGURE 119. Tokelau Island house, Fakaofu atoll. Photograph, Gordon McGregor, courtesy of the Bernice P. Bishop Museum.

The Tongan is an ardent individualist, strongly in favor of "Tonga for the Tongans." Immigration of foreigners to Tonga has been discouraged by a law that prohibits them from owning land. About one-fifth of the land is uninhabitable, and the density of population is very uneven throughout the rest of the area, as shown by Table 2.

TABLE 2

POPULATION

District or Island	Area of Inhabited Islands, Square Miles	Density per Square Mile 1900	1918	1938
Niuafo'ou Island	19.4	56	58	67
Niuatoputapu Island	7.2	99	115	113
Vava'u (district)	46.0	100	123	176
Ha'apai (district)	19.8	265	311	366
'Eua Island	33.7	13	12	14
Tongatapu Island	100.3	76	96	145

The population of Tonga is increasing steadily because of a high birth rate and good health conditions. Tongans are essentially agriculturists. To insure full cultivation of the land for both subsistence farming and raising copra and fruits for export, each male Tongan at the age of 16 years is entitled to lease 8¼ acres of land for cultivation, at about $1.60 a year, on condition he plants 200 coconuts within a year. He can also have 132 square yards of land in his village as a house site, without charge. There is no scarcity of land in the kingdom; and there is no housing problem. A family can construct its own house, with the help of a few friends, from materials readily at hand.

THE LOW CORAL ISLANDS

Scattered throughout 1,000,000 square miles of the central Pacific, for the most part south of the Equator, are some 60 groupings of low,

FIGURE 120. Group of Singave women and children on Fortuna Island, Photograph E. C. Burrows, courtesy of the Bernice P. Bishop Museum.

flat, coral islands (Fig. 121). Excluding the sixteen Gilbert Islands (see Chapter 10), these have a combined area of 311 square miles; but over 70 per cent of the land is concentrated on Christmas Island (see Table 3).

These islands represent practically every type of sand and coral formation, from the saucer-shaped, sandy "pancake" (such as Baker, Fig. 122, Jarvis, or Vostok) with no lagoon to the reef-enclosed lagoon with almost no dry land. They also have a great range of rainfall, from the meager amount that falls on dry, barren Malden, to the copious precipitation on drenched Washington Island, which has turned the former salt lagoon into a fresh-water lake and whose lush vegetation has formed peat bogs. Some, like Kingman Reef, have only a tiny speck of dry land. Others have long ribbons of reef, along which are dots or ridges of sand, with various kinds of vegetation.

As the rainfall increases, there is a progressive improvement and advance in the type of soil and vegetation. The driest islands have grass and low herbs scattered over gray sand; those with moderate rainfall have dry, scrubby forest and groves of coconut palms, beneath which is light brown, sandy loam; finally the wet islands have a luxuriant growth of trees, with moss on their bark and bird's nest ferns perched in their branches, and beneath which the rich, dark, fern-covered soil is always moist. All these are found at elevations of 5 to 20 feet, built up of fragments of reef rock, coral, and the skeletons of marine plants and animals. The land is highest at the crest of the abruptly sloping beach, especially on the windward side; from this it slopes gradually down to the edge of the lagoon or the center of the "pancake."

Under best conditions man finds life difficult on low coral islands. There is little or no fresh water in the soil. It is usually so brackish that visitors to the islands will not drink it. Many of the Polynesian inhabitants, however, prefer it to the tasteless rainwater, which generally is caught and stored. Few food plants will grow, except on the wettest of the islands. During dry periods both food and drink disappear. This region also is subject to violent storms, which blow down houses and coconut palms, ruin crops, and may even cause waves to wash completely over the low surface. And yet on such islands we find concentrations of population as high as 660 per square mile. For the entire Ellice group the number probably exceeds 470 per square mile (or 1.4 acres per person), and this is increasing steadily. The drier Gilbert Islands, with an average of 244 persons per square mile (2.6 acres per person), already have been forced to transfer part of their surplus population to the formerly uninhabited Phoenix Islands.

The Phoenix Islands settlement scheme was begun in 1937, with a grant from the British Colonial Development and Welfare Fund. The Phoenix Islands became a part of the Gilbert and Ellice Islands Colony on March 18, 1937, and the fund was used to buy leases held by outside interests. In 1937 Sydney Island, rechristened Manra, had its 7500 coconut palms apportioned among 260 Gilbertese settlers; and the 15,000 coconut palms on Hull Island, called Orona, were alloted to 432 colonists. Meanwhile 58 Gilbertese were sent to Gardner

Island, renamed Nikumaroro, to clear portions of the forest and plant coconut palms. It was estimated that these three islands could accommodate a maximum of 900, 1100, and 1000 natives, respectively. By 1948 the first two groups of colonists had increased naturally to 299 and 558, and there were 84 persons on Gardner. After 400

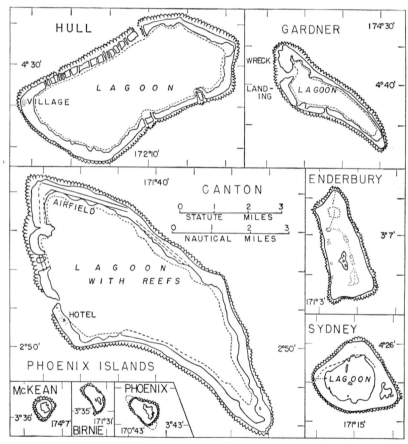

Figure 121. Islands of the Phoenix group.

colonists have been settled on Gardner, no more persons will be taken to these islands, the extra room being left for normal increase. Attempts have been made, without much success, to grow coconut palms on tiny Birnie, Phoenix, and McKean islands. If they succeed, these islands will be made use of by the populations of the three colonized islands to grow additional food.

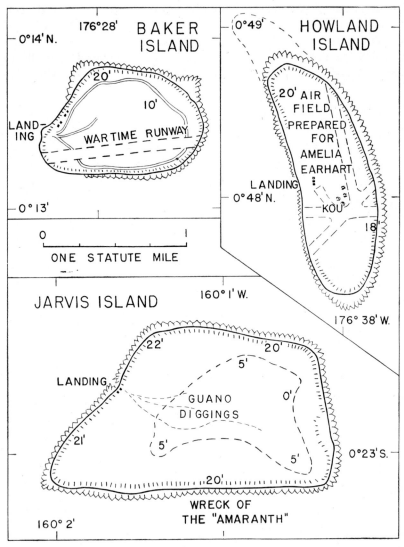

FIGURE 122.   Baker, Howland, and Jarvis islands.

The next contemplated transfers, to relieve population pressure in the Gilbert and Ellice islands, will be made to the British Northern Line Islands.   Christmas Island has already been purchased for that purpose.   There are an estimated 140,000 coconut palms on Fanning, 200,000 on Washington, and 300,000 on Christmas, with additional acres that could be planted. These three islands produce up to 2500 tons of copra a year. They could care for a large number of surplus people, if need be.

Efforts have been made to obtain the use of uninhabited islands in Fiji for colonists from small, overcrowded coral islands. The Banaban inhabitants of Ocean Island, who were forced from their island and their homes and crops destroyed by the Japanese, have been settled happily on Rabi (ram'-bee) Island in the Fiji group.

TRANSPORTATION

One of the chief problems throughout the South Pacific is shipping and other means of transportation. Perishable commodities cannot be marketed from numerous small, scattered islands, unless ships run frequently, regularly, and carry cargo at not too great expense. During 1949 only two steamships made regularly scheduled trips between this entire region and markets in New Zealand, visiting only six ports. Schooners, with uncertain schedules, visited others, some islands not oftener than once or twice a year.

The construction of airfields on several of the islands, as a result of war activities, has given considerable encouragement to air transportation. One line runs a plane every two weeks from Auckland to Rarotonga (Cook Islands), touching at Tonga, Apia (Samoa), and Aitutaki (Cook Islands), within this area. A French line, from New Caledonia to Tahiti, also stops at Aitutaki.

During the last half century the people of this region have given up much of their native culture, and have become increasingly dependent upon the foreign administration. Populations are increasing steadily, because of improved health conditions. Better education, motion pictures, and closer contact with the outside world have tended to make the indigenous people less satisfied with their own surroundings. In order to improve their conditions they must have more income. This means more exports; and the circle comes back to a growing need for better transportation, and the opportunity to make a fair profit in an available market.

"Experts" may say that these people would have been happier and better off had they been left untouched by foreign civilization. But it would be difficult for them to turn back now. The immediate solution seems to lie in better crops and better transportation, perhaps in part by air, to better markets. What the future may hold for them no one can foretell.

TABLE 3

STATISTICAL SUMMARY OF THE CENTRAL PACIFIC ISLANDS

Tonga (Principal Islands from North to South)

Island	Maximum Elevation, Feet	Area, Square Miles	Population 1931	Population 1937
Niuafo'ou*	853	19.4	1,291	1,229†
Tafahi*	2000	1.3	47⎫	
Niuatoputapu (Keppel's Island)*	350	5.7	743⎭	829
3 small islands		0.2	......	......
Vava'u Group		(56.1)	(7,643)	8,158
Fonualei*	600	0.75	......	......
Late*	1700	6.7	......	......
Kapa	345	2.3	517	......
Pangaimotu	290	3.4	354	......
Hunga	245	1.85	228	......
'Uta Vava'u	670	34.6	5,313	......
54 small islands	290	6.5	1,231	......
Ha'apai Group		(50.1)	(6,410)	6,856
Kao*	3380	4.8	......	......
Tofua*	1670	21.4	......	......
Fonuafo'ou (Falcon Island)*	(variable)		......	......
Ha'ano	100	2.5	972	......
'Uiha	100	2.1	745	......
Foa	100	5.1	907	......
Lifuka	100	4.4	1,751	......
19 islets up to	200	3.7	528	......
Lulunga group to (20 islets)	140	2.2	935	......
Nomuka group to (12 islets)	166	3.5	572	......
'Otu Tolu group (3 islets)	71	0.4	......	......
Hunga Ha'apai*	400	0.25	......	......
Hunga Tonga*	490	0.15	......	......
28 islets up to	180	1.9	......	......
Tongatapu Group	270	99.2	12,357	15,274
'Eua	1078	33.7	348	444†
'Ata*	1165	0.9	......	......
Total		268.9	28,839	32,790

* Island of volcanic formation.

† Inhabitants evacuated from Niuafo'ou, December, 1946, because of violent volcanic eruption; being settled on 'Eua.

TABLE 3 (Continued)

SAMOA

Island	Maximum Elevation, Feet	Area, Square Miles	Population	Density per Square Mile	Political Administration
Western Samoa (1946)					
Savaii	6094	703	18,380	27.1	Trusteeship
Apolima	472	2			of
Manono	197	3	50,380	113.5	New
Upolu	3608	430			Zealand
Total		1138	69,030	60.7	
American Samoa (1950)					
Tutuila (and Aunuu)	2141	54	15,621	266.7	United
Ofu (and Nuu)	1587	2			States
Olosega	2095	1.5	2,817	136.8	of
Tau	3056	15			America
Rose islet	10	0.3	. . . . .	. . . . .	
Total		72.8	18,438	232.6	
Total for all Samoa		1210.8	87,468	71.0	
Swains Island		1.25	164	116	Administered by American Samoa

WALLIS AND FUTUNA

Island	Maximum Elevation, Feet	Area, Square Miles	Population, 1948		Density per Square Mile
			Indigenous	Foreign	
Uvea (Wallis)	470	23.1	5700	35	248
Reef islets	200	1.3	. . . .	. .	. . .
Hoorn Islands					
Futuna	2500	24.7	2500	5	101
Alofi	1200	11.4	. . . .	. .	. . .
Total		60.5	8200	40	134

TABLE 3 (*Continued*)
COOK ISLANDS

Island	Maximum Elevation, Feet	Area, Square Miles	Population, March 1948				
			Indigenous		Foreign		Total
			Male	Female	Male	Female	
"*Lower Cook Group*"							
Aitutaki	450	6.1	1,282	1,216	7	3	2,508
Atiu	394	10.9	687	588	6	6	1,287
Mauke	100	7.1	322	442	6	3	773‡
Rarotonga	2110	25.8	2,714	2,578	166	91	5,549‡
Mangaia	554	27.3	910	952	7	2	1,871‡
(High Cook Island)		77.2	5,915	5,776	192	105	11,988
Manuae and Te Au o Tu		2.3	18	10			28
Takutea		0.45	....	....	...	...	......
Mitiaro		4.0	95	125	...	...	220‡
"*Northern Cook Group*"							
Penrhyn (Tongareva)		6.2	369	331	...	...	700
Rakahanga		1.55	168	155	2	...	325
Manihiki		2.0	214	235	4	1	454
Pukapuka		2.0	335	332	6	1	674
Nassau		0.45	....	....	...	...	......
Suvarov (Suwarrow)		1.0	....	....	...	...	......
Palmerston		1.55	34	33	...	...	67
Low Cook Islands		21.5	1233	1221	12	2	2,468
Total for Cook Islands		98.7	7148	6997	204	107	14,456

‡ In 1947 the population of Canton Island was 81 British subjects and about 150 Americans. The remaining population of the Phoenix Islands on these two dates were British (in 1931 workmen from the Gilbert and Ellice islands; in 1947 Gilbertese colonists). The small American colony on Enderbury arrived in 1938 and was withdrawn in 1942.

TABLE 3 (*Continued*)
ELLICE ISLANDS

Island	Area, Square Miles	Population		Density per Square Mile	
		1931	1947	1931	1947
Nanumea	1.5	770	746	515.4	499.4
Nanumanga	1.1	424	524	395.0	488.1
Niutao	1.0	645	644	660.6	659.5
Nui	0.8	410	490	524.8	627.2
Vaitupu	2.15	720	728	332.7	336.3
Nukufetau	1.1	394	524	341.7	454.3
Funafuti	1.1	413	528	384.7	490.5
Nukulaelae	0.7	178	282	253.7	402.0
Niulakita	0.15	40	21	245.2	129.2
Total	9.6	3,994	4,487	416.8	468.2

TOKELAU ISLANDS

Atafu	0.8	356	460	445	575
Nukunono	2.1	268	375	128	179
Fakaofo	1.0	478	581	478	581
Total	3.9	1,102	1,416	282	363

PHOENIX ISLANDS

Canton	3.5	.....	230‡	.....	65.7
Enderbury	2.3	.....	.....	.....	....
Birnie	0.1	.....	.....	.....	....
Phoenix	0.2	.....	.....	.....	....
Sydney (Manra)	1.7	16	294	9.9	182.9
Hull (Orona)	1.5	15	530	9.9	351.2
Gardner (Nikumaroro)	1.6	.....	79	.....	49.4
McKean	0.2	.....	.....	.....	....
Total	11.1	31	1,133	2.8	102

‡ In 1947 the population of Canton Island was 81 British subjects and about 150 Americans. The remaining population of the Phoenix Islands on these two dates were British (in 1931 workmen from the Gilbert and Ellice islands; in 1947 Gilbertese colonists). The small American colony on Enderbury arrived in 1938 and was withdrawn in 1942.

TABLE 3 (*Continued*)
Line Islands

Island	Area, Square Miles	Population		Density per Square Mile	
		1931	1947	1931	1947
American Equatorial Islands					
Howland	0.73	.....	.....	.....	....
Baker	0.65	.....	.....	.....	....
Kingman Reef	0.01	.....	.....	.....	....
Palmyra	0.50	.....	@ 100	.....	@ 200
Jarvis	1.74	.....	.....	.....	....
Total	3.63	.....	@ 100	.....	@ 27.5
British Northern Line Islands					
Washington	2.9 ⎫	467	158	30.6	54.9
Fanning	12.4 ⎭		259		20.9
Christmas	222.7	38	52	0.2	0.4
	238.0	505	469	2.1	2.0
British Southern Line Islands					
Malden	11.25	@ 25	.....	2.2	....
Starbuck	8.1	.....	.....	.....	....
Caroline	1.45	@ 20	.....	14	....
Vostok	0.1	.....	.....	.....	....
Flint	1.0	@ 30	.....	30	....
	21.9	@ 75	.....	3.4	....
Low Coral Islands (including low islands in Cook and Samoa groups)	311.18	8093	10,218	36	31

@ = approximate.

REFERENCES

Cook Islands

Beaglehole, Ernest, *Islands of Danger,* Progressive Publication Society, 212 pp., Wellington, 1944. (Pukapuka and Nassau Islands.)

Beaglehole, Ernest and Pearl, "Ethnology of Pukapuka," *Bernice P. Bishop Museum Bull.* 150, 419 pp., 6 plates, 55 figures, Honolulu, 1938.

Buck, Peter H. (Te Rangi Hiora), "The Material Culture of the Cook Islands (Aitutaki)," *Board of Maori Ethnographic Research Memoirs,* Vol. 1, Wellington, 1926.

―――― "Ethnology of Manihiki and Rakahanga," *Bernice P. Bishop Museum Bull.* 99, 238 pp., 11 plates, 109 figures, Honolulu, 1932.

―――― "Mangaian Society," *Bernice P. Bishop Museum Bull.* 122, 207 pp., 1 figure, Honolulu, 1934.

―――― "Arts and Crafts of the Cook Islanders," *Bernice P. Bishop Museum Bull.* 179, 533 pp., 16 plates, 275 figures, Honolulu, 1944.

Marshall, Patrick, "Geology of Mangaia," *Bernice P. Bishop Museum Bull.* 36, 48 pp., 3 plates, 3 figures, map, Honolulu, 1927.

―――― "Geology of Rarotonga and Atiu," *Bernice P. Bishop Museum Bull.* 72, 75 pp., 5 plates, 13 figures, Honolulu, 1930.

Wilder, Gerritt Parmile, "Flora of Rarotonga," *Bernice P. Bishop Museum Bull.* 86, 113 pp., 8 plates, 3 figures, Honolulu, 1931.

Tonga

Gifford, E. W., "Tongan Society," *Bernice P. Bishop Museum Bull.* 61, 352 pp., 1 plate, 3 figures, Honolulu, 1929.

Hoffmeister, J. Edward, "Geology of Eua, Tonga," *Bernice P. Bishop Museum Bull.* 96, 93 pp., 22 plates, 6 figures, Honolulu, 1932.

McKern, W. C., "Archaeology of Tonga," *Bernice P. Bishop Museum Bull.* 60, 123 pp., 6 plates, 49 figures, Honolulu, 1929.

Wood, A. H., *History and Geography of Tonga,* 108 pp., C. S. Sumers, Nuku'alofa, Tonga, 1932, 1938.

Niue Island

Leob, Edwin M., "History and Traditions of Niue," *Bernice P. Bishop Museum Bull.* 32, 226 pp., 13 plates, 5 figures, 1926.

Thomson, Basil, *Savage Island: an Account of a Sojourn in Aiue and Tonga,* London, 254 pp., ill., 1902.

Samoa

Buck, Peter H. (Te Rangi Hiora), "Samoan Material Culture," *Bernice P. Bishop Museum Bull.* 75, 724 pp., 56 plates, 338 figures, Honolulu, 1930.

Christophersen, Erline, "Flowering Plants of Samoa," *Bernice P. Bishop Museum Bull.* 128, 221 pp., 32 figures, Honolulu, 1935.

Coulter, John W., "Land Utilization in American Samoa," *Bernice P. Bishop Museum Bull.* 170, 48 pp., 2 pls., 7 figs., Honolulu, 1941.

Daly, R. A., *The Geology of American Samoa*, Carnegie Institution of Washington Publication No. 340, pp. 95–145, Washington, D.C., 1924. (Also papers by Chamberlin and Mayor in the same publication.)

Dulles, Foster R., *America in the Pacific, a Century of Expansion*, 229 pp., Houghton Mifflin Co., Boston, 1938. (American Samoa.)

Keesing, Felix M., *Modern Samoa: Its Government and Changing Life*, 506 pp., Allen and Unwin, London, 1934.

Mead, Margaret, *Coming of Age in Samoa*, 297 pp., New York, 1929, 1936 (Blue Ribbon Books).

—— "Social Organization of Manua," *Bernice P. Bishop Museum Bull.* 76, 218 pp., Honolulu, 1930.

Setchell, William A., *American Samoa: I. Vegetation of Tituila Island. II. Ethnobotany of the Samoans. III. Vegetation of Rose Atoll.* Carnegie Institution of Washington Publication No. 341, 275 pp., Washington, D.C., 1924.

Stearns, Harold T., "Geology of the Samoan Islands," *Geol. Soc. Amer. Bull.* 56, pp. 1279–1332, maps, illustrations, 1944.

WALLIS AND HOORN ISLANDS

Burrows, Edwin G., "Ethnology of Futuna," *Bernice P. Bishop Museum Bull.* 138, 239 pp., 11 plates, 37 figures, Honolulu, 1936.

—— "Ethnology of Uvea (Wallis Island)," *Bernice P. Bishop Museum Bull.* 145, 176 pp., 8 plates, 29 figures, Honolulu, 1938.

—— "Topography and Culture of Two Polynesian Islands," *Geogr. Rev.*, Vol. 28, pp. 214–223, maps, illustrations, 1938.

Stearns, Harold T., "Geology of the Wallis Islands," *Geol. Soc. Amer. Bull.* 56, pp. 849–860, 1945.

THE ATOLLS

Bryan, E. H., Jr., *American Polynesia and the Hawaiian Chain*, Star-Bulletin Publishing Co., Honolulu, 1939, 1942. (Extensive bibliography.)

Christophersen, E., "Vegetation of Pacific Equatorial Islands," *Bernice P. Bishop Museum Bull.* 44, Honolulu, 1927.

Ellis, Albert F., *Adventuring in Coral Seas*, 2nd ed., Angus and Robertson, Ltd., Sydney, 1937.

Emory, Kenneth P., "Archaeology of the Equatorial Islands," *Bernice P. Bishop Museum Bull.* 123, Honolulu, 1934.

Macgregor, Gordon, "Ethnology of Tokelau Island," *Bernice P. Bishop Museum Bull.* 146, Honolulu, 1937.

Wentworth, C. K., "Geology of the Equatorial Islands," *Bernice P. Bishop Museum Occasional Papers*, Vol. 9., No. 15, Honolulu, 1931.

15

New Zealand

ROBERT G. BOWMAN

THE SELF-GOVERNING DOMINION OF NEW ZEALAND IS A REMOTE insular Pacific outpost of the Commonwealth of Nations[1] and the home of less than 2,000,000 people, mostly of British extraction. Its major physical components are two large, mountainous islands, together with a number of adjacent lesser islands and islets (Fig. 123). Various outlying island clusters and isolated fragments of land dispersed over 6,000,000 square miles of ocean between the equator and the frozen fringe of Antarctica have also been annexed to the Dominion, most of them during the twentieth century. New Zealand proper, or the "heartland" of the Dominion, includes North and South islands (44,281 and 58,092 square miles, respectively), Stewart Island (670 square miles), and the Chatham Islands, which lie across 450 miles of open ocean to the east (372 square miles). North, South, and Stewart islands together have a latitudinal spread of about 13° (34° 30′ to 47° 20′ south) or 900 statute miles, and a longitudinal spread of slightly more than 12° (166° 10′ to 178° 20′ east), which in these latitudes corresponds to about 600 statute miles. They lie about 1200 miles east-southeast of Australia, 1600 miles north of Antarctica, 6000 miles west of Chile, and 4000 miles south-southwest of Hawaii. The total land area of the Dominion is reported to be 103,934 square miles (exclusive of Antarctic claims), which is about the same size as the states of Colorado or Illinois, and a little larger than the United Kingdom.

GEOLOGY

Land seems to have persisted in the New Zealand area at least since early Paleozoic time, yet also to have varied importantly in area, out-

[1] Until recently, the "British Commonwealth of Nations."

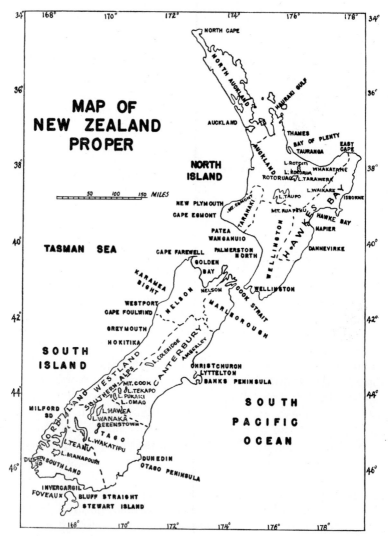

FIGURE 123.   Political map of New Zealand proper.

line, and elevation through successive geologic ages. Periods of marked crustal stability, gentle regional warping, slow subsidence, or gradual denudation have been interrupted at times by diastrophic revolutions of magnitude and intensity. These tectonic crises have caused relatively rapid buckling, shattering, and displacement of the earth's crust along the southwestern margins of the Pacific basin, forming mountains of various types and dimensions, and occasionally resulting in the outpouring of vast quantities of lava, ash, and other volcanic debris, with notable changes in the outlines and surface features of the islands. The most important periods of mountain building appear to have been in the early Cretaceous and late Tertiary. In the interval between these two major periods of disturbance all the coal formations and most of the limestones in the Dominion were laid down. The soils and most of the valuable gold concentrations, on the other hand, are definitely post-Tertiary developments.

Ancient crystalline rocks (principally granites) and metamorphosed Paleozoic sediments outcrop in many parts of South Island. A relatively broad belt of fine-grained graywacke and argillite (Trias-Jura?) forms the mountain backbone of Canterbury and Marlborough provinces and persists through a narrower zone in North Island at least as far as Hawke Bay. Similar rocks outcrop in the interior of North Island and in North Auckland Peninsula. Younger and weaker sedimentary rocks flank the mountains here and there, and accumulations of recent alluvium, mostly coarse gravel, often mask the underlying rock formations in the larger river valleys as well as some of the plains bordering the sea. In mid-Tertiary, numerous volcanic outbursts took place in South Island. The most violent activity occurred in the vicinity of Banks Peninsula and Dunedin, where the partly eroded remnants of old volcanoes form bold headlands and deep, sheltered harbors. All volcanoes in South Island are now classed as extinct.

Tertiary rocks occupy most of North Island, with the exceptions noted above. Because of relatively greater susceptibility to erosion they now outcrop in areas of generally more subdued topography than is characteristic of the older, harder rocks of the interior of South Island and their northern outliers in Wellington and Hawkes Bay provinces. The Pleistocene, which brought widespread glaciation to the elevated interior of South Island followed by the spreading of vast sheets of loose rock debris over the adjacent plains, was marked by intensification of volcanic activity in North Island and the accumulation of thick sheets of basalt, rhyolite, pumice, and similar extrusive materials.

Pleistocene and Recent deposits and oscillations of sea level have profoundly influenced the economic life and pattern of present-day New Zealand, perhaps more directly and importantly than those of all other geological ages combined. The lowland plains and valley alluvium were formed then, or else greatly modified. Placer gold was concentrated in useful deposits, and secondary enrichment of the famed Hauraki lodes took place. Regional uplift of the land increased stream gradients, which since that period have not had time to carve their valleys to grade and therefore provide many advantageous sites for the harnessing of water power. Coastal subsidence, furthermore, has provided valuable harbors through the drowning of some of the mouths of old river valleys and the breaching of ancient crater rims by the sea.

The major outpourings of volcanic materials in Pleistocene and Recent time have been in the vicinity of Hauraki Gulf and the Thames Peninsula near Auckland, on the interior plateau around Lake Taupo, and in western Taranaki. Certain volcanoes are still active, especially in the interior where Ruapehu and Ngauruhoe have both produced spectacular eruptions in late years. Frequent earthquakes provide further evidence of the geologic youth of portions of New Zealand. Examples of such earth movements are the Murchison "quakes" in 1929 in South Islands and at Hawke Bay in 1931 in North Island.

RELIEF

South Island is considerably more mountainous than North Island (Fig. 124). Over half its surface is dominated by the imposing Southern Alps, with included valleys and structural basins. By contrast, little more than one-tenth of North Island is truly mountainous, if foothills and dissected plateau country are excepted. The Southern Alps unquestionably deserve prominent rank among the world's more spectacular mountain ranges. Their precipitous, serrated crests rise more than 2 miles above sea level near the center of the island, and elsewhere stand mostly above 5000 feet. At least seventeen peaks reach elevations of 10,000 feet or more and give birth to large streams of glacial ice. The highest of these peaks is Mt. Cook, called "Aorangi" (The Cloud Piercer) by the native Maoris. The snow-capped, gale-lashed summit of this mountain towers 12,349 feet above sea level, and its flanks nourish six important glaciers.

The mountains of North Island for the most part are lower and less snowbound in winter, but nevertheless are quite impressive. The extensions of the Southern Alps in the eastern part of the island attain elevations of 5000 feet or more in places and ordinarily are capped with snow in winter. Still more imposing are the graceful volcanic cones of Mt. Ruapehu (9175 feet), Mt. Ngauruhoe (7515 feet), and Tongariro (6458 feet), which loom above a volcanic plateau near the center of the island, and Mt. Egmont (8260 feet) in western Taranaki. Ruapehu and Egmont have summit craters that contain small frozen lakes.

The extensive mountain regions of these two large islands, although

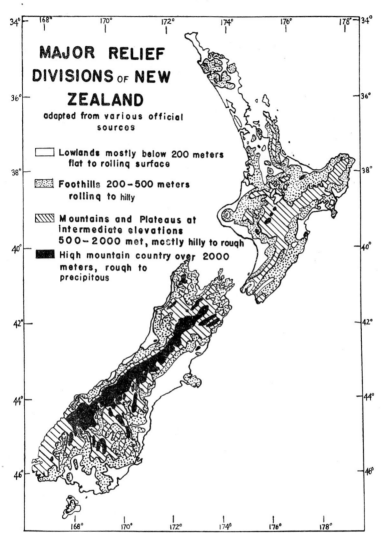

Figure 124. Relief map of New Zealand.

they inhibit agricultural development and close settlement, are playing an increasingly important role in the economic and recreational life of the Dominion. Lumbering and mining are carried on here and there in lower elevations, and a number of excellent hotels, chalets, and huts cater to the growing tourist industry. Also the mountains, interior valleys, and basins, where they are well-vegetated, serve as natural storehouses of water for domestic and industrial use by cities

and towns on the adjacent plains, for irrigation, and for the generation
of hydroelectric power.   In addition they play an important part in
flood control.

Plateaus are not extensive, numerous, or exceptionally high in New
Zealand.   There are only two worth mentioning here, Fjordland, in
the extreme southwest of South Island, and the volcanic plateau
in the interior of North Island.   Both stand at elevations ranging from
about 2000 to 4000 feet.   The climate of Fjordland is rather bleak and
the surface generally barren, and hence there are few permanent
occupants.   North Island has been settled, rather thinly to be sure,
in certain parts where the soils are somewhat more mature and surface
water or ground water can be tapped economically.   Dairying, stock
raising, tourism, and afforestation are the chief economic activities of
North Island upland.

The lowland plains, with their relatively deeper and more extensive accumulations of alluvium, their greater accessibility, and
their more genial climate, are naturally the areas of densest settlement
and premium resource in New Zealand.   Some of their physical limitations from the standpoint of productivity and population carrying
capacity, on the other hand, are small size; scattered distribution; soils
that locally are excessively thin, immature, stony, swampy, salty, or
acid; flooding; sometimes lack of first-class sea outlets; and inferior
hinterlands.

The preeminent lowland of North Island is the Waikato District
south of Auckland, on the whole perhaps the richest and most productive part of the Dominion, agriculturally speaking. Others of
special value through their combination of size and quality are the
Thames lowland just east of the Waikato; the crescent-shaped plains
bordering the Bay of Plenty, Hawke Bay, and Cook Strait; the
triangular Gisborne lowland; the rectangular Hutt Valley northeast
of Wellington; the gently sloping and exceptionally fertile plains that
encircle Mt. Egmont volcano in Taranaki; and the Dannevirke Valley
between Wellington and Napier.   South Island counterparts of these
relatively superior lowlands are the Canterbury Plains, stretching without interruption for nearly 150 miles along the east coast between
Amberley and Waimate; the Balclutha lowland and interior valleys of
Otago; the Oreti and Waimea plains in Southland; and the Blenheim
and Nelson hinterlands in Marlborough and Nelson provinces.   The
narrow coastal terraces and river valleys in Westland Province generally have inferior agricultural and pastoral lands owing mainly to
"sour" soils and excessively wet climate.   Their placer gold deposits,
coal seams, and stands of valuable native timber, however, form the

bases for other important economic activities, supplemented by commercial fishing and to a lesser extent tourism.

COASTS AND HARBORS

The coastline of New Zealand is relatively long in proportion to its area. It is also rather irregular, especially in North Auckland, Marlborough, and western Southland (Fjordland), where bays and gulfs, sounds, and fjords, respectively, indent the shoreline deeply. Near Auckland this is a distinct advantage, for it provides that city and its productive Waikato and Thames hinterlands with a commodious harbor and a sheltered anchorage large enough and deep enough to accommodate all the fleets of the world at one time. Much of the "advantage" of the indentations of Marlborough and Fjordland however, is wasted—in Fjordland practically all of it—because the hinterlands are so poor. The narrow inlets of Banks and Otago peninsulas, on the other hand, provide Christchurch (via Lyttelton) and Dunedin with well-protected outlets to the sea; and Southland has a fair harbor at The Bluff. Nelson harbor is rather small and shallow, and Westland's river-mouth harbors at Hokitika, Greymouth, all Westport are handicapped by restricted deep-water docking space gravel bars across their sea outlets, and exposure to storm winds, shore currents, and waves. Wellington has a fairly good anchorage and approach, but its deep-water docking space is limited. Napier, Wanganui, New Plymouth, and several other ports with attractive lowlands in their neighborhood have to contend with relatively straight, exposed shorelines, with shoal water, and with shifting river-mouth deposits.

Auckland is both the largest city and the commerical capital of the Dominion, and as such has strong political influence. This influence is due partly to the fact that it has the most spacious and generally most useful harbor, and in addition the richest tributary lowland in the Dominion. It also enjoys the commercial advantage of being situated nearest the sea link between the United States and Australia. Furthermore, Auckland is the logical New Zealand terminal for Pan-American Airways planes on the increasingly important trans-Pacific run between the United States and Australasia, and the main port of call for Australian and New Zealand planes on the Australia–New Zealand air link.

DRAINAGE AND WATER SUPPLY

Although the rivers of New Zealand are mostly short, shallow, and swift-flowing, they have served advantageously as avenues of interior exploration and settlement in the past and are now primary sources of domestic, industrial, irrigation, and hydroelectric water supply. A number furnish attractive sites for port development at or near the coast. The beds and terraces of several are the leading sources of placer gold; others function as important tourist attractions because of their natural beauty, boating facilities, and sportfishing. Most, on the other hand, have obstructions in the form of sand spits or gravel bars across their mouths and rapids or falls inland that make them practically useless for inland navigation. Some race through deep gorges where their banks are almost unapproachable. Others sprawl out over mile-wide gravel beds and thereby render substantial tracts of land valueless for cultivation, although for the same reason they are relatively easy to ford and in addition supply New Zealand with a well-nigh inexhaustible reserve of gravel for construction purposes. In South Island the principal streams east of the mountain divide are, from north to south, the Wairau, Clarence, Waimakariri, Ashburton, Rakaia, Rangitata, Waitaki, Clutha, and Mataura. Of these, the Rakaia is especially important as a source of irrigation water for South Canterbury, and the gravel bed of the Clutha is noteworthy for its reserves of placer gold. West of the main divide the principal streams are the Buller and the Grey in Westland. Their valleys are of special importance economically because of the coal measures that outcrop along them and for the gold in their stream gravels.

The rivers of North Island, like those of South Island, drain more or less radially outward from the high interior. They are not particularly important except as sources of water for domestic and stock use, as power development sites, and as tourist attractions. The Waikato and the Mangahao feature hydroelectric stations. The Wanganui, the Rangitikei, and the Manawatu, draining into Cook Strait, have considerable volume and fairly reliable flow, and hence are likely to figure importantly in the future. There are no sizable streams in North Auckland or along the east coast of the island.

The many large and small lakes in New Zealand deserve at least brief mention because of their great natural beauty and wide tourist appeal, their varied scientific interest, and their utility in connection with water storage for power development and flood control. In South Island there are nine large sheets of fresh water, ranging from 10 to 50 miles in length and to 5 miles wide. All are ponded behind moraines left by Pleistocene glaciers in valleys east and south of Mt. Cook. Lake Coleridge in west-central Canterbury is an important hydroelectric power site. Lake Tekapo, Pukaki, and Ohau occupy parallel depressions on the floor of the Mackenzie Basin in southwestern Canterbury at elevations of 1500 to 2400 feet above sea level. Because of their volume, high level in summer (when they are fed by melting snows), elevation, and proximity to plains with deficient rainfall as well as east-coast cities and towns, they are of considerable importance as sources of irrigation water, hydroelectric power, and domestic and industrial water supplies. Lakes Hawea, Wakatipu, and Wanaka in western Otago and Manapouri and Te Anau in western Southland are perhaps especially distinguished for the beauty of their natural setting. Some of the smaller lakes, like the high-level tarns occupying glacial cirques in Fjordland and the forest pools that provide perfect mirror images of near-by glaciers and snow-capped mountains in Westland, are just as picturesque, if less useful.

In North Island lakes are fewer, and the surrounding topography is generally more subdued, but such lakes as there are also have their attractions and uses. Taupo, the largest body of fresh water in New Zealand, has an area of 238 square miles and a maximum depth of 534 feet. It is situated near the center of the island in a broad depression on the volcanic plateau and has a surface elevation of 1250 feet. It is also the site of an important hydroelectric power development, and a world-famed tourist and sportfishing center. Waikareomoana to the east is perhaps the most scenic of all North Island lakes, as well as a hydroelectric power development site. The cluster of lakes about Rotorua, including lake Rotorua, Rotoiti, and Tararewa, is best known as a tourist center that combines with its lake appeal the attraction of several colorful Maori settlements, thermal activity in the form of geysers and hot springs, and sulphur baths.

GLACIERS AND GLACIATION

Except for some small, remnant, mountain glaciers near the summit of Mt. Ruapehu and a scattering of abandoned cirques and moraines at lower elevations, North Island has few attractions for the student of glacial history. In South Island, however, Pleistocene glaciers bit deeply and widely into the rock ramparts of the Southern Alps, roughening the topography here and smoothing it there in response to varying rock hardness, degree of rock fracture, flowage patterns in the ice streams, and other influences. East of the main divide, where the descent is (and was then) more gradual, the huge streams of glacial ice pouring down from high-level sources of nourishment fanned out and coalesced sufficiently at one time to form an icecap nearly 250 miles long and 100 miles wide. Later, as the accumulations of ice shrank in response to warmer temperatures or decreased precipitation in their source regions, they left behind immense quantities of coarse outwash material to be reworked and redeposited by torrents issuing from the rotting remnants of the ice mass. Great piles of morainic debris, ice-scoured ledges, striae, and boulder erratics are other evidences of former glacial activity.

Today only shrunken remnants of these once great Pleistocene glaciers remain in the upper reaches of the huge troughs their predecessors occupied and helped to sculpture. Still they are impressive, and attract numerous visitors to the region. They also help to maintain the level of lakes and regulate the flow of streams. Largest glacier is the Tasman (Fig. 133), on the eastern side of the Cook Range. This ice stream is 18 miles long, more than a mile wide through most of its length, and more than 1200 feet thick some 3 miles above its toe. Others of note on the eastern slopes of the main divide are the Murchison (11 miles), the Mueller and Godley (each about 8 miles), and the Hooker (slightly over 7 miles). On the western slopes the more important are the Fox (9¾ miles) and the Franz Josef (8½ miles). Owing to steeper gradients and heavier precipitation west of the divide, these last two glaciers descend within 700 feet of sea level, where their terminal faces abut upon luxuriant tree ferns, mosses, and flowering vines in the west-coast rainforest.

CLIMATE AND CLIMATIC CONTRASTS

The climate of New Zealand may be broadly described as cool-temperate and marine or oceanic. Thus it is rather similar to the climate of South Chile, Tasmania, and the northwest coast of North America, including parts of Washington, British Columbia, and southern Alaska (Köppen symbols: *Cfb*). Characteristic features are mild winters and cool summers, abundant rainfall fairly evenly distributed throughout the year, prevailing westerly winds, frequent passage of cyclonic storms, and little snow except in the higher elevations and latitudes. The normally marked excess of precipitation over evaporation means that runoff is substantial, all major streams and lakes are permanent though subject to fluctuations in level, and soil moisture is ordinarily plentiful.

These are the main climatic generalities. Since they are generalities, none should be applied indiscriminately to all parts of a land with such marked regional diversity as New Zealand, or all of them to any one part. A few examples will serve to illustrate the need for such caution (Fig. 125). Westland is excessively wet, with an average rainfall of more than 100 inches. Parts of the central Otago and extreme southwest Canterbury, on the other hand, are remarkably dry, with an average annual rainfall of less than 20 inches. Intense,

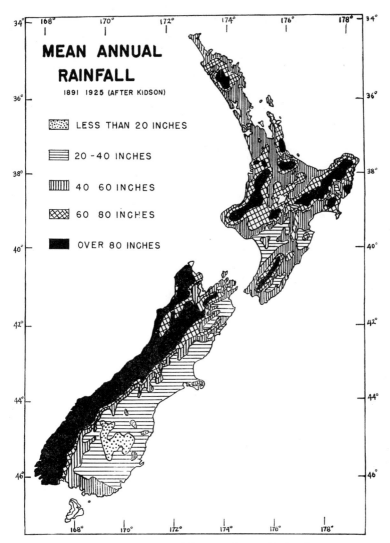

MEAN ANNUAL RAINFALL

1891 1925 (AFTER KIDSON)

LESS THAN 20 INCHES

20 -40 INCHES

40 60 INCHES

60 80 INCHES

OVER 80 INCHES

FIGURE 125.   Rainfall map of New Zealand.

persistent sunlight and desiccating foehn winds in Canterbury also cause the rainfall to be less effective in terms of soil moisture and plant growth than the same or even a somewhat less amount in northern Canada, southeast Australia, or Kansas.   The driest parts can probably be classed as desert.   Yet the horizontal distance between this water-deficient region and areas to the west that receive over 200 inches a year is less than 40 miles.

North Auckland, furthermore, has a subtropical climate whereas the more elevated parts of the Southern Alps and the southwestern extremities of the Dominion are subarctic. Nelson and Napier are sunny and mild, but Fjordland is cloudy and bleak. Auckland City has an average of one day of damaging frost a year and no snow, whereas Gore in Southland averages 109.2 days of damaging frost a year and snow and ice blanket the flanks of Mt. Cook to depths of several hundred feet in many places. By way of additional contrasts, Wellington is usually windy and the Bay of Plenty is usually calm. And the day-to-day (and in some respects season-to-season) weather in Christchurch is more intemperate than temperate.

The controls responsible for the varied patterns of weather and climate in the Dominion are: (1) latitude, which causes the northern parts to be several degrees warmer than the southern as a consequence of the annual decrease in insolation with increasing latitude; (2) altitude, which in South Island especially produces marked contrasts in temperature and atmospheric pressure; (3) the barrier effect of high mountains, more specifically the Southern Alps, which partly screen the eastern slopes of South Island from rain, and at the same time help to induce heavy precipitation on western exposures by initiating upward displacement of conditionally unstable air masses approaching via the Tasman Sea; (4) prevalence of westerly winds in these latitudes, which in combination with the mountain barrier tends to accent the contrasts between east- and west-coast climates; (5) cyclonic storms, which move generally from west to east and buffet the more exposed parts of Westland, Fjordland, and Southland; and (6) small land area in an oceanic setting, which permits moisture-laden winds to penetrate nearly all parts of the islands, and tempers the extremes of winter cold and summer heat.

Of less importance as climatic controls are: (1) ocean currents, which move northward along the eastern and western shores of New Zealand yet vary but slightly in their surface temperatures as they do so; (2) tropical cyclones, which are infrequent in this region and penetrate only the northern parts of the Dominion proper and then only after their intensities have been substantially reduced; and (3) removal of forests by man, which has significant effects on microclimates in the cleared areas, especially on surface temperatures, wind velocity near ground level, evapotranspiration, and soil moisture.

SOILS

Most New Zealand soils are immature. They also tend toward acidity, primarily owing to the copious rainfall of the Dominion and secondarily to the acidic composition of some parent materials. The majority of the soils have developed on fairly steep mountain slopes or on flood-plain deposits under forest cover, the principal exception to flood-plain deposits being the soils of some of the tussock grasslands. The soils of perhaps half the total land area may be classified as lithosols and shallow soils of the rough, stony youthful mountain or plateau country. The rest of the area includes such varied soil associations as podzols and podzolic soils (chiefly in South Island); alluvial soils developed on recent stream deposits; the sour "pakihi" soils of the tussock grasslands; rendzinas in the limestone country fringing

FIGURE 126.   Upper Waimakariri Valley from Sugar Loaf Mt. near Cass. Note frost formations in foreground, the wide shingle flats along the river, and the dense growth of beach forest on the midslopes.

Hawke Bay on the south and in parts of North Auckland; reddish-brown soils of the low-rainfall zone in central Otago; bog, half-bog, and ground-water podzols of some of the poorly drained coastal lowlands and interior swamplands; and coastal sands.

Because of the generally high relief of the land surface, the preponderance of "skeletal" soils, the relative paucity of large, contiguous tracts of land with soils of substantial depth and natural fertility, as well as other environmental limitations, it is doubtful if more than 40 per cent of the Dominion is suited to intensive, continuous cultivation. This does not mean, however, that there is a deficiency of reasonably good land at hand to provide for the basic needs of the present population of the Dominion, and perhaps ultimately several times as many. But it does indicate that opportunities for expanding the cultivated area are rather severely limited by the physical qualities of the land.

NATIVE AND NATURALIZED FLORA

The peculiar features of much of the native flora of New Zealand have aroused scientific curiosity throughout the world from the beginnings of exploration. New Zealand has been isolated from land masses of continental size at least since Tertiary time, with the result that its plants reflect a high degree of endemism although earlier land

FIGURE 127. Tussock grassland south of Lake Pukaki, Mackenzie Basin, South Island.

connections with southeast Asia (Malaysia) and southern Chile through Antarctica are suggested by strong affinities between the respective floristic elements of these regions. The basic ingredients of New Zealand's flora appear to be Malayan, since the great majority of the vascular plants—flowering plants, conifers, ferns, and lycopods—show direct or indirect relationships with those of Malaya. Interspersed and to some extent hybridized with these early Malayan migrants are at least 250 species of plants now peculiar to Australia, Tasmania, and New Zealand. These may have come in with the Malayan element or have been carried to New Zealand by ocean currents, winds, or birds. A third element, called Antarctic, is represented by some 70 species of vascular plants closely related to elements in the flora of southern South America and islands in the Southern Ocean fringing Antarctica. Among these are the "beeches" (*Nothofagus*), fuchsias, broadleafs, laurels, and ourisias.

Three principal botanical regions have been identified in the Dominion: a northern region extending southward to the 38th parallel of latitude, containing nearly 100 species peculiar to the north such as the kauri (*Agathis australis*), mangrove (*Avicennia officinalis*), and pohutukawa (*Metrosideros excelsa*); a central region from 38° south to 42° south, less distinctive in its plant associations; and a southern region with a substantial representation of Antarctic elements.

Native plant associations are separated for convenience of description into forest, grassland, scrub, and bog or swamp types. The forests are of three main types: coniferous forest, subdivided into kauri and podocarp assemblages with the kauri restricted to the northern part of North Island and the podocarp rather spottily distributed elsewhere; broadleaf forest of mixed species, characteristic of central and southern parts of North Island; and beech forest, dominated by one or more species of the genus *Nothofagus* and characteristic of the mountains and foothills, especially east of the main divide. The native grasslands are dominated by tussock grasses of the generas *Festuca*, *Poa*, and *Danthonia*, with which are sometimes a variety of shrubs, herbs, and ferns. They are most widespread in Otago, Canterbury, and the interior of North Island, where their range has recently been extended through clearing of the scrub and subsequent invasion of the scrublands by tussock associations. Scrub formations are well developed on exposed coasts, on the smaller islands, on the higher mountains above timberline, on certain swamp, bog, pumice, and clay lands, and on some rather fertile soils as a consequence of forest removal by volcanic or human agency. Bog-swamp vegetation, which contains many distinct species and genera, is often found in poorly drained depressions near the seacoast, on the volcanic plateau in the interior of North Island, on the Canterbury Plains, and in scattered localities elsewhere in the lowlands.

A substantial number of the indigenous plants have proved beneficial in the economy of New Zealand, both in Maori times and since European colonization began. The rimu and totara are podocarps that have proved to be of considerable value for lumber. Also prized for this purpose is the kauri "pine," although only a few small, scattered stands of this once-widespread monarch of the northern forests remain today, practically all in State-owned preserves. The Maori ate the edible roots of the native bracken fern and a New Zealand type of flax (*Phormium tenax*), as well as the kumara or sweet potato and a variety of other plant foods and plant substances. Most of the original forests have by now been lumbered off or destroyed in the process of clearing land for agriculture and grazing, except in southern Westland and western Southland. In the future, New Zealand will have to depend largely on plantations of introduced species of trees for its supply of wood and wood products.

FIGURE 128. Rainforest on the slopes of Mt. Egmost, Taranaki Province. This is about the 4000-foot level.

At least 500 species of plants embracing 261 genera and 63 families, recently introduced through human agency, have now become naturalized in New Zealand. Many more might be cited that have not yet become naturalized or adapted fully to local conditions of soil and climate. Sixty-four of these species are classified as "widespread and abundant," and of these nearly a third are grasses.

Statistics, however, are inadequate to give an impression of the important role introduced plants play in the modern economy of New

Zealand or of the changes they have wrought in the appearance of most of its landscapes. Extensive tracts of land have been practically denuded of their indigenous vegetation and replaced by an essentially alien flora. Even larger areas now feature blends of native and alien species. Tens of thousands of acres of once-forested country have been converted to dairy and sheep pastures consisting in the main of European grasses and clovers. Many thousands of acres of tussock grassland have been converted to plantations of Monterey pine (*Pinus radiata*) and other fast-growing, introduced softwoods. Shelterbelts and hedgerows of Monterey cypress (*Cupressus macrocarpa*) line many roadsides, paddock boundaries, and homesteads in various parts of the Dominion.

Some plant introductions, moreover, have been beneficial and some harmful. Plantations of valuable trees have been established, pastures have been improved, and homes and gardens have been beautified. But hosts of weeds are eclipsing useful species of plants on carelessly tended land. One such plant is gorse from Scotland, a yellow-flowered, thorny shrub.

FAUNA

The only land mammals native to New Zealand are two species of bats. Sea mammals in coastal waters include the fur seal, sea lion, sea elephant, sea leopard, several species of whales, and porpoises. Birds were plentiful in the early days of settlement, but forest clearing, grass fires, indiscriminate shooting, and introduced predators like the rat, cat, stoat, and weasel have taken a heavy toll. Most unusual of the native birds perhaps are the flightless (but not wingless) kiwi, weka, kakapo parrot, and takahe or rail. In addition, the kea has gained notoriety as an alleged killer of sheep, the tui is beautiful and musical, the huia is distinctive because it is the only known species of avifauna in which the bills of the two sexes are markedly different, and the wry-billed plover has a curious bill turned to one side. Cormorants or shags are abundant, and penguin species are so numerous that New Zealand is generally regarded as the center of dispersal of this sartorially elegant bird. Largest and certainly one of the most interesting of the extinct birds is the ostrichlike moa, of which there seem to have been at least twenty-one species. The tallest attained a height of 12 feet or more. When and why these giants died out or were killed off is unknown, but it is possible that the agents of their destruction were pre-Maori (Moriori) hunters, apparently the first human beings to reach New Zealand.

There are some fifteen species of lizards native to the Dominion and, in addition, the lizardlike tuatara (*Sphenodon punctatus*), which has the distinction of being the only surviving representative of the order Rhynocephalia. It has a rudimentary third eye, and is found only in New Zealand, and today on but few of the smaller islands. Two species of frogs represent the amphibians, but over three hundred species of fish have been identified, some of which are peculiar to New Zealand. No snakes have been found anywhere in the country.

One of the peculiarities of the invertebrates is the scarcity of butterflies despite the prevalence of moths. Native bees, ants, dragonflies, beetles, and other orders also represent the insects, and a species of native spider lives on or near the sea beaches.

Profound changes have been wrought in the fauna since the arrival of the first shipload of permanent European settlers. Prior to that time the only mammals introduced by human agency were Maori dogs and rats, and pigs liberated in 1773 by the English explorer Captain James Cook. With large-scale settlement came sheep, cattle, horses, and many other domesticated animals. Other faunal introductions now well acclimatized are songbirds, deer, chamois, thar, or European mountain sheep, trout, pheasants, quail, starlings, English sparrows, German owls, and skylarks. Many accidentally introduced insect pests have also become well established, like the cabbage moth that first appeared in 1930. Animal pests in addition to some of the birds listed above are rabbits, shoats, and weasels. Deer are a nuisance at times in parts of the interior where they browse or graze on mountain pastures otherwise suitable for sheep. Government hunters are occasionally sent to cull out surplus deer, sometimes thousands in a single year.

THE PEOPLE

MAORI ANTECEDENTS AND CULTURE

No one knows for sure when New Zealand was first visited by man, or who that original discoverer was, or whence he came. Archeological discoveries and ancient Maori legends, however, indicate that when the first Maoris arrived the east coast of North Island was already the abode of a primitive gathering and hunting people who appear to have lived in cave shelters and then, or earlier, subsisted in part on the flesh of the giant moa birds. These "true" aborigines the Maori invaders called Moriori or "inferior people." They seem to have been dislodged early and driven to South Island and the Chatham Islands by their more numerous, aggressive, technologically superior, and better-organized Maori conquerors. Gradually they were even here hunted out, exterminated, or absorbed into the Maori population, the last identifiable member of their tribe dying a natural death in the Chatham Islands in 1933.

Maori origins are similarly obscure, for until relatively recently these migrant Polynesian islanders had no written language and their legends are often vague. From somewhere in southern Asia, it is thought they infiltrated into the mid-Pacific to the Tonga Islands, which they called "Hawaiki," and considered their ancestral home. According to Maori legend, New Zealand was first discovered in the middle of the tenth century A.D. by Kupe, one of their ancestral heroes. On his return to Hawaiki, Kupe reportedly told of his discovery, and his sailing directions for reaching the new land presumably were handed down orally for several generations without any effort to follow them up. In the twelfth century Toi, a Tahitian chief, and his grandson are said to have reached "Aotearoa" (New Zealand) and settled there, taking wives from earlier settlers (?) and becoming the progenitors of mixed Polynesian tribes. Then in the fourteenth century the great Maori fleets arrived, bringing with them a variety of seeds for planting in addition to dogs and rats. Behind the migration, it is suggested, were pressure of population on food resources and social revolt in their islands of earlier adoption, Hawaiki. In a relatively short time after their arrival in North Island we are told that they had penetrated to nearly all parts of the main islands, named practically all distinctive features, and established well-defined tribal boundaries.

The Maoris prior to their migrations to New Zealand were already skilled navigators, fearless warriors, and expert agriculturalists. They had to make drastic changes in many of their living habits in New Zealand, however, for it was quite a different environment from their earlier tropical home. These adjustments they seem to have made fairly quickly and successfully. They learned how to build more substantial dwellings, make warmer clothing, and use new types of food. Of their traditional plant foods, only the kumara (sweet potato) could be grown successfully in New Zealand, and there not in all areas. To supplement their diet they came to rely on such local products as bracken fern root, and fish from the rivers, lakes, and ocean. Native flax supplied fiber for clothing and cordage. They soon developed great skill in wood carving, using mostly the workable wood of the totara tree. They also manufactured fine tools and weapons from native greenstone, and their fortifications such as trenches, moats, and palisades reveal a degree of military engineering skill scarcely approached by any other "primitive" group in the world. The basic social unit was the family, but in their system of land tenure and field cultivation they were communistic, like other Polynesians. Chieftainship was hereditary. Intertribal warfare and to some extent cannibalism were popular and were glorified by much ceremonial, until the disturbing influence of Westernization drastically altered their patterns of social behavior.

Early contacts between the Maoris and European explorers, traders, missionaries, and subsequently settlers were usually friendly and mutually advantageous after the inevitable preliminary skirmishes. But as a variety of social injustices, land seizures, and acquisition of native land through subterfuges grew more common, increasing friction and later open hostility developed. The Maori wars of 1860-1870 resulted almost inevitably in victory for the better-armed and better-organized whites and the subjugation of the natives. From then until practically the end of the nineteenth century, the Maoris decreased in numbers and for a time even seemed destined to become extinct. But a succession of increasingly conscientious New Zealand governments, together with the surprising resiliency, patience, and able leadership of the Maoris themselves, helped pave the way eventually for major land and social reforms. These have since reversed the earlier trend toward extinction, and between 1896 and 1936 the Maori population appears to have more than doubled, until they number about 100,000. They have made substantial strides in scientific dairying, sheep farming, and agriculture, and have won at least the important preliminary rounds in their effort to gain full social and economic privileges and representation.

Most Maoris continue to live in small village communities on native preserves in North Island. About one person in twenty in the Dominion is classed as a Maori, and in Auckland Province, one in nine. They have been increasing in number two-and-a-half times as fast as whites, but Maori blood is becoming increasingly dilute. Probably less than half of those officially classed as Maori are now of pure Maori descent. Their principal handicaps—to generalize and oversimplify these somewhat—are lack of sufficient good-quality land to which they have clear title and on which they can realize their agricultural capabilities; a certain measure of political, economic, and social division within their own ranks, causing disunity with respect to objectives and leadership; inferior educational facilities; inadequate health services; relatively poor housing; and a continued sense of inferiority that no laws in themselves can entirely erase. It is worth noting, however, that an ever-increasing number of Maori leaders are winning high distinction in their fields of specialization, including politics, anthropology, art, and literature, and that the contributions and sacrifices of the world-famed Maori Battalions of the First and Second World Wars were perhaps second to no other equivalent group.

EUROPEAN DISCOVERY, EXPLORATION, AND SETTLEMENT

Credit for the discovery of New Zealand by a European is generally accorded the Dutch sea captain, Abel Janszoon Tasman, although the geographer Francoys Jacobszoon Visscher, who accompanied Tasman on his famous voyage of discovery in Australasian waters, appears to have played an equally important role in the discovery of the country. On the morning of December 13, 1642, the majestic peaks of the Southern Alps rose out of the watery wastes to the east. Coasting northward to what is now called Golden Bay, they attempted a landing, but this effort was repelled by hostile Maoris, who killed four of the boat's crew. Later the exploring party drifted aimlessly in Cook Strait for six days in miserable weather, and then for nine days moved northward in continued bad weather along the west coast of North Island to Three Kings Islands. From there they returned to their base at Batavia in Java, discovering on their way Tonga and Fiji.

One hundred and twenty-seven years passed before a European again visited New Zealand's shores. He was the English navigator and explorer, Captain James Cook. Between 1769 and 1777, Cook visited the islands on five different occasions, during which he proved that they were not part of a great southern continent, made frequent landings, collected valuable rock and plant specimens, and mapped the coasts with such accuracy that it is said some of his charts can be used safely for navigation in New Zealand today. Cook, like Tasman, left his name indelibly engraved on maps of New Zealand (that is, Tasman Glacier, Cook Strait, and Mt. Cook). The two explorers together helped fix the position and determine the shape and outline of New Zealand for the first time on maps of the world.

The next fifty years witnessed many voyages to New Zealand waters, as well as the beginnings of small-scale settlements in the north, where missionaries and whalers developed early bases at the Bay of Islands and made important discoveries in the south. Most of these southern discoveries were made by sealers out of Sydney, but some were made by organized scientific expeditions. One of the expeditions was led by George Vancouver in 1791, when Dusky Sound was surveyed and the Snares Islands and Chatham Islands were discovered. Another was guided by d'Urville in 1826, when additional coastal detail was mapped.

Inland exploration began in earnest soon after the beginning of the nineteenth century with the missionary travels of Samuel Marsden and penetrations by various traders in the north and scoutings by sealers and traders in the south. The discovery of gold lured more people to the scene. Work by botanists, geologists, and other scientists have added to our knowledge of the country.

The period between 1840 and 1880 was essentially a period involving the beginnings of organized settlement and the expansion of the inland frontier. The overwhelming majority of the settlers came from England and Scotland. Before 1840 New Zealand remained essentially the domain of independent traders and missionaries, partly because no organizing genius had yet appeared on the scene to direct group settlement and win government backing for colonization.

The first important group settlements were sponsored by the New Zealand Company, which in 1840 sent out an advance party to Port Nicholson (Wellington). In spite of conflicting interests and agonizing delay, the Company was eventually granted 1,250,000 acres of land by the government, and the right to arrange for immigrants. Various difficulties later forced the company out of business in 1855, but not before permanent colonists had been planted at strategic locations such as New Plymouth, Wanganui, Wellington, and in fact all other large, modern centers in North Island except Auckland. In 1848 and 1850 two South Island colonies were organized on a similar pattern by Scotch Presbyterian and Church of England pioneers at Dunedin and Christchurch, respectively. Partly through the good fortune of rich gold discoveries in the 1860's in their vicinities and partly through the swift development of back-country sheep runs, both colonies quickly became economically sound.

The major gold discoveries of the 1860's soon followed. These discoveries served two particularly useful ends. First, they produced local accumulations of capital for reinvestment; and in the second place they helped to lure thousands of prospective settlers to New Zealand. These, in turn, created greater local demand for food and other basic consumer goods, and thereby gave agriculture, livestock farming, and the economy in general an important boost. South Island early gained economic and political leadership over North Island largely as a result of these rich gold discoveries, its physical advantages for sheep farming, and its freedom from Maori troubles. These advantages prevailed until the disastrous depression of the 1880's, an economic catastrophe that all but prostrated New Zealand, a young country heavily loaded with external debt, inexperienced in "high finance," and not entirely through its own choosing saddled with a highly vulnerable economy engrossed in primary production for overseas markets. Its economic structure was thus hit early and hard.

After the depression of the 1880's important changes took place in the pattern and focus of settlement in the Dominion. Refrigerated shipping and cold storage gave New Zealand a previously unsuspected opportunity to market fresh meat, eggs, butter, and cheese in the distant but lucrative markets of Great Britain, in particular, and of industrial Europe in general. Liberalism in government, land reform, and the organized labor movement got under way. North Island soon and understandably surged ahead in population, value of farm

FIGURE 129.   Cattle grazing on rich pasture in the Waikato District near Hamilton, North Island.

production, foreign trade, city growth, and political influence. Auckland and Wellington rapidly assumed leadership largely because of their favorable geographical positions, port advantages, and productive hinterlands. The economic stimulus of the First World War brought additional rapid development in land industries. The population of the Dominion as a whole almost doubled in a quarter of a century (1895–1921), rising from 700,000 to 1,200,000. A growing structure of transport, industry, commerce, and professional services was evident; and while more land was still being taken up and improved for farming, opportunities for employment were becoming even more numerous and more rewarding in the expanding urban centers of the Dominion.

Then came another more or less unexpected economic setback that had similarly severe repercussions on the growth of settlement, the world-wide depression of the 1930's. This like its late-nineteenth century predecessor hit New Zealand early and heavily, owing chiefly to the Dominion's dependence on exports of a narrow range of primary products to limited overseas markets, and to its large external debt. Expansive optimism quickly gave way to pessimism with the onset of price collapses. Land values were sharply reduced, and many farmers soon faced financial ruin. Unemployment, even in so thinly populated and ordinarily productive country, reached a frighteningly high level. Wage rates dropped, and near chaos prevailed until the government was finally forced to take drastic steps to "cushion" the disaster. This time, as before, in the 1880's, economic crisis brought small farmers and urban workers closer together, and led to a powerful resurgence of the Labor Party, culminating shortly in political victory.

By 1940 New Zealand was well on the road to economic recovery. However, the Dominion was by that time also embroiled in a war of global dimensions. When that war was won, continued sovereignty was assured, at least for a time. New Zealand's economic prospects would now seem to be less simply defined, increasingly dependent on "triangular" international trade, and yet on the whole freer of outside price manipulations. A rocky economic road appears to lie ahead, but that is nothing new to New Zealanders!

POPULATION DISTRIBUTION

Intercensal statistics for 1939 show a total population for the Dominion of 1,701,566 with only a slight excess of males over females. Of this population, nearly two-thirds (65 per cent) resided in North Island. About 95 per cent were in New Zealand proper, and of this 95 per cent the Maori population constituted about 5 per cent (88,450). The remaining 76,852 people (mostly natives) in the Dominion lived in the Mandated Territory of Western Samoa, the Cook Islands, Niue, the Tokelau Islands, and the Kermadecs. All the so-called outlying islands and the Ross Dependency in Antarctica were uninhabited in 1939.

The four provinces of North Island reportedly contained a total of 1,064,064 people in 1939, about 54 per cent living in Auckland Province and 31 per cent in Wellington Province, with the remaining 15 per cent about evenly divided between Hawkes Bay and Taranaki, provinces without large cities comparable to Auckland and Wellington. South Island had a population of 560,650, of which number 42 per cent were listed as residents in Canterbury Province, 27 per cent in Otago, 13 per cent in Southland, and 10½ per cent in Nelson; the remaining 7½ per cent were about equally divided between Marlborough and Westland Provinces. As in North Island, the two provinces with large urban centers (Canterbury and Otago) contained a majority of the island's population.

New Zealand's population is more widely dispersed than those percentages might at first seem to indicate. There are to be sure only four "large" urban concentrations—Auckland (221,500 in 1939), Wellington (157,900), Christchurch (135,400), and Dunedin (82,800). They contain 54 per cent of the total population of the Dominion, but they are well spaced from north to south. All are ports except Christchurch, which has good rail connections to the near-by port of Lyttelton. In addition to these four major urban centers there are ten of lesser size that also are well scattered. North Island has seven of the ten: Hamilton (20,800), Gisborne (16,300), Napier (19,400), Hastings (18,900), New Plymouth (19,300), Wanganui (26,100), and Palmerston North (25,300). In South Island Nelson (14,000), Timaru (19,300), and Invercargill (26,500) are secondary centers. Elsewhere there are numerous smaller towns and villages. The rural population is on the whole well dispersed throughout the productive parts of each province, although it is denser in the agricultural areas of the Dominion than in the pastoral areas, and denser in the lowlands than in the highlands.

The density of population for the Dominion proper in 1939 was 15.71 persons per square mile. If we exclude from consideration the areas of lakes, rivers, harbors, estuaries, rugged mountains, sterile or nearly sterile soils, and other essentially unoccupied (and largely unoccupiable) country—in all perhaps one-third the total area—the density of population per square mile of effectively *occupied* land was 23.6. If we further exclude the populations of all cities, towns, and villages that contain over 300 people, we find that the strictly *rural* population density is 9.3 persons per square mile of effectively occupied land. This average rural density varies widely of course, being roughly sixteen times as great in the dairy farming as in the sheep farming districts, and one hundred and forty times as great in market-gardening areas as in sheep-farming areas. Yet even in the most densely populated rural districts, there is no "crowding" comparable to that prevailing on fertile flood plains in many parts of the Orient, where rural densities of a thousand or more persons per square mile may be encountered.. We must remember, however, that the teeming low lands of East Asia produce almost wholly for local markets, whereas New Zealand farms produce a greater volume of goods for export than for local consumption.

The standards of living of these Oriental subsistence farmers are also far below those of New Zealand's farm (and city) populations. Many times the present number of people might *subsist* on the farm lands and grazing lands of New Zealand, but it is not likely that closer settlement would permit many more people to live on them without marked reduction of living standards. Merely to have more people living more poorly on the same amount of land hardly seems a desirable goal. It would also appear that the opportunities for lucrative employment are currently greater in the cities and towns of the Dominion than in the rural districts. No appreciable expansion of the occupied area, incidentally, is likely to take place, for practically all the land that seems to be of any existing or potential value is already occupied and in use for one purpose or another.

The racial composition of New Zealand's population, if we exclude the Maoris and natives in the annexed and outlying islands, is remarkably homogeneous. The overwhelming majority are of British (hence white or Caucasian) extraction, mostly English and Scotch. "Alien" races in 1936 included 2899 Chinese, 1235 Syrians, and 1157 Indians. The Maoris are the only numerically significant non-European minority in the New Zealand population.

THE ECONOMY

RESOURCE ADVANTAGES

The New Zealand environment has a number of distinct advantages in primary production, a sphere of economic activity in which the nation has become highly specialized and highly efficient. One such asset is its unusually large assortment of soil types, which among other things favors the development of varied assemblages of pasture plants. Some are better suited to winter grazing, others to summer grazing. Nearly every province also contains a variety of soils that are favorable for the growth of a wide range of different field, truck, and orchard crops. Even the poorest soils in the country will ordinarily yield some income from light grazing and forestry. This applies to the soils developed on steep hill slopes in western Canterbury and on recent volcanic ash deposits in North Island. The menace of soil erosion on such steep hill slopes, however, cannot be disregarded. Many of these slopes are probably better suited to forestry than grazing, although the income from grazing may be substantially greater over a short period of time.

Another environmental advantage is the rather mild, moist climate that prevails in most parts of the islands. Like the English climate that it approximates, it is admirably suited to the growth of highly nutritious pasture grasses and clovers. Winters are not severe enough as a rule to require barns for the protection of livestock, and this helps to reduce production costs. Where winters are severe enough to damage or arrest the growth of pasture plants (as in parts of western Canterbury, Otago, and Southland) turnips, marrows, or other types of supplementary stock feed can be grown during the warmer months of the year and stored for winter use. The climate of the lowlands also permits the cropping of oats, wheat, mangolds, and lucerne or alfalfa, as well as a variety of green fodder crops that help to maintain milk supplies during the drier months in the dairying districts.

Other important assets of the physical environment are a scattering of metallic ore deposits, particularly gold; sources of light, heat, and power, essentially coal and water; a limited quantity but a rather considerable variety of valuable native timbers; inadequately surveyed, but apparently considerable fish and shellfish populations in coastal waters; and scenic attractions that in many instances transcend even the glowing descriptions of tourist leaflets and alone lure a substantial number of free-spending tourists to the Dominion.

Let us examine the structure and regional differentiation of New Zealand's present-day economy in greater detail, however, and see if we can gain greater insight into some of the more important economic problems that currently confront the Dominion as well as additional basis for forecast.

REGIONAL SPECIALIZATIONS IN AGRICULTURE AND GRAZING

North Island on the whole is much better adapted to grazing than to agriculture (Fig. 129). Nearly all the crops produced on the island are fed to livestock. Dairying and sheep farming predominate. There is perhaps no finer sheep country in the world than the rolling limestone downs of Hawkes Bay Province, which is also noted for horse breeding. It is also claimed that many dairy farms in North Island produce more butterfat per acre than farms in any other part of the world growing all their own stock food. This is not all due to favorable topography, soil, climate, and plant complex. Much of the credit must go to the knowledge, skill, and foresight of the farmers, to wide use of fertilizers, scientific pasture improvement and management, good transport facilities, and efficient marketing. The area of principal attraction for dairy farming in North Island is undoubtedly the Waikato district south of and yet conveniently tributary to Auckland, with Taranaki Province a close second. Both are major exporters of butter and milk powder.

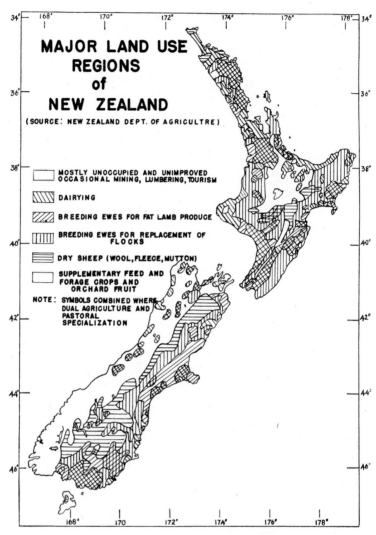

FIGURE 130.　Land use in New Zealand.

The total area of orchards is roughly the same in the two islands, but orchard specialties differ somewhat from place to place. Auckland Province, for example, is the only one that produces citrus fruit on a commercial scale, mostly oranges and lemons. Other areas tend to specialize in apples, pears, peaches, grapes, or other fruit, though in general each province produces most of the ordinary orchard fruits somewhere within its boundaries.

South Island has a substantially larger total area of cropland and a greater proportion of its occupied land under crops. Regional specialization in agriculture and grazing is to be noted in the Nelson hinterland (apples, pears, grapes, tobacco, hops); Canterbury Plains (fat lambs, mutton, crossbred wool, wheat and oats, root crops); central Otago (fruit); Southland and Westland (dairying); Mackenzie Basin (merino sheep for fine, long staple wool and ewes for replacement of flocks); and Banks Peninsula (fruit). There has been little change in the total area devoted to arable cash crops since 1900; in fact, the tendency is for this area to contract slightly. In a sense New Zealand farmers grow crops more through necessity than by choice.

The general characteristics of the farming-grazing economy of New Zealand may be summarized as follows:

(1) Emphasis on livestock, largely sheep and cattle, which produce 90 per cent of the gross value of farm production.

(2) Heavy dependence of livestock production on export markets (mostly Great Britain), to which go over 70 per cent of such products.

(3) The emphasis in livestock farming on native grasslands (especially the tussock complex) and improved swards of introduced grasses and clovers, with less than 3 per cent of the total area of cropland used for the production of supplementary feed.

(4) The wide use of the latest and most advanced scientific methods of herd and flock management, pasture improvement, and fertilization.

(5) Mechanization of many phases of farm production.

(6) Exceptionally high output per unit of labor and unit of land.

(7) The contrast between large land holdings in the hill country and substantially smaller properties (as a general rule) in the lowlands, and the greater proportion of relatively small holdings in North Island than in South Island.

(8) The approximate balance between freehold land tenure and leasehold (mostly Crown).

FORESTRY

Both the area and the value of New Zealand's native forests have diminished greatly since the early days of settlement. This is due to a number of circumstances, but mostly to the clearing of forests to make room for agricultural and pastoral settlements, and secondarily to lumbering operations. Vast tracts of valuable timber have been burned off directly or cut and then fired without thought of using the timber, or of the future forest needs of the nation. Nearly two-thirds of the original stand are gone, and most of the remainder consists of low-grade forests (mostly overmature), or is too inaccessible or too diffused in small stands for commercial use. Almost a million acres of forest plantations have been established in the government program designed to meet existing needs for forest products and at the same time insure adequate future supplies. The drain continues, however, since new growth is restoring only a fraction of the annual cut of well over 300,000,000 board feet. Various programs, public and private, are under way to halt the downward trend in commercial

FIGURE 131. Town of Gisborne, North Island, looking east toward Poverty Bay.

timber reserves. Among these programs are state acquisition and reforestation of cutover, indigenous forest land; thinning, pruning, and otherwise improving state plantations of exotic trees; establishment of state-owned demonstration sawmills, box factories, planing mills, wood-preserving plants, and the like to promote more efficient cutting and milling; the substitution wherever possible of log sales for block disposal of standing timber; expansion of privately owned plantations; control of insect damage; and better fire protection.

Of the native trees, the most valuable for commercial purposes are rimu, kahikatea, totara, matai, beech, and kauri. The most valuable of the exotic species are Douglas fir, western yellow (ponderosa) pine, *insignis* (Monterey) pine, Corsican pine, lodgepole pine, and western red cedar. Timber exports in 1938 were valued at £177,831 as against timber imports valued at £622,396.

MINING

The most important mining regions in New Zealand are in Westland and Otago provinces in South Island and in the Hauraki region in North Island. Both coal and placer gold are mined extensively in the Grey and Buller valleys of Westland. Placer gold is also being dredged in Clutha Valley in central Otago and phosphates are mined in that province. The Hauraki region produces gold and silver from secondary quartz deposits. Other areas of specialization include the Onekaka region adjacent to Golden Bay in Nelson (iron ore); the Lake Wakatipu region in Otago (tungsten ore); North Auckland (mercury ore and kauri gum); Southland (platinum); Rotorua and Lake Taupo area (sulfur); New Plymouth (petroleum); and Nelson (granite and marble). The total value of mineral production in 1938 was £4,014,515, with coal accounting for over half this figure, gold about one-fourth, and building stone about one-eighth. Gold led all mineral exports in value, followed by kauri gum, coal, and silver.

Future prospects in the field of mining do not appear to be exceptionally bright, although the possibility of discovering new, workable deposits of a variety of minerals cannot be discounted, either in localities where some mining has already taken place or in new mining areas. There is enough proven coal (ranging from lignite to anthracite) in the Dominion to meet household, transport, and industrial fuel requirements for several decades at least and at the same time support a modest iron and steel industry. The first iron and steel works in New Zealand is located at Onekaka. Some 13,000,000 tons of 40 to 50 per cent iron ore has been proven in the area, and extensive deposits are known elsewhere.

FISHERIES

The most productive commercial fishing grounds in the New Zealand area have been relatively shallow waters (less than 40 fathoms) close in to the coasts. It must be admitted, however, that little scientific study of the prospects for deep-water fishing has so far been made. Edible subtropical and cold-water fishes abound in shallow waters at least, and as many are caught ordinarily as can be profitably marketed in the Dominion. In northern waters the snapper is the most valuable single element in the commercial catch. Tarakiki are taken in substantial numbers in Hauraki Gulf, Bay of Plenty, Hawke Bay, Cook Strait, and off the coasts of Canterbury and Otago. Several species of flounders are caught in various shallow, sheltered waters. Blue cod constitute much of the southern line catch, and groper and kapuku are taken on lines from North Cape to Stewart Island. Sardines or pilchards are known to be present in large shoals off parts of the coast, but as yet no regular sardine fishery has been established. The value of these fish for oil and fertilizer is of course widely recognized.

FIGURE 132. Lyttleton harbor from the northwest. Note flanks of dissected volcano. Harbor is submerged valley cut across crater of old volcano.

The value of the total fish catch in the season 1938–1939 amounted to £531,082, including shellfish and whales. In the same season the value of fish and shellfish exports was £171,570. The industry provides employment for about 2200 fishermen (less than half on full-time) and about 400 people in other part-time and full-time work related to fishing, such as canneries. Over 300 vessels are engaged more or less regularly, and three times as many in part-time work related to fishing, such as canneries. Over 300 vessels are engaged more or less regularly, and three times as many in part-time commercial fishing.

Sport fishing is active in the fresh and salt waters of the Dominion. It is not an idle boast that these waters offer some of the finest sport fishing to be found anywhere in the world. Lake Taupo is now the habitat of well-acclimated rainbow trout brought in from North America, weighing up to 20 pounds, and Mackinaw trout, Atlantic salmon, and other fish have been introduced.

Fishing in the coastal waters off Auckland Province for such big-game fish as tarpon, shark, and swordfish likewise attracts sportsmen from both inside and outside New Zealand. A world's record black marlin swordfish (976 pounds) was caught in 1926 off the Bay of Islands.

FIGURE 133.   Tasman Glacier, looking northwest; Cook Range at left.

MANUFACTURING INDUSTRIES

It is perhaps a common misconception that manufacturing is entirely a recent development in New Zealand. From almost the earliest days of settlement, remoteness forced, or at least strongly encouraged, a variety of local manufactures. Among them were textile and boot manufacturing, milling of grain and flax, rendering of whale oil, and the making of spars for ships. With the advent of refrigeration came meat freezing, butter factories, and cheese factories. Processing of farm products still accounts for a large proportion of the total factory output.

Many new manufacturing industries have been established and many older ones considerably expanded as a result of the stimulus of wartime demands and the government program of industrialization as a means of reducing imports, "cushioning" or spreading the impact of price fluctuations, and decreasing the risks of unemployment. Whether or not this will prove to be an expensive program in the long run and place excessively heavy burdens on primary production is still a hotly debated question in New Zealand, just as in Australia, where a similar trend is evident. Among the new or relatively new manufacturing industries in New Zealand are motor assembly and related manufacturers, chemicals, printing, hosiery, paper manufacture, woodworking, house furnishings, fertilizers, radio assembly, confectionery, tobacco products, and during the Second World War especially, shipbuilding, small arms manufacture, and other wartime essentials. Ample supplies of cheap, well-reticulated, hydroelectric power and the general aptitude of New Zealanders for most factory labor help to balance such obvious disadvantages as relatively small-scale production for limited markets and high wage rates.

By 1938 there were some 17,500 "factories" in New Zealand, employing a total of more than 123,500 factory workers. The value of factory output (based on incomplete factory coverage) was reported as £113,691,556. Auckland and Wellington provincial districts, with 55 per cent of the total population of the Dominion, contributed 60 per cent of the factory output. It should be noted in this respect, however, that Auckland District, the undisputed leader among manufacturing centers, includes the large, rich Waikato dairy region that both supplies and processes over half the dairy products of the Dominion.

TRANSPORT AND COMMUNICATION

In 1939 there were 3319 miles of state-owned railway line, and this included nearly all the mileage in the country. The gauge of the lines is narrow (3 feet 6 inches). Both rails and rolling stock are of light construction by comparison with American standards, but the lines provide reasonably adequate service for the tasks required of them. An ever-increasing mileage is being electrified. The Railways Department operates its own telephone and telegraph system. There were only 198 miles of private rail lines reported in 1937, mostly serving collieries and sawmills. Cities are served in addition by tramway (street car) and bus lines.

Road mileage at the beginning of 1939 totaled a little more than 52,000 miles, of which nearly two-thirds was surfaced. The coverage and condition of the road net are on the whole quite good, considering the roughness of much of the topography and numerous local hazards such as landslides, earthquakes, washouts, floods, and the attack of storm waves along the coast.

Trans-oceanic steamship lines ordinarily provide regular freight, mail, and passenger service between New Zealand and Australia, Great Britain, Canada, and the United States.   Auckland, Wellington, Lyttelton, and Dunedin together account for over 70 per cent of the entering tonnage of overseas shipping, the remainder being distributed among some eighteen lesser ports of entry.   Of entering tonnage in 1938, about half was registered in the United Kingdom and one fourth

Figure 134.   Alluvial lowlands near Gisborne, North Island.

in other British countries, including Australia, New Zealand, and Canada.   The remainder was chiefly American, Norwegian, Japanese, Dutch, or German shipping.

Coastwise and inter-island connections are maintained by New Zealand's "mosquito" fleet, which in 1940 numbered about 300 vessels averaging 55 tons net.   Only one of these vessels weighed over 2500 tons.

Commercial aviation is a comparatively recent development in the Dominion.   Little had been accomplished in this direction prior to 1933, when the government approved and financed a scheme for establishing a chain of airports.   By March, 1939, however, there were fifty-five licensed airdromes.   Three local commercial companies were then in operation, and by late 1940 the inter-island, trans-island,

Auckland-Sydney, and Auckland–San Francisco runs were becoming more or less routine. The Second World War helped to speed up the development of commercial as well as military aviation, and today New Zealand has a fairly well equiped system of commercial air lines.

Postal service, telephone, and telegraph lines, and radio communications effectively link all important parts of the Dominion proper, and rates are low. The smaller islands, when occupied, are served by radio and occasional mail boats. Ocean cables have linked the Dominion with Australia since 1876 and with Vancouver Island in Canada since 1902.

THE POLITICAL PROSPECT

It is readily apparent that the smallest and the remotest of the three Dominions of the Commonwealth of Nations, "down under" is neither a land of unlimited opportunity nor a poor relation. It is certainly not a land that is capable of easing measurably the enormous population pressures in the Orient by simply opening its doors to immigrants from those crowded regions. On the other hand, it is quite likely that New Zealand will experience gradual increases in population, industrial enterprise, and political stature. There appears to be some room for more people, more factories, even more farms in the areas already given to farming. New Zealand has achieved an enviable reputation in the world as a highly efficient primary producer, as a pioneer in the realm of social security, as a staunch defender of human rights in war as well as in peace, and as one of the most scenic, hospitable, and healthful countries anywhere on earth.

REFERENCES

Beaglehole, J. C., *The Discovery of New Zealand,* Department of Internal Affairs, Wellington, 1939.

Belshaw, Horace (editor), *New Zealand,* University of California Press, Berkeley, 1947.

Belshaw, H., D. O. Williams, and F. B. Stephens, *Agricultural Organization in New Zealand,* Melbourne University Press, Melbourne, 1936.

Buck, Peter, H., *Vikings of the Sunrise,* Frederick A. Stokes, New York, 1938.

Clark, Andrew H., *Invasion of New Zealand by People, Plants and Animals: The South Island,* Rutgers University Press, New Brunswick, 1949.

Cockayne, L., *New Zealand Plants and Their Story,* Government Printer, Wellington, 1927.

Condliffe, J. B., *New Zealand in the Making,* Allen and Unwin, London, 1930.

Cotton, C. A., *Geomorphology of New Zealand, Part I, Systematic*, Dominion Museum, Wellington, 1922.

Cowan, James, *Settlers and Pioneers*, Department of Internal Affairs, Wellington, 1940.

Cumberland, K. B., *Soil Erosion in New Zealand*, Soil Conservation and Rivers Control Council, Wellington, 1944.

Falla, R. A., "The Outlying Islands of New Zealand," *New Zealand Geographer*, Vol. 4, pp. 127–154, October, 1948.

Finlay, A. Martin, *Social Security in New Zealand*, Whitcombe, and Tombs, Wellington, 1943.

Firth, Raymond, *Primitive Economics of the New Zealand Maori*, Routledge, London, 1929.

Geog. Rev., American Geographical Society, New York. (See especially the articles in this journal by Kenneth B. Cumberland, "Canterbury Landscapes," Vol. 30, No. 1, 1940; "A Century's Change," Vol. 31, No. 4, 1941; "Contrasting Regional Morphology and Soil Erosion," Vol. 34, No. 1, 1944. These three articles emphasize landscapes and destructive exploitation of natural resources in New Zealand.)

Guthrie-Smith, H., *Tutira, the Story of a New Zealand Sheep Station*, 2nd ed., W. Blackwood and Sons, London, 1926.

Introduction to New Zealand, Government Printer, Wellington, 1946.

Kidson, E., "The Climatology of New Zealand," *Handbuch der Klimatologie*, Vol. VI, Berlin, 1932.

McClymont, W. G., *The Exploration of New Zealand*, Department of Internal Affairs, Wellington, 1940.

Milner, I. F. G., *New Zealand's Interests and Policy in the Far East*, Institute of Pacific Relations, New York, 1940.

Nash, Walter, *New Zealand, a Democracy That Works*, Duell, Sloan and Pearce, New York, 1943.

New Zealand Geographer, Christchurch, New Zealand Geographical Society.

New Zealand Journal of Science and Technology, Wellington.

New Zealand Official Yearbook, Government Printer, Wellington.

Oliver, W. R. B., *New Zealand Birds*, Fine Arts (New Zealand) Ltd., Wellington, 1930.

Pascoe, J. D., *Unclimbed New Zealand*, Allen and Unwin, London, 1939.

Phillipps, W. J., *Fishes of New Zealand*, Avery, New Plymouth, 1940.

Somerset, H. C. D., *Littledene, a New Zealand Rural Community*, Council for Educational Research, Wellington, 1938.

Sutch, W. B., *Recent Economic Changes in New Zealand*, Institute of Pacific Relations, Auckland, 1939.

Sutherland, I. L. G. (Editor), *The Maori People Today*, Institute of Pacific Relations, New York, 1940.

Transactions of the Royal Society of New Zealand, Wellington.

Vaile, E. Earle, *Pioneering the Pumice*, Whitcombe and Tombs, Auckland, 1939.

Wood, F. L. W., *New Zealand in the World*, Department of Internal Affairs, Wellington, 1940.

16

Indonesia

ANTHONY E. SOKOL

THE NAME INDONESIA, AS APPLIED TO A GEOGRAPHIC AREA, IS SUFFI-
ciently new in literature to require definition. In this book it denotes
the vast archipelago situated between Asia and Australia, on the one
hand, and the Indian and Pacific oceans on the other. It includes
not only most of what once was called the Dutch East Indies, but
also the British part of Borneo and the Portuguese portion of Timor;
it excludes, however, New Guinea and its adjacent islands. The term
Indonesia was introduced by the German ethnologist Bastian, in
analogy to Polynesia, Micronesia, etc., but to him it also comprised
the Philippines, British Malaya, Formosa, and even Madagascar. The
name *United States of Indonesia* was first adopted by the nationalists
of the East Indies for their country, which became independent December 27, 1949. It included all the former Netherlands East Indies except
Dutch New Guinea. Originally there were sixteen states in Indonesia,
but by August, 1950, these had merged into a Federal system. President Soekarno proclaimed it the new Republic of Indonesia.

By whatever name these islands are known, they remain the world's
largest archipelago and one of its foremost equatorial regions. Their
importance is due primarily to two factors, their relative position and
their productiveness.

Lying between two continents and two oceans, Indonesia, together
with the neighboring Malay Peninsula, controls the lines of communication in one of the strategically most vital parts of the world. In
the hands of the Japanese, the archipelago constituted a thoroughly
effective block to all allied traffic between those regions; in times of
peace the islands have performed their role as stepping stones of international commerce for more than 2000 years.

The fertility of Indonesia's soil, its even and comparatively pleasant

460

climate, and its intelligent population have combined to make it one of the great treasure houses, producing a large share of the world's needs in raw materials.

Moreover, the interest of all nations is directed to Indonesia because it offers the absorbing example of a people emerging from the passive role of a colony into the consciousness of unity and nationhood, with the concomitant desire for independence and the demand for freedom from foreign domination.

GEOGRAPHIC LOCATION, AREAS, AND POPULATIONS

The Indonesian Archipelago lies astride the equator, extending from about 95° to 135° east longitude, and about 6° north to 11° south latitude. It is almost 3000 miles long and more than 1000 miles wide. Its total area, land and sea, is thus about equal to one-half of Europe, geographically excluding Russia, or roughly the area of the United States. The innumerable islands constituting the archipelago are usually divided into the groups shown in Table 1.

TABLE 1

INDONESIAN ARCHIPELAGO

	Area, Square Miles	Population,* Millions
I. The Greater Sunda Islands		
A. Sumatra, with adjacent islands	185,000	10
B. Java and Madura	50,000	50
C. Borneo and adjacent islands	290,000	3.5
D. Celebes and adjacent islands	85,000	4.5
II. The Lesser Sunda Islands, including Bali, Lombok, Sumbawa, Sumba, Flores, Timor, etc.	35,000	4.5
III. The Moluccas or "Spice Islands," including Halmahera, Ceram, etc.	20,000	1
Total	665,000	75

* Figures for the areas of the various islands vary considerably, first because of inaccuracies in the estimates, but also because some include the adjacent islands while others do not; some exclude the British part of Borneo and the Portuguese part of Timor, others include the whole islands. Population figures are only estimates, since the last general census was taken in 1930. New Guinea is not treated systematically here, as it is included in Chapter 6. It will be mentioned, however, whenever it is needed for purposes of comparison or contrast.

In addition to this geographic division, the Dutch usually divide the archipelago along administrative lines, into Java and Madura on the one hand, and the outer islands, comprising everything else, on the other. Events after the Second World War have brought about entirely new groupings, however, as indicated in the section on political developments.

TOPOGRAPHY AND GEOLOGICAL STRUCTURE

The general structure of the archipelago may perhaps be best understood as the product of a polarity, or the effect of two major forces, exerted by the two neighboring continents. In matters of geology, climate, fauna, flora, and population, the influence of Asia is the most pronounced, though that of Australia is by no means negligible. In all these respects Indonesia represents a gradual transition from one extreme to the other, from an almost purely Asiatic region to a predominantly Australian one, with intermediary steps combining both to a certain degree.

The map (Fig. 135) shows that the large western islands, Sumatra, Java, and Borneo, stand on a shallow submarine platform that is a direct continuation of the Asiatic mainland, with which they were connected until comparatively recent times. There is evidence indicating that a land bridge existed between Sumatra and the Malay Peninsula as late as the second century of the Christian era. Borneo must have become separated at a very much earlier period, and it is doubtful that Celebes has ever been connected with either of the other large islands. Likewise, the eastern part of the archipelago forms a part of the Australian landshelf, whereas Celebes and the Moluccas are separated from both by deep sea channels.

Other structural elements largely responsible for the formation of the archipelago are the two main mountain ranges that run through most of the islands and meet each other in the region of the Moluccas. The western, being an extension of the Indo-China Mountains that branch off from the Himalayas, extends from the northern tip of Sumatra through Java and the Lesser Sunda islands, with a branch running north to the Moluccas and Celebes; it is sometimes called the Sunda Arc. The other, the Sulu Arc, reaches southward from Japan through the Philippines into the Moluccas. Both contain many volcanoes, active and extinct, that make the Indonesian Archipelago the most volcanic region on earth. As a result of the progressive depression in the eastern part of the Sunda Fold, the land masses along its course decrease in size from west to east. Generally speaking, the mountains drop off abruptly toward the Indian Ocean—in western Sumatra and southern Java—with great depth of the sea close to the shore, whereas on the other side the slope is much more grad-

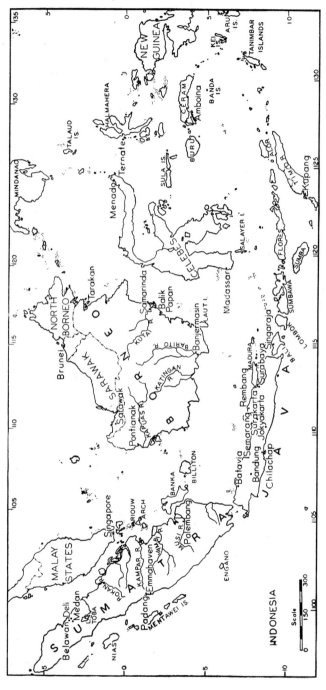

FIGURE 135. Map of Indonesia.

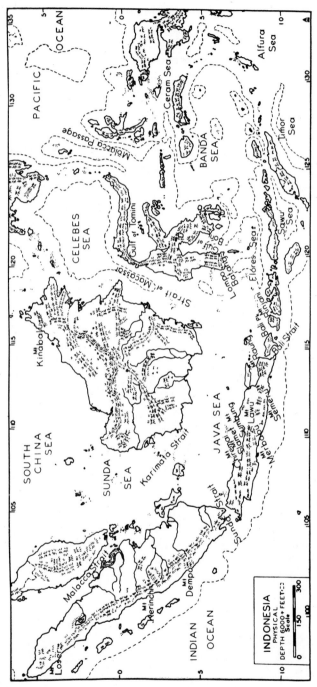

FIGURE 136. Physical features of Indonesia.

ual, ending in extensive flatlands and bordering on shallow inner seas. In consequence, the archipelago is like a vast bowl, formed by the two folds, out of which rises the great land mass of Borneo, which differs from the other islands by being entirely non-volcanic (Fig. 136).

The geological composition of the islands is very complicated and offers a wide range from the youngest to the oldest formations and deposits. Ancient rock occurs more or less widely distributed over the archipelago, with large Tertiary strata in between. Because of the volcanic nature of the region, these formations are often covered to a great depth by recent volcanic ejecta. In the tropical climate, with its copious rainfall, these surface materials, rich in nutritive substances, decompose rapidly and are distributed by the rivers over the lower regions, where they build up extremely fertile soil. Generally speaking, therefore, rich soil is found in the islands wherever there are volcanoes of comparatively recent origin, as in most parts of Java. But where the soil is composed of non-volcanic, older material, it is as poor as in other tropical areas, where the constant washing away of soluble elements is not counteracted by new fertile deposits. Naturally, this difference in fertility goes far to explain the variations in the distribution of the population and the range of civilization found in Indonesia.

CLIMATE

Lying within the tropical zone, Indonesia has days of almost equal length throughout the year and uniformly high temperatures. But because of the insular character of the region, the heat rarely exceeds 80° F. Moreover, as the temperature decreases by about 1° F for every 335 feet of elevation, the higher locations have a cooler and more agreeable climate by day, with occasional frosts occurring at night at the highest altitudes. Average seasonal and daily variations in temperature are small, except in the mountains. As a rule, the temperature in this area depends more on the altitude of a place than on its geographic location or on the season of the year.

The proximity of the continents renders the archipelago the most typical monsoon region of the world. Wind and rainfall are regulated by the alternating monsoons, which are also responsible for any seasonal variations. In general, the West monsoon, blowing from November to January, and from west to northwest, is that of the rainy season, whereas the East monsoon, blowing from east to southeast, usually brings less rain. In most of the archipelago rainfall is copious and humidity is high. But as one approaches Australia, a regular dry season becomes more clearly marked. Atmospheric pressure is rather uniform, and winds rarely rise above a gentle breeze. The months between the monsoons have variable winds and usually bring heavy thunderstorms, with showers of as much as 2 inches of rain per hour.

TABLE 2

AVERAGE TEMPERATURE AND RAINFALL

Place*	Elevation, Feet	Average Yearly Temperature, °F	Average Yearly Rainfall, Inches	Average Humidity, Per Cent
Batavia, Java	25	79.3	75	82
Buitenzorg, Java	800	76.5	170	80
Bandung, Java	2350	72.5	80	78
Tosari, Java	5600	60.6	80	79
Gede, Java	9900	48.0	120	84
Medan, Sumatra	80	78.0	80	83
Padang, Sumatra	20	79.5	180	80
Palembang, Sumatra	30	79.9	100	82
Pontianak, Borneo	10	80.1	130	83
Balikpapan, Borneo	3	78.4	90	85
Menado, Celebes	20	79.1	110	82
Macassar, Celebes	5	79.1	115	80
Amboina, Moluccas	10	79.3	140	83
Kupang, Timor	150	80.1	55	73

* English spelling of Indonesian names is followed here throughout. But since many maps and books use the Dutch spelling, the following simple rules should be kept in mind:

Dutch		English
oe	=	*u* or *oo*
aoe	=	*au* or *ou*
dj	=	*j*
tj	=	*ch*
j	=	*y*

For instance, Soerabaja = Surabaya
Tjilatjap = Chilachap

Malay or Indonesian words are usually accented on the next to the last syllable.

Land and sea breezes, the influence of the coastal configuration, or the presence of large mountain massifs, frequently counteract and sometimes even reverse the general pattern caused by the monsoons. For instance, rainfall usually increases as one nears the mountains, an altitude of 4000 feet being the zone of maximum precipitation. In consequence, local differences are quite pronounced and limit the value of generalizations. But despite the generally high temperature and humidity, the climate of the archipelago is not unsuitable for white people if proper caution is maintained, especially as a periodic escape from the hot lowlands into the cooler mountain regions is easily possible under modern conditions.

TABLE 3

DISTRIBUTION OF RAINFALL (1940)

	Jan.	Feb.	Mar.	Apr.	May	June	July	Aug.	Sept.	Oct.	Nov.	Dec.
Batavia	28.5	10.5	7.5	5.5	6.5	2.0	0.75	0.5	0.2	0.1	1.8	7.5
Palembang	7.0	11.0	9.0	8.0	8.0	3.5	4.0	4.1	1.1	2.3	8.0	9.0
Balikpapan	10.0	7.5	11.5	7.0	22.5	12.0	9.5	8.5	3.0	0.8	6.5	7.5
Macassar	51.5	27.0	12.5	9.0	4.0	0.7	0.0	0.0	0.0	0.0	2.5	19.0
Kupang	15.5	10.0	11.0	2.0	0.0	0.0	0.0	0.0	0.0	0.0	0.5	8.5

FLORA AND FAUNA

As is to be expected, the vicinity of the two continents has a strong effect on plant and animal life in the archipelago. This relationship was first pointed out by the English naturalist, Alfred Russel Wallace, who, about a century ago, tried to systematize the situation by drawing a line separating the two main regions from each other. Somewhat later the German zoologist, Max Weber, drew another line of separation, thus establishing three distinct divisions, one of Asiatic and one of Australian predominance, with an intermediary area between them. Investigations have proved that such marked separations do not exist and that the distribution of fauna and flora in the archipelago is not in entire correlation. All that can be maintained is that Indonesia is a region in which Asiatic, Australian, and endemic types intermingle, and that plants and animals from one of the continents occur more frequently as one nears the continent in question. But for a very general appraisal of the fauna and flora of the archipelago the two "lines" still have a certain value. (See Fig. 137.)

Geological formation, soil, climate, altitude, and the activity of man all combine to make for an exceedingly rich and varied vegetation and numerous species of animals. Thus, for instance, 45,000 varieties of ferns and phanerograms, belonging to 3000 genera, have been found in Indonesia and the Philippines. In Java alone 6000 varieties are known to exist; Borneo can boast of 780 species of orchids. Under favorable conditions, growth becomes unbelievably luxuriant; the vines called rattan sometimes reach a length of close to 1000 feet, bamboo stalks grow to a circumference of 30 inches, some palm leaves attain a size of 40 feet, and the archipelago also produces the largest known flower, rafflesia, more than 3 feet in diameter.

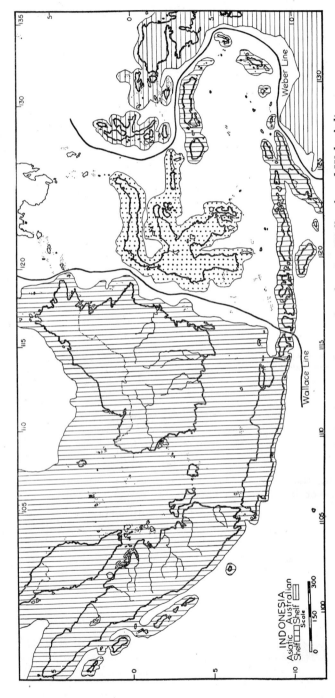

FIGURE 137.   Continental shelfs of Asia and Australia, showing Wallace's and Weber's lines.

Wherever nature is still undisturbed by man and favorable soil conditions obtain, the equatorial sea climate of the lowlands produces the tropical rainforest. Toward the ocean shore this rainforest passes into the coastal forest, which, near river mouths and swampy shores, is composed mostly of mangrove and nipa palms. As the ground rises, a number of species found in the lowlands gradually disappear and are replaced by others, including oak, chestnut, rhododendron, berries, and many flowers. Still higher up, the zone of conifers and mountain casuarina is reached. The mountain flora, reminiscent of the temperate zone, goes up to about 10,000 feet, but trees and shrubs occur almost right to the snow line that lies around 15,000 feet of altitude. Only a few peaks in New Guinea rise above that line.

In the southeastern part of Indonesia, which feels the influence of the dry Australian climate, the rainforest is replaced either by a monsoon or seasonal forest or by a park-like landscape of grassland with occasional trees.

As a result of the influence of man, genuine primeval vegetation is now rare in the archipelago, except for the impenetrable swamps of the coastal regions. Clearing land for cultivation, especially the wasteful system of shifting agriculture, practiced by the more primitive tribes destroys the forest and replaces it with shrubs and grass, particularly the tall and tough alang-alang. In Java and other settled areas the forests have, of course, given way to permanently and regularly cultivated fields. There are some government-controlled forests, especially of teak, which are protected against the incursions of agriculture.

Among the numerous useful plants found in the archipelago, many are of foreign origin and have been introduced in comparatively recent times. Some of them have assumed great importance in the economic life of Indonesia, and frequently the immigrant plants have almost ousted the native flora of a certain region. Fruits of many different kinds flourish in abundance on the various islands, but few of them grow wild. Among them the banana, pineapple, durian, mango, mangosteen, tamarind, apple, citrus fruit, breadfruit, papaya, berries, and guava are the most widely cultivated, and beans and squash are of major importance among vegetables.

The fauna of Indonesia reflect more clearly than the flora the tripartite division mentioned above. But even here the transition from one extreme to the other is only gradual, and the individual islands show striking differences among each other.

Like the vegetation, the animal life of the archipelago is exceedingly rich in species and shows a great variety of forms. It is known to comprise at least 650 species of mammals, 2000 species of birds, more than 300 varieties of snakes, 250 amphibians, hundreds of fish species, and well over 250,000 insect species. In addition to the faunal types of Asia and Australia, the archipelago has many unique types of its own, occurring especially in the intermediary zone.

Zoologically, Sumatra, Borneo, and Java resemble the Malay Peninsula. But whereas the orangutan and the gibbon occur in Borneo and Sumatra, they are not found in Java; Sumatra has the largest

FIGURE 138.   View of Garoet Mountain, a volcano, and Garoet Valley, with inundated rice fields near Ngamplang, Java. Photograph courtesy K.P.M. Lines.

number of ape species, Borneo fewer, and Java still fewer. The wild ox (banteng) is common in Java and is found also in Borneo, but not in Sumatra; elephants are native in Sumatra, found in Borneo, but not in Java. Tigers are numerous in Java and Sumatra, but not in Borneo, and the Malayan bear is missing in Java. The one-horned rhinoceros still lives in Java and southern Sumatra; the bulk of Sumatra knows only the two-horned type. The tapir lives in Sumatra, but is unknown elsewhere; the leopard or panther is found only in Java.

In addition to these large animals, the islands abound in smaller ones, such as deer, of which the mouse deer and the barking deer are of special interest. Wild pigs, found almost everywhere, do great damage to crops—one reason why tigers are still tolerated in densely populated Java. There are many kinds of monkeys on all the western islands but none in the Moluccas or in New Guinea. In addition to these, squirrels, lemurs, hares, bats, flying foxes, rats, and mice are numerous in most parts of the archipelago.

The western part of the archipelago is also rich in bird life, though not so rich as the eastern portion. Among the species found are the peacock, argus pheasant, hornbill, duck and other waterfowl, several varieties of kingfishers, pigeons, parrots, and cockatoos, and numerous sea birds.

Crocodiles of various types are common all over the archipelago, and there are many varieties of tortoises, turtles, lizards, frogs, and toads. Among the lizards, the chichaks and the geckos are valued in human habitations as insect catchers; the now-famous monitor or dragon lizards of Komodo, discovered by Europeans only in 1911, grow to a length of 10 feet and attack even large animals. Although there are many poisonous species and pythons found among the snakes in the islands, they do not, as a rule, constitute a grave danger to human life.

As pests they are far outdistanced by the tremendous number of insects, flies, mosquitoes, leeches, scorpions, and centipedes. But there are also many beautiful species of butterflies and interesting beetles of various kinds.

The seas around the islands, and their inland waterways, teem with life, such as fish, mollusks, crustaceans; in the eastern parts the dugong, or sea cow, is still found occasionally. The coral reefs and lagoons are particularly rich in marine life, but there are also sharks and octopuses to be found in all parts of the sea.

In contrast to the western islands, New Guinea, the Key and the Aru islands, and Timor are almost purely Australian in the nature of their animal life, despite the differences in climate. Large mammals are completely lacking, but some primitive species occur, such as the kangaroo and other marsupials and the egg-laying anteater, which are entirely absent from the rest of the archipelago. On the other hand, these regions are preeminently the home of the bird-of-paradise, of which there are many and gorgeous varities, the cassowary, and numerous parrots and parakeets. Vultures, pheasants, or jungle fowl, however, are lacking.

Celebes, the Moluccas, and the eastern Lesser Sunda Islands form the transitional belt. Of these, Celebes is zoologically the most interesting as it contains species that occur nowhere else in the archipelago but have close relatives as far away as Europe and Africa. Among the unique types of Celebes are the hogdeer, the dwarf buffalo, and a special type of baboon. The Moluccas are poor in mammals, but abound in birds and butterflies.

Most of the domesticated animals, such as the water buffalo or carabao, cattle, goats, and sheep, as well as dogs and cats, have been brought into Indonesia from outside.

MINERAL RESOURCES

The potential mineral resources of Indonesia have not yet been fully explored, but it is believed that they are enormous and include many "strategic materials." As most of the deposits are found in the outer islands—Java being comparatively poor in workable minerals—systematic prospecting has barely started; moreover, difficulties of transportation and labor supply make working of the mineral wealth of the less-developed islands impossible or unprofitable.

Nevertheless, a great variety of minerals are known and are being exploited even now (Fig. 141). Chief among them is petroleum, which is found mainly in Sumatra, Borneo, and Java, with minor fields in Ceram, New Guinea, and Timor; but new fields are frequently located. The petroleum found in the archipelago is quite plentiful, but its importance is further increased by the fact that this is the only source of liquid fuel in practically the entire East Asiatic and Australian region. Next in significance is tin, which is mined in the islands of Banka, Billiton, and the Riouw Archipelago. This region, together with the Malay Peninsula, supplies the major portion of the world's demand for tin.

Indonesia also has considerable reserves of coal, located mostly in Sumatra and Borneo. Some of it is of excellent quality, but little of it is exported. Iron ore occurs in Celebes, South Borneo, and Sumatra, but has as yet received little attention. Of growing importance are bauxite, located in the Riouw Archipelago and Celebes, and manganese, found in Sumatra. Besides these, there are less extensive deposits of nickel and copper, both in Celebes, wolframite, in Banka and Billiton, sulfur, iodine, asphalt, platinum, gold, silver, and diamonds.

PEOPLES

The great majority of the peoples of Indonesia belong to the Malayan race, which shows predominantly Mongoloid traits. But within this racial group there are many differences in detail, and there are also peoples of entirely different racial characteristics to be found there. The bulk of the Malayans live in the western islands and gradually thin out toward the east. In New Guinea and adjacent islands the Papuans are the dominant race, with small groups of Negritos in the interior. In the Moluccas and the eastern Lesser Sunda Islands, a mixture of all these races is found.

The Malayans or Malays themselves may be divided into two main groups, the proto-Malays or Earlier Malays,[1] and the deutero-Malays or Later Malays. It is assumed that the proto-Malays, who show some

FIGURE 139.   Rice and settlement near Fort de Kock, Sumatra.
Photograph courtesy K.P.M. Lines.

Caucasoid heritage, came to the islands from the Asiatic mainland, perhaps 8000 years ago. They probably displaced most of the original population, composed largely of Negritos, or drove them into the more inaccessible parts of the large islands. Perhaps 4000 to 6000 years later a new wave of invaders from Asia, with more definitely Mongolian traits, arrived in the archipelago. They, in turn, drove the earlier immigrants into the interior, and they themselves settled in the more desirable regions of the large islands. There was, however, much mingling of the various groups involved so that it is sometimes difficult to draw sharp lines of racial division.

[1] Formerly the term *Indonesian* was sometimes applied to this group in particular.

As a result of these consecutive migrations and replacements the latest arrivals, the deutero-Malays, occupy most of the lower regions of the large western islands, but are also found scattered throughout the archipelago. The Earlier Malays occupy mainly the interior highlands of Sumatra, Borneo, Celebes, and many of the smaller islands.

TABLE 4

THE PRINCIPAL TRIBAL DIVISIONS
IN THE INDONESIAN ARCHIPELAGO

Race or Tribe	*Location*	*Approximate Number*
Deutero-Malays (Later Malays)		
Achinese	North Sumatra	1,000,000
Coastal Malays	East Sumatra, Borneo, coast islands	4,500,000
Menangkabaus	West-central Sumatra	2,000,000
Sundanese	West Java	11,000,000
Javanese	Central Java	33,000,000
Madurese	East Java and Madura	5,500,000
Balinese	Bali, Lombok	2,000,000
Macassarese }	Southern Celebes }	3,500,000
Buginese }	East Coast of Borneo }	
Proto-Malays (Earlier Malays)		
Rejang-Lampong	Southern Sumatra	1,000,000
Bataks	Central Sumatra	1,500,000
Dayaks	Borneo	3,000,000
Tarajas	Central Celebes	1,000,000
Menadonese	Northern Celebes	1,000,000
Alfurs	Moluccas	1,000,000
Alorese	Lesser Sunda Islands	4,500,000
Papuas	New Guinea, adjacent islands	1,000,000

In appearance all the Malays show a great similarity. Usually they are of small stature (5 feet, 2 or 3 inches) and slender build, with brown skin, dark eyes, straight or wavy hair, but little body hair, a flat face, broad nose, and lips of medium thickness. In character they are sedate and phlegmatic but proud, polite, and well mannered, poised and dignified, and of graceful bearing; they are intelligent, adaptable, and artistically gifted. To most of them, work is not a virtue but a necessity, money not an aim in itself but a readily expendable commodity. They do not like to exert themselves beyond the demands of mere subsistence, but have a great capacity for enjoyment in the form of festivities, gambling, or just idling.

But within this comparative similarity there are also striking differences. From the gentle, orderly, and easygoing Javanese to the aggressive and fanatical Achinese of Sumatra, the diligent, thrifty, and energetic, but hot-tempered Madurese, and the democratic and self-reliant Menangkabaos, there are many intermediary stages, just as there are between the highly sophisticated and complex civilization of the Javanese and Balinese and the primitive backwardness of the Dayak or Alfur headhunters, or between the advanced agriculture and the highly developed irrigation system of Java or Balai to the outworn and wasteful methods practiced in Borneo and some of the other islands.

In number as well as in civilization the races of Java are the predominant group. Together with their racial brothers of Sumatra, they also form the driving elements in Indonesian aspirations for political independence.

Almost 90 per cent of the Indonesians are Mohammedans by religion. However, their Mohammedanism is strongly mixed with older animistic beliefs and is usually less fanatical in Indonesia than in some other countries. Many of the tribes of the interior of the larger islands are still pagans. In Bali a form of Hinduism, blending Brahmanism and Buddhism with Chinese and indigent animistic influences, has been preserved. Wherever Islam prevails, Christianity has made little progress. Only some of the pagan tribes of Sumatra and Borneo have been christianized after long missionary efforts, but in some places, such as Ambon or Menado, the people were converted long ago. Altogether there are about 2,500,000 Christians in the islands.

In addition to the native peoples, there are about 1,250,000 Chinese in Indonesia, some of whom have lived there for many generations without, however, losing their racial and cultural identity. As a rule the Chinese represent the retail merchant and craftsman classes, fulfilling an economic function that seems to be distasteful to most of the Malays. Chinese are found all over the archipelago, even in the remotest sections, where they often come as pioneers of a more advanced civilization. Because of the financial hold some of them have over the natives, they are frequently disliked. In former years many Chinese accumulated great riches, but the newest immigrants usually come as coolies to work in the plantations and mining enterprises of the outer islands.

The 250,000 Europeans who lived in Indonesia in 1940 included the half castes or Eurasians who were always legally—and partly even socially—grouped with the Whites. The bulk of the Europeans are, of course, the Dutch, who filled the upper strata of governmental, business, agricultural, and industrial positions. The majority of the Whites are concentrated in Java, where living conditions are most favorable to them. In contrast to other colonizers, the Dutch often remained all their lives in the Indies, returning to Holland only for a vacation or to pursue their studies there.

Among foreign Orientals in the archipelago, the Japanese, though small in number, were accorded equal status with the Europeans and

FIGURE 140. Balinese dancing girl. Photograph, Netherlands Information Bureau.

were, before the Second World War, gradually gaining economic ascendancy. Arabs, although also small in number and representing another class of retail merchants, are for religious reasons regarded with respect by the natives. Other groups, such as Indians, are insignificant in numbers and influence. But although Europeans and foreign Orientals together constitute only 2 per cent of the total population of Indonesia, they have controlled among themselves the larger portion of the national income.

The density and distribution of the population within the archipelago show great variations, reflecting the fertility of the various islands. Java, with some 1000 people per square mile, is one of the most densely populated areas of the world, whereas Borneo is one of the most sparsely settled regions. As is natural in a predominantly agricultural country, most people live in small villages, and larger towns are comparatively rare.

LANGUAGES

Except for the Papuans, the Indonesians speak a language that belongs to the widespread Malayo-Polynesian linguistic stock. Yet despite this basic relationship, there are some 250 dialects that are mutually incomprehensible, and range from the thoroughly cultivated, complicated, and rich Javanese to the much less-developed tongues of the primitive tribes. Counteracting this linguistic diversity, a simplified form of the Malay language—the native tongue of the Malays of Malacca and the eastern coasts of Sumatra—is the *lingua franca* of the East Indies.

ECONOMIC LIFE

In consequence of the favorable conditions prevailing there, Indonesia before the Second World War was the most profitable colonial empire of its size. The large quantities of raw materials, vegetable and mineral, more than paid for the needed imports of manufactured goods and the return on foreign investments. The war disrupted the economic life of the Indies, and it may be some time before a situation will be reached that can again be termed "normal." This is true not only because of the unsettled political situation but also because some of the products of the archipelago, which formerly constituted the bulk of its export and income, are no longer in as much demand as they were. The development of chemical substitutes may reduce the need for rubber and quinine; Indonesian sugar has been less in demand for a long time, and so has coffee. But because of the favor of circumstances and the adaptability of man to new conditions, the Indies have weathered several such crises in the past. Sugar and coffee themselves together with indigo, replaced spices as the main export products in the eighteenth century; rubber, tin, and oil have taken the place of sugar and coffee during the twentieth. It is reasonable to assume that the world will continue to need materials that the soil of Indonesia can furnish better or in larger quantities than other regions of the earth. After a period of uncertainty, the country will surely regain its place as one of the important sources of tropical raw materials, however different they may be from those produced in the past. Moreover, a population of over 70,000,000 constitutes a sizable market for the industrial goods of the West, and its value will increase as the living standards of the Indonesians improve.

Conditions are too much disturbed and unsettled to permit a clear picture of Indonesian economic life to be drawn. This description, therefore, must be based chiefly on the situation as it existed before the war, such changes as are discernible in peacetime being noted.

AGRICULTURE

Numerous factors determine the nature of the agricultural production of Indonesia. For instance, the purpose: Is the crop grown for domestic consumption, chiefly as food, or for exports? The method: Is the crop grown by natives in their own fields or on special plantations? The soil: Is the crop grown on fertile and well-irrigated soil, as found chiefly in Java, or on the poorer soil that predominates in the outer islands?

Native food crops consist chiefly of rice (the basic food in the western islands), maize or corn, cassava (the source of tapioca), coconut, sago (the staple food of the eastern islands), peanuts, soybeans, sweet potatoes, vegetables, and fruits. These are cultivated by the natives, usually according to age-old methods, though sweet potatoes and maize have been introduced into the country only comparatively recently. None of these crops is grown on plantations.

The production of the large plantations or estates is governed almost exclusively by export needs. It includes primarily sugar, rubber, tea, coffee, cinchona, oil palms, agave, cocoa, and the better grades of tobacco. Some of these crops require a smooth-functioning organization, including scientific research and constantly improved production methods, careful financing and marketing, all of which need considerable capital. However, native production has assumed a large share of certain export crops, especially of rubber and coffee. Other crops have always been grown by small native producers; among them are pepper, coconuts (copra), kapok, and low-grade tobacco. In general, the share of the native population in the production of export crops has steadily risen; although it was only 9 per cent in 1900, it had reached more than 40 per cent in 1940.

The same gradual increase is also noticeable in the part played by the outer islands, in the cultivation of export crops, but outside of Java, Bali, and part of Sumatra, native agriculture is still mostly of the

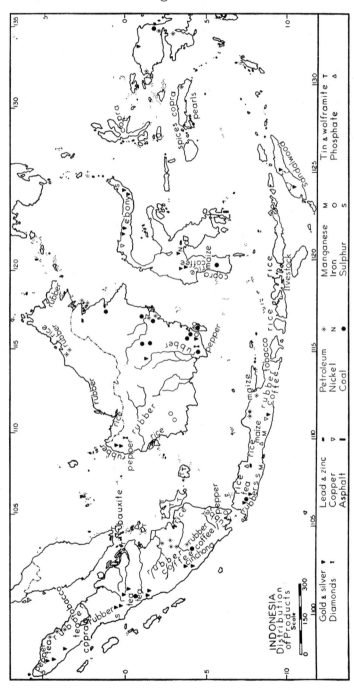

FIGURE 141. Distribution of products in Indonesia.

primitive type, extensive rather than intensive, wasteful of space, and able to maintain a very sparse population.

The principal food crop of Indonesia, rice, is grown, wherever conditions permit, in "wet" or irrigated fields (*sawahs*). Only where that is impossible is *ladang* or dry culture resorted to, giving paddy of inferior quality. Rice fields are found in the alluvial plains of the large western islands, especially in Java, where they even cover the hills to an altitude of 4000 feet. Sometimes secondary crops are planted between the harvesting and the planting of the rice, but in the mountains rice cultivation continues almost uninterrupted.

Despite the intensive rice culture, however, Java cannot produce enough for her rapidly growing population, which increases about 600,000 per year; and rice, usually of an inferior quality to that grown in Java, has to be imported. One of the chief problems in Indonesia is that the population increase of Java keeps ahead of the increase in food production. With practically all arable land already under cultivation (60 per cent of the total area), the immediate problem seems to be to find improved rice strains, or some other high-yielding crops, and to introduce improved methods of cultivation in place of the traditional ones. Attempts to settle Javanese in the outer islands, especially Sumatra, where conditions similar to those of Java are found in some places, have met with only very limited success in the past.

TABLE 5

CULTIVATED AREAS AND YIELDS OF CHIEF CROPS
IN JAVA AND MADURA (1939)

	Harvested Area, Acres	Yield, Tons
Rice	10,000,000	9,000,000
Maize	5,000,000	1,900,000
Cassava	2,500,000	8,400,000
Sweet potatoes	500,000	1,500,000
Peanuts	600,000	200,000
Soybeans	300,000	300,000

Before the Second World War the government of the Netherlands Indies tried to protect the land of the natives against economically stronger groups by forbidding the sale of land to foreigners. But government-owned land and parts of the land cultivated by the natives could be leased to Europeans and foreign Orientals for the raising of export crops or for industrial purposes, yet only in such a way that it would not seriously interfere with the cultivation of food crops. Actually, only about one-tenth of the cultivated area of Java was occupied by plantations.

Among the plantation crops for export (Fig. 142), sugar used to take first place. By extensive research and the application of scientific production methods, Java-grown cane achieved the highest yield in sugar. It is often grown on irrigated land in rotation with other crops, the sugar being milled in Java itself and the surplus exported mainly to India, Japan, and Europe. Java is still, next to Cuba, the most important sugar exporter of the world.

However, the supremacy of sugar as the main export crop has been challenged by rubber. Its cultivation is not limited to Java, nor is it grown only on foreign-controlled estates. Despite the restrictions imposed on the cultivation of rubber and other crops, for the purpose of maintaining prices, Indonesia furnished some 40 per cent of the world's supply of that commodity, the bulk of it going to the United States. Rubber production, distributed practically over the entire Archipelago, covers a larger area than any other export crop; for commercial purposes, only *Hevea brasiliensis* or the Para rubber tree is grown.

Next in importance as an export crop is tea, 90 per cent of which is grown on estates lying in the middle altitudes of 1200 to 6000 feet. Most of it is sold to Australia and New Zealand. Coffee, also one of the "hill cultures," is among the oldest export products of the archipelago, as indicated by the name "Java" for a good cup of coffee. Reduced by a leaf disease about 1900, the coffee crop never quite recovered its former importance. Good tobacco is grown around Jokyakarta in Java, but it ranks second to the product of the estates around Deli in Sumatra, which furnish the famous "cover" or "wrapper leaf" for high-quality cigars.

One of the best known products of the archipelago is the bark of the cinchona tree, from which quinine is extracted. Introduced about a hundred years ago from South America, it is now grown mainly in Java, on estates owned and operated by the government, which also has a quinine factory and an experimental station at Bandung. The trees grown here yield two to three times the amount of quinine produced by the trees in Peru. Rapidly growing in importance is the estate cultivation of oil palms, located chiefly in Sumatra, whose output of palm oil—in quantity as well as quality—has already outdistanced that of West Africa, whence it was introduced to the Indies. Other products of value in the world market are kapok, cultivated chiefly in Java by the natives, hard cordage fibers, copra, gutta percha, and spices, especially black and white pepper, grown mainly by natives in Sumatra, cloves, nutmeg and mace, and various vegetable oils and fats.

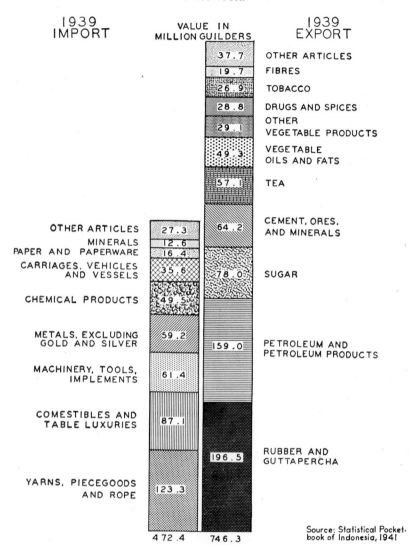

FIGURE 142. Prewar imports and exports of Indonesia.

Among the products of the forests of Indonesia, teak has first place, but only a comparatively small part of it is available for export. Other valuable timbers exploited in the archipelago are ebony, iron wood, and sandalwood. Rattan for wicker chairs, gum dammar, copal, and other resins, varieties of wild rubber, mangrove bark for tanning, and various other useful products are also exported. However, owing to conditions in the outer islands, systematic exploitation has not been attempted, though it would increase the output considerably. The value of forests for the country lies not only in the number of usable products but also in their hydrological and orological functions. The Second World War affected Indonesian agriculture and all other forms of economic life adversely. It is estimated that, on the average, production in 1950 was at least 25 per cent lower than before the war, and it will be some time before a new normal pattern is reestablished.

An important contribution of the Dutch to life in the archipelago is the organization of numerous and excellent scientific institutions for the purpose of studying and improving agricultural methods, and of disseminating agricultural information among the population.

CATTLE BREEDING

Although some of the Indonesians are excellent cattle breeders, the proportion of livestock to the population for the archipelago is very small.

TABLE 6

LIVESTOCK IN INDONESIA IN 1940, IN 1000's

	Java	*Sumatra*	*Borneo*	*E. Indonesia*	*Total*
Horses	219	36	0 5	455	710.5
Cows, bulls, oxen	3588	382	31	599	4600
Buffaloes (carabaos)	1925	391	34	827	3177
Goats	5161	337	19	433	5950
Sheep	1780	43	2.1	65	1890.1
Hogs	166	356	154	591	1267

Farmers in the archipelago use cattle chiefly as draft animals; meat production is of secondary importance, and a dairy industry hardly exists. The best cattle come from Madura, Bali, and Sumbawa, which is also the home of the small Indonesian horse. The small number of pigs in Java is explained by the fact that the population is predominantly Mohammedan. Sheep are not raised for their wool, but only for slaughtering. Animal hides and skins form a considerable part of the export from the islands. By combating diseases and introducing better stock, the government is improving the livestock.

FISHERIES

Considering the importance of fish as a source of food for the native population, the fishing industry must be said to be gravely underdeveloped. Natives all along the coasts fish, but generally only as a by-trade, and only in Madura and Bagan-Si-Api-Api on the east coast of Sumatra has fishing reached large-scale proportions. Just before the Second World War, however, the Japanese began to put the fishing industry on a more systematic basis by introducing modern equipment. On the other hand, the raising of fish in local ponds and in irrigated rice fields between harvests is fairly well developed and adds greatly to the natives' supply of proteins. In the eastern part of the archipelago, pearl and shell fishery is carried on, mostly by Arabs or Japanese.

TABLE 7

PER CAPITA FOOD CONSUMPTION IN JAVA (1940)

	Yearly Average, Pounds	Calories per Diem		Yearly Average, Pounds
Rice	191	790	Vegetables and fruit	130
Cassava	350	600	Fish	13
Maize	81	320	Meat	6.5
Sweet potato	70	110	Milk	2
Soybeans	12	50	Sugar	15
Peanuts	6	45		

MINING

In view of the mineral wealth of the archipelago, the mining industry naturally has an increasingly important place in its economy, mining products representing about one-third of the value of Indonesian exports (Fig. 142). Of greatest significance are, of course, the oil fields and the tin mines. The oil fields are exploited chiefly by the Royal Dutch Company, a subsidiary of the Shell interests, and by the American Standard Oil concerns. The most important refineries are located in Balik Papan, Borneo. The mining of tin is to a large extent in the hands of the government; the tin is usually smelted locally and refined in the Netherlands or in Singapore. Most of the coal mines are also owned by the government and supply

TABLE 8

MINERAL PRODUCTION OF INDONESIA IN PREWAR YEARS

Petroleum (1938)		7,500,000 tons
Tin	(average 1936–1939)	33,000 "
Coal	" " "	1,300,000 "
Bauxite	" " "	192,000 "
Phosphate	" " "	24,000 "
Sulphur	" " "	14,000 "
Manganese ore	" " "	10,000 "
Asphalt	" " "	5,000 "
Nickel (exported in 1940)		57,000 "
Gold		4,500 pounds
Silver		40,000 "

primarily domestic needs. Gold and silver are mined chiefly by Chinese and refined locally. The exploitation of bauxite has been undertaken with considerable success. The introduction of modern, mechanized production methods might greatly facilitate mining and perceptibly increase production in Indonesia. Moreover, artificial restrictions on production has often limited the output of minerals as well as of certain export crops.

INDUSTRY

Industry in the western sense of the word is still in its infancy, but the two World Wars and the depression of the 1930's forcefully indicated the need of making Indonesia less dependent on the import of essential manufactured goods and the need of obtaining a more balanced economy. As a rule, finished products maintain their prices better than agricultural or mineral raw materials. The Indies, therefore, are especially hard hit during a depression and in times of war they cannot obtain western machinery and equipment at any price. In consequence, a promising beginning has been made of introducing various light industries, for which the natives show considerable aptitude, whereas a heavy industry will hardly ever be successful in this tropical country. More systematic efforts to utilize available water power for industrial purposes may be of great help in the future.

In general, most of the industrial activity is in the service of local agriculture or mining, either for domestic use or for export, and is usually carried on by the same companies that produce the raw material. Of great significance, however, is also the developing textile industry, which, in time, may make the country self-sufficient in this respect.

With very few exceptions, the native home industries aim only at supplying the local markets with clothing, foodstuffs, dwellings, and household furniture. Only the weaving of hats and batik work, both centered in Java, are also done for export. But the batik industry, like most of the other native arts and crafts, is in danger of being commercially ousted by the cheaper machine-made imported product and of being artisitically ruined by the undiscriminating taste of tourists, who have little appreciation for the real value of the things they buy.

COMMERCE

Before the Second World War the wholesale trade of Indonesia was mostly in the hands of Europeans, primarily the Dutch, whereas the intermediary trade was divided among Europeans, Chinese, Arabs, and Japanese. The share of the native element in the archipelago's trade was limited almost entirely to the retail trade in the native markets or *pasars*.

As long as Holland followed a monopolistic trade policy, most of Indonesia's products were shipped to the mother country, whence they were distributed to the various markets of the world. In more recent times, however, the Dutch have adhered to a policy of free trade and the Open Door, which has tended to make the archipelago almost independent of Holland in its trade, shipment being made more and more directly from the producing area to the ultimate consumer.

TABLE 9

COMPOSITION OF EXPORTS, 1910 AND 1939, IN PERCENTAGES

	Estate Crops	Native Agricul- tural Products	Mining	Other Goods
1910	57	21	16	6
1939	42	25	30	4

THE SHARE OF JAVA AND MADURA IN IMPORTS AND EXPORTS

	Java		Outer Islands	
	Imports	Exports	Imports	Exports
1930	64.5	50	35.5	50
1939	70	36.5	30	63.5

Since about 1930 the share of the United States in the consumption of Indonesian products has increased considerably, whereas Japan has succeeded in more than doubling its imports into the island. Before the Second World War about two-thirds of the total export went to Europe and the United States, about one-fifth to other Asiatic countries; of the imports, two-fifths came from Europe, one-eighth from the United States, and one-third from Asiatic countries, the remainder being distributed between Australia and Africa.

TABLE 10

INDONESIA'S SHARE IN THE WORLD EXPORT
OF CERTAIN COMMODITIES (1939), IN PERCENTAGES

Quinine (production)		91	Palm oil (export)		24
Pepper	(export)	86	Tin	"	20
Kapok	"	72	Tea	"	19
Rubber	"	37	Bauxite	"	7
Fibers	"	33	Coffee	"	5
Coconut products	"	27	Sugar (production)		6

As far as export is concerned, Indonesia has a near monopoly in some commodities; in others, it furnishes an important part of the world demand; in still others, the quality produced there is higher than that of other regions.

As a colonial country, Indonesia has been to a large extent dependent for its economic development on foreign capital, and will probably remain in that position for some time to come. Naturally, the major part of that capital came from Holland, with Great Britain and the United States together investing only about one-tenth of the Dutch share; the largest part of the investment was in petroleum, with rubber a close second, and sugar third.

TRANSPORTATION AND COMMUNICATION

Favorably situated with regard to the main traffic lanes between Europe, Africa, India, and China, on the one hand, and Asia and Australia, on the other, with a considerable foreign trade, Indonesia is well connected with the rest of the world by regular lines, Dutch and others, and by numerous tramp steamers. Although the general configuration of the islands does not make for many good natural harbors, there is nevertheless available a sufficient number of well-developed modern ports with all necessary facilities for refueling and rapair work. Since 1888 the inter-island traffic has been maintained chiefly by the *Koningklijke Paketvaart Maatschappij* (K.P.M., or Royal Packet Navigation Company), which before the Second World War owned over 130 vessels with a total of about 350,000 gross tons. Its services were supplemented by other Dutch and British companies and by the numerous native vessels that ply between the islands.

Many of the large rivers of Sumatra and Borneo are navigable for a considerable distance, and in fact often represent the only means of transportation in these areas. In the other islands rivers are usually too short for ships of any size to navigate.

Aviation is well developed, the islands being dotted by airfields, though at present many of these are in need of repair. The leading Dutch air transportation concern was the K.L.M., which maintains regular flights to and from the Netherlands, whereas the K.N.I.L.M. (Royal Netherlands Indies Airways) ran services within the archipelago.

In Java the railroad system is well developed, totaling more than 3000 miles, and taking care of about two-thirds of the commercial transport needs; half of it is owned by the government. In Sumatra there are only about 1200 miles of railroads; the other islands have almost none.

For the economic life of Indonesia the automobile has proved to be of the utmost importance, especially in areas that cannot maintain an expensive railroad. At the beginning of 1940 there was a total of about 90,000 motor vehicles of all kinds in service in the archipelago. In Java and Sumatra they had at their disposal an excellent network of good roads, and even in the other islands there was a good beginning of systematic road building.

The archipelago is well connected with the rest of the world by radio and cable; telegraph and telephone service is highly developed in the more densely settled areas.

GOVERNMENT

Before the Japanese invasion in 1942 the government of the Netherlands Indies consisted of an executive branch, composed of the Governor General, who was appointed by the Netherlands Crown, the "Council of the Indies" of five members chosen by the Crown and the Netherlands Cabinet, and a colonial Cabinet of eight, chosen by the Governor, except for the Ministers of War and Navy, who were appointed directly by the Crown. The legislative branch was composed of the *Volksraad* (People's Council), which, first created in 1916, gradually developed from an advisory to a co-legislative body and formed the nucleus of an Indonesian Parliament.

The administrative branch consisted of the members of the Civil Service, comprising eight governors, many residents, assistant residents, controllers, and minor officials. The higher ranks were mostly filled by Dutch and Eurasians (30,000), the lower by natives (180,-000). Parallel to this organization was that of the native rulers or regents. In Java alone there were still four sultans and seventy other native princes (rajahs) nominally ruling over the natives, whereas 60 per cent of the outer islands were governed in this indirect manner (340 native states and regencies). Each native ruler, however, had a Dutch official at his side who actually controlled all governmental acts. Under the native ruler there were district chiefs of various ranks down to the village head man. The affairs of the villages are usually managed by these head men and a council of elders, elected by the village assembly of all male adults.

The Japanese occupied Indonesia for four years. After their expulsion at the close of the Second World War the Dutch tried to come to some kind of understanding with the natives to reestablish the ties between the Netherlands and Indonesia. After much fighting and long-drawn-out negotiations, which eventually caused the intervention of the United Nations, a settlement was finally reached, and on December 27, 1949, Dutch rule officially ended in Indonesia.

The political structure that takes its place is the Netherlands-Indonesian Union, composed of the Kingdom of the Netherlands on the one hand and the Republic of Indonesia on the other. The new union does not prejudice the status of either country as an independent and sovereign state. At the head of the union is the queen. Ministerial and parliamentary conferences are to assure a maximum of cooperation between the two partners for the promotion of common interests, especially in foreign relations, defense, finance, and economic matters. A Court of Arbitration is set up for the settlement of disagreements between the two.

At first the new nation was called the United States of Indonesia and was a federation composed of some sixteen states. However, the number of states was soon reduced, and in August, 1950, the remaining states joined to form a new government called the Republic of Indonesia. Batavia was renamed Jakarta, an old Indonesian name, and Jokyakarta (or Jogjakarta) was designated the capital of the Republic of Indonesia.

This arrangement does not change the political status of British Borneo or Portuguese Timor. Moreover, the Dutch part of New Guinea is to remain under the control of the Netherlands temporarily.

Borneo is divided politically into the large former Dutch part and the smaller British portion, which consists of British North Borneo, Sarawak, and Brunei. The first, with an area of 30,000 square miles and a population of some 350,000, is the only territory in the world still administered by a chartered company. Sarawak, founded by James Brooke of British-Indian extraction in 1842, covers about 50,000 square miles, has a population of 500,000, and is still ruled by the white descendants of the founder. Brunei is the smallest of the three British-protected states, with only 2500 square miles and some 40,000 people, ruled by a rajah of Malay ancestry.

HISTORY

The Indonesian Archipelago may well be one of the cradles of mankind, as is indicated by the finding in Java of the remains of *Pithecanthropus erectus,* the "erect ape man," who lived during the Pliocene age. Little is known about the history of the archipelago until about the beginning of the Christian era. At that time the various Malay tribes were well settled there and had developed their culture to a comparatively high degree, when there began an influx of merchants and adventurers from India who, bringing with them the superior civilization of their country, gradually established themselves as rulers and as the upper caste in many parts of Indonesia. After several centuries of amalgamation and adaptation, during which Chinese influences were also added, a new Indonesian culture was developed. Though based primarily on Hinduism, it had nevertheless a distinctly Indonesian flavor. In time some of the kingdoms gained ascendancy over their neighbors until empires grew up, some of which gained control over large parts of the archipelago and even land beyond it. About the thirteenth century conflicts with China, and the rapid spread of Islam, caused a decline in Hindu culture and of the native kingdoms. When the Portuguese arrived in the archipelago, in the early sixteenth century, the empires had declined in power and could offer no effective resistance to the new invaders.

The Portuguese did not come to the Indies with the intention of founding a new colony, but only to trade and to carry on a Holy War against their old enemies, the Arabs, who had previously controlled the trade between the Orient and Europe. The religious fervor of the Portuguese often antagonized the natives, and, when the Dutch arrived in the archipelago in 1596, Portuguese power was already waning. Within a few years, the Hollanders established themselves as the strongest naval power in the Indies, using their favorable position to gain for themselves a monopoly of the trade in spices, the commodity that had first attracted European nations to the archipelago. Uniting their efforts in the Dutch East India Company in 1602, the Dutch established several bases in the Far East and eventually made Batavia the headquarters of a commercial empire comprising all of East Asia.

Although the Dutch were interested only in trade and showed little inclination to interfere in native life, religious or political, they became involved more and more in the internal affairs of the islands. To keep up profits, the Dutch East India Company had to subdue uncooperative native princes, dictate prices, and levy tributes, until it emerged, almost against its will, as the virtual ruler of Java. Since spices alone did not assure sufficient profits, the Dutch began to interest themselves in Java's agriculture, introducing coffee, sugar, and indigo as revenue-producing crops. But rising expenses, a corrupt administration, and diminishing returns finally led to the collapse and dissolution of the Company in 1799. The Dutch government took over the control of its possessions, but, as a result of the Napoleonic Wars, which brought Holland under French domination, the archipelago actually passed into English hands. Java was conquered in 1811, Thomas S. Raffles becoming lieutenant governor of the island. He instituted a number of reforms in the administration of the Indies, many of which were retained by the Dutch even after they returned to Java at the end of the Napoleonic period.

From 1870 on, the welfare of the natives became a definite governmental concern. Private enterprise was encouraged to take over agricultural development from the government. At the same time, the outer islands were opened to direct Dutch rule, although several long wars had to be fought before all of them were brought under control. These wars absorbed whatever financial surplus the colonies could produce, so that from 1877 on they made no direct financial contribution to the mother country.

Under the new policy the number of European enterprises increased rapidly, but so did the native population. Yet since the growth in their number was not matched by a corresponding increase in available foodstuffs, the natives became poorer and more ready to work for low wages, assuring the western ventures good profits.

By 1900 another change in the Dutch attitude toward the Indies occurred with the institution of the "Ethical Policy," which recognized native welfare as the chief aim of the government, relegating the profit motive to a secondary place. Under this policy the Dutch sought to improve not only the economic status of the population, but also its social and cultural well-being, by introducing fair labor laws, making western education available to the natives, etc. Although at first this was done in a paternalistic way, without consulting the natives themselves, the new attitude gradually led to a development of democratic institutions, giving the Indonesians themselves a voice in the management of their own affairs. In 1922 a change in the Netherlands constitution abrogated the term "colonies" and made the Indies an integral part of the Kingdom of the Netherlands. From then on, cautious, slow, and often reluctant steps were taken to prepare the country for some form of autonomy in the future. By that time, however, the natives, once they had become acquainted with western ideas and conditions, had become restive and impatient. Indonesian nationalism was growing fast, and soon the Indonesians were demanding complete independence and freedom for Indonesia. Reforms of various kinds and strict governmental measures succeeded in keeping the movement under control up to the time of the Japanese invasion in 1942.

Never having thought it wise to arm the native population, the Dutch were too weak to withstand the attack of a determined and well-equipped enemy. After a heroic but brief resistance, the Indies passed under the complete control of the conqueror. Japanese anti-White propaganda coincided with the natural desire of the Indonesians for independence, with the result that the return of the Dutch after the war was not welcomed by the population. After much discussion and some clashes between the two parties, independence for Indonesia was finally achieved in 1949.

CIVILIZATION

In view of the great diversity of cultural levels among the peoples of the archipelago, it is difficult to generalize about their civilization. The highest form of civilization is found, of course, in Java, where during the Hinduistic period architecture, sculpture, literature, and music reached a very impressive level of achievement, as documented by such monuments as the Borobudur temple, the Chandi Mandut, the ruins of the Dieng Plateau, and many others. In literature the Javanese translations of the great Indian poems are outstanding, but there are also numerous original works of merit, in Javanese as well as in Malay and Buginese. Javanese music reached a high degree of perfection and is still played by the native *gamelans* or orchestras. The theater found its finest expression in the *wayang* plays, shadow or puppet plays that even now hold their own against the competition of western movies as a popular entertainment. The performance of these traditional plays by living persons is restricted to the princely courts, where the arts of the past have found a shelter; Jokyakarta and Surakarta, the seats of the two most important remaining native rulers of Java, are still the center of Javanese culture and tradition. One of the best-known art forms of Indonesia is the dance, for which Bali has become especially famous. Among the crafts that still flourish there as well as in Java, weaving, carving in wood and other material, tortoise shell work, terra cotta figures, gold and silver work are noteworthy; but most famous of the industrial arts of Java is batik, the painting in wax on cloth.

Even among the otherwise rather primitive and backward tribes of the outer provinces, an amazing artistic sense is often evinced, as indicated by the elaborate houses built in some parts of Sumatra, the weaving done in many other islands, and the weapons, boats, household goods, and religious symbols.

Basically, the social organization of most of the Indonesians is similar and surprisingly democratic. But it is often topped by the autocratic rule of some sultan or rajah, who frequently belongs to another racial group. Although most of the Indonesians have adopted the patriarchial system, some tribes, such as the Menangkabaus, still practice matriarchy, according to which relationship is counted only on the mother's side. In the western part of the Archipelago, the position of women is rather high and, at least in Java, they have taken an active part in the nationalist movement. Cannibalism, formerly prevalent in New Guinea and adjacent islands, is nowadays practically stamped out, as is head hunting, which used to be practiced among the Dayaks of Borneo and numerous other tribes.

This great diversity of cultures as well as of language makes the development of a common Indonesian national civilization, with common ideals and similar goals, exceedingly difficult. The same obstacles hindered the spread of popular education by western models and made it quite expensive. As a result, literacy in Indonesia is at a low level. However, the existing schools, from the lowest to the several institutions of college rank, established within the last few decades are of a recognized high quality. The problem of education is one of the most important among the many and difficult ones that face Indonesia, if the country is to develop into a democracy, as this term is understood in the West. It is here that western aid may be of the greatest value.

TABLE 11
CITIES OF INDONESIA

Java	Population	Outer Islands	Population
Batavia	600,000	Palembang, Sumatra	125,000
Surabaya	450,000	Medan, Sumatra	90,000
Semarang	250,000	Padang, Sumatra	60,000
Bandung	200,000	Macassar, Celebes	100,000
Surakarta	200,000	Menado, Celebes	35,000
Jokyakarta	150,000	Banjermasin, Borneo	80,000
Malang	100,000	Balikpapan, Borneo	35,000
Pekalongan	80,000	Pontianak, Borneo	50,000
Buitenzorg	80,000	Ambon (Amboina), Moluccas	20,000
Kudus	65,000	Singaraja, Bali	15,000
Cheribon	65,000	Ternate, Halmahera	7,500
Megelang	60,000		

REFERENCES

Boeke, J. H., *The Structure of Netherlands Indian Economy*, Institute of Pacific Relations, New York, 1942.

British Admiralty, *A Manual of Netherlands India*, London, 1920.

Broek, J. O. M., *Economic Development of the Netherlands Indies*, Institute of Pacific Relations, New York, 1942.

Brouwer, H. A., *Geology of the Netherlands Indies*, The Macmillan Company, New York, 1925.

Callis, H. G., *Foreign Capital in Southeast Asia*, Institute of Pacific Relations, New York, 1942.

Cator, W. L., *The Economic Position of the Chinese in the Netherlands Indies*, Chicago, University of Chicago Press, 1936.

Cole, Fay-Cooper, *The Peoples of Malaysia*, New York, D. Van Nostrand Company, 1945.

Daniel, Hawthorne, *Islands of the East Indies*, G. P. Putnam's Sons, New York, 1944.

De Klerck, E. S., *History of the Netherlands East Indies*, W. L. & J. Brusse, Rotterdam, 1938.

De Leeuw, H., "Sumatra, Economic and Geographic," *Bull. Geogr. Soc. Philadelphia*, Vol. XXVIII, 1930.

Department of Economic Affairs, Netherlands Indies Government, *Statistical Pocket Book of Indonesia*, Batavia, 1947.

Emerson, R., "The Netherlands Indies and the United States," *World Peace*, 1942.

Emerson, R., L. Mills, and V. Thompson, *Government and Nationalism in Southeast Asia*, Institute of Pacific Relations, New York, 1942.

Furnivall, J. S., *Netherlands India: a Study of Plural Economy*, The Macmillan Company, New York, 1944.

Honig, Pieter, and Frans Verdoorn (Editors), *Science and Scientists in the Netherlands Indies*, prepared under the auspices of the Board for the Netherlands Indies, Chronica Botanica, Waltham, Mass., 1945.

Hyma, A., *The Dutch in the Far East: a History of the Dutch Commercial and Colonial Empire*, George Wahr, Ann Arbor, 1942.

Kennedy, Raymond, *The Ageless Indies*, Longmans, Green & Company, Toronto, 1942.

Kennedy, Raymond, *Islands and Peoples of the Indies*, Smithsonian Institution, Washington, D.C., 1943.

Nederlandsch Aardrijkskungige Genootschap, *Atlas Van Tropische Nederland*, Batavia, 1938.

Netherlands Indies Government, *100 Pages of Indonesian Economics*, Batavia, 1947.

Pelzer, K. J., *Population and Land Utilization, Economic Survey of the Pacific Area*, Institute of Pacific Relations, New York, 1941.

Sheltema, A. M. P. A., *The Food Consumption of the Native Inhabitants of Java and Madura*, Batavia, 1936.

Sitsen, P. H. W., *The Industrial Development of the Netherlands Indies*, New York, 1942.

Vandenbosch, A., *The Dutch East Indies: Its Government, Problems, and Politics*, University of California Press, Berkeley, 1941.

Van Gelderen, J. J., *The Recent Development of Economic Foreign Policy in the Netherlands East Indies*, Longmans, Green & Company, Toronto, 1939.

Van Valkenberg, S., "Java: the Economic Geography of a Tropical Island," *Geogr. Rev.*, Vol. XV, New York, 1925.

Vlekke, B. H. M., *Nusantara: a History of the East Indian Archipelago*, Harvard University Press, Cambridge, 1943.

Wickizer, V. D., and M. K. Bennett, *The Rice Economy of Monsoon Asia*, Stanford University, Food Research Institute, 1941.

17

The Kuril and Ryukyu Islands

WALTER R. HACKER

In giant steps the Asiatic continent descends to the floor of the Pacific Ocean. These steps are arranged in concentric zones from the Bering Sea to Indonesia. Built of the same material as the land mass, they indicate the breaking down into segments of the outer part of the continental mass against the resistant foundation of the Pacific basin. These broken blocks of the earth's crust have been tipped, with upswellings and volcanic extrusions occurring along their outer edges and compensative subsidence in their middle areas.

In the outermost zone the central depressions are completely submerged, and only the highest sections of the uplifted margins rise above the level of the sea. Like garlands fastened to the rim of the continent they form peninsulas and island chains encompassing marginal seas. Thus the Alaska Peninsula, the Aleutian, and the Komandorskie islands, separate the Bering Sea from the Pacific; a similar relationship exists between Kamchatka, the Kuril Islands, and the Sea of Okhotsk; Sakhalin, Hokkaido, Honshu, and the Sea of Japan; Korea, Kyushu, the Ryukyu Islands, and the East China Sea. These flooded basins with their elevated rims resemble huge sinter terraces around the mouth of a geyser.

Beyond the island festoons, the suture between the peripheral blocks and the floor of the Pacific basin is marked by a series of deep ocean trough. In the Tuscarora Deep of the Kuril Trench 28,000 feet have been sounded, the Ryukyu Trench off Okinawa is 24,700 feet in depth, and 34,800 feet have been sounded in the Ramapo Deep off the east coast of Honshu. Gravity determinations have shown that the entire zone is inside an area of incomplete isostatic adjustment. The ocean troughs are characterized by distinct mass deficiency whereas the islands are lying in a belt of positive isostatic anomaly. As a result, tectonic activity must be expected to be intensive. It finds its expression in the crowding of seismic epicenters, in the frequency of earthquakes, and in the volcanic nature of most of the islands.

FIGURE 143. Reproduction of an old map of the Kuril Islands, from Georg Wilhelm Steller, *Beschreibung von dem Lande Kamtschatke*, herausgegeben von J. B. S. (cherer), Johann G. Fleischer, Frankfort and Leipzig, 1774.

THE KURIL ISLANDS

Separating the Sea of Okhotsk from the Pacific Ocean, the Kuril Islands form the link between Kamchatka and Hokkaido. They consist of thirty-two islands and major rocks extending over a distance of about 650 miles (Fig. 144). Their area is about 2900 square miles. The northernmost island, Shimushu To, is separated by the Shimushu Kaikyo or Kuril Strait from Kamchatka; Nemuro Kaikyo separates the westernmost island, Kunashiri Shima, from Hokkaido. Table 1, arranged from north to south, gives the islands with their approximate area and the main volcanoes with their elevations.

RELIEF

With the exception of Shimushu To and the group of low flat islands
lying between the Nemuro Peninsula and Shikotan To, all the islands
are mountainous and of recent volcanic origin. Shimushu To consists
of the same sedimentary and metamorphic rocks as southwestern Kamchatka and belongs with it in the zone of Tertiary folds. No extrusive
material is to be found. In contrast with the other islands with their

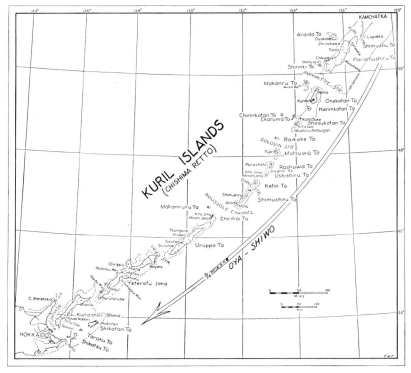

FIGURE 144. Map of Kuril Islands.

prominent volcanic cones, Shimushu does not rise above 623 feet.
Numerous little streams have sculptured its surface into low ridges,
and isolated hills are mainly covered with grass, scrub, and lichens.
Here and there patches of dwarfed willows, alders, and pines can be
found.

Kuril Strait, which separates Shimushu from Kamchatka, is about 6
miles wide, but rocks and reefs narrow the navigable channel to about
half that distance. The strait is very shallow and the tides set through

TABLE 1

KURIL ISLANDS

Islands	Area, Square Miles	Volcanoes	Elevation, Feet
Shimushu To*	89	. . . .	. . . .
Paramushiru To*	562	Taisho Dake†	3885
		Chikura Dake	5957
		Shiriyajiri†	5894
Araido To	46	Oyakoba Yama†	7654
Shirinki To	½	Shirinki Yama†	2459
Onekotan To	121	Nemo Dake	3344
		Kuroishi Yama†	4367
Makanru To	21	Makanru Dake	3830
Harimukotan To	16	Harimukotan†	3975
Shasukotan To	34	Kuro Dake†	3097
		Kita Iwo†	2707
Ekaruma To	5½	Ekaruma Dake†	3868
Chirinkotan To	1	Chirinkotan†	2418
Mushiru Retsugan	?	. . . .	. . . .
Raikoke To	1¼	Raikoke Dake†	1808
Matsuwa To	20	Fujo Dake†	4872
Rashuwa To	25	Porochoto Dake†	3137
Ushishiru To, Kita Jima Minami Jima	1½	Minami Jima D.†	1307
Ketoi To	35	Ketoi Dake†	3845
Shimushiru To	126	Shimushiru	4462
		Aron Dake†	1881
		Milne Mt.	5013
Chirihoi To, Black Brothers	7	Kita Fuji†	2265
		Minami Fuji	2496
Makanruru To, Buruton Jima	2	Makanruru Dake	2900
Uruppu To*	298	Uruppu Fuji†	4389
		Shirata Yama	4375
Yetorofu or Etorofu Jima*	930	Moyoro Yama†	3687
		Chirippu Yama†	5210
		Berutarube D.†	4008
Kunashiri Shima*	444	Chacha Dake	6051
		Rouse Nobori†	3005
Shikotan Shima*	70	. . . .	. . . .
Taraku To	4	. . . .	. . . .
Shibotsu Shima	17½	. . . .	. . . .
Yuri Shima	2½	. . . .	. . . .
Akiyuri Shima	½	. . . .	. . . .
Shuisho To	3½	. . . .	. . . .

* Inhabited.

† Active.

Glossary: Kaikyo, K., St. = strait; suido = channel; to, shima, jima = island; dake, D., **Yama, fuji** = mountain.

it at great speed, causing heavy rips over the shoals and along the reefs.

Of non-volcanic origin also is the group of islands that extend north-eastward from Cape Notsu (Noshap Zaki), the easternmost point of the Nemuro Peninsula. Like this peninsula and the adjacent section of Hokkaido, they represent remnants of abrasion surfaces at various levels that truncate folded Tertiary rocks. They were once connected with the mainland, but the waves made breaches and scoured out channels across the narrow tongue of land, forming five islands and numberless islets, reefs, and rocks.

An 11-mile wide channel, Shikotan Suido, separates the eastern-most of these islands from Shikotan To. Geologically, this island represents an intermediate type with recent volcanic rocks breaking through and covering in part the folded Mesozoic and Tertiary strata, but without any volcanic cones being preserved. Its highest elevation is a roundish-topped hill of basaltic rock near the northern coast rising 1211 feet above the sea. This classes Shikotan To as the lowest of all the volcanic islands. It differs from the others also in its much gentler relief, which makes it quite suitable for cattle raising. None of the other islands has an equally indented coastline. There are innumerable coves and bays, the larger of which form well-protected harbors for small fishing craft. Chief among these are the harbors of the fishing villages of Shakotan and Horobetsu on the north coast and Notoro on the southwest coast.

The main group of islands, from Araido To in the northeast to Kunashiri Shima in the southwest, is volcanic in origin and appearance. It is one of the most active and most recent volcanic zones on the earth. Out of more than forty volcanoes, twenty-two have been recorded as active to some degree. Activity varies from violent eruptions at short intervals with ejections of lava, rocks, ashes, and flames to a solfataric stage where only steam and gases are emitted. In general, the activity seems to have been decreasing in intensity in the last fifty years.

The volcanoes seem to be arranged at irregular intervals along sev-eral more or less parallel lines. At the northeastern end of the inner-most line lies the perfectly shaped cone of Oyakobe Dake, the loftiest peak in the Kuril Islands, which is 7654 feet high. To this same line belong the 2418-foot high Chirinkotan Dake, also reported active at some time, and the now-extinct lava domes of Makanru To and Makanruru To. Continuations of this inner zone are the volcanoes of the Shiretoko Peninsula of eastern Hokkaido. The volcanoes of the other lines rise either as individual cones above the sea, as do Shirinki

Yama, Ekaruma Dake, Raikoke Dake, and Minami Jima Dake in the Ushishiru group and Kita Juji in the Chirihoi group, or are connected by lava flows and other volcanic sediments to form larger islands. On the largest islands, Yetorofu Jima, Paramushiru To, Kunashiri Shima, and Uruppu To, the volcanoes rest upon an erosion surface of andesitic and besaltic rocks. Where low and narrow landbridges of sedimentary rocks connect two volcanic cones, the islands so formed assume the typical shape of a "ladyfinger," as Shasukotan To. Ocean currents have contributed to the building of these islands by carrying the loose sands and ashes from shore to shore.

The younger volcanoes have not yet been greatly modified by surface erosion and are of regular conical shape. To this type belong the islands of Chirinkotan, Ekaruma, and Raikoke, among others. Along the shores the surf has carved steep cliffs and bizarre forms out of the poorly consolidated material. Some of the smallest islands seem to be just starting their rise above the sea in a beginning stage of their formation. Other groups of rocks, like Avos Rocks, Srednoi Rocks, and Mushiru Rocks, may be interpreted as mere ruins of former cones destroyed by violent explosions and the work of the sea.

Sometimes secondary cones are rising out of old craters, for example, Chacha Dake (St. Anthony's Peak, 6050 feet) on Kunashiri Shima, which is the second highest peak in the islands, and Kuroishi Yama (Blakiston Peak, 4367 feet) on southern Onekotan To. Broughton Bay, at the northeastern end of Shimushiru To, is a volcanic caldera. The sea breached the rim of the caldera and created a crescent-shaped basin connected only by a narrow passage with the open water. The secondary cone of the volcano, Uratman, protrudes on the eastern side of the bay.

At the western end of the island chain, Kunashiri Shima extends into the wide bay formed by the two peninsulas, Shiretoko and Nemuro, of eastern Hokkaido. Nemuro Strait is 8 to 16 miles wide, but continuously shifting sand banks and frequent fogs are a hazard to navigation. Across the deep 12-mile wide Kunashiri Suido lies the largest and most important island of the whole group, Yetorofu Jima.

On these two last-named islands volcanic features are least pronounced and fluvial-erosion forms predominate. On Kunashiri Shima the volcano, Rouse Nobori (3005 feet), has been observed in eruption, but at present only hot springs and fumeroles issue from its base. Sulphur deposits in its ruined crater had been worked in the past but are now exhausted. Other sulphur deposits occur on the shores of Lake Ponto on the west coast. On Yetorofu Jima, three volcanoes have been reported as active: Moyoro Yama (3689 feet) at the northeastern end of the island, Chirippu Yama (5210 feet) on the west coast, and Berutarube Dake (4008 feet) in the south. At the foot of Berutarube Dake sulphur had also been mined for some time. Filling the space between these peaks and many extinct volcanoes, there are, on both islands, large stretches of low, well-timbered ridges, separated by broad swampy valleys. Along the coast traces of marine terraces can be seen.

The only large indentation in the coast of Kunashiri Shima is the bay of Tonari at the southwest end of the island. The bay offers suitable anchorage for the fishing vessels that visit the island during the summer months. The coast of Yetorofu Jima, on the other hand, is characterized by several deep bays formed by protruding volcanic cones, mainly on the northern side of the island; namely, Naibo Wan, Rubetsu Wan, Shana Wan, and Bira Wan, named for the main settlements on those bays. The chief harbor and the administrative center of the island is Shana, with a permanent population of several hundred persons that is greatly increased during the fishing season. None of the bays are well sheltered, but they offer a fair protection during the summer months when the prevailing winds and comparative freedom from fog make this coast the leeward side of the island. The best anchorage, particularly during the winter months, is provided by the deep, 6-mile-wide Hittokappu Bay on the southwest side of the island. It was here that the Japanese fleet assembled in December, 1941.

CLIMATE

In latitude, the Kuril Islands span from 51° North at Kuril Strait to 43½° North at Nemuro Channel. But the climate of the islands is controlled to a lesser degree by latitude than by the fact that they are situated on the western side of the Pacific and in proximity to the largest of all land masses. In such a location, the definite seasonal change in the direction of the prevailing winds and the presence of a cold ocean current alongside the islands become the decisive climatic factors.

The importance of these factors in producing a severe climate is best shown by comparing the climate of the Kuril Islands with that of other areas lying in the same latitude. Although the contrast between both sides of the Pacific is great, it becomes remarkable when the western side of the Eurasian continent is compared with the eastern side. Whereas the Kuril Islands have a subarctic climate (*Dfc* of the Köppen system) that makes them a marginal area for human habitation, France experiences mild winters in its marine west-coast climate. (See Table 2.) In the latitude of Kunashiri one may enjoy in Europe the subtropical mediterranean climate of the Italian and French Riviera. The two columns representing the Eurasian continent graphically illustrate what is probably the greatest climatic difference between any areas situated in the same latitude.

TABLE 2

COMPARISON OF CLIMATES IN SAME LATITUDE

Lat., N		West Eurasia East		West North America East		Lat., N
		British Isles, *Cfb*	Kamchatka, *Dfc*	British Columbia, *Cfb*	Labrador, *Dfc*		
51°		Strait of Dover	Kuril Strait	Queen Charlotte Sound	Strait of Belle Isle		51°
	Atlantic Ocean	France, *Cfb,* *Csa*	Kuril Island, *Dfc*	Pacific Ocean	Vancouver Island ⎫ Washington ⎬ *Cfb,* Northern ⎪ *Csb* Oregon ⎭	Newfoundland ⎫ Nova Scotia ⎬ *Dfb* Maine ⎭	Atlantic Ocean	
43½°		French Riviera	Nemuro Channel	Coos Bay, Oregon	Portland, Maine		43½°
		Mediterra- nean, *Csa*	Japan, *Cfb,* *Dfb, Cfa*	California, *Csb*	Southeastern United States, *Cfb*		

In winter the weather is dominated by the almost constantly blowing monsoon winds and by the frequent occurrence of cyclonic storms. Because of the Aleutian low in the east-northeast, the midwinter isobars cross the islands generally in a meridional direction. As a result, from October until March, the prevailing winds blow from the northwest, bringing cold air from the continent. Gales are quite frequent.

Having picked up moisture while blowing across the Sea of Okhotsh, the winter monsoons cause heavy and frequent precipitation on the islands, particularly on their windward side. From the end of October until the end of April or early May, the precipitation is mainly in the form of snow or graupel. Snow cover is present from November until April. The heaviest snowfalls are caused by the cyclonic storms, which come from North China and Manchuria and pass across the islands in great numbers during the winter months. Great wind velocities are common during these cyclonic disturbances.

With the weakening and retreat of the continental anticyclone the prevailing winds change gradually, during April and early May, from a westerly to a southerly and finally to a east-southeasterly direction. In contrast to the winter monsoons, the summer monsoons are much more moderate in force and constitute by themselves no hazard for navigation. Also gales are very infrequent during the summer months.

The chief difficulty for navigation along and between the islands in summer is the dense fog that shrouds the islands almost continuously during the height of this season. As a result there is little sunshine in summer, particularly on the Pacific side, and the air temperature is greatly depressed. Shana has only three months with mean temperatures over 50° F, Table 3, and an August average of only 66° F, although it lies on the Sea of Okhotsk and experiences, even in summer, days with bright sunshine. The summer fog is caused by the cold Oya-Shiwo Kamchatka current that undercuts the warm southeasterly monsoon laden with moisture.

Table 3 gives the more important climatic data for Shana on the northwestern shore of Yetorofu Jima. It must, however, be borne in mind that Shana has, because of its favorable location, about the mildest climate of any spot in the Kuril Islands and cannot be considered as representative of the climate of the islands as a whole. With only 3 months over 10° C and 4 months under 1° C, Shana, and with it the rest of the Kuril Islands, has a humid subarctic climate or a *Dfc* climate in Köppen's classification.

TABLE 3

CLIMATIC DATA FOR SHANA, YETOROFU JIMA (1903–1929)

(Temperature in ° C)

	Year	Jan.	Feb.	Mar.	Apr.	May	June	July	Aug.	Sept.	Oct.	Nov.	Dec.
Mean air temperature	4.2	5.5	7.0	4.6	1.4	5.2	9.2	13.7	15.8	13.3	8.8	3.0	2.3
Mean max. temp.	7.9	2.7	3.8	0.9	5.1	9.6	13.5	17.9	19.9	17.4	12.5	6.1	0.4
Mean min. temp.	0.4	8.7	10.9	8.8	2.1	1.0	4.9	9.8	11.8	9.0	4.5	0.4	5.3
Absolute max. temp.	30.8	8.6	8.8	11.5	21.3	24.0	27.3	30.7	30.8	26.7	20.9	17.6	12.2
Absolute min. temp.	24.6	23.2	24.6	24.5	12.4	6.1	3.7	1.5	1.1	1.2	4.1	8.6	15.1
Relative humidity	82	82	84	83	80	80	85	88	88	83	78	77	77
Cloudiness*	7.8	9.0	8.3	7.3	7.3	7.5	7.4	8.0	7.5	7.1	7.1	8.6	9.0
Precipitation, mm.	1031	94	54	62	65	78	59	74	99	97	111	131	108
Number rainy days	224	27	20	18	15	15	13	16	14	16	19	25	28

* Percentage of sky covered on a scale from 1 to 10.

VEGETATION

The climatic classification given for the Kurils applies only to the lower elevations of the islands, whereas the higher slopes rise above the climatic timberline with the temperature of the warmest month remaining below 10° C. But even with summer temperatures high enough to permit growth of trees, timberland is, nevertheless, very scarce and limited to a few localities. Only on the 4 larger islands in the south are the more protected hillsides covered with groves of trees. The species are, in general, identical with those found on Kamchatka: spruces and some larches mixed with birches, aspen, and mountain ashes; willows and alders along the streams are also characteristic for this subarctic forest.

In places the species cross the timberline in stunted and dwarfed forms and invade the tundra zone of the higher elevations, where they are found in association with the dwarf stone pine (*Pinus pumila*) amidst the short grasses, lichens, and mosses.

Various kinds of sedges, rushes, and grasses are found on the swampy floors of the valleys among dense growths of the short bamboo grass, sasa. The low shrubs of the ericaceous genera,*Vaccinium, Andromeda,* and *Chamaedaphne,* are quite common, and their berries are a very important food item for wild animals and birds. In early summer the somberness of the landscape is mitigated by the arrival of a number of wild flowers like buttercups, forget-me-nots, daisies, pinks, lilies, irises, and several others.

The wind-swept slopes along the shores are covered with a dense shrubby vegetation that, in places, is almost impenetrable. Umbelliferous plants predominate, associated with ferns and species of the nettle, pea, rose, and sunflower families, among others.

Captain H. G. Snow, commenting upon the vast fields of kelp that entangle the islands, says that probably in no other part of the world is there a greater luxuriance in the growth of seaweed. Some of the islands are surrounded by an unbroken belt of floating forests of algae a mile wide and reaching down about 18 fathoms (108 feet). Red and green algae are represented, but most numerous are various types of giant brown algae of the families Laminariaceae and Fucaceae, which sometimes measure 140 to 150 feet in length. They develop very rapidly in early summer and attain their fullest growth in July. But by the end of August much of it has been broken off, and large quantities are thrown up on the shore and rot on the beaches or drift off with the currents. These kelp beds have been the favorite resort of the sea otter because, here, they could find abundant food and refuge in stormy weather since the force of the winds is broken over the kelp patches. In summer Japanese fishermen gather seaweed from the vicinity of the islands in the south, dry it on the beaches, and ship it to Japan and to China where, under the name of K'un-pu, it is used as a source of iodine and potash, and in the preparation of some medicines.

ANIMAL LIFE OF SEA AND LAND

The chief economical value of the Kuril Islands at one time was in the sea otter and seal fisheries. Sea otters (*Latax lutris* or *Enhydra lutris* a, monotypic genus), once existed in great numbers about the reefs and kelp beds all along the island chain. The furs of the sea otter were famous for their fine quality, and they brought high prices. By indiscriminate hunting the animals have been all but killed off or driven away. They are now so rare and so difficult to approach that commercial hunting has not paid since the end of the nineteenth century.

The northern fur seal (*Arctocephalus ursinus* or *Callorhinus alascanus*) experienced a similar fate. In the seventies of the nineteenth century it was estimated that as many as 30,000 seals each summer frequented the rookeries on Mushiru Retsugan, Raikoke To, and Srednoi Rock in Suride Kaikyo. They congregated in June and would remain until October, when the first heavy snow would drive them away. After several years of indiscriminate slaughter the seals abandoned the rookeries, and they are now so rare that hunting is seldom profitable.

With the sea otters and the fur seals driven off, the sea lions (*Eumetopias stelleri*) remain as the only occupants of the islands rookeries. They visit the breeding grounds every summer in great numbers up to 100,000 or more, and their habits are similar to those of the fur seal. But they are, at present, of no commercial value.

Very common all along the islands are the hair seals (*Phoca vitulina*). In contrast to the sea lions and the fur seals, the hair seals do not associate in rookeries, but lie alone or in small groups on low rocks or rocky ledges. They are of little commercial value and are rarely hunted.

Whales and porpoises visited the Kuril Islands in the past in great numbers, the bays and straits being favorite feeding grounds for them. Of the dolphin family, Delphinidae, killer whales (*Orcinus orca*) and black whales (*Globiocephala melas*) have been extensively hunted for their bones, oil, skin, and blubber. Among the toothless whales (suborder Mysticeti), the right whale (*Balaena japonica*) is only occasionally encountered offshore; the blue whale (*Balaenoptera musculus*), the sulphur-bottom whale (*B. sulphureus*), the humpback whale (*Megoptera nodosa*), and the gray-back whale (*Rachionectes glaucus*) were once very common about the coasts of the islands and have been extensively hunted for their blubber and "whalebone."

There are only a few species of land mammals native on the Kuril Islands, but among them several kinds that yield excellent furs. On Shimushu To and Paramushiru To, black and brown varieties of the Kamchatka bear (*Ursus arcticos*) were formerly quite numerous, but are very scarce nowadays. On the same islands and on Onekotan To lemmings occur in great numbers, and in places the ground is honeycombed by the holes burrowed by these small rodents. Several varieties of foxes are still very plentiful on most of the islands. The foxes of the northern islands are identical with those of Kamchatka and have very fine furs. Those of the southern islands are the same as those on Hokkaido, but their furs are of poorer quality. The richest mammalian fauna is to be found on Yetorofu Jima and Kunashiri Shima. Bears, foxes, land otters, wolves, martens, sables, hares, and squirrels existed in great numbers and were much hunted. It was in search of these valuable furs that the Japanese and Russian traders penetrated into the islands. Most of these animals are now very rare, and the fur trade is of little importance.

The Kuril Islands are rich in number and species of birds. The greatest number of land birds is found on the southern islands, which are wooded and offer an abundant supply of insects and berries. Woodpeckers, swallows, swifts, wagtails, wrens, crows, falcons, and eagles are among the most common. Ground-breeding birds like the puffins, auks, and guillemots are prevalent on the islands of the central group, especially on those that do not have land mammals. They arrive in late spring and leave in early fall. Most common of all the birds is the burgomaster gull. Found breeding on all the islands, it is a veritable bird of prey, not only feeding on fish and small birds but also stealing the eggs of other birds, especially those of the guillemot.

Although to a lesser degree than on Sakhalin, a number of birds, like ducks, geese, swans, divers, and others, stop at the Kuril Islands, a station in their migratory route to breeding grounds farther north.

The greatest economic wealth of the Kuril Islands lies in their fish and fisheries. The streams of the islands teem with salmon and salmon trouts at certain seasons while the shelf zone around the northern and southern islands belong to the richest fishing grounds on earth. Vast shoals of herring and sardines pass, at times, over these banks, whereas cod, halibut, and rockfish belong to the most common types which can be fished all year. Since the water around the central island group is very deep and the ocean floor is sandy and rocky, there are particularly no fish in this area. Canneries exist in several islands, the largest ones on Paramushiru To and Shikotan Shima. Work in these canneries brings several thousand Japanese to the islands during the summer. In winter the fishing fleets operate mostly from harbors on Hokkaido.

THE INHABITANTS

Before the arrival of Japanese settlers, most of the islands were settled by a native population known as the Kuril Ainu. They lived in small hamlets along the shores and on the banks of the streams, gaining their subsistence by hunting land animals and birds with bow and arrow, catching fish in the streams and coastal waters, killing sea otter and seals for their meat and skins; they supplemented their diet with bird eggs, berries, roots, and mussels. The contents of sea otter intestines, when stewed, were considered a delicacy. Their clothes were made of birdskins, seal hides, and other furs, and of a coarse material made from tree bark. They had no domesticated animals except the dog. The Ainu, in spite of lacking some of the higher cultural elements, did possess a plank boat lashed with whale sinew.

The inhabitants of the southern islands closely resembled the Ainu of Hokkaido; those of the northern islands showed more Mongoloid features, suggesting a mixture with the Aleuts and the peoples of Kamchatka. They had, however, preserved in their culture a number of elements that seem to indicate that they came originally from more southern regions. In contrast to their northern neighbors, the Ainu are not fond of raw seafood, oil, or blubber, but prefer the meat of land animals and birds. More of them are hunters than fishermen.

Contact with their new masters, the Russian and the Japanese, quickly reduced the number of the Kuril Ainu and their racial vigor. Strong liquor, small pox, syphilis were as devastating here as in many other territories. There are only a few hundred natives left on the islands; most of them work in Japanese canneries.

DISCOVERY AND OWNERSHIP

Nothing was known in the western world of the islands north of Japan proper before the seventeenth century. It is doubtful that the Japanese themselves had, at this time, anything more than very vague information about the islands. In 1643, the Dutch East India Company sent an expedition north of Japan under the command of Maerten Gerritszoon Vries. He discovered Sakhalin and the islands that are now known as the Kurils. Shortly afterwards, Russian Cossacks, coming from the north along the coast of Kamchatka, learned of the existence of the islands. They gave the islands their present name, which is probably derived from the word "kurit," to smoke. By the end of the seventeenth century Russian fur traders had established stations on Kamchatka and had come in contact with the natives of the adjacent islands. In 1729 Vitus Bering sailed the St. Gabriel through the Kuril Strait on his way back to Okhotsk. In the *Beschreibung von dem Lande Kamtschatka* George Wilhelm Steller in 1774 gave the first description of the Kuril Islands. He said that the natives of these islands spoke a language unlike Japanese or the language of the Itelmi of Kamchatka.

The Japanese seem to have been rather reluctant to extend their rule over the islands. By the end of the eighteenth century they claimed only the three southern islands, Shikotan Shima, Kunashiri Shima, Etorofu Jima, as part of their domain. The northern islands, on the other hand, were exploited by the Russian-American Company. In 1795 this company had established a station on Uruppu To and, in 1830, took formal possession of the northern and central islands and put them under Russian protection. In 1873 Japan turned Sakhalin over to the Russians and obtained in exchange the whole of the Kuril Island group. The Japanese gave the islands the name Chi Shima, which means Thousand Islands. At the conclusion of the Second World War the Russians came into possession of the islands as far south as Etorofu Jima; Shikotan Shima and Kunashiri Shima remained under Japanese control.

THE RYUKYU ISLANDS[1]

Separating the East China Sea from the Pacific Ocean, the Ryukyu Islands extend over a distance of about 650 miles between Taiwan and Kyushu. The islands are arranged in a wide arc between the 24th and 30th parallels, with an average distance of 500 miles from the China coast (Fig. 145). Not all the islands between Taiwan and Kyushu are considered as belonging to the Ryukyu Retto.[2] The northern-most islands, the Osumi Gunto, are, by tradition, a part of Japan proper and are included in the Kagoshima prefecture of Kyushu. Tokara Kaikyo or Colnett Strait, 75 miles south of Kyushu, becomes the northern boundary of the Ryukyus. On the southwestern end of the chain, a 75-mile stretch of water separates Yonaguni Shima from the coast of Taiwan.

Japanese maps show fifty-five islands in the Ryukyu Retto, covering an area of about 1300 square miles. The islands are arranged in three groups, northern, central, and southern, separated by broad straits. There is, however, no consistency in naming these groups and their

---

[1] Ryukyu is the Japanese transcription of the two characters used in writing the name of the islands. The Chinese transcription would be Liu-ch'iu. Both characters refer to precious stones and have been chosen by Chinese literati to represent phonetically the name under which the islands are known by the natives. Other spellings, however, like Riukiu, Liukiu, Lewchew, Loochoo, Luchu, are also frequently found in literature. Englebert Kaempfer wrote, in 1690, of the Riuku or Liquejo Islands. Another Japanese name for the islands, introduced more recently, is Nansei Retto or Southwestern Islands.

[2] Retto, like gunto and shoto, means archipelago, group, cluster, chain, string of islands.

subdivisions. The more commonly used names of the subdivisions and of the major islands in each group are given in Table 4, together with their highest elevation and the areas of the larger islands. The Tokara Retto and Amami Gunto belong to the Kagoshima prefecture; the Okinawa and Saki Shima Gunto constitute the Okinawa prefecture, with the city of Naha on Okinawa as the administrative seat.

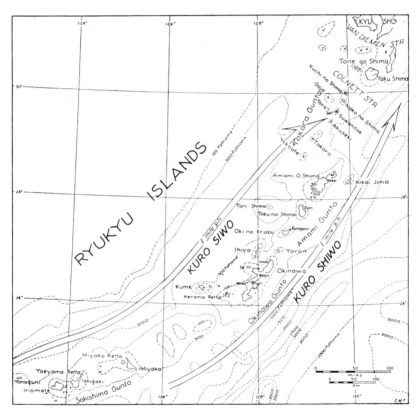

FIGURE 145. Map of Ryukyu Islands.

Geologically, the islands fall into three more or less parallel zones. The inner zone consists of recent volcanic material, lavas, and ashes, with each volcanic cone rising as an individual island above the sea. All the islands of the Tokara Retto, plus the Bird Island or Tori Shima in the Amami Gunto, belong in this category. Three of them, Nakano, Suwanose, and Akuseki, are active volcanoes; the first two mentioned are the highest elevations in the Ryukyu group. These volcanoes are comparatively small and low, but steep slopes and an abrupt rise from the ocean make them impressive landmarks. This volcanic zone finds its continuation in the Kaimon volcanic region of southern Kyushu.

TABLE 4

THE RYUKYU RETTO

			Elevation, Feet
Northern Ryukyu, or Tokara Retto, or Linschoten Islands		Kuchino Shima	2066
		Nakano Shima	3215
		Suwanose Shima	2621
		Akuseki Shima	1926
Central Ryukyu	Amami Gunto	Kikai Shima	692
		O Shima (310 square miles)	2297
		Tori Shima	264
		Takuno Shima	2113
		Okino Erabu Shima	807
	Okinawa Gunto	Okinawa Shima (510 square miles)	1650
		Ie Shima	
		Tori Shima	77
		Kume Shima	1070
		Kerama Retto	
Southern Ryukyu, or Saki Shima Gunto	Miyako Retto	Miyako Shima	378
	Yaeyama Retto	Ishigaki Shima (94 square miles)	1726
		Ioiomoto Shima (118 square miles)	1542
		Yonaguni Shima	

Gneiss, schists, phyllites, and other Paleozoic metamorphic rocks predominate in the folded mountains of the central zone. Submergence left the summits of the mountain belt to form most of the islands of the Amami Gunto and the Okinawa Gunto groups. The islands are more hilly than mountainous and only a few of them rise above 2000 feet. As in most of the Ryukyu Islands, suitable agricultural land is at a minimum. Thus marine terraces, stretches of level land between the rolling hills, and the gentler hillsides themselves are intensively cultivated.

The third zone is, in general, built of Tertiary rocks, most commonly uplifted coral limestone. Okinawa consists partially of these Tertiary limestones that become the dominant rock in the southern Ryukyu. Ishigaki and Ioiomoto Shima are very hilly and possess only little level land. Miyako Shima is the lowest and flattest of all the major islands, but, being built mainly of porous limestone and having no mountains to catch the rain and give rise to streams, Miyako Shima suffers from a scarcity of surface water that is a serious handicap for agriculture. As a result, the whole Saki Shima group is thinly populated.

It is of major importance for the topography and the cultural development of the islands that the February isotherm of 20° C (68° F) for the surface water crosses the Ryukyu Islands in the vicinity of Amami O Shima. As a consequence, coral reefs partly surround the islands of the central group. All the islands of the southern group are almost entirely encircled by reefs, which make an approach extremely difficult. The islands of the Tokara group, which are more easily accessible, offer little or no incentive for human occupation.

CLIMATE

Meteorological data are given in Table 5 for two weather stations in the Central Ryukyu Islands, for which observations over a long period of years have been made, Nase, on O Shima, and Naha, on Okinawa. To judge from data available for southern Kyushu and northern Taiwan, the northern Ryukyu and most, if not all, of the islands of the Saki Shima group fall into the same climatic province. There is, however, the possibility that some of the southernmost islands lie within the tropical climate belt. Farther out in the Pacific Ocean, the northern boundary of the tropical climate belt swings somewhat poleward, as is to be expected. There is a small island about 430 miles east of Ishigaki Shima and, in the same latitude, with the name of Oki Daito Shima or Rasa Island, for which observations over a period of three years are available. With an average temperature for the coolest month of 19.3° C (66.7° F) this island falls definitely into the tropics classification.

The Ryukyu Islands have a pronounced warm and cool season, although the cool season can hardly be called a winter. Owing to the distance of the islands from the continent, the winters are, on the average, 6° C warmer, in corresponding latitudes, than on the coast of China. Snow-covered mountains are a familiar sight in Chekiang, but snow and hore frost are unknown in these islands.

From October until the beginning of April, the winter monsoon blows over the islands with northerly wind directions prevailing. The force of the winds is in general strong, and they are heavily laden with moisture. At Nase, rain showers occur in winter on the average of two out of three days, and the percentage of sky obscured by clouds is extremely high. Frequently the winds assume gale force and may blow for days in undiminished fury. As a result, the sea around the islands is usually rough in this season, and sailing between the islands and north to Kyushu is hazardous.

TABLE 5
METEOROLOGICAL DATA FOR THE CENTRAL RYUKYU ISLANDS
(Temperatures, °C. Precipitation, mm.)
NASE, O SHIMA (1897–1926)

	Year	Jan.	Feb.	Mar.	Apr.	May	June	July	Aug.	Sept.	Oct.	Nov.	Dec.
Mean temp.	20.8	14.3	14.2	16.2	19.4	21.8	25.3	27.4	27.5	26.0	22.7	19.3	15.9
Mean max. temp.	24.4	17.6	17.3	19.6	22.9	25.7	28.9	31.2	31.2	29.8	26.4	22.7	19.2
Mean min. temp.	17.7	11.2	11.2	13.0	16.1	18.5	22.3	24.2	24.4	23.0	19.5	16.2	12.8
Precipitation	3169	200	211	211	261	320	407	246	332	269	306	231	176
Rainy days	237	23	21	20	19	19	20	18	20	20	19	17	2

NAHA, OKINAWA (1916–1925)

	Year	Jan.	Feb.	Mar.	Apr.	May	June	July	Aug.	Sept.	Oct.	Nov.	Dec.
Mean temp.	22.2	15.8	16.1	17.7	21.0	23.3	27.0	28.3	28.1	26.7	24.0	20.8	17.6
Mean max. temp.	25.5	19.2	19.5	21.2	24.4	26.7	30.2	31.8	31.2	29.9	27.3	24.2	20.8
Mean min. temp.	18.8	12.4	12.6	14.1	17.5	19.9	23.8	24.8	24.9	23.4	20.7	17.3	14.3
Precipitation	1960	139	123	151	132	259	202	185	186	174	162	135	112
Rainy days	171	17	17	19	17	18	16	9	9	8	10	15	16

RASA ISLAND (1923, 1925, 1926)

	Year	Jan.	Feb.	Mar.	Apr.	May	June	July	Aug.	Sept.	Oct.	Nov.	Dec.
Mean temp.	24.0	19.4	19.3	20.4	22.2	25.0	26.5	28.6	28.8	28.0	25.9	23.9	20.5
Mean max. temp.	26.8	22.7	23.8	23.9	25.5	28.0	29.2	30.7	30.3	29.6	28.0	26.3	23.9
Mean min. temp.	20.8	15.8	15.6	16.6	18.5	21.2	23.4	26.1	25.9	25.2	22.7	21.2	17.1
Precipitation	1297	108	56	79	105	74	161	104	114	285	93	66	52
Rainy days	178	15	13	13	13	16	17	18	15	18	14	13	13

In late spring the islands come under the regime of the summer monsoon. The prevailing winds change to a southerly and southeasterly direction, bringing warm and humid air from the Pacific. There are, in general, fewer rainy days in summer; cloudiness is also markedly less. But summer is also the main season for typhoons that sweep over the islands each year in great numbers, causing heavy damage to trees, buildings, and shore installations. Because of these storms the summer precipitation exceeds that of any other season. During one day of a typical typhoon storm, 262 millimeters (10.3 inches) of precipitation were measured at Naha.

With winter month averages dropping below 18° C (64.4° F) the islands have a humid subtropical climate (*Cfa* in the Köppen system);

only the highest elevations rise into the *Cfb* zone, with summer month averages remaining below 22° C (71.6° F).

FLORA AND FAUNA

The mild winters and abundant rainfall throughout the year bring about a luxuriant growth of plants handicapped only in the smaller islands by the nearness of the sea. Since the hilly nature of the islands limits the expansion of land under cultivation, there are still large areas of native vegetation preserved.

Owing to the moderate height of the islands, there are no distinct vegetation life zones discernible. More conspicuous are variations caused by differences in the type of bedrock, particularly between the limestone and the shale and schist areas.

A characteristic plant association will be found along the sea cliffs and sandy beaches, consisting of various palms, cycads, woody and herbaceous vines, a large number of succulent plants, grasses, sedges, and others. Along the shores of the southernmost islands stretches of mangrove forests exist.

The Ryukyu Islands have, for a long time, served as a bridge over which plants migrate between Taiwan and the Japanese Islands. As a result, the native flora of the islands presents a composite picture, having many elements in common with Japan, Taiwan, and, through Taiwan, with South China. But there are also noticeable differences among the floras of these areas. The islands do not share with Taiwan plants that are distinctly tropical nor representatives of the high mountain flora. There are also a number of endemic species that are either limited to the group as a whole or to individual islands.

The heavily wooded areas of the Ryukyu Islands are of the mixed subtropical monsoon forest type, composed of conifers, evergreen and deciduous broad-leaf trees, a number of palms, various species of bamboo, several members of the banana family, and numerous ferns and tree ferns. The most common coniferous tree is the Ryukyu matsu (*Pinus luchuensis*, Mayr.), which is found on most of the islands. Perhaps the most conspicuous element in the native flora is the so-called sago palm (*Cycas revulata*, Thunb.), which reaches its northern limit here. There exists in places a dense shrub and undergrowth vegetation, in the composition of which sumacs, rhododendrons, camellias, barberries, *Ficus*, the shrubbery calamus palm, various bamboos, ferns, and tree ferns have an important part.

In contrast to the rich plant life, the fauna of the islands is extremely poor in number of species. The mammals are represented by rats and bats and, on the larger islands, by boars and deer. The majority of the islands, however, are infested with a deadly poisonous snake, called habu, which claims many victims every year.

INHABITANTS

Engelbert Kaempfer, in 1691, made the following remarks about the Ryukyu islanders: "The inhabitants which are for the most part either husbandmen or fishermen, are a good natured merry sort of people, leading an agreeable contented life, diverting themselves, after their work is done, with a glass of rice beer, and playing upon their musical instruments, which they for this purpose carry out with them into their field." Commander Perry, in 1853, called these people "industrious and inoffensive," and found "these islands . . . . fertile beyond measure . . . as pleasant as any in the world."

According to recent visitors to the islands, the character of the people has not changed. The problem of making a living, however, became much more difficult. By natural growth and immigration the population of the islands has greatly increased since then while the production of food has not kept up with the home demand.

There are about 570,000 souls living in the Ryukyu Islands, a remarkably large number considering the smallness of the islands and the limited amount of arable land. Since there exist only minor industrial establishments that can provide the islanders with employment, and since trade with the outside world is very well, three quarters of the population have to derive their living from agriculture. The rural density, therefore, is very high, and the holdings of an individual family is, on the average, less than two acres. In the past many farmers secured additional income, which could be spent to buy more foodstuffs, by home manufacturing, the products of which could readily be sold on the home market and even exported to China and Japan. Home industry in the islands has suffered greatly in competition with machine goods manufactured in Japan.

As a result of these changes, the islands have ceased to be self-supporting, and an increasing number of islanders have been forced to emigrate each year to Japan to look for work in industry and trade. Another obstacle in the way of securing a sufficient amount of food is the fact that the islanders are, by tradition and preference, rather poor fishermen. This seems to refute Kaempfers statement to the contrary. The hazards that the coral reefs present to fishermen in the waters around the islands are perhaps responsible for this character trait.

The Ryukyu islanders, however, are excellent farmers. Wherever suitable land could be found they have taken it under intensive cultivation. Agriculture is carried on in terraced fields, and great care is taken to keep the terraces and irrigation ditches in good·condition. In the absence of sufficient animal dung, human excreta are diligently collected and returned to the fields, as is done in China. This regular application of manure has preserved and frequently improved the original fertility of the soil. In contrast to the dark humus-rich loams of the paddy fields, commented upon by many an observer, the uncultivated hillsides are covered by a much-leached reddish laterite.

AGRICULTURE

The subtropical climate of the islands permits the growing of a great variety of food plants. The need to feed a dense population

Figure 146. Village in Okinawa. Official U.S. Navy Photograph.

has taught the islanders to select those plants and to evolve those techniques of agriculture that enable them to realize the largest possible yield from the land. More than two-thirds of the arable land are given to the cultivation of the three staple crops—sweet potato, rice, and sugar cane. The sugar cane, which is being grown predominantly as a cash crop, has increased its acreage at the expense of rice to meet the rising cash outlays of the farmer. However, because of primitive methods of preparation and the competition from Taiwan, the amount exported is small.

More acreage is used for sweet potatoes than for rice because of the hilly nature of the islands and the rather common occurrence of permeable subsoils that do not hold the water for paddies but are very suitable for tuberous crops. The yield in bushels per acre and the caloric value per acre of the sweet potato are higher than for any other crop. The sweet potato exceeds rice in bushels per acre at a ratio of about 8–1. As in other areas of dense population, sweet potatoes are now grown in fields previously planted with rice or are grown in rotation with rice. Since the sweet potato has a lower protein content than rice, a protein deficiency is frequently observed in

FIGURE 147.   An Okinawa family in the village
of Taria.   Official U.S. Navy Photograph.

these areas. To remedy this deficiency, more beans and peanuts should be grown. By a combination of these crops the highest possible food value per acre can be obtained. This practice is also followed in the Ryukyu Islands, where increasing amounts of green beans and peanuts are planted in rotation with rice and sweet potatoes.

The winters are mild enough so that two rice crops can be obtained. The first crop is planted in the seed beds as early as February or March. Two weeks to a month later, the transplanting of the seedlings into the well-prepared and fertilized paddy fields takes place. This crop can be harvested in June or July, and at about the same time the seedlings of the second crop are transplanted. The second crop, harvested in November or December, is frequently followed by a crop of tubers or leafy vegetables.

None of the cultivated tubers native in southeast Asia, like the Chinese yam (*Dioscorea batatas*) and the Chinese taro (*Sagittaria sagittifolia*), have the high nutritional value of the sweet potato; they are nevertheless frequently planted, partly by tradition, partly for their particular flavor. In addition, the roots of the lotus (*Nelumbo nucifera*), water chestnuts (*Eleocharis tuberosus*), water plantains (*Alisma plantago*), and the fruits of the water caltrop (*Trapa bicornis*) are obtained from permanent ponds not readily drained for the rice fields. Other vegetables commonly grown in small quantities by individual farmers are radishes, turnips, melons, and eggplants. Cooking oil is pressed from the seeds of rape, and sago is obtained from the pith of the cycas. Bamboo yields edible shoots and material for building and for all kinds of utensils.

With most of the farmer's time and labor spent for the production of staple foods, little attention is given to fruit trees although a great variety of them can be grown on the islands. There exist no well-tended orchards, but some kinds of fruit trees are found around most homesteads. Characteristic fruits grown on the islands are: bananas, Chinese pears (*Pyrus pyrifolia*), Japanese persimmons (*Diospyros kaki*), loquats (*Eriobotrya japonica*), kumquats (*Fortunella japonica*), lichees (*Litchi chinensis*), longans (*Euphoria longana*), Chinese dates (*Ziziphus jujuba*), and Buddha's hands (*Citrus medica var. sarcodactylis*). The fruits of the Chinese olive tree (*Canarium album*) are eaten as a vegetable, and a cooking oil is pressed from the seeds. Preserved fruits, either dried or prepared with syrups or molasses, are eaten as confection and also exported to Japan. Tobacco is planted in small patches. Rows of tea bushes are grown along the trails and on the reddish soils of the hillsides. But there is also an import of better-grade tea from Formosa.

Primitive liquor stills are a common sight on the islands, where a variety of distilled beverages are produced. Sake is made by distilling malted and fermented rice mash. Arrack is prepared from cane-sugar molasses and by distilling toddy obtained from the unopened inflorescences of various palms. Other liquors are made from fermented fruit juices, especially banana juices.

ANIMAL INDUSTRIES

It is only natural that under the crowded conditions on the islands domesticated animals have been secondary sources of food. Most common are hogs, ducks, and chickens. The hog is retained mainly as a scavenger and a middleman to transform coarse, indigestible sub-stances into human food. Ducks are largely self-supporting in creeks and ponds. The sale of chicken eggs gives the farmer a quick cash income. Water buffalos are work animals; they are sold to the butcher only when they can be replaced by a younger and stronger animal. Frequently on the islands two or more farmers share in the ownership and use of one buffalo.

MINERALS

The islands are rather poor in mineral resources. There are some low-grade coal seams and small bodies of iron ore on Okinawa, and sulfur is found on several islands. On Rasa Island phosphate rock is commercially extracted by a Japanese company. Salt is produced from sea water, and salt evaporators are built on tidewater flats near Shimorabu on Okinawa.

DOMESTIC MANUFACTURES

The islanders are not only resourceful farmers but also good crafts-men and artists. Their skill is shown in the construction of their homes, in the manufacture of various fabrics, in the weaving of mats, screens, hats, and in the making of all the tools and utensils that they need in the house and in the fields. Proof of their artistic talent are the beautiful designs of their textiles, the quality of their pottery and lacquer. They were noted for the production of particularly durable vermilion-colored lacquer ware that was exported in large quantities to Japan.

CITIES

Almost all trade with the outside world is handled by the two ports Naha and Nase. Naha is the largest and most important town in the islands. It has a population of about 66,000 and is, as stated previously, the administrative center for the Okinawa and Saki Shima Gunto. It is located on the southwest coast of Okinawa between a shallow bay to the north and the mouth of the Asato River to the south. There are three railroads leading out of the city: one across the isthmus to the Japanese naval base Yonabaru on Nagagusuku Bay on the southeast coast; a second to the town Mima south of Naha; and a third one in a northern direction some distance along the west coast. A few miles east of Naha lies the old capital of Okinawa, Shuri. This city has a population of about 20,000 and has preserved with its many shrines, temples, memorial gates, and well-built homes much of its historical charm.

Third in size and importance is the port Nase, the largest town of O Shima. It lies in the northern part of the island in one of the deep bays of the much-indented coastline. The southern part of O Shima and the island opposite it to the southwest comprised another Japanese naval reservation.

VILLAGE LIFE AND CULTURE

The majority of the islanders live in small villages and hamlets along the coast or in the valleys in the midst of their fields. In the way they build their homes they show the composite character of their civilization. The Ryukyu Islands have served not only as a bridge for the migration of plant species but also for the movement of peoples and the transmittal of material and spiritual culture traits. In their racial features they show affinities to Malaysian and Proto-Japanese stocks with subsequent admixture of Chinese and Japanese blood. Their language, which is closely related to Japanese, seems to have evolved from an old Japanese dialect and at the same time preserved many ancient forms.

FIGURE 148. Native mother and child in Okinawa. Official U.S. Navy Photograph.

Chinese elements in their culture are the use of bricks and tiles in the construction of their houses, the erecting of brick walls around courtyards, the making of arched bridges and gateways, type of musical instruments, the calendar, the administrative hierarchy and its symbols of power. Of Japanese origin are the floor plan of many houses with all the rooms arranged on one floor; the Cha-shitsu, the room in which the Cha-no-yu (tea ceremony) is held; the thickly thatched roofs either of the shichu-zukuri (hipped) or irimoya (hipped with gables) type; building the house upon a raised floor; the custom of wearing wooden sandals; and the *go* play. Also Buddhism was introduced into the islands from Japan, but it exerts, nowadays, little influence upon the people. Many of the temples are abandoned and in a state of decay. To arrange funeral processions is about the only function left to the monks.

The Ryukyu Islands seem to have enjoyed political independence under the rule of native dynasties since ancient times. The islanders developed a comparatively high civilization and maintained friendly and mutually benefiting relations with their neighbors to the north and to the west. In 1372 the Chinese extended their rule over the islands under the first emperor of the Ming dynasty without, however, removing the local royal dynasty. At the beginning of the seventeenth century the Daimo of Satsuma annexed the northern islands, including O Shima, to his domain and collected annual tribute from the islands that remained in possession of the native dynasty. To strengthen her position in the islands and to prevent other powers from gaining a foothold in them, the Japanese occupied all the islands in 1879, dethroned the king, and established a new perfecture under the name of Okinawa as an integral part of the empire. After the Sino-Japanese War, the Chinese had to recognize this status in 1895. At the end of the Second World War, the islands came under American administration; in 1950 their future disposition had not been decided.

REFERENCES

Chamberlain, B. H., "The Luchu Islands and Their Inhabitants," *Geogr. Jour.*, Vol. V, 1895.

Climatic Atlas of Japan, Imperial Meteorological Bureau, Tokyo, 1929.

Geological Atlas of Eastern Asia, Imperial Geology Survey, Tokyo, 1929.

Goldschmidt, R., *Neu-Japan. Reisebilder aus Formosa, den Ryukyuinseln, Bonininseln, Korea und dem sudmandschurischen Pachtgebiet*, Berlin-Dahlem, 1927.

Haushofer, K., *Japan und die Japaner*, Teubner, Leipzig, 1933.

The Japan Yearbook, Japan Yearbook Office, Tokyo. Annual. Since 1933 published by Foreign Affairs Association, Japan.

Kudo, Y., "Flora of the Island of Paramushir," *Jour. Col. Agr. Hokkaido Univ.*, Vol. II, 1922.

Leavenworth, C. S., "History of the Loochoo Islands," *Jour. Chin. Brit. Royal Asiatic Soc.*, Vol. XXXVI, 1905.

Merrill, E. D., *A Bibliography of Eastern Asiatic Botany*, Arnold Arboretum of Harvard University, Jamaica Plain, Mass., 1938.

Milne, John, "A Cruise among the Volcanoes of the Kuril Islands," *Geol. Mag.*, 1879.

Miyabe, K., *The Flora of the Kurile Islands*, Memoirs Boston Society of Natural History, Vol. 4, 1890.

Newman, Marshall T., and Ransom L. Eng, *The Ryukyu People: a Cultural Appraisal*, Annual Report of the Smithsonian Institution for 1947, pp. 379–405, Washington, 1948.

Okada, T., "The Climate of Japan," *Bull. Central Meteor. Observ. Japan*, Vol. IV, No. 2, Tokyo, 1931.

Perry, Commander M. C., *Narrative of the Expedition of an American Squadron to the China Seas and Japan, 1852–1854*, Washington, 1856.

Richthofen, F.v., *Geomorphologische Studien aus Ostasien*, Berlin, 1904.

Rosinski, H., "Japan," *Handbuch der Geogr. Wissensch.*, Athenaion, Potsdam, 1931.

Simon, Edmund M., *Beiträge zur Kenntnis der Ryukyu Inseln*, Leipzig, 1914.

Snow, H. J., *Notes on the Kuril Islands*, John Murray, London, 1897.

────── *In Forbidden Seas*, Edward Arnold, London, 1910.

Statistical Yearbook of Japan, Statistical Bureau, Tokyo. Annual.

Tatewaki, M., "Vascular Plants of the Middle Kuriles," *Bull. Biogeogr. Soc. Japan*, Vol. IV., pp. 257–334, 1934.

Uyehara, Yukuo, "Ryukyu Islands, Japan," *Econ. Geog.*, Vol. IX, pp. 395–405, 1933.

Wolf, Laurence G., "A Glimpse of Okinawa," *Jour. Geogr.*, Vol. 47, pp. 41–51, February, 1948.

18

Islands of the Eastern and Northern Pacific

OTIS W. FREEMAN

THE ISLANDS DISCUSSED IN THIS CHAPTER ARE IN THE EASTERN AND northern Pacific Ocean at varying distances off the west coasts of the American continents, most of them in excess of 300 miles, except the easternmost Aleutians. All the islands are of volcanic origin except for part of the Aleutian group, in which occur older rocks overlain by recent lavas and pyroclastic materials. When discovered by Europeans, all the islands were uninhabited by man except for the Aleutians. In general the islands described are small and are separated by vast distances, and this isolation attracted harmless and peculiar marine animals that survived on these unknown spots long after they had disappeared from regions familiar to man. Perhaps the uniqueness of the pelagic mammals is the chief unifying factor about these islands.

Off South America are Juan Fernandez, San Felix, San Ambrosio, the Gelapagos Islands, and Malpelo Island. Sala-y-Gomez is also included because, although much closer to Easter Island than to South America, it was never inhabited or considered a part of Polynesia. Off central America and Mexico are Cocos, Clipperton, the Revilla Gigedo Archipelago, and Guadalupe Island, and in the far north the Aleutian, Pribilof, and Commander islands. St. Lawrence Island, St. Mathew Island, Hall Island, and the two Diomede Islands are also located in the Bering Sea but will not be described. They all belong to the United States except the westernmost Diomede Island.

GALAPAGOS ISLANDS

The Galapagos (Spanish for turtle) Islands were named by Dampier in 1684 for the giant tortoises found there. Discovered by the Bishop of Panama, Fray Tomas de Berlanga, in 1535, the islands became the resort of buccaneers, for whose supposed buried treasure many expeditions have searched. The pirates and later the whalers ate the huge, fat turtles, which were the more welcome because the animals remained alive for weeks on shipboard without attention, and their fat would not spoil in the tropics as do butter and lard for which it was a substitute. Ecuador occupied the islands in 1837, and after

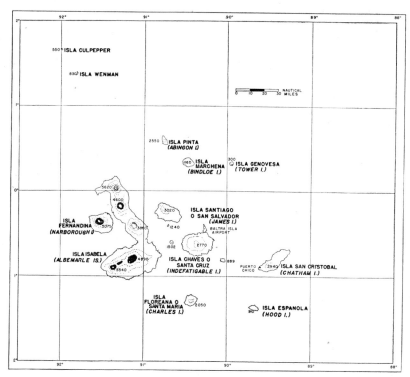

FIGURE 149. The Galapagos Islands.

employing them for a time as a penal colony, made efforts to colonize the group. However, the attempts were not very successful, and the population is small. In 1942, during the Second World War, the United States obtained the right to establish air and naval bases in the Galapagos Islands; they helped to guard the Pacific entrance to the Panama Canal 800 miles northeast. Among the installations was a large air base constructed on Baltra Island, a small neighbor to Charles or Floreana Island. The bases were deactivated in 1946.

The Galapagos Islands extend for 100 miles on each side of the equator between the longitudes of 89° to 92° west, located about 550 to 700 miles off the coast of South America (Fig. 149). There are fifteen islands, six of which are large, and in addition numerous rocks and islets. Authorities differ in regard to the area of the islands, some figures going above 3000 square miles and as low as 1868 square miles, but about 2870 square miles is usually accepted. Officially the group is named the Territory of Colón of Ecuador or the Archipelago de Colón. Islands of the group have been given names commemorative of the time of Columbus, but the English names persist; and, in addition, the original Spanish names, although obsolete, are sometimes used. For example, the largest island, which accounts for nearly two-thirds the area of the group, is called Albemarle by the English, Santa Gertrudis by the Spanish, and Isabella by the Ecuadorians. In a similar way, Charles is known both as Floreana and as Santa Maria, and Indefatigable has been called both Chaves and Santa Cruz. Unofficially the Galapagos are sometimes called Las Isles Encantadas (Haunted Islands).

Albemarle or Isabella Island is boot-shaped, and the roughly rectangular foot is about 45 by 20 miles in size, with the major axis lying in an east-west direction. To this is joined, by a low isthmus, a peninsula about 55 by 15 miles in dimensions, extending towards the northwest. Other islands and their sizes are Indefatigable (Santa Cruz), about 25 by 15 miles with Baltra Island lying close to its north shore; Narborough (Fernandina), nearly 15 miles in diameter; Charles (Santa Maria or Floreana), about 9 by 5 miles; Chatham (San Cristóbal), about 24 by 8 miles; James (San Salvador or Santiago), 20 by 10 miles; Bindlee (Marchena), 8 by 5 miles; Hood (Española), 5 to 6 miles in diameter; Abingdon (Pinta), 6 by 3 miles; Barrington (Santa Fe), 5 by 3 miles; and Duncan (Pinzon), Jervis (Rabida), Tower (Genovesa), Wenman, and Culpepper, which are 1 to 3 miles in diameter. Tortuga (Brattle) and Roca Redondo are other small islands less than a mile in diameter.

The islands, wholly of volcanic origin, are located above sets of intersecting fissures near the side of the Albatross Plateau. Darwin declared there were over 2000 volcanoes, mostly cinder cones, in the group, but only a score are truly large volcanoes. Most of the islands consist of one big volcano, but Chatham and James have two each, and Albemarle possesses six major volcanoes. Parasitic cinder and ash cones are scattered all about on the slopes of the large volcanoes, and many lava flows have broken through the sides of the cones. Known eruptions occurred in 1814, 1825, 1897 (James Island), 1925 on

Albemarle, 1928 on Abingdon, 1937 and 1949 on Narborough. All the larger islands have peaks of considerable height, the summit of Albemarle reaching an elevation of 4700 feet; that on Narborough 4320 feet, James 2700 feet, Chatham 2490 feet, and Indefatigable 2296 feet.

The lower parts of the islands up to elevations of around 600 to 800 feet are covered with flows of exceedingly rough, bare lava, or by broken volcanic rocks covered with a tangle of spiny cactus and thorn bushes that make travel exceedingly difficult. Furthermore, the blocks of lava and the cinder beds are so pervious that the always scanty rainfall sinks underground at once and flowing water is unknown on most of the islands; and the securing of drinking water under these conditions is a problem. Above 800 to 1000 feet in elevation rainfall increases, with almost daily showers during the rainier season. The abundant rainfall causes rapid decomposition of the volcanic rocks and the development of a clay soil, which, although thin, holds moisture, and on which trees, ferns, and other plants grow that help to conserve the water resources. Here springs and pools of water occur. However, below the zone of misty woods weathering is slow, and any water trickling into the region quickly disappears in the loose, porous rock.

The climate is not a normal one for the equatorial region because the cold Peru (Humboldt) Current and upwelling of cold water reduce the surface temperature of the ocean to as low as 60° F off the coast of southeast Albemarle, whereas the water temperature is 80° F on the other side of the island. Lowland temperatures average about 70° to 72° F, but may rise above 90° F. The temperature drops about 1° F for 300 feet of ascent, and the middle slopes at an elevation of 1500 feet have an average temperature of about 66° F. Higher in the mountains, where clouds and fogs predominate, the day temperatures often fall below 60° F, and night temperatures are still colder. The steady, southeast trade winds blowing from the cool ocean are drier than usual for the latitude, and the lowlands never have much rain. The rain that falls comes mostly from January to April, but completely rainless years have been known. The uplands are rainy, and although records are lacking, it has been estimated from the character of the vegetation, etc., that the rainfall is around 48 inches annually. The rainfall results from convectional showers and orographic effects on the trade winds, and the bulk of the precipitation falls from February to May, with mists and light rains continuing to drench the soil during the so-called summer of June to January. The southeast islands (Chatham and Charles) have more rainfall, which begins at lower elevations than on islands further northwest.   On all the islands the southeast side of the mountains is rainier than the lee-ward side.   The most soil and vegetation likewise occur on the south-east slopes and extend to lower levels there.   The low and young volcanic islands have no soil and few plants.   Although the islands are bisected by the equator, coral reefs do not occur.   Their absence re-sults from the temperature of the cold Peru Current which is below that at which corals grow.

The native flora and fauna are most interesting to naturalists, and have been studied by numerous scientific expeditions, including Charles Darwin in the *Beagle* in 1835, Alexander Agassiz in the *Albatross* in 1891, and several others.   The Galapagos Islands are one of the world's best examples of the effect of isolation on organic forms, and many of the conclusions of Darwin and Wallace concerning evolution were based on evidence from this group.   The native wild-life is remarkably tame, the birds and animals never having learned to fear man because the islands were uninhabited when discovered.

Of about 600 plant species native to the Galapagos Islands, nearly 40 per cent are endemic.   Mangrove trees fringe low shores, but the dry, lower lava slopes are barren.   Two species of cacti (*Opuntia* being usually the larger) and thorny shrubs form the principal vege-tation up to elevations of about 800 feet, at which level begin dense forests of rather slender trees seldom over 30 feet tall that include the spiny *Mimosa, Acacia,* and *Castila*.   With these are mingled many ferns, about sixty species being recognized, and creepers.   Above the forests, at elevations of 1600 to 2000 feet, the summit domes are usually rounded and covered with grass on which wild cattle and donkeys graze.   Soil has developed where the forests and grasslands occur, and, although running water is scarce, the clay holds ground water and there are small springs and pools for the animal life.   Heavy mists soak the grass and herbage so that animals can go a long time between drinks.   Tortoises take several days at their slow pace to reach water, and where the creatures still exist their paths radiate outward from the drinking places.

Much of the animal life is peculiar to the Galapagos Islands; for example, according to Darwin, all but one of twenty-six species of land birds are endemic, and a few species are restricted to only one island.   The huge land tortoises are found only in these islands, which also possess the only sea-going iguana (*Amblyrhynchus*) in the world.   A small rodent is the only mammal.   The effects of isolation are shown by the land tortoises, of which there were fifteen species, each island with any tortoises having its own species, except on Albemarle, home of the biggest specimens. On Albemarle there were originally five species that apparently resulted from the five largest volcanoes on the island being once separate islands that were not united until after a peculiar species had developed on each of the islands. The sea tortoises and marine iguana are similar in all the islands. Several species of seals and a sea lion are found in the Galapagos, and before it was exterminated by hunters there was a herd of fur seal. Insects are abundant and furnish food for many of the birds. Among the birds are hawks, owls, martins, flycatchers, doves, a finch, cuckoo, and the mockingbird. Most of the birds are related to species found in Central and South America, but one, a sandpiper, is known elsewhere only in the Hawaiian Islands. Of forty-six genera of birds, twenty-eight are water birds including gulls, frigate birds, cormorants, boobies, pelicans, and ducks, which can wander freely throughout the Pacific. There is a species of penguin that doubtless migrated from the Antarctic by way of the Peru Current. The same species of large albatross that lives off Cape Horn nests on the islands.

The land tortoises, for which the islands were named, were once very numerous. They lived in both the dry lower zone and the upper moist zone, preferring the moist zone. They grew to weigh 400 pounds and had a life span that sometimes may have lasted 400 or 500 years. Their meat is delicious, the fat a good substitute for butter, and the liver when fried in the animal's fat is a great delicacy. Because the creatures are easily captured and can survive without food for weeks at sea, it early became the custom for whalers to stop at the Galapagos Islands and take on tortoises for food. Records show that 189 whaling ships took away more than 13,000 tortoises between 1831 and 1868; and it is thought that whalers may have removed more than 100,000 in all. In addition, settlers killed thousands for their oil that could be sold for food and for sport without using the carcasses. Dogs have killed many also, and pigs devour the eggs. Of fifteen species of land tortoises, eight have been exterminated and the numbers of the seven surviving species have been greatly reduced.

The marine iguanas live on seaweed and formerly went to their feeding grounds in vast herds, but like the tortoises their numbers have been much reduced. The marine iguanas when mature were 3 or 4 feet long and weighed up to 15 or 20 pounds, but they were not relished for food by human beings. Land lizards, both large and small, also live in the islands. The flesh of the land iguana, once common but now rare, is eaten and tastes much like chicken. The large land iguana sometimes was 4 feet long, and part of the cause for their increased scarcity is that they are killed and eaten by dogs and pigs. Snakes occur on four islands and are each of a different species.

Fish, which are plentiful among the islands, include rock cod, dolphin, devil fish, sharks, and mullet. Crab and big crayfish, called lobsters, are common; more of both fish and shellfish could be caught for mainland markets.

Wild cattle, donkeys, goats, pigs, dogs, and cats, which descended from animals introduced by colonists who later abandoned their homesteads, live on many of the islands. The cattle are hunted for their hides and tallow, and the pigs and goats for food. Turtle oil is also exported.

Small deposits of sulfur and guano have been discovered and have been produced in a minor way.

SETTLEMENT

Between 1000 and 2000 people live in the Galapagos Islands, and about 700 of them are on Chatham (San Cristobal) Island, which is favored by good anchorages and better soil and water than most of the group. It has been inhabited since 1869, and the chief settlement, Progresso, located 4 miles from Wreck Bay, has about 400 to 500 people. There is an estate on which livestock are kept, and two crops per year of corn, potatoes, fruit, and coffee can be raised. Hides and coffee are exported. Albermarle (Isabella) Island supports about 400 inhabitants who graze cattle and grow corn, tobacco, fruit, vegetables, and a little sugar cane on the south part of the big island, which is wooded and green. Most of the island consists of barren lava flows and ash heaps and is unused. The people live in tiny villages of huts roofed with thatch or sheet iron near the small plantations located in areas of soil not covered by recent lava. Charles (Floreana or Santa Maria) Island has a population of about 20, some of whom are engaged in hunting the wild cattle of the island. Water is scarce, but Post Office Bay was an anchorage for whalers who, when homeward-bound, picked up the mail left in a cask fastened to a post. Most of the other islands are utterly barren and unpopulated. A penal settlement existed for some time on Charles, but the island has been abandoned for many years, except for some of the cleared land now used by settlers. Several families reside on Santa Cruz or Indefatigable Island. Efforts to colonize the Galapagos Islands have had little success, and it seems unlikely that a large population can ever be supported because of the scarcity of suitable farm land and water supplies.

JUAN FERNANDEZ

The Juan Fernandez Islands, named for their Spanish discoverer, are now owned by Chile and consist of the two principal islands of volcanic origin separated by 84 miles of ocean. Mas-a-Tierra (landward) is at about latitude 33° 35′ south, and longitude 78° 50′ west, some 360 miles west of Valparaiso. Mas-Afuera (farther out from the mainland) is at latitude 33° 45′ south and longitude 80° 45′ west. Both islands are much-eroded ancient volcanoes believed to be of Tertiary age.

Mas-a-Tierra has a very irregular shape and is 13 miles long by 4 miles wide. The framework of the island is a curving central ridge from which narrow, steep-sided ridges descend to the sea, ending in great cliffs against the base of which the waves break. The valleys between the ridges are generally narrow, have a steep slope, level land being a rarity; and on the north coast some valleys terminate in open bays, between which cliffs of 1000 feet high may occur. The eastern half of the island is roughest and highest, culminating in a peak 3090 feet high called El Yunque (the anvil) because of its shape; it rises from the coast in less than a mile. The eastern half of the island has a humid climate and the valleys are well forested; the southwestern portion is to leeward, and is drier. The valleys are not occupied by permanent streams, and the vegetation is mainly grass and herbs, devoid of trees. Weather records kept at Cumberland Bay on the north coast show an agreeable temperature and small annual range, February having a mean of 66.9° F and August of 54° F. Frost is never known, the coldest recorded temperature being 38.8° F. The mean annual rainfall is about 40 inches, 80 per cent coming from April to September. No doubt this is exceeded considerably at higher elevations. Damp fog hangs about the mountain summits much of the year, even during the dry season.

Mas-Afuera is a compact, oval-shaped island, about 7½ miles north-south and 4½ miles broad. It rises toward the south to a peak 6562 feet high. The shores are rocky and precipitous with many stacks and an offshore reef, which make landing difficult and dangerous. The west side of the island is highest, dropping off abruptly to sea level with cliffs 4000 to 5000 feet high The main valleys are narrow and often have waterfalls near their head. All drain to the east and have been eroded to sea level, but those on the west are short and of the hanging-valley type. There are no harbors or safe anchorages. Between 1909 and 1913 a penal settlement was maintained, but since its abandonment the island has usually been uninhabited.

Much of the flora of the Juan Fernandez Islands is unique; out of 142 species of plants, two-thirds are endemic. Among the trees was sandalwood, which is unknown in America and occurs elsewhere only in the Indian and west Pacific regions, and is now probably extinct on Juan Fernandez because men were unrestrained in their cutting of the rare species. The native palm (*Juania australis*) grows only in these islands and has been much depleted because of its handsome wood. The dry part of Mas-a-Tierra has thickets of xerophytic shrubs, grass, and introduced weeds. The lower zone in the humid parts of both Mas-a-Tierra and Mas-Afuera contains many ferns, including some endemic species, along with some native trees and bushes; the middle zone has the best forests, located chiefly in the valleys about 1000 to 2200 feet in elevation; the topmost belt consists of meadow and an alpine zone. Among the ferns in the foggy upper forest zone is a tree fern related to a Fijian species and another that is endemic. Many other plants are connected with distant Pacific islands rather than with the South American mainland. The middle forest zone is composed largely of an endemic myrtle tree (*Myrceugenia fernandeziana*) and the tree fern (*Dicksonia berteroana*). A magnolia-like tree (*Lactoris fernandeziana*) is the sole representative of its genus in the world. Other endemic plants are the *Gunnera*, with leaves like a gigantic rhubarb, which are sometimes 6 to 10 feet in diameter, and the cabbage tree (*Dendroseris littoralus*), named for the shape of its leaves. The upland meadows on Mas-Afuera include many ferns and, according to Skottsberg,[1] become alpine above 3500 feet with a Magellanic flora.

There are no endemic land mammals, but sea lions exist, although much reduced in numbers. There are a few land birds and numerous sea birds. The introduced goat has severely damaged native vegetation, and cats have killed many of the birds.

For many years Juan Fernandez, the legendary home of Robinson Crusoe, was visited only temporarily by pirates, whalers, and sailors. However, finally a garrison was installed at the Bay of San Juan Bautista (Cumberland Bay), and for a time a penal settlement was located there. Lack of any considerable area of level or gently sloping land has been a factor in the failure of efforts at farming, although some cattle are raised and the wild goats are hunted. The present population of about 450 is engaged chiefly in lobster fishing and the processing of the catch.

The large crustacean, *Palinurus frontalis*, is popularly called a

[1] Carl Skottsberg, "The Islands of Juan Fernandez," *Geogr. Rev.*, Vol. 5, pp. 362–383, 1918.

"lobster," although closer to a crayfish. It is related to the spiny lobster of Florida but lacks the big claw of the ordinary North American variety. It is native only to Juan Fernandez, and the sterile islands of San Felix and San Ambrosio 500 miles to the north. The creatures may reach a length of 2½ feet and may weigh 10 or 12 pounds apiece. The lobsters are much appreciated in Chile and in Buenos Aires. Thousands are shipped alive to market, and two canneries process the remainder of the catch. About 80,000 lobsters are taken annually. To protect the industry, no lobster longer than 10 inches can be kept by the fishermen.

There are many fish in near-by waters, including a huge species of cod, but little has been done to utilize them.

SALA-Y-GOMEZ

Sala-y-Gomez consists of three rocky islets at about latitude 26° 28′ south and longitude 105° 28′ west, 205 miles east of Easter Island, and like Easter is claimed by Chile. Sala-y-Gomez was discovered in 1793 by a Spanish commander of that name. It is uninhabited. The main island rises from a spur of the Albatross Plateau and is less than one-half mile long, running northwest to southeast, and 400 yards wide. It is a remnant of a volcano most of which has been eroded by the waves. The high point is estimated at 98 feet above sea level, most of the island being no more than heaps of stones barely above the water. There are a few low bushes, and frigate birds nest on the island.

SAN FELIX AND SAN AMBROSIO ISLANDS

San Felix, in latitude 26° 15′ south, longitude 80° 7′ west, and its companion San Ambrosio 10 miles eastward, are uninhabited isles of volcanic origin belonging to Chile. The islands are 500 miles west of Caldera, Chile, 500 miles north of Juan Fernandez (Mas-a-Tierra), and due east from Easter Island and Sala-y-Gomez.

The islands are situated above a fissure near the eastern edge of the Albatross Plateau, and rise from nearby depths of 3 miles, giving an indicated height for the volcanoes of 16,000 to 18,000 feet above the floor of the ocean.

San Felix is a rather low, crescent-shaped island about 2 miles long east and west by 500 to 1000 yards wide. There are cones at either end of the crescent; that on the west end of the ridge is about 630 feet high, and that on the east end is a little lower and forms small, inaccessible Gonzales Island, which is separated from San Felix by a shallow, narrow strait. Steam still comes from the crater on San Felix.

San Ambrosio attains an elevation of 1570 feet and is about 2 miles long by half a mile broad, with precipitous cliffs 800 feet high along the northern shore.

San Felix and San Ambrosio were once the resort of a great herd of the southern fur seals, but sealers practically exterminated the animals many years ago. Later, lobsters were caught for mainland consumption, but this fishery became depleted and has been abandoned. Fish are abundant and and attract flocks of sea birds, which nest on the islands, but even the number of birds has been much reduced through man's activities. There is little soil, the vegetation is sparse, and water is in scant supply.

COCOS ISLAND

Cocos is a palm-fringed, mountainous island covered with dense evergreen vegetation as the result of a tropical rainy climate. It lies in latitude 5° 32′ north, longitude 87° 2′ west, 295 miles southwest from Costa Rica, which has owned the island since 1888, 540 miles from Panama, and about 400 miles northeast of the Galapagos Islands, from which it differs greatly in climate. The supposed site of treasure carried from Peru and buried to escape the buccaneers, Cocos Island has been the locale of many expeditions to unearth the treasure; but, if such has been discovered, the finders have not advertised their good fortune! Usually there is a resident or two on the island living in a haphazard fashion, but there are no settlements or industries.

Cocos, of volcanic origin, is about 3 by 4½ miles in size, with an area of about 12 square miles. There are two summits, one 2788 feet and the other 1574 feet above sea level; and the surface slopes from these towards the coastline, which for three-fourths of its circuit consists of sheer cliffs rising about 600 feet above the water. The climate is very rainy, and the streams draining the interior often end in waterfalls that tumble off the cliffs into the sea. This results from the ocean waves usually being a more effective agent of erosion than the streams so that hanging valleys are developed. Where the streams flowed over weak rocks in their lower courses the mouths of the valleys were worn to sea level. At Wafer and Chatham bays on the north coast the stream mouths have been drowned to form the principal harbors.

Of about 100 plants described from Cocos, about 10 are unique to that island. Turtles and fish are abundant in the ocean around the island. Wild pigs, descended from introduced ones, are found.

CLIPPERTON

Clipperton is a lonely isle belonging to France at latitude 10° 18' north and longitude 109° 13' west at a strategic location in this air age, 660 miles southwest of Acapulca, 1270 miles northwest of the Galapagos Islands, and 1500 miles west of Costa Rica. The island was named for John Clipperton, a mate on the ship of the English navigator, William Dampier, who with others deserted Dampier and became a pirate using the isle named for him as headquarters. Clipperton was claimed for the United States under the Guano Act in 1856 but was not occupied by Americans. It was later annexed by France, then claimed by Mexico, which maintained a garrison there for several years; but after arbitration by the king of Italy, it was awarded to France in 1931.

Clipperton is an atoll whose narrow coral rim is 8 to 20 feet high and about 5 miles in circumference, with a brackish lagoon occupying the center. Near the southeast of the island is Clipperton Rock, an exposure of volcanic rock called trachyte, which has become partly phosphatized.[2] Sea birds nest on the island and interaction between bird guano and the limestone rock has produced calcium phosphate, which has been worked at intervals. Exports of 200 tons per annum were reported, but the deposits are apparently nearly exhausted.[3] Vegetation is scanty, consisting of low weeds, clumps of grass, and a few coconut palms. Clipperton has prospective value as an air base although inadequate anchorages and the lack of any passage through the rim into the lagoon have prevented its use as a fueling station by steamships.

MALPELO ISLAND

Malpelo Island and associated rocks are at about latitude 4° north, longitude 81° 34' west, and 260 miles west of Buenaventura, Colombia, to which country the island belongs. It is little more than a rock, a mile long, reaching 846 feet above sea level, and barren except for a few bushes. It is the remnant of a volcano, and a number of stacks just above the water near by.

[2] J. J. H. Teall, "A Phosphatized Trachyte from Clipperton Atoll," *Geol. Soc. Quart. Jour.*, Vol. LIV, pp. 230–233, 1898.

[3] W. J. Wharton, "Note on Clipperton Atoll," *Geol. Soc. Quart. Jour.*, Vol. LIV, pp. 228–229, 1898.

REVILLA GIGEDO ARCHIPELAGO

The Mexican-owned archipelago of Revilla (ruh-véeya) Gigedo (hee-gáy-do) consists of Isla de Socorro, the largest, Clarion Island, 6 by 2 miles and second in size, and two smaller islands, Roca Partida and San Bernadicte. All the islands are of volcanic origin, and Clarion rises to an elevation of 1000 feet. The group is about 300 miles south of Magdalena Bay and 400 to 500 miles west of Manzanilla; Clarion is nearly 150 miles west of the others. The flora is rather poor but includes many flowering plants. Clarion has snakes and lizards that are peculiar to the island. There are several species of land birds and many species of sea birds. Fish, crabs, and shellfish are numerous near the shores. Many big green sea turtles come to the patches of sandy beach to lay their eggs; they are often caught for food.

GUADALUPE ISLAND

The island of Guadalupe, a part of Mexico, is about 150 miles west of Baja California and nearly 180 miles southwest of San Diego. It is a rugged, old volcanic island 20 miles long by 6 miles wide; erosion has developed steep cliffs along the shore. The island rises to a height of 4500 feet above the sea from depths of about 7500 feet. The dry lower slopes supported only low brush and herbage, but the upper heights, commonly enshrouded in clouds and mists, favored a wonderful growth of forests, in which pines, cypress, oak, and palms flourished. Species found only on this island of Guadalupe indicate that it is wholly oceanic in origin. Fully 140 endemic plant species have been described from Guadalupe. Originally there was a rich variety of land birds. Unfortunately both goats and cats were introduced. Free of enemies, the goats increased to thousands and ate almost every living thing, and the cats destroyed the native birds. The rich green ground cover has almost disappeared, along with the young trees, and unless the goats can be exterminated the mature trees will finally perish and a unique flora will disappear.

Marine mammals were once abundant on Guadalupe. On three rookeries there was a herd of at least 100,000 fur seals (*Arctocephalus townsendi*) related more closely to the southern than to the northern varieties; in addition there were many elephant seals or sea elephants, and sea lions. Between the years 1800 and 1830 at least 200,000 fur sealskins were taken from Guadalupe, most of which went into the oriental trade. Left unhunted, the few survivors increased to several thousand, only to be exterminated in a final slaughter of several thousand animals about 1880.

The ungainly elephant seal, named from the snout that on old males may be 16 inches long, once resorted to many oceanic islands and coasts, including those of Lower California, but the huge, fat, harmless creature has apparently been exterminated everywhere in the Pacific, except for the last remnant of several hundred survivors on Guadalupe Island (Fig. 150). The island has been made a game preserve by

FIGURE 150. The northwest corner of Guadalupe Island, with a herd of elephant seals on the beach at the base of precipitous cliffs. Photograph courtesy of the Alan Hancock Foundation.

Mexico, but permits have been given for the slaughter of some of the animals for their oil. For a time a Mexican garrison was stationed in Guadalupe, but usually the island is uninhabited.

ALEUTIAN ISLANDS

The sweeping arc of the Aleutian Islands extends over 1000 miles beyond the Aleutian Peninsula and so far towards Asia that the westernmost island, Attu (Fig. 151), is as far west of Honolulu in degrees of longitude (but not in miles) as that city is west in degrees from

San Francisco. The Aleutians were an unfamiliar part of United States territory to most Americans before the Second World War, but the occupation of Attu and Kiska (Fig. 152) by the Japanese in 1942, the recapture of the islands by United States forces in 1943, and the establishment of naval bases and air bases made the Aleutians better known, so that the islands have become something more than just a name on the map to many of our citizens. Strong bases on Unalaska, Umnak, and Adak islands and minor bases elsewhere in the group were established before or during the Second World War, and these now serve as outposts in the defense system of the United States. The

FIGURE 151.   Aerial view of Attu, Aleutian Islands.   Official U.S. Navy Photograph.

Aleutians were discovered by Vitus Bering in 1741. They were once a part of Russian America, title passing to the United States in 1867 when our country purchased Alaska from Russia.

GEOLOGY

The Aleutian Islands, which are the seaward portion of the Aleutian arc, represent the peaks of mountains most of whose mass is submarine. The islands above sea level are mainly, sometimes wholly, constructed of lava and pyroclastic materials, but there are occurrences of older sediments and other rocks that resulted from folding and uplifting of the strata along a zone of weakness in the crust. Offshore is a fore-deep, the Aleutian Deep, about 25,200 feet in depth, which parallels the Aleutian mountain arc. The volcanoes have developed at intervals along major fractures associated with the mountain development. Nearly fifty large volcanoes, many of which are active, and many more small cones are known in the Aleutian Islands. There have been scores of eruptions reported in the nineteenth and twentieth centuries, including Okmok Volcano on Umnak Island, which erupted in 1945, and Akutan, a 4200-foot volcano 27 miles northeast of Dutch Harbor, which erupted in 1947 and 1949. Two of the most active volcanoes are Shishadin (9387 feet high), sometimes called "Smoking Moses," on Unimak Island, and Makushin, over 5000 feet high, on Unalaska Island. Bogoslof is a volcanic island of the pyroclastic type west of Unalaska, and since its discovery in 1790 it has repeatedly changed its shape and

FIGURE 152. Cloud-capped Kiska Volcano, elevation 4000 feet on Kiska Island in the Aleutians. Official U.S. Navy Photograph.

size, even becoming two islands for a time, as the result of explosive eruptions and wave erosion. Oddly enough a big herd of sea lions on Bogoslof have been little affected by the frequent and vigorous eruptions. According to G. D. Robinson of the U.S. Geological Survey there have been at least 225 recorded volcanic eruptions along the Aleutian arc, including the mainland, since Alaska was discovered by the Russians.

The islands are typically of irregular shape with steep cliffs that rise abruptly from the sea, and there are few safe harbors. The interiors generally consist of very rugged mountains that attain heights of several thousand feet, and some islands are practically one volcano. The larger islands supported icecaps in the glacial period, and glaciers and snow still cover the higher peaks. There are many swift rivers and waterfalls. Some of the islands have areas of lowlands that are commonly dotted with small glacial lakes. The wet tundra is a handicap to travel.

The Aleutian Islands have an area of 6821 square miles of which Unalaska has 1074 square miles, Adak, 289, Agattu, 109, Amchitka, 171, Attu, 311, and Kiska, 125.

DIVISIONS

The chain of the Aleutian Islands consists of about 20 large islands, some 50 small ones, and scores of islets, making perhaps 150 islands of all sizes, which extend in a curving arc nearly 1200 miles long and about 20 to 50 miles broad. From east to west they include the Fox Islands of which 3 (Unimak, Unalaska, and Umnak) are large; and 6 smaller ones make up the Krenitzin group, of which only Akun and Akutan are inhabited. Next are the Islands of the Four Mountains, really 5 islands, of which 3 have peaks 8156 feet, 7500, and 5281 feet in elevation, respectively. There are 4 islands without a group name: Yunaska, 3118 feet high; Chagulak, smallest but highest of the four with its summit at 3750 feet; Amukta, 3450, and Seguam, 2098 feet. Next are the Andreanof Islands, Amlia, Atka (4852 feet), which is the largest and has a native village, Great Sitkin (5740 feet), Adak (3900 feet), and its close neighbor Kagalaska, Kanaga (4416 feet), Tanaga (6975 feet), and 6 small islands, one of which, Gareloi, is 5334 feet in elevation. Then come the Rat Islands, Semisopachnoi, Amchitka, Kiska, and 5 smaller islands, none of which were inhabited before the Second World War, and some small rocky islets. Submarine peaks have been reported beyond Attu.

Unimak is the largest island, 65 miles long and 25 miles broad, and encompasses about 2000 square miles, close to one third the area of the entire chain. It is separated from the Alaska Peninsula by False Pass, or Isanotski Strait, which is narrow and shallow. There are two active volcanoes of which Mt. Shishadin (9387) is the highest peak in the Aleutians, and there are other high volcanic peaks, Mt. Pogromni, 6500 feet high, Isanotski (Ragged Jack), 8088 feet, and Round Top, 6155 feet, each of the last two having glaciers. The Unimak Pass between the big island and the Krenitzin group is the chief strait for vessels entering Bering Sea, although some take Akutan Pass east of Unalaska Island. Once well populated, Unimak now has few inhabitants. Once caribou grazed on the island, but they have been exterminated.

Unalaska is the most important and the second largest Aleutian island (1074 square miles). The island has an irregular shape, and the eastern portion is more mountainous than the western peninsula. Mount Makushin contains a deposit of sulfur in its crater. On Constantine Bay on the northeast shore is the village of Dutch Harbor, which before the Second World War had a population of a few hundred but was the chief trading center of the Aleutians. Dutch Harbor is now the site of an important air and naval base, and the headquarters of the U.S. Coast Guard vessels of the Bering Sea patrol, who among other duties guard the herd of fur seals on their winter migrations. Dutch Harbor has a strategic location, is close to the main entrances into Bering Sea from the West Coast, and by direct air routes the base is 2046 miles from Pearl Harbor, 1653 from Midway Island, 1261 to Petropavlovsk, Kamchatka, 1084 to Sitka, and 1707 miles to Seattle. There is a salmon cannery on the north shore of Unalaska and a native village of Kashega on the south coast.

Umnak, third in size of the Aleutians, was once well populated, but now only a small settlement, Nisholski, is located near the west end of the island. Fort Glenn was established as an air base on the east end of the island during the Second World War.

CLIMATE

The climate of the Aleutians is a succession of unpleasant weather. Cyclonic storms with winds of gale violence, sudden squalls, low clouds, dense fogs, and drizzling rain or driven snow for days on end result from the interaction of warm and cold air masses coming together near the contact between the warm Japan Current and the cold Kamchatka and Aleutian currents. The interaction provides the air masses, both of which are humid, with strong differences in temperature. Mean annual temperatures are about 40° F; the annual range is small, from about 30° F in the coldest month to 50° F in the warmest month. Sea-level temperatures as low as zero are unknown. The annual rainfall at sea level is 24 to 48 inches, and considerably more at higher elevations. Some stations report 250 rainy days per year with frequent strong gales and heavy fogs. In general the climate is of the marine type, wet and cool, rather than cold. However, the wind, rain, mists, fog, high humidity, and general lack of sunshine combine to make such disagreeably raw weather that the mild temperatures and moderate annual rainfall are of small benefit. The islands are ice-free and open to navigation the entire year, but storms and fog are treacherous. Commonly thought of as located far north, actually the Aleutians are nearly a thousand miles south of the Arctic Circle and in the same latitude as London and Berlin.

FLORA

The flora of the Aleutians is poor, only 480 species having been described of which a high percentage consists of grasses and sedges.

There are no indigenous trees in the Aleutian Islands perhaps because the gales and fogs make the climate unsuitable. Plants, some of which have showy flowers, are fairly plentiful in protected valleys. They include low willows, birches, and other shrubs, some of which have edible berries, various grasses, and herbs. The uplands and ridges are largely devoid of plant growth except for the simplest sorts, like moss and lichens. Sheep and cattle find the grazing adequate during summer, but the difficulty of curing hay for winter and the raising of any crops, except a few hardy vegetables, have prevented the establishment of a livestock industry.

FAUNA

The land fauna is unimportant, but the sea life is present in great abundance. The chief land mammal is the blue fox, which trappers introduced on some islands for its fur. The birds are spectacular. Many species are present in large numbers although the original vast flocks have been somewhat reduced, in part by foxes preying on the young birds and eggs. There is an abundance of sea mammals—several species of whales, sea lions, seals, dolphins, porpoises, and formerly the walrus. Once there were great herds of sea otter, now very rare, because their valuable fur led to intense hunting of the animals. Because the taking of sea otter is now prohibited, the animals have begun to be seen again in herds of several hundred on their feeding grounds among the kelp beds. Sea lions and whales are much less numerous than formerly because of persistent hunting. The most valuable sea lion is the *fur seal* of the Pribilof Islands that was once hunted in the Aleutians during its migrations.

Fish are abundant, including cod, halibut, herring, salmon, mackerel, and rock fish. King crabs, sometimes weighing 20 pounds each, and true crabs, shrimps, and other shellfish can be caught in the shallow water or along the shores.

THE PEOPLE

The Aleutians are the only islands included in this chapter on which native inhabitants lived before their discovery by Europeans. The Russians found probably 20,000 or 30,000 Aleuts living in villages along the chain of islands. The climate was unpleasant, but the abundance of food available from the sea made the Aleutians attractive to the natives. Aleuts are a separate people from the American Indians and Eskimos, although some authorities think they are distantly related to the Eskimo, to whose culture and language theirs are somewhat similar. The Aleuts are short and sturdy, with black hair and eyes, and a swarthy complexion. They made boats called bidarkas of driftwood covered with skins that resemble the Eskimo kayak, hunted the sea mammals with harpoons, and dressed in the skins of animals and birds. Their villages were located along beaches on which boats could land in rough seas, where there was a supply of fresh water, and in areas like sand spits and necks of land suitable for defense. Today the villages are often placed near river mouths where salmon can be caught during their runs. Nearly everything used by the Aleuts came from the sea; the marine mammals, fish, birds, and shellfish were their food supply, and driftwood and whalebones were the raw materials for the framework of their communal houses. Family-sized houses were sometimes built of sod. Stones for implements, grass for weaving baskets, brush for fuel, and a few berries and greens for food were the principal items that came from the land.

The Aleuts resisted the Russian traders but were defeated after thousands had been killed. Their hunters were then put to work, almost like slaves, in pursuit of the sea otter and other sea mammals for the benefit of their conquerors. Disease and hardships wiped out whole villages until by 1867 only a thousand-odd Aleuts survived. Today, aside from the military, only about 3000 people live in the Aleutian Islands of whom possibly half are Aleuts, with mixed blood accounting for part of the remainder. The census reports over 5000 Aleuts. Many, however, do not live in the Aleutian Islands, but in the Pribilofs and on the mainland of Alaska.

PRESENT SITUATION

The Aleutian Islands are important strategically as air and naval bases but are of small economical importance today. Fox-fur farming is an industry on some islands, a few sheep are grazed, and there are a few small gardens. A whaling station is located on Akutan Island, and a salmon cannery on Unalaska Island. The Japanese formerly caught and canned in floating canneries quantities of crab meat from the Aleutians. Americans paid no attention to this industry until after the Second World War, but king crabs are now canned by an American firm. The crabs are also now marketed fresh in Pacific Coast cities.

PRIBILOF ISLANDS

The Pribilof Islands were discovered in 1786 by a Russian captain of that name who had seen the herds of fur seals heading north into the fogs of Bering Sea in the spring. His search was successful when he found the breeding grounds of the animals on the isolated islands. The Pribilofs are about 200 miles north of Unalaska and about 200 miles off the mainland of Alaska. They became a part of the United States with the purchase of Alaska in 1867.

There are two chief islands 40 miles apart: St. Paul, 13 miles long with an area of 35 square miles, and St. George, 10 miles long with 27 square miles. Otter Island (4 square miles) and Walrus reef, which contains only 64 acres of land but is occupied by immense numbers of birds, are near St. Paul. The islands are hilly and of volcanic origin, with Bogoslof crater on St. Paul, 600 feet in elevation, being the high point. There are no harbors. Climatically, the year has two seasons, a cool, rainy, foggy summer, and a cold dry winter, without any appreciable spring or fall. The scanty vegetation includes ferns, mosses, grasses, a creeping willow, and small bushes. These islands in the midst of the cold Bering Sea have sterile land, but a large variety of sea animals in vast numbers resort there during the brief summer. Originally among these were fur seals, sea otters, walrus, sea lions, and dozens of species of sea fowl, but the sea otters have now vanished. Blue foxes and a few reindeer have been introduced by man.

The northern fur seal (*Otaria* [*Callorhinus*] *ursina*) had its main rookeries on the Pribilof and Commander islands, and once the number of fur seals on the Pribilofs was estimated at 5,000,000. The males, called bulls, in full maturity weigh 400 to 500 pounds each; the females, called cows, are much smaller and average about 80 pounds in weight. The animals are of polygamous habit, and during the summer big bulls possess harems that average about thirty cows. The young are called pups, and the young males for a few years are called bachelors, who until they reach large size are unable to secure a harem or maintain a place on the beach against the more powerful and older bulls. In the fall the entire Pribilof herd ranges far south towards Hawaii, living all winter entirely at sea and feeding on squid and small fish, to return in the spring or early summer to the Pribilof beaches. The Commander herd, which is much smaller, swims south to about the latitude of southern Japan before returning.

During the migration of the fur seals to and from the Pribilofs, vessels of the U.S. Coast Guard accompany the herd and protect the animals against poachers. After severe losses from pelagic sealing operations from about 1890 to 1910 that threatened the fur seals with extermination and reduced their numbers to 127,000 in 1911, a treaty was signed in 1911 between the United States and Great Britain, Russia and Japan, by which these countries forbade their citizens to engage in pelagic sealing in return for a share in the proceeds from the sale of sealskins. Japan denounced the treaty as of 1941 and no longer receives any part of the income. Under protection the fur seals in the Pribilofs have increased to well over 2,000,000 animals, of which 80 per cent are at the St. Paul rookery and the remainder on St. George. About 65,000 skins, all from bachelor seals, are taken annually, which does not interfere at all with the increase of the herd. The pelts are prepared for market in St. Louis, Missouri, and sold at auction there. The natives eat some of the meat, but more of it is fed to blue foxes whose fine coats provide additional income to the government.

Only agents of the United States and workmen and their families engaged in the butchering of the fur seals and care of the skins can reside in the Pribilof Islands, which have been a fur-seal reservation since 1868. Most of the few hundred residents who live on St. Paul are Aleuts brought in as workmen. They are provided with schools, churches, hospital, and comfortable living quarters, and occupy four or five villages.

COMMANDER ISLANDS

The Commander (Komandorski) Islands, belonging to Russia, are located 200 miles west of Attu and about 140 miles off the Kamchatka Peninsula. There are two large islands, Bering of 607 square miles and 69 miles by an extreme width of 28 miles, and Copper (Medny) of 180 square miles, together with several uninhabited islets or rocks. The Commanders are similar to the Aleutians in the mountainous character of the islands, the high point being 2200 feet in elevation, and in having mild temperatures, frequent storms, and no trees. Like the Aleutians also, the Commanders are noteworthy for the abundance and character of their sea life. Most remarkable was a close relative of the tropical manatee, called Steller's sea cow, which sometimes grew to a length of 25 feet with a weight of 3 tons. It grazed on the pastures of seaweed. The animal was unique, being found only on these islands. Having no fear of man, and being perfectly harmless, it was soon exterminated for the sake of its oil. Sea otters and a herd of probably 1,000,000 fur seals once considered the Commanders their home, but their numbers have been much reduced. Now protected by the Russian government, the surviving fur seals are slowly increasing. Sea lions and many species of sea birds are still numerous in the Commander Islands. The people, a mixture of Russian and Aleut, number several hundred. The port of Nikolskoe on the west side of Bering Island is the only settlement of importance.

REFERENCES

Agassiz A., "General Sketch of the Expedition of the Albatross from February to May 1891," *Harvard University Bull. Museum Comp.* Zool. 23, pp. 1–89, 1892.
———— "Reports on the Scientific Results of the Expedition to the Eastern Tropical Pacific," *Harvard University Museum Comp. Zool. Memoirs,* Vol. 33, 1906.
Beebe, William, *Galapagos, World's End,* G. P. Putnam's Sons, New York, 1924.
———— *The Arcturus Adventure,* G. P. Putnam's Sons, New York, 1926.
Chubb, L. J., "Geology of Galapagos, Cocos and Easter Islands," *Bernice P. Bishop Museum Bull.* 110, Honolulu, 1933.
Kroeber, A. L., *Floral Relations among the Galapagos Islands,* University of California Publication in Botany, Vol. VI, No. 9, pp. 199–220, 1916.
McBride, George M., "The Galapagos Islands," *Geogr. Rev.,* Vol. 6, pp. 229–239, 1918.
National Resources Committee, *Regional Planning, Part 7, Alaska,* U.S. Government Printing Office, Washington, 1938.
Robinson, G. D., "Exploring Aleutian Volcanoes," *Natl. Geogr. Mag.,* Vol. 94, pp. 509–528, October, 1948.
Schmitt, Waldo L., "A Voyage to the Island Home of Robinson Crusoe," *Natl. Geogr. Mag.,* Vol. 54, pp. 353–370, September, 1928.
Skottsberg, Carl, "The Islands of Juan Fernandez," *Geogr. Rev.,* Vol. 5, pp. 362–383, 1918.
Stewart, A., "A Botanical Survey of the Galapagos Islands," *Proc. Calif. Acad. Sci.,* Vol. IV, No. 1, pp. 7–252, 1911.
Teall, J. J. H., "A Phospatized Trachyte from Clipperton Atoll," *Quart. Jour. Geol. Soc.,* Vol. 54, pp. 230–233, 1898.
Walker, Ernest P., *Alaska America's Continental Frontier Outpost,* War Background Studies No. 13, Smithsonian Institution, Washington, 1943.
Wharton, W. J., "Note on Clipperton Atoll," *Quart. Jour. Geol. Soc.,* Vol. 54, pp. 228–229, 1898.
Willis, Bailey, and H. S. Washington, "San Felix and San Ambrosio, Their Geology and Petrology," *Bull. Geol. Soc. Amer.,* Vol. 35, pp. 374–384, 1924.

19

Trade, Transportation,
and Strategic Location in the Pacific

CHARLES M. DAVIS

THE TRADE THAT FLOWS ACROSS THE PACIFIC CONSISTS FOR THE MOST
part of exchange between the nations that border on the ocean. The
major part of it is *intercontinental* in nature, that is, it carries Asiatic
commodities to America and American commodities to Asia. A
smaller part is truly *oceanic*, in that it carries products that originate
in the oceanic environment, on the islands or the immediate continental shores. North America and Asia are two of the three most important commercial regions of the world; the trade that moves between
them reflects the differences between the nations on either side of the
ocean.

INTERCONTINENTAL TRADE

The United States is a nation of high living standards and cor-
respondingly high labor costs; its production, therefore, is very expensive by world standards. However, American industry is amaz-
ingly efficient so that some types of goods, especially machinery and
automobiles, are made more cheaply here than anywhere else and can
be sold in competition, notwithstanding the wages paid to workmen
in the United States. The country possesses most of the necessary
industrial raw materials but must import some essential commodities
such as tin and rubber. In the western Pacific area only two nations,
Japan and Australia, have efficient and extensive industrial systems.
The industrial system of Japan is based on cheap labor but lacks many
raw materials; that of Australia possesses most of the materials but
lacks the population for a large domestic market for its products.

545

The exports that the United States sends out in Pacific trade are of two general kinds, vehicles and machinery that are produced so efficiently by the industrial system and raw materials such as cotton, petroleum, and tobacco. (See Tables 1 and 2 for destinations and values.) The imports are chiefly raw materials from tropical agriculture and metals or ores that are not produced in sufficient amounts within the United States to meet domestic requirements.

Asiatic materials are vital to the industry of the United States. Of 100 leading groups of imports into the United States, 56 are supplied at least in part from East Asia, and in 23 of these groups Asiatic sources ranked first.[1] Three of the four largest groups, rubber, tin, and silk, come principally from Asia. Across the Pacific trade routes come rubber, tin, fibers, lead, zinc, oils, alloy metals, and ores. Because much of the productive capacity of the United States is located in the eastern part of the country, many of these products, particularly those originating in the East Indies, are shipped by way of the Indian and Atlantic oceans; and a great deal of the transpacific shipping is routed through the Panama Canal rather than to west coast ports.

Canada in terms of its living standards and production costs resembles the United States more than any other country, but it lacks the large domestic market, the industrial equipment, and some of the raw materials. Exportable Canadian commodities are chiefly ores and foodstuffs, not very well suited to Pacific trade.

The countries of western South America have a minor share in the intercontinental trade of the Pacific. The greater parts of their populations have little purchasing power, and their raw material exports, chiefly nitrate, copper, and iron ore, move by way of the Panama Canal to Atlantic ports in the United States and Europe; seldom do they cross the Pacific.

Except for Australia and New Zealand, the nations of the Asiatic side of the Pacific are in a period of transition and disruption. Some are recovering from war damage, others are passing through political changes out of states of feudalism and colonial exploitation. Although their climatic peculiarities and natural resources remain unaltered, there is little reason to believe that the characteristics of trade in the future will be the same as they were in the past.

Before the Second World War the foreign trade of *China* was small in proportion to its immense population. Eighty per cent of the people are small farmers and have little purchasing power. China, prior to the war, imported rice and sugar, cotton goods, petroleum,

[1] Gunther Stein, *American Business with East Asia*, U.S. Paper No. 3, 10th Conference of the Institute of Pacific Relations, New York, 1947.

iron and steel, machinery, and vessels. Its exports were principally agricultural products, silk, oils, soybeans, and animal derivatives. Of this trade the United States supplied somewhat less than one-fifth of the imports and took more than one-fifth of the exports. At the close of the war there came a tremendous increase in the value of the trade, and for a few years the United States supplied more than half the imports. Unfortunately by 1949 American trade with China declined materially with mounting inflation and change in the form of Chinese government.

Hong Kong, a British colony near Canton, occupies a unique position in Chinese trade. Under the stable conditions of British law the commercial facilities of Hong Kong are much better developed than those of China itself. To Hong Kong are shipped goods of many kinds destined for the Chinese market, making the colony one of the world's greatest transshipment ports. Hong Kong is an import rather than an export station in the Pacific, and the great disproportion between trade moving into and out of this port is evident on Tables 1 and 2.

Japan, during the 75 years before the Second World War, had transformed her economic system from self-sufficing agriculture to industry and world trade. Because there were few raw materials in the country this industry was developed chiefly upon the efficiency and cheapness of her labor. The most important commodity that originated entirely within Japan was raw silk; this and a certain amount of manufactured silk goods constituted more than one-fifth of the exports. Some tea was sent out, but most of the remainder of the exports consisted of articles manufactured in Japan from imported raw materials. Chief among them was cotton cloth, rayon, woolens, metal goods, and articles made of wood. Raw cotton and wool constituted one-third of the import value, and much of the remainder was made up by fertilizers, metals, ores, scrap iron, and fuels necessary to the industrial process. In the Japanese trade before the war, the United States, China, and India were the principal suppliers as well as the chief markets. Of the imports, the United States furnished one-third, China one-sixth, and India one-tenth; of the exports, the United States and China took one-fifth each and India somewhat less than one-tenth. To support this world trading industry Japan built up a merchant marine and a program of government subsidy that enabled Japanese products to compete effectively in the world's markets. The dependence of Japanese industry and of the people whom it supported upon access to foreign raw materials and markets was the principal reason that Japan went to war.

The Japanese industrial system was shattered by the Second World

War; factories were destroyed, the merchant marine was annihilated, and world trading network broken up.   After the war the country was occupied and its industry was revived along lines dictated by the occupational authorities.   Japanese industry and trade will be beset with many difficulties.

The Philippines occupy a special position in Pacific trade because they have been under the protection of the United States, and their production has been stimulated and conditioned by the requirements of the American market.   Their exports are agricultural commodities of tropical climatic conditions and cheap labor: raw sugar, coconut products, abaca (hemp), and tobacco.   The imports are rice from

FIGURE 153.   Midway Island, one of the "stepping stones" of the principal Pacific airway.   The airstrip and its facilities occupy most of the space on this tiny islet.   Photograph courtesy of the Pan American World Airway.

Indo-China and wheat and dairy products from the United States and Canado, machinery, vehicles, and manufactured goods.   Prior to the Second World War the United States took 82 per cent of the exports and supplied 78 per cent of the imports, and continues to dominate Philippine trade.

Malaya and the East Indies are a treasure house of commodities valuable and necessary to industrial nations.   Much of the world's rubber and tin comes from this area, and it is an important source of sugar, coffee, tea, rice, spices, tobacco, kapok, petroleum, copra, and minerals.   Singapore, the commercial center, is closer to New York by way of Suez than by way of Panama.   Because of this fact and also because of European political control, much of the produce moves by way of the Indian and Atlantic oceans rather than over the Pacific. Less than one-third of the tin imported into the United States from southeastern Asia comes by way of the Pacific coast; only 5 per cent of the rubber is shipped over the Pacific and of this almost all goes by way of the Panama Canal to east coast and Gulf ports.

Australia and New Zealand are significantly different from the other Asiatic-Pacific countries. Both of them are inhabited by people of European background and of high living standards. These conditions are maintained by selective immigration and by regulated production and trade designed to protect the domestic market and to insure foreign markets for exportable goods. These facts, together with membership of these two countries in the British Commonwealth, directs a large share of the trade towards Great Britain and other nations in the Commonwealth, and therefore it moves through the Indian and Atlantic oceans rather than the Pacific. The exports of both countries are principally agricultural and pastoral products: from Australia, wool, wheat, meats, and hides; from New Zealand, wool, dairy products, meats, and hides. The Australian industrial production is intended chiefly for the home markets of both countries, and little of it is sent out. The imports are machinery, petroleum, textiles, drugs, and chemicals.

The Pacific trade of these countries is largely with the United States, and together, Australia and New Zealand are second only to the Philippines as a Pacific source region for American industry. Wool and hides are the principal commodities sent to the United States; in addition Australia ships small amounts of lead ore, lead, and zinc. In return Australia and New Zealand take from the United States an almost equal value in machinery, automobiles and parts, petroleum, and tobacco.

OCEANIC TRADE

The trade of the Pacific oceanic islands is of much less importance than the intercontinental trade. With the exception of Hawaii, their total island population is small, their resources are relatively insignificant, and the trading distances are great.

Hawaii, the crossroads of the Pacific, is commercially the most important of the island groups. It occupies a strategic position, contains a relatively large and mixed population, and is part of the commercial and industrial system of the United States. Production in the islands is centered on two great tropical crops, pineapples and sugar, produced by large-scale modern methods and intended for export to

Figure 154. Harbor of Honolulu. The palatial passenger ship belongs to the Matson lines. Photograph courtesy of the Hawaii Visitors Bureau.

TABLE 1

IMPORTS FOR CONSUMPTION INTO THE UNITED STATES FROM
PACIFIC COUNTRIES AND AREAS, CALENDAR YEAR 1948*

Country or Area	Value, U.S. Dollars	Principal Items
Australia	131,811,039	Wool, lead, hides, and skins
New Zealand	32,774,464	Wool, hides, and skins
British West Pacific islands	94,463	Cocoa, coffee, tea
French Pacific islands	1,741,084	Ferroalloys
Western Pacific islands	854,380	Oil seeds, miscellaneous
Hong Kong	3,644,001	Furs, oil seeds, fibers
Japan	59,681,025	Raw and manufactured silk, cotton manufactures
China	117,439,790	Furs, oils and wax, fibers
Philippines	227,503,278	Oil seeds, fibers, sugar
Burma	1,699,884	Lead
Siam	49,200,487	Rubber, tin
French Indochina	3,265,117	Rubber
Netherland Indies	76,161,224	Rubber, tin

Source: Report FT 120, Department of Commerce, Bureau of the Census, Washington, 1949.

the mainland. In return the Hawaiian Islands import from the mainland all types of manufactured goods, petroleum, and food. There is a very important asset represented in the islands by tourists whose expenditures constitute an invisible item of Hawaiian export.

TABLE 2

EXPORTS OF DOMESTIC MERCHANDISE FROM THE UNITED STATES TO PACIFIC COUNTRIES AND AREAS, CALENDAR YEAR 1948*

Country or Area	Value, U.S. Dollars	Principal Items
Australia	113,844,905	Vehicles and machinery, petroleum and petroleum products, tobacco
New Zealand	33,912,208	Vehicles and machinery, petroleum and petroleum products, tobacco
British West Pacific islands	923,591	Miscellaneous
French Pacific islands	3,052,735	Vehicles, petroleum and petroleum products, textiles
Western Pacific islands	65,599	Foods and grains
Hong Kong	82,897,384	Medicines and chemicals, vehicles, textiles
Japan	322,850,020	Foods, raw cotton, fertilizers
China	239,786,584	Raw cotton, foods, vehicles, and machinery
Philippines	465,903,571	Textiles, foods, vehicles, and machinery
Burma	4,520,983	Vehicles and machinery
Siam	16,333,318	Vehicles, medicines
French Indochina	14,304,997	Vehicles, petroleum, textiles, medicines
British Malaya	81,847,971	Textiles, vehicles
Netherland Indies	91,501,559	Vehicles and machinery, food, cotton manufacturing

* *Source:* Report FT 420, Department of Commerce, Bureau of the Census, Washington, 1949.

French Pacific islands consist of New Caledonia and the island groups around Tahiti known as French Oceania. New Caledonia contains important resources of ores including nickel, chrome, and several other ferroalloy metals. Previous to the Second World War these were shipped to France, the United States, and Japan, and coffee, copra, and pearl shells were exported to France. Imports of manufactured goods and foods came principally from France and Australia, and to a smaller extent from the United States. French Oceania exports chiefly tropical agricultural products, vanilla and copra, and phosphate fertilizers from the island of Makatea. The return imports are foods, textiles, machinery, and petroleum. This trade before the war was fairly equally divided between France and the United States, except for the phosphates that were shipped principally to Japan.

The British West Pacific islands include as main components eastern New Guinea, the Solomons, western Samoa, and the Fijis. The trade of all these island groups has the common factor that copra is one of the chief items and that Australia is the principal destination of exports and source of imports. In addition, New Guinea produces gold and rubber; Nauru and Ocean Islands, phosphate; and the Fijis, sugar and bananas. The imports to the islands are varied; machinery, petroleum, lumber, prepared foods, and spirits are important items.

TRADE ROUTES

The most important trade route in the Pacific originates on the California coast and terminates at Manila (Fig. 155). This route follows as nearly as practicable a great circle of the earth, the shortest path between two points northward along the Canadian Pacific coast, skirting the Aleutians, and southward along the Asiatic shore. This great circle characteristic is poorly illustrated on an ordinary map centered on the ocean, but a globe shows that the shorelines of western America and eastern Asia form a nearly straight line and that the shortest steaming track is one that follows the shorelines rather closely. Along this route are the great ports of the Pacific. On the American side Los Angeles, San Francisco, Seattle, Portland, and Vancouver all share in this traffic. Yokahama is the first port of call on the Asiatic end of the route. Its volume of commerce both from Pacific as well as Asiatic trade before the Second World War made Yokahama the fourth largest port of the world. Kobe, also in Japan, was third in the world in its prewar tonnage, and its neighbor, Kobe, just across the bay, was eighth. Shanghai, Hong Kong, and Manila lie along the southward continuation of the route.

Ships that pass through the Panama Canal loaded for Asiatic ports find that a great circle course takes them northward along the American coast, somewhat south of the North Pacific track but shorter by a few hundred miles than by way of Hawaii. This route has the advantage that Canal shipping can call at the west coast ports with only short detours from the sailing track.

For other routes than the northern one, Hawaii is the hub of Pacific trade. These islands, the most important insular stations of the Pacific, are located on the sailing tracks from the American west coast to south

Pacific ports. Steamers from Panama may take this somewhat longer route in winter to avoid the storminess of the Aleutians. Prior to the Second World War the combined tracks from the west coast to Hawaii carried nearly as much tonnage as the North Pacific route, and that from Hawaii to Japan only slightly less. If to this volume is added

FIGURE 155. Shipping routes of the Pacific. The solid lines indicate the most important commercial trade routes, the dotted lines, other tracks.

the traffic from the Canal to Asia by way of Hawaii as well as that destined for Australia and New Zealand, it is evident that more Pacific tonnage passes through Hawaii than any other single location in the Pacific, making Honolulu the most important oceanic port of call. This does not mean, however, that Honolulu is the greatest of the Pacific ports because much of this cargo is not unloaded or handled in the Hawaiian Islands but is only in transit to its ultimate mainland destination. Honolulu, however, is the only important Pacific port that owes its prominence solely to Pacific trade. The great mainland ports, both on the American and the Asiatic shores, derive large shares of their commerce from trade that has not traversed the Pacific.

Goods are carried across the Pacific by two classes of ships, the liner and the tramp. The liners are commonly larger and faster vessels that operate on fixed routes and schedules; the tramps are smaller and slower ships that pick up bulk cargoes wherever these are available. On the Pacific routes there is an excess of westbound volume over eastbound, and this excess is taken by tramp vessels that continue from Asia to Europe and America by way of the Indian and Atlantic oceans. Because it is uneconomical for liner shipping to call at small island ports these are usually served by tramps. The flexibility of schedule and the unspecialized nature of tramp shipping are of importance in transporting bulk cargoes of low value, but these advantages are declining in the demand for faster service and specialized facilities for handling and preserving cargoes.

All the populated island groups of the Pacific require some kind of ocean connections. The Hawaiians, the Fijis, Samoa, and Tahiti are regular ports of call for liner shipping, and most of the others are served by tramps as cargoes accumulate. Inter-island transportation within groups themselves is ordinarily accomplished by smaller steamers, motor ships, and auxiliary schooners. In parts of the ocean, particularly the western Pacific, this secondary shipping suffered damage and decay during the war years, and its slow replacement has delayed the economic recovery of these areas.

AIR TRANSPORTATION

Transpacific air travel became established in 1935 with the development of aircraft capable of flying the required distances. The earliest of these were the *Clipper* seaplanes designed to take off and land on water and to carry enough fuel for flights of more than 2000 miles. After the Second World War, with landing strips constructed on the important islands, these seaplanes were replaced by more economical land planes (Fig. 156). The earliest air routes across the Pacific could not take advantage of the ability of aircraft to fly great circle courses for several reasons. The north Pacific near the Aleutians is a stormy area, suitable landing facilities are rare, and stations are difficult to supply by shipping. The longer routes were then more practicable, and along them the United States had already acquired the "stepping stones" for waystations.

The original airway across the Pacific utilized only those stopping places under United States sovereignty. Its route was from San Francisco to Manila by way of Honolulu, Midway (Fig. 153), Wake, and Guam. When matters of reciprocal rights were adjusted between the nations, this route continued to the Asiatic mainland. An offshoot of this airway, serving Australia and New Zealand, branches at Hawaii and reaches Auckland and Sydney by way of Canton, Suva in the Fijis, and Noumea in New Caledonia. There have been added several variations to this route, including direct flights from Midway and Wake to Tokyo and service to Hawaii from Seattle and Los Angeles. During the Second World War all transpacific flying was under government control. After the cessation of hostilities official planes were the most numerous on the Pacific airways. For this official transportation Guam is the western Pacific hub, and into it feeds air traffic from Japan and the Philippines. From Guam to Hawaii the route passes through the islands of the late Japanese mandate with a stop at Kwajalein in the Marshalls, to Johnston Island southwest of Hawaii, and on to Honolulu. Since the war a fourth route has been added, approximating the great circle of the north Pacific. It passes overland from Seattle to Anchorage, Alaska, and thence southeastward to Japan, with a refueling stop in the Aleutians.

In addition to these principal transpacific air routes there are many shorter and local schedules flown in and around the ocean. Air strips constructed during the war are the chief landing points, and smaller and older planes the principal vehicles. This traffic is the air counterpart to inter-island shipping and will maintain itself wherever local traffic makes it profitable.

STRATEGIC LOCATIONS

In peace the Pacific is a highway that carries goods from one nation to another; in war it is a route over which some will attack and others will defend. Islands that lie between the mainlands by the accident of their locations become parts of the plans and aspirations of the border nations, acquiring or losing significance with changes in strength and purpose and with technological developments.

During the first half of the nineteenth century there was little interest in ownership of oceanic islands; their populations and resources were so insignificant that few were claimed. Whaling and trading captains had landed on scores of them and recorded the facts of their discoveries, but, in general, governments neglected to formalize these claims. In 1872 Germany declined the offer of a protectorate over the

Fijis, and in 1877 Great Britain similarly refused to assume the protection of Samoa. In the later decades, however, the change from sail to steam navigation made coaling stations imperative, and the rise of Japan and Australia as important world areas brought increased value to the possession of the specks of land in this great ocean. By 1900

FIGURE 156. Transpacific air Routes. Major routes are indicated by solid lines; secondary by dotted lines.

all the islands with considerable populations had been added to the empires of the world powers, and many others had been acquired for their guano and phosphate deposits or as cable stations. The acquisitions of the United States were scattered but important. In 1898 and 1899 Hawaii had been annexed upon petition of its government; western Samoa was obtained by an agreement with Germany and Great Britain; and an indefinite trusteeship over the Philippines and possession of Guam were results of the Spanish War. The tiny islet of Midway had been claimed and occupied in 1867, and Wake in 1899. In addition, the United States retained, but did not actively assert, claims to several uninhabited islands of the Line group between Hawaii and Samoa. In 1935, when transpacific aviation was being planned and pioneered, these claims were resurrected and supported by occupations establishing sovereignty over Kingman, Palmyra, Baker, Howland, and Jarvis islands and joint use with Great Britain of Canton and Enderbury. Thus were acquired the steppingstones of two air routes; one to the Orient by way of Hawaii, Midway, Wake, Guam, and the Philippines; the other from Hawaii, by way of the Line Islands and Samoa to Australia (Fig. 156).

The location of islands greatly favors America in military strategy. From Hawaii to Asia and Australia are island groups that may be offensive bases or defensive strongholds, but from Hawaii to the American coast lie 2000 miles of open water. Until 1941 this distance was considered to be the extreme operating range of a surface fleet, and, therefore, if a strong force remained based at Hawaii, no hostile fleet could safely attack the western coast of the United States. As a consequence of the war, Japan received a mandate over all the German possessions in the Pacific north of the equator. These, the Carolines, the Marianas, and the Marshalls are of little commercial value but form a screen extending 2000 miles into the ocean before Japan. Before 1941, war in the Pacific was foreseen principally as a conflict of surface ships and submarines. On the part of the United States the operations were to consist of a gigantic and costly task of island sweeping, whereby the fleet bases could be moved forward until Japan, the only probable enemy, was blockaded and troops could be brought in for an invasion. Japan, from her point of view, hoped that the island screen would afford the small bases and air strips, thereby making such an advance too slow and costly to be maintained. The role of airpower in a sea campaign was well understood, but its decisive significance could not be appreciated until late in the decade of 1930.

Location for a powerful primary naval base must provide a spacious harbor in which a fleet can maneuver under air attack, airfields for protection, land for the extensive shops, docks, arsenals, and stores, and ordinarily a neighboring city from which to draw the manpower necessary to operate the base.[2] Such situations are rare indeed on the Pacific islands; of the American possessions only Hawaii offers most

[2] William Herbert Hobbs, *The Fortress Islands of the Pacific*, p. 19, Edwards Brothers, Ann Arbor, Mich., 1945.

of these qualities. Pearl Harbor became our primary base, the center of the line of our naval frontier extending from the secondary bases of Dutch Harbor in the Aleutians to Pago Pago in western Samoa. The Japanese had no comparable situations in the low atolls and isolated high islands of their screen. They improvised a base at Truk in the Carolines, where a large atoll with its reefs provided protection and small islets inside the lagoon gave situations for short air strips and for naval installations. Truk was useful only so long as the Japanese held the air above it, and it was abandoned by the fleet when air supremacy was lost.

The importance of strategic Pacific locations in the Second World War can be illustrated by a brief review of the operations. The Japanese intended to seize Malaya and perhaps India, hold them for their own purposes, and make the recovery of these areas so costly to the Allies that a settlement would result whereby Japan would retain all or some of these conquests. Australia was the only important location of Allied manpower and resources in the Pacific area, and to become the base of operations would need great support from the United States. To interrupt shipping between Australia and the United States, the Japanese occupied the Melanesian arc from New Guinea to the Southern Solomons, but were prevented by the Battle of the Coral Sea from gaining the important positions of the Fijis and New Caledonia. This failure to isolate Australia was disastrous for Japan. The Allied plan of retaliation was to attack the homeland of Japan rather than attempt the reconquest of Indonesia. By way of the stepping stones of New Guinea, the Philippines, and Okinawa, the forces under General MacArthur came within striking distance of Japan proper. North of the equator the island screen of the Marshalls and the Carolines, so tactically important in a purely surface war, was ineffective against superior air strength, and an attempt to enlarge it by an occupation of Midway resulted in another naval disaster for Japan. The very number of the islands was a disadvantage; it permitted the Allies to attack the weaker of them and then neutralize the stronger by air power. The low atolls of the Marshalls and Carolines were difficult to defend although the high islands such as the Marianas, the Palaus, and Iwo Jima were bitterly and fanatically contested from strong points excavated into their surfaces. Command of the air enabled the Allies to push advanced bases far forward. The atoll of Ulithi, south of Yap, was made into a temporary base by warehouse ships and tankers that anchored in the quiet waters of its lagoon and supplied the combat ships. An extremely effective submarine campaign from these bases and later by air from the Philippines cut off

Japan from the petroleum and other resources of her Malayan conquests. Of the western Pacific islands, the Marianas were the most
important strategically, for from them the B 29 planes could reach the
Japanese homeland. From Okinawa and the Marianas Japan was
forced within her inner defences; she was cut off from supply; the
navy was destroyed; the industrial plant was being demolished by
incendiary bombing and the two atomic bombs were a double coup
de grâce.

In these campaigns across the Pacific, the primary strategic locations
were Pearl Harbor, which assured the coast of the United States; Australia, which was the primary base of operations; and the Marianas,
from which destruction was brought to the Japanese homeland.

PROBLEMS OF THE UNITED STATES IN THE PACIFIC

The conclusion of the war brought new responsibilities to the United
States. For strategic reasons the United States has assumed control
of the Micronesian islands formerly mandated to Japan. The total
area of these islands scattered over a wide ocean is quite small, and
their combined populations is less than 150,000. The immediate tasks
of refocusing their limited trade from Japan to the United States, of
setting up workable governments, and of educating the people are well
on the way to completion and offer few difficulties in their accomplishment. Of much greater significance are the problems of Japan. It
seems obvious that these 70,000,000 people cannot live by agriculture
alone, and their productive and commercial systems have been shattered by the war. In planning its reconstruction several grave circumstances must be considered. Silk is no longer so important as it was
in prewar times; the Japanese shipping is largely destroyed; some of
the principal markets are no longer dependent upon Japanese goods.
Above these material questions are two that involve the future position
of Japan in the world. First, would a strong, industrialized Japan
ever again become an enemy of the United States across the Pacific?
Second, would an industrialized and friendly Japan become a bastion
of strength against some other Asiatic enemy as England was the
fortress of democracy against a Nazi Europe?

Index